NEW INSIGHTS
INTO ASTROLOGY

NEW INSIGHTS
into ASTROLOGY

Sex is a T-Square
Number Symbolism
Harmonics
Aspects
Asteroids
Research

NONA GWYNN PRESS

Excerpts from *Name Your Baby* by La Reina Rule
Copyright © 1963, 1966, 1986 by Bantam Books,
a division of Bantam Doubleday Dell Publishing Group, Inc.
Used by permission of Bantam Books,
a division of Bantam Doubleday Dell Publishing Group, Inc.

International Standard Book Number 0-935127-12-7

Cover design by Maria Kay Simms

Published by ACS Publications
P.O. Box 34487
San Diego, CA 92163-4487

First Printing, April 1993

Dedication
To everyone whose birth patterns contributed to the writing of this book,
but particularly to my husband, Sy, and to my children, Edward and Gwynn.

Acknowledgment

My thanks to Diane Cramer who, while writing drafts of her own recently released book on medical astrology, managed to find the time and patience to word process the many drafts of mine.

Contents

Tables

Figures

Introduction

Sex is a T-Square

The T-Square has been libeled, as have all difficult aspects. Without tension there would be no release of tension. A Grand Trine creates a harmonious state which does not seek energy release (unless this configuration is connected to an inharmonious aspect). Therefore, an orgasm, the culmination and release of tension and hopefully the end result of sex, is the product of a T-Square, not a Grand Trine. (My reasoning is purely deductive—no statistical study having been done to this effect.)

I must add, after defending with my best argument the much maligned T-Square[1] (or Cosmic Square[2] for that matter), accomplishments of a nature other than sexual accompany this interaction. People with so-called "difficult" aspects (square, opposition and, sometimes, conjunction) must seek release of the tension inherent in these aspects by being active. This activity may cause their careers, their gardens or the public good to flourish. There can, of course, be negative results. The energy expressed is disruptive, but there would be no fulfillment without force, and force is disruptive. A career is not furthered, society altered or a garden planted without disruption. Trines and Grand Trines[3] have their place, but that is, for the most part, connected to a square or T-Square where the soft aspects can "grease the wheels" for the hard ones. (Of course, sometimes they "grease the skids" instead.)

Though "energy" and "force" are operative words, my belief is not that the aspects, or planets, affect our behavior but rather that they reflect it and us. Our destiny is not imposed upon us. It is an expression of what we already are or have been.

I am writing this book to express my ideas, which frequently differ from those of other astrologers. Perhaps some background on my evolution into and as an astrologer might help.

In July of 1966 when Neptune, unbeknownst to me, was about to make a station within a degree of a square to my Aquarius Ascendant (also unknown to me), my mother gave me a coupon to send away for a six-month astrological prediction. She had gotten hers and thought it was remarkable. I got mine and, though it said things that were true like "You're going through a difficult time now," I figured they knew anybody who sent for a six-month prediction must be going through a difficult time.

My first positive reaction to astrology occurred in 1968 when I read *Linda Goodman's Sun Signs.* Having previously read (in addition to my six-month prediction) Sun sign forecasts in the newspapers and never finding one forecast that came true, I thought people who believed in astrology were gullible, illogical and unscientific. I scanned Linda Goodman's book to be *au courant* and to disprove astrology. Instead, I wept at her description of Sagittarians because it reminded me so much of my Sagittarian mother, father and son. (Having three close members of your family with their Suns in the same sign is something to weep about in itself.)

Despite my tears, the description wasn't completely applicable to both my parents and my son. For instance, Goodman characterizes Sagittarians as extravagant. My mother and father were extravagant, but my son is not. I later discovered that my father's Venus (Venus relates to love and money) is in Sagittarius, my mother's is in Aquarius and my son's is in Capricorn. Capricorn is a sign which is not extravagant, so my son's having his Venus in that sign explained his carefulness with both love and money. The more I read and the more I knew the rest of the chart, the more there seemed to be something to astrology.

In December of 1968, around when Goodman's book was beguiling me, Neptune was in Scorpio, exactly opposition my Mercury at the end of Taurus. By January of 1970 it hit my Moon at 00° Gemini and then struck my 02° Gemini Sun in January of 1971.

In June of the latter year my son went away for a few weeks, and the awareness of my children's impending independence was intensified. The thought, "Now it's my turn," came over me. Deciding that what I wanted for my turn was to learn astrology and not having the time to take classes, I bought a book designed as an astrological home study course. The following aspects were within 01° of being exact. Jupiter and Neptune were opposition my Moon, and Saturn was conjunct my Mercury and before the month was out, conjunct my Moon, approaching my Sun. A year later, after I had started taking astrology classes, an astrologer read my chart and remarked, "A colossal thing happened in June 1971. Transiting Jupiter and Neptune were opposition your natal Sun and Moon, while transiting Saturn was conjunct them."

What happened was that my life changed irrevocably. Transiting Saturn was in my third house of the mind, while transiting Neptune and Jupiter were in my ninth of higher education. (All references are to the Placidus House system.) Without knowing these aspects, I decided to structure (Saturn) my mind (Mercury and third house) through education (Jupiter and ninth house), regarding astrology (Neptune). (Saturn was conjunct my Mercury, approaching my Sun and Moon, at the time of the decision.) And I was going to do it at home (Mercury rules my fourth house). As observed before, hard aspects such as the square, opposition and conjunction are disruptive, but disruption is only negative when it blocks instead of releasing. Under these "colossal" aspects I was released by becoming aware of the need to separate (Saturn) from my children (Mercury also rules my fifth house) and do my own thing (Sun and Moon).

During a period of over seven years Neptune made varying hard aspects to my Sun, Moon, Venus, Mars, Jupiter, Neptune, Midheaven, Moon's Nodes, Vertex and East Point in mutable signs.[4] I became Neptunized." Those to whom it has happened will know what I'm talking about—the others probably won't. At first I thought I might be losing my mind. However, with three planets, the Vertex and South Node in Virgo and Saturn in Aquarius in the twelfth house close to my Ascendant, I approached astrology critically— Neptune or not.

In December of 1972 I heard Charles Emerson lecture. At the end of his talk he spoke about an organization, the National Council for Geocosmic Research, and of the fact that astrology, with the advent of computers, could be tested scientifically now, as it never could be in the past. He said those who wanted to take part in this astrological research should speak to him after the lecture. Hearing the clarion call, I presented myself for service, joined NCGR and soon became research chairman of the New York Chapter.

March 11, 1974, with transiting Neptune stationary retrograde 03' away from an exact square to my Mars, the New York Chapter began a research project that was to continue for several years. We had gained access to the birth and death information on everyone who committed suicide in New York City from 1969-1973. Chapter 6 includes a reproduction of the summary of that study which appeared in the *Journal of Geocosmic Research,* Vol. 2, No. 2.

With Neptune square my Jupiter within a degree, I spoke on the Suicide Project at an NCGR Conference in March of 1976. Geoffrey Dean, who was writing a book on astrological research called *Recent Advances in Natal Astrology,* heard me speak and asked me to write an article about the project so he could include our research in his book. I did, and it was the basis for my later article in the *Journal.* Dean also gave me a sample of his book which I "critiqued" without his solicitation. The unexpected result was a request for me to read the entire book and follow suit. I agreed and became one of his eight collaborators. Then, in October 1977, with Neptune squaring my Jupiter within a degree again, Neil Michelsen asked me to edit Joan Negus' book and workbook, *Basic Astrology: A Guide for Teachers and Students.*

The aspects have been noted because so many astrologers consider that a square or an opposition (even if it isn't in a T-Square) has to be bad, particularly if the square or opposition involves Neptune. As for Jupiter, which figured in the last two events, it relates to publishing and rules my Midheaven (career), so under aspects to my Jupiter from Neptune (astrology) I began either collaborating on, editing or writing astrological literature. Rather than being negative, these aspects have been very positive.

1978 was the year *Recent Advances, Basic Astrology* and my article on suicide appeared. I began writing my own book May 21, 1979 at 07:21 PM EDT in Forest Hills, New York. This book is about my research—some experimental like the

Suicide Project, some observational like my ongoing study of lunations, begun in March 1976. Another continuing study is one on harmonics, especially individual harmonic charts, that was initiated after my hearing John Addey speak at a conference in England in September of the same year. From the harmonic analysis an involvement with number symbolism developed. Solar, and other returns, are also analyzed. Asteroids, or minor planets, have been the basis for additional investigation. These six subjects, as well as Uranian planets, are discussed in the succeeding chapters.

This discussion is not absolute. One of my different ideas is that astrologers do not always know what is going to happen and should not let the predictive power of astrology seduce them into thinking otherwise. I've heard astrologers say, "That marriage is definitely going to break up," or "They shouldn't get married—it will never work." We may be able to describe a person and a relationship by looking at the aspects, interaspects and composite chart[5], but we cannot be certain what that person is going to do or what is going to happen to that relationship. Complicating the problem is the fact that each planet and house has at least three meanings. When our eighth house is activated, we don't know if we're going to inherit money, die or have a great sexual experience. To me the goal of astrology is to understand ourselves—not necessarily to know which of the three it's going to be.

Even if we were able to distinguish which of the meanings of the planets was activated at a particular time, there might be other planets operating that are unknown to us now, as Neptune, Uranus and Pluto were unknown to people a few hundred years ago. More importantly, there are purposes that are unknown to us— reasons we are here, expressing the patterns of our charts. That marriage which the astrologers thought would never last or should never occur may be the most important purpose in the lives of the couple. And that purpose may express itself most forcefully through a T-Square.

Astrology is not an absolute science. Science isn't even absolute. We can only lift the veil a little. The purpose of my book is to share the methods which have helped me catch a glimpse of what is hidden.

## CHAPTER ONE

Number Symbolism

Astrology is an expression of number symbolism. The degree of a planet or point is significant, as is the number of degrees between planets, points, and planets and points. An aspect is merely a number of degrees separating numbers, and the power of astrology is in the numbers. A radical departure from traditional astrology, but those are my beliefs after extensive study.

The Meaning of Numbers

But what do the numbers mean? If we knew their correspondence to the planets and signs, as astrologers we would know their meaning. In February of 1978 I heard Joseph Mark Cohen speak at an NCGR lecture. He said that the numbers relate to the houses of the natural zodiac, so 1 is the first house, Aries and Mars; 2 is the second house, Taurus and Venus; etc.[1] Also, Cohen stated 1 is like the conjunction; 2, the opposition; 3, the trine; etc. The number would be like the aspect which results from the division of that number into 360°.

I began to experiment with this system and found it worked. The number 3, Mercury and Gemini do flow like the trine. The number 6 is Mercury again, but not as flowing, since it corresponds to Virgo and the sextile. Accepting that the Moon is like the square was difficult until I thought of the structure of the home and the responsibility of the mother. What could be more "squarish" than that? Even the cycle of the Moon is divided into four cycles. And, people with 4 prominent in their charts do appear to be under the auspices of the Moon, Cancer and the square. 5 is the fifth house, Leo, the Sun and the quintile. How appropriate that the quintile, which is associated with creativity, should correlate to the house, sign and planet of creative self-expression. Numerologists usually consider 7 serious, responsible and associated with "sacred and religious matters."[2] Marriage can be a religious sacrament, and nothing is more serious and responsible than marriage (seventh house), unless it's motherhood which often comes with marriage. As for the septile, my studies indicate it pertains to partnership. 8 represents power and money which certainly bring to mind the eighth house, Scorpio and Pluto. Also, I have found the semisquare and sesquiquadrate[3] prominent in eighth house matters. As for 9—our decimal system has expanded to its full extent when it reaches 9, and the ninth house, Sagittarius and Jupiter refer to expansion. Regarding the novile, or nonile, it is associated with completion, and 9 completes the single digit cycle. The basis for Indian astrologers' correlating 9 to the marriage partner may be that the marriage partner can be a completion of the self. 10 is very solid like Capricorn and Saturn, while 11 is very erratic like Aquarius and Uranus. 12 is reminiscent of the twelfth house, Pisces and Neptune, and semisextiles and quincunxes[4] relate to circumstances that are very nebulous, or Neptunian, if you will.

The complete sequence would be as follows:

Table I - Number Correlations

#	House	Sign		Planet		Aspect		# of Degrees	
1	1st	Aries	♈	Mars	♂	Conjunction	♂	360°	(0°)
2	2nd	Taurus	♉	Venus	♀	Opposition	☍	180°	
3	3rd	Gemini	♊	Mercury	☿	Trine	△	120°	
4	4th	Cancer	♋	Moon	☽	Square	□	90°	
5	5th	Leo	♌	Sun	☉	Quintile	Q	72°	
6	6th	Virgo	♍	Mercury	☿	Sextile	✶	60°	
7	7th	Libra	♎	Venus	♀	Septile	S	51° 25'42.8"	
8	8th	Scorpio	♏	Pluto	♇	Semisquare (Octile)	∠	45°	
9	9th	Sagittarius	♐	Jupiter	♃	Novile (Nonile, Nonagon)	N	40°	
10	10th	Capricorn	♑	Saturn	♄	Decile (Semiquintile)	⊥	36°	
11	11th	Aquarius	♒	Uranus	♅	Undecile	U	32° 43'38.1"	
12	12th	Pisces	♓	Neptune	♆	Semisextile	⋎	30°	

OTHER SYSTEMS OF ASTRO-NUMEROLOGY
Of course, there are other systems of astro-numerology. Another schema declares that 1 is the Sun and 2 is the Moon, which is similar to saying 1 is Mars and 2 is Venus, since the Sun and Mars are masculine and positive, while the Moon and Venus are feminine and negative (no value judgment intended). The correspondence to the houses of the natural zodiac, however, with the whole spectrum given above of signs and aspects as well as planets, I find most beneficial.

REDUCTION

If the number is above 12, I reduce it to a number from 1-12 (23 = 2 + 3 = 5), and use the corresponding house, sign, planet and aspect. Multiple digit numbers, though, do have a somewhat different meaning because they contain several numbers—23 will primarily have the meaning of 5, but with a coloration of 2 and 3. Of the 2 and 3, 2 will be more prominent because it is the initial number. (Since you do not start reducing to a single digit after 9, some numbers occur less frequently. 10, 19 and 28 will be 10, not 1; 11 and 29 will be 11, not 2; 12 will be 12, not 3.)

DEGREE INTERPRETATION

Reading interpretations of the degrees is helpful. Sepharial's translation of "La Volasfera," which is included in a book called *The Degrees of the Zodiac Symbolized* by Charubel, is particularly good.

The symbols attributed to the degrees in the various degree books are usually expressive of the numbers' correspondence to the houses of the natural zodiac. For instance, the symbol in "La Volasfera" for 01° Aries reads, *"A strong man standing, dressed in skins, or heavy, loose, and coarse material—the shoulders almost bare. In his hand he bears a club. The figure suggests a Hercules.*[5] What could be more double Aries (Aries for the sign and Aries for the number) than that!

I also consult *Degrees of the Zodiac* which has no symbols and which is a synthesis by Esther V. Leinbach of six different authorities. Leinbach has not just synthesized, she has modernized—no swords or sceptres, cavaliers or camels in her book. She says that the authorities tend to agree, but when they don't the degree may be "less stringent."[6]

After much experimentation, I read the degree that is given. In other words, if a planet is past the halfway mark, I do not go to the next degree—03°59' is still 03°. Leinbach, who studied the degrees for ten years, also uses the degree that is given, thus substantiating my independent conclusion.

The degrees of the Ascendant, Sun and Moon are the most important, but every planet or point will be influenced by its degree. However, it is necessary to keep in mind the nature of the planet or point and apply the interpretation to that nature.

As for the separations between the planets, points, and planets and points, they can now be seen. Many computer programs, including the one I use with my computer, list angular separations. Astro Computing Services (now known as Astro Communications Services) offers the option of angular separations instead of midpoints on the natal chart. (Midpoints can be ordered as a supplement.) From my studies it seems that non-aspects are as important as aspects, or rather that there is no such thing as a non-aspect. Each separation has its own meaning.

The meaning is defined by the number of degrees in the separation. For instance, with a separation of 1 (as with a position of 1), the planets involved describe the person himself—his own persona. (The degree separation between planets at say 02°45' and 04°30' of a sign is 01°, not 02°.) As for 0, it contains the void. If there is a 00° separation, nothing is separating the planets and points, except the minutes which are of secondary importance. The planets and/or points will work together, either successfully or unsuccessfully, according to their respective natures.

On the other hand, there is usually a feeling of lack associated with a planet or point that is at 00° of a sign. Often the native will overcompensate to fill this void. Also, the quality of the sign may be intensified, since there is no number to qualify that quality.

Zero added to another number, i.e., $1 + 0 = 10$, adds the power of the void to that number. Saturn, the 10 planet, is a combination of the Mars energy (1) and the need to fill the void (0), often by overcompensation.

MINUTES AND SECONDS

The degrees are of primary significance, but the minutes are also important. I have found that the interpretations (using the same system as for the degrees) are more appropriate if you do not go to the next minute when the seconds are past 30" or .5. Astro now lists the positions of the planets in degrees, minutes and seconds and the positions of the points and asteroids in degrees and minutes with one decimal place. For instance, my Sun is rounded off to 02° Gemini 35' in the chart (see Figure 1), but is listed as 02°34'51"[7] in the upper left-hand corner of Astro's black-and-white Natal Chart (BNC). I consider my Sun as 02° Gemini 34', which is actually the Sun's degrees and minutes at my birth. As for the separations, Astro rounds them off to the closer minute. To know if this is the accurate minute you yourself would have to subtract one position from the other, including either the seconds or the fraction of the minute in this operation. When the fraction of a second is past .5, Astro lists the following second, but even the seconds are meaningful and shouldn't be rounded off. When the data has been accurate enough for me to use the seconds, they have followed the same schema as the degrees and minutes.[8]

IMPROVED INTERPRETATION

Incidentally, I am much more stable and much less scattered than the archetypal Gemini. A great deal of this difference is attributable to the combination of 2 (Taurus) with Gemini. When the numbers are not taken into account the signs (as well as the houses, planets and aspects) are often misinterpreted.

Once the house, sign, planet and aspect corresponding to the number is known, not only their general meanings, but their meanings in the individual chart should be considered. For instance, the stability and persistence which in general are associated with the #2 correlates are individualized, in regard to my 02° Gemini Sun, by my second house, Taurus, Venus and oppositions. (I prefer Placidus house cusps.) My second house has Aries on the cusp and Uranus, ruling my Ascendant, in it. Taurus is in my second and third house, and Mercury, the ruler of my Sun and Moon, is in Taurus. My Venus is in Gemini in the fourth house; rules the third house, Mercury and eighth house; and is exactly square the Vertex, semisquare Uranus and sesquiquadrate Mars. Exact oppositions are the East Point to the South Node, and the Antivertex to Jupiter.[9] That stability and persistence is shown to be very much related to me personally (Aries cusp, Ascendant rulership, aspects to Ascendant ruler and Mars, oppositions of East Point and Antivertex). Those

Figure I – Natal Chart of the Writer

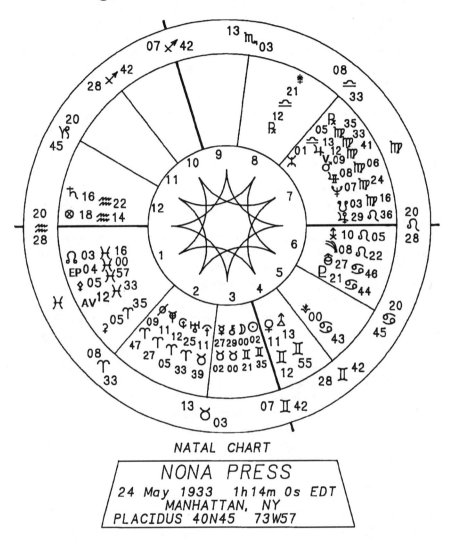

NATAL CHART

NONA PRESS
24 May 1933   1h14m 0s EDT
MANHATTAN, NY
PLACIDUS 40N45   73W57

qualities are also emphasized (Taurus in natural house, Sun and Moon rulership, aspect to Vertex), and connected to the #3 correlates (third house Taurus, Taurus Mercury, third house rulership, oppositions to South Node and Jupiter ruled by Mercury). It's no wonder I've concentrated on writing this book for the last thirteen years!

ORBS

The aspects designated as exact are aspects within a degree. As the term is used here, aspects within a degree are those where the planets and/or points are either at the number where the aspect is exact or the adjacent numbers. (I use this orb at least through the first 12 aspects. See pages 110-11 for greater detail.) This is not a 01° orb—it can be almost 02°. In the 30° sequence one planet or point may be at the beginning of a degree, and the other, at the end of the following degree.

The same degree is extremely powerful, but the one before or after seems to have a sympathetic vibration. Similarly, a person usually starts to "feel the effect" when a transiting planet goes into the degree before an aspect to his chart, though the planet may be almost two degrees away from that aspect. Classical aspects with a larger orb have some effect, but it is the exact within a degree aspects, classical or not, that are incisive. (Exact within a degree symmetrical patterns [planetary pictures] are sometimes formed from aspects with a larger orb—thus accounting for the effect of these inexact aspects.)

Combining Positions and Separations

To illustrate how the numbers of separations are combined with those of positions, there is the following example (see Figure II which, for the purpose of simplification, is an abbreviated chart). A man has his Mars at 14° Cancer 07', Mercury at 14° Cancer 19' and Sun at 17° Cancer 17' in the fifth house. Mars is separated by 00°11' from Mercury, and Mercury is separated by 02°58' from the Sun. If you like, an equation, ♂ (14♋07) 00°11' ☿ (14♋19) 02°58' ☉ (17♋17) 5th house, can be written.[10] As already mentioned, the degrees are of primary significance. The degree represents the principle of the position or separation, while what that principle relates to is the minute. Some key words for this equation could be: **Energy or assertion** (children or creativity - home - in relation to marriage) the void - in relation to the unusual or odd - **communication** (children or creativity - home - in relation to career) one's own money - in relation to home - **life force** (wife's earning capacity - home - in relation to wife's earning capacity) in the sphere of children or creativity. Expressing this combination of principles, this man earns money by selling on the street (Mercury is the god of roads) the pictures which his wife creates in their home, surrounded by their six children (five of theirs and one of hers by a previous marriage).

INDIVIDUAL MEANINGS

The general zodiacal meanings of the numbers have been recorded, but their meanings in the individual chart should be evaluated as well. Though the corresponding house, sign, planet and aspect are considered when evaluating the individual meaning of a number, particular attention should be paid to the corresponding planet (placement, rulerships, aspects). For instance, this man's Venus, corresponding to 2, the number of the separation between his Mercury and Sun, is in Gemini in the third house and rules his third and eighth houses. Again, money (Venus) is associated with creativity or the ego (Sun) and communication or merchandizing (Mercury, Gemini, third house placement, third house rulership) and the wife's money (eighth house rulership). Venus is semisquare the Sun within a degree, connecting money (also love) to the ego (Sun) by an 8, Scorpio, Pluto principle, and the wife's money is highlighted once more.

Figure II – Abbreviated Chart of Man

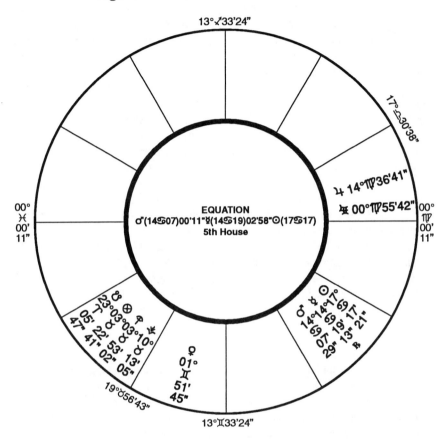

The other correspondences to 2—the second house, Taurus and the opposition—would be examined also. In the second house are the South Node in Aries and the Part of Fortune, Uranian planet Kronos, and asteroid Vesta in Taurus. How fitting that the Moon's Nodes, which are associated with close relationships, should figure in the delineation of this man's working partnership with his wife. Kronos, which is things above average, Vesta, which is vested interests, and the Part of Fortune, which is just what its name implies, being in Taurus in the second house reinforces the message—particularly since this partnership produces a lot of money! There is only one exact opposition within a degree, the Ascendant opposition Apollon (a Uranian planet), completing the picture since Apollon refers to commerce and trade.

I use asteroids and Uranian planets because they also give additional information that is highly significant. What has been written about number symbolism, in regard to the planets and points, is relevant to them too. Asteroids are minor planets, but Uranian planets may not be planets at all—just sensitive points. In the

Appendices, there are Asteroids with Glyphs and Uranian Planet Key Words. Many of the key words, but not their mythological associations, are from *Rules for Planetary Pictures* by Hans Niggemann. (I was one of the Uranian Society members who, at the suggestion of Bill Meridian, met bi-monthly from October 3, 1981 to January 15, 1983 to contribute observations on the Uranian planets that differed from the delineations recorded in *Rules*.)

The separation between Mars and the Sun has not been included in the equation because Mercury is between them, but that separation would be analyzed too. This man's Sun is 03°09' away from his Mars, and he is also very aggressive (Mars) in his merchandizing and communication (3), particularly regarding his own philosophies (9). His Mercury, corresponding to 3, is in Cancer in the fifth house, again bringing in the home and children. Mercury rules his fourth and seventh houses, once more emphasizing the home and wife. Mercury is exactly conjunct Mars, and sextile Jupiter in the seventh house. The sextile is a Virgo-type aspect of work and service, and Jupiter rules his tenth house of the career. (The third house, Gemini and exact trines would be noted too.)

Of course, the entire fifth house, where this equation is placed, could be considered in terms of children. The Mercury and Mars at 14° Cancer in the fifth house, sextile Jupiter at 14° Virgo in the seventh house, can relate to a male (♂) child. This man has a son from a previous marriage who is a Sagittarian (♐). (Also, 14 = 5 = children.)

Other Examples

Some other instances of how the numbers and their correlations can help in the interpretation of a chart are the following. My Jupiter is in the seventh house, which seems to indicate that it refers to the husband. However, Jupiter rules my tenth and is at 13° which equals 4, and both my father (4) and my mother (10) were Sagittarians, ruled by Jupiter. A client has Mercury in the tenth at 13° which equals 4, and both her father (10) and mother (4) were Virgos, ruled by Mercury. Also, her Mercury is 04°07' from her Midheaven, with the 04° referring to the mother and the Midheaven referring to the father. As for her Venus, it is in the ninth house 07°54' from her Mercury in the tenth. Her first husband has a Taurus Sun and Libra Ascendant (Venus) and a Virgo Moon (Mercury); her second has a Libra Moon and a Virgo Midheaven and stellium, including his Ascendant and Moon Rulers. The house placements and rulerships of her Venus and Mercury don't indicate that these planets refer to the partner, but the 07° separation between these planets does. (The 07° separation [or separation reduced to 07°] may relate to exact aspects of the partner instead of his or her personal points.) The additional 54' between her Mercury and Venus show a relationship of the partner principle (7) to the foreign (5 + 4 = 9), and both her husbands are foreign (her father was foreign-born). The additional 07' between her Mercury and Midheaven show a relationship of the mother principle (4) to the partner (7), which there is. (The principle of the degree is relating to the principle of the minute.)

Other Associations

Interestingly enough, 7 corresponds to the septile (51°25'42.8"), and the critical degrees, which are based on this sevenfold division of the zodiac, were used medically (51 = 6) by astrologer-doctors to determine the time of a crisis. 7 is associated with marriage (seventh house, Libra), which is involved with service (6), and which certainly is always at a "critical" stage.

As for the "7-year itch," it relates more to the number 7 than it does to the square in the Saturn Cycle at approximately seven years. Sometimes Saturn exactly squares the degree it held at the marriage or beginning of a relationship after six years, but it is commonly at seven years that there is a problem.

Synastry and Composite and Relationship Charts

Numerological analysis of the separations between two people's planets and points is very enlightening. Composite charts, which are based on the midpoints of these separations, can also profit from a consideration of the numbers.

The composite chart of my husband and myself has Jupiter at 00° Scorpio and Mars at 02° Scorpio in the fifth house of children. (For simplicity's sake, only the degrees are being considered.) We have a son, mine by a previous marriage, and a daughter, the product of this present marriage. Our son, who is a Sagittarian, is described by composite Jupiter at 00° Scorpio. Composite Jupiter is sextile within a degree the composite Moon in the third house at 29° Leo. This boy has a Cancer Ascendant, and 29° Leo is the position of his Moon. The composite Moon is exactly opposition the composite Midheaven at 29° Aquarius, which is conjunct composite Pallas at 28° Aquarius. Pallas is an asteroid that relates to perception, and our son had mixed dominance, a perceptual problem. The lack or problem is indicated by the 00°. Also, 29° equals 11 (Uranus) which is erratic, and 28° equals 10 (Saturn) which can be limiting, both of which the problem was. As for Jupiter's being in Scorpio, this sign is appropriate because our son has Pluto exactly semisquare his East Point. Our daughter is described by composite Mars at 02° Scorpio. She is a Leo, with Scorpio rising and a Taurus (2) Moon, and her Mars is exactly semisextile her Sun and North Node and quintile her Ascendant. Composite Mars is exactly inconjunct, or quincunx, the composite North Node at 02° Gemini[11] in the twelfth house, and our daughter has her Mercury (Gemini) exactly square her Moon in Taurus (2), and her Neptune (twelfth house) in Scorpio exactly square her Sun. She was an actress (twelfth house) who earned money (2) by communicating (Gemini) in association with others (North Node). She is the director of development at a motion picture company (twelfth house) who earns money (2), by choosing what scripts (Gemini) to film, in association with others (North Node). Also, composite Venus, which correlates to 02°, is exactly conjunct the composite twelfth house cusp. By the way, though the fifth house relates to children in general, it particularly relates to our children, since our daughter has a Leo Sun and our son, a Leo Moon.

Relationship charts, which are based on the time and space midpoints (rather than the degree midpoints) between charts, are similarly enhanced.

Planetary Pictures

Planetary pictures are also more precisely interpreted when the numbers are taken into account. The houses, signs and rulerships, contrary to what most cosmobiologists[12] believe, should be considered too.

For instance, two people have the planetary picture ♅ = ☿/♀ (Uranus is conjunct, opposite, square, semisquare or sesquiquadrate the midpoint of Mercury and Venus). Reinhold Ebertin gives the following definition for this picture: "Inventive ability, the gift of getting ideas, an appreciation of the necessity of reform, rhythms, periods, numbers, symbols. - A mathematician, a public speaker full of ideas and quick at repartee."[13]

The first person's Mercury/Venus midpoint is at 26° Pisces 43' in her seventh house. She has Uranus at 10° Taurus 52' in the eighth house, semisquare to the midpoint. Uranus rules the sixth house, the midpoint at 26° equals 8 and there is a 44° separation, equaling 8, between the planet and the midpoint. This woman had erratic (Uranus), nebulous (Pisces) money (Taurus) problems regarding her father (10). She now works (10 and sixth house) with her husband (seventh house), and there are erratic (Uranus), nebulous (Pisces) problems regarding her husband's money (eighth house, and midpoint and separation between planet and midpoint equaling 8).

The second person's Mercury/Venus midpoint is at 17° Pisces 19' in his seventh house, while Uranus is conjunct this point at 16° Pisces 54', also in the seventh. The separation between the planet and midpoint is 00°. 16° equals 7 which is his wife in particular and his partnerships in general. Here Uranus rules the seventh house. The man is a musician ("rhythms, periods, numbers, symbols") who is involved in musical (Pisces) partnerships, and he has an *idealistic* (Pisces) marriage to a wife with an Aquarius (Uranus) Ascendant. (Pisces can be idealistic, as well as nebulous, and some of the picture's *energies* being expressed through a personal point of the partner—Aquarius Ascendant—helps.) The midpoint 17° Pisces 19' should be taken into account. 17 equals 8 which relates to the partner's money, but which, particularly since the midpoint (8) and planet (7) are exactly conjunct, also adds great Scorpionic power to the musical and marriage partnerships.

This woman and this man are both "full of ideas and quick at repartee," but in one instance there is emphasis on money and the father or career (Uranus in Taurus, equaling 10) and in the other, emphasis on musical and idealistic partnership (Uranus in Pisces, equaling 7). Both midpoints are in Pisces in the seventh house and equal 8 (Scorpio), but in the first case 8 is the addition of 2 and 6 (a Taurus and Virgo influence) and in the second case, 1 and 7 (an Aries and Libra influence). The minutes add greater shading. In each case the numbers (in combination with the houses, signs and rulerships) help the astrologer determine how the meaning of the picture will manifest.

(The numerological method may seem complex, but so is life and so are people. Using timed charts is more complicated than using solar charts, but it is much more informative. The numbers refine our interpretations even further.)

Regarding the orb in planetary pictures, I take aspects to the midpoint that are within a degree. The aspects are the conjunction, opposition, square, semisquare and sesquiquadrate, and, as explained before, "within a degree" means at the degree where the aspect is exact or the adjacent degrees (see pages 5-6). I discontinued using a 01° orb after finding descriptive pictures eliminated with it, while not finding non-descriptive pictures added with the aspects within a degree technique. (The average orb with this technique is $01^1/_2°$.)

Moreover, contrary to what many astrologers say, all planetary pictures are not "equal." A conjunction equaling the midpoint is different from an opposition, square, semisquare or sesquiquadrate equaling it. A planetary picture formed by a Grand Trine is different from one formed by a T-Square. Again, the difference is in the numbers. A T-Square, since it is composed of an opposition ($^1/_2$ of the zodiac) and 2 squares ($^1/_4$ of the zodiac), is both Taurean and Cancerian. A planetary picture formed by a T-Square combines these qualities too. A Grand Trine, since it is composed of 3 trines of 120° (which is $^1/_3$ of the zodiac), is very Mercurial, very Geminian—flowing like the quicksilver that is Gemini's metal. A Grand Trine planetary picture partakes of this Mercurial quality. (Of course, the 120° of the separation gives the Mercuriality a Neptunian cast.)

Examining a House

Speaking of 3's, an examination of the third house in terms of writing and communication may be in order. When examining a house even the cusp should be considered. My third house cusp is 13° Taurus 03' (13 = 4 = home). The separation between the cusp and Mercury is 13°, again emphasizing the home. Mercury is at 27° Taurus 01' (27 = 9 = publishing). Mercury is 03° from the Moon (3 = writing). The Moon is at 00° Gemini 21' (00° = the void and usually the desire to fill it). The Moon is 02° from the Sun, which brings in the idea of values and possibly money. The Sun is at 02° Gemini 34' which again equals values and money. The Sun is 05° from the fourth house cusp, equaling creativity. An evaluation that comes out of this numerological analysis of the third house is: creative writing in the home which will be published and which will express values and perhaps make money. (The minutes of the cusps, planets and separations between them reinforce this interpretation. What the principle of the degrees relates to is the minutes.)

Applying vs. Separating and Dexter vs. Sinister

Now for another analysis. There have long been questions as to whether an aspect is different when it is applying, as opposed to separating, and dexter (right), as opposed to sinister (left).[14] My feeling is that the differences which have been noted are mainly attributable to the fact that the angular separation in exact aspects is different from the angular separation in inexact aspects. For instance, a square will equal 9 when it is exact, 8 when it is at 89° and 10 when it is at 91°. Of course, an applying, separating, dexter or sinister square can be either 89° or 91°, so the difference is just coincident with the application or separation, and right or left position.

Possibly though, since an applying aspect in the natal chart will become exact in the progressed chart when the native is young and impressionable, the applying aspect may have greater consequence. Incidentally, the concept of progressions— a day is equivalent to a year—has long seemed "odd." However, studying number symbolism, you realize that 1 day is similar to 1 month, is similar to 1 year. All 1s are related, so are all 2s, etc.— that is why a day for a year progressions work.

Significance of Birth Time and Date

And all numbers are significant—not just the numbers in the horoscope. The birth time is very meaningful. The time gives the quality of that moment. A person or event is born at that time because the person or event is in sync with that moment. 01:14 AM is recorded on my birth certificate. This is Daylight Saving Time. When this fabricated time is in effect, it represents what is external, while Standard Time represents what is internal, or what is behind the surface. The 1 o'clock Daylight Saving Time indicates that externally I am assertive. The 12 o'clock Standard Time, which is behind it, indicates that internally I am idealistic. What is behind the assertiveness is often idealism.

On page 6 I wrote, "The degree represents the principle of the position or separation, while what that principle relates to is the minute." In the case of time, I've found the hour is analogous to the degree, while the minute of time is analogous to the minute of arc. Therefore, the external principle of my birth time is first house, Aries, Mars, conjunction, in relation to fifth house, etc. In general, this principle could be assertiveness in relation to children or creativity. The internal principle is twelfth house, Pisces, Neptune, semisextile, in relation to fifth house, etc. In general, this principle could be idealism in relation to children or creativity. The correlated factors in my chart give information as to what these principles mean to me in particular. For instance, both my Mars and Neptune are in Virgo in the seventh house. This placement indicates that the assertiveness, and idealism on which it is based, are in service to others. The Mars is at 09°, so the assertive service to others is expansive. The Neptune, on which the assertiveness is based, is at 07°, so the idealistic service to others is shared. Since this assertive idealistic service is in relation to children or creativity, my Sun must be considered. My Sun is at 02° Gemini in the third house, so the assertive idealistic service could be in relation to persistent communication either with my children or through my creativity. Further analysis of the #1, #12 and #5 factors in my chart would give greater detail.

The birth date should be taken into account too. My birth date is May 24, 1933, with May being the 5th month, 24 equaling 6, and 1933 equaling 7 (1 + 9 + 3 + 3 = 16 = 7). The year is analogous to the degree or hour. The month is analogous to the minute of arc or time, and the day, which is the most specific, to the second of arc or time. The principle of my birth date is seventh house, etc., in relation to fifth house, etc., in regard to sixth house, etc., which in general could be partnership in relation to children or creativity, in regard to service. (As always, study the chart for particularity.) Note the similarities between my birth time and birth date.

Numerology

I look at the numbers separately, but they may be added together. Numerologists sum the month, day and year of birth to get the Life Path or Path of Destiny. In my case the sum would be 9, the Jupiter number. My Jupiter is in the seventh house at 13° Virgo, and the major purpose and meaning in my life has been service (Virgo) through marriage (seventh house) and motherhood (13 = 4). The other 9-equivalencies should be noted for further detail.

You can take the numerological Personal Year, which is the addition of the current year to the sum of your birth month and day, and find the correspondence as well. (You can use any of the traditional numerological techniques and apply the prescribed astrological analogue for added insight into these techniques.)

Reflections of the Zodiacal Numbers

Also, your age at the time of an event—marriage, birth, death, etc.—is significant and relates, in terms of your age, to the house, sign, planet and aspect that correspond to that number. For instance, I was eighteen years of age at the time of my first marriage, so the ninth house, Sagittarius, Jupiter and novile in my natal chart will demonstrate what that age meant to me. (There will be a coloration of 1 and 8, with the initial number, 1, being more prominent.) The separation between your age and the age of another person follows suit. The separation between my age and my second husband's is nine years, two months and twenty-seven days, emphasizing the 9 correlates again. The principle is 9 (completion), in relation to 2 (love), in regard to 9 (completion).

Another reflection of the numbers of the zodiac is the number of people at a gathering. For three and a half years I belonged to a group of eleven astrologers and one psychiatrist who met once a month to discuss astrological counseling problems. When there were twelve of us present, the group was very Neptunian. When several people left, and there were only eight, there was a Scorpionic influence and greater dynamism (the semisquare had replaced the semisextile). As the number of people changed, the vibration of the group changed.

In similar fashion, the numerical sequence of events or people in your life is described by the zodiacal analogy. Your first love affair or marriage is usually more Martian; your second, more Venusian; your third, more Mercurial, etc. Of course, the individual chart must be considered—your Mars might be in Taurus, and your Venus in Aries, affecting the analysis. Your first love affair or lover, marriage or marriage partner, is represented by your first house, Aries, Mars, conjunction; your second, by your second house, Taurus, Venus, opposition. Your second lover might be your first husband. In relation to love affairs, he is represented by the second house; in relation to marriage, by the first. Though the seventh is the house of the marriage partner, the first house, along with Aries, Mars and the conjunction, illustrates what the principle of the number 1 means to you. Your first husband or marriage is, therefore, described generally by your seventh house and specifically by your first.

Primacy of Numbers

Number symbolism is the principal factor in the revelation of what is hidden. Our lives are made up of numbers— the positive and the negative, the spaces that are filled and the ones that are vacant—the bodies and the separations between them. It is by analyzing the numbers that we come to know the measure of our lives and of ourselves. That is the reason why I have tried to reveal the primacy of numbers and their primary connection with the zodiac in Chapter 1 (1st house, Aries, Mars, conjunction).

CHAPTER TWO

Harmonics

It is fitting that harmonics should be the subject of Chapter 2 (2nd house, Taurus, Venus, opposition). Harmonics are very much allied to number symbolism, since they are just another way of looking at the numbers, and what better way to evaluate (2nd house, Taurus, Venus) anything than from a point opposite it (opposition).

Harmonics is a term borrowed from music and science, that in the case of astrology refers to the 360° circle and its divisions or aspects. The 1st harmonic of the 360° chart is 360°, or the division of 360 by 1, and equates to the conjunction of the planets and/or points. The 2nd harmonic of the 360° chart is 180°, or the division of 360 by 2, and equates to the opposition. The other harmonics follow this same pattern. For harmonics 1-12 the results of the divisions of 360° can be seen under the heading "# of Degrees" on page 2.

Harmonic Devices

There are various devices for finding which planets and/or points are separated by the aspect of the harmonic. For instance, the 5th harmonic magnified chart, circular dial, planet sort or graph will reveal the factors which are either conjunct or 72° or 144° apart by showing them as conjunct. The 72° aspect is the quintile, which is $^1/_5$ of 360°, and the 144° aspect is the biquintile, which is $^2/_5$ of 360°. 144° is the only multiple of 72° that occurs before 180°. Usually, the closer angular separations, less than 180°, are considered. 216° (which is $^3/_5$ of 360°) would be 144°, and 288° (which is $^4/_5$ of 360°) would be 72°, on the other side of 180°.

The angular separations or arclengths of the harmonics from 1-16, including their multiples, are as follows:

Table II – Arclengths

HARMONIC	1	2	3	4	5	6	7	8
1	360° (0°)							
2	180°							
3	120°							
4	90°	180°						
5	72°	144°						
6	60°	120°	180°					
7	51°25'42.8"	102°51'25"	154°17'08.5"					
8	45°	90°	135°	180°				
9	40°	80°	120°	160°				
10	36°	72°	108°	144°	180°			
11	32°43'38.1"	65°27'16.3"	98°10'54.5"	130°54'32"	163°38'10"			
12	30°	60°	90°	120°	150°	180°		
13	27°41'32.3"	55°23'04.61"	83°04'36.92"	110°46'09.2"	138°27'41"	166°09'13.8"		
14	25°42'51.4"	51°25'42.8"	77°08'34.29"	102°51'25"	128°34'17"	154°1'08.5"	180°	
15	24°	48°	72°	96°	120°	144°	168°	
16	22°30'	45°	67°30'	90°	112°30'	135°	157°30'	180°
MULTIPLES	1	2	3	4	5	6	7	8

The underlined arclengths are the ones unique to that harmonic

THE MAGNIFIED CHART

The magnified chart is constructed by translating the longitude of the planets and points into absolute longitude, which begins with 00° Aries, and multiplying those numbers by the number of the harmonic. (My Sun is 02° Gemini 34'50.88", which is 62°34'50.88" in absolute longitude. This is the translation of my Sun's four-place decimal position. With computer precision, 62°34'50.88" X 5 = 312°54'15.12", or 12° Aquarius 54'.) As a result a new chart is created. This new chart can be used for the purpose of seeing aspects. For instance, all conjunctions within 05° in the 5th harmonic chart will be either conjunct, quintile or biquintile within 01° in the original chart. (The original positions have been multiplied by 5.) However, aspects can be seen much more easily in other forms. Planet sorts and graphs for harmonics, as well as circular dials, display the aspects without magnification. The construction of graphs and dials will be outlined in the latter half of this chapter.

Magnification of meaning is another purpose for which the magnified chart can be used. What the magnified chart gives you, which the other aspect finders cannot give you, is a complete transformation of the chart. It is as if a high intensity magnifying glass had been placed over the original chart. And the consequent transformation, with its new degrees, signs, houses and aspects, is descriptive of the meaning of that harmonic in relation to the original chart.

Meanings of the Harmonics

After studying harmonics since September 1976, I have concluded that the meanings of the harmonics are essentially the same as the meanings of the numbers. Some examples are the 5th and 15th harmonic. The 5th harmonic is the quintile aspect, and like 5 it corresponds to the 5th house, Leo and the Sun and would focus on creativity, children, love affairs and entertainment. The 15th harmonic is the quindecile aspect (not the sextile), but like 15 it corresponds to the 6th house, Virgo and Mercury and would focus on physical health, work, service and criticality. The second column of Table IV, on page 36, gives references of the harmonics.

Calculation of Magnified Charts

Before explaining how I came to this conclusion, let me explain further how to calculate harmonics and discuss some problems connected with them. As illustrated, the harmonic mathematical procedure is merely a matter of translating the zodiacal longitude of the planets and points into absolute longitude (beginning with 00° Aries), multiplying those numbers by the number of the harmonic, and then translating the resultant numbers back to zodiacal longitude. If a number is larger than 360°, before translating to zodiacal longitude, multiples of 360 are subtracted until the number is less than 360°. The following table gives 60 multiples of 360, which should be all you'll need.

Table III – 360° Multiples

1.	360	16.	5760	31.	11160	46.	16560
2.	720	17.	6120	32.	11520	47.	16920
3.	1080	18.	6480	33.	11880	48.	17280
4.	1440	19.	6840	34.	12240	49.	17640
5.	1800	20.	7200	35.	12600	50.	18000
6.	2160	21.	7560	36.	12960	51.	18360
7.	2520	22.	7920	37.	13320	52.	18720
8.	2880	23.	8280	38.	13680	53.	19080
9.	3240	24.	8640	39.	14040	54.	19440
10.	3600	25.	9000	40.	14400	55.	19800
11.	3960	26.	9360	41.	14760	56.	20160
12.	4320	27.	9720	42.	15120	57.	20520
13.	4680	28.	10080	43.	15480	58.	20880
14.	5040	29.	10440	44.	15840	59.	21240
15.	5400	30.	10800	45.	16200	60.	21600

To calculate the harmonics without multiplication, *Harmonic Chart Tables* by John Addey can be used. He gives a table for the degrees and one for the minutes, and by simple addition the harmonic positions can be derived. I first availed myself of these tables but later ordered the harmonic positions for over 500 charts from Astro because they calculate the seconds. (When only the degrees and minutes are considered, my 24th harmonic Sun is 02° Gemini 00', instead of 01° Gemini 56' when the degrees, minutes and seconds are calculated.) With a calculator the procedure, including computing the seconds, is relatively easy, particularly with a calculator that converts from decimals to degrees, minutes and seconds. A calculator or my computer is what I now use for asteroids whose positions are not offered by Astro. (100-year custom ephemerides of these asteroids are offered.) My investigation of asteroids is discussed in Chapter 3.

Accuracy

Though harmonic computation is simple, accuracy in the original positions is especially important because any error in them is magnified in the harmonic chart. There are those who would argue that ephemerides and birth data aren't accurate enough, even without magnification, for consideration of the minutes of the planets and cusps. However, some ephemerides now list the minutes with one decimal place,[1] and charts ordered from Astro give the minutes and seconds of the Sun, Moon and planets and the minutes with one decimal place of the points and asteroids. Also, in the harmonic options, four-place decimal listing of the positions is available. Neil Michelsen, to assist me in my research, has provided me with four-place decimal listing of the positions of the planets, points, cusps, asteroids Ceres, Pallas, Juno, Vesta and Chiron and Uranian planets in all the charts, harmonic or otherwise, that I have ordered. (The translation of the four-place decimals could occasionally be one second more or less than the translation of the up to fourteen-place decimals that the computer is calculating internally.) Since December 1, 1989, Astro's planetary calculations of Sun through Pluto have been based on the Jet Propulsion Laboratories' ephemeris data. Since 1984, the JPL data has been used by the US Almanac Office.

DELTA T CORRECTION

In regard to ephemerides, another factor to consider is that many are based on Ephemeris Time, which assumes that the rotation of the Earth is constant. Since it is not, the Delta T Correction must be made. Delta T is the difference between Ephemeris Time and Universal Time, also known as Greenwich Mean Time. *The American Ephemeris for the 20th Century* is based on Universal Time, so if this ephemeris is used the Delta T Correction does not have to be made. The perturbations in the Earth's rotation must be observed to determine exactly what the Delta T is. Analysis of observations of lunar occultations of stars, eclipses of the Sun, and transits of Mercury has resulted in revised values for Delta T. The last observed value is +55.5816s for July 1, 1987. Since the summer of 1987, when this new data became available, Astro has been implementing it. A new edition of *The American Ephemeris* with this new data, and the new JPL data, was published at the beginning of 1988. (The new edition implemented the new JPL data before the chart services did.)

GEOMETRIC POSITIONS

Geometric positions of the Sun, Moon, planets and asteroids will further promote exactitude. The geometric positions are where the Sun, Moon, planets and asteroids really are. The apparent positions, which are what most astrologers use, are where these bodies appear to be. When we look at the sky we are seeing where the bodies were at the time the light left that body to travel to Earth. The further a body is from the Earth, the longer its light takes to travel to Earth. It takes the light of Pluto approximately four hours, so what we are getting with the apparent position of Pluto is where Pluto was four hours ago. Consequently, the natal geometric positions are always further along in the zodiac, unless the body is retrograde.

In 1972 when Neil Michelsen first began processing orders at his newly-founded Astro Computing Services, all charts were calculated geometrically because the geometric positions are the astronomically correct ones. In the Fall of 1975, due to complaints from some client-astrologers used to calculating from the apparent positions in ephemerides, Neil changed to apparent positions. No one noticed, other than the "complainants" and myself. As a result of my noticing, Neil restored the geometric option, but this restoration is one of astrology's best-kept secrets! Neil referred to this option as the "Nona Press Option" because I am the only one who knows about it. Hopefully, the publishing of my book will make other people aware of the greater accuracy of the geometric positions. Certainly, it will make them aware that there is such an option.

There is one other astrologer who uses geometric positions. I first discovered that someone shared my predilection, upon hearing the English astrologer Geoffrey Cornelius speak at a conference in the summer of 1980. Cornelius casts charts, as I do, for the exact minute and second of events. He said that if the geometric positions are used, the chart is exactly synchronous with the event. He gave the following examples. In the Wedding of Princess Anne at the exact moment that the name "Father" in the phrase "In the name of the Father" was pronounced, the Sun was on the Midheaven to the second. In the coronation of Elizabeth II at the exact moment the crown was placed on Elizabeth's brow, Jupiter was on the Midheaven to the second. Perhaps, the reason that both Cornelius and I have come to the same conclusion is that we are both involved with the synchronicity of the moment.

And, perhaps geometric charts are "an idea whose time has come." In *Asteroid-World: Fall 1987,* Zip Dobyns writes of casting charts for Earth conjunctions with Venus, Mars, Saturn, Uranus and Pluto. These are geocentric charts with heliocentric planetary positions added. (Earth conjunctions as seen from the Sun are the same as Sun oppositions as seen from the Earth.) Zip says differences of up to 19 minutes were found for the timing of the aspects when the ACS geocentric ephemerides with apparent positions were compared to the later ACS heliocentric ephemeris with geometric positions. The geometric positions, which yielded an impressive number of exact aspects to the angles, were used.

All my ACS charts are calculated geometrically, with the exception of some of the asteroids in some of the charts. My computer is not programmed to calculate geometrically,[2] and it is difficult to determine the Astronomical Unit (A.U.) distances of the asteroids without a computer. Therefore, the asteroids other than the twenty Astro offers for individual charts, are not always calculated geometrically. (The twenty asteroids are Ceres, Pallas, Juno, Vesta, Chiron, Amor, Dembowska, Diana, Dudu, Eros, Frigga, Hidalgo, Icarus, Lilith, Pandora, Pittsburghia, Psyche, Sappho, Toro and Urania.)

There is a new option, called *Many Interesting Asteroids*, which has 468 asteroids listed in zodiacal sequence for any birth time and date between 1880 and 2005. This option can be ordered with geometric positions, and the asteroids are now listed with the one-place decimal. All of these asteroids in my charts which have been magnified, and in the Figures, have the geometric positions.

The difference between the geometric and the apparent positions of the Sun, Moon, planets and asteroids is seconds. In planet and asteroid returns, the seconds difference between the geometric and apparent position of the planet or asteroid can make degrees differences in the angles. The asteroids for which returns are calculated by Astro are Ceres, Pallas, Juno, Vesta and Chiron. Returns of the True Lunar Node, Halley's Comet (for this century), Transpluto,[3] the Uranian planets and Dark Moon Lilith[4] are also cast.

My geometric charts, calculated by Astro, are now with nutation (wobble of the Earth) correction, which I have found a valuable refinement. Even the Uranian planets, Transpluto, Dark Moon Lilith and Halley's Comet have this correction.

In calculating Dark Moon Lilith, whether geometric or apparent, Astro uses an astronomical orbit. The difference between Astro's positions and those of the published ephemerides can be more than three degrees. I have compared the non-astronomical positions with the astronomical positions and found the latter far superior. An improvement in the calculation of the positions of the Uranian planets went into effect at Astro in May 1989. I have also found these new positions preferable, and the Figures, and any charts that have been magnified, have this improvement. (The *Uranian Transneptune Ephemeris 1850-2050*, with these improved calculations by Neil Michelsen, was published the summer of 1989 by Fritz Reider Uranian Publications.)

TIMING

As for the contention that birth data is not accurate enough to make fine distinctions, it is true that if the time is recorded only to the minute, the natal position of a planet that moves 1 degree per day can not be accurate to the second. 60 minutes of arc per day divided by 1440 minutes of time per day equals .0416666 or 00'02"30 or $02^1/_2$ seconds of arc per minute of time. If a planet moves $^1/_2$ a degree per day, it would move $01^1/_4$ seconds each minute, so you probably could get the correct second. The 1st harmonic chart equates to the natal chart. For the 2nd-11th harmonic positions of a planet that moves a degree a day, you could get the correct minute. The 12th harmonic position would be outside the limit.

However, when the time of an event is recorded to a second of time, the natal positions of the planets, at least theoretically, can be accurate to a second of arc. The 2nd-719th harmonic positions of planets that move a degree a day could be accurate to a minute of arc. The 720th harmonic positions would be outside the limit (60 x 12).

In the recent past the most accurate birth time one could expect was the hour. Now we have the minute, but the seconds are not recorded at birth or at most events. An exception is those events, such as airplane crashes, stock market transactions, input and output of computer data, which are recorded electronically. In the future, the second may be what is expected. In the meantime, I, like Cornelius, have recorded the exact hour, minutes and seconds of events that I have observed. The greater accuracy in the chart is revealing. The minutes of the angles change, since the Midheaven usually moves about 15' of arc in one minute of time. The degree is the principle, and the minute (the second also) is what that principle relates to, so the meanings of the angles change.

As explained previously, even the time of the event has meaning. (The hour would then be equivalent to the degree.) During a wedding I attended, the ring was given at 01:23:35 PM, and the pronouncement was made at 01:25:52 PM. The time of the ring-giving correlates to the 1st house, Aries, Mars, conjunction principle, in relation to the 5th house, Leo, Sun, quintile, in regard to the 8th house, Scorpio, Pluto, semisquare. The time of the marriage pronouncement correlates to the 1st house, Aries, Mars, conjunction principle, in relation to the 7th house, Libra, Venus, septile, in regard to the 7th house, Libra, Venus, septile. Consequently, I thought pregnancy would be an imminent occurrence. The transiting positions of the correlated factors would give greater information. However, the 8 (3 + 5) points to regeneration. The repetition three times of the number 5, and the addition of 2 + 3 to make 5 puts the emphasis of the partnership (2 + 5 and 5 + 2) on children. The 1s give the immediacy. Of course, this prediction was not told to the couple, yet within two months the bride was pregnant.

As for the objection that we don't know when the moment of marriage is, I consider the moment of completion of the pronouncement as the moment. Nevertheless, as in the example above, I often record several different moments. At Jewish weddings I have recorded the moment of the breaking of the glass. Each different time is descriptive of the different event.

For the birth of a baby, the baby's complete emergence would seem the time. Some astrologers contend that the first breath is the time of birth, and surely this moment is significant. However, according to *Principles and Practice of Obstetrics* the baby breathes before it is born, and it is considered born even with asphyxia. On the other hand, at its emergence the baby has been born, as a new entity, into the world. With my own children, I was awake at both deliveries and looked at the clock on the wall when the doctor said at the first delivery, "You have a baby boy," and at the second delivery, "You have a baby girl." The time I saw on the clock was the same as the time on the birth certificate. Unfortunately, I was not aware of the importance of the seconds at that time.

I have one case of an accurately timed death. Usually the recorded time of death is the time certified by the doctor or ambulance attendant and so is later than the death. In this case, the person died at home with most of his family around the bed. One of his sisters heard the death rattle cease. The sister looked at their mother who had been feeling his pulse as she held his hand. She nodded, and the sister knew that meant he was dead. She looked at the bedroom clock, and the time was 01:35 AM. One of the daughters ran to the living room to look at the clock on the video cassette recorder, which has to be accurate to record TV programs, and the time was 01:36 AM. The death was assumed to be 01:35:30 AM. The seconds may not be exact, but they are sufficiently accurate for us to believe that the minutes are.

For several years I've recorded, usually to the second, the times of ordinary occurrences, as well as of special events. Among what has been recorded are the times of the beginning and end of all phone calls made and received by myself and most of the times of my sending, receiving and reading material, visiting places and buying products. Also, I've observed the times other people have experienced such occurrences and persuaded them to keep track of at least special events to the second.

When reading material I will sometimes record, not just the second of beginning the material, but the second of reading a particular word within the material. When recording the time of entering a place, I consider the moment of crossing the threshold as the moment of entry. The time of purchase is taken to be the moment the goods are paid for, or the moment the goods are in hand if the exchange of money for goods is made simultaneously. If the goods are sent, they would come under your domain the moment they cross your threshold. When recording the time of the beginning of a show, I usually consider the dimming of the lights as the moment of beginning, but if the lights are not dimmed, the moment might be that of the music playing or the curtain going up. The time gives the flavor of each moment. Sometimes what you're recording is the time of looking at your watch, but that moment has its flavor too.

Recording the hours, minutes and seconds of these seemingly less important events, I have found that their times follow the same numerical patterns as the times of major events. "Seemingly" qualifies "less important" because I'm beginning to suspect that there are no unimportant events. What seems to be unimportant may be important on a symbolic level.

Something else that I have done is set the alarm on a calculator or digital watch to buzz at the hour, minute and second of my Solar Return. (Other people have been persuaded to do the same with their own Solar Returns.) What is occurring at that moment is reflective of the meaning of the Solar Return. (The Sun's Return is synchronous with the occurrence.)

To insure accuracy, before setting the alarm, call "Time" to get the exact seconds. If the calculator or watch can't be set to the second, adjust the time accordingly, i.e., for 08:28:14 PM the clock can be set 14 seconds slow, so that when the alarm rings at 08:28 the time will really be 08:28:14.

Of course, it could be contended that the birth time may be inaccurate, so the Solar Return time may be too. As for my time, it is accurate since my mother was awake when I was born and noted the time, and her notation is the same as that recorded on my birth certificate. Nevertheless, the time was only recorded to the minute, so that time and the Solar Return time, assuming that the birth observer recorded the closer minute, may be off by as much as half a minute. This possible inaccuracy is not a valid argument against trying to be as accurate as possible, so as not to compound the inaccuracy.

The alarm technique need not be restricted to Solar Returns. The observation of other astronomical events—Lunar Returns, an eclipse or lunation, the conjunction of two planets, the crossing of an angle by a planet—is also worthwhile. If the time of the event is only known to the minute, the observation of that time can be valuable too.

More and more, the times of non-astronomical events are being supplied at least to the minute. When you purchase items at some stores the register receipt records the time of the purchase to the minute. (Sometimes the name of the salesperson and cashier will be included.) The times of long distance and credit calls are listed on your bills. Many answering devices tell the time of incoming calls. Of course, some of these times are rounded off to the closer minute, and the internal clocks which supply them may be inaccurate. (I have noted some registers which have not been adjusted for Daylight Saving Time or vice versa.) However, in the process of timing, these mechanical time keepers can be of assistance. One way is in showing the interweaving of events. Your answering device may be recording a call for you while you are purchasing an item. The synchronicity of these two events may help you to understand their synonymity—the equivalence of their meanings.

EXACT COORDINATES

When studying the meaning, whether numerical or synchronistic, of the exact hour, minutes and even seconds, you will not need the exact coordinates, since the time will be the same in the entire time zone. However, to calculate the most accurate chart possible, you will need them. Topographic maps can be used to find these exact coordinates for a birth or other event.

My realization of what a difference a slight difference in coordinates can make occurred as follows. When my chart and my children's charts were first done by Astro, the coordinates they were using for Manhattan, our birthplace, were longitude 73°W57' and latitude 40°N45'. Later, when these charts were run again (with new options), Astro had changed their coordinates for Manhattan to longitude 73°W59' and latitude 40°N46'. There were slight differences in the personal points of these charts, changing some even to a different degree (when the minutes were close to the beginning or end of a degree). According to my system of number symbolism, the original numbers were more appropriate, so I had the charts redone with the original coordinates. When I later looked at a topographic map, my coordinates were 73°W59' and 40°N45', and my children's were 74°W00' and 40°N45'. I recast the charts but decided to continue using the original charts which had the less western longitude. With less western longitude, the angles are a couple of minutes of arc later. My recollection is that there were several additional seconds of time which I didn't record when my children were born. (This may well have been the case with my mother and my birth.) The additional seconds of time would have resulted in a couple of additional minutes of arc—hence, my preference for the less western longitude. (This example illustrates the importance of recording both the exact seconds and the exact coordinates.)

IMPROVED CALCULATIONS

Another occasion I had to see improvement from small differences was in 1980 when Astro made their calculation of the outer planets even more accurate than it had been. With the recalculated charts there were differences in some of the minutes and the more accurate minutes were more fitting. The new JPL data, of course, has produced even greater precision.

In the past there weren't telescopes to observe astronomical phenomena. Now there are. In the future, telescopes will probably be even more accurate. The fact that we weren't so observant or accurate in the past is no argument against our being so observant and accurate in the present and even more so in the future.

My Discovery of Harmonics

Having discussed some of the problems of accuracy in astrology in general and harmonic charts in particular, I'm ready to give you a little background on my discovery of harmonics. I first learned about harmonics when John Addey spoke about them in New York in April 1973. I then bought his book, *Astrology Reborn*, but the lecture and the book dealt with the distribution of the Suns of 7,302 Doctors of Medicine and 1,970 British Clergy. (Another purpose for which harmonics can be used is to discover if there is a harmonic distribution characteristic of a particular group.) The strongest amplitude (percentage of the mean distribution) of the Suns of the doctors is in the 12th harmonic. The strongest amplitude of the Suns of the British Clergy is in the 7th harmonic. (The 1st harmonic has the highest amplitude in a study of 7,012 US Clergy.) Addey believed the numbers have symbolic meaning but told me he didn't know their correlation to the planets. His analysis of the solar factor in many charts was interesting, but how did one apply this analysis to an individual chart? In September 1976 at an astrology conference in England, I heard Addey speak about individual harmonic charts. Ever since, I have been doing and studying these harmonic magnifications of natal charts and find them one of the best means to "lift the veil a little."

Individual Harmonic Charts

Speaking about individual harmonic charts, Addey said that the harmonic of your age corresponds to that year of your life. In other words, there is no harmonic for the first year of life. When you become 1—that is the 1st harmonic, which is the natal chart. 2 years of age is described by the 2nd harmonic. Addey's procedure was to place the harmonic planets around the natal chart, or to make a separate chart starting with the harmonic Ascendant as the Ascendant and adding 30° for each subsequent house cusp. I followed his procedure but also tried making a separate chart starting with the harmonic Midheaven on the Midheaven, and adding 30° for each subsequent house cusp.

I tested these harmonic charts and discovered they worked. They didn't describe the year before or after, and they responded to transits. The placement of the harmonic planets around the natal chart was most effective. The reason may be that the harmonic is a view of the original chart and as such should always be looked at in conjunction with it. However, when, in addition to the natal chart with the harmonic positions around it, the Ascendant and Midheaven Equal Houses Charts are used, they are very helpful. The harmonic positions of the planets are the same. It is just the house cusps which are different, giving a different emphasis or focus to the chart.

ASCENDANT AND MIDHEAVEN EQUAL HOUSE CHARTS

The Ascendant Equal House Chart is more related to the personal life, while the Midheaven Equal House Chart is more related to the public life. There is further information on these differences in Table IV on pages 36-37. For instance, the 2nd harmonic (which has the correlation of 2, 2nd house, Taurus, Venus, opposition) refers to money, possessions, love, values and relationship. The 2nd Harmonic Ascendant Equal House Chart would be consulted for a supplementary description of love, values in regard to personal matters, and personal relationships, while the 2nd Harmonic Midheaven Equal House Chart would be consulted for a supplementary description of money, possessions, values in regard to public matters, and public relationships. These descriptions apply to both the year, and the principle, of that number.

FACTORS

The harmonic charts were done at first with the original four asteroids (Ceres, Pallas, Juno and Vesta), in addition to the ten planets, Ascendant, Midheaven, Nodes and Vertex. Then, the East Point, Part of Fortune, Uranian planets, and Transpluto (⊖)[3] were added, and I found the interpretations better with them, than without. Later, other asteroids, Dark Moon Lilith (∅)[4] and Halley's Comet (↑) were included, and the interpretations were made even more specific. The following eight Figures (III-X) have these factors. (See Appendices 1 and 2 for glyphs) The natal charts include the forty-seven asteroids synopsized in Chapter 3, and the harmonics include the original four, Chiron and six personal name asteroids. The six personal name asteroids have names that correspond to those of the people involved. The personal name asteroid study is discussed in Chapter 3. The positions of the bodies and points, whether or not they are in a Figure, are given throughout the book, so that the reader will be aware of the exact positions and aspects.

First Test: 1st and 2nd Marriage

In testing experimental techniques like harmonics, it is necessary to experiment on people you know well. As my first test of the harmonic charts, I predicted what my 18th and 24th harmonics would be like, based on what my first and second marriages were like (the first was when I was 18, and the second was when I was 24 years of age).

For my 24th harmonic (see Figure III), my prediction was that with the harmonic positions placed around my natal chart there would be a lot of emphasis on my seventh house, on Leo and Libra and on the Sun, which is the ruler of my seventh house. My 24th harmonic Sun is 01° Gemini 56', conjunct my natal Sun at 02° Gemini 34' (and my natal Moon at 00° Gemini 21', equaling my Sun/Moon midpoint). The 24th harmonic Ascendant is in Leo, and the 24th harmonic Midheaven is in Libra. (I found the harmonic Midheaven indicates the main purpose of the year or of the harmonic principle.) That harmonic Midheaven, plus two planets and two asteroids (harmonic Pallas and harmonic Juno), fall in my natal seventh house. (The other asteroid in the seventh house is a personal name asteroid that was not being used at the time of my first test.) Juno relates to marriage, and Pallas, to the law, and it is a legal marriage. The harmonic Sun is also exactly opposition harmonic Zeus, a Uranian planet, at 02° Sagittarius 03' and trine the harmonic Vertex and Antivertex at 01° Aquarius 22'. (In even-numbered harmonics, the Vertex and Antivertex are conjunct, as are the Nodes.) Zeus is associated with reproduction, and the Vertex, with fate, and it is a productive marriage—there was a child—which was probably fated.

My first marriage (the 18th harmonic, see Figure IV) was not a "partnership," so I didn't believe there would be as much emphasis on my seventh house and Libra. I thought there would be on Leo and my fifth house because a child was the main product of that marriage. The 18th harmonic Midheaven is in Leo, and only two Uranian planets (harmonic Zeus and harmonic Cupido) fall in my seventh house.

These Uranian planets are appropriate, since Cupido relates to marriage, Zeus, as already mentioned, relates to procreation, and it was a procreative marriage. In my fifth house, harmonic Uranus is exactly conjunct harmonic Ceres,[5] and sudden (Uranus) maternity (Ceres) occurred—I became pregnant a month and $^1/_2$ after my marriage. As for Libra, harmonic Zeus, Vesta, Venus and Admetos are in that sign. (There are no personal points.) Vesta is an asteroid associated with vested interests, and Admetos is a Uranian planet associated with stoppage or "going around in circles." Vesta, Venus and Admetos are in the eighth house, with Pluto there also but in Scorpio. Natally Venus and Pluto are in the 9th harmonic (40° apart). In the 18th harmonic, which is a multiple of the 9th, Venus and Pluto are still close (09°), but Admetos has now come between them, conjunct their midpoint. Venus combined with Pluto is often an obsessive love, while Admetos added to that combination might indicate being unable to break out of a repetitive cycle of obsessive love. (Though my progressed chart for the time of this marriage shows appropriate aspects for marriage, with the progressed Sun exactly trine my natal Ascendant, and the progressed Moon exactly trine my natal Venus, the 18th harmonic is appropriate on a deeper level.)

URANIAN PLANETS—POSITIVE INTERPRETATIONS

It is important to not just use the negative interpretations of the Uranian planets. In my 24th harmonic, harmonic Admetos is exactly square the harmonic Midheaven. In this case Admetos is close to Venus and Kronos, rather than to Venus and Pluto, and Kronos is a Uranian planet interpreted as "everything above average." I have noticed an association of Admetos with music (perhaps because practising and playing an instrument require "going around in circles"), and my second husband is a musician. In this same harmonic, harmonic Mercury,though not exactly conjunct harmonic Hades, is separated from it by 01° (plus minutes). Mercury is the ruler of my natal Sun and Moon (as well as the harmonic Sun), and Hades is a Uranian planet related to antiquity. What is described therefore may be a marriage (Sun and Moon) which has a karmic or past-life context (Hades).

THE PARTNER'S HARMONIC

The partner's harmonic should be examined too.[6] My second husband was 33 years old when we were married. His 33rd harmonic (see Figure V) emphasizes his natal seventh house, with the harmonic Node there at 11° Pisces 08' (conjunct my natal Antivertex at 12° Pisces 33'). Libra is emphasized with harmonic Venus, Ceres and the Part of Fortune in that sign. His natal fifth house is activated by the harmonic Midheaven at 11° Capricorn 27' and harmonic Uranus at 18° Capricorn 06' falling there. Also, harmonic Uranus is conjunct his natal Sun/Moon midpoint at 17° Capricorn 49'. In this marriage, not only did my husband eventually acquire his own child (fifth house), but he immediately became a father (Capricorn) to a stepchild (Uranus and 11°). The emphasis on my husband's Sun/Moon midpoint is appropriate because not only does the Sun/Moon midpoint refer to marriage, but his Sun/Moon midpoint equals my Sun/Moon midpoint.

Figure III – 24th Harmonic around Natal Chart of the Writer

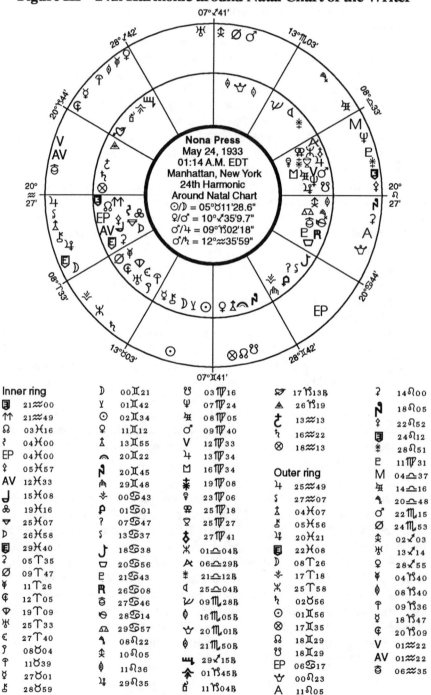

Nona Press
May 24, 1933
01:14 A.M. EDT
Manhattan, New York
24th Harmonic
Around Natal Chart
☉/☽ = 05°♉11'28.6"
♀/♂ = 10°♐35'9.7"
♂/♃ = 09°♑02'18"
♂/♄ = 12°♒35'59"

Inner ring							
🝐	21♒00	☽	00♊21	☊	03♍16	♋	17♑13R	?	14♌00
⇈	21♒49	Y	01♊42	♆	07♍24	⟁	26♑19	N	18♌05
♌	03♓16	☉	02♊34	⛢	08♍05	♏	13♒13	♀	22♌52
?	04♓00	♀	11♊12	♂	09♍40	♄	16♒22	🝐	24♌12
EP	04♓00	♎	13♊55	V	12♍33	⊗	18♒13	✳	28♌51
♀	05♓57	♎	20♊22	♃	13♍34			P	11♍31
AV	12♓33	N	20♊45	M	16♍34	Outer ring		M	04♎37
J	15♓08	♏	29♊48	✳	19♍08	♃	25♒49	⛢	14♎16
☊	19♓16	⚹	00♋43	♀	23♍06	S	27♒07	⚹	20♎48
▽	25♓07	P	01♋01	♀	25♍18	♐	04♓07	♂	22♏15
☽	26♓58	?	07♋47	☿	25♍27	♂	05♓56	Ø	24♏53
🝐	29♓40	S	13♋37	☿	27♍41	♃	20♓21	♈	02♐03
?	05♈35	J	18♋38	⛢	01♎04R	🝐	22♓08	♅	13♐14
Ø	09♈47	▽	20♋56	⋏	06♎29R	☽	08♈26	♀	28♐55
♀	11♈26	P	21♋43	✳	21♎12R	⚹	17♈18	♀	04♑40
☽	12♈05	R	26♋08	☽	25♎04R	♅	25♈58	◊	08♑40
♀	19♈09	☉	27♋46	♇	09♏28R	♄	02♉56	♈	09♑36
♅	25♈33	⊖	28♋14	◊	16♏05R	☉	01♊56	♉	18♑47
∊	27♈40	♎	29♋57	♅	20♏01R	⊗	17♊35	♀	20♑09
?	08♉04	♌	08♌22	◊	21♏50R	☊	18♊29	V	01♒22
♈	11♉39	♏	10♌05	ᛘ	29♐15R	☊	18♊29	AV	01♒22
☿	27♉01	◊	11♌36	⛰	01♑45R	EP	06♋17	⊖	06♒35
♃	28♉59	♃	29♌35	☿	11♑04R	♒	00♌23		
						A	11♌05		

07°♐41'
28°♑42'
20°♑44'
20° ♒ 27'
08°♏33'
13°♏03'
13°♉03'
28°♊42'
20°♋44'
08°♊33'
20° ♌ 27'
13°♍03'
07°♊41'

Figure IV – 18th Harmonic around Natal Chart of the Writer

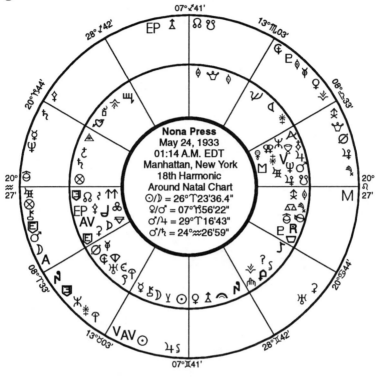

Inner ring

🝛	21≈00	☽	00♊21	☋	03♍16	⟋	17♑13ᴿ	♅	09♋56
⇞	21≈49	⚹	01♊42	♆	07♍24	⬠	26♑19	?	10♋30
☊	03♓16	☉	02♊34	⯓	08♍05	⚷	13≈13	M	18♌28
⚹	04♓00	♀	11♊12	♂	09♍40	♄	16≈22	⬆	00♍36
EP	04♓00	⚷	13♊55	V	12♍33	⊗	18≈13	♃	22♍46
⚶	05♓57	⟋	20♊22	♃	13♍34			∅	26♍09
AV	12♓33	⯒	20♊45	⊔	16♍34	**Outer ring**		♆	00♎17
⌿	15♓08	♏	29♊48	⯝	19♍08	⯓	25≈42	⚷	01♎32
⯒	19♓16	⯐	00♋43	⯞	23♍06	⊗	28≈11	⯝	12♎58
▽	25♓07	♇	01♋01	♇	25♍18	⟋	11♓57	♀	21♎41
☽	26♓58	?	07♋47	⚸	25♍27	🝛	24♓06	⚹	26♎00
🝛	29♓40	⟋	13♋37	⚶	27♍41	♂	24♓11	◐	29♎00
?	05♈35	☌	18♋38	⛢	01♎04ᴿ	☽	06♈19	ⴹ	01♏08
∅	09♈47	⯐	20♋56	⯘	06♎29ᴿ	A	08♈19	♁	07♏36
⚹	11♈26	ⴹ	21♋43	⯝	21♎12ᴿ	⯒	13♈33	☊	28♏52
♁	12♈05	⯒	26♋08	⬦	25♎04ᴿ	🝛	18♈09	☋	28♏52
♀	19♈09	◐	27♋46	♏	09♏28ᴿ	⚸	19♈28	⚷	10♐35
♅	25♈33	◑	28♋14	◐	16♏05ᴿ	⚶	21♈38	EP	12♐13
⚵	27♈40	⯝	29♋57	⯝	20♏01ᴿ	♈	29♈42	⚶	17♑09
⟋	08♉04	⬆	08♌22	◑	21♏50ᴿ	V	16♉01	♄	24♑42
♈	11♉39	⚷	10♌05	⯲	29♐15ᴿ	AV	16♉01	♅	06≈35
♀	27♉01	◐	11♌36	⯰	01♑45ᴿ	☉	16♉27	♆	13≈17
⚷	28♉58	♃	29♌35	⯒	11♑04ᴿ	♃	04♊22	◐	19≈56
						⟋	05♊20		

Figure V – 33rd Harmonic around Natal Chart of Sy Press

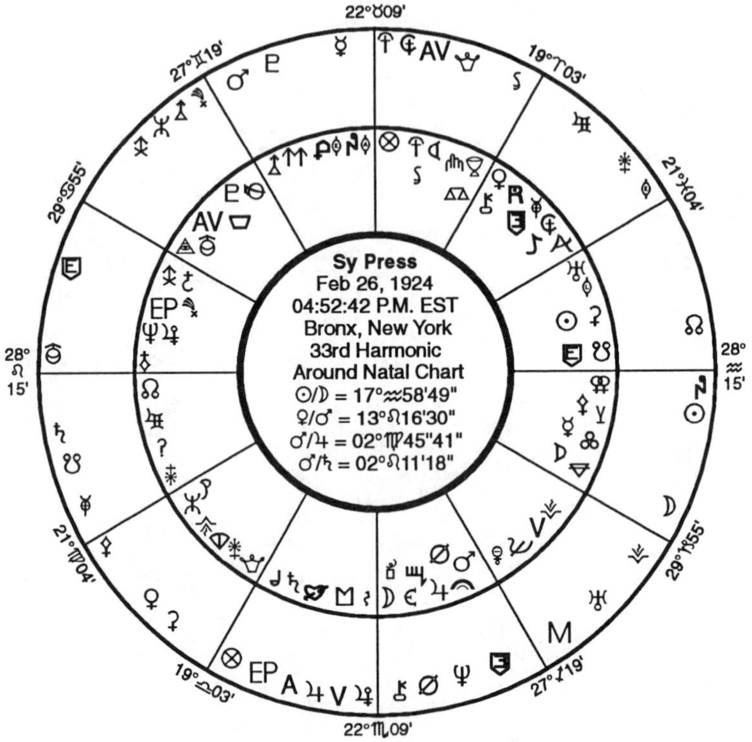

22°♉09'
19°♈03'
21°♓04'
28° ♒ 15'
29°♑55'
27°♐19'
22°♏09'
19°♎03'
21°♍04'
28° ♌ 15'
29°♋55'
27°♊19'
Sy Press
Feb 26, 1924
04:52:42 P.M. EST
Bronx, New York
33rd Harmonic
Around Natal Chart
☉/☽ = 17°♒58'49"
♀/♂ = 13°♌16'30"
♂/♃ = 02°♍45"41"
♂/♄ = 02°♌11'18"

Inner ring

☊ 02♍09
⯡ 03♍05℞
? 13♍01℞
⚹ 17♍10℞
⚳ 24♍25℞
⯤ 27♍26
⯧ 29♍19℞
⯢ 29♍43
✳ 16♎20℞
♕ 17♎29℞
J 24♎43℞
♄ 02♏07℞
⯨ 03♏37
M 03♏43
⚸ 16♏07℞
☽ 28♏35
⯣ 03♐30
∈ 04♐28
⯥ 07♐52
♃ 17♐36
Ø 18♐14
⌒ 20♐23
♂ 24♐22

⚵ 29♐34
⯦ 18♑57
V 20♑22
⯬ 22♑39
D 05♒13
▽ 10♒36
♣ 16♒27
☿ 18♒13
Y 20♒32
⚴ 21♒39
⚤ 21♒40
E 01♓06
☋ 02♓09
☉ 07♓03
⚷ 14♓01
⚶ 16♓37
♅ 16♓54
A 23♓40
⚳ 01♈21
J 02♈56
⯠ 05♈04
Ǝ 07♈49
R 13♈29

♀ 16♈25
⚷ 18♈04
⚖ 20♈10
⚱ 21♈49
⯰ 26♈24
ɑ 28♈52
ϛ 03♉24
⚲ 04♉07
⊗ 19♉47
⚶ 27♉01
⯎ 04♊19
⚶ 05♊24
⯏ 05♊33
↑↑ 07♊57
⯫ 08♊18
⊖ 03♋32
♇ 10♋22℞
▽ 15♋03℞
AV 20♋22
⊖ 23♋30℞
▲ 28♋29℞
ξ 00♌38℞
⯩ 03♌02℞

⯪ 13♌34℞
EP 17♌18
⚴ 17♌51℞
♆ 18♌30℞
⚵ 20♌05℞

Outer ring

♄ 09♍54
☋ 11♍08
⯠ 17♍22
⚴ 24♍47
♀ 02♎04
⚷ 12♎43
⊗ 23♎01
EP 00♏56
A 02♏23
♃ 11♏03
V 12♏36
⚴ 19♏22
⚷ 26♏20
Ø 01♐50
♆ 10♐52
Ǝ 18♐08
M 11♑27

♅ 18♑06
⯬ 27♑52
☽ 13♒17
☉ 22♒39
⯎ 22♒54
☊ 11♓08
⚶ 28♓28
✳ 29♓25
⯡ 11♈48
ϛ 22♈17
♕ 07♉09
AV 12♉36
⚳ 15♉02
⚲ 16♉19
☿ 01♊12
♇ 12♊23
♂ 24♊28
⯪ 27♊31
⯫ 04♋03
⯤ 05♋50
⯩ 10♋20
E 06♌32
⊖ 25♌45

PRIMARY ISSUES

Just as the Sun/Moon midpoint will be more highlighted for some people (such as my second husband and myself), other factors will be more highlighted for other people. By the same token, I am not suggesting that if a marriage produces children there will be an emphasis on Leo and the fifth house in the relevant harmonic; or that if a marriage does not produce children, there will not be. It is a matter of knowing what are the primary issues of the relationship and of associating these issues with the symbolism of the houses, the signs, the planets and the numbers in the charts.

AGE NUMBERS

In terms of the number of my age, my first marriage (occurring at 18) relates to the number 9, with a coloration of 1 and 8, and my second marriage (occurring at 24) relates to the number 6, with a coloration of 2 and 4. The zodiacal associations thereof—the house, sign, planet and aspect associated with the number—are pertinent. They are pertinent in the natal, and in the harmonic magnification of the aspect.

Further Tests

As a further test, I asked a friend to predict the salient features of both the harmonic chart that coincided with her age at her first marriage and the harmonic chart that coincided with her age at her second marriage. This experiment was equally successful. Continuing my experiments, I predicted what the harmonics would be like at past ages, before calculating the harmonics of those ages, and predicted what events would occur at future ages, after calculating the harmonics of those ages.

My Procedure

My procedure, after placing the harmonic positions around the natal chart, was, and is, to note the signs, houses and degrees of the harmonic Ascendant, Midheaven, Sun and Moon, the emphasized houses, the aspects, and some of the planetary pictures. "Planets" is meant to refer as well to the other bodies, such as asteroids, Uranian planets, Transpluto, Dark Moon Lilith and Halley's Comet included in these harmonic charts.

HARMONIC CONJUNCTIONS

The conjunctions of the harmonic planets and/or personal points to each other are especially important. The conjunctions within the same number of degrees as the number of the harmonic will show the harmonic aspects that are within a degree in the radix chart. The conjunctions that are from the degree of a planet or point to the degree before or the one after will show what is especially highlighted in a particular harmonic. Sometimes, three or more planets and/or points that are not conjunct from one degree to another in the harmonic chart are equidistant from each other and so would be highlighted by virtue of their symmetry (planetary pictures by conjunction). Also, observe major configurations (T-Squares, Grand Trines, Yods, etc.).

HARMONIC CONFIGURATIONS

Configurations in harmonic charts, as in unmagnified charts, have the qualities of the houses and signs with which they are associated. For instance, the Yod is a combination of a sextile and two quincunxes, and it is this combination which gives the Yod its fated quality. The houses (6 and 12) and the signs (Virgo and Pisces), associated with these aspects, have a karmic quality. With the sixth house and Virgo, there is a necessity for service; with the twelfth house and Pisces, a necessity for spiritual development. The sextile ties the planets together in relation to work or physical health, while the quincunx or semisextile connects them in relation to nebulousness or mental health. As for the T-Square, it is a combination of the maternalism or emotionality of the 4 and the possessiveness or persistence of the 2. You are superimposing other harmonics on the harmonic, but I think such overlaying is valid. The particular harmonic chart is highlighted in terms of these overlays and their principles.

HARMONIC PLANETARY PICTURES

I also calculate the harmonic Sun/Moon, Venus/Mars, Mars/Jupiter and Mars/Saturn midpoints, place their positions (with degrees, minutes and seconds) in the center of the wheel, and look for the planetary pictures. These planetary pictures superimpose the 8th harmonic on the particular harmonic being studied. However, since harmonics encompassed within the 8th harmonic are different from the 8th and from each other, record whether the planet or personal point equaling the midpoint is conjunct, opposition, square, semisquare or sesquiquadrate. The 1st, 2nd and 4th harmonics are tied to the 8th by the fact that they are multiples of it, but, as mentioned before, not all planetary pictures are "equal." The conjunction will have an Arian quality; the opposition, a Taurean one; the square, a Cancerian; and the semisquare and sesquiquadrate, a Scorpionic quality. If these planetary pictures are formed from aspects, notice which ones they are. (A Grand Trine planetary picture is different from a T-Square planetary picture.) Also, in what sign and house and at what degree does the midpoint fall? Consider similarly the planet or personal point at the midpoint. As an example, in my 18th harmonic (see Figure IV), harmonic Admetos, which can be stoppage, equals by opposition the harmonic Sun/Moon midpoint. The midpoint of the Sun/Moon is at 26° Aries 23' in my natal second house and Admetos is at 26° Libra 00' in my natal eighth house. (The marriage was terminated.) The principle of the degree still relates to the minute, but with the harmonics, it is more difficult to know if the minute is correct (see pages 18-24 on the importance of accuracy). Also, the East Point (referring to the self) and Uranian Planet Vulcanus (referring to fated happenings) equal by a sesquiquadrate the Sun/Moon midpoint.

HARMONIC IN RELATION TO NATAL

Then, the aspects, especially conjunctions of harmonic planets and personal points to natal planets and personal points, are observed. My 18th harmonic Venus at 21° Libra 41' is conjunct my natal Juno (marriage) at 21° Libra 12' ℞, opposition 18th harmonic Juno at 21° Aries 38'. Sometimes major configurations will be formed between harmonic positions and natal ones. My 18th harmonic Moon at 06° Aries

19' and Ascendant at 08° Aries 19' are sextile my 18th harmonic Mercury at 06° Aquarius 35', with all three quincunx my natal Neptune at 07° Virgo 24' (Yod). The 07° would link the 06° and 08°, and my natal Apollon at 08° Virgo 05' and Mars at 09° Virgo 40' should be included, since they are conjunct my natal Neptune. (Apollon is a Uranian planet that I associate with the Greek and Roman god Apollo. Mythological associations, I have discovered, are very helpful in the interpretation of the Uranian planets. See Uranian Planet Key Words in the Appendices.) Interestingly, my first husband, whom I married when I was 18 years old, has a Cancer Sun (harmonic Moon), a Virgo Moon (harmonic Mercury), a Pisces Ascendant (natal Neptune) and an Apollon and Mars which connect prominently (either by exact aspects or by rulerships) with his Moon, Mercury and Ascendant.

NATAL TO HARMONIC PLANETARY PICTURES

Also noted are pictures formed between the natal planets or points and the harmonic Sun/Moon, Venus/Mars, Mars/Jupiter and Mars/Saturn midpoints. In my 18th harmonic, the harmonic Sun/Moon midpoint equals by conjunction my natal Uranus, by square my natal Transpluto (a projected planet more Plutonian than Pluto), by semisquare my natal Venus, and by sesquiquadrate my natal Vertex.

HARMONIC TO NATAL PLANETARY PICTURES

Reversing the process, look at which harmonic planets and points equal the natal Sun/Moon, Venus/Mars, Mars/Jupiter and Mars/Saturn midpoints. In my 18th harmonic, harmonic Pallas (relating to law) equals by sesquiquadrate my natal Sun/Moon midpoint. In my 24th harmonic, the harmonic Sun (ruler of my natal seventh house) equals by conjunction my natal Sun/Moon midpoint. In my second husband's 33rd harmonic, harmonic Uranus (ruler of his natal seventh house) equals by conjunction his natal Sun/Moon midpoint. My 18th harmonic Sun does not equal my natal Sun/Moon midpoint, and in the harmonic of my first husband's age at the time of our marriage, the ruler of his natal seventh house does not equal his natal Sun/Moon midpoint. My first marriage was not a "seventh house marriage," so I didn't expect this seventh house emphasis. In the harmonic of my first husband's age at the time of his second marriage, the ruler of his natal seventh house still does not equal his natal Sun/Moon midpoint, but does equal his natal Mars/Jupiter midpoint by sesquiquadrate. (A lot of children were the product of this marriage.)

FOUR MAJOR MIDPOINTS

The Sun/Moon midpoint is always noted because it relates to the combined archetypes of man and woman (more specifically husband and wife or father and mother). The Sun, through its association with the life force, is the archetype for the father and husband, while Saturn refers to the father as the authority figure. The Venus/Mars midpoint is always noted because it relates to the combination of love and sex—another important "concept." Mars, through its assertion of energy which can be sexual energy, relates to sex, while Pluto's reference to sex is on the deeper level of regeneration. As for Venus, when it is combined with Mars it seems to act more like a carnal second-house, than a conjugal seventh-house, Venus. (The Venus/Mars midpoint can sometimes be energy directed towards making money, instead of love-sex.) The Mars/Jupiter midpoint is considered because it refers to birth, as well as to "successful creative activity" in general.[7] The Mars/Jupiter midpoint is associated with birth, since birth is the expansion (Jupiter) of the self (Mars) and of the sexual energy (Mars). The Mars/Saturn midpoint is recorded because it describes energy (Mars) being applied to the career (Saturn), as well as the limitation (Saturn) of energy (Mars). Applying your energy to a particular career is a limitation or channeling of your energy. The Mars/Saturn midpoint is prominent in regard to marriage too. Limiting yourself to one person, as in marriage, is a restriction (Saturn) of energy, particularly sexual energy (Mars). The situation of these planetary combinations in the natal chart and their other references would augment this attribution of meaning to them.

It is also meaningful if these midpoints are equal to each other—whether harmonic to harmonic or harmonic to natal. My 18th harmonic Sun/Moon midpoint equals by square my natal Venus/Mars midpoint, showing the importance of love and sex in the marriage which occurred during that year.

OTHER MIDPOINTS

Though the Sun/Moon, Venus/Mars, Mars/Jupiter and Mars/Saturn midpoints are always calculated for their intrinsic interest and for consistency, other midpoints are considered when they are relevant, either because of position or meaning. For example, my 18th harmonic Venus/Pluto midpoint was noted because it equals by opposition my 18th harmonic Sun/Moon midpoint—descriptive of a marriage based on compulsive love. My natal and harmonic Sun/Uranus midpoints were noted because the Sun and Uranus are the rulers of my natal seventh and first houses. Despite the fact that the Sun/Moon midpoint is the marriage midpoint, the Sun and Uranus have a special connection to marriage for me. (In general, the midpoint of planets ruling houses is connected to the affairs of the houses the planets rule.)

ORB

The conjunctions that indicate which planets and personal points are in a particular harmonic aspect are observed, but all the aspects, major configurations and planetary pictures recorded are from the degree of the planet or point to the degree before and the degree after. These exact aspects, configurations and pictures focus on what is significant in that year or principle. Always relate the harmonic positions back to the natal chart. What do the planets mean to the individual—in what signs and houses are they placed, what do they rule, and what exact aspects do they form natally?

General Views

As mentioned before, the Ascendant Equal House Chart and Midheaven Equal House Chart can be erected, but before discussing their different perspectives, there are some general views I want to express.

The 13th harmonic has been variously described as "esoteric or karmic astrology" or "manifest destiny." I think these attributions are due to the 13th harmonic's correlation to the fourth house, with its reference to the endings of all matters or the final outcome.

Regarding another contention about harmonics by some astrologers, I do not agree that only some of the harmonics, such as the 1st, 2nd, 3rd, 4th, 6th and 8th are operative for the mass of people, while the 5th, 7th and 9th are operative only for the spiritually enlightened. In my experience, all the harmonics are operative for everyone! Those who profess that harmonics are hierarchical, also contend that only the 1st, 2nd, 4th, 8th, and 16th harmonics are harmonics of manifestation. According to this theory, the 5th, 7th and 9th harmonics are describing only potentialities, not manifestations. According to my observations of transits, progressions and Solar Arcs,[8] in relation to both magnified charts and the harmonic aspects from which they derive, all harmonics are harmonics of manifestation. The 5th harmonic creativity manifests when a work of art or a child is created; the 7th harmonic balance manifests when a marriage or other partnership is formed; the 9th harmonic higher mind manifests when a law is administered or a book published. Each harmonic has both ethereal and mundane qualities. The 2nd harmonic is mundane in regard to money and possessions, but ethereal in regard to values and love. The 4th harmonic is expressed concretely as the home or more nurturing parent, but nebulously as the quality of maternalism. As for the 8th harmonic, the partner's money and legacies are substantive, while regeneration and transformation are not.

Ascendant and Midheaven Perspectives

Now that my view—all harmonics are operative—has been stated, it's time to discuss how they operate from the different perspective of the Ascendant and of the Midheaven. The Ascendant Equal House Chart relates more to the private domain and the Midheaven Equal House Chart relates more to the outer world. The harmonic planets around your natal chart relate to you in general, rather than to you from a particular perspective.

See the following table for references of the harmonics and for Ascendant and Midheaven Equal House applications of these references. The table gives just a few. Other references of the house, sign and planet associated with the number would apply. Also, if a reference that has been listed as personal is public in the particular case, or vice versa, use the other frame of reference. The Midheaven Equal House Chart, derived as it is from the Midheaven, has a great deal to do with the career, status and parentage. Parentage can be related to the personal life, but regarding status in the world, parentage is related to the public life. The natal chart too can be set up with Ascendant equal houses to highlight you in regard to your personal life; Midheaven equal houses, to highlight you in regard to your public life. Since the meanings of the harmonics are the same as the meanings of the numbers, the second column, REFERENCE, of this table can be used in general to interpret a number, house, sign, planet and aspect. (Substitute "Self" for "Natal Chart," as a reference of 1, 1st house, Aries, Mars and conjunction.)

Table IV – Harmonic References — A and M Equal House

HARMONICS	REFERENCE
1	Natal Chart
2	Money; possessions; love; values; relationship (opposition--aspect of relationship).
3	Lower mind; lower education; near travel; communication; siblings.
4	Maternalism; more nurturing parent; home; foundation; endings of all matters.
5	Creativity; children; love affairs; romance; entertainment.
6	Physical health; work; service; criticality; siblings of 4th house parent.
7	Marriage; partnership; partners; open enemies; artistry.
8	The partner's money; legacies; sex; death; regeneration; transformation.
9	Higher mind; higher education; distant travel; law; publishing; in-laws; completion.
10	Paternalism; more authoritative parent; employers; career; status; goal.
11	Hopes and wishes; humanitarianism; originality; friends; organizations.
12	Mental health; spirituality; nebulousness; secret enemies; siblings of the 10th house parent*; institutions.
13	References of 4, with a coloration of 1 and 3, i.e., maternalism (4) with a secondary emphasis on the self (1) and communication (3).
14	References of 5, with a coloration of 1 and 4, i.e., children (5) with a secondary emphasis on the self (1) and maternalism (4).
15	References of 6, with a coloration of 1 and 5, i.e., service (6) with a secondary emphasis on the self (1) and children (5).
16	References of 7, with a coloration of 1 and 6, i.e., marriage (7) with a secondary emphasis on the self (1) and service (6).

*There is no implication that the siblings of your tenth house parent are your secret enemies. In fact, your secret enemies may sometimes be within yourself.

ASCENDANT EQUAL HOUSE

Personal Life

Love; values in regard to personal matters; personal relationships.

Lower mind; personal communication; siblings in regard to the personal life.

Maternal qualities in the personal life; more nurturing parent in regard to the personal life; home; foundation; endings in the personal life.

Creativity in terms of children and love affairs; children in regard to the personal life; romance; personal entertainment.

Physical health; personal service and criticality; siblings of 4th house parent in regard to the personal life.

Marriage partnerships; marriage in regard to the personal life; partners and open enemies, in regard to the personal life; personal artistry.

Sex; death; regeneration; transformation.

Higher mind; in-laws in regard to the personal life; personal completion, as in marriage.

Paternal qualities in the personal life; more authoritative parent and employers, in regard to the personal life; personal goal.

Hopes and wishes in regard to the personal life; originality in the personal life; friends in regard to the personal life.

Mental health; spirituality; nebulousness in the personal life; secret enemies and 10th house parent's siblings, in regard to the personal life.

References of 4, with a coloration of 1 and 3, in regard to the personal life; the final outcome in regard to the personal life.

References of 5, with a coloration of 1 and 4, in regard to the personal life.

References of 6, with a coloration of 1 and 5, in regard to the personal life.

References of 7, with a coloration of 1 and 6, in regard to the personal life.

MIDHEAVEN EQUAL HOUSE

Public Life

Money; possessions; values in regard to public matters; public relationships.

Lower education; near travel; public communication; siblings in regard to the public life.

Maternal qualities in the public life; more nurturing parent in regard to the public life; foundation; endings in the public life.

Creativity in terms of career or goal; children in regard to the public life; public entertainment, such as theatre.

Work; public service and criticality; siblings of 4th house parent in regard to the public life.

Business partnerships; marriage in regard to the public life; partners and open enemies, in regard to the public life; public artistry.

The partner's money; legacies.

Higher education; distant travel; law; publishing; in-laws in regard to the public life; public completion, as in the career.

Paternal qualities in the public life; more authoritative parent and employers, in regard to the public life; career; status; public goal.

Hopes and wishes in regard to the public life; humanitarianism; originality in the public life; friends in regard to the public life; organizations.

Nebulousness in the public life, which could be expressed as music, art, photography, film or astrology; secret enemies and 10th house parent's siblings, in regard to the public life; institutions.

References of 4, with a coloration of 1 and 3, in regard to the public life; the final outcome in regard to the public life.

References of 5 with a coloration of 1 and 4, in regard to the public life.

References of 6, with a coloration of 1 and 5, in regard to the public life.

References of 7, with a coloration of 1 and 6, in regard to the public life.

With the Ascendant and Midheaven Equal House Charts, planets and points around angles, and planets and points exactly conjunct intermediate cusps are highlighted in that particular frame of reference. ("Planets" includes Uranian planets, asteroids and other bodies.) The degrees and signs of the personal points, and particularly the Ascendant, should be considered. The Ascendant is the chart's self or persona. A comparison of the harmonic houses in which these personal points are posited is enlightening. Exact conjunctions to the natal chart and where the harmonic Ascendants fall in that chart should be noted as well. The different emphases placed by the Ascendant and Midheaven equal houses on the harmonic aspects, particularly the conjunctions and the multiple aspects are significant.

Examples of my 5th, 7th, 9th and 18th harmonics to illustrate the procedure follow. The examples deal with particular concerns of particular harmonics from particular perspectives, suggesting possible interpretations. Other concerns of that harmonic could be interpreted as well—also obviously, other astrological meanings could be attributed to houses, signs and planets.

5TH HARMONIC

As stated (Table IV), the 5th Harmonic Ascendant Equal House Chart describes creativity more in terms of one's love affairs and children, while the 5th Harmonic Midheaven Equal House Chart describes creativity more in terms of one's career or goal.

The Ascendant of my 5th Harmonic Ascendant Equal House Chart is 12° Virgo 18', implying a combination of idealism (12°) and service (Virgo), or nebulousness and criticality, as regards love affairs and children. The Ascendant is exactly conjunct my natal Vertex and Jupiter in my seventh house, referring to the fated (Vertex) completion (Jupiter) through partnership (seventh house), already expressed in my natal chart. The harmonic Sun is at 12° Aquarius 54' in the harmonic sixth house, but exactly conjunct the sixth house cusp, combining the principles of service (sixth house) and children (fifth house). The 12° Aquarius 54' position suggests unusual (Aquarius) and fanciful (12°) children. The harmonic Moon is at 01° Aquarius 45' in the harmonic fifth house—unusual (Aquarius) again, but assertive (01°) now. The harmonic Midheaven is at 08° Virgo 27' in the harmonic twelfth house, reiterating the Ascendant's combination of 6 and 12, with the addition of 8 now. In other words, the goal or even paternalism (Midheaven), within the personal context of the 5th harmonic, combines service, nebulousness and transformation.

The derived Ascendant of my 5th Harmonic Midheaven Equal House Chart is 08° Sagittarius 27', exactly conjunct my natal Midheaven at 07° Sagittarius 41'. The sign of Sagittarius shows that education and publishing are important for creativity in terms of my career or goal. The number 8 may refer to research, and the number 7, to partnership. The harmonic Sun is now in the harmonic third house, relating to writing on technical (Aquarius) and esoteric (12°) astrology. The harmonic Moon is in the harmonic second house, stressing values; and the harmonic Ascendant is in the harmonic tenth, stressing goals.

As also stated (Table IV), the 5th Harmonic Ascendant Equal House Chart describes one's children in regard to the personal life, while the 5th Harmonic Midheaven Equal House Chart describes one's children in regard to the public life. From the public perspective then, the careers of my children are relevant. For instance, the 12° Aquarius 54' position of the Sun in the third house then describes the fact that my daughter was an actress (12) and is a film (12) and television (11) director of script (3) development, and my son is a space (12) communications (3) process engineer (11).

As mentioned, the multiple aspects are significant. There is a series of aspects that is highlighted in the Midheaven, but not in the Ascendant, Equal House Chart. The series and the planets and points in it are highlighted by exact conjunctions to cusps. The aspects are Neptune at 07° Gemini 01' semisextile Jupiter at 07° Cancer 52', semisextile Uranus at 07° Leo 45', semisextile the Midheaven at 08° Virgo 27'. This series of Neptunian aspects, forming two Virgoan aspects and one Cancerian aspect (three semisextiles, forming two sextiles and one square), with Neptune, Jupiter, Uranus and the Midheaven in the series, epitomizes my creativity in my career or goal and my children in regard to the public life. (The fact that Jupiter rules my natal Midheaven, and Neptune and the Midheaven are in an exact square natally, shows what these three factors mean to me.) The pictures formed by these aspects, such as Uranus equals Jupiter/Midheaven by conjunction, and Jupiter equals Uranus/Neptune by conjunction, would be noted. (The harmonic also describes what happened at the age corresponding to the number of the harmonic. My mother married when I was five years old and again when I was seven years old, and the 5th and 7th harmonics, respectively, describe these events.)

7TH HARMONIC

The 7th Harmonic Ascendant Equal House Chart describes marriage partnerships, while the 7th Harmonic Midheaven Equal House Chart describes business partnerships. Addey has related the 7th harmonic to one's creations, [9] and a marriage or business partnership is one's creation of a new entity—the partnership. The comparison of the Ascendant and Midheaven Equal House Charts will focus on the differences between the personal and public partnership. Conjunctions of harmonics to charts other than the natal chart can be significant.

The Ascendant of my 7th Harmonic Ascendant Equal House Chart (see Figure VI) is 23° Gemini 14', exactly conjunct my composite Ascendant with my present husband and my composite and relationship Sun with my former husband.[10] The 23° Gemini Ascendant of this Ascendant Equal House Chart signifies the importance to me, in marriage partnerships, of creative (5) communication (Gemini). This Ascendant falls in my natal fourth house, emphasizing my home and foundation. The derived Ascendant of my 7th Harmonic Midheaven Equal House Chart (see Figure VII) is 23° Aries 51', exactly conjunct my composite and relationship Sun with my partner in astrological research. The 23° Aries derived Ascendant of this Midheaven Equal House Chart signifies the importance to me, in business partnerships, of creative (5) assertiveness (Aries). This Ascendant falls in my natal second

Figure VI – 7th Harmonic Ascendant Equal House Chart

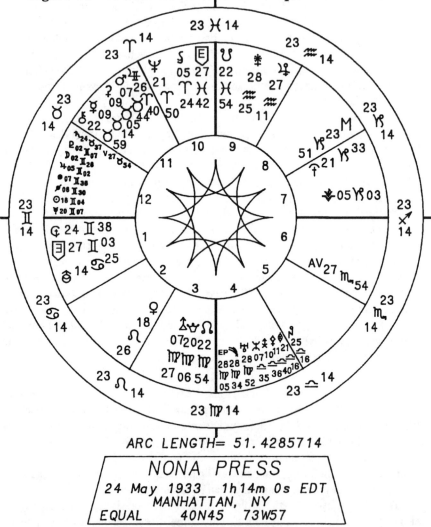

ARC LENGTH= 51.4285714

NONA PRESS
24 May 1933   1h14m 0s EDT
MANHATTAN, NY
EQUAL   40N45   73W57

house, emphasizing my values and/or money. Harmonic Neptune at 21° Aries 50' and Apollon at 26° Aries 39' straddle the 23° Aries Ascendant, describing my astrological partnerships now and my artistic partnerships in the past (I was a textile designer). Apollon is a Uranian planet that relates to science, art and music through its association with the Greek and Roman god Apollo.

Not only business partnerships, but partners in regard to the public life, can be described by the 7th Harmonic Midheaven Equal House Chart. Therefore, the Neptune-Apollon on the 23° Aries derived Ascendant also describes the fact that my husband is a musician. The 5 (23°), in reference to my husband's career or goal, may relate to public entertainment, since my husband plays in the musical theatre. (When

Figure VII – 7th Harmonic Midheaven Equal House Chart

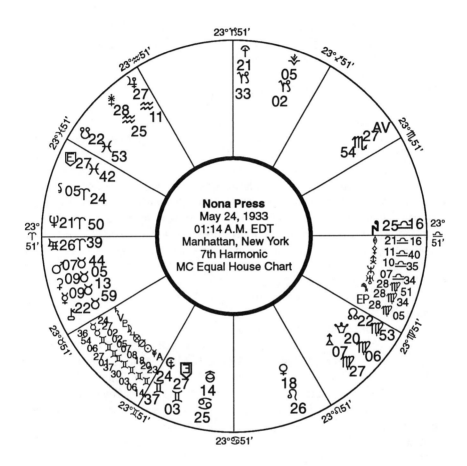

the seventh harmonic equal house charts are thought of as the partner in regard to the personal or public life, the Ascendant and first house describe him, and the Descendant and seventh describe his partners.)

After the Ascendant of the Ascendant Equal House Chart is compared to the derived Ascendant of the Midheaven Equal House Chart, other comparisons are made. The harmonic Sun is at 18° Gemini 03' and the harmonic Moon is at 02° Gemini 27', falling, from the personal perspective, in the harmonic twelfth house. This sign and placement indicate that empathetic (twelfth house) communication (Gemini) is a necessary part of my marriage partnerships. (Also, my husband is a musician with his Sun in Pisces and Mercury exactly opposition Neptune.) The 18°

of the Sun implies an emphasis on the higher mind, and the 02° of the Moon, on values. From the public perspective the harmonic Sun and Moon fall in the harmonic second house, indicating that communication (Gemini) on values or money (second house) is a necessary part of my business partnerships. There is a conjunction of the harmonic Moon at 02° Gemini 27' and harmonic Pluto at 02° Gemini 06', conjunct my natal Sun at 02° Gemini 34', connoting emotional obsessiveness in partnerships. (This harmonic conjunction shows that natally my Moon and Pluto are about three minutes away from an absolutely exact septile—21' is 7 X 03'.) The harmonic Ascendant at 23° Gemini 14', from the public perspective, also falls in the harmonic second house, but exactly conjuncts the third house cusp, highlighting communication again—possibly writing—in my business partnerships. The harmonic Midheaven at 23° Capricorn 51', from the personal perspective, falls in the harmonic eighth house, exactly conjunct the eighth house cusp, highlighting transformation (eighth house) in my marriage partnerships. Or, the harmonic Midheaven from the personal perspective may relate to my husband's career (Midheaven and Capricorn) being involved with other people's money (eighth house—he's also a musical contractor) in the theatre (5). Usually finances would be associated with business partnerships; however, a great deal of my husband's work is done at home and so becomes very personal and very much involved with our marriage partnership. The fact that the Ascendant of my Ascendant Equal House Chart and the Midheaven of my Midheaven Equal House Chart are exactly quincunx shows a connection (a Neptunian one) between the personal and public perspectives, in regard to my partnerships.

A major configuration (which is highlighted in both the 7th Harmonic Ascendant, and Midheaven, Equal House Chart) is a Grand Trine of the North Node at 22° Virgo 53' trine Kronos at 21° Capricorn 33' and the Midheaven at 23° Capricorn 51', trine Chiron at 22° Taurus 59' and Saturn at 24° Taurus 36'. The Uranian planet Kronos is related to authority in general. More specifically, Chiron (the first of the "other asteroids" that I added later) is associated with being a foster parent (Chiron was one to many of the Greek heroes). The theatre contractor is an authority who, since he is custodian of the musicians, has a Chiron-like quality. My husband's being a foster parent to my son and a custodian of the musicians, from the personal standpoint, could be indicated by the house placements in my Ascendant Equal House Chart. See Figure VI (the North Node is in the 3rd house, exactly conjunct the 4th; Kronos is in the 7th, close to the 8th, with the Midheaven in the 8th, exactly conjunct the 8th; and Chiron is in the 11th, exactly conjunct the 12th, with Saturn in the 12th, exactly conjunct the 12th). My husband is a humanitarian and self-sacrificing father figure to both my son and the musicians. My husband's being a foster parent to my son and a custodian of the musicians, from the public standpoint, could be indicated by the house placements in my Midheaven Equal House Chart. See Figure VII (the North Node is in the 5th house, exactly conjunct the 6th; Kronos is in the 9th, close to the Midheaven; and Chiron is in the 1st, exactly conjunct the 2nd, with Saturn in the 2nd, exactly conjunct the 2nd). My husband supported my son, and the contractor is paymaster to the musicians. The planetary pictures formed by this Grand Trine, such as the Midheaven equals by opposition the Saturn/Node midpoint, and Chiron, Saturn equals by opposition the Midheaven/Node midpoint, would be recorded. The different placements of midpoints are relevant too.

Only the planets and points that are conjunct and trine within a degree have been included in this Grand Trine, but if other planets and points are conjunct these Grand Trine planets and points within 07°, these conjunctions would be noted. (These conjunct planets and points would be in the 7th harmonic, i.e., forming septiles natally.) Harmonic Chiron and Saturn are conjunct the harmonic Vertex (a fated point) within 07°, and the harmonic North Node is conjunct the harmonic East Point and Uranus within 07° (Uranus relates to step-children).

As stated, the 7th harmonic describes the fact that my mother married when I was seven years old. Her marriage brought me a stepfather or foster parent. Her marriage when I was five years old had also brought me a stepfather, but that marriage was short-lived and, therefore, my having a stepfather was too. The marriage that occurred when I was seven lasted for twenty-five and a half years, only ending with the death of my stepfather. My gaining a stepfather at seven years of age would be described from the personal perspective by the 7th Harmonic Ascendant Equal House Chart; from the public perspective, by the 7th Harmonic Midheaven Equal House Chart. The fact that Chiron for me could be expressed as a stepfather is prefigured in my natal chart where it is exactly conjunct my Mercury, the ruler of my Sun, Moon and fourth house. To me, the fourth house, and so the Moon, represents my father. I too, brought a stepfather to my son (Mercury is also ruling my fifth house and Cancer is in it).

9TH HARMONIC

The 9th Harmonic Ascendant Equal House Chart describes personal completion, as might occur through marriage, while the 9th Harmonic Midheaven Equal House Chart describes public completion, as might occur through the career. (The 10th harmonic describes the career, particularly when the harmonic is seen from the Midheaven perspective.)

The Ascendant of my 9th Harmonic Ascendant Equal House Chart is 04° Aries 09', exactly conjunct my natal Ceres in my first house. Ceres relates to nurturing, as does the number 4, while the sign of Aries energizes this emphasis on motherhood in relation to my personal completion. The harmonic Sun is at 23° Libra 13' in the harmonic seventh house. The harmonic Sun is exactly conjunct the harmonic Antivertex at 23° Libra 00'.[11] Their conjunction shows that natally the Sun and Antivertex are just about a minute away from an absolutely exact novile (13' is just a little more than 9 X 01'). This harmonic conjunction lends an air of fatedness (Antivertex) to completion (9th harmonic) through personal partnerships (seventh house and Libra). (I think the Vertex and Antivertex refer to a higher purpose in life [or to the career, as a mundane expression of that higher purpose], which may be why the Vertex and Antivertex are associated with fate.) The harmonic Sun equals 5 and rules the fifth house in the Ascendant Equal House Chart, as well as the harmonic East Point,[12] bringing in the importance of creativity (children) in regard to this personal completion. (The East Point is like the Ascendant but is how you are, rather than how you act or react.) The harmonic Moon is at 03°Libra 09' in the harmonic sixth house, but exactly conjunct the harmonic seventh house. 03° emphasizes communication or duality. The importance of marriage is stressed by both the Sun and Moon being in the sign of Libra, and their respective placement in and conjunction to the seventh house. In this case Libra and the seventh house refer to marriage partnerships, rather than business partnerships, because we are dealing with the perspective of the Ascendant Equal House Chart.

The signs of the Sun and Moon, but not the placements, would be the same in the Midheaven Equal House Chart. In that chart (since the derived Ascendant is 09° Virgo 14') the Moon is in the harmonic first house, and the Sun, in the harmonic second house. This placement, in reference to completion through the career, emphasizes the self, and money, or values in regard to public matters. The sign of Libra would here refer to business partnerships. The 09° Virgo Ascendant indicates the importance of the higher mind (09°) and analytical thinking (Virgo) in this completion. This Ascendant is exactly conjunct my natal Mars in the seventh house, activating energy (Mars) in partnerships (seventh house).

The harmonic Midheaven at 09° Gemini 14' is in the third house of the Ascendant Equal House Chart, indicating that my goal or career (Midheaven), in regard to personal completion, is communication (Gemini and third house) of the higher mind (09°). The harmonic Ascendant at 04° Aries 09' is in the seventh house of the Midheaven Equal House Chart, indicating that my self or persona (Ascendant), in regard to public completion, is assertive (Aries) and maternal (04°) in partnerships (seventh house).

In the Ascendant Equal House Chart, Mercury at 03° Virgo 17' forms a Yod with the Ascendant at 04° Aries 09' and Vulcanus[13] at 05° Aquarius 17'. The Yod is sometimes called the Finger of God because of its fated quality. This quality would be involved with the self (Ascendant) and powerful (Vulcanus) communication or duality (Mercury). Mercury is also exactly trine Jupiter at 02° Taurus 11', bringing in expansiveness, and semisextile the Moon at 03° Libra 09', reaffirming maternalism. Mercury is in the harmonic fifth house, exactly conjunct the sixth house. Vulcanus is in the harmonic eleventh house, exactly conjunct the eleventh. As regards personal completion, Mercury relates to children (fifth house), combined with service (sixth house and Virgo) and communication (03°). As for Vulcanus, it reiterates the emphasis on children (05°) and adds an unusual or erratic quality (Aquarius and eleventh house). On a secondary level of consideration (that of rulership) Mercury rules the third house and the Midheaven (in Gemini) and itself, the sixth house and Chiron (in Virgo), influencing communication, goals, service and foster parenting. The inclusion of Chiron, with its connotation of foster parenting, makes the interpretation more specific. In my personal completion, which may be through marriage, a stepfather will play a role—my second husband is stepfather to my son from my first marriage.

In the Harmonic Midheaven Equal House Chart there is no longer the exact conjunction to cusps. Now, Mercury is in the harmonic twelfth house, and Vulcanus is in the harmonic fifth house. As regards public completion, Mercury relates to public nebulousness, which could be expressed as music, art, dance, photography, film or astrology (twelfth house), combined with analytical thinking (Virgo) and public communication, which might be writing (03°). As for Vulcanus, it suggests that creativity in the career or goal (fifth house) may be expressed in technical astrology (Aquarius). On a secondary level of consideration, Mercury rules the derived Ascendant, itself, Chiron and the Midheaven, influencing the persona, communication, foster parenting and the career or parent. Chiron is also the teacher and wounded healer, so what may be more specifically expressed is that completion in the career is through communication which teaches and heals.

A harmonic also shows what the number, house, sign, planet and aspect associated with it mean to the person whose harmonic it is. For instance, since my 9th harmonic shows what Sagittarius means to me, that harmonic is descriptive of the fact that **both** my parents were Sagittarians. Mercury being exactly trine Jupiter and semisextile the Moon describes the duality (Mercury) of this Sagittarianism (Jupiter), connected with nurturing (the Moon). In the public perspective, the symbolism of Mercury's twelfth house position is fulfilled by my mother being a dancer and my father being an artist working a great deal in the theatre. Both did "creative writing." As for Aquarius in the fifth in the public perspective, they were innovative regarding creativity in their careers. They were also Chiron-type figures—my father taught me art and in general was a wounded healer to me, and my mother adopted a son.

Something else shown by my 9th harmonic is that harmonic Venus at 10° Capricorn 50' and harmonic Pluto at 15° Capricorn 34' are in a novile aspect natally. In the 9th Harmonic Midheaven Equal House Chart, they are in the harmonic fifth house, indicating creativity in the career or goal (Midheaven perspective and Capricorn). The 9th harmonic, from the perspective of the Midheaven, can refer to publishing. This novile aspect between Venus and Pluto, which in another context could be personal completion through obsessive love, in this context could be publishing of harmonic research (Venus is associated with harmony, and Pluto, with research). Venus is also associated with values, and numbers are values, so the publishing of research on numbers or numerical positions would be appropriate. The rulership by Venus of the ninth house, Jupiter and Ceres could show productivity (Ceres) and publishing (ninth house and Jupiter) affected by these values. The rulership by Venus of the second house, Sun, Antivertex, Moon and Poseidon could show destined (Antivertex) creativity (Sun), intuition (Moon), esoterica (Poseidon)[14] and public relationships (second house) affected by these values. The rulership by Pluto of the third house and Uranus supports the idea of research (Pluto) affecting writing (third house) and technical astrology (Uranus). This association is further reiterated by the Moon (ruled by Venus) being the ruler of the eleventh house and exactly semisextile Mercury. A reading might be spiritual astrology (semisextile) connects writing (Mercury) and intuition (Moon), concerning technical astrology (eleventh house). I have already been involved in the publishing of the *Asteroid Names & Nodes* and the *Ephemeris of Diana* (the asteroid). Anticipating Chapter

3 on asteroids, let me add that my 9th harmonic Diana is at 02° Pisces 46', exactly quincunx the harmonic Moon, sextile harmonic Jupiter (Finger of God) and opposition harmonic Mercury. (Regarding the Ephemeris, the Moon connection may symbolize the fact that in Roman mythology Diana was the goddess of the moon.) These booklets are both astrological and technical and have many numerical positions. If you're reading these words in book-form, the publishing of the harmonic research has followed.

The natal positions of my Venus and Pluto establish a precondition for this 9th harmonic expression. Venus is at 11° Gemini 12' in my fourth and rules my third house of writing, while Pluto is at 21° Cancer 43' in my sixth, exactly conjunct that cusp, and rules my ninth house of publishing.

18TH HARMONIC

The 18th harmonic is a multiple of the 9th harmonic, and so repeats some of its aspects and planetary pictures. 18 also adds up to 9, and so the 9th harmonic's references are ascribed to it. The colorations of 1 and 8 are applicable. (Of course, the references are derived from the corresponding house, sign and planet.) Completion was the goal of my marriage at 18 years of age. Higher education was emphasized by my giving up mine to further that of my husband. There was distant travel—a move to a different state—and marriage is a matter of law.

The Ascendant of my 18th Harmonic Ascendant Equal House Chart (see Figure VIII) is 08° Aries 19', with the Moon at 06° Aries 19' close to that angle. The fourth house cusp at 08° Cancer 19' is conjunct Uranus at 09° Cancer 56'. My marriage transformed (8) and disrupted (Aries) my life, as well as home (Moon close to the Ascendant, and Uranus in Cancer, conjunct the fourth house cusp). Ceres at 10° Cancer 30' would be pulled in because it is exactly conjunct Uranus. Not only was there sudden maternity, but I was separated by the marriage from my own mother (Ceres, and an exact conjunction from the harmonic Moon to my natal Ceres). The Ascendant of my 18th Harmonic Ascendant Equal House Chart falls in my natal first house, exactly conjunct the second house cusp, emphasizing the self, combined with love or with values in regard to personal matters. The derived Ascendant of my 18th Harmonic Midheaven Equal House Chart falls in my natal ninth house. This Ascendant (see Figure IX) is 18° Scorpio 28', with the Nodes and Hades in Scorpio, bracketing the Ascendant. After moving out of state (natal ninth house), I worked (public perspective) for a large (9) insurance company (Scorpio). Hades, being another name for Pluto and for the underworld, has an association with Scorpio. The Nodes show the connection between this underworld and the self or persona (Ascendant) of this year or principle.

The harmonic Sun at 16° Taurus 27' emphasizes values or love (Taurus), combined with partnership (7). The Sun is exactly conjunct the harmonic Vertex and Antivertex, showing the fated quality of this marriage. (The fact that the Sun rules my natal seventh house should not be forgotten.) In the Ascendant Equal House Chart the harmonic Sun, Vertex and Antivertex are in the second house, and the Sun rules the fifth house and Midheaven. The emphasis from the personal perspective is on a fated love, concerning a child. In the Midheaven Equal House

Chart the harmonic Sun, Vertex and Antivertex are in the sixth house and the Sun rules the Midheaven. The emphasis from the public perspective is on fated work concerning a career. Work and career were particularly emphasized that year because, other than one summer job, I had never worked before.

The harmonic Moon at 06° Aries 19' emphasizes assertiveness (Aries), combined with service (06°). In the Ascendant Equal House Chart the harmonic Moon is in the twelfth house and rules the fourth house, Uranus and Ceres. The emphasis from the personal perspective is on nebulousness in the personal life, in relation to the home (fourth house) and sudden (Uranus) motherhood (Ceres). In the Midheaven Equal House Chart the harmonic Moon is in the fifth house and rules the ninth house, Uranus and Ceres. The emphasis from the public perspective is on creativity in the career (fifth house) in relation to work (Ceres) for an organization (Uranus) out of state (ninth house). (Ceres translates from motherhood to productivity or work.)

The harmonic Midheaven at 18° Leo 28' emphasizes creativity (Leo), combined with completion (9). In the Ascendant Equal House Chart the harmonic Midheaven is in the fifth house, emphasizing creativity in terms of love affairs and children. In the Midheaven Equal House Chart the harmonic Ascendant (08° Aries 19') is in the fifth house, emphasizing creativity in terms of the career or goal. (Parentage, regarding status in the world, is also associated with the Midheaven Equal House Chart.)

The repetition in the 18th harmonic of the Venus-Pluto 9th harmonic aspect was mentioned on page 27. The 18th harmonic Venus and Pluto, from the personal perspective, fall in the harmonic seventh house, emphasizing marriage partnerships; from the public perspective, in the harmonic twelfth house, emphasizing the imminent dissolution of the partnership. (Around my natal chart they fall in my natal eighth house, emphasizing obsessiveness.) Another pertinent observation is that in the 18th harmonic the Sun and Moon are 40° apart. This is the 9th harmonic separation or aspect, and having it between these bodies in this harmonic indicates that completion (9th harmonic) was being sought that year (when I was 18) through marriage (Sun and Moon).

Regarding the repetition of planetary pictures, the Sun/Moon midpoint equals the Venus/Pluto midpoint in both the 9th and the 18th harmonic; but in the 9th, the East Point and Vulcanus don't equal the Sun/Moon and Venus/Pluto midpoints, while in the 18th, they do. At nine years of age I didn't have a fated marriage. The different events are indicated too by the different houses and signs.

FOCUS

In the comparison of the Ascendant and Midheaven Equal House Charts, the focus has been on the harmonic positions of certain factors—the Ascendant, Midheaven, Sun and Moon, as well as the points and bodies (including asteroids and Uranian planets) that conjunct cusps or are in multiple aspects. There has been this focus because these positions (along with the conjunctions that show the harmonic aspects) are the most important. However, all the positions are descriptive and contribute to the delineation of the particular harmonic.

Figure VIII – 18th Harmonic Ascendant Equal House Chart

ARC LENGTH= 20.0000000

NONA PRESS
24 May 1933   1h14m 0s EDT
MANHATTAN, NY
EQUAL   40N45   73W57

A OR M PERSPECTIVE IN RELATION TO NATAL

The houses of either the Ascendant or Midheaven Equal House Chart, together with the bodies and points, can be put around the natal chart, as is often done with the placement of Solar Returns around the natal chart. Outside the harmonic ring (which is around the natal chart), the cusps of the equal house chart are placed on projecting lines. Along with the cusps, the numbers of the cusps are given in circles, as ③ 23° Leo 14', which is the third house cusp of the Ascendant Equal House Chart in my 7th harmonic (see Figure X). The third and fourth house cusps and part of the second house of my 7th Harmonic Ascendant Equal House Chart fall in my natal seventh

Figure IX – 18th Harmonic Midheaven Equal House Chart

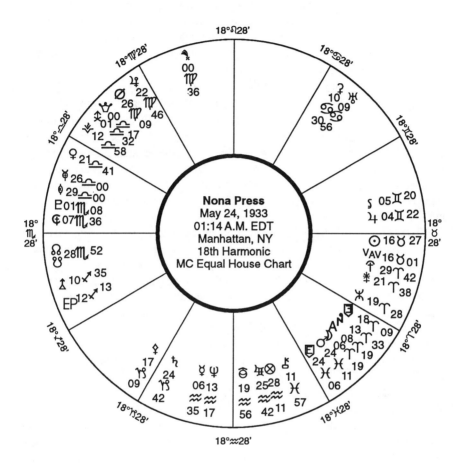

house. Emotional communication of personal values is what a marriage partnership means to me (7th harmonic in the Ascendant perspective in relation to the natal chart).

To give some other possible interpretations of Ascendant perspective 7th harmonic houses falling in the natal seventh house, there is the following. The first and second harmonic houses falling in the natal seventh house indicates that what is significant in the marriage partnership is the self and values. Both my former and present husband have this combination, but the former has the first and second cusps falling in his seventh, while the present has only the second cusp, accentuating for my present husband values more than self. (Note accent on values for all three of us.) The fourth and fifth harmonic houses falling in the natal seventh suggests that what is sought in the marriage partnership is emotional, or maternal, self-expression. The ninth and tenth harmonic houses falling in the natal seventh might mean that what is expected in the marriage partnership is the attainment of the higher mind and the goal. The other combinations would follow suit. (To illustrate the significance of harmonic houses falling in natal houses, the natal seventh house was chosen, but all the natal houses would be similarly affected.)

CHART COMPARISON FROM DIFFERENT PERSPECTIVES

Harmonics are very helpful in synastry (chart comparison). If planets or points in one person's 7th harmonic chart are conjunct within 07° planets or points in another person's 7th harmonic chart, when the radix charts are compared those conjuncting planets or points are either conjunct or in a 7th harmonic interaspect[15] within a 01°. (The word planets, as used here, is not limited to them.) Of course, in any harmonic, if the conjuncting planets or points are at the same degree or from one degree to the next, there is an even more powerful connection between the charts.

To see if you have these interaspects, instead of placing your Ascendant Equal House Chart around your natal chart, you can place it around someone else's Ascendant Equal House Chart and see the conjunctions, as well as the other aspects that are formed. (These other aspects should be exact.) You could also place your Midheaven Equal House Chart around someone else's Midheaven Equal House Chart. If the harmonic is the 7th, and the relationship is a business partnership, or you want to see the marriage from the perspective of business or the public life, you would use the Midheaven Equal House Charts. Planets and personal points around angles are particularly important. Conjunctions to cusps highlight those areas of life.

For instance, when my 7th Harmonic Ascendant Equal House Chart (see Figure VI) is placed around my husband's, my harmonic Venus in the second house is conjunct his harmonic seventh cusp exactly. On the contrary, when my 7th Harmonic Midheaven Equal House Chart (see Figure VII) is placed around my husband's, my harmonic Vesta in the ninth house is conjunct his harmonic seventh cusp exactly. From the personal perspective, love and personal values are highlighted, and from the public perspective, vested interests. Similarly, the Ascendant of my 7th Harmonic Ascendant Equal House Chart falls in the fifth house of his comparable chart, while the derived Ascendant of my 7th Harmonic Midheaven Equal House Chart falls in the tenth house of his comparable chart. Intermediate cusps, particularly when they are conjuncted, are considered as well. The second house cusp of my 7th Harmonic Ascendant Equal House Chart is exactly conjunct his harmonic sixth house Venus, which rules his harmonic fourth and ninth houses and Sun. From this perspective, love (second house) in my marriage partnership is highlighted by service-oriented love (Venus in the sixth) in his marriage partnership, which relates to expansive nurturing of children (rulerships). The second house cusp of my 7th Harmonic Midheaven Equal House Chart is conjunct his harmonic eleventh house Antivertex and Mars, which rules his harmonic Midheaven and Jupiter. From this

Figure X – 7th Harmonic Ascendant Equal House Cusps around Natal Chart

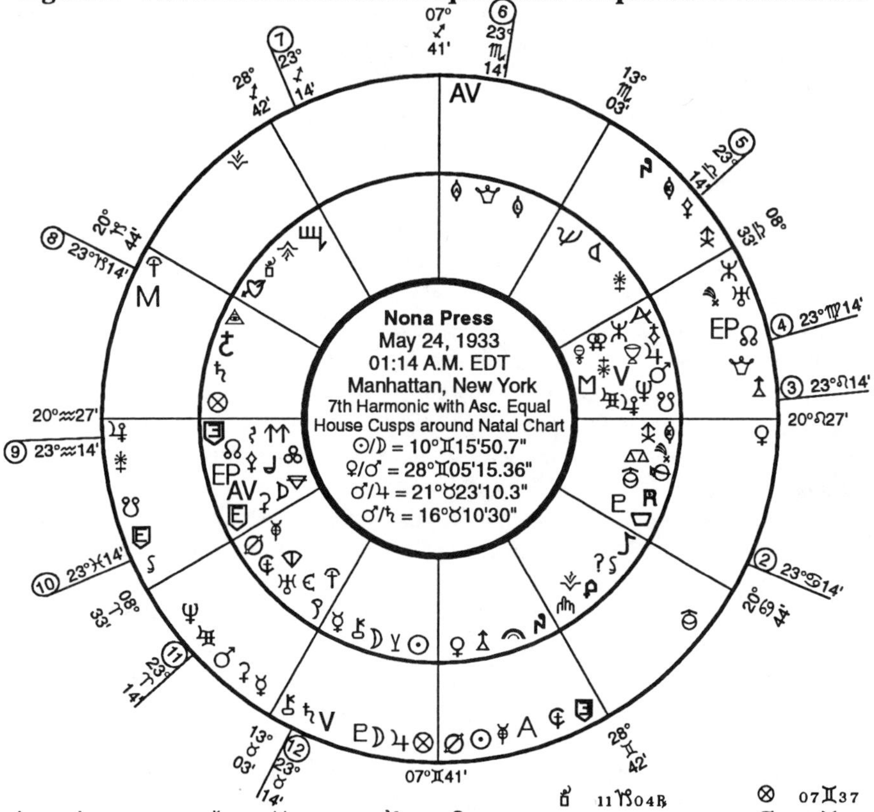

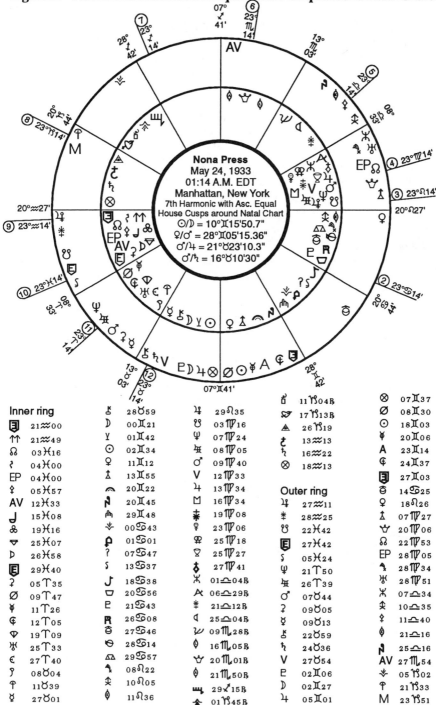

Inner ring

Ǝ	21♒00
↑↑	21♒49
☊	03♓16
ʔ	04♓00
EP	04♓00
⚴	05♓57
AV	12♓33
J	15♓08
♣	19♓16
▽	25♓07
D	26♓58
E	29♓40
⚳	05♈35
Ø	09♈47
⚶	11♈26
₵	12♈05
▽	19♈09
♅	25♈33
∈	27♈40
ʕ	08♉04
Ϙ	11♉39
☿	27♉01
⚷	28♉59
☽	00♊21
Ɣ	01♊42
☉	02♊34
♀	11♊12
⚵	13♊55
⌒	20♊22
N	20♊45
ᙏ	29♊48
⩛	00♋43
P	01♋01
?	07♋47
ʃ	13♋37
J	18♋38
ᗜ	20♋56
♇	21♋43
R	26♋08
ϴ	27♋46
⊖	28♋14
ΔΔ	29♋57
⚸	08♌22
⚵	10♌05
⌽	11♌36
♃	29♌35
☋	03♍16
♆	07♍24
⛢	08♍05
♂	09♍40
V	12♍33
♃	13♍34
M	16♍34
✳	19♍08
⚵	23♍06
⚮	25♍18
⏄	25♍27
⚴	27♍41
ⵣ	01♎04℞
⩕	06♎29℞
✳	21♎12℞
◖	25♎04℞
ψ	09♏28℞
⌽	16♏05℞
♕	20♏01℞
⌽	21♏50℞
ɯ	29♐15℞
⇑	01♑45℞
ȸ	11♑04℞
⚸	17♑13℞
▲	26♑19
ƈ	13♒13
♄	16♒22
⊗	18♒13

Outer ring

♃	27♒11
✳	28♒25
☋	22♓42
E	27♓42
ʃ	05♓24
♆	21♈50
⛢	26♈39
♂	07♉44
⚳	09♉05
☿	09♉13
⚷	22♉59
♄	24♉36
V	27♉54
♇	02♊06
☽	02♊27
♃	05♊01
⊗	07♊37
Ø	08♊30
☉	18♊03
⚶	20♊06
A	23♊14
₵	24♊37
Ǝ	27♊03
ϴ	14♋25
♀	18♌26
⚵	07♍27
♕	20♍06
☊	22♍53
EP	28♍05
⚸	28♍34
♅	28♍51
ⵣ	07♎34
⚳	10♎35
⚴	11♎40
⌽	21♎16
N	25♎16
AV	27♏54
⩛	05♑02
Ϙ	21♑33
M	23♑51

perspective, money (second house) in my marriage partnership is highlighted by unusual fated assertiveness (Antivertex and Mars in the eleventh) in his marriage partnership, which relates to career expansion (rulerships). (This contact between our 7th Harmonic Midheaven Equal House Charts could also be read as relating to parentage.) The degrees and signs of the planets and cusps would, of course, be considered.

Chart Comparison of Different People

Instead of comparing Ascendant and Midheaven harmonic perspectives, you could compare people by placing your harmonic chart around the harmonic chart of each person. With my 7th Harmonic Ascendant Equal House Chart placed around my ex-husband's, my harmonic tenth house cusp and part of my harmonic ninth house fall in his harmonic seventh house. With my 7th Harmonic Ascendant Equal House Chart placed around my husband's, my harmonic third house cusp and part of my harmonic second house fall in his harmonic seventh house. (Note the correspondence to my harmonic third house cusp and part of my harmonic second house falling in my natal seventh house.) The Ascendant of my aforementioned harmonic chart falls in the tenth house of my ex-husband's comparable chart, while this Ascendant falls in the fifth house of my husband's comparable chart. As mentioned, planets and personal points around angles are significant. With my ex-husband there is a cluster around the tenth house, while with my husband there is a cluster around the fourth. (One-half of the former cluster is included in the latter cluster.)

Equidistant on the tenth house cusp of my ex-husband's 7th Harmonic Ascendant Equal House Chart are my 7th harmonic Chiron, Saturn, Vertex on one side and my 7th harmonic Pluto, Moon, Jupiter, Part of Fortune on the other. The tenth cusp is 00° Gemini, with the Chiron - Part of Fortune ranging from 22° Taurus to 07° Gemini. Chiron, Saturn, Vertex refer to the fact that in our marriage my ex-husband, who is a Cancerian, was like a foster parent or teacher to me. (He was literally a teacher too.) The Pluto-Moon conjunction has already been described as connoting emotional obsessiveness in partnerships. A lot of the obsessiveness was concerning our son—a Sagittarian (Jupiter)—and he was the most fortunate (Part of Fortune) result of the partnership. Equidistant on the fourth house cusp of my husband's 7th Harmonic Ascendant Equal House Chart are my 7th harmonic Chiron, Saturn, Vertex on one side and my 7th harmonic Mars, Ceres, Mercury on the other. The fourth cusp is 17° Taurus, with the Mars - Vertex ranging from 07° Taurus to 27° Taurus. Here I believe the Chiron, Saturn, Vertex refer to the fact that in marrying me my husband became a foster parent to the son from my previous marriage. As for the Mars, Ceres, Mercury, he married a Geminian (Mercury) mother (Ceres) of a boy (Mars).

My harmonic Mars at 07° Taurus and harmonic Saturn at 24° Taurus surround my husband's 7th harmonic Saturn and Mars at 14° Taurus and 20° Taurus (equidistant on either side of the fourth cusp at 17° Taurus). Natally, his Mars and Saturn are in a 7th harmonic aspect, while my Mars is in a 7th harmonic aspect to his Saturn, and my Saturn is in a 7th harmonic aspect to his Mars. His Antivertex at 22° Taurus and my Vertex at 27° Taurus are also in 7th harmonic aspect to each other, giving a fated quality. There is a partnership (7th harmonic) in the home (fourth cusp), involving responsibility to this son, as well as energy applied to the career (Mars-Saturn in both charts). The career is personalized by being in the home. (Interestingly, our daughter has 7th harmonic Mars and Saturn equidistant on the tenth house cusp of her 7th Harmonic Ascendant Equal House Chart.)

MAJOR CONFIGURATIONS

The way in which a major configuration in one chart ties in with the other chart is important too. A major configuration in my 7th harmonic, which is mentioned on pages 42-43, is the Grand Trine of the North Node (22° Virgo 53'), trine Kronos, Midheaven (21° Capricorn 33', 23° Capricorn 51'), trine Chiron, Saturn (22° Taurus 59', 24° Taurus 36'). In relation to my ex-husband's 7th harmonic chart in the Ascendant perspective, my harmonic Chiron, Saturn is 07° away from a conjunction to his harmonic tenth house cusp at 00° Gemini. In relation to my husband's 7th harmonic chart in the Ascendant perspective, my harmonic Chiron, Saturn is exactly conjunct his harmonic Antivertex at 22° Taurus and Mars at 20° Taurus. (The 21° of my Kronos pulls in the 20° of his Mars.) These conjunctions were already discussed in reference to equidistance on the angles, but in the case of my husband another point of the Grand Trine is highlighted as well. My harmonic Kronos, Midheaven (authority) is exactly conjunct his harmonic Juno (goddess of marriage) at 24° Capricorn. My 7th harmonic Grand Trine may help my husband give expression to his 7th harmonic Mars-Saturn aspect—through his being a foster parent (Chiron) to my son.

REFERENCES TO THE NATAL

Though you are comparing one person's harmonic chart to another's, references to the natal chart of either party are relevant. As an example, 22° Taurus (the degree of my husband's 7th harmonic Antivertex) is the degree of his natal Midheaven, and 27° Taurus (the degree of my 7th harmonic Vertex) is the degree of my natal Mercury, ruler of my Sun and Moon. 07° Gemini (the degree of his 7th harmonic Mercury) is the degree of my natal fourth house cusp. Also, references other than degree conjunctions are significant. Natally my husband's Sun is exactly opposition my Neptune. This interaspect can result in idealization. My husband's 7th harmonic Neptune equals by an opposition my 7th harmonic Sun/Moon midpoint, while my 7th harmonic Sun equals by a sesquiquadrate his 7th harmonic Sun/Moon midpoint. It is now his Neptune and my Sun that are emphasized, but the principle of idealization is still operative. (Natally my Sun equals by a sesquiquadrate my husband's Sun/Moon midpoint, so this 7th harmonic picture is a continuation of the natal picture.)

The closer to exactitude, aspects or planetary pictures are natally, the more likely they will continue throughout the harmonics. The deviation from exactness increases as the harmonic number is increased—double the harmonic number, double the deviation. Natally my ex-husband's Sun equals by a semisquare my Sun/Moon midpoint, but since the natal deviation from exactitude is over three-quarters of a degree, the picture does not continue in the 7th harmonic, or even lower harmonics. Interestingly, his 7th harmonic Moon equals by a semisquare my 7th harmonic Sun/Moon midpoint. The fact that his Sun is emphasized natally, while his Moon is emphasized in the 7th harmonic, may indicate that, though he exerted a dominance over me, he was *in the marriage* the reflector rather than the emanator.

Harmonics in Reference to Event Charts

Other references of harmonics are to event charts. The 7th harmonic would be germane to the chart of the first meeting, or the chart of the marriage if the relationship comes to that. The transiting positions are activating the harmonic ones, as well as the natal. Note particularly the angles and the personal points. (The East Point, West Point, Antivertex and Vertex are additional angles.)

The four events given as examples are the meeting of and the marriage to my first and my second husband. The charts were not rectified. Before becoming aware of the importance of astrology, I sensed the importance of time and noted the timing of events. The time of meeting my first husband is accurate to the minute because he came up to me at the end of a college class which always ended at the same moment with the ringing of a bell. The times of meeting my second husband and the two marriages are within five minutes of being exact. The three harmonic charts mentioned are 7th Harmonic Ascendant Equal House Charts.

MEETING — 2ND HUSBAND

When my present husband and I met, the transiting South and North Node were exactly conjunct the fourth and tenth cusp of his 7th harmonic chart, while transiting Apollon, Jupiter was exactly conjunct the North Node, fourth cusp of my 7th harmonic chart. (See Figure VI.) Apollon is associated with the Greek and Roman god Apollo, who is linked with the Sun. This "Sun" connection is especially appropriate for the meeting of my future husband and myself, since I have Leo on my natal seventh cusp, and he has Leo on his natal first cusp and Apollon exactly conjunct his natal North Node in the first house. Transiting Apollon and Jupiter activated the major configuration in my 7th harmonic—the Grand Trine of the North Node, fourth cusp, trine the Kronos, Midheaven, trine Chiron, Saturn (activating as well my husband's 7th harmonic Juno and Mars, Antivertex). There was a transiting asteroid exactly conjunct the first cusp and Hades[16] of my aforementioned chart and another transiting asteroid conjunct within 07° (septile) and moving towards the seventh cusp of his aforementioned chart. These asteroids are precisely descriptive of the event which occurred because the asteroid which was conjunct the first cusp, Hades of my 7th harmonic chart of marriage is the asteroid with the name of my husband, and the asteroid which was moving towards the seventh cusp of my husband's 7th harmonic chart of marriage is the asteroid with my name. These asteroids at 25° Gemini 54' and 11° Leo 01' were exactly semisquare each other—the eighth house, Scorpio, Pluto aspect. The asteroid with the first name of our daughter and the middle name of myself is another factor in my 7th harmonic Grand Trine which was activated. (The first name is the prime indicator of the person.) This asteroid is at 20° Virgo, conjunct the North Node and fourth cusp at 22° Virgo and 23° Virgo, and pulled into the Grand Trine by Kronos at 21° Capricorn. Also, the transiting asteroid with the name of my son (my husband's stepson-to-be) at 15° Cancer 20' equaled by a semisquare my natal Sun/Moon midpoint, which equals my husband's by a sesquiquadrate. (The names of my son and his father, my former husband, are the same.)

The NCGR Asteroid Committee's study on personal name asteroids is discussed in Chapter 3. There the names of these asteroids are given, and their correspondence to the names of the people is explained. In this chapter, I am alluding to name asteroids because they make interpretations of natal, harmonic and transiting charts so specific.

MEETING — 1ST HUSBAND

When my former husband and I met, the transiting North Node, Ascendant, East Point on one side and the transiting South Node, Descendant, West Point on the other were exactly conjunct my 7th harmonic name asteroid of this husband, West Point on one side and my 7th Harmonic East Point, Uranus on the other. (See Figure VI.) The transiting North Node, Ascendant, East Point were also exactly conjunct my natal name asteroid of this husband. (Since the name of our son is the same, there would be a reference to him, too.) The transiting fourth and tenth cusp were exactly conjunct the Vertex and Antivertex of this husband's 7th harmonic chart, while transiting Venus, Saturn and Cupido (marriage) were exactly conjunct the North Node, fourth cusp of my 7th harmonic chart. Of course, with the conjunction to the North Node, my 7th Harmonic Grand Trine was activated in this case too. The transiting asteroids that are precisely descriptive of the event which occurred are the asteroid with my name at 19° Aries 09'℞, exactly trine the asteroid with my former husband's name at 19° Sagittarius 21', and both exactly trine Pluto at 19° Leo 12'. At our meeting we (our name asteroids) were compulsively (Pluto) swept away (exact Grand Trine). The Pluto was exactly conjunct my 7th harmonic Venus at 18° Leo 26', my natal seventh house cusp at 20° Leo 27' and my former husband's natal Sun/Moon midpoint at 18° Leo 58'. In the transit chart the asteroid with my name, and Admetos at 21° Aries 10'℞, equaled the Sun/Moon midpoint at 20° Cancer 41' by a square, while an asteroid at 06° Virgo 56' with a name equivalent to mine equaled this midpoint by a semisquare. (Our study indicated that the name of an asteroid does not have to be exactly the same as the name of a person for the asteroid to represent that person.) The Admetos in this case does seem to point to the termination (Admetos) through me (my name asteroids) of that first marriage (Sun/Moon midpoint) that was eventually to result from this meeting.

MARRIAGE — 2ND HUSBAND

When my present husband and I were married, the transiting first house cusp was exactly conjunct my 7th harmonic Cupido, Juno—both related to marriage. (See Figure VI.) Also, transiting Juno was conjunct my 7th harmonic Jupiter to the minute and exactly opposite his 7th harmonic Cupido to the minute. Jupiter is appropriate because not only is it expansive, but it is concerned with law, as is marriage.[17] My 7th harmonic Grand Trine (which ties in with my husband's 7th harmonic Juno and Mars, Antivertex) was activated once more—this time by transiting Apollon, Mercury being exactly conjunct my 7th harmonic North Node, fourth house cusp. Mercury is appropriate because of the marriage certificate or document, and Apollon is appropriate because of its, and our, already mentioned Leonine associations. The transiting Mars, Vertex was exactly conjunct my husband's 7th harmonic South Node. The transiting Moon, asteroid with the name of our daughter-to-be two years hence (same as my middle name) was exactly conjunct his 7th harmonic Vertex, name asteroid. The transiting Moon, asteroid with our daughter's name (22° Scorpio 07', 23° Scorpio 03'), which conjuncted his 7th harmonic Vertex, name asteroid (22° Scorpio 40', 23° Scorpio 49'), conjuncted his natal fourth house cusp (22° Scorpio 09') as well. The transiting asteroid with my name at 01° Virgo 04' was square my 7th harmonic Pluto, Moon conjunction at 02° Gemini and his 7th harmonic East Point at 01° Sagittarius 06'. Transiting Pluto and Zeus at 00° Virgo equaled by a semisquare, Kronos at 29° Taurus 12'℞ equaled by a sesquiquadrate, and Venus and Poseidon at 13° Libra and the asteroid with a name similar to the name of my son (his stepson) at 15° Libra 46' equaled by a conjunction, the transiting Sun/Moon midpoint at 14° Libra 42'.

As for the natal Sun/Moon midpoints of my second husband and myself, my 7th harmonic Moon and Pluto and his 7th harmonic East Point equal them. These midpoints, which equal each other, were further activated by the Second Marriage Chart. The asteroid with my name at 01° Virgo in the seventh house equaled my natal Sun/Moon midpoint at 01° Gemini by a square, and his natal Sun/Moon midpoint at 17° Capricorn by a sesquiquadrate. Also, Pluto and Zeus at 00° Virgo in the seventh house equaled my Sun/Moon midpoint. The asteroid with a name equivalent to mine was at 17° Capricorn 48'℞ in the eleventh house, equaling my midpoint by a sesquiquadrate, and his by a conjunction. The asteroid with his name was at 17° Cancer 06' in the fifth house, equaling my midpoint by a semisquare, and his by an opposition. The asteroid with a name similar to the name of my son (his stepson) at 15° Libra 46' was in the eighth house, equaling my midpoint by a sesquiquadrate. The asteroid with my husband's name, the one with an equivalent to my name, and the one with a similarity to my son's name, were in a T-Square. (Including himself in the "we," my son always said "when we got married.") This T-Square was connected to what I consider another major configuration—a square combined with two sesquiquadrates. The exact square of Pluto, Zeus and my name asteroid to my natal Sun/Moon midpoint, and their exact sesquiquadrates to my husband's natal Sun/Moon midpoint and to the asteroid with a name equivalent to mine, forms such a powerful pattern. This pattern I had found significant, only to discover that another astrologer, Alan Epstein, had come to the same conclusion. He dubbed this configuration the Fist of God because it seems even more likely to be externally manifested than the Yod or Finger of God (a sextile combined with two quincunxes) which he had been studying.

Though the Sun/Moon midpoint is descriptive of marriage, not every couple will find such prominent tie-ins between this midpoint and the marriage chart. The fact that the natal Sun/Moon midpoints of my husband and myself equal each other makes this midpoint particularly important for us. However, our transiting name asteroids in this Second Marriage Chart equaling our "original" marriage midpoints makes "the story" even more specific (our name asteroids), as well as more than "transitory."

MARRIAGE — 1ST HUSBAND

When my former husband and I were married, the transiting Part of Fortune was exactly conjunct his 7th harmonic Vulcanus, Juno, while transiting Vulcanus was exactly conjunct my 7th harmonic first cusp, Hades. (See Figure VI.) Other exact aspects from the First Marriage Chart to our 7th harmonic charts are as follows. The transiting South Node and North Node were across the first cusp and seventh cusp, Pluto of his 7th harmonic chart. In relation to my 7th harmonic chart, transiting Apollon was conjunct my daughter's first name (my middle name) asteroid, North Node, fourth cusp; transiting Kronos was conjunct my Chiron, Saturn; and transiting Mercury was conjunct my Kronos, Midheaven; all activating my exact harmonic Grand Trine. Conjunct my harmonic South Node, tenth cusp was transiting Ceres, while conjunct my harmonic East Point, Uranus was transiting Cupido, and conjunct my harmonic Pluto, Moon was the transiting Antivertex. Transiting Venus was conjunct his harmonic Antivertex, fifth house cusp of his 7th harmonic chart. (The child we were to conceive— a boy with Venus exactly opposite his Ascendant—was, I believe, the main purpose of the marriage.) My transiting name asteroid at 02° Cancer 41'℞ was semisextile my 7th harmonic Pluto, Moon conjunction at 02° Gemini and sextile my first husband's 7th harmonic Sun, Pallas, Admetos conjunction at 01° and 02° Taurus. His transiting name asteroid at 02° Aries 44' was sextile my 7th harmonic Pluto, Moon conjunction and semisextile his 7th harmonic Sun, Pallas, Admetos conjunction. Our transiting name asteroids were exactly square. My role in the marriage was a Lunar one (02° Cancer), while his was a Martian one (02° Aries). The houses add greater detail—my asteroid was in the twelfth, and his was in the tenth. Of course, the degree of the name asteroids is Taurean, and so, stubbornly fixed in both cases. Transiting Cupido at 27° Virgo 46' (conjunct my 7th harmonic East Point and Uranus at 28° Virgo) and Dark Moon Lilith at 29° Gemini 31' (conjunct his 7th harmonic Vertex at that degree), equaled the transiting Sun/Moon midpoint at 13° Aquarius 16' by sesquiquadrates. The inexact square of Cupido and Dark Moon Lilith is pulled together by their exact sesquiquadrates to the Sun/Moon midpoint, forming a Fist of God. Dark Moon Lilith is supposedly a moon whose shadow is seen on the sun every six months. Though very skeptical about its use, I did find upon investigation that it has the seductive quality of a siren and represents hidden fascinations. The hidden fascination of the marriage (Cupido and Sun/Moon midpoint) was like a beguiling siren whose song we could not resist (Dark Moon Lilith).

As for my first husband's natal Sun/Moon midpoint at 18° Leo, which my 7th harmonic Venus equals by a conjunction, the First Marriage Chart further activated it. The eighth house Moon (ruler of the First Marriage Chart) at 19° Aquarius 42', my name asteroid at 02° Cancer and his name asteroid at 02° Aries equaled by an opposition, a semisquare and a sesquiquadrate, respectively, his Sun/Moon midpoint. Since his natal Mars/Saturn midpoint at 17° Leo is conjunct his natal Sun/Moon midpoint, the harmonic Venus and transiting name asteroids equaled his natal Mars/Saturn midpoint as well. As for my natal Sun/Moon midpoint at 01° Gemini, which my 7th harmonic Pluto, Moon equals by a conjunction, the First Marriage Chart further activated it. The Antivertex at 02° Gemini 06', the North Node at 00° Pisces 39', the Ascendant at 15° Cancer 30', Juno at 16° Capricorn 11' and the asteroid with a name similar to my first husband's and our son's at 16° Libra 56'[18] equaled by a conjunction, square, semisquare, sesquiquadrate and sesquiquadrate, respectively, my Sun/Moon midpoint. The Ascendant, the Juno in the seventh house (exactly conjunct the cusp) and this name asteroid in the fourth house were in an exact T-Square. Connected to the T-Square was a Fist of God, formed by the Antivertex at 02° Gemini being exactly sesquiquadrate Juno and this name asteroid. The Antivertex was then square the asteroid with my second husband's name at 03° Pisces 07'and the North Node at 00° Pisces in the ninth house, with the latter exactly sesquiquadrate the 16° Libra asteroid with the name similar to my first husband and son's, forming another Fist of God. What we have here are two interlocking Fists of God, with the common factors being the Antivertex and this name asteroid of my first husband and son. (Both configurations are connected to the T-Square.) The asteroid with my second husband's name, exactly conjunct his natal South Node and my natal North Node, equaled his natal Sun/Moon midpoint at 17° Capricorn by a semisquare. This emphasis on the name asteroid of my second husband within the First Marriage Chart implies to me that within this chart are not only signs of the dissolution of the first marriage, but also signs of the subsequent marriage that would ensue from it.

OTHER DESCRIPTIVE FACTORS

Though I stated that the angles and the personal points are particularly important, and the name asteroids are particularly explicit, the "rest" is descriptive too. In my 7th harmonic I have Neptune at 21° Aries and Kronos at 21° Capricorn, forming a square. In my first husband's 7th harmonic he has Saturn at 20° Cancer and Ceres at 19° Libra, forming a square. Combining our squares, we have a Cosmic Square. It could be said that in relation to partnership (7th harmonic) I have a Neptunianism (which can be expressed as idealization or deception or involvement with art, music or spirituality), that is greater than average (Kronos). On the other hand, my first husband in relation to partnership (7th harmonic) has a Saturnineness (which can be expressed as responsibility or separateness), that is related to nurturing (Ceres). He had been separated from his own mother, and the final outcome of our marriage was his unsuccessful attempt to separate me from our son. (The Ceres myth is relevant, though her separation was from a daughter.) With our squares interacting (the square is a Lunar aspect, and the issue was maternal), the negative expression of my 7th harmonic Neptune square Kronos and his 7th harmonic Saturn square Ceres was manifested.

The transits at the times of our meeting and marriage supported this manifestation. At the time of our meeting, our Cosmic Square was exactly aspected by the transiting asteroid with my name at 19° Aries and Admetos at 21° Aries (conjunct my harmonic Neptune at 21° Aries) opposite transiting Juno at 22° Libra—my natal Juno is at 21° Libra—(conjunct his harmonic Ceres at 19° Libra, square my harmonic Kronos at 21° Capricorn and his harmonic Saturn at 20° Cancer). At the time of our marriage our Cosmic Square was exactly aspected by transiting Admetos at 20° Aries (conjunct my harmonic Neptune at 21° Aries) opposite transiting Neptune at 21° Libra (conjunct his harmonic Ceres at 19° Libra) square transiting Mercury at 20° Capricorn (conjunct my harmonic Kronos at 21° Capricorn, opposite his harmonic Saturn at 20° Cancer). The positions at 20° pull in those at 19°. (Transiting Mercury was also tied into my 7th harmonic Grand Trine.) On the contrary, in my second husband's 7th harmonic only the Sun at 19° Libra similarly activates my 7th harmonic square. At the time of our meeting none of the bodies considered thus far similarly set off this square. At the time of our marriage only transiting Vesta at 21° Aries did so. Vesta could have been indicating that in this case vested interests in music were what was being expressed by my greater than average Neptunianism in relation to marriage (my second husband is a musician).

SUMMATION

The transiting charts in the four cases are descriptive of the events. The charts of the meetings have within them the seed of the marriages that were to follow. There are some factors which are frequently featured, such as the fourth house cusp and Nodes. In each of the eight interchanges (4 events x 2 people) either one or the other is featured—usually both. The four event charts activated my 7th harmonic North Node, fourth house cusp, which in turn activated my 7th harmonic Grand Trine. In general, the fourth house cusp is appropriate because in marriage the base or foundation, as well as the literal home, is usually changed. In general, the Nodes, which are the points at which the Moon crosses the apparent path of the Sun, are appropriate because they are close connections, especially between a man (Sun) and a woman (Moon). The North Node and fourth house cusp being conjunct in my 7th Harmonic Ascendant Equal House Chart makes this symbolism particularly fitting for me. Another repeated factor is the linkage of transiting Mercury and Apollon. In the Second Marriage Chart, they are exactly conjunct in the seventh house. In the First Marriage Chart, they are exactly trine, with the Mercury in the seventh house, and the Apollon in the third. In the First Meeting Chart, Mercury and Apollon are also exactly conjunct, but in the sixth house. Apollon relates to the Greek and Roman god Apollo (hence the Sun), and Mercury, to communication and documents—so they are appropriate in meetings and marriages. But they are particularly so for me and my husbands, since natally Mercury rules my Sun, Moon and Venus, and my seventh house Neptune, Mars, Jupiter, South Node and Vertex, as well as my Apollon, which is exactly conjunct my Neptune and Mars.

Though the four event charts have been related to the seventh harmonic, which specifically describes partnership, they also relate to other harmonics. The fifth is relevant because there were children and romance. The ninth is also because marriage is legal, and completion is usually sought in a marriage relationship.

Multiple Connections between Harmonics

Looking at the exact multiple conjunctions among the 5th, 7th and 9th harmonics is revealing. My 7th harmonic Grand Trine, which was activated by the four event charts, is connected to the 5th and 9th harmonics. In the Ascendant perspective, 5th harmonic Zeus (reproduction) in the fifth house is conjunct 7th harmonic Kronos (things above average), Midheaven (goal) in the seventh and eighth house, respectively. 9th harmonic Chiron (healer) in the sixth house is conjunct the 7th harmonic name asteroid of my daughter and North Node in the third house, and the fourth cusp. Considering other exact aspects, this 9th harmonic Chiron is trine 9th harmonic Ceres in the second house and 7th harmonic Chiron in the eleventh house and Saturn in the twelfth. (Kronos at 21° Capricorn pulls in the 20° bodies, such as the name asteroid of my daughter at 20° Virgo and Ceres at 20° Taurus.) The multi-leveled combination shows the following. Children (5th harmonic, Zeus and fifth house) are the above average goal (Kronos, Midheaven) of marriage (7th harmonic and seventh house) and sex (eighth house). Completion (9th harmonic) is through service (sixth house) as a healer (Chiron) in marriage (7th harmonic) connections (name asteroid and Node) that highlight communication (third house) in the home (fourth house cusp). Completion (9th harmonic) is also through nurturing (Ceres) love (second house) in marriage (7th harmonic) with a healer or foster parent who is a humanitarian, self-sacrificing, or literally Pisces, father (Chiron and Saturn in the eleventh and twelfth house). The Grand Trine would give a flowing quality. Naturally, the degrees and signs would give more detail.

These harmonics will also relate to the harmonic of the marriage age. In comparisons of exact conjunctions from the harmonic of the marriage age to the 5th, 7th and 9th harmonics, there are appropriate conjunctions to the 5th in terms of children, to the 7th, in terms of marriage, and to the 9th, in terms of completion or legality.

My second marriage occurred when I was 24 years of age, and some examples of exact conjunctions from my 24th harmonic to my 5th, 7th and 9th harmonics are as follows. In the Ascendant perspective, my 24th harmonic Descendant is conjunct my 5th harmonic Sun in the sixth house, conjunct the sixth cusp (combining the principles of the sixth and fifth). The Sun is the ruler of the 5th harmonic twelfth house, as well as of the Uranus in the eleventh and Saturn in the twelfth. Through my marriage at 24 years of age (24th harmonic Descendant), my son (5th harmonic Sun) became a stepchild of a Piscean father (5th harmonic Uranus in the eleventh and Saturn in the twelfth). My 24th harmonic asteroid with my second husband's name in the seventh house is conjunct my 7th harmonic Cupido and Juno (which are marriage) in the ninth house, and partnership is emphasized with this husband. My 24th harmonic Saturn in the ninth house is conjunct my 9th harmonic Jupiter in the first house, and Jupiter is the ruler of the 9th harmonic ninth house. In this second marriage responsible completion is emphasized.

There are some positions in the 5th, 7th and 9th harmonics that are exactly conjuncted by both the 18th and 24th harmonics. As an example, my 7th harmonic Cupido and Juno at 27° and 28° Aquarius, respectively, are activated by my 18th harmonic Part of Fortune at 28° Aquarius and by my 24th harmonic asteroid with my second husband's name at 27° Aquarius.

Just the conjunctions have been considered, but other exact aspects are relevant. In my 24th harmonic that name asteroid is opposite harmonic Juno at 28° Leo (my second husband's natal Ascendant) and quincunx harmonic Neptune at 27° Virgo (my husband is a Pisces). Also, 24th harmonic Ceres at 14° Leo and Uranus at 13° Sagittarius are semisextile and quincunx, respectively, my natal asteroid with his name at 13° Cancer. He did marry a mother (Ceres) with Aquarius rising (Uranus), who brought him a stepchild (Uranus).

Harmonic Midpoint Connections

Looking at the midpoints in the harmonic of the marriage age in relation to those in the 5th, 7th and 9th harmonics is also fruitful. Midpoint interchanges with the marriage partner, and natal correspondences, should be considered. Four major midpoints are listed in the center of the wheels of my 24th harmonic (Figure III), my 18th harmonic (Figure IV), my 7th harmonic (Figure X), and my present husband's 33rd harmonic (Figure V).

Focusing on the Sun/Moon and Venus/Mars midpoints and the 7th and 9th harmonics, there are the following examples. My 24th harmonic Venus/Mars midpoint at 10° Sagittarius equals my 7th harmonic Sun/Moon midpoint at 10° Gemini by an opposition. This equation is supported by my 24th harmonic Venus/Mars midpoint equaling (by a sesquiquadrate), and my 7th harmonic Sun/Moon midpoint equaling (by a semisquare), my natal Venus/Mars midpoint at 25° Cancer. With my present husband and me, there are several Sun/Moon and Venus/Mars midpoint interchanges between the harmonics of our respective ages at the time of our marriage and our 7th and 9th harmonics. His 33rd harmonic Venus/Mars midpoint at 13° Leo equals my 7th harmonic Venus/Mars midpoint at 28° Gemini by a semisquare. My 24th harmonic Sun/Moon midpoint at 05° Taurus equals his 7th harmonic Sun/Moon midpoint at 04° Scorpio by an opposition. As for the 9th harmonic, his 33rd harmonic Sun/Moon midpoint at 17° Aquarius equals my 9th harmonic Venus/Mars midpoint at 18° Aquarius by a conjunction. These midpoints both equal his 9th harmonic Venus/Mars midpoint at 03° Libra by a sesquiquadrate. My 24th harmonic Venus/Mars midpoint at 10° Sagittarius equals his 9th harmonic Sun/Moon midpoint at 10° Gemini by an opposition. This last interchange equals my natal Venus/Mars midpoint at 25° Cancer, by a sesquiquadrate from my 24th harmonic Venus/Mars midpoint, and by a semisquare from his 9th harmonic Sun/Moon midpoint. To compound matters, his 9th harmonic Sun/Moon midpoint at 10° Gemini equals my 7th harmonic Sun/Moon midpoint at that same degree by a conjunction. The connection of the 7th and 9th harmonics is appropriate because we sought completion (9th harmonic) in our marriage (7th harmonic). The marriage (7th harmonic) was also legal (9th harmonic). As mentioned, the Sun/Moon midpoint is particularly relevant to our relationship because natally our Sun/Moon midpoints equal each other. (Only the midpoints and the aspects by which they equal each other have been considered. An analysis of the houses, signs and degrees would give further insight.)

With my former husband and me, there are several Sun/Moon and Venus/Mars midpoint interchanges between the harmonics of our respective ages at the time of our marriage and our 7th and 9th harmonics. My 18th harmonic Sun/Moon midpoint at 26° Aries equals his 7th harmonic Sun/Moon midpoint at 12° Gemini and my 7th harmonic Sun/Moon midpoint at 10° Gemini by a semisquare. This equation is supported by my 18th harmonic Sun/Moon midpoint equaling (by a square), and my 7th harmonic Sun/Moon midpoint equaling (by a semisquare), my natal Venus/Mars midpoint at 25° Cancer. As for the 9th harmonic, his 30th harmonic Venus/Mars midpoint at 29° Aquarius equals my 9th harmonic Sun/Moon midpoint at 13° Libra by a sesquiquadrate. My 18th harmonic Sun/Moon midpoint at 26° Aries equals his 9th harmonic Venus/Mars midpoint at 26° Libra by an opposition. This last interchange equals my natal Venus/Mars midpoint at 25° Cancer by a square from my 18th harmonic Sun/Moon midpoint and his 9th harmonic Venus/Mars midpoint. Another reference to the natal is my 9th harmonic Venus/Mars midpoint at 18° Aquarius equaling his natal Sun/Moon midpoint at 18° Leo by an opposition. Also, his 9th harmonic Venus/Mars midpoint at 26° Libra equals my 7th harmonic Sun/Moon midpoint at 10° Gemini by a sesquiquadrate. The connection of the 7th and 9th harmonics is appropriate because, though the marriage (7th harmonic) didn't last, we sought completion in it, and it was legal (9th harmonic).

DIFFERENCES BETWEEN THE CONNECTIONS

This connection of the 7th and 9th harmonics with my first husband, however, is different from that with my second husband. With my first husband there is Venus/Mars midpoint to Sun/Moon midpoint, rather than Sun/Moon midpoint to Sun/Moon midpoint, and sesquiquadrate, rather than conjunction, between the midpoints.

In general, there are differences between the interchanges with my first husband and those with my second husband. There are not as many interchanges with the former as with the latter, but what the interchanges are is more important than how many there are. Most of the interchanges with my first husband tie in with my natal Venus/Mars midpoint, which equals my natal Uranus at 25° Aries by a square. This configuration can refer to sudden attractions which don't last. (The interchanges with my second husband, that tie in with my natal Venus/Mars midpoint, do so through my natal Venus at 11° Gemini—a more benign influence.) The two interchanges with my first husband that do not tie in with my natal Venus/Mars midpoint are as follows: his 30th harmonic Venus/Mars midpoint at 29° Aquarius equaling my 9th harmonic Sun/Moon midpoint at 13° Libra by a sesquiquadrate, and my 9th harmonic Venus/Mars midpoint at 18° Aquarius equaling his natal Sun/Moon midpoint at 18° Leo by an opposition. 29° Aquarius is exactly square my natal Mars/Saturn midpoint at 28° Scorpio, and 18° Aquarius is not only exactly opposite his natal Sun/ Moon midpoint at 18° Leo, but his natal

Mars/Saturn midpoint at 17° Leo. Though Mars can energize the Saturn, often Saturn inhibits the Mars instead. My ex-husband works with his second wife, which can be a positive expression of his natal conjunction of the Sun/Moon and Mars/Saturn midpoints. The importance of relating everything back to the natal chart should be realized.

OTHER COMPARISONS

In the examples given of midpoint interchanges, the harmonic of my marriage age and of the marriage ages of my first and second husband have been analyzed in relation to our 7th and 9th harmonics and natal charts. Instead, the harmonic of my marriage age could be compared to the harmonic of each of their marriage ages. In fact, you can compare the harmonic of your age to the harmonic of the age of an important person in your life at any point to see what is going on between you at that time. The focus has been on the midpoints, but it could be on the entire chart instead.

13th Harmonic as the Final Outcome

Another fruitful consideration is of the 13th harmonic in relation to other harmonics and to the natal chart. The 13th harmonic is the final outcome, as well as maternalism, the more nurturing parent, the home and the foundation (4)— particularly regarding the self (1) and communication (3). You can look, for instance, at the connections between the 13th harmonic and the 7th to see the final outcome of marriage, and between the 13th and 5th to see the final outcome of love affairs, creativity and children. Of course, first look at the 13th harmonic to see what it shows about the final outcome in general. If you're investigating marriage, look at the partner's 13th and 7th harmonics too. It isn't always possible to know the final outcome ahead of time, but these investigations will certainly help.

To illustrate how the 13th harmonic might be studied, particularly in relation to the 7th harmonic of marriage, especial consideration is given to the asteroids with the names of my two husbands, two children and myself. This choice has been made because when the general symbols of marriage, such as Venus, Juno and Cupido, are combined with the specific symbols of people— asteroids with their names— a specific, rather than a general, story is told. The harmonic houses mentioned are from the personal perspective of the Ascendant Equal House Chart.

MY 13TH HARMONIC

In my 13th harmonic, the asteroid with my ex-husband's name at 25° Pisces is exactly semisextile Jupiter at 26° Aquarius and the Descendant at 26° Aries and quincunx the Venus, Ascendant conjunction at 25°, 26° Libra, and Cupido at 24° Leo. These are all Neptunian aspects and so can be deceptive and dissolving, as well as idealistic. The sign of the asteroid is Neptunian too. The Venus, Ascendant and Cupido form a Yod, or Finger of God, with the name asteroid. The asteroid with my husband's name at 27° Sagittarius is exactly sextile Jupiter and the Venus, Ascendant conjunction. These are aspects of criticality and service. The name asteroid is in an exact Grand Trine with the Descendant at 26° Aries and Admetos at 28° Leo. As mentioned, Admetos can be neverending, or "till death do us part." Tied in with the Descendant (which is particularly related to the partner, and the asteroid with the name of the partner) in a flowing aspect in the 13th harmonic, this interpretation seems appropriate. This name asteroid is also exactly square the Part of Fortune at 27° Virgo. The square, being a maternal aspect, is very powerful but may indicate some conflict. This conflict may be between my husband's philosophy and thinking (name asteroid in Sagittarius at 27° in the 3rd house) and my integral, analytical philosophy and spirituality (Part of Fortune in Virgo at 27° in the 12th house), in regard to my final outcome (my 13th harmonic). (The Part of Fortune, being a combination of the Ascendant, Sun and Moon, is a point of integration as well as of Fortune.)

As an example of exact connections between my 13th and 7th harmonic, 13th harmonic Jupiter at 26° Aquarius is conjunct 7th harmonic Cupido, Juno at 27°, 28° Aquarius, while 13th harmonic Venus, Ascendant at 25°, 26° Libra is conjunct the 7th harmonic asteroid with my name at 25° Libra, forming an exact Grand Trine with the 7th harmonic asteroid at 27° Gemini that has the name similar to my son's. (Though my son's name is the same as his father's, I discovered, and discuss in Chapter 3, that when a name asteroid is approximate it may describe one approximately-named person more than it does another.) Until 1985 when another asteroid was named, the name of this asteroid also most closely approximated the name of my daughter. The final outcome (13th harmonic) of marriage (7th harmonic) seems to be auspicious (Jupiter), in relation to marriage (Cupido, Juno) and loving (Venus, Ascendant) in relation to me (my name asteroid) in harmonious connection to my children (similar name asteroid). The fact that the exact trine of the 13th harmonic connects with the Grand Trine of the 7th harmonic confirms the flowing aspect of the marriage harmonic.

MY 2ND HUSBAND'S 13TH HARMONIC

In my husband's 13th harmonic, the asteroid with my name and Dark Moon Lilith at 26°, 27° Cancer (I fascinate him) is exactly sextile Mercury and the North Node at 26°, 28° Virgo (I am a double Gemini). The name asteroid, Dark Moon conjunction forms an exact Grand Trine with Saturn at 27° Scorpio, and the South Node at 28° Pisces. Though not pulled into the Grand Trine, Chiron at 24° Scorpio is shown to be natally in exact 13th harmonic aspect to Saturn; and Cupido, Antivertex at 22°, 24° Pisces is shown to be natally in exact 13th harmonic aspect to the South Node.

Interaspects can be studied. As an example of exact connections between my second husband's 13th and my 7th harmonic, his 13th harmonic Vesta at 24° Libra is conjunct my 7th harmonic asteroid with my name at 25° Libra (activating my 7th harmonic Grand Trine in air); his 13th harmonic Saturn at 27° Scorpio is conjunct my 7th harmonic Antivertex at 27° Scorpio (activating his 13th harmonic exact Grand Trine in water); and his 13th harmonic Mercury and North Node at 26°, 28° Virgo are conjunct my 7th harmonic East Point, Uranus at 28° Virgo. Close by, his 13th harmonic Vertex at 24° Virgo is conjunct my 7th harmonic North Node, fourth cusp at 22°, 23° Virgo, which is trine Kronos, Midheaven, trine Chiron, Saturn, with our daughter's name asteroid pulled into the Grand Trine by Kronos. This is my 7th harmonic exact Grand Trine in earth which is always being activated by event and other charts. Also, his 13th harmonic Cupido, Antivertex at 22°, 24° Pisces is conjunct my 7th harmonic South Node, tenth cusp. His harmonic for the final outcome and for maternalism combines with mine for marriage with an emphasis on vested interests (Vesta), close connections (Nodes), Destiny (Vertexes), communication (Mercury) and marriage (Cupido). The highlighted Chiron, Saturn aspect in my 7th harmonic reinforces the Chiron, Saturn aspect in his 13th harmonic. Chiron, Saturn has been mentioned before in reference to my second husband's being a foster parent to my son. This manifestation, through our marriage, is part of the final outcome (13th harmonic) for my second husband. The final outcome and other references of 13 particularly regard the self (1) and communication (3), and our marriage is one of communication of self to each other. Our mutual activation of each other's individual harmonic Grand Trines is conducive to this expression because the trine is the aspect of communication.

On the other hand, my 7th harmonic asteroid with my name is exactly quincunx his 13th harmonic Antivertex, semisextile his Chiron and square his asteroid with my name. In regard to marriage (7th harmonic), my self-expression (my name asteroid in the fifth house) may be dissolved (Neptunian aspects) in relation to my second husband's final outcome (13th harmonic) as the preordained (Antivertex) foster father (Chiron) he became through me (my name asteroid). (My 7th harmonic name asteroid's exact quincunx to the Chiron, Saturn in my 7th harmonic Grand Trine in earth foreshadows this manifestation.) The square between my 7th harmonic asteroid with my name at 25° Libra and his 13th harmonic asteroid with my name at 26° Cancer is a maternal aspect, but this aspect may indicate, in regard to the final outcome (his 13th harmonic), some conflict between his perception of me as a mother (Cancer and 26°) and my perception of me as a wife (Libra and 25°), in regard to marriage (my 7th harmonic). (26° relates to the mother through Scorpio's reference to regeneration.) In contrast, his 7th harmonic asteroid with my name at 00° Cancer is exactly trine my 13th harmonic asteroid with my name at 29° Aquarius. (It seems as if a combination of hard and soft aspects is best.)

DISCRIMINATION BETWEEN HUSBANDS
The already mentioned conjunction of my 13th harmonic Jupiter at 26° Aquarius to my 7th harmonic Cupido and Juno at 27° and 28° Aquarius pulls in my 13th harmonic name asteroid at 29° Aquarius. It is these 7th harmonic positions of Cupido and Juno that are mentioned as being exactly conjuncted by appropriate positions in both my 18th and 24th harmonics (the years of my marriages). However, in the Ascendant perspective, my 18th harmonic asteroid with my former husband's name is at 24° Pisces in the 12th house, not tying in from one degree to the next with these positions, while my 24th harmonic asteroid with my present husband's name is at 27° Aquarius in the 7th house, exactly conjunct these positions. Also, 24th harmonic Jupiter at 25° Aquarius is exactly conjuncting its 13th harmonic position at 26° Aquarius.

OTHER CONSIDERATIONS
The relationship of other harmonics to the 13th and 7th could be considered. For instance, my 13th harmonic Jupiter and asteroid with my name at 26° and 29°

Aquarius (conjunct my 7th harmonic Cupido and Juno at 27° and 28° Aquarius) is exactly conjunct my 9th harmonic Saturn at 27° Aquarius. Completion through responsibility (9th harmonic Saturn) in marriage (7th harmonic Juno and Cupido) may have as its end result my expansion (13th harmonic asteroid with my name, and Jupiter).

In relation to the natal charts, my 13th harmonic Jupiter and asteroid with my name at 26° and 29° Aquarius (conjunct my 7th harmonic Cupido and Juno at 27° and 28° Aquarius), are exactly conjunct my husband's natal 7th house cusp at 28° Aquarius, opposite my natal Cupido at 29° Leo, conjunct his natal Ascendant. Cupido moves slowly, but my natal Moon at 00° Gemini is exactly square it, making this Uranian planet of marriage and family personal for me in an emotional way (Moon and square).

13th Harmonic as More Nurturing Parent

Though the 13th harmonic has been treated in terms of the final outcome, it also describes maternalism and the more nurturing parent, particularly in terms of the self and communication. To give an example, my father was my more nurturing parent, or at least was perceived as such by me. With my 13th harmonic Ascendant at 26° Libra, exactly conjunct Venus at 25° Libra, he was an artist, and our main communication was concerning art. In fact, he was my art teacher. He was also a double Sagittarius (Sun and Moon in Sagittarius), which is expressed in the exact trine to 13th harmonic Jupiter at 26° Aquarius. The 13th harmonic will also connect appropriately with that more nurturing parent's chart and with the factors in the offspring's chart which describe that parent. This Ascendant, Venus conjunction is exactly square his natal East Point at 25° Capricorn (we were separated) and opposition my natal Uranus at 25° Aries (he was an unusual parent). Uranus is the ruler of my natal Ascendant, as well as of the asteroid with the personal name closest to my father's name. (Details are given in Chapter 3.) This asteroid is conjunct my Ascendant, and I always identified with my father. This name asteroid and my Ascendant are also exactly trine (communication aspect) my name asteroid in my fourth house of the father. When we rediscovered each other, it was like finding someone who speaks your language in a land of strangers. To help you decide if it is your father or your mother who is the fourth house parent, you can use the 4th, 10th and 13th harmonics. The 4th describes the more nurturing parent in general terms, rather than in specific terms of communication.

Reiteration

There will be some who will argue that placing one harmonic over another and over natal charts will add too many factors. But it is through these accretions that what is significant is seen. Certain degrees, certain bodies or personal points, certain houses and certain aspects will be repeated again and again. And harmonics, which highlight particular principles and magnify them so that small differences loom large, are particularly suited to this accretionary process. And small differences bring us to the question of twins.

Twins

Several astrologers have studied twins in relation to the 13th harmonic and have said that the differences between twins can be seen particularly in relation to this harmonic. My studies indicate that all of the harmonics will distinguish between twins—each harmonic according to its own principle. The 13th harmonic being the final outcome, as well as maternalism or emotionality particularly regarding the self and communication, is an important principle and so shows significant differences. But the other harmonics are important principles too and show significant differences as well.

An example to illustrate my contention is the following case of identical male twins born seven minutes apart. The exact coordinates for the place of their birth were used. A listing of the harmonics from 1-30 is given in Figure XI for the older twin; in Figure XII, for the younger. The 1st harmonics are the natal charts. The positions in the listing are rounded off to the closer minute.

BIRTH TIME

Using my system of astro-numerology, differences are seen even before the natal chart or harmonics are considered. The first twin was born at 06:05 AM, and the second was born at 06:12 AM. Daylight Saving Time was in effect, so Standard Time was 05:05 and 05:12 AM. According to my studies, Daylight Saving Time is what is external, and Standard Time is what is internal. Though externally the twins don't seem the type to seek the limelight, they are both musicians who are performers (5). However, the first-born twin (05:05—Leo in relation to Leo) is more concerned with performing on stage and continued playing in rock-and-roll bands for nine years after the second-born twin (05:12—Leo in relation to Pisces) had decided he would never play in them again. Rather than play rock-and-roll on the road, the latter chose to play jazz, blues and weddings in New York. In our era there is more potential for being a super-star in rock-and-roll, than in jazz or blues, and the competition is such that until you've made it, "the Road" is your venue. (Often, after you've made it too.)

NATAL CHARTS

The natal charts support this distinction. The Ascendant of the older twin is 23° Taurus 56', while the Ascendant of the younger twin is 26° Taurus 11'. Again with the first-born twin, we have the emphasis on performance (23 = 5, and 5 in the 56 minutes). With the second, instead we have a Scorpionic emphasis (26). Considering the ten planets, four asteroids, eight Uranian planets, Transpluto, Nodes, Vertexes, East Point and Part of Fortune, there are three differences in house positions. Uranus is in the third house with the traveling twin, while Uranus is in the second house with the stay-at-home twin. Kronos (authority) is in the first house with the twin who wants to be famous, while it is in the twelfth house with the twin who just wants to be comfortable. Saturn is in the sixth house of the first-born twin who is more sickly, while it is in the fifth house of the second-born twin who doesn't really like the life of a performer. Also, the first-born twin has Kronos exactly conjunct his Ascendant, and Venus at 06° Taurus 12' exactly conjunct the East Point at 06° Taurus 50'. (Venus is the ruler of the Ascendant.) Both of these conjunctions would incline more to performance. Note that the principle of the East Point (6) relates to performance (5), with the 5 made even more powerful by the addition of the 0. Then, the Moon of the first twin is 13° Scorpio 14', instead of 13° Scorpio 18'—again the emphasis on 5 for the twin who wants "to shine." Degree symbolism, such as is given in Sepharial's translation of "La Volasfera" also helps discriminate. The symbols should not be taken literally, but metaphorically.

13TH HARMONICS

As for the 13th harmonic, 13 years is how old the twins both were when they began playing rock-and-roll—a reflection of a harmonic's reference to the happenings during the year of that age.

When their 13th harmonics are compared, the most outstanding difference is between the Ascendants. (Considering the Ascendants, Midheavens, Vertexes, East Points and Parts of Fortune, which are the factors that are particularly different between the harmonic charts of one twin and the other, gives the greatest contrast.) The harmonic Ascendant of the first-born twin is 11° Pisces 20', while the harmonic Ascendant of the second-born twin is 10° Aries 29', conjunct harmonic Vulcanus at 11° Aries 24', the natal twelfth house cusp at 09° Aries 03' and harmonic Pluto at 08° Aries 25'.

Re the first-born twin, the persona of his 13th harmonic can be described as erratic (11°) nebulousness or musicality (Pisces). Re the second-born twin, the persona of his 13th harmonic can be described as stable (10°) assertiveness (Aries), tempered by the conjunctions mentioned. The conjunction to Vulcanus would reinforce not only the intensity, but the subterranean quality of Pluto because Vulcan lived and worked under the ground. The twelfth house is concerned with the hidden also. Regarding the references of the 13th harmonic, the younger twin has a greater submerged emotional intensity (Ascendant conjunct Vulcanus, natal twelfth, and Pluto) than the older twin. (One of the references of the 13th harmonic is emotionality.) The twin with this powerful quadruple conjunction feels he is closer to their mother then his brother is—a reflection of the 13th harmonic's reference to the more nurturing parent. With the Ascendant equal house cusps placed around the 13th harmonic and natal chart of each twin as in Figure X, a different area emphasis is created by the Ascendants being one sign away from each other. As regards 13th harmonic concerns, the power and fated happenings related to Vulcanus (Vulcan was the Roman god of fire and metal-working) affect each twin differently. For instance, harmonic Vulcanus which the younger twin has exactly conjunct his harmonic Ascendant, emphasizing the persona, the older twin has exactly conjunct his harmonic second house cusp, emphasizing "Love; values in regard to personal matters; personal relationships." See Table IV. Also, the older twin has harmonic Uranus and Juno falling in his natal sixth house, with Juno exactly conjunct the natal sixth cusp and Uranus exactly conjunct the natal seventh cusp. The younger twin has harmonic Juno falling in the natal fifth house and harmonic Uranus in the natal sixth house, with no conjunctions to cusps. For the older twin, a greater emphasis is placed on marriage in the final outcome because

Figure XI
Harmonics 1-30 for Older Twin
Bronx, New York May 9, 1952 6h 5m 0s EDT

	1st	2nd	3rd	4th	5th	6th	7th	8th	9th	1Øth
☉	18 ♉ 43	7 ♋ 26	26 ♌ 10	14 ♎ 53	3 ♐ 36	22 ♑ 19	11 ♓ 02	29 ♈ 46	18 ♊ 29	7 ♌ 12
☽	13 ♏ 14	26 ♊ 28	9 ♒ 43	22 ♍ 57	6 ♉ 11	19 ♐ 25	2 ♌ 39	15 ♓ 53	29 ♎ 08	12 ♊ 22
☿	23 ♈ 00	16 ♉ 00	9 ♊ 00	2 ♋ 00	25 ♋ 00	18 ♌ 00	11 ♍ 00	4 ♎ 00	27 ♎ 00	20 ♏ 00
♀	6 ♉ 13	12 ♊ 25	18 ♋ 38	24 ♌ 51	1 ♎ 04	7 ♏ 16	13 ♐ 29	19 ♑ 42	25 ♒ 55	2 ♈ 07
♂	7 ♏ 34	15 ♊ 07	22 ♑ 41	0 ♍ 14	7 ♈ 48	15 ♏ 21	22 ♊ 55	0 ♒ 28	8 ♍ 02	15 ♈ 35
♃	2 ♉ 31	5 ♊ 02	7 ♋ 33	10 ♌ 03	12 ♍ 34	15 ♎ 05	17 ♏ 36	20 ♐ 07	22 ♑ 38	25 ♒ 08
♄	9 ♎ 02	18 ♈ 04	27 ♎ 05	6 ♉ 07	15 ♏ 09	24 ♉ 11	3 ♐ 12	12 ♊ 14	21 ♐ 16	0 ♋ 18
♅	11 ♋ 04	22 ♎ 08	3 ♒ 12	14 ♉ 16	25 ♌ 20	6 ♐ 24	17 ♓ 28	28 ♊ 32	9 ♎ 36	20 ♑ 40
♆	19 ♎ 35	9 ♉ 10	28 ♏ 45	18 ♊ 20	7 ♑ 55	27 ♋ 31	17 ♒ 06	6 ♍ 41	26 ♓ 16	15 ♎ 51
♇	19 ♌ 07	8 ♑ 13	27 ♉ 20	16 ♎ 26	5 ♓ 33	24 ♋ 39	13 ♐ 46	2 ♉ 52	21 ♍ 59	11 ♒ 06
A	23 ♉ 57	17 ♋ 54	11 ♍ 51	5 ♏ 48	29 ♐ 45	23 ♒ 42	17 ♈ 39	11 ♊ 36	5 ♌ 33	29 ♍ 30
M	2 ♒ 14	4 ♐ 27	6 ♎ 41	8 ♌ 55	11 ♊ 09	13 ♈ 22	15 ♒ 36	17 ♐ 50	20 ♎ 04	22 ♌ 17
☊	26 ♒ 54	23 ♑ 49	20 ♐ 43	17 ♏ 37	14 ♎ 31	11 ♍ 26	8 ♌ 20	5 ♋ 14	2 ♊ 08	29 ♈ 03
⚷	12 ♑ 14	24 ♎ 27	6 ♌ 41	18 ♉ 55	1 ♓ 08	13 ♐ 22	25 ♍ 35	7 ♋ 49	20 ♈ 03	2 ♒ 16
⚳	3 ♉ 02	6 ♊ 04	9 ♋ 05	12 ♌ 07	15 ♍ 09	18 ♎ 11	21 ♏ 13	24 ♐ 14	27 ♑ 16	0 ♓ 18
⚴	26 ♓ 01	22 ♓ 03	18 ♓ 04	14 ♓ 06	10 ♓ 07	6 ♓ 09	2 ♓ 10	28 ♒ 12	24 ♒ 13	20 ♒ 14
⚵	19 ♒ 01	8 ♑ 03	27 ♏ 04	16 ♎ 05	5 ♍ 07	24 ♋ 08	13 ♊ 09	2 ♉ 11	21 ♓ 12	10 ♒ 14
⚶	2 ♍ 17	4 ♒ 34	6 ♋ 51	9 ♐ 08	11 ♉ 25	13 ♎ 42	16 ♓ 00	18 ♌ 17	20 ♑ 34	22 ♊ 51
⊗	6 ♌ 05	12 ♐ 10	18 ♈ 14	24 ♌ 19	0 ♑ 24	6 ♉ 29	12 ♍ 34	18 ♑ 38	24 ♉ 43	0 ♎ 48
V	24 ♎ 58	19 ♉ 56	14 ♐ 53	9 ♋ 51	4 ♒ 49	29 ♌ 47	24 ♓ 45	19 ♎ 43	14 ♉ 40	9 ♐ 38
E	6 ♉ 50	13 ♊ 40	20 ♋ 30	27 ♌ 20	4 ♎ 10	11 ♏ 00	17 ♐ 50	24 ♑ 40	1 ♓ 31	8 ♈ 21

	11th	12th	13th	14th	15th	16th	17th	18th	19th	20th
☉	25 ♍ 55	14 ♏ 38	3 ♑ 22	22 ♒ 05	10 ♈ 48	29 ♉ 31	18 ♋ 14	6 ♍ 57	25 ♎ 41	14 ♐ 24
☽	25 ♑ 36	8 ♍ 50	22 ♈ 04	5 ♐ 18	18 ♋ 33	1 ♓ 47	15 ♎ 01	28 ♉ 15	11 ♑ 29	24 ♌ 43
☿	13 ♐ 00	6 ♑ 00	29 ♑ 00	22 ♒ 00	15 ♓ 00	8 ♈ 00	1 ♉ 00	24 ♉ 00	17 ♊ 00	10 ♋ 00
♀	8 ♉ 20	14 ♊ 33	20 ♋ 46	26 ♌ 58	3 ♎ 11	9 ♏ 24	15 ♐ 37	21 ♑ 49	28 ♒ 02	4 ♈ 15
♂	23 ♏ 09	0 ♋ 42	8 ♒ 16	15 ♍ 49	23 ♈ 23	0 ♐ 56	8 ♋ 30	16 ♒ 04	23 ♍ 37	1 ♉ 11
♃	27 ♓ 39	0 ♉ 10	2 ♊ 41	5 ♋ 12	7 ♌ 43	10 ♍ 13	12 ♎ 44	15 ♏ 15	17 ♐ 46	20 ♑ 17
♄	9 ♑ 20	18 ♋ 21	27 ♑ 23	6 ♌ 25	15 ♒ 27	24 ♌ 28	3 ♓ 30	12 ♍ 32	21 ♓ 34	0 ♎ 36
♅	1 ♉ 44	12 ♌ 48	23 ♏ 52	4 ♓ 56	16 ♊ 00	27 ♍ 04	8 ♑ 08	19 ♈ 12	0 ♌ 16	11 ♏ 20
♆	5 ♉ 26	25 ♏ 01	14 ♊ 36	4 ♑ 11	23 ♋ 46	13 ♒ 21	2 ♍ 56	22 ♓ 32	12 ♎ 07	1 ♉ 42
♇	0 ♋ 12	19 ♏ 19	8 ♈ 25	27 ♌ 32	16 ♑ 38	5 ♊ 45	24 ♎ 51	13 ♓ 58	3 ♌ 04	22 ♐ 11
A	23 ♏ 27	17 ♑ 24	11 ♓ 21	5 ♉ 18	29 ♊ 15	23 ♌ 12	17 ♎ 09	11 ♐ 06	5 ♒ 03	29 ♓ 00
M	24 ♊ 31	26 ♈ 45	28 ♒ 58	1 ♑ 12	3 ♏ 26	5 ♍ 40	7 ♋ 53	10 ♉ 07	12 ♓ 21	14 ♑ 35
☊	25 ♓ 57	22 ♒ 51	19 ♑ 45	16 ♐ 40	13 ♏ 34	10 ♎ 28	7 ♍ 23	4 ♌ 17	1 ♋ 11	28 ♉ 05
⚷	14 ♏ 30	26 ♌ 44	8 ♊ 57	21 ♓ 11	3 ♑ 25	15 ♎ 38	27 ♋ 52	10 ♉ 06	22 ♒ 19	4 ♐ 33
⚳	3 ♈ 20	6 ♉ 21	9 ♊ 23	12 ♋ 25	15 ♌ 27	18 ♍ 29	21 ♎ 30	24 ♏ 32	27 ♐ 34	0 ♒ 36
⚴	16 ♒ 16	12 ♒ 17	8 ♒ 19	4 ♒ 20	0 ♒ 22	26 ♑ 23	22 ♑ 25	18 ♑ 26	14 ♑ 27	10 ♑ 29
⚵	29 ♐ 15	18 ♏ 16	7 ♎ 18	26 ♌ 19	15 ♋ 20	4 ♊ 22	23 ♈ 23	12 ♓ 24	1 ♒ 26	20 ♐ 27
⚶	25 ♏ 08	27 ♈ 25	29 ♍ 42	1 ♓ 59	4 ♌ 16	6 ♑ 33	8 ♊ 50	11 ♏ 07	13 ♈ 24	15 ♍ 42
⊗	6 ♒ 53	12 ♊ 57	19 ♎ 02	25 ♒ 07	1 ♋ 12	7 ♏ 17	13 ♓ 21	19 ♋ 26	25 ♏ 31	1 ♈ 36
V	4 ♋ 36	29 ♑ 34	24 ♌ 32	19 ♓ 30	14 ♎ 27	9 ♉ 25	4 ♐ 23	29 ♊ 21	24 ♑ 19	19 ♌ 16
E	15 ♉ 11	22 ♊ 01	28 ♋ 51	5 ♍ 41	12 ♎ 31	19 ♏ 21	26 ♐ 11	3 ♒ 01	9 ♓ 51	16 ♈ 41

	21st	22nd	23rd	24th	25th	26th	27th	28th	29th	30th
☉	3 ♒ 07	21 ♓ 50	10 ♉ 33	29 ♊ 17	18 ♌ 00	6 ♎ 43	25 ♏ 26	14 ♑ 09	2 ♓ 53	21 ♈ 36
☽	7 ♈ 58	21 ♏ 12	4 ♋ 26	17 ♒ 40	0 ♎ 54	14 ♉ 09	27 ♐ 23	10 ♌ 37	23 ♓ 51	7 ♏ 05
☿	3 ♌ 00	26 ♌ 00	19 ♍ 00	12 ♎ 00	5 ♏ 00	28 ♏ 00	21 ♐ 00	14 ♑ 00	7 ♒ 00	0 ♓ 00
♀	10 ♉ 28	16 ♊ 40	22 ♋ 53	29 ♌ 06	5 ♎ 18	11 ♏ 31	17 ♐ 44	23 ♑ 57	0 ♓ 09	6 ♈ 22
♂	8 ♐ 44	16 ♋ 18	23 ♒ 51	1 ♎ 25	8 ♉ 58	16 ♐ 32	24 ♋ 05	1 ♓ 39	9 ♎ 12	16 ♉ 46
♃	22 ♒ 48	25 ♓ 19	27 ♈ 49	0 ♊ 20	2 ♋ 51	5 ♌ 22	7 ♍ 53	10 ♎ 24	12 ♏ 54	15 ♐ 25
♄	9 ♈ 37	18 ♎ 39	27 ♈ 41	6 ♏ 43	15 ♉ 44	24 ♏ 46	3 ♊ 48	12 ♐ 50	21 ♊ 52	0 ♑ 53
♅	22 ♒ 24	3 ♊ 28	14 ♍ 32	25 ♐ 37	6 ♈ 41	17 ♋ 45	28 ♎ 49	9 ♒ 53	20 ♉ 57	2 ♍ 01
♆	21 ♏ 17	10 ♊ 52	0 ♑ 27	20 ♋ 02	9 ♒ 37	29 ♌ 12	18 ♓ 47	8 ♎ 22	27 ♈ 57	17 ♏ 33
♇	11 ♉ 18	0 ♎ 24	19 ♒ 31	8 ♋ 37	27 ♏ 44	16 ♈ 50	5 ♍ 57	25 ♑ 03	14 ♊ 10	3 ♏ 17
A	22 ♉ 57	16 ♋ 53	10 ♍ 50	4 ♏ 47	28 ♐ 44	22 ♒ 41	16 ♈ 38	10 ♊ 35	4 ♌ 32	28 ♍ 29
M	16 ♏ 48	19 ♍ 02	21 ♋ 16	23 ♉ 29	25 ♓ 43	27 ♑ 57	0 ♐ 11	2 ♎ 24	4 ♌ 38	6 ♊ 52
☊	25 ♈ 00	21 ♓ 54	18 ♒ 48	15 ♑ 42	12 ♐ 37	9 ♏ 31	6 ♎ 25	3 ♍ 20	0 ♌ 14	27 ♊ 08
⚷	16 ♍ 46	29 ♊ 00	11 ♈ 14	23 ♑ 27	5 ♏ 41	17 ♌ 55	0 ♊ 08	12 ♓ 22	24 ♐ 36	6 ♎ 49
⚳	3 ♓ 38	6 ♈ 39	9 ♉ 41	12 ♊ 43	15 ♋ 45	18 ♌ 46	21 ♍ 48	24 ♎ 50	27 ♏ 52	0 ♑ 54
⚴	6 ♑ 30	2 ♑ 32	28 ♐ 33	24 ♐ 35	20 ♐ 36	16 ♐ 38	12 ♐ 39	8 ♐ 41	4 ♐ 42	0 ♐ 43
⚵	9 ♏ 28	28 ♍ 30	17 ♌ 31	6 ♋ 33	25 ♉ 34	14 ♈ 35	3 ♓ 37	22 ♑ 38	11 ♐ 39	0 ♏ 41
⚶	17 ♒ 59	20 ♋ 16	22 ♐ 33	24 ♉ 50	27 ♎ 07	29 ♓ 24	1 ♍ 41	3 ♒ 58	6 ♋ 15	8 ♐ 32
⊗	7 ♌ 41	13 ♐ 45	19 ♈ 50	25 ♌ 55	2 ♑ 00	8 ♉ 05	14 ♍ 09	20 ♑ 14	26 ♉ 19	2 ♎ 24
V	14 ♓ 14	9 ♎ 12	4 ♉ 10	29 ♏ 08	24 ♊ 06	19 ♑ 03	14 ♌ 01	8 ♓ 59	3 ♎ 57	28 ♈ 55
E	23 ♉ 31	0 ♋ 21	7 ♌ 11	14 ♍ 01	20 ♎ 52	27 ♏ 42	4 ♑ 32	11 ♒ 22	18 ♓ 12	25 ♈ 02

Figure XII
Harmonics 1-30 for Younger Twin
Bronx, New York May 9, 1952 6h 12m 0s EDT

	1st	2nd	3rd	4th	5th	6th	7th	8th	9th	10th
☉	18 ♉ 43	7 ♋ 27	26 ♌ 10	14 ♎ 54	3 ♐ 37	22 ♑ 21	11 ♓ 04	29 ♈ 48	18 ♊ 31	7 ♌ 15
☽	13 ♏ 18	26 ♊ 36	9 ♒ 55	23 ♍ 13	6 ♉ 31	19 ♐ 49	3 ♌ 07	16 ♓ 26	29 ♎ 44	13 ♊ 02
☿	23 ♈ 00	16 ♉ 01	9 ♊ 01	2 ♋ 01	25 ♋ 02	18 ♌ 02	11 ♍ 02	4 ♎ 03	27 ♎ 03	20 ♏ 04
♀	6 ♉ 13	12 ♊ 26	18 ♋ 39	24 ♌ 52	1 ♎ 05	7 ♏ 19	13 ♐ 32	19 ♑ 45	25 ♒ 58	2 ♈ 11
♂	7 ♏ 33	15 ♊ 07	22 ♑ 40	0 ♍ 14	7 ♈ 47	15 ♏ 21	22 ♊ 54	0 ♒ 27	8 ♍ 01	15 ♈ 34
♃	2 ♉ 31	5 ♊ 02	7 ♋ 33	10 ♌ 04	12 ♍ 35	15 ♎ 05	17 ♏ 36	20 ♐ 07	22 ♑ 38	25 ♒ 09
♄	9 ♎ 02	18 ♈ 04	27 ♎ 05	6 ♉ 07	15 ♏ 09	24 ♉ 11	3 ♐ 12	12 ♊ 14	21 ♐ 16	0 ♋ 18
♅	11 ♋ 04	22 ♎ 08	3 ♒ 12	14 ♉ 16	25 ♌ 20	6 ♐ 24	17 ♓ 28	28 ♊ 32	9 ♎ 36	20 ♑ 40
♆	19 ♎ 35	9 ♉ 10	28 ♏ 45	18 ♊ 20	7 ♑ 55	27 ♋ 30	17 ♒ 06	6 ♍ 41	26 ♓ 16	15 ♎ 51
♇	19 ♌ 07	8 ♑ 13	27 ♉ 20	16 ♎ 26	5 ♓ 33	24 ♋ 39	13 ♐ 46	2 ♉ 52	21 ♍ 59	11 ♒ 06
A	26 ♉ 12	22 ♋ 23	18 ♍ 35	14 ♏ 46	10 ♑ 58	7 ♓ 09	3 ♉ 21	29 ♊ 32	25 ♌ 44	21 ♎ 55
M	3 ♒ 56	7 ♐ 51	11 ♎ 47	15 ♌ 43	19 ♊ 39	23 ♈ 34	27 ♒ 30	1 ♑ 26	5 ♏ 22	9 ♍ 17
☊	26 ♒ 54	23 ♑ 48	20 ♐ 43	17 ♏ 37	14 ♎ 31	11 ♍ 25	8 ♌ 19	5 ♋ 14	2 ♊ 08	29 ♈ 02
⚷	12 ♑ 14	24 ♎ 27	6 ♌ 41	18 ♉ 55	1 ♓ 08	13 ♐ 22	25 ♍ 35	7 ♋ 49	20 ♈ 03	2 ♒ 16
⚳	3 ♉ 02	6 ♊ 04	9 ♋ 06	12 ♌ 08	15 ♍ 10	18 ♎ 11	21 ♏ 13	24 ♐ 15	27 ♑ 17	0 ♓ 19
⚴	26 ♓ 02	22 ♓ 03	18 ♓ 05	14 ♓ 06	10 ♓ 08	6 ♓ 09	2 ♓ 11	28 ♒ 12	24 ♒ 14	20 ♒ 15
⚵	19 ♒ 01	8 ♑ 03	27 ♏ 04	16 ♎ 06	5 ♍ 07	24 ♋ 09	13 ♊ 10	2 ♉ 11	21 ♓ 13	10 ♒ 14
⚶	2 ♍ 17	4 ♒ 34	6 ♋ 51	9 ♐ 09	11 ♉ 26	13 ♎ 43	16 ♓ 00	18 ♌ 17	20 ♑ 34	22 ♊ 51
⊕	6 ♌ 05	12 ♐ 10	18 ♈ 14	24 ♌ 19	0 ♑ 24	6 ♉ 29	12 ♍ 34	18 ♑ 38	24 ♉ 43	0 ♎ 48
V	26 ♎ 14	22 ♉ 27	18 ♐ 41	14 ♋ 55	11 ♒ 08	7 ♍ 22	3 ♈ 35	29 ♎ 49	26 ♉ 03	22 ♐ 16
E	8 ♉ 38	17 ♊ 16	25 ♋ 54	4 ♍ 32	13 ♎ 10	21 ♏ 48	0 ♑ 26	9 ♒ 04	17 ♓ 42	26 ♈ 20

	11th	12th	13th	14th	15th	16th	17th	18th	19th	20th
☉	25 ♍ 58	14 ♏ 42	3 ♑ 25	22 ♒ 09	10 ♈ 52	29 ♉ 36	18 ♋ 19	7 ♍ 03	25 ♎ 46	14 ♐ 30
☽	26 ♑ 20	9 ♍ 38	22 ♈ 57	6 ♐ 15	19 ♋ 33	2 ♓ 51	16 ♎ 09	29 ♉ 28	12 ♑ 46	26 ♌ 04
☿	13 ♐ 04	6 ♑ 04	29 ♑ 05	22 ♒ 05	15 ♓ 05	8 ♈ 06	1 ♉ 06	24 ♉ 06	17 ♊ 07	10 ♋ 07
♀	8 ♉ 24	14 ♊ 37	20 ♋ 50	27 ♌ 03	3 ♎ 16	9 ♏ 30	15 ♐ 43	21 ♑ 56	28 ♒ 09	4 ♈ 22
♂	23 ♏ 08	0 ♋ 41	8 ♒ 15	15 ♍ 48	23 ♈ 21	0 ♐ 55	8 ♋ 28	16 ♒ 02	23 ♍ 35	1 ♉ 08
♃	27 ♓ 40	0 ♉ 11	2 ♊ 42	5 ♋ 13	7 ♌ 44	10 ♍ 15	12 ♎ 46	15 ♏ 16	17 ♐ 47	20 ♑ 18
♄	9 ♑ 19	18 ♋ 21	27 ♑ 23	6 ♌ 25	15 ♒ 26	24 ♌ 28	3 ♓ 30	12 ♍ 32	21 ♓ 33	0 ♎ 35
♅	1 ♉ 44	12 ♌ 48	23 ♏ 52	4 ♓ 56	16 ♊ 01	27 ♍ 05	8 ♑ 09	19 ♈ 13	0 ♌ 17	11 ♏ 21
♆	5 ♉ 26	25 ♏ 01	14 ♊ 36	4 ♑ 11	23 ♋ 46	13 ♒ 21	2 ♍ 56	22 ♓ 31	12 ♎ 06	1 ♉ 42
♇	0 ♋ 12	19 ♏ 19	8 ♈ 25	27 ♌ 32	16 ♑ 38	5 ♊ 45	24 ♎ 51	13 ♓ 58	3 ♌ 04	22 ♐ 11
A	18 ♐ 07	14 ♒ 18	10 ♈ 30	6 ♊ 41	2 ♌ 53	29 ♍ 04	25 ♏ 16	21 ♑ 27	17 ♓ 39	13 ♉ 51
M	13 ♋ 13	17 ♉ 09	21 ♓ 05	25 ♑ 00	28 ♏ 56	2 ♎ 52	6 ♌ 47	10 ♊ 43	14 ♈ 39	18 ♒ 35
☊	25 ♓ 56	22 ♒ 51	19 ♑ 45	16 ♐ 39	13 ♏ 33	10 ♎ 27	7 ♍ 22	4 ♌ 16	1 ♋ 10	28 ♉ 04
⚷	14 ♏ 30	26 ♌ 44	8 ♊ 57	21 ♓ 11	3 ♑ 25	15 ♎ 38	27 ♋ 52	10 ♉ 05	22 ♒ 19	4 ♐ 33
⚳	3 ♈ 21	6 ♉ 23	9 ♊ 25	12 ♋ 27	15 ♌ 29	18 ♍ 30	21 ♎ 32	24 ♏ 34	27 ♐ 36	0 ♒ 38
⚴	16 ♒ 17	12 ♒ 18	8 ♒ 20	4 ♒ 21	0 ♒ 23	26 ♑ 24	22 ♑ 26	18 ♑ 27	14 ♑ 29	10 ♑ 31
⚵	29 ♐ 16	18 ♏ 17	7 ♎ 18	26 ♌ 20	15 ♋ 21	4 ♊ 23	23 ♈ 24	12 ♓ 26	1 ♒ 27	20 ♐ 28
⚶	25 ♏ 08	27 ♈ 26	29 ♍ 43	2 ♓ 00	4 ♌ 17	6 ♑ 34	8 ♊ 51	11 ♏ 08	13 ♈ 25	15 ♍ 43
⊕	6 ♒ 53	12 ♊ 57	19 ♎ 02	25 ♒ 07	1 ♋ 12	7 ♏ 17	13 ♓ 21	19 ♋ 26	25 ♏ 31	1 ♈ 36
V	18 ♋ 30	14 ♒ 44	10 ♍ 57	7 ♈ 11	3 ♏ 24	29 ♉ 38	25 ♐ 52	22 ♋ 05	18 ♒ 19	14 ♍ 33
E	4 ♊ 58	13 ♋ 36	22 ♌ 14	0 ♎ 52	9 ♏ 30	18 ♐ 08	26 ♑ 46	5 ♓ 24	14 ♈ 02	22 ♉ 40

	21st	22nd	23rd	24th	25th	26th	27th	28th	29th	30th
☉	3 ♒ 13	21 ♓ 56	10 ♉ 40	29 ♊ 23	18 ♌ 07	6 ♎ 50	25 ♏ 34	14 ♑ 17	3 ♓ 01	21 ♈ 44
☽	9 ♈ 22	22 ♏ 40	5 ♋ 59	19 ♒ 17	2 ♎ 35	15 ♉ 53	29 ♐ 12	12 ♌ 30	25 ♓ 48	9 ♏ 06
☿	3 ♌ 07	26 ♌ 08	19 ♍ 08	12 ♎ 08	5 ♏ 09	28 ♏ 09	21 ♐ 09	14 ♑ 10	7 ♒ 10	0 ♓ 11
♀	10 ♉ 35	16 ♊ 48	23 ♋ 01	29 ♌ 14	5 ♎ 27	11 ♏ 41	17 ♐ 54	24 ♑ 07	0 ♓ 20	6 ♈ 33
♂	8 ♐ 42	16 ♋ 15	23 ♒ 49	1 ♎ 22	8 ♉ 56	16 ♐ 29	24 ♋ 02	1 ♓ 36	9 ♎ 09	16 ♉ 43
♃	22 ♒ 49	25 ♓ 20	27 ♈ 51	0 ♊ 22	2 ♋ 53	5 ♌ 24	7 ♍ 55	10 ♎ 26	12 ♏ 56	15 ♐ 27
♄	9 ♈ 37	18 ♎ 39	27 ♈ 41	6 ♏ 42	15 ♉ 44	24 ♏ 46	3 ♊ 48	12 ♐ 49	21 ♊ 51	0 ♑ 53
♅	22 ♒ 25	3 ♊ 29	14 ♍ 33	25 ♐ 37	6 ♈ 41	17 ♋ 45	28 ♎ 49	9 ♒ 53	20 ♉ 57	2 ♍ 01
♆	21 ♏ 17	10 ♊ 52	0 ♑ 27	20 ♋ 02	9 ♒ 37	29 ♌ 12	18 ♓ 47	8 ♎ 22	27 ♈ 57	17 ♏ 32
♇	11 ♉ 18	0 ♎ 24	19 ♒ 31	8 ♋ 37	27 ♏ 44	16 ♈ 50	5 ♍ 57	25 ♑ 03	14 ♊ 10	3 ♏ 17
A	10 ♋ 02	6 ♍ 14	2 ♏ 25	28 ♐ 37	24 ♒ 48	21 ♈ 00	17 ♊ 11	13 ♌ 23	9 ♎ 34	5 ♐ 46
M	22 ♐ 30	26 ♎ 26	0 ♍ 22	4 ♋ 18	8 ♉ 13	12 ♓ 09	16 ♑ 05	20 ♏ 01	23 ♍ 56	27 ♋ 52
☊	24 ♈ 58	21 ♓ 53	18 ♒ 47	15 ♑ 41	12 ♐ 35	9 ♏ 29	6 ♎ 24	3 ♍ 18	0 ♌ 12	27 ♊ 06
⚷	16 ♍ 46	29 ♊ 00	11 ♈ 14	23 ♑ 27	5 ♏ 41	17 ♌ 54	0 ♊ 08	12 ♓ 22	24 ♐ 35	6 ♎ 49
⚳	3 ♓ 40	6 ♈ 42	9 ♉ 44	12 ♊ 46	15 ♋ 48	18 ♌ 49	21 ♍ 51	24 ♎ 53	27 ♏ 55	0 ♑ 57
⚴	6 ♑ 32	2 ♑ 34	28 ♐ 35	24 ♐ 37	20 ♐ 38	16 ♐ 40	12 ♐ 41	8 ♐ 43	4 ♐ 44	0 ♐ 46
⚵	9 ♏ 30	28 ♍ 31	17 ♌ 33	6 ♋ 34	25 ♉ 35	14 ♈ 37	3 ♓ 38	22 ♑ 40	11 ♐ 41	0 ♏ 43
⚶	18 ♒ 00	20 ♋ 17	22 ♐ 34	24 ♉ 51	27 ♎ 08	29 ♓ 25	1 ♍ 43	4 ♒ 00	6 ♋ 17	8 ♐ 34
⊕	7 ♌ 41	13 ♐ 45	19 ♈ 50	25 ♌ 55	2 ♑ 00	8 ♉ 05	14 ♍ 09	20 ♑ 14	26 ♉ 19	2 ♎ 24
V	10 ♈ 46	7 ♏ 00	3 ♊ 14	29 ♐ 27	25 ♋ 41	21 ♒ 54	18 ♍ 08	14 ♈ 22	10 ♏ 35	6 ♊ 49
E	1 ♋ 18	9 ♌ 56	18 ♍ 34	27 ♎ 12	5 ♐ 50	14 ♑ 28	23 ♒ 07	1 ♈ 45	10 ♉ 23	19 ♊ 01

his natal seventh house cusp and his harmonic Juno, which both refer to marriage, are highlighted in the 13th harmonic.

OTHER HARMONICS

However, if you want to focus on marriage, you should look at the 7th harmonic; and if you want to focus on the career, the 10th harmonic. Whichever harmonic is chosen, a comparison of exact major configurations is helpful.

Choosing the 10th harmonic and considering exact major configurations with the Ascendant, Midheaven, Vertex, East Point or Part of Fortune, the first-born twin has a Yod and a Grand Trine, while the second-born twin has a Grand Trine.

The differences between the Grand Trines are revealing. The older twin's Grand Trine is East Point (08° Aries 20'), trine Sun (07° Leo 11'), trine Vertex (09° Sagittarius 38'), while the younger twin's Grand Trine is Ascendant (21° Libra 55'), trine Cupido, Pallas (19° Aquarius 45', 20° Aquarius 15'), trine Vesta (22° Gemini 51'). With the first-born twin, we have the Solar quality, that was noticed in his birth time and natal chart, reiterated in the 10th harmonic in terms of his career. If you put his 10th harmonic planets and points in the Midheaven Equal House Chart (which is particularly related to the career) the harmonic East Point falls in the fifth house, the harmonic Sun, in the ninth house, and the harmonic Vertex, in the first house. This twin not only performs and travels, but writes many of the songs he performs, and his primary goal is to have the songs published. His combination of factors which relate to the self (East Point, Aries, first house), to performance (Sun, Leo, fifth house) and to travel and publishing (Sagittarius, ninth house, 09°) supports this manifestation. As for the second-born twin's Grand Trine (placing the 10th harmonic planets and points in the Midheaven Equal House Chart), the harmonic Ascendant falls in the eleventh house, the harmonic Cupido, Pallas in the third house, and the harmonic Vesta, in the seventh house. Though this twin is working in a bank now, he is studying to become a computer programmer. His combination of factors which relate to the self (Ascendant), to banking (Vesta, 20°) and to computer programming (Pallas, Aquarius, eleventh house) supports this manifestation. The exact conjunction of Pallas and Cupido, of course, shows that natally Pallas and Cupido are in a 10th harmonic aspect within 2 minutes of exactitude. (Pallas and Cupido are actually in a 2nd harmonic aspect natally—each harmonic picks up the harmonics divisible in it.) Natally, Pallas is at 26° Pisces 01', and Cupido is at 25° Virgo 58'. The first-born twin would have this exact opposition, but it would not exactly aspect his natal Ascendant at 23° Taurus, while it would the second-born twin's natal Ascendant at 26° Taurus. The second-born twin's working in a bank is also appropriate for this 26° Taurus Ascendant. (The Plutonian quality noted in this twin's 13th harmonic is too.)

As for the older twin's 10th harmonic Yod, it is Ascendant (29° Virgo 29'), Transpluto (00° Libra 48'), quincunx the North Node (29° Aries 03') and Ceres (00° Pisces 17'). Interestingly, while the second-born twin has Vesta in a major configuration (Grand Trine) with his 10th harmonic Ascendant, and he works in a bank, the first-born twin has Ceres in a major configuration (Yod) with his 10th harmonic Ascendant, and the only job he has had outside of music has involved food (Ceres).

The 10th harmonic focuses on paternalism as well. For the older twin this major involvement of Ceres with the 10th harmonic may indicate that he perceives their mother as the more authoritative, more distant, parent. The younger twin has Ceres exactly sextile his 13th harmonic Ascendant, and, as mentioned before, he perceives himself as closer to their mother. He also perceives his brother as closer to their father. Unfortunately, I was only able to interview the younger twin and so have only his perception. The mother might be the 13th harmonic for both twins, but the younger twin might identify with her more. The younger twin's 13th harmonic Uranus is exactly square his 13th harmonic East Point, while the older twin's 13th harmonic Uranus is exactly square his 13th harmonic Vertex. The mother is an Aquarian, so the Uranus may represent her. The East Point, in contrast to the Vertex which is "fated" happenings, is the self, so the East Point aspect may represent the younger twin's identification with the mother. There is a conjunction of his 13th harmonic East Point at 22° Leo 14', and the older twin's 10th harmonic Midheaven at 22° Leo 17'. Their mother has an exact conjunction to these points from her natal Neptune at 21° Leo—21° (twin) Leo (Sun, Son). Sun will sometimes mean son— a word that isn't it, but sounds like it—because astrology is often metaphorical, instead of literal.

As explained before, other harmonics can be related to the 13th harmonic to see their final outcome. The first-born twin has a 13th harmonic exact Saturn, Mercury conjunction at 27° Capricorn 23', 28° Capricorn 59'. His 10th harmonic Ascendant at 29° Virgo 29' exactly aspects not only this conjunction, but his 13th harmonic Midheaven at 28° Aquarius 58', East Point at 28° Cancer 50' and Part of Fortune at 00° Cancer 03'. These connections could relate to his having finally decided to return to New York to concentrate on writing and publishing his songs. The younger twin, though having written songs before, is not that interested in writing any longer. With his 13th harmonic Saturn and Mercury at 27° Capricorn 22' and 29° Capricorn 04', he doesn't have an exact Saturn, Mercury conjunction. His 10th harmonic East Point at 26° Aries 20' exactly aspects the 13th harmonic Saturn, but not the Mercury and not any of the other four personal points which are the most discriminating.

INTERVALS OF TIME

As a final comment, my studies show that the separation between the age of one person and another is significant. Usually, it is the number of years that is the principle, and what that principle relates to is the number of months, which in turn applies to the number of days. In the case of the twins, the number of hours, which is 0, would be the principle, and what that principle relates to is the number of minutes, which in turn applies to the number of seconds. The house, sign, planet and aspect references would be relevant. But aside from these references, since it is the number that is paramount, different periods of time are interchangeable. An interval which is expressed as minutes between the birth of one twin and the other can be expressed as months, as well as days or years, in their lives. In other words, the 7 minute time separation between the birth of the older twin and the younger has translated into other time separations with intervals of 7 between events in the life of the older twin and the younger. For instance, the older twin met the girl he wanted to marry (and married) almost 7 months before the younger twin met the girl he wanted to marry. (I suspect that the separation between the births is closer to 6 and $^3/_4$ minutes, than 7, because the interval in regard to a number of other events has also been "almost 7.")

RELEVANCE OF ALL HARMONICS

Hopefully, this brief analysis of twins will illustrate the fact that it is not just the 13th harmonic which discriminates between twins, or between people or events in general. Just as all the numbers are relevant, all the harmonics are—each according to its own meaning.

Intervals of Space and Time

And, an interval of space, since the number is paramount, can equate to an interval of time. In the harmonic chart of one's age, I've noticed that the number of degrees between bodies and/or personal points, or between them and natal angles, equates to the number of months after one's birthday that an important event occurs. The particular harmonic bodies and personal points and natal angles would be relevant to the particular event.

MONTHS FROM BIRTHDAY TO MARRIAGE

For instance, my second husband and I were married August 30, 1957, six months and four days after his 33rd birthday, February 26, 1957. In his 33rd harmonic chart (see Figure V), his harmonic Sun (natally the ruler of his Ascendant and posited in his seventh house) is approximately 06° before his natal seventh house cusp; his harmonic Moon is approximately 06° before my natal Ascendant (I figured prominently in this event); his harmonic Midheaven is approximately 06° before his harmonic Uranus (natally the ruler of, and posited in, his seventh house); and his harmonic Kronos (head of the family) is approximately 06° before his natal Midheaven and a square to his harmonic Sun.

To be exact, there were six months, four days, one hour, seven minutes and eighteen seconds between my husband's birth time (not Solar Return time) on his 33rd birthday and the time of our marriage on our marriage day. This birth time, which has been rectified from the 05:00 P.M. EST given me by my husband's mother, is 04:52:42 P.M. EST. As explained in endnote 6, I consider it valid to use this rectified time in my research because there was no time on the birth certificate, the time given me was "rounded off," and the rectification was done long before his chart was used for my research. The time of the marriage pronouncement, as I recall, was 07:00 PM EDT, which would have to be changed to 06:00 PM EST to equate to his birth time. You would add to the harmonic positions 06°07.8323925', which is 06° for the six months and 07.8323925' for the four days, one hour, seven minutes and eighteen seconds.[19]

These computations, which are not done by Astro, are done by my calculator from positions with four-place decimals, except for the asteroids (other than Ceres, Pallas, Juno, Vesta and Chiron) with one-place decimals, and Transpluto, Dark Moon Lilith and Halley's Comet with none. The seconds are included to better demonstrate these new concepts and to illustrate the importance of the greatest possible exactitude.

The addition is as follows: 33rd harmonic Sun (22° Aquarius 39'43.56") + 06°07.8323925' = 28° Aquarius 47'33.5", exactly conjunct his natal Descendant (28° Aquarius 15'15.12"); 33rd harmonic Moon (13° Aquarius 17'54.6") + 06°07.8323925' = 19° Aquarius 25'44.5", exactly conjunct my natal Ascendant (20° Aquarius 27'44.28"); 33rd harmonic Midheaven (11° Capricorn 27'42.84") + 06°07.8323925'= 17° Capricorn 35'32.7", exactly conjunct 33rd harmonic Uranus (18° Capricorn 06'42.84") and his natal Sun/Moon midpoint (17° Capricorn 49'3.3"); 33rd harmonic Kronos (16° Taurus 19'22.08") + 06°07.8323925' = 22° Taurus 27'12", exactly conjunct his natal Midheaven (22° Taurus 09'55.8") and square 33rd harmonic Sun (22° Aquarius 39'43.56"). Notice that the harmonic Sun is about a half a degree past its conjunction to the minute, while the harmonic Midheaven is about a half a degree before its conjunction to the minute. A mixture of some conjunctions applying to and some separating from 00' of exactitude and some at 00' of exactitude, is typical.

The name asteroids are particularly descriptive. For the marriage of my husband and myself, exact aspects of my name asteroid and his will be used to demonstrate this assertion. In my husband's 33rd harmonic chart, the asteroid with my name is at 22° Aquarius 54'12", conjunct the Sun at 22° Aquarius 39'43.56", in an exact Grand Trine with the Part of Fortune at 23° Libra 01'28.9" and Mars at 24° Gemini 28'21.36". By the time of our marriage, this harmonic asteroid had "progressed" to 29° Aquarius 02'1.94", conjunct my husband's natal seventh house cusp at 28° Aquarius 15'15.12". This seventh house emphasis is repeated in the harmonic of my age when we married. In my 24th harmonic chart (see Figure III) the asteroid with my husband's name is at 27° Aquarius 07'42", conjunct his natal seventh house cusp. By the time of our marriage three months and six days after my birthday, this harmonic asteroid had progressed to 00° Pisces 20'44.7", square my harmonic Sun at 01° Gemini 56'25.44" (he has Leo on his first cusp, and I have it on my seventh), which is conjunct my natal Sun/Moon midpoint at 01° Gemini 27'58.6", opposite harmonic Zeus at 02° Sagittarius 03'22.68". (As mentioned before, it was a fruitful marriage.) As for my harmonic asteroid with my name, it is at 18° Leo 05'06", sextile the Part of Fortune at 17° Gemini 35'53.5" and Nodes at 18° Gemini 29'36.24". By the time of our marriage, this harmonic asteroid had progressed to 21° Leo 18'8.74",[20] conjunct my natal seventh house cusp at 20° Leo 27'44.28", again pointing to marriage. As for my husband's harmonic asteroid with his name, it is at 22° Aries 17'06", sextile his harmonic asteroid with my name. By the time of our marriage, this harmonic asteroid with his name had progressed to 28° Aries 24'55.9", semisextile his harmonic asteroid with a name equivalent to mine at 28° Pisces 28'18", Juno (marriage) at 29° Pisces 25'27.84", and sextile his natal Descendant.

My husband's progressed name asteroid was also semisquare (Pluto aspect) his harmonic Pluto (12° Gemini 23'20.4"), in his exact harmonic Cosmic Square of that planet opposite Neptune (10° Sagittarius 52'26.4"), square Saturn, South Node (09° Virgo 54'16.56", 11° Virgo 08'20.4"), opposite North Node (11° Pisces 08'20.4"). This major configuration might add the responsibility of Saturn, the intensity of Pluto and the idealism of Neptune. Interestingly, my husband has a Pisces Sun and a Scorpio Moon, so the Neptune and Pluto may represent him. The activation of a major harmonic configuration is always significant, but in this case there is a multiple effect because harmonic Pluto is in an exact Grand Trine with the harmonic Moon (13° Aquarius 17'54.6") and harmonic Ceres (12° Libra 43'41.16") and in a series of exact connecting Yods with the harmonic Midheaven (11° Capricorn 27'42.84"), Jupiter, Vertex (11° Scorpio 03'2.52", 12° Scorpio 36'28.08"), the South Node (11° Virgo 08'20.4") and Apollon (11° Aries 48'58.32"). As previously explained, in regard to marriage Apollon is particularly important for me and my husband. Its shining, as well as the expansiveness of Jupiter, the emotionality of the Moon and the nurturing of Ceres, are added. The South Node is in an exact Grand Trine with the Midheaven and Antivertex (12° Taurus 36'28.08"). An interpretation could be that close connections (South Node) are purposeful (Midheaven) and fated (Antivertex). The South Node's being in an exact Cosmic Square with Saturn, the North Node, Pluto and Neptune has already been mentioned. The Midheaven and Antivertex are in exact T-Squares. The Midheaven is square Apollon and Ceres, while the Antivertex is opposite Jupiter, Vertex and square the Moon. These additional configurations repeat the principles of Apollon, Jupiter, the Moon and Ceres as listed above, but now in the more forceful form of squares and oppositions.

A REPEATED SEPARATION
When you scan the harmonic chart and notice that there is a repeated separation between bodies and/or personal points, or between them and natal angles, you can deduce that an important event will occur in that number of months. Which planets, asteroids, personal points and natal angles are involved will help you determine what the event will be. Of course, several planets, asteroids and/or personal points at the same or contiguous degrees will make for a multiple, and so even stronger, activation. One major configuration progressing to another is particularly powerful.

YEARS FROM BIRTHDAY TO WILLS
As stated, the number is paramount, and so, different periods of time are interchangeable. Therefore, a separation can represent a number of days or a number of years, rather than a number of months. The harmonic chart of the age at which you were married, for instance, is a harmonic related to that marriage, and the end of that age does not end the relevance of that harmonic chart to that marriage. The approximate 06° separations in my second husband's 33rd harmonic (see Figure V), which refer to our marriage approximately six months after his 33rd birthday, also refer to our writing our wills approximately six years after this birthday. Of course, I had no awareness of harmonics or astrology at that time. Later, at the beginning of my study of astrology, for research purposes I made lists of important events, and the signing of the wills was the only important event I recorded for 1963. The wills were signed February 3, 1963, and their main purpose was to state my wishes that

if something happened to me, my second husband would get custody of my son from my previous marriage. Our lawyer said that, though our wills were not binding in this regard, the wishes of a deceased mother had decided weight with the court. Not knowing the time of the signing, I shall use just the number of years and days. Considering a degree for a year, the amount of change in 1 day is less than 10 seconds of arc because there are 60 minutes of arc divided by 365 days—366 days in leap years. (365.24219879 days is not used because the progression is from one birthday and time to the next birthday and time, rather than from the degree, minute and second of the Sun to the same degree, minute and second of the Sun. Experimenting with the use of the Solar Return time for harmonic progressions, I found that it did not work as well as the birth time.)

The increment of 05°56.219178',[21] which equates to the five years and 342 days that had elapsed since my second husband's 33rd birthday, brings the harmonic Sun to 28° Aquarius 35'56.7", exactly conjunct his natal Descendant. The Sun represents children (and can be "the son"), and the Descendant represents the partner. This same increment brings the harmonic Moon to 19° Aquarius 14'7.75", exactly conjunct my natal Ascendant. The Moon represents the mother, and the Ascendant, the self. The harmonic Midheaven comes to 17° Capricorn 23'55.9", exactly conjunct his harmonic Uranus and natal Sun/Moon midpoint. The Midheaven is purpose, as well as career; Uranus relates to the stepchild; and the Sun/Moon midpoint, to marriage. Harmonic Kronos, with this increment, is at 22° Taurus 15'35.2", exactly conjunct his natal Midheaven and square the harmonic Sun. Kronos is the head of the family, and the Sun, "the son." Harmonic Chiron comes to 02° Sagittarius 16'14.4", in exact opposition to harmonic Mercury and to my natal Sun. Chiron relates to stepparents; Mercury, to documents; and my Sun, to "my son." The progressed harmonic aspects of our marriage were repeated at the signing of our wills. Though I didn't mention the Chiron aspect when discussing the marriage, this aspect was in effect and describes the marriage as well because our signing the marriage document made my second husband the stepfather to my son.

PERSISTENCE OF HARMONIC RELEVANCE

The relevance of a harmonic chart to a marriage which occurred at that age does not end with the termination of that marriage. (The same would be true for another important event that occurred and was terminated.) My first marriage was when I was eighteen. There were six years, 98 days, 17 hours and 46 minutes between my 18th birthday and my second marriage

$$\frac{98.740277}{365} = \frac{x}{60'} = 16.231278'$$

so the increment is 06°16.231278'. There were eight years, 65 days, 13 hours and 14 minutes between my 18th birthday and my daughter's birth

$$\frac{65.5513888}{366} = \frac{x}{60'} = 10.746129'$$

so the increment is 08°10.746129' (366 days is used in this equation because my daughter was born July 28, 1959, and from my birthday May 24, 1959, to my birthday May 24, 1960, is 366 days).

In my 18th harmonic chart (see Figure IV), progression of the asteroid with my second husband's name at 05° Gemini 20'48" by a degree for a year from my 18th birthday to when I married my second husband brings the asteroid to 11° Gemini 37'1.88", in an exact opposition to the 18th harmonic Vulcanus and East Point (10° Sagittarius 35'47.76", 12° Sagittarius 13'1.56") and square to 18th harmonic Chiron (11° Pisces 57'32.76"). My second husband (name asteroid) was the fated (Vulcanus) partner (opposition to East Point) who became the stepfather (Chiron) to my son from my first marriage. Progression of the 18th harmonic Ascendant at 08° Aries 19'20.28" to the time of my marrying my second husband brings the Ascendant to 14° Aries 35'34.1", exactly conjunct the 18th harmonic asteroid with my name at 13° Aries 33'48". Thus, another axis of the self and partner is activated. Progression of the 18th harmonic asteroid with the name of my daughter by my second husband at 00° Libra 17'30" to the time of my giving birth to her brings the asteroid to 08° Libra 28'14.77", exactly conjunct the 18th harmonic Descendant. Within the harmonic of the age that I married my first husband, the symbols of my second husband, myself, and our daughter are appropriately configured to foretell and depict that second marriage, which is relevant to the first.

To show more examples of degree for a year progressions, in my 24th harmonic chart (24 was my age at the time of my second marriage) there are several separations that are approximately 02°, equating to the two years between my 24th birthday and the birth of our daughter (see Figure III). Progressing the harmonic asteroid with my name at 18° Leo 05'06" from my 24th birthday to the time of the birth of our daughter brings it exactly conjunct my natal seventh house cusp at 20° Leo 27'44.28". The 02° separation from this harmonic asteroid to my natal seventh house cusp was mentioned in regard to the three months and six days after my birthday that I married my second husband. Our meeting had been one month and seven days after my birthday. Using a degree for a month progressions, at both the time of the meeting and of the marriage, the harmonic asteroid with my name is exactly conjunct my natal seventh house cusp. Using a degree for a year progressions, two years and two months (the time between my 24th birthday and the birth of this child) is halfway between, in other words in numerical symmetry with, the meeting and the marriage. Progressing harmonic Jupiter at 25° Aquarius 49'33.6" from my 24th birthday to the time of the birth of our daughter brings it exactly conjunct the harmonic asteroid with my second husband's name at 27° Aquarius 07'42". Jupiter is the ruler of the fifth house in the Ascendant Equal House Chart (children and love affairs). Using a degree for a month progressions, at the time of our meeting, the harmonic asteroid with my second husband's name is also activated by an exact conjunction from harmonic Jupiter.

In my second husband's 33rd harmonic chart, there are several separations that are approximately 02°, equating to the two years between his 33nd birthday and the birth of our daughter (see Figure V). The harmonic East Point is approximately 02°

before the harmonic Ascendant, both in Scorpio, the sign of reproduction. Harmonic Transpluto is in Leo approximately 02° before his natal Ascendant in Leo, and Leo relates to children, and Transpluto is like Pluto, only more so. Harmonic Saturn (paternalism) is approximately 02° from the harmonic South Node. They are both in the Cosmic Square, referred to on pages 74-75, that involves Pluto, the planet of reproduction. (Major configurations that have a span of several degrees are prime candidates for the occurrence of events when the span is bridged.) Progressing the prior factors in these approximate 02° separations to the succeeding factors, the former are exactly conjunct the latter. As for the progressed harmonic name asteroids, the one with my name is still in the exact Grand Trine with the harmonic Part of Fortune and Mars, while the one with his name is still exactly opposite the harmonic Part of Fortune and has moved exactly sextile Mars. (See degree for a month progressions.)

A FITTING SEPARATION

Though the harmonic chart of the age at which you were married is relevant to that marriage, the 7th harmonic is relevant to marriage in general. The separation equivalent to the age at which you were married will relate to that marriage. As a result, a separation of 24° in my 7th harmonic (see Figure X) will relate to my second marriage. The harmonic and natal planets, personal points, asteroids, Uranian planets and other bodies that are exactly aspected, especially conjuncted, will be particularly descriptive of that relationship.

For instance, at the time of my second marriage my 7th harmonic Cupido (family) at 27° Aquarius 11'14.64" and Juno (marriage) at 28° Aquarius 25'1.2" had progressed to 21° Pisces 27'28.5" and 22° Pisces 41'15", conjunct my 7th harmonic South Node at 22° Pisces 53'38.04" and tenth cusp in the Ascendant perspective at 23° Pisces 14'11.04".[22] The progressed Cupido and Juno were square my 7th harmonic Ascendant, Hades (23° Gemini 14'11.04", 24° Gemini 37'39.72"). At the same time my 7th harmonic Ascendant had come to 17° Cancer 30'24.9", semi-square my Sun/Moon midpoint (01° Gemini 27'58.6"), and opposite my husband's (17° Capricorn 49'3.3"). My 7th harmonic Mars at 07° Taurus 44'23.28", Ceres at 09° Taurus 05'15.36" and Mercury at 09° Taurus 13'51.96" had progressed to 02° Gemini 00'37.16", 03° Gemini 21'29.2" and 03° Gemini 30'5.84", conjunct my 7th harmonic Pluto, Moon conjunction (02° Gemini 06'37.8", 02° Gemini 27'44.28") and my natal Sun (02° Gemini 34'50.88"), ruler of my seventh house. My 7th harmonic Chiron at 22° Taurus 59'2.76" and Saturn at 24° Taurus 36'36.72" had progressed to 17° Gemini 15'16.6" and 18° Gemini 52'50.6", conjunct my 7th harmonic Sun (18° Gemini 03'57.24"), ruler of my seventh house. My 7th harmonic Vertex at 27° Taurus 54'3.96" had progressed to 22° Gemini 10'17.8", conjunct my 7th harmonic Ascendant, Hades. The Ascendant, Hades conjunction has already been related to a karmic connection; the Pluto, Moon conjunction, to emotional obsessiveness in partnerships; the Mars, Ceres, Mercury conjunction, to my being a Geminian mother of a boy. As for the Chiron, Saturn, it is part of my, by this time, well-known 7th harmonic Grand Trine that refers to foster parentage. These factors were highlighted in the meeting and marriage charts previously discussed.

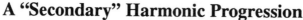

A "Secondary" Harmonic Progression

Another type of harmonic progression is one that Susan Town has been using. Susan, an astrologer who has been working on harmonics, told me of her method, and I tried it to good effect. This harmonic progression is an interpolation between two consecutive harmonics. It is like secondary progressions, where you interpolate between the planetary positions on one day and the next, only instead you interpolate between the planetary positions in one harmonic and the next. My previously stated method is more like Solar Arc progressions, where you add the Solar Arc, though, rather than the Solar Arc which is sometimes a little more or less than a degree for a year, I add a degree for a year or a month. With harmonic charts, the degree for a year method works better than the Solar Arc, though I use Solar Arc progressions as well as secondary progressions (a day for a year) to progress the natal chart. Just as you can use both Solar Arc and secondary progressions with natal charts, you can use both my method and Susan's with harmonics, which is what I now do. Susan sets up the harmonic charts at month intervals from one birthday to the next, using the decimal part of a year. Experimenting with her method, I set up charts for important events, such as my marriage to my second husband, rather than monthly charts.

OUR MARRIAGE HARMONIC PROGRESSIONS

With my marriage to my husband the harmonic interpolation is between my 24th and my 25th harmonics. There is the equivalent of one degree between one harmonic and the next. What you want to discover is what proportion of the 60 minutes of arc has elapsed between the birthday and the event, including times. There were 98 days between my 24th birthday and our marriage day, plus 17 hours and 46 minutes between 01:14 AM EDT (my birth time) and 07:00 P.M. EDT (our marriage time) so the harmonic is equivalent to 24°16.231278'

$$\frac{17 \cdot 46}{24} = .7402777; \quad \frac{98.7402777}{365} = \frac{x}{60'} = 16.231278'.$$

As explained, 365 days is used because the progression is from one natal birth time to the next. My natal positions would then be multiplied by this harmonic, and the product would be their progressed harmonic positions at the time of the marriage. This is the same increment that was used with the 7th harmonic (see page 78), only in that case the increment was added, not multiplied. (The numbers of the increment themselves have meaning, whether added or multiplied. Translated into degrees, minutes and seconds, the increment is 24°16'13.8".)

There were 185 days between my second husband's 33rd birthday and our marriage day, plus 1 hour, 7 minutes and 18 seconds between 04:52:42 PM EST (his birth time) and 06:00 PM EST (our marriage time changed to standard time to equate to his birth time) so the harmonic is equivalent to 33°30.418641'

$$\frac{1 \cdot 7 \cdot 18}{24} = .0467361; \quad \frac{185.0467361}{365} = \frac{x}{60'} = 30.418641'.$$

The natal positions would then be multiplied by this harmonic, and the product would be their progressed harmonic positions at the time of the marriage. The degree and minutes with decimals can be translated to a single harmonic number with decimals. For instance, 33°30.418641' becomes 33.5069773 when the 30.418641' is divided by 60'.

Originally, I did these harmonic progressions by calculator from natal positions with four-place decimals, except for the asteroids (other than Ceres, Pallas, Juno, Vesta and Chiron) with one-place decimals, and Transpluto, Dark Moon Lilith and Halley's Comet with none. Later, Astro added the option of Progressed Harmonics, and the charts were recast. When positions are multiplied, the greater accuracy of internal calculation by computer to fourteen digits is especially advisable. (Of course, the multiplications are of the geometric positions of the planets.) Even the 468 asteroids in *Many Interesting Asteroids* are calculated to this degree of accuracy. Also, Astro *now* calculates the South Node and Antivertex separately from the North Node and Vertex. The North Node and South Node, as well as the Vertex and Antivertex (which in the even-numbered harmonics are conjunct and in the odd-numbered harmonics are opposition), in the progressed harmonics can be in any separation.

The progressed positions can be put around the harmonic of the age, i.e., 24th (which in turn would be around the natal chart), or a separate Ascendant or Mid-heaven Equal House Chart could be drawn. The Ascendant Equal House Chart would be for the personal perspective, and the Midheaven Equal House Chart, for the public one. These charts are analyzed as are other harmonic charts, noting the conjunctions, particularly those that are exact within the chart and from the chart to the natal chart. Of course, houses, signs, degrees, aspects (especially, major configurations), midpoints, and bodies and points around angles and exactly conjunct intermediary cusps would give further information and emphasis.

In the following progressed harmonic charts, the asteroids included (other than Ceres, Pallas, Juno, Vesta and Chiron) are the six personal name asteroids already mentioned. These charts are Ascendant Equal House Charts. For simplicity, the positions are listed without seconds.

In my progressed 24th harmonic chart, the exact conjunctions are Apollon (Sun figure) and Dark Moon Lilith (Moon figure) at 27° Scorpio 02' and 27° Scorpio 31'; Saturn (father) and the South Node (close relationships) at 28° Cancer 32' and 29° Cancer 57'; Vulcanus (power) and the asteroid with my husband's name at 24° Pisces 07' and 25° Pisces 09'; and Zeus and Admetos (both husbands of loyal wives) at 07° Capricorn 14' and 07° Capricorn 46'.

In my husband's progressed 33rd harmonic chart (see Figure XIII), the Antivertex (fated happenings) and Juno (marriage) are conjunct at 08° Cancer 34' and 08° Cancer 58'. This exact Antivertex, Juno conjunction is in an exact Grand Trine and Cosmic Square. The Grand Trine is with Mars at 08° Scorpio 30' and Pallas at 07° Pisces 51', exactly conjunct his natal Sun. Pallas relates to legalities; and Mars, to the son he was gaining through this legal marriage. The Cosmic Square is with Ceres at 07° Aries 08', Vertex at 09° Aries 49', the East Point at 10° Capricorn

32' and Venus at 10° Libra 24'. Ceres relates to nurturing; the Vertex, to fated happenings; The East Point, to the self; and Venus, to love and in this case to fatherhood because it rules the Libra 10th house cusp. Note that the Vertex and Antivertex, as well as the North Node (28° Taurus 16') and South Node (29° Aquarius 32'), are exactly square, placing an emphasis on fated happenings and close relationships.

Another exact square in my husband's progressed harmonic is of Chiron at 05° Sagittarius 29' and Halley's Comet at 05° Virgo 14'. Chiron, as mentioned, relates to the stepfather, while Halley's is a powerful activator.

Since Halley's Comet is so dynamic, it should be discussed in more detail. Though all comets may be activators, Halley's has the activating quality of an eclipse. I've found that the literal meanings of factors relate to their metaphorical meanings, and comets seem almost like a metaphor for the solar system. As *The Random House College Dictionary* states, comets have a "highly eccentric orbit" (evoking Uranus). As *The Columbia Encyclopedia* states, comets "reflect" (like the Moon), "as well as radiate light" (like the Sun), have a head of "rock or sand interspersed with gaseous matter" (evoking Saturn and Neptune) and are "nebulous in character" (like Neptune). As for Edmund Halley, he was the "first astronomer to predict the return of a comet"—the one given his name—and Halley's Comet is particularly related to prediction. He was the official astronomer-royal of England, and Halley's Comet is related to governments, particularly to the government of England. He conducted original studies of Mercury and Venus, as well as catalogued stars, and Halley's Comet is innovative.

The Ascendant of my husband's progressed 33rd harmonic chart is 17° Capricorn 32', exactly conjunct my husband's natal Sun/Moon midpoint, which equals mine by a sesquiquadrate. (His natal Venus, Chiron, and Juno, daughter's name asteroid, as well as North Node, Apollon, and stepson's name asteroid, South Node, and my natal Sun and Nodes, also equal this midpoint.)

As for harmonic midpoints, the Sun/Moon, Venus/Mars, Mars/Jupiter and Mars/Saturn midpoints (with degrees, minutes and seconds) are placed in the center of the wheel, when it is drawn by hand. (The same is done with these midpoints in the unprogressed harmonic chart.) My husband's progressed 33rd harmonic Sun/Moon midpoint is 13° Cancer 53'50". (Since the midpoints are being given with the seconds, the factors will be also.) The progressed factors which equal this midpoint are his North Node (28° Taurus 16'42.6") by a semisquare, his South Node (29° Aquarius 32'0.2") by a sesquiquadrate, his Dark Moon Lilith (12° Aries 46') by a square, and his Uranus (13° Cancer 59'19.32") by a conjunction. Dark Moon Lilith represents hidden fascination. The progressed South Node is exactly conjunct my husband's natal Descendant. The Nodes, symbolizing close relationships, are particularly important for my husband and me because natally our Nodes are exactly conjunct, but reversed across our first and seventh houses. Uranus is important for us because it is the ruler of his natal Descendant and my natal Ascendant. The 13° Cancer of this Sun/Moon midpoint and Uranus is notable too because it is the position of my natal asteroid with the name of my husband. This point also equals

Figure XIII – Progressed 33rd Harmonic
Ascendant Equal House Chart of Sy Press

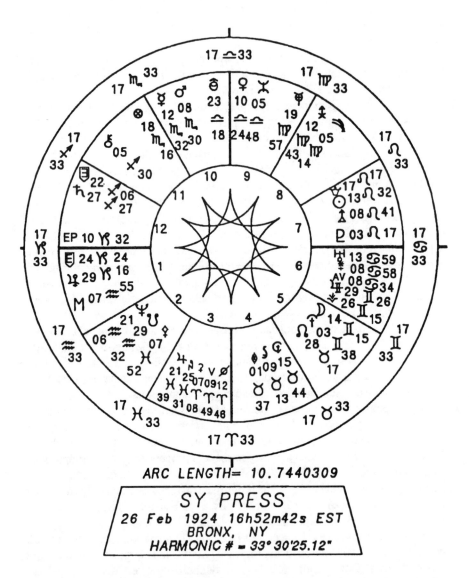

ARC LENGTH= 10.7440309

SY PRESS
26 Feb 1924 16h52m42s EST
BRONX, NY
HARMONIC # = 33° 30'25.12"

by a sesquiquadrate our conjunct natal Mars/Saturn midpoints at 28° Scorpio. As I've mentioned, the Mars/Saturn midpoint is important in marriage because restriction (to a specific person) of the sexual energy is what is pledged in marriage. There is also a possible reference to the structuring of energy (Mars) for the career (Saturn), rather than the usual interpretation of inhibition (Saturn) of the energy (Mars).

When there are name asteroids of the people involved, the midpoint of these asteroids is relevant. My husband's progressed 33rd harmonic midpoint of the asteroid with his name and the asteroid with my name is 17° Aries 22'03", exactly conjunct the progressed fourth house cusp and equaling our natal Sun/Moon midpoints. His progressed Ascendant (17° Capricorn 32'59.28") equals by a square, his progressed Kronos (03° Gemini 37'35.04") equals by a semisquare, and his progressed Mars/Saturn midpoint (02° Sagittarius 58'30") equals by a sesquiquadrate, this progressed midpoint of our name asteroids. The Ascendant is the persona of the chart, Kronos is the "head of the family," and the Mars/Saturn midpoint relates to marriage. My progressed 24th harmonic midpoint of the asteroid with my husband's name and the asteroid with my name is 17° Gemini 32'51", exactly sextile his comparable midpoint. My progressed Sun (18° Gemini 52'11.28") equals by a conjunction, and my progressed North Node (18° Virgo 39'0.72") equals by a square, this progressed midpoint of our name asteroids. The Sun is a symbol of the husband, and the ruler of my natal seventh house cusp, and the Nodes have to do with close relationships.

THE PROGRESSED HARMONIC IN RELATION TO THE HARMONIC

An added consideration would be the relationship of the progressed harmonic and the harmonic, i.e., the progressed 33rd harmonic and the 33rd harmonic—to what and from what have the progressed positions come. My husband's progressed 33rd harmonic Ascendant has come to 17° Capricorn 32', exactly conjunct his natal Sun/ Moon midpoint (marriage) at 17° Capricorn 49'. This progressed Ascendant has come from its 33rd harmonic position at 02° Scorpio 23', exactly conjunct his natal Saturn at 02° Scorpio 07'℞ which is in an exact natal T-Square with his name asteroid at 03° Taurus 24', Kronos at 04° Taurus 07' and Zeus at 03° Leo 02'℞. In other words, his 33rd harmonic Ascendant had already activated his natal configuration which relates to him (his name asteroid) being "above average" (Kronos) in his responsibility (Saturn) to "creation" (Zeus). At another level of meaning, the stepson he was acquiring at our marriage is a Sagittarian, and Zeus is identified with Jupiter. (This natal T-Square refers as well to my husband's career [Saturn] being in the theatre [Zeus in Leo] as a contractor [Kronos]. Kronos refers to authority, but with an unusual quality— see key words.)

ONE PERSON'S PROGRESSED
HARMONIC IN RELATION TO ANOTHER'S

Also, exact conjunctions of my husband's progressed 33rd harmonic positions and my progressed 24th harmonic positions would be descriptive of our marriage. My husband's progressed 33rd harmonic Ascendant at 17° Capricorn 32' was conjunct my progressed 24th harmonic Venus at 18° Capricorn 11'. My progressed 24th harmonic Ascendant at 07° Scorpio 47' was conjunct his progressed 33rd harmonic Mars at 08° Scorpio 30', opposition his progressed 33rd harmonic name asteroid at 09° Taurus 13', conjunct my progressed 24th harmonic Descendant. As for my 24th harmonic asteroid with his name, it had progressed to 25° Pisces 09', conjunct his progressed 33rd harmonic asteroid with my name at 25° Pisces 31'. These asteroids were already conjunct in our unprogressed harmonics (27° Aquarius 07', 22° Aquarius 54'), but the conjunction was not exact from one degree to the next. Though at the time of our marriage, the asteroid with my name appears to be separating from the exact conjunction, it was not. My husband's harmonic asteroid with my name had been progressing longer, since his birthday was approximately three months before mine; however, my harmonic asteroid with his name had been progressing faster and so was about to overtake his.[23] In fact, the exact conjunction of our name asteroids to the minute was to occur just three days after our marriage.

The separation between my husband's natal asteroid with my name and my natal asteroid with his name is 39°18', so the asteroids are in 9th harmonic aspect to each other (40°). They are conjunct in the 9th harmonic chart, but not exactly— my husband's harmonic asteroid with my name is at 08° Scorpio 58', and my harmonic asteroid with his name is at 02° Scorpio 40'. Strangely, the particular natal separation between these asteroids, which results in this inexact conjunction in the 9th harmonic chart, results in an exact one when the harmonics of the respective marriage ages are progressed to the day of the marriage. What harmonic is this? Not only are the harmonics different but they are progressed different lengths of time because of the time between the birthdays. What a complex combination of factors is required to conjoin at the same time these two name asteroids and the two people they represent.

Naturally, the other exact aspects to this progressed conjunction would augment the description of our marriage and of us (our name asteroids). In my husband's progressed 33rd harmonic, the asteroid with my name (25° Pisces 31') was semisquare the asteroid with his name (09° Taurus 13'), sextile the asteroid with the name of his stepson (24° Capricorn 24') and square Vesta (26° Gemini 14'). Our marriage, and the son that came with it, brought commitment (Vesta) to my husband. In my progressed 24th harmonic, the asteroid with my husband's name (25° Pisces 09') was conjunct Vulcanus (24° Pisces 07'), trine Halley's Comet (25° Scorpio 32'), semisquare Vesta (11° Taurus 51'), sesquiquadrate Neptune (10° Scorpio 18') and semisextile the Moon (24° Aries 46'). (My secondary progressed Moon was 24° Aries 42' at the time of my marriage.) As mentioned, Halley's Comet is a powerful activator. Our marriage, and my forceful (Vulcanus) husband (his name asteroid), brought commitment (Vesta) to me. He is a Neptunian-type (Sun in Pisces) and Lunar-type (Moon in the fourth house, exactly square his Ascendant). He is a musician as well, and so has vested interests (Vesta) in music (Neptune). Vesta is both vested interests and commitment, and another key word for Neptune is fascination. Neptune and the Moon were exactly sextile and sesquiquadrate the asteroid with my name at 09° Virgo 55'. The fascination (Neptune) was mutual, and I was an artist (Neptune) who was already a mother (Moon).

BRACKETING OF THE ANGLES

As stated, bodies and points around angles are highlighted, and the Ascendant-Descendant is the axis of relationship.

In conclusion (considering the planets, personal points, Uranian planets, and the asteroids and other bodies mentioned), in my progressed 24th harmonic, Neptune (10° Scorpio 18') was the closest to the Ascendant (07° Scorpio 47'). Vesta (11° Taurus 51') and the Antivertex (04° Taurus 02') were the closest to the Descendant, bracketing it equally within ten minutes of arc. As for my husband's progressed 33d harmonic, the East Point (10° Capricorn 32') and name asteroid of his stepson (24° Capricorn 24') were the closest to the Ascendant (17° Capricorn 32'), bracketing it equally within five minutes of arc. Closest to the Descendant was Uranus at 13° Cancer 59' (the degree of my natal asteroid with his name), and Uranus will always be associated with marriage for him, since natally he has Uranus in the seventh house and Aquarius on its cusp. As an example of degree symbolism, 13° has the references of 4 (among which are the final outcome and maternalism) with a coloration of 1 (the self) and 3 (communication). Also, Uranus was 03°33' from the Descendant at 17° Cancer 32'—appropriate for marriage to a double Gemini with Aquarius Rising.

Technical Discoveries

Having discussed harmonic progressions, I shall now share a potpourri of little technical discoveries I have made while studying harmonics. These discoveries have certainly been made by, or known to, others, but to me they were revealed, as if for the first time.

NATAL SEPARATION
CORRELATES TO HARMONIC CONJUNCTION

Noticing that in a man's 23rd harmonic chart, Venus and Mars are conjunct within one minute of arc and that in his natal chart the separation between Venus and Mars is 15°39', I said to myself, "Divide 15°39' into 360° and see if you get 23." I did, and the answer was "Yes" (actually, 23.003195). I realized that you can know when planets, etc., will be conjunct in a harmonic by figuring their separation and dividing it into 360. (However, the result of this division will not always be close to an integral harmonic, and so they may not be conjunct in any integral harmonic.) There is a Table of Basic Harmonic Arclengths in John Addey's *Harmonic Chart Tables* (which is also in *Astrologer's Guide to the Harmonics* by James S. and Ruth E. Williamsen) that enables you to see without division. The separations given are 15° for the 24th harmonic and 15.6522°, or 15°39'08", for the 23rd harmonic. I prefer the more precise 15.652174° or 15°39'7.83", but the tables are good for scanning. With more accurate calculation, the natal separation between this man's Venus and Mars turns out to be 15°39'16.9", and the harmonic positions, rather than being Mars at 14° Pisces 41' and Venus at 14° Pisces 42', are Venus at 14° Pisces 47'40" and Mars at 14° Pisces 51'9.7". Nevertheless, this natal separation is still close to the separation which produces conjunction in the 23rd harmonic, and this man moved in with his girlfriend when he was 23 years old.

HARMONIC ASPECT AND INTERASPECT PATTERNS

Another discovery I made is that there are also discernable patterns regarding when someone's harmonic planets will aspect your harmonic planets or midpoints. For planets, you can read instead personal points, Uranian planets, asteroids or other bodies. (Of course, this pattern would apply to your own harmonic planets aspecting your harmonic planets or midpoints.) As already mentioned, if natally someone's planets equal your midpoints exactly, these pictures will continue throughout at least the lower harmonics. However, if natally someone's planets do not equal your midpoints, they may equal them in different harmonics in a predictable manner. For instance, if natally someone's Ascendant is 70° away from your Sun/Moon midpoint, his 9th harmonic Ascendant will equal your 9th harmonic Sun/Moon midpoint by a square to the midpoint. The explanation is that 80° is a separation in the 9th harmonic (double 40°, the basic 9th harmonic separation), and 70° is a quarter or three-quarters of the way between 40° and 80°, or, in other words, square to the midpoint. (The same would be true of 10°, 30°, 50°, 90°, 110°, 130° and 150° from the natal midpoint.) To discover with other harmonics what is square to the midpoint, or planet, divide the basic harmonic separation by four. That quotient, that quotient times 3, that quotient plus the basic separation, etc., are the answers.

To continue musings on when aspects will occur in the harmonics, exact natal conjunctions, if they are exact enough, will be repeated throughout the harmonics. Any deviation from exactness will be multiplied by the number of the harmonic, so the persistence of a conjunction, or other aspect, will be in direct correlation to the degree of its precision. Exact natal oppositions will be shown as conjunctions in the 2nd harmonic and in all harmonic multiples of 2. In the odd-numbered harmonics, these exact natal oppositions will be shown as oppositions. Exact natal trines will be shown as conjunctions in the 3rd harmonic and in all harmonic multiples of 3. In the 2nd harmonic and in the 2 harmonics between the harmonic multiples of 3, these exact natal trines will be shown as trines. As for exact natal squares, they will be shown as conjunctions in the 4th harmonic and in all harmonic multiples of 4. In the 2nd harmonic these exact natal squares will be shown as oppositions, and in the 3rd harmonic these exact natal squares will be shown as squares. In the 3 harmonics between the harmonic multiples of 4, the pattern is square, opposition, square. Exact natal quintiles and biquintiles will be shown as conjunctions in the 5th harmonic and in all harmonic multiples of 5. In the 2nd, 3rd, 7th, 8th and 12th harmonics, the exact natal quintiles will be shown as biquintiles, while in the 4th, 6th, 9th and 11th they will be shown as quintiles. For the cycle of the exact natal biquintiles, substitute in the sentence above the word quintiles for biquintiles, and vice versa. The patterns for the other aspects can be deduced from these. The repeat of the pattern is according to the aspect's harmonic number, i.e., the square or 4th harmonic will repeat its sequence after every 4 harmonics, the 5th, after every 5. The sequence is based on the repeated addition of the aspect's angular separation (basic harmonic separation). For instance, in the 5th harmonic chart the square will be shown as a square because in the 4th harmonic chart it is shown as a conjunction, and $00° + 90° = 90°$. The aspect keeps "hopscotching" around the different harmonic circles .

Despite this predictability, if you see an aspect within a harmonic chart, you won't necessarily know what natal aspect it represents. Double the harmonic number is shown as an opposition; triple, as a trine; and quadruple, as a square. As a result, in the 5th harmonic chart, for example, an opposition will be representing not only an opposition, but other natal aspects in the 10th harmonic; a trine, not only a trine, but other natal aspects in the 15th harmonic; a square, not only a square, but other natal aspects in the 20th harmonic (5 x 2 = 10; 5 x 3 = 15; 5 x 4 = 20). Naturally, if the natal aspects are not exact, new harmonic aspects will be formed.

An example of a natal aspect that is exact enough to be repeated in a harmonic multiple is the following. My Venus (11° Gemini 12') and Ascendant (20° Aquarius 27') are natally in a 13th harmonic aspect. In my 13th harmonic chart, Venus is at 25° Libra 39' exactly conjunct the Ascendant at 26° Libra 00'. At 13 years of age I met my first love and sold my first drawing—love and art are both Venusian concerns. In my 26th harmonic chart, Venus is at 21° Taurus 19', exactly conjunct the Ascendant at 22° Taurus 01'. At 26 years of age my daughter was born, and Venus can represent the daughter. Through the conjunctions in the harmonics the repeated patterns of your life are seen. The principles of the degrees and what they apply to (the minutes and seconds if accurate enough), combined with the signs, give information as to the particular manifestation. Of course, the houses, rulerships and exact aspects will add more detail. In my 26th harmonic, Venus is the ruler of the Sun, which in the Ascendant perspective is in the fifth house of children. The Venus, Ascendant conjunction is exactly trine Jupiter (expansion), as well as square Zeus (procreation). Reference to the natal chart gives further insights, and this harmonic Venus, Ascendant conjunction is exactly opposite my natal asteroid with the name of my daughter, as well as square (Lunar aspect) my natal Ascendant.

NATAL ABSOLUTE LONGITUDE
CORRELATES TO HARMONIC CYCLES

There are also harmonic cycles related to the absolute longitude of a natal planet, etc. For instance, my natal Moon is at 00° Gemini 21'6.48" which is 60°21'6.48" in absolute longitude. If you divide 60°21'6.48" into 360°, the result is 05°57'54.09", which is close to six. Every six years my harmonic Moon comes back to the same position or close to it. In the 7th harmonic my Moon is at 02° Gemini 27'44.28", and in the 13th harmonic my Moon is at 04° Gemini 34'22.08". The cycle is an emotional one because it is a cycle of the Moon. My ages at my marriages (18 and 24) were six years apart, and other emotional events have followed this six-year cycle. When planets are 60° apart (instead of a planet being at 60° in absolute longitude), these planets are conjunct every six years but may be in a completely different sign and natal house each time.

Another observation was that my natal Sun/Moon midpoint at 01° Gemini 28' (this was before I calculated to the second) was repeated to the minute in my 42nd harmonic and that the position in my 2nd harmonic was repeated to the minute in my 43rd harmonic, etc. There was a pattern of repetition that occurred every 41 harmonics. Wondering if every position, whether planet, etc., or midpoint, is repeated in some harmonic, I calculated what my harmonic Sun/Moon midpoints would be if my natal Sun/Moon midpoint were 01° Gemini 29'. 83 harmonics were computed without an exact to the minute repeat. In the 42nd harmonic, the Sun/Moon midpoint was close at 02° Gemini 10', and in the 83rd harmonic, this midpoint was close at 02° Gemini 52'. Thinking in terms of the harmonics as representative of years of one's life, if my Sun/Moon midpoint were 01° Gemini 29', instead of 01° Gemini 28', it would never repeat to the minute in my lifetime. Of course, when calculated to the second, my natal and harmonic Sun/Moon midpoints are different. My natal Sun/Moon midpoint is 01° Gemini 27'58.6" and my 42nd harmonic Sun/Moon midpoint is 01° Gemini 35'4.56". Though the midpoint no longer repeats to the minute, the observation is still valid. Not all natal positions have the same potential for repetition in the harmonics. Some positions may have cycles that are elliptical and reappear, whereas others may have cycles that are hyperbolic and appear only once, at least in this lifetime.

Summation: Magnification of Integral Harmonics

In summation, my discoveries on magnification in regard to integral harmonics are the following. The harmonics follow cycles whose patterns can be traced. Each harmonic focuses on a different area or quality of life, as well as on that year of life. The "planets," signs, houses, aspects and degrees that are highlighted in that harmonic give the characteristics of that quality and of that year in the particular life.

Arc Transform Charts

One more topic I would like to treat, before discussing harmonics as aspects, is magnification in regard to fractional harmonics, or arc transform charts. These charts were introduced by James S. Williamsen. Actually, they are based on the fact that the division of 360° by the angular separation between two planets, will give the harmonic in which the two planets will be conjunct. This is what I discovered in the case of the man whose Venus and Mars are conjunct in the 23rd harmonic. However, as mentioned, not all planets will be conjunct in any integral harmonic. For the arc transform, the angular separation is counted forward in the zodiac (i.e., Aries to Sagittarius, not Sagittarius to Aries) and divided into 360°. What Williamsen proposed is to multiply the natal positions by the resultant harmonic, whether it is integral or not. The two planets are then exactly conjunct to the second in a magnified chart which is very descriptive of the relationship of the two planets.

THE DIFFERENCE BETWEEN
INTEGRAL AND FRACTIONAL HARMONICS

My perception of the difference between integral and fractional harmonics is illustrated by the following. The 4th harmonic corresponds to the Moon, etc., and the 5th harmonic corresponds to the Sun, etc., while the arc transform of the Sun and Moon corresponds to the combination of these two planets. Also, the integral harmonic charts are general expressions of the principles of the numbers, while the arc transform charts are specific expressions of those principles. The integral harmonic charts are equivalent to the degrees, while the arc transform charts are equivalent to the degrees, in relation to the minutes, in regard to the seconds. (The fractional harmonic can be converted to degrees, minutes and seconds.) In this respect the arc transform charts are like the progressed harmonic charts. My 24th harmonic chart is for me descriptive of the principle of 6, while my 24th harmonic chart progressed to the time of my marriage (24°16'13.8") is for me descriptive of the principle of 6, in relation to the principle of 7, in regard to the principle of 4. (The interpretation could be service, in relation to marriage, in regard to the foundation or final outcome. The individual numbers give additional shading.) In like fashion, my 24th harmonic chart reflects in general the year when I was 24 years of age, while my 24th harmonic chart progressed to the time of my marriage reflects in particular the event which occurred at that time.

Before giving examples of arc transform charts, I find it necessary to answer a statement regarding them made by Geoffrey Dean. The statement, which is preceded by a definition of A as "angular separation between any two planets," is as follows: "Furthermore there appears to be no reason why an arc transform based on 360/(360-A) should not be equally valid, in which case the total number of charts is doubled."[24] The reason why an arc transform based on 360/(360-A) should not be equally valid is that this calculation does not produce an exact conjunction in the harmonic chart, while an arc transform based on 360/A does. The exact conjunction shows that the planets in question are in the exact harmonic which corresponds to their exact angular separation, and that's what arc transforms and harmonics are all about. In fact, I believe that the arc transform is the bridge between the two main purposes of harmonics—to know the aspects and to transform the chart by magnification. The exact angular separation or aspect is calculated, and from this exact angular separation the exact harmonic is derived, and then the radix chart is transformed by multiplication (or magnification) of this chart by this harmonic. These exact aspects and harmonics may not be the ones with which we are familiar, but they are the "true" ones nevertheless. The inexact aspects and harmonics are like background music for these major leitmotifs.

THE IMPORTANCE OF ACCURACY

As with the harmonic progressions, originally I did the arc transforms by calculator. Later, Astro added the option of Arc Transforms or Fractional Harmonics, and the charts were recast. With a harmonic based on the exact separation between planets, the greater accuracy of internal calculation by computer to fourteen digits is especially advisable. (Of course, my exact separations are of the geometric positions of the planets.) Even the 468 asteroids in *Many Interesting Asteroids* are calculated to this degree of accuracy. Also, Astro *now* calculates the South Node and Antivertex separately from the North Node and Vertex. The North Node and South Node, as well as the Vertex and Antivertex (which in the even-numbered harmonics are conjunct and in the odd-numbered harmonics are opposition), in the fractional harmonics can be in any separation.

Sun-Moon Arc Transform

The arc transform of the Sun and Moon is particularly important because the Sun-Moon separation (like the Sun/Moon midpoint) deals with the man and the woman (husband and wife, father and mother), the ego and the emotion, the conscious and the unconscious. (As mentioned, Saturn refers to the father as the authority figure, while the Sun, through its association with the life force, is the archetype for the father and husband.) Other references of the Sun and Moon combination, and its situation in the natal chart, would augment this list of equivalencies.

The separation between my Sun and Moon is 02.2290916° (02°13'44.73"), and that separation divided into 360° gives the 161.5007666 harmonic or 161°30'2.76". (This exact separation and harmonic are calculated by computer to fourteen digits and printed out to seven-decimal places.) This fractional harmonic correlates to the concerns of the number 8, but because the fractional harmonic can be translated into degrees, minutes and seconds, the correlation becomes more specific. A possible reading is transformation, in relation to thought, in regard to values. (Greater shading is obtained from the individual numbers.) The separation between the Sun and Moon, which can represent what is literally separating the parents, husband and wife, etc., also has a specific meaning. The meaning of the harmonic and the meaning of the separation are connected. As the harmonic is derived from the separation, the meaning of the harmonic is derived from the meaning of the separation. In this case (02°13'44.73"), the principle of the separation is values, in relation to maternalism, in regard to transformation. (Individual meanings of these numbers are shown by their zodiacal correlations in the natal chart.)

As with other harmonic charts, the arc transform chart can be placed around the natal chart, or a separate Ascendant or Midheaven Equal House Chart can be drawn. The arc transform chart placed around your natal chart is from the perspective of you in general; the Ascendant or Midheaven Equal House Chart, from the perspective of your personal or your public life, respectively.

When my Sun and Moon are multiplied by the harmonic derived from their separation, these planets are at 26° Aries 51'18.36". As far as the relationship of the Sun and Moon archetypes is concerned, this degree, minute and second, combined with the sign, is especially significant to me. Transformation through self-assertion, in relation to service, in regard to completion is a probable interpretation.

With the arc transform chart placed around my natal chart, my arc transform Sun-Moon is exactly conjunct my Uranus at 25° Aries 33'7.2" in my second house. This conjunction brings a quality of unusualness to my combination of the Sun and Moon, particularly in the sphere of values and money. This unusualness would relate not only to a combination of my husband and myself but also to a combination of my father and mother.

From the perspective of my personal life, the Sun-Moon is in the fourth house (see Figure XIV). In my personal life, there is an emphasis on maternalism, the home and the foundation in respect to man-woman relationships, the ego and emotion, conscious and unconscious. These combinations are unusual (natal conjunction to Uranus).

From the perspective of my public life, the Sun-Moon is in the ninth house. In my public life, there is an emphasis on higher education, publishing and law in respect to man-woman relationships, the ego and emotion, conscious and unconscious. These combinations are unusual (natal conjunction to Uranus).

As mentioned, the Sun and Moon combination in the natal chart would be relevant. My Sun and Moon are in Gemini in the third house, with the Sun exactly square the Nodes in Pisces and Virgo. For me, duality in close relationships, as well as communication through work in the arts or the occult, would be a part of the combination of these two planets. For instance, for me the communication of astrology combines Sun-Moon archetypes, such as the conscious and unconscious. And, because this is the 161.5007666 harmonic (161°30'2.76"), that communication is always in the light of transformation, in relation to thought, in regard to values.

Bodies or points that are conjunct in the arc transform chart are natally either conjunct or in the same fractional harmonic as the two planets on which the arc transform is based. Certainly for my Sun-Moon arc transform, I would not consider conjunctions within the same number of degrees as the number of the harmonic (in this case 161°), but a 03° or 04° orb does seem to be effective, especially when the planets are in an exact planetary picture. However, the conjunctions from the degree to the degree before or after are the most descriptive (in this case natally these aspects would be no more than 30" of arc from exactness).

For simplification, the positions, other than those of the Sun-Moon, are being given without the seconds. Nevertheless, the seconds of the other bodies and points, if their positions are accurate, are important too. In the following arc transform charts, the asteroids included (other than Ceres, Pallas, Juno, Vesta and Chiron) are the six personal name asteroids already mentioned.

In my Sun-Moon Arc Transform Chart, the exact conjunctions are Mercury (communication) and Halley's Comet (powerful activator) at 00° Scorpio 52' and 01° Scorpio 17'; Apollon (Sun figure), Vertex ("fate" or higher purpose) and Saturn (father figure) at 02° Pisces 24', 03° Pisces 07', and 04° Pisces 27'; asteroid with the name of my first husband/son (them) and Zeus (procreation) at 07° Leo 20' and 08° Leo 56'; and South Node (close relationships) and Part of Fortune, Ascendant (integrated persona) at 03° Capricorn 19' and 04° Capricorn 54'. (The Part of Fortune is always conjunct the Ascendant in the Sun-Moon Arc Transform Chart.) The combination of man and woman (conscious and unconscious) for me is decribed by the combination of the meanings of the conjuncting bodies and points. For instance, the combination of man and woman (conscious and unconscious) for me involves communicative power (Mercury, Halley's Comet) and radiant dedication to a higher purpose, such as paternalism (Apollon, Vertex, Saturn). Added to Apollon's radiance are that Uranian planet's primary Gemini, and secondary Aquarius, quality. (See Uranian Planet Key Words.) Apollon, Saturn, the South Node and Zeus are also highlighted in my progressed 24th harmonic chart.

The conjunction of an arc transform body or point to its natal position emphasizes that body or point. My arc transform name asteroid is at 21° Gemini 45', exactly conjunct my natal name asteroid at 20° Gemini 45', emphasizing the nominal identification of the self.

The Ascendant and Midheaven, and the placement of the Midheaven in the Ascendant Equal House Chart and the Ascendant in the Midheaven Equal House Chart, should always be noted.

Of course, exact aspects, particularly major configurations, are important. Pay especial attention to major configurations around the angles, and major configura-

Figure XIV – Sun-Moon Arc Transform Chart
of the Writer

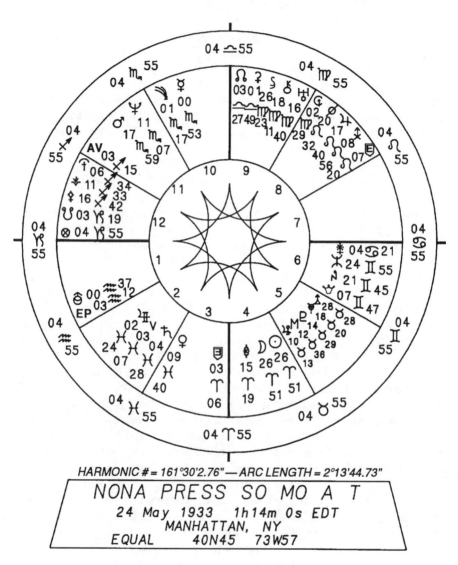

HARMONIC # = 161°30'2.76" — ARC LENGTH = 2°13'44.73"

NONA PRESS SO MO A T
24 May 1933   1h14m 0s EDT
MANHATTAN, NY
EQUAL   40N45   73W57

tions of the Sun-Moon and of the significant name asteroids. If they are available to you, the best name asteroids would be those with your name, your husband's or wife's, your mother's, your father's, your childrens', your lovers'. Studying the asteroids with the names of your lovers in the Sun-Moon arc transform will help you to decide if they'll become your marriage partners.

In my Sun-Moon Arc Transform Chart, from the personal perspective, there is an exact Cosmic Square on the angles. The South Node (03° Capricorn 19'), Part of Fortune, Ascendant (04° Capricorn 54') are opposite Juno (04° Cancer 20'), 7th cusp (04° Cancer 54'), square North Node (03° Libra 27'), 10th (04° Libra 54') and square the asteroid with the name similar to the name of my first husband/son (03° Aries 06'), 4th (04° Aries 54'). (Note that in my Sun-Moon Arc Transform [as in my husband's progressed 33rd harmonic], the North Node is exactly square the South Node, and the Vertex is exactly square the Antivertex.) This exact Cosmic Square is connected to three exact interconnecting Fists of God, with the South Node, Part of Fortune, Ascendant and the asteroid, 4th cusp sesquiquadrate Jupiter at 17° Leo 39'; the asteroid, 4th and Juno, 7th sesquiquadrate Mars at 17° Scorpio 58'; and the North Node, 10th and South Node, Part of Fortune, Ascendant sesquiquadrate Admetos at 18° Taurus 19'. These major configurations indicate the importance of close relationships involving marriage, parenthood, and a person with the name of my first husband/son. The Mars adds assertiveness, and Jupiter, expansion. As for Admetos, it has an association with roots. If those roots are not established, termination of the relationship may ensue.

SUN-MOON ARC TRANSFORM IN RELATION TO OTHER CHARTS

Connections between the Sun-Moon Arc Transform Chart and other charts are also meaningful. My arc transform Sun-Moon is exactly conjunct my 18th harmonic Sun/Moon midpoint at 26° Aries 23'36.4". 18 years old was my age when I married my first husband. As for some exact connections to his natal chart from my Sun-Moon Arc Transform Chart, there are the following. My arc transform South Node (03° Capricorn 19') and Part of Fortune, Ascendant (04° Capricorn 54') are conjunct his Juno at 03° Capricorn 59'ʀ. My arc transform Venus at 09° Pisces 40' is conjunct his Uranus, East Point at 09° Pisces 22'ʀ, 10° Pisces 40'. My arc transform Jupiter (17° Leo 39') is conjunct his name asteroid at 16° Leo 16' and his Sun/Moon midpoint at 18° Leo 58'35". These connections bespeak the marriage partners we became.

I've found that, in relation to the Sun-Moon Arc Transform Chart, the Sun/Moon midpoint is especially significant. Not only does my arc transform Jupiter equal my first husband's natal Sun/Moon midpoint, but there are additional planetary pictures. Equaling his Sun/Moon midpoint are my arc transform Mars (17° Scorpio 58'), by a square; my arc transform Admetos (18° Taurus 19'), by a square; my arc transform South Node (03° Capricorn 19'), Part of Fortune, Ascendant (04° Capricorn 54'), by a sesquiquadrate; my arc transform Juno (04° Cancer 20'), by a semisquare; my arc transform North Node (03° Libra 27'), by a semisquare; and my arc transform asteroid with the name similar to his and our son's (03° Aries 06'), by a sesquiquadrate. This name asteroid is exactly conjunct their name asteroid (02° Aries 44') at the time of the marriage. These planetary pictures reiterate the likelihood of marriage, with the Admetos perhaps referring to the termination of this marriage.

Equaling my second husband's natal Sun/Moon midpoint at 17° Capricorn 49'3.3" are my arc transform Antivertex (03° Sagittarius 15'), by a semisquare; my arc transform Apollon, Vertex (02° Pisces 24', 03° Pisces 07'), by a semisquare; and my arc transform Hades (02° Virgo 29'), by a sesquiquadrate. The arc transform Apollon and Hades equal my Sun/Moon midpoint at 01° Gemini 27'58.6" by squares. These planetary pictures point to a relationship with higher purpose (Antivertex, Vertex) and Sun associations (Apollon). The Hades could add karmic or past-life references. My arc transform Apollon, Vertex are exactly conjunct my second husband's South Node at 02° Pisces 09' and my North Node at 03° Pisces 16'. The exact reversal of our natal Nodes, and their equaling our natal Sun/Moon midpoints, is the strongest contact between our charts. (The activation of this contact has been mentioned repeatedly.) Also equaling his Sun/Moon midpoint natally are his Juno, daughter's name asteroid, Venus, Chiron, Apollon and stepson's name asteroid. Since our natal Sun/Moon midpoints equal each other, most of these bodies equal my natal Sun/Moon midpoint. Also, my natal Sun equals by a sesquiquadrate his natal Sun/Moon midpoint (I am bringing the shining of the Sun to his marriage midpoint). My first husband's natal Sun equals by a semisquare my natal Sun/Moon midpoint (he is bringing the shining of the Sun to my marriage midpoint). Perhaps it is the shining of the *son* which my first husband is bringing to me, which I in turn am bringing to my second husband.

SUN-MOON ARC TRANSFORM
SIGNIFYING SUN AND MOON PEOPLE

The Sun-Moon Arc Transform Chart relates not only to the native but also to those people signified by the Sun and Moon. Both the Ascendant and the Midheaven Charts reflect the natal charts of those relevant people. This reflection is in regard to those factors which are emphasized and/or associated similarly in the natal charts of those people, i.e., the father and mother, and husband and wife.

In the arc transform and natal charts, placements, rulerships, exact aspects and the involvement of "personal points" and name asteroids show emphasis and/or associations. (The "points" most individual or "personal" to the person are the Ascendant, Midheaven, Vertexes, East Point, Part of Fortune, Sun and Moon.) For example, in the Ascendant Equal House Chart, with my arc transform Sun-Moon in the fourth house in Aries, the symbolism of the Moon is emphasized (natural house placement), in association with the symbolism of Mars (Aries). In the Midheaven Equal House Chart, with my arc transform Sun-Moon in the ninth house in Aries, and the Sun of that arc transform Sun-Moon ruling the derived Ascendant, the symbolism of Jupiter (ninth house) is emphasized, in association with the symbolism of Mars (Aries and Ascendant). This Lunar and Jupiterian emphasis, in relation to Martian symbolism, is shown in the charts of my father and mother, husbands and myself.

My father had his natal Moon at 22° (Moon number) exactly conjunct (Mars aspect) his Sun and sesquiquadrate his Mars. The sign of his Sun and Moon is Sagittarius, and the ruler of his ninth house is exactly conjunct his Ascendant. My mother had her natal Aries Moon in her first house, exactly conjunct her Aries Ascendant, with Cancer on the cusp of her fourth house. Her Sun and Jupiter in Sagittarius are exactly conjunct (Mars aspect) in the ninth house, which her Jupiter rules. Her Mars in Sagittarius is also in the ninth house. My second husband has his natal Moon in the fourth house exactly square (Moon aspect) his Ascendant in Leo. His Mars and Jupiter are in his fourth house in Sagittarius, and his Mars is the ruler of his ninth house. His Jupiter is in an exact Grand Trine with his Sun ruler, which is exactly conjunct his East Point. My first husband has his natal Moon in the seventh house with their ruler in Cancer exactly conjunct his Mars in Cancer. The Moon ruler and Mars are exactly sesquiquadrate his Ascendant and quincunx his Midheaven in Sagittarius, while his Jupiter is exactly square that Midheaven. As for me, my natal Moon, which is two degrees from my Sun, rules the planet that is exactly quincunx my Ascendant. Also, my name asteroid, which is exactly trine my Ascendant, is in my fourth house. My Mars is at 09° (Jupiter number), and my Jupiter is at 13° (Moon number). My Jupiter, the ruler of my Midheaven, is exactly opposition my Antivertex in the first house.

Another example of the Sun-Moon Arc Transform Chart reflecting the natal charts of the relevant people is the following. With the Ascendant in Capricorn, and Saturn exactly conjunct the Vertex in Pisces, the symbolism of Saturn is emphasized, in association with the symbolism of Mars (Ascendant) and Neptune (Pisces). The Vertex, which helps to emphasize Saturn, also takes part in its combined symbolism. (Though treated separately, each example is not completely discrete. The symbolism of the Moon emphasized in the previous example is connected with this example through the association with the symbolism of Mars shared by both examples.)

My father had his natal Ascendant and East Point in Capricorn, and his Sun, Moon and Saturn in the twelfth house, with his Moon exactly opposite his Neptune. His Vertex is exactly trine his Saturn. The ruler of his Sun, Moon and Saturn, as well as his name asteroid, are in the tenth house, with the name asteroid exactly semisquare his Ascendant. My mother had her natal Midheaven in Capricorn exactly square (Moon aspect) her Aries Antivertex, East Point in the twelfth house, and semisextile (Neptune aspect) her name asteroid. Her Mars is at 12° (Neptune number), and her Neptune is in Cancer exactly quincunx (Neptune aspect) her Sun and Sun ruler conjunction. My second husband has his natal Ascendant at 28° (Saturn number) exactly square (Moon aspect) his Moon at 28°, ruling his Antivertex. His Saturn is exactly opposite his name asteroid. His Sun is in Pisces ruling his Ascendant and his exact East Point, Neptune conjunction. My first husband has his natal Saturn exactly conjunct his Moon, with their ruler in Cancer exactly conjunct Mars in Cancer. The Moon-Saturn ruler and Mars are exactly sesquiquadrate his Ascendant in Pisces and quincunx (Neptune aspect) his Midheaven at 13° (Moon number). His first-house East Point (10°—Saturn number) and Antivertex are also in Pisces, with his Antivertex exactly quincunx (Neptune aspect) his name asteroid. His Neptune at 12° (Neptune number) is exactly trine his Midheaven. As for me, Pisces is intercepted in my natal first house, while my Neptune, ruler of my East Point and Antivertex in the first house, is exactly square (Moon aspect) my Midheaven. My East Point is at 04° (Moon number), my Antivertex is at 12° (Neptune number), while my Saturn is in the twelfth house.

Another example of the Sun-Moon Arc Transform Chart reflecting the natal charts of the relevant people is the following. In the Ascendant Equal House Chart, with my arc transform Nodes in an exact major configuration conjuncting the angles, the symbolism of the Nodes is emphasized in association with the angles. In the Midheaven Equal House Chart, with my arc transform Nodes still in a major configuration that has the South Node conjuncting the Ascendant, the symbolism of the Nodes is still emphasized in association with an angle. The Nodes of the Moon, being the points at which the Moon crosses the apparent path of the Sun, are associated with the Sun and the Moon. In the Midheaven Equal House Chart, the arc transform South Node and Ascendant are in the fifth house, reiterating the Sun association. (Again, though treated separately, each example is not completely discrete.)

My father had his natal Nodes in Capricorn-Cancer across his first-seventh houses. His North Node is in an exact conjunction with his Ascendant and Part of Fortune, and his Mars is exactly quincunx that stellium. Since the Part of Fortune is a combination of the Ascendant, Sun and Moon, its exact conjunction to his Ascendant also reflects the Nodes' association with the angles in my arc transform chart and the Nodes' association with the Sun and Moon in general. My mother had her natal Nodes in Aries-Libra across her first-seventh houses. The exact conjunction of her Moon and Ascendant and their both being at 05° (Sun number) also reflect the Nodes' association with the angles in my arc transform chart and the Nodes' association with the Sun and Moon in general. My second husband has his Nodes across his first-seventh houses. His Sun's rulership of, as well as his Moon's exact aspect to, his Ascendant also reflect the Nodes' particular and general association. My first husband has his Nodes in Libra-Aries in 23° (Sun number). The ruler of his Ascendant is in Leo, with the ruler of his Moon, as well as Mars, in Cancer at 14° (Sun number) in the fifth house exactly sesquiquadrate his Ascendant. This Sun and Moon association with the Ascendant also reflects the Nodes' particular and general association. As for me, my natal Nodes are across my first-seventh houses, with my North Node exactly conjunct my East Point at 04° (Moon number). (My arc transform Vertex and Saturn conjunction at 03° and 04° Pisces is exactly conjunct my natal North Node and East Point conjunction at 03° and 04° Pisces.) The East Point is an additional angle. My Nodes are exactly square (Moon aspect) my Sun. The Sun's exact aspect to the Nodes, as well as the North Node's exact conjunction to the East Point, also reflect the Nodes' association with the angles in my arc transform chart and the Nodes' association with the Sun and Moon in general.

SIMILARITIES IN THE LIVES OF SUN AND MOON PEOPLE

Having shown how the Sun-Moon Arc Transform Chart relates to the natal charts of the people signified by the Sun and Moon, I'll give an instance of how it describes similarities in the lives of those people.

The arc transform examples, from the public perspective, can refer to a career in the arts. More specific indications in the Midheaven Equal House Chart are the following. Jupiter is rising 05° from the 12° Leo derived Ascendant. Jupiter rules the fifth house, as well as Vesta (vested interests) in the fourth house, but exactly conjunct the fifth. Jupiter is exactly semisextile (Neptune aspect) Uranus and Chiron in the second house of money. Uranus' position refers to the fact that money is usually earned in the arts as an independent free lance; Chiron's position, to the fact that the earning is usually accompanied by a seeking after knowledge and truth. The ruler of that Uranus is Mercury in the third house of writing. Neptune is in the third, exactly conjunct the fourth cusp. The ruler of Neptune and the fourth is conjunct the Midheaven by 01°+ minutes. My parents, husbands and myself all are or have been free lances in the arts. My parents were both involved in show business. My mother was a dancer, singer, actress and lyricist. My father was an artist who did set and costume designing and caricatures for the theatre. He also wrote poems, though they were not published, and plays, though they were not produced. My second husband is a musician and musical contractor, working primarily in the theatre. He has also written music, and his contracting involves much "paperwork." My first husband was a teacher and is an art dealer. I was an artist (doing caricatures for the theatre, among other things) and am now an astrologer, writing a book.

SUN-MOON ARC TRANSFORMS OF SUN AND MOON PEOPLE

The Sun-Moon Arc Transform Charts of the people signified by the Sun and Moon should be considered. Which brings me to my second husband's Sun-Moon Arc Transform Chart. The separation between his Sun and Moon is 98.4655624° (98°27'56.02"). This separation divided into 360° gives the 3.6561006 harmonic or 03°39'21.96"—communication, in relation to idealism or nebulousness, in regard to communication. As always, take into account the shading of the individual numbers. It is interesting that with the arc transform of his Sun and Moon in a 3+ harmonic, he chose to marry a double Gemini.

When his Sun and Moon are multiplied by this harmonic, they are both at 02° Virgo 17'24". This degree, minute and second, combined with the sign, is particularly important to him, as far as the relationship of the Sun and Moon archetypes is concerned. Values of service, in relation to transformation, in regard to service might be a possible interpretation (the individual numbers give greater detail). His arc transform Sun-Moon is exactly conjunct his natal North Node (02° Virgo 09'20.52"), Apollon (03° Virgo 05'7.08"ʀ) and my natal South Node (03° Virgo 16'14.16") and square my natal Sun (02° Gemini 34'50.88"). To reiterate the magnitude of this activation: the exact reversal of our natal Nodes, and their tie-in with our natal Sun/Moon midpoints, is the strongest contact between our charts; besides his natal Nodes, his natal Juno, daughter's name asteroid, Venus, Chiron, Apollon and stepson's name asteroid equal his natal Sun/Moon midpoint, which equals mine; and besides my natal Nodes, my natal Sun equals his natal Sun/Moon midpoint. Also, in his Sun-Moon Arc Transform Chart, the North Node at 16° Libra 17'47.76" is exactly semisquare his arc transform Sun-Moon and equals both our natal Sun/Moon midpoints.

From the perspective of my husband's personal life (Ascendant Equal House Chart of the Arc Transform), the Sun-Moon is in the twelfth house, exactly conjunct the twelfth house cusp (connecting the eleventh with the twelfth). In his personal life, there is an emphasis on idealism and self-sacrifice (connected with the unusual) in respect to man-woman relationships, the ego and emotion, conscious and unconscious. These combinations are concerned with close connections and Sun symbolism (natal conjunction to the North Node and the Uranian planet Apollon). Apollon is associated with the Greek and Roman god Apollo, who is linked with the Sun.

A major configuration that my husband has in his arc transform chart is an exact T-Square of the asteroid with my name (25° Scorpio 11'), opposite Transpluto (25° Taurus 00'), Saturn (25° Taurus 31'), square Cupido (24° Leo 01') and Neptune (26° Leo 24'). This T-Square indicates an emphasis on an idealistic (Neptune) marriage (Cupido) that is obsessively (Transpluto) responsible (Saturn). There could also be a dissolving (Neptune) of the responsibility (Saturn). This emphasis, though in a chart descriptive of the relationship of the Sun and Moon, especially relates to me because my name asteroid is in the T-Square. As outlined before, in my natal chart Pisces (Neptune) is intercepted in my first house; my Neptune, the ruler of my East Point and Antivertex in the first house, is exactly square my Midheaven (Saturn); and my Saturn is in the twelfth house (Neptune). Cupido and Transpluto, the other factors in the T-Square, are also emphasized in my natal chart. My Cupido is exactly square my Chiron and Moon and exactly semisquare my asteroid with my husband's name; my Transpluto, ruled by the Moon, is exactly sextile my Mercury, Chiron. Mercury is very prominent in my chart because it rules my stellium in Gemini (including my Sun and Moon and the asteroid with my name) and my stellium in Virgo (including Neptune). The houses, signs and degrees of the planets in my husband's arc transform T-Square are also descriptive of me. For instance in the Ascendant perspective, which is the more personally descriptive, Transpluto and Saturn are in the eighth house (my natal Pluto is exactly quincunx my Ascendant); Cupido and Neptune are in the eleventh house (Aquarius is the sign of my natal Ascendant); the asteroid with my name is in the second house (the ruler of my natal Ascendant is in my second house).

The midpoint of significant name asteroids should be noted. In my husband's Sun-Moon Arc Transform Chart, the midpoint of the asteroid with my name (25° Scorpio 11') and the asteroid with his name (02° Leo 07') is 28° Virgo 39'38". Equaling the midpoint by a conjunction is Ceres (nurturing) at 27° Virgo 46'; by an opposition, Juno (marriage) at 27° Pisces 51'; by a square, Zeus (procreation) at 29° Gemini 50'; by a sesquiquadrate, the Antivertex (a fated point) at 13° Taurus 34'; by semisquares, the South Node (close connections) at 14° Leo 23' and the Dark Moon Lilith (fascination) at 14° Scorpio 09'.

As explained, the arc transform chart can be placed around the natal chart. The arc transform chart is then related to you in general, rather than to your personal life or to your public life in particular. With my husband's Sun-Moon Arc Transform Chart placed around his natal chart, arc transform Cupido and Neptune are in his natal twelfth house, and arc transform Transpluto and Saturn are in his natal tenth house. The twelfth house relates to music, and the tenth, to the career. Though we are not looking at the arc transform chart from the public perspective, these are valid references in terms of my husband in general. Not only is he a musician, but his mother and father at one time owned a music store and operated it together—a more mundane expression of these energies. Other manifestations of the twelfth house are art and the occult. The third leg of the T-Square is the arc transform asteroid with my name. This asteroid falls in my husband's natal fourth house, and I was an artist and am an astrologer.

The arc transform Ascendant is significant and would be placed in the harmonic ring around the natal chart, as well as in the Midheaven Equal House Chart which has an Ascendant derived from the Midheaven. The Ascendant of my husband's Sun-Moon Arc Transform Chart is 02° Libra 01'55.92". This Ascendant indicates that the persona of this chart, which describes the relationship of the Sun and Moon archetypes for him, is very much preoccupied with partnership (Libra). In fact, the preoccupation is with values of partnership, in relation to the self, in regard to paternalism.

Conjunctions and connections between arc transform charts should be noted. Considering my husband's and my Sun-Moon Arc Transform Charts from the Ascendant perspective, there are the following exact conjunctions activating my Cosmic Square on the angles. His arc transform 4th cusp (02° Capricorn 01') conjuncts my arc transform South Node, Part of Fortune, Ascendant (03° Capricorn 19', 04° Capricorn 54'); his arc transform Part of Fortune, Ascendant (02° Libra 01') conjuncts my arc transform Ceres, North Node, 10th cusp (01° Libra 48', 03° Libra 27', 04° Libra 54'); and his arc transform 7th cusp, asteroid with our daughter's first name/my middle name (02° Aries 01', 02° Aries 02') conjuncts my arc transform asteroid with the name similar to my son's (03° Aries 06').

ARABIC PARTS

As mentioned, the Part of Fortune is always conjunct the Ascendant in the Sun-Moon Arc Transform Chart. The reason is that the definition of the Part of Fortune is "a zodiacal point which is equally distant from the Ascendant as the Moon is from the Sun in longitude.[25] In this arc transform chart there is no distance between the Sun and the Moon, so there is no distance between the Part of Fortune and the Ascendant. The same would be true of the Part of Spirit. The formula of the Part of Spirit is $A + \odot - D$, while the formula of the Part of Fortune is $A + D - \odot$.

Though the names of the Arabic Parts are evocative, I think the Parts relate to the meanings of the planets and points in them. For instance, the Part of Fortune, being a combination of the Ascendant, Sun and Moon, relates to the persona, ego and emotion. (The Sun and Moon refer to the male and female principles, too.) The Part of Spirit is the same combination, but its formula ($A + \odot - D$) places more emphasis on the Moon, since that is the factor which is subtracted. (Perhaps, when the native is born with the Sun below the horizon, placing more emphasis on the Moon, the names of the Parts should be reversed.) The Part of Destiny ($M + \odot - D$) and the Part of Status ($M + D - \odot$) have ancestors as one of their concerns. Similarly, two of the concerns of Parts with Mercury or Jupiter in them are writing and travel.

Sun-Moon Arc Transform Transit

While studying my husband's arc transform of his Sun and Moon, I realized that this arc transform, falling between his 3rd and 4th harmonics, would be the same as a secondary-type harmonic progression between the time he was three and four years old. The harmonic is 3.6561006 or 03°39'21.96". The equation

$$\frac{39'21.96"}{60'} = \frac{x}{365}$$

when solved is 239.4765. Therefore, the day and time to which this arc transform, or harmonic progression, equates would be 239 days, 11 hours, 26 minutes and 9.6 seconds after his third birthday

$$.4765 = 28'35.4"; \quad \frac{28'35.4"}{60'} = \frac{x}{24} = 11.436 \quad \text{or 11h 26m 9.6s.}$$

That day would be October 24, 1927 at 04:18:51.6 AM EST, as his birthday and time is February 26, 1924 at 04:52:42 PM EST.

Since a harmonic progression is descriptive of what is happening at that time in a person's life, I wondered what was happening at that time in my husband's life. His parents are dead, so they couldn't be questioned, and he was only three and a half years old, so he couldn't remember. Though not able to discover what, if anything, happened to him even around that time, I looked in the ephemeris to see the transits, and they were most intriguing. I then had the chart drawn by Astro for 04:18:51 AM EST in the Bronx, New York, my husband's birthplace. Strangely, like our Arc Transform Sun-Moon Charts, this transit chart is very much tied into the factors in our natal charts that relate to marriage and to the strongest connections between our natal charts.

The transiting Moon, Antivertex (16° Libra 16'13.08", 16° Libra 23'42.72") were in an exact Cosmic Square with the Vertex (16° Aries 23'42.72"), Pluto (17° Cancer 09'1.8"ʀ) and asteroid with daughter's first name/my middle name (18° Capricorn 01'06"). This transiting Cosmic Square activated his exact natal T-Square with Juno (marriage), asteroid with daughter's first name/my middle name (16° Libra 20'46.32"ʀ, 17° Libra 29'24"ʀ), Venus and Chiron—stepfather (16° Aries 25'35.76" and 18° Aries 04'14.52") and Sun/Moon midpoint (17° Capricorn 49'3.3"). The transiting Moon, Antivertex, Vertex, Pluto and name asteroid all equaled his natal Sun/Moon midpoint—the Moon, Antivertex and Vertex by squares, Pluto by an opposition, and the name asteroid by a conjunction. The transiting Moon, Antivertex, Vertex and Pluto all equaled my natal Sun/Moon midpoint (01° Gemini 27'58.6")—the Moon and Antivertex by a sesquiquadrate, and the Vertex and Pluto by semisquares.

The transiting Dark Moon Lilith at 03° Pisces 00' also equaled his natal Sun/Moon midpoint and was exactly conjunct his natal South Node at 02° Pisces 09'20.52" (conjunct his natal asteroid with the name of my son at 01° Pisces 06'24") and my natal North Node at 03° Pisces 16'14.16". This exact reversal of our Nodes is across our natal first and seventh houses, so it relates to marriage. My second husband's asteroid with the name of my son being involved with these Nodes, and our Sun/Moon midpoints, shows my son's involvement with our marriage. When my husband and son met for the first time, they "took" to each other as if they'd known each other all their lives. Their instant affinity could be described by this transiting Dark Moon Lilith's conjunction to the natal Nodes and the name asteroid.

Since this massive tie-in of our natal Sun/Moon midpoints with our natal Nodes, etc., is the strongest contact between our charts, how appropriate that it should be activated by the transits of the day and time which equate to the arc transform of my husband's Sun and Moon. These transiting positions also exactly aspected positions in our relationship chart—in brief, the Sun and Juno at 16° and 18° Libra, Vesta at 17° Aries, Pluto at 18° Cancer, the East Point and North Node at 00° and 01° Gemini, the South Node at 01° Sagittarius and Neptune at 00° Virgo.

The transiting Ascendant (06° Libra 01'6.96") was exactly opposition my natal Ceres—nurturing (05° Aries 35'2.04"). In other words, I am the mother figure who is the wife (conjunction of Ceres to Descendant). That Descendant was exactly semisquare my natal Ascendant (20° Aquarius 27'44.28").

Another interesting link is that the transiting North Node (19° Gemini 50'39.12") was exactly conjunct my natal asteroid with my name (20° Gemini 45'12"), opposition the transiting asteroid with a name close to my son's and our daughter's (20° Sagittarius 06'54") and, of course, the transiting South Node, and square the transiting asteroid with my name (19° Pisces 23'54"), in an exact T-Square. Incidentally, the transiting North Node was exactly trine my husband's natal Mercury (18° Aquarius 13'6.6"); and transiting Mercury (23° Scorpio 32'22.92") was exactly trine transiting Jupiter (24° Pisces 46'22.08"℞); and, as you no doubt by this time know, I am a double Gemini—Sun and Moon. (The excessiveness of the Jupiter planet bespeaks the excess of the Mercury sign.)

My arc transform of my Sun and Moon, falling between my 161st and 162nd harmonics (the 161.5007666 harmonic), is also the same as a secondary-type harmonic progression. Unfortunately, since I shall not live to be 161 years old, the arc transform of my Sun and Moon cannot be equated to a day and time during my life. However, I thought if this chart (which would be in the year 2094) were calculated, it might also be descriptive of connections between my husband's and my chart, even though it would be past our lifetimes. Once this thought had occurred to me there was no alternative but to pursue it. Not having ephemerides for this year, I sent to Astro for the chart of November 22, 2094 at 06:56:57 PM EST.

$$.5007666 = 30'2.76"; \quad \frac{30'2.76"}{60'} = \frac{x}{365} = 182.77983 \text{ days};$$

$$.77983 = 46'47.39''; \quad \frac{46'\,47.39''}{60'} = \frac{x}{24} = 18.715933 \text{ or } 18h\,42m\,57.36s;$$

birth date and time + days, years, hours, minutes and seconds,

May 24,	1933	at	00:14	AM EST
+182	161		18:42:57.36	
Nov. 22,	2094		18:56:57.36	EST
			06:56:57.36	PM EST

If the number of days brings the date past December 31, a year is added to the year column; if the number of hours brings the time past midnight, a day is added to the day column.

This transit chart (see Figure XV) has the ten planets, four original asteroids (Ceres, Pallas, Juno, Vesta), Chiron, eight Uranian planets, Transpluto and Dark Moon Lilith. (In the title of the chart, SO stands for Sun; MO, for Moon; A T for arc transform; and TR, for transit.) The fifteen other asteroids,[26] which since the fall of 1983 Astro Computing has offered for inclusion in charts, are only for the 20th century. Since my ephemerides are also only until the year 2000, and Astro's *Many Interesting Asteroids* are only until 2005, I could not add the name asteroids, which are so helpful in the analysis of relationships. As for Halley's Comet, its positions are only available from December 31, 1899, to January 10, 1997. Despite the fact that this unequal number of factors makes a comparison of the two transit charts inequitable, I shall attempt to make one.

COMPARISON OF ARC TRANSFORM TRANSITS

In the transit chart which is equivalent to my Sun-Moon Arc Transform Chart, the Part of Fortune (18° Capricorn 25'35") and Admetos (15° Cancer 38'35.88"ʀ) tie in with my husband's aforementioned Cosmic Square in the transit chart which is equivalent to his Sun-Moon Arc Transform Chart. The Part of Fortune is a "fortunate" point of integration of the persona, ego and emotion. Admetos has a stick-to-it-ive quality which can relate to never-ending as well as ending. Supporting the never-ending interpretation is the fact that Admetos is in the first house, in Cancer—a house associated with the self, and a sign associated with "holding on."

The 06° Libra Ascendant and 08° Libra East Point of my husband's transit chart is exactly conjunct the Mars (07° Libra 41'32.28") of my transit chart. The fourth house Mars rules the eleventh house, as well as Cupido (family) and Pluto (regeneration). This interaspect conjunction is exactly square the Ascendant (08° Cancer 38' 11.4") of my transit chart, with the 07° Mars pulling in the Midheaven (06° Cancer 57' 48.6") of my husband's transit chart. Another emphasis on the angles is the exact conjunction of the IC (16° Virgo 43' 33.24") of my transit chart and the Venus (17° Virgo 07' 7.32") of his transit chart. The twelfth house Venus rules the Libra Ascendant, East Point, Moon, Antivertex, Mars and Sun, as well as the Taurus eighth house, Chiron and Kronos. (The Moon and Antivertex are in the aforementioned Cosmic Square.)

Another link is the South Node and asteroid with a name close to our daughter's and my son's (19° Sagittarius 50'39.12", 20° Sagittarius 06'54") in my husband's

Figure XV – Transit Chart equivalent to
Sun-Moon Arc Transform Chart of the Writer

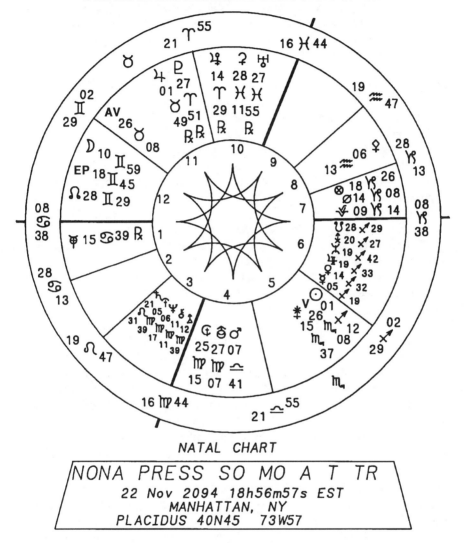

NATAL CHART

NONA PRESS SO MO A T TR
22 Nov 2094 18h56m57s EST
MANHATTAN, NY
PLACIDUS 40N45 73W57

transit chart being exactly conjunct Apollon, Poseidon and Zeus (19° Sagittarius 32'56.4", 19° Sagittarius 41'31.92", 20° Sagittarius 27'16.56") in mine. As mentioned, Apollon relates to Sun symbolism; Poseidon, to a Super-Neptunism; and Zeus, to procreation. In my transit chart, this stellium is exactly opposite the East Point (18° Gemini 45'57.6"), the self, and trine Saturn, the father (21° Leo 31'27.84"), which is exactly conjunct my natal Descendant (20° Leo 27'44.28"). My husband became the stepfather to my son and the father to our daughter.

CONNECTIONS TO OTHER CHARTS

Connections to the natal and other charts are also important. From the transit chart, which is equivalent to my Sun-Moon Arc Transform Chart, to my natal chart some of the exact conjunctions are the Antivertex (26° Taurus 08'57.84") conjunct my Mercury (27° Taurus 01'58.8"), ruler of my Sun, Moon, IC, Venus and fifth house cusp, as well as my seventh house stellium; the twelfth house cusp (02° Gemini 29'6.36") conjunct my Sun (02° Gemini 34'50.88"), ruler of my Descendant; the Moon (10° Gemini 59'25.44") conjunct my Venus (11° Gemini 12'18.36"), ruler of my Mercury; and the third-ninth cusps (19° Leo-Aquarius 47'8.16") across my Descendant-Ascendant (20° Leo-Aquarius 27'44.28"). The transiting Sun (01° Sagittarius 12'1.44") is exactly opposite my natal Sun and Moon (00° Gemini 21'6.48") and equals my natal Sun/Moon midpoint (01° Gemini 27'58.6"). The transiting Sun/Moon midpoint is 06° Virgo 05'43.4", exactly conjunct Kronos, Neptune (05° Virgo 38'46.32", 06° Virgo 16'44.76") and my natal Neptune (07° Virgo 24'20.16"), opposition my husband's natal Sun (07° Pisces 03'1.44"). The most prominent major aspect between my husband's and my natal planets is my Neptune exactly opposite his Sun. This natal opposition, which can result in idealization, was written about in reference to my husband's and my 7th harmonic charts, so this transit chart is repeating the symbolism not only of our natal charts, but of our harmonics of marriage. This opposition is exactly square my natal Midheaven-IC (07° Sagittarius-Gemini 41'34.44"), activating the symbolism of father and mother, as well as of career and home.

As with other charts, I look at the Sun/Moon, Venus/Mars, Mars/Jupiter and Mars/Saturn midpoints. The Mars/Jupiter midpoint in my transit chart is 19° Cancer 45'29". Kronos (05° Virgo 38' 46.32") and Mercury (05° Sagittarius 19'15.96") equal both the Sun/Moon and Mars/Jupiter midpoints. This connection shows again the importance to me of children (Mars/Jupiter), in regard to man-woman relationships (Sun/Moon). Kronos denotes the head of the family, and Mercury is the ruler of the Moon, East Point, North Node, Kronos, Neptune, Chiron and twelfth and fourth cusps. Also, Mercury can represent me, a double Gemini, and Neptune can represent my husband, a Pisces with Neptune in the twelfth house, exactly conjunct his East Point.

SIGNIFICANCE OF SMALL DIFFERENCES IN NATAL CHARTS

These transit charts that equate to my Sun-Moon Arc Transform Chart and to my husband's are good examples of how a little difference in natal charts can be significant. In the fall of 1985 Astro began to use the "true" obliquity of the ecliptic, rather than the "mean" obliquity. The true obliquity is obtained by adding the nutation in obliquity to the mean obliquity. In my chart the difference from mean to true is a plus seven seconds of arc. Also, at that time there was the implementation of revised values for Delta T—in my case a plus one second of time. In the fall of 1987, the nutation (wobble of the Earth) correction was applied to the Moon. Again there were seconds differences. The Sun-Moon Arc Transform is based on the separation between these two bodies, so seconds differences in their positions resulted in seconds difference in the harmonic. Since 60 minutes of arc is equivalent to 365 days, seconds difference in the harmonic made days difference in the transit chart. (Of course, the differences between the "mean" and "true" positions, etc., are small by comparison to the differences between the apparent and geometric positions.)

Venus-Mars Arc Transform

Arc transforms of other combinations of planets can be calculated to good effect. (It is advantageous to compare the arc transform chart of one combination with the arc transform chart of another, particularly in regard to the conjunctions between the charts.) The Venus-Mars Arc Transform Chart describes the relationship of love and sex, which Venus and Mars combined represent. Naturally, this correspondence is not the only possible one. There is some relation to marriage, with Mars and Venus being the rulers of the first-seventh houses in the natural zodiac. Venus and Mars can also represent the daughter and the son, as well as energy directed towards making money. In regard to the daughter and son, the arc transform chart reflects those factors which are emphasized and/or associated similarly in their natal charts. The Venus-Mars Arc Transform Charts of a mother and father may reflect different factors of their children, or reflect the same factors in different ways.

As always, the situation in the natal chart—in this case the house, sign and degree position, the rulerships and exact aspects of Venus and Mars—would add meanings specific to the particular person.

The arc transform of my Venus and Mars is in the 4.0690816 harmonic (04°04'8.69"). The harmonic is derived from the separation between natal Venus and Mars. When my natal Venus and Mars are multiplied by this harmonic, they are both at 19° Capricorn 44'21.12". The numerical principles of the separation, of the harmonic, and of the arc transform Venus-Mars position are significant. The arc transform of my second husband's Venus and Mars is in the 1.4518977 harmonic (01°27'6.83"). When his natal Venus and Mars are multiplied by this harmonic, they are both at 23° Aries 50'58.92". Appropriately, my husband's arc transform Venus-Mars at 23° Aries equals by a semisquare the midpoint of my arc transform Venus-Mars at 19° Capricorn and my arc transform Sun-Moon at 26° Aries.

CONNECTIONS TO OTHER CHARTS

Connections to the natal charts of the native and of significant people are appropriate. Activation of their natal Venus/Mars midpoints by the Venus-Mars Arc Transform Charts is descriptive. For instance, my arc transform South Node equals by an opposition my former husband's natal Venus/Mars midpoint; and my arc transform Pluto (obsession) equals by a sesquiquadrate, and my arc transform North Node equals by a semisquare, my present husband's natal Venus/Mars midpoint. Though both the North and the South Node refer to close relationships, the South Node symbolizes relationships from the "past." (The activation of other midpoints, such as the natal Sun/Moon midpoints, tells more of the story.)

PROCEDURE

Look for the bodies and points that are conjunct in the Venus-Mars Arc Transform Chart. They are the ones that are natally either conjunct or in the same fractional harmonic as Venus and Mars. The Sun, Moon, Ascendant and Midheaven, and the placement of the Midheaven in the Ascendant Equal House Chart and the Ascendant in the Midheaven Equal House Chart, should always be noted.

Of course, exact major configurations around the angles are outstanding. Important as well are exact aspects and interaspects of arc transform Venus-Mars and of significant name asteroids. My husband has no major configurations involving his arc transform Venus-Mars at 23° Aries 50'58.92". His arc transform Uranus (23° Leo 40'53.04") is exactly trine his arc transform Venus-Mars, but it takes my arc transform South Node (23° Sagittarius 40'14") to connect with this aspect and change it into a Grand Trine. (His arc transform Venus-Mars being brought into a major configuration helps to integrate the meaning of these planets.) This Grand Trine refers not only to the suddenness of our passionate love, but to his gaining through a close relationship with me (my South Node) a stepson (Uranus), who is Venusian (Venus-Mars—the boy [Mars] natally has Venus exactly opposite his Ascendant). Also, Venus rules the seventh house in my husband's Ascendant Equal House Chart, so his arc transform Venus-Mars could be describing a son (Mars) who is brought by the wife (seventh house). Another connection from my Venus-Mars Arc Transform Chart that changes an exact trine in my marriage partner's Venus-Mars Arc Transform Chart into a Grand Trine is my Chiron (00° Sagittarius 03'59.76"), trine his Hades (01° Aries 58'53.4") and his asteroid with the name of my son (00° Leo 44'00") and the South Node (02° Leo 15'21"). Chiron, as stated many times, refers to the stepfather; Hades and the South Node can refer to past-life connections; and the asteroid with the name of my son refers to him.

Similarities between charts, as well as interaspects, are notable. A similarity between the Venus-Mars Arc Transform Charts of my husband and myself is that the Ascendants are both in Scorpio. His is 05° Scorpio 14'59.64" and mine is 13° Scorpio 59'14.64". Interestingly, his minutes are the same as my seconds, and his seconds are the same as my minutes. The principle of his degree combines the Solar archetypes of the #5 with the Plutonian archetypes of the Scorpio sign, in relation to the Solar archetypes of the #14, in regard to the Solar archetypes of the #59; while the principle of my degree combines the Lunar archetypes of the #13 with the Plutonian archetypes of the Scorpio sign, in relation to the Solar archetypes of the #59, in regard to the Solar archetypes of the #14. Also, our Venus-Mars arc transform Ascendants are 08°44'15" apart, repeating in the degree and minute the Scorpio symbolism of our love-sex combinations.

Transformation of the Natal Figure

Another relevant consideration is the natal positions from which the arc transform positions have come. By noting what the arc transforms have come from and to, you see how what was indicated in the natal chart is made more specific in the arc transform chart.

Though this consideration is always relevant, it is particularly obvious in the harmonic between the 1st and 2nd harmonics. In this harmonic, most of the natal relationships are maintained, so if within those original relationships planets or points are introduced, the transformation of the natal figure by them is especially outstanding. For instance, natally my husband has the asteroid with the name of my son at 01° Pisces 06'24", the South Node at 02° Pisces 09'20.52", the Sun at 07° Pisces 03'1.44", Ceres at 14° Pisces 01'19.56" and Uranus at 16° Pisces 54'45", all in the seventh house. This placement could indicate a stepson being brought to him by his wife. In my husband's Venus-Mars Arc Transform Chart, the asteroid with the name of my son is 00° Leo 44'00"; the South Node, 02° Leo 15'48"; the Sun, 09° Leo 21'45.36"; Ceres, 19° Leo 29'5.28"; Uranus, 23° Leo 40'53.04"; and Pluto, 25° Leo 44'5.28". Considering the natal positions coming to the harmonic positions in the Ascendant Equal House Chart, there is the following. The asteroid with the name of my son and the South Node have come from the sign Pisces in the seventh house—empathy associated with the wife—to Leo in the ninth house—children associated with expansion (also, the son is a Sagittarian). The Sun, Ceres and Uranus have come from the sign Pisces in the seventh house —empathy associated with the wife—to Leo in the tenth— children associated with paternalism. Pluto (regeneration) has been added at the end of the Leo group. Pluto has come from the sign Cancer in the eleventh house—maternalism associated with stepchildren—to Leo in the tenth house—children associated with paternalism. The natal and arc transform numerical positions are also important. As one example, Pluto has come from 10° Cancer 22' 31.44"—paternalism combined with maternalism, in relation to maternalism, in regard to maternalism—to 25° Leo 44' 5.28"—the wife combined with children, in relation to regeneration, in regard to children.

Venus-Mars Arc Transform Transit

The day and time to which my Venus-Mars Arc Transform Chart equates is June 18, 1937 at 05:22:44.4 AM EST. (The chart was drawn by Astro for 05:22:44 AM EST for Manhattan, New York.) What event, if any, occurred in my life at that time, I don't know. However, this transit chart, like my Venus-Mars Arc Transform Chart, highlights the factors in my natal chart that for me describe the relationship of Venus and Mars. (For simplification, the positions are being given without the seconds.)

For instance, just as the transit charts equivalent to my second husband's and my Sun-Moon Arc Transform Charts connect appropriately with our natal Sun/Moon midpoints, the transit chart for this time connects appropriately with our natal Venus/Mars midpoints. Tying in with my natal Venus/Mars midpoint at 25° Cancer 26' is an exact transiting T-Square of Jupiter (25° Capricorn 34'℞), opposition Pluto (27° Cancer 26'), square the Moon (26° Libra 27'). (Jupiter equals by an opposition, and the Moon, by a square, my natal Venus/Mars midpoint.) This connection can refer to the fact that for me love-sex (Venus-Mars) is related to an expansive (Jupiter), obsessive (Pluto) emotionality (Moon). Tying in with and equaling my husband's natal Venus/Mars midpoint at 20° Aquarius 24' are the following transiting factors—the asteroid with the name of his stepson at 19° Aquarius 46'℞ (conjunction), Mars at 20° Scorpio 05'℞ (square) and Saturn at 04° Aries 26' (semisquare). These interconnections can refer to the fact that my husband became the father (Saturn) to the boy (Mars) with that specific name (name asteroid). Of course, not only the natal Venus/Mars midpoints are important. For example, the transiting asteroid with the name of my husband is 17° Cancer 10', equaling our natal Sun/Moon midpoints.

As for the Ascendant of the transit chart equivalent to my Venus-Mars Arc Transform Chart, it is 08° Cancer 49' exactly conjunct the Ascendant of the transit chart equivalent to my Sun-Moon Arc Transform Chart at 08° Cancer 38'. Not only does this degree with this sign indicate that for me the combinations of both love-sex and husband-wife are emotionally obsessive, but the coincidence in these two charts of this degree and sign indicates that for me love-sex and husband-wife coincide.

The day and time to which my husband's Venus-Mars Arc Transform Chart equates is August 10, 1925 at 03:29:53 PM EST. What event, if any, occurred in his life at that time, I don't know. However, this transit chart, like his Venus-Mars Arc Transform Chart, highlights the factors in his natal chart that for him describe the relationship of Venus and Mars.

For instance, transiting Cupido (20° Leo 14') equals by an opposition, and transiting Hades and Admetos (04° Aries 07'℞ and 06° Aries 52'℞) equal by a semisquare, his natal Venus/Mars midpoint. This connection can refer to the fact that for him love-sex (Venus-Mars) is related to a marriage (Cupido) that is karmic and steadfast (Hades and Admetos). Also, the marriage was to a *previously* married wife who brought him a *previously* fathered son—Hades. That these degrees particularly refer to me is indicated by the fact that my natal seventh house cusp is 20° Leo 27' and my natal Ceres is 05° Aries 35'. (There are also interesting connections between our transit charts.) As for my natal Venus/Mars midpoint, the transiting asteroid with the name of my son (24° Cancer 15') and Transpluto—Super-Pluto (24° Cancer 58') equal it by a conjunction, and transiting Mercury (09° Virgo 25') and transiting Vulcanus—power (10° Gemini 31') equal it by semi-squares. These interconnections can refer to the fact that I was the wife (Mercury rules the seventh), who brought the transforming (Transpluto) boy with that specific name (name asteroid) to this powerful (Vulcanus) connection.

Another interesting feature of this transit chart is that the asteroid with the name of my husband is 26° Leo 37', exactly conjunct the asteroid with my name at 27° Leo 22' and Mars at 28° Leo 43'. This triple connection (which is exactly conjunct my husband's natal Ascendant at 28° Leo 15') is exactly conjunct Juno, Neptune (28° Leo 45', 28° Leo 46') in his Sun-Moon Arc Transform Transit Chart. These conjuncting bodies and points form exact multiple aspects with the Vertex-Antivertex (26° Scorpio-Taurus 08') and North Node-South Node (28° Gemini-Sagittarius 28') in my Sun-Moon Arc Transform Transit Chart (see Figure XV). Also, in my husband's Venus-Mars Arc Transform Transit Chart (as in his Sun-Moon A T TR Chart), Dark Moon Lilith activates our natal Sun/Moon midpoints and reversed Nodes. This time the Dark Moon, instead of being 03° Pisces 00', exactly conjunct my North-his South Node, is 03° Gemini 25', exactly conjunct my

Sun at 02° Gemini 34'. Finally (as in his Sun-Moon A T TR Chart), there is an exact conjunction to my natal name asteroid at 20° Gemini 45'—this time from the Descendant at 21° Gemini 24'.

Conclusion

For this analysis of arc transform transit charts, the focus has been on my husband's and mine. However, the arc transform transit charts that I have done for other people have been equally revealing.

There have probably been synchronous events at the times of the transit charts, but even if there haven't been literal events, astrology is metaphorical as well as literal, and these charts are metaphors for what the principle of the combined factors means to the native.

In other words, the transit chart which is equivalent to an arc transform chart, reflects, as does the arc transform, the principles of the particular combined factors (i.e., Sun-Moon). And arc transforms are the perfect expression of the two main purposes of harmonics—to know the aspects and to transform the chart by magnification. Arc transforms are this perfect expression because they are, in a magnified form, the exact aspect or angular separation. The question of orbs for the aspect becomes obsolete. At the risk of a pun—if, as they have been called, harmonics are waves, then arc transforms are the wave of the future.

Harmonics as Aspects

Now to discuss harmonics as aspects in the radix chart, rather than as magnifiers of the radix bodies with the magnified results placed either around the radix chart or in a separate chart.

The harmonics equate to the aspects, with the first harmonic being the conjunction, and the second (360 divided by 2), the opposition. Addey calls the 1st harmonic "the fundamental."[27] The "basic" harmonics are the 2nd through 180th without the multiples of their arclengths (or angular separations). The fractions representing these separations have the harmonic as the denominator and 1 as the numerator. (The fractional harmonics, or arc transforms, always have 1 as the numerator too, only they have the fractional, rather than the integral, harmonics as the denominator.) Reading the Williamsens' book, *Astrologer's Guide to the Harmonics,* you discover that from the 2nd harmonic to the 180th, covered in the book, the total of integral harmonics and their multiples is 16,110.[28] The multiples would have the harmonic as the denominator and the number of the multiple as the numerator. Between the angular separations of 02° and 04°, practically every minute of arc has its own basic harmonic—some minutes more than one, which is very specific! (From the 04° separation on, the harmonics are not always basic, and more than one harmonic is often listed for a separation.) When bodies or points are in the angular separations between 02° and 04°, their harmonics and meanings are very specific.

ORB

Naturally, in these higher harmonics where the intervals of the harmonics are a minute apart, my "within a degree" orb would not apply. In fact, after the 16th harmonic, my "within a degree" orb would become increasingly non-functional, since the average of my orb is $01\frac{1}{2}°$, and the angular separation of the 16th harmonic is less than $01\frac{1}{2}°$ different from the angular separation of the 17th harmonic.

SPECIFIC HARMONICS AND MEANINGS

An example of specific harmonics and meanings is the following. A 02°15'00" separation between two planets will place them in the 160th harmonic ($\frac{1}{160}$), which will correspond to the seventh house, Libra, Venus. The principle of the separation is second house, Taurus, Venus, opposition (2), in relation to sixth house, Virgo, Mercury, sextile (15). A 02°14' separation between two planets will place them either in the 161st harmonic or the 160th, depending upon the number of seconds. Which separation is the closer will be the deciding factor. The angular separation of the 161st harmonic ($\frac{1}{161}$) is 02°14'9.69". Therefore, the integral harmonic of a 02°14'30" separation would be the 161st, even though its fractional harmonic would be 160.5948 (360/02°14'30"). With the fractional harmonics (arc transforms) there is no question of orb because they are exact. The 161st harmonic would correspond to the eighth house, Scorpio, Pluto. The principle of the separation would still be second house, Taurus, etc., but in relation to fifth house, Leo, etc. (As explained before, the coloration of the individual numbers is considered.)

HIERARCHY OF HARMONICS

When planets or points are not in angular separations where every minute has its own basic harmonic, the separations may relate to both specific and general harmonics. The specific may be more exact, but the general may take precedence. When you are dealing with the integral harmonics, I believe there is a hierarchy, with the 30° aspects in the first 12 harmonics being at the highest echelon, and the other harmonics in the first 12 being next. Without reduction, the first 12 harmonics equate to the 12 houses, signs, etc. Of the first 12, the 1st, 2nd, 3rd, 4th, 6th and 12th harmonics are given priority because when they are "within a degree" the planets or points in these harmonics are at the same or the adjacent numbers. And when they are, they are visibly picking up the archetypes of the numbers. Of the other harmonics in the first 12 (5th, 7th, 8th, 9th, 10th and 11th), the 8th harmonic is given greater emphasis by me. The reasons are that I can also visually observe it in the chart and that its effect is very powerful. The power may come not only from the Pluto association, but from the fact that the 8th harmonic is a sub-harmonic of the 2nd and 4th harmonic, as well as of the 1st.

To explain, a sub-harmonic of a harmonic is one whose arclength is divisible into the arclength of the harmonic (45° is divisible into 180° and 90°). The number of the sub-harmonic is a multiple of the number of the harmonic (8 is 4 x 2 and 2 x 4), or said in reverse, the number of the harmonic is divisible into the number of the sub-harmonic. If the original aspects are considered with magnification and are close enough to exactitude, those planets that are shown as conjunct in the magnified harmonic will be shown as conjunct in the magnified sub-harmonics. If the original aspects are considered in condensed forms, such as planet sorts, graphs and circular dials, the planets shown as conjunct in the harmonic will be shown as conjunct in the sub-harmonics too. Each additional sub-harmonic will add its aspects to the conjunctions of the previous harmonics. However, when the aspects are considered without magnification or condensation, they are separate. Nonetheless, there is a similar vibration when one harmonic is a multiple of another, even though each harmonic has a different reference because of its number. For instance, the 2nd and 3rd harmonics are the primary harmonics—even and odd, hard and soft. The multiples of the 2nd harmonic have a hard vibration, while the multiples of the 3rd have a soft one. The 6th and the 12th are in both series and so have a mixed vibration (6 is 2 x 3 and 12 is 2 x 6 or 3 x 4). The other harmonics, besides the 2nd and 3rd, with prime numbers—the 5th, 7th, 11th, 13th, etc.—do not fit into either series and so start their own series. Their multiples share their vibrations but may also have the vibration of one of the series (10 is 5 x 2 and so has the quality of 5, but also the quality of the 2 series).

Returning to our hierarchy, after the 12th harmonic, the "basic" harmonics (with 1 in the numerator) follow, and then the harmonics after the 12th with 2-12 in the numerator. If none of these conditions apply, then the more exact aspect is of greater rank.

The "basic" harmonics after the 12th harmonic are given precedence because the basic harmonics have a special significance. The number of the denominator refers to the number of the numerator, so with 1 as the numerator, the meaning of the denominator is referring to itself (1). In other words, $^1/_5$, the fraction representing the basic 5th harmonic separation, is creativity, children, love affairs and entertainment (5), in reference to itself or its own nature (1). The basic harmonics relate to the fundamental meanings of the harmonics, so the quintile ($^1/_5$ or 72°) would express the fundamental meaning of the 5th harmonic.

The harmonics with 2-12 in the numerator come next in the hierarchy because they are still referring to the 12 houses, signs, etc. $^2/_5$, the fraction representing the double 5th harmonic separation, or biquintile (144°), would be creativity, etc. (5), but in reference to money, values and love (2).

Angular Separations

Now that the hierarchy of the harmonics has been outlined, the meanings of the different angular separations of some harmonics must be outlined as well. The procedure used with these harmonics will serve as a guide for the procedure to be used with the others.

5TH HARMONIC SEPARATIONS

Though 72°, the 5th harmonic separation, refers to creativity, children, love affairs and entertainment, the principle of the degree separation (since 72 adds up to 9) is ninth house, Sagittarius, Jupiter and the novile. If the separation is the classic 72°, the aspect would have a Sagittarian quality. If the separation is 71°, it would still refer to creativity, etc., but have a Scorpionic quality; if 73°, a Capricornian one. 72°

has a coloration (its individual numbers) of seventh house, Libra, Venus, septile, and second house, Taurus, Venus, opposition. Perhaps, this double Venus coloration, as well as the creativity reference, is why the 5th harmonic sometimes relates to talents. (As mentioned, the meaning of the harmonic is derived from the meaning of the separation.) 71° would have the coloration of seventh house, etc., and first house, etc., while 73° would have the coloration of seventh house, etc., and third house, etc. Since I take aspects from one degree to the adjacent degrees (22° aspects 21° and 23°), with sufficient minutes the separation could sometimes be 70°. (An aspect with less than a 01° orb necessarily fits the criterion; with more than a 02° orb, it does not; between a 01° and 02° orb, the aspect has to be checked to see if it does or does not. As stated, the average orb is $01^1/_2$°.) The 70° separation would have a Libran quality, but with the addition of the power of the void (0), often resulting in the need to fill it. The 144° separation, which is the double quintile or biquintile ($^2/_5$), is still associated with Leonine matters, but in reference to money, values and love. There would be a Sagittarian quality, but with an Arian as well as a double Cancerian coloration. 143° would have a Scorpionic quality, but with Arian, Cancerian and Geminian coloration. The 142° and 145° separations would follow suit. The first number is most prominent, so the Arian is the most prominent coloration in these biquintile separations. The last number is next in importance, with the initial and final number surrounding the number in-between.

A 5TH HARMONIC EXAMPLE

As an example of how to apply this technique, a client has in her natal chart a 5th harmonic separation of 71°17' between her Moon at 16° Capricorn 58' and her Mars at 05° Scorpio 41'. The aspect, being in the 5th harmonic, refers to entertainment among other things, and she is a professional drummer, which even today is unusual for a woman. There would be a Scorpionic quality because the degree of the separation adds up to 8, but with a Libran and Arian coloration. The power of Scorpio is appropriate for a drummer. The principle of the degree would apply to the minute—Scorpio principle in relation to Scorpio. The aspect is between Moon and Mars, which could be the assertive woman, which a female drummer must certainly be in her playing. The sign of Mars is Scorpio, reaffirming the separation's Scorpio principle in relation to Scorpio. While the integral harmonic gives a general reference, the principle of the degree in relation to the minute (whether of the separation or of the position) gives a specific manifestation. The 5th harmonic's general reference to entertainment is made more specific in the 05° Scorpio 41' position of Mars. She did play in Broadway theatre, which is an appropriate manifestation for the Leo number in relation to the Leo number. The degree and sign of a position are often combined in their expression. The sign of the Moon is Capricorn, showing a possible connection to the career; however the position of the Moon is 16° Capricorn 58'—the partnership principle in relation to nurturing. With the degree of the Moon at 16, adding up to 7, and the separation between the Moon and Mars being 71°17' with two 7s in it, this aspect relates to the man she married, as well as to her career. Her husband has a Cancer Ascendant with an Aries Moon.

The other exact aspects, rulerships and placements of the Moon and Mars in her radix chart would be taken into account also. The general meanings of the numbers in the Moon-Mars aspect have been given, but for further detail, the individual meanings as expressed in her radix chart should be considered. In the Moon-Mars aspect, the numbers 5 (harmonic) and 8 (separation) are emphasized, and so her fifth and eighth houses, signs, planets and aspects should be examined. As one instance, her Pluto (8) is in Leo (5), reiterating the connection between these numbers. Other quintiles and biquintiles are particularly pertinent. What occurs in this examination is a repetition and further explication of important themes and connections.

This numerical method discriminates between people with the same signs, houses and aspects and explains why these factors do not work the same way for everyone. Slight differences in time and place (or just differences in time, as was shown with the twins) will result in different manifestations. Fortunately, after a while, thinking numerically becomes quite spontaneous.

9TH HARMONIC SEPARATIONS

To continue this examination of the harmonic aspects: $^1/_9$, the fraction representing the basic 9th harmonic separation, is the higher mind, higher education, distant travel, legal matters and expansion (9), in reference to itself or its own nature (1). The separation is 40°, so the principle is the home, more nurturing parent, emotions and all endings, with the additional power of the void (0). Perhaps, this combination of expansion and endings is why the 9th harmonic relates to completion. Judgment is another word connected with Sagittarius—bringing to mind the Last Judgment which is certainly a completion. Indian astrologers say the 9th harmonic chart describes the marriage partner. My observation is that the 9th harmonic chart describes whatever completes you, which could be a career, rather than a marriage partner. Of course, the 9th harmonic reference to legal matters is relevant to marriage, or to a career if a contract is signed. The 80° separation, which is the double novile or binovile ($^2/_9$), would still be associated with Sagittarian matters (9), but in reference to money, values and love (2). Also, now there would be a Scorpionic quality (80), instead of a Cancerian one (40). 160°, the quadruple novile or quadrinovile, would have a Libran quality, with an Arian and Virgoan coloration. (Don't negate the power of the 0s.) This $^4/_9$ aspect would still be Sagittarian (9), but in reference now to the home, more nurturing parent, emotions and all endings (4). 38°, 39°, 41°, 78°, 79°, 81°, 158°, 159° and 161° separations would have their own connotations within the 9th harmonic context. 120°, the triple novile ($^3/_9$), is subsumed in the 9th harmonic, but is more specifically the 3rd harmonic aspect ($^1/_3$). It therefore refers to Geminian matters and, since its separation is 120°, has a Piscean quality—emphasized by the power of the void.

7TH HARMONIC SEPARATIONS

The 7th harmonic refers to marriage, partnership, partners and open enemies. The basic 7th harmonic separation is 51°25'42.8", so the principle is service, in relation to marriage, in regard to service, and the colorations thereof. $^2/_7$, the double septile, would still be associated with marriage, etc., but in reference to money, values and love. The double septile or biseptile separation is 102°51'25", so the principle is idealism (with a coloration of the self and love, surrounding the void), in relation to service, in regard to marriage. (Though the colorations are not always given, they are always relevant.) $^3/_7$, the triple septile, would still refer to marriage, etc., but in reference to communication, etc. The triple septile or trisuptile separation is 154°17'8.5", so the principle is status, in relation to power (with a coloration of the self and the other), in regard to power. The particular degree and minutes of your separation would change the principle and what it relates to for you, while maintaining its reference to Libran matters.

It is more difficult to determine if the 7th harmonic aspect is within orb—at the same or adjacent degrees. For instance, if a planet were at 10° Cancer 20'20", an exact bisuptile would be formed at 23° Libra 11'45" (a 102°51'25" separation). A planet from 22° Libra 00'00" to 24° Libra 59'59", would be considered within range, since to me the contiguity of the numbers is more important than the distance.

Proportionate Orb vs. "Within a Degree" Orb

John Addey says that the orb should be proportionate to the harmonic. He suggests 12° to 15° for the conjunction and states that if the orb for the conjunction (the 1st harmonic) is 12°, then the orb for the opposition (the 2nd harmonic) should be 06°; the orb for the trine should be 04°; the square, 03°; the quintile, 02°24'; the sextile, 02°; the septile, 01°43'; the semisquare, 01°30'; the novile, 01°20'; the decile, 01°12'; the semisextile, 01°; the quindecile or 15th aspect, 00°48'. The multiples, such as the quincunx or inconjunct (150°) which is the 5th multiple of the semisextile (30°), would have the same orbs.[29] (According to his scheme, the undecile would be 01°05'; the 13th aspect, 00°55'; the 14th aspect, 00°51'; and the 16th aspect, 00°45'.)

I have worked with this system and found the orbs too wide for the 1st-6th harmonics. Using Addey's 12° orb for the 1st harmonic, you are picking up the 30th-180th harmonics, since the 30th harmonic has a 12° separation and the 180th has a 02° separation, with the other harmonics having separations in-between. (Using my orb for the 1st harmonic you are not picking up any of these harmonics, since my orb is never larger than 01°59'59".) And these higher harmonics fit the symbolism of their numbers' reference to one of the 12 houses, signs, etc., rather than fit the symbolism of 1, first house, Aries, Mars, conjunction.

On the other hand, for some of the harmonics after the 6th harmonic, I have found Addey's orbs too narrow. His orbs for the septile, semisquare, novile, decile, undecile, semisextile, 13th, 14th, 15th and 16th aspects have eliminated aspects that are very descriptive. Of the first 12 harmonics (which are the primary ones, since they simply without any reduction equate to the 12 houses, signs, etc.), the last 4 are the only ones for which Addey gives orbs that are smaller than the average of mine. My orb, which is 01°30' on an average, is closest to his orb for the semisquare, which is 01°30'. The difference is that Addey's orb would allow $01^1/_2$° on either side of exactitude, while mine might be 01° on one side and 02°, or 01°59'59", on the other.

OVERLAPPING OF HARMONICS

With my orb, from the 11th harmonic on there may be an overlapping of orbs, causing an overlapping of harmonics; however, Addey's orb from the 15th harmonic on mandates an overlapping of orbs, causing an overlapping of harmonics. His orb for the 15th harmonic is 00°48', while his orb for the 16th harmonic is 00°45'. The basic separation for the 15th harmonic is 24°00', while the basic separation for the 16th harmonic is 22°30'. There is a 00°03' overlapping of the orbs. With each successive harmonic, as the interval gets smaller, the overlapping is greater.

When two harmonics overlap, whether within a chart or between charts, I believe both harmonics may be in effect. However, as stated, I give priority to the first 12 harmonics, and, of those, precedence to the "obvious" harmonics.

To give an example of two harmonics being in effect at the same time with my orb, a friend's Uranus at 28° Aries 54' is in both a 12th and a 13th harmonic aspect (or interaspect) to my Mercury at 27° Taurus 01'. Adding the harmonic separation to the earlier position, with the 12th harmonic the exact aspect falls at 28° Taurus 54', while with the 13th harmonic it falls at 26° Taurus 35'. Thus my Mercury in relation to my friend's Uranus is between the 12th and 13th harmonics, closer to the 13th. This bracketing effect is usually present when it is two contiguous harmonics that are in question. Despite the 13th harmonic being closer, priority is given to the 12th. These harmonics are very appropriate because my friend and I are involved in astrological pursuits (12th harmonic, as well as Mercury and Uranus), but there is an emotional quality to the relationship (13th harmonic).

Though greater weight is given to the obvious 30° aspect and its multiples (where the adjacency of the numbers can be seen), after much experimentation I believe the archetypes of the numbers, even when their adjacency is hidden, are still operative.

Mini-Study of Harmonic Interaspects

In the process of coming to this conclusion, not only were harmonic positions and angular separations within charts ordered from Astro, but harmonic interaspects, or angular separations between charts, were ordered from Cosmic Patterns, another computer service. This service lists ten planets and the Ascendant in 121 combinations, beginning with Sun to Sun and ending with Ascendant to Ascendant. Each combination is listed with its angle. If the angle falls in a harmonic interaspect from the 1st-16th, that harmonic interaspect, and that interaspect's orb and strength is given. Addey's proportionate orb is used, and the strength is based on that orb (0 orb is 1.00 strength).

In doing tallies of these interaspects between various people, I discovered that, since each harmonic interaspect was separate from every other harmonic interaspect, the proportionate orb did not allow an equal chance of occurrence to each harmonic. For example, the 2nd harmonic interaspect, the opposition, was separate from the 1st harmonic interaspect, the conjunction. The 2nd harmonic had an orb of 06°; the 1st harmonic, an orb of 12°. The opposition, like the conjunction, has only 1 chance of occurring in 360°, so making its orb $\frac{1}{2}$ the orb of the conjunction gives it $\frac{1}{2}$ the chance of occurring.

Of course, when Addey proposed the proportionate orb, he was considering the 1st harmonic as being included in the 2nd. In this way with the 06° orb in the 2nd harmonic, there would be 1 chance for the opposition to occur and 1 chance for the conjunction to occur—the equivalent of the 12° orb for the conjunction alone. The computer service did not include in a harmonic the harmonics divisible in it, such as the 1st harmonic in the 2nd, and yet used the proportionate orb.

In a harmonic chart, sort, graph or dial, all the harmonics divisible in the harmonic, i.e., the harmonics in their sub-harmonic, are shown as conjunct. As a result, these devices are not a good choice if the purpose is to know the individual harmonic aspects and to see which are occurring more frequently. The angular separations are a good choice, but you need an orb which gives each aspect an equal chance to occur.

EQUAL CHANCE ORB

An equal chance orb, starting with 12° for the conjunction, would have to have 12° for the opposition; 06° for the trine and square, since each has 2 places at which it can occur—120° and 240°, and 90° and 270°, respectively; 03° for the quintile (biquintile); 06°, the sextile; 02°, the septile (biseptile, triseptile); 03°, the semi-square (sesquiquadrate); 02°, the novile (binovile, quadrinovile); 03°, the decile (tridecile); 01°12', the undecile; 03°, the semisextile (quincunx); 01°, the 13th aspect; 02°, the 14th aspect; 01°30', the quindecile or 15th aspect; 01°30', the 16th aspect. (When there are names for the multiples, those names are in parens.) The table of harmonic arclengths on page 16 should make these figures clear. The underlined arclengths are the ones unique to that harmonic. After the 2nd harmonic they would be repeated on the other side of 180°. Thus, the semisextile would have 4 places to occur—12° orb divided by 4 = 03° orb.

Contrary to this equal chance orb, with Addey's proportionate orb (unless the harmonics divisible in a harmonic are included), there are 2 x as many conjunctions as oppositions, squares, semisquares, (sesquiquadrates) or 16th harmonic aspects; 1.5 x as many conjunctions as trines or noviles (binoviles, quadrinoviles); 1.25 x as many, as quintiles (biquintiles); 3 x as many, as sextiles or semisextiles (quincunxes); 1.16 x as many, as septiles (biseptiles, triseptiles); 2.5 x as many, as deciles (trideciles); 1.1 x as many, as undeciles; 1.08 x as many, as 13th harmonic aspects; 2.33 x as many, as 14th harmonic aspects; and 1.87 x as many, as 15th harmonic aspects. Sextiles and semisextiles (quincunxes) are the most discriminated against; then, deciles (trideciles); next, 14th aspects; followed by oppositions, squares, semisquares (sesquiquadrates) and 16th aspects; then 15th aspects; next, trines and noviles (binoviles, quadrinoviles); followed by quintiles (biquintiles); then septiles (biseptiles, triseptiles); next, undeciles; and, finally, 13th aspects.

Also, with my "within a degree" orb or with any other constant orb (such as the 01° orb that most people use with the harmonic dials) the aspects would not have an equal chance of occurring. The trine, square or sextile would have a 2 x greater chance of occurring than the conjunction or opposition; the quintile (biquintile), semisquare (sesquiquadrate), decile (tridecile), or semisextile (quincunx), 4 x ; the septile (biseptile, triseptile), novile (binovile, quadrinovile) or 14th aspect, 6 x ; the 15th or 16th aspects, 8 x ; the undecile, 10 x ; and the 13th aspect, 12 x .

With the constant orb, some short division could easily "equalize" the chances of occurrence. Or, barring such division, though the comparative frequency of the aspects in a chart (or between charts) can not be tallied, the frequency of a particular aspect in a chart (or between charts) as compared to the frequency of that aspect in another chart (or between charts) can. (If certain aspects are discriminated against in one chart, they will be equally discriminated against in the other chart.)[30]

COMPARATIVE FREQUENCY OF INTERASPECTS

Despite this comparability of the charts I wanted to know the comparative frequency of the interaspects. Realizing that the computer service's use of Addey's proportionate orb for separate interaspects had skewed my tallies, I made graphs with the harmonics on the y-axis and the orbs on the x-axis and entered the number of interaspects that fit into each harmonic at each orb. In this way I was able to see, for instance, those conjunctions within 06° that would be included in the 06° orb of the oppositions—thus equalizing, without the use of the equal chance orb outlined above, the chances of these interaspects occurring.

In the following mini-study, these interaspects are between myself and six people, between one of those people and another person, and between another couple. My interaspects are with two husbands, two children, one friend and one acquaintance. The interaspects between one of those people and another person are those of my first husband with his second wife. The other couple are married business associates of mine. Though eight sets of interaspects, involving ten people, is a very small number, it is suggestive. With the exception of the married business

Table V
Interaspects of First Wife with

First Husband				Second Husband			
#	Harmonics			**#**	Harmonics		
(16)	10			(11)	7	14	
(15)	1	7		(10)	2	4	
(14)	5			(9)	6		
(12)	6	13		(8)	9		
(10)	2			(7)	5 13 15 16		
(9)	4	8		(6)	1 10 12		
(8)	12			(5)	8		
(7)	11	15		(4)	3		
(6)	16			(3)	11		
(5)	14						
(4)	9.						
(0)	3						

associates, these are people I know well. And in the study of yourself and people you know well, you have the advantage of your intimate knowledge.

Addey's method (including harmonics in their sub-harmonic) and orb are used in this mini-study. Though his method and orb are not the ones I recommend, this comparison of the frequency of harmonics between charts is valid within its own terms. The results are interesting.

With my second husband, the 7th and 14th harmonics have the most aspects, with a count of 11. The 2nd and 4th are next, with 10; 6th, 9; 9th, 8; 5th, 13th, 15th and 16th, 7; 1st, 10th and 12th, 6; 8th, 5; 3rd, 4; 11th, 3. With my first husband, the 10th harmonic has the most aspects, with a count of 16. The 1st and 7th are next, with 15; 5th, 14; 6th and 13th, 12; 2nd, 10; 4th and 8th, 9; 12th, 8; 11th and 15th, 7; 16th, 6; 14th, 5; 9th, 4; 3rd, 0. In fact, since a picture is worth a thousand words or numbers, the visual presentation of the frequency of occurrence is on the previous page.

Note that the frequency of occurrence of the 7th harmonic is high in both sets of interaspects but that with my first husband the 10th harmonic is the highest. Though 10, the Saturn number, relates to responsibility, it also relates to separation, which is what occurred very early in the marriage. There was also a parent-child syndrome operative between us that would be described by the prominence of the 10th harmonic. Note that the 1st harmonic is coupled with the 7th, instead of, as with my second husband, the 2nd and 4th following close behind the 7th and 14th. 1 brings in a Martian element, while 2 brings in a Venusian one, and the opposition, the 2 aspect, is called the aspect of relationship. As for the fact that the 14th harmonic is highlighted with my second husband, 14 equals 5, and the 5th is one of the highest harmonics with my first husband. The prominence of harmonics that refer to children (5) equates to the fact that both marriages produced children. Another interesting observation is that with my first husband the 3rd harmonic has no incidence, and the 9th harmonic has the next least incidence. The 3rd harmonic has to do with communication—there was little—the 9th, with law and completion— our legal commitment of marriage did not complete us, and so we did not complete it.

Which harmonics have the same number of occurrences, and what that number is, is important too. Of course, if other factors were added, the number of occurrences would change, but in terms of the ten planets and Ascendant with this orb these are the numbers which apply. For instance, with my second husband, the 7th and 14th harmonics having the same number of incidences describes the fact that in the marriage, children (5) and partnership (7) are very much aligned. The upbringing of the children was shared before such sharing was fashionable—which brings up the fact that the number of occurrences is 11, the number of the avant-garde. The 5th, 13th, 15th and 16th harmonics all have 7 incidences, which combines the concepts of children, home, service and partnership. The fact that the number of occurrences is 7 stresses partnership again.

The harmonic order with my two children is as follows:

Table VI
Interaspects of Mother with

#	Son Harmonics			#	Daughter Harmonics		
⑫	4	9		⑬	4	16	
⑪	2	8		⑪	2	9	14
⑩	3	10		⑩	1	7	
⑨	13			⑨	11	15	
⑧	5	6		⑦	13		
⑦	15			⑥	5	8	
⑥	1	14		⑤	10	12	
④	7	12		④	3	6	
③	11	16					

With both of my children the 4th harmonic is the highest harmonic. In my son's case that position is shared with the 9th harmonic, and in my daughter's, with the 16th. The prominence of the 4th harmonic is appropriate because I had previously decided that for both my son and my daughter the fourth house represents the mother. The combination of the 4th and the 9th harmonics in my son's case is apt, since, as a result of his perceptual problems, we were much involved in "higher education" (9)—including remedial assistance at several universities. As mentioned, the number of occurrences is pertinent. The number is 12, which (with a shading of the self and values) stresses the nebulousness of the problems. (Accompanying the perceptual problems was mental brilliance.) The combination of the 4th and the 16th in my daughter's case is apt, since we are involved figuratively in a partnership (7). The number is 13, which stresses intuition, with a shading of the self and communication. Our partnership is a partnership of intuition, where the insights of one act as a powerful stimulant to the insights of the other. The 3rd harmonic is in the lowest category, but the 9th is in the second highest. The 3rd has an incidence of 4, again connecting communication with intuition; the 9th has an incidence of 11, connecting the higher mind with sudden flashes of insight. (Uranus rules electricity.)

The harmonic order with my friend and my acquaintance is as follows:

Table VII
Interaspects of Woman with

#	Friend Harmonics					#	Acquaintance Harmonics				
⑬	2	7				⑬	9				
⑫	14					⑪	11	12			
⑪	4					⑨	15				
⑩	5	11				⑧	1	13			
⑨	3	8	16			⑦	5				
⑧	1	6	10	13	15	⑤	6	8	10	14	16
⑦	12					④	3				
⑥	9					③	2	7			
						②	4				

The "partnership" that there is with my friend, there is not with my acquaintance—observe the leading position of the 7th harmonic with my friend, as opposed to the trailing position of the 7th harmonic with my acquaintance. The relationship with my acquaintance is mostly involved with the higher mind, astrology and esoterica, and 9,11 and 12 are the harmonics that have the highest frequency of occurrence. The number of occurrences of the 11th and 12th harmonics is 11, emphasizing astrology again. The other harmonics, their positions and number of occurrences are equally descriptive.

The harmonic order of the interaspects of my first husband and his second wife are on the left. Those of the married business associates of mine are on the right. Though these interaspects are juxtaposed, the interaspects of my first husband and his second wife would be compared to those of my first husband and myself.

Table VIII

#	Interaspects of 1st Husband with 2nd Wife Harmonics	#	Interaspects of Husband with Wife Harmonics
(12)	15	(16)	8
(9)	6 7 19 11	(15)	4
(8)	2	(12)	6 10
(7)	1 8 10 12 16	(11)	5 12
(6)	15 14	(10)	2 3
(5)	3 4	(8)	13 14 15
(3)	13	(7)	7 11
		(6)	9
		(4)	1
		(1)	16

Note that the 15th harmonic is the highest harmonic between my first husband and his second wife, and they do work (6) together and have several children (1 and 5). Also, though the 3rd harmonic is low, it does have an incidence of 5, as opposed to an incidence of 0 in the case of myself and my first husband. The 9th harmonic is second highest instead of being second lowest, and the 1st harmonic is not as prominent as it is with my first husband and myself. Between the other husband and wife, the 8th harmonic is the highest harmonic. They are business associates, and for business associates the partner's money is an especially important factor. I can not comment on the other meanings of 8, since the couple are just acquaintances. The 4th harmonic is the second highest, and they work (15 occurrences) in the home (4). Relatively, the 7th harmonic is not that high, but it does have an incidence of 7 and is coupled with the 11th harmonic. Their partnership (7) involves technological astrology (11).

It should be clear that not all husband-wife interaspects have a prominence of the 7th harmonic, though that harmonic relates to partnership, and that not all parent-child interaspects have a prominence of the 4th or 10th harmonic, though those harmonics relate to parentage. It is the quality of the relationship, rather than the category, that is symbolized.

COMPARISON WITH A CONSTANT ORB

As explained earlier, though with a constant orb such as mine the relative position of a harmonic aspect (or interaspect) cannot be determined, the frequency of a harmonic aspect (or interaspect) in one case, compared to the frequency in other cases, can. The results of these tallies can also be compared to the results of the previous tallies. However, with my orb (from one degree to the next), there would be less incidence of harmonic aspects (or interaspects) than with Addey's, since the harmonic aspects (or interaspects) are not included in their sub-harmonic aspects (or interaspects). Also, for these first 16 harmonics the average of my orb would be less than the average of Addey's orb.

With my orb the comparison of the frequency of harmonic interaspects between myself and my first husband, second husband, son, daughter, friend and acquaintance is as follows:

Table IX

| | Interaspects of Woman with | | | | | |
Harmonics	1st Hus. #	2nd Hus. #	Son #	Daughter #	Friend #	Acquaint. #
1	3	0	0	1	2	0
2	1	2	2	2	2	0
3	0	1	3	1	0	1
4	1	1	2	3	1	2
5	6	3	6	3	5	3
6	7	3	2	0	1	4
7	8	8	4	9	9	3
8	4	3	7	2	3	3
9	4	10	8	9	4	12
10	7	3	2	1	1	4
11	7	3	4	9	10	16
12	4	3	3	2	3	7
13	13	9	9	8	9	9
14	2	7	5	4	7	6
15	4	5	5	9	5	7
16	3	7	3	12	6	3

With my first husband the 10th harmonic is still highlighted because there is more incidence of that harmonic with him than with anyone else. Compared to my second husband who has 3 occurrences, he has 7. (The number of occurrences of a harmonic is important here too—in terms of my orb now.) The 6th harmonic is also emphasized with my first husband, and his criticality (natal Moon in Virgo) was an issue in the marriage. Again, compared to my second husband who has 3 occurrences, he has 7 (separation [10th harmonic] and criticality [6th] in our marriage [7]). In the case of my first husband, the 1st harmonic remains prominent in comparison to the other cases. In my second husband's case, though the incidence of the 1st harmonic (0) is not that different from most of the other cases, it is different from the incidence (3) in my first husband's case. Also, there are 2 occurrences of the 2nd harmonic for my second husband, compared to 1 occurrence for my first husband. Both my first and second husband have an incidence of 8 for the 7th harmonic, which is "equivalent" to the incidence for my daughter and friend (9), with whom I also have partnerships. These scores are much higher than those for my son and acquaintance (4 and 3) with whom I do not have partnerships. The 5th harmonic is not so emphasized for my second husband as for my first (3 compared to 6). On the other hand, the 14th harmonic, which also refers to children, is more emphasized for my second husband than for my first (7 compared to 2). With my first husband there is still no incidence of the 3rd harmonic, and the 9th with him continues low (4), compared to the 9th with most of the others. There are 1 incidence of the 3rd harmonic and 10 incidences of the 9th harmonic with my second husband. As for the 11th harmonic, my second husband with just 3 occurrences is well below the average of the 6 people. (My first husband has 7 occurrences.)

Could this low incidence of the 11th harmonic explain the stability with my present husband? With him, the 11th harmonic's having 3 occurrences could be the avant-garde or erratic related to our thinking, while with my ex-husband, the 11th harmonic's having 7 occurrences could be the avant-garde or erratic related to our marriage. Using Addey's orb, my present husband and I do have 11 occurrences of the 7th and 14th harmonics, which I correlated to our being avant-garde (11 occurrences) in our sharing the upbringing of the children (7th and 14th harmonics). A particular area of a relationship being avant-garde or erratic (11 occurrences) is not the same as the relationship's having a high or low incidence of the avant-garde or erratic (11th harmonic).

The 4th harmonic remains comparatively highlighted with my son and daughter (though my acquaintance has the same incidence as my son). The 9th continues high with my son, and the 16th, the highest with my daughter. The number of occurrences of the 16th harmonic with my daughter is 12, relating to the intuition in our partnership. 12, the Neptune number, is nebulous and esoteric and so can also relate, like 4, the Moon number, to intuition. The 16th, 15th and 4th harmonics are higher with my daughter than with the other people, highlighting partnership, analysis and intuition in our relationship. The 3rd and 8th harmonics are higher with my son than with the other people, highlighting communication and transformation in our relationship.

The 7th harmonic is still high with my friend, compared to my acquaintance (9 occurrences compared to 3). With my acquaintance the higher mind, astrology and esoterica continue to be emphasized. The 9th, 11th and 12th harmonics are the only ones where he, compared to the other people, has the highest incidence. Also, with him there are 0 occurrences of the 1st and 2nd harmonics, while with my friend there are 2 occurrences of both. (Several astrologers have told me they've never seen a substantial relationship, unless, considering the ten planets, there was at least one interaspect of a conjunction or an opposition within an orb of 2 degrees. That orb is similar to mine, which averages $01^1/_2$ degrees.)

SUMMATION

In summation, this comparison of the frequency of harmonic interaspects highlights differences in the relationships of the people involved. The comparison of the frequencies with my orb to the frequencies with Addey's orb is also enlightening. With my orb, the difference in the number of occurrences is not as great. (My orb is smaller, and the harmonics are not included in their sub-harmonics.) However, for the most part, the differences are repetitive of those produced by the larger, more inclusive orb. The orb of influence of harmonics is probably not discrete, but one tries to find the orb which is most reflective of the most intense influence. My "within a degree" orb, I think, reflects such an influence, especially in the first 16 harmonics.

However, my working in this mini-study with the first 16 harmonics is because they were the ones the computer service computed, not because I think they are the only ones that are meaningful. With the higher harmonics there are often combinations of harmonics in effect simultaneously, and such combinations are meaningful too.

Specific and General Harmonics

As mentioned before, when angular separations do not have a basic harmonic for every minute of arc, the separations may have both specific and general harmonics associated with them. The specific provide more detail. The general harmonics are often those that take precedence in the hierarchy of harmonics. In this hierarchy the 30° aspects in the first 12 come first, the other harmonics in the first 12 are next, the basic harmonics after the 12th follow, and then the harmonics with 2-12 in the numerator— to what the harmonic refers—come next. If the separation fits in none of these categories, or if more than one fits in them, then the more exact, and so more specific, harmonic has priority. The fractions are reduced to the lowest common denominator. The following is to illustrate the dichotomy of general and specific harmonics.

My Sun, ruler of my seventh house, is 75°40'5.88" ($^4/_{19}$) from my second husband's Uranus, ruler of, and posited in, his seventh house. My Sun is 75°55'49.8" ($^4/_{19}$) from his Neptune, which is exactly conjunct his East Point and Cupido (self and marriage-family). These separations and harmonics are related to the stepson (Uranus), which I brought my Pisces husband (Neptune) through our marriage (East Point, Cupido and Sun, seventh house). The Williamsens' book lists the exact arclengths of the harmonics. For 75°40'08", the listing closest to the separation between my Sun and my husband's Uranus, the 157th harmonic ($^{33}/_{157}$) is given. For 75°56'15", the listing closest to the separation between my Sun and his Neptune, the 128th harmonic ($^{27}/_{128}$) is given. However, the 19th harmonic ($^4/_{19}$), which is given for 75°47'22", would take precedence over the 157th harmonic ($^{33}/_{157}$) and the 128th harmonic ($^{27}/_{128}$) because the numerator 4 is from 2-12, and so supersedes the numerators 33 and 27. With my orb, for the Sun-Neptune separation the 14th harmonic ($^3/_{14}$) would be picked up, but it would be a background influence, since it doesn't fit into one of the first three categories, and since the 19th harmonic ($^4/_{19}$) is more exact. There is also the 24th harmonic ($^5/_{24}$), given for 75°00'00", which may be a background influence for both separations. The 24th is a sub-harmonic of the 12th, 8th, 6th, 4th, 3rd, 2nd and 1st harmonics, producing a similar vibration. The question of the power of multiples or divisions of harmonics is discussed on pages 110-11.

24 was my age when my husband and I were married, emphasizing for us the number 24, and so, the 24th harmonic. There are other appropriate interaspects between my husband and myself that are definitely in the 24th harmonic. My Jupiter in the seventh house is 75°00'31.32" ($^5/_{24}$) from his Moon in the fourth. For 75°00'00", the listing closest to the separation between my Jupiter and his Moon, the 24th harmonic ($^5/_{24}$) is given. There is no harmonic that is competitive with it, so it would be the only integral harmonic associated with that separation. In another interaspect my Jupiter is 15°19'18.8" ($^1/_{24}$) from his Ascendant. For 15°19'09", the listing closest to the separation between my Jupiter and his Ascendant, the 47th ($^2/_{47}$) is given. However, the 24th harmonic, or $^1/_{24}$, would take precedence over the 47th harmonic ($^2/_{47}$) because with the numerator being 1, the harmonic is basic.

Despite the fact that in the case of his Ascendant and my Jupiter the 24th harmonic (being basic) takes precedence, the 47th (being closer) gives more specific detail. For instance, the 24th harmonic ($^1/_{24}$) would correlate to work (6), with a shading of money, values, love (2) and home (4), in reference to itself (1); while the 47th harmonic ($^2/_{47}$) would correlate to free-lancing (11), with a shading of home (4) and partnership (7), in reference to money, values, love (2). My second husband's Ascendant describes him. My Jupiter in the 7th can describe a successful husband or marriage. My husband is successful as a musician and musical contractor, who earns our money through working free-lance from our home. Both harmonics are needed for a proper description. The 24th harmonic, with its correlation to work, is more general, while the 47th, with its correlation to free-lancing, is more specific.

Description of People

Returning to the first 12 harmonics, I have the following observations. The 7th harmonic aspects, like 7th harmonic charts, are descriptive of the partner. Given the ten planets, Ascendant, Midheaven and North Node, whose angular separations Astro lists, in my natal chart there are nine 7th harmonic aspects. Each aspect is reflective of either personal points, important positions or exact aspects in both my second, and first, husband's natal chart. My Sun is 102° 07'6.6" ($^2/_7$) from my

Ascendant, and my second husband has his Ascendant, East Point and Neptune (the ruler of his Sun) in Leo, while my first husband has both the ruler of his Ascendant and his name asteroid in Leo, as well as his Sun in the fifth house. My Moon is 51°22'41.8" ($^1/_7$) from my Pluto, and my second husband has his Moon in Scorpio in the fourth house, exactly square his Ascendant, while my first husband has his Pluto in Cancer, exactly trine his Uranus, which is exactly conjunct his East Point. Also, he has a Cancer Sun. My Moon is 103°58'44" ($^2/_7$) from my Saturn, and my second husband's Saturn is in Scorpio (see previous 7th harmonic aspect), exactly opposite his name asteroid in the ninth house (see succeeding 7th harmonic aspect), while my first husband's Saturn is exactly conjunct his Moon. My Moon is 103°13'27" ($^2/_7$) from my Jupiter, and my second husband has Jupiter in the fourth house in an exact Grand Trine with Venus, and the East Point, Neptune (the ruler of his Sun). My first husband has Jupiter exactly square his Midheaven in Sagittarius (which is exactly trine his Neptune, ruler of his Ascendant and East Point), and exactly sextile his Mercury and Mars in Cancer. My Mercury is 102°38'38" ($^2/_7$) from my Mars, and my second husband has Virgo (ruled by Mercury) in his first house (ruled in the natural zodiac by Mars), while my first husband has Mercury (the ruler of his Moon) exactly conjunct his Mars. (This aspect refers also to the previous 7th harmonic aspect.) Three more 7th harmonic aspects connect to the three 7th harmonic aspects with my Moon. They are Jupiter 152°47'48" ($^3/_7$) from Saturn, Jupiter 51°50'45.6" ($^1/_7$) from Pluto, and Saturn 155°21'25" ($^3/_7$) from Pluto. These aspects reinforce the Lunar aspects already discussed. My final 7th harmonic aspect is my Uranus 52°16'53" ($^1/_7$) from my North Node. My second husband's North Node, which is exactly trine his name asteroid, is ruled by Mercury in Aquarius; and Mercury is exactly opposite his East Point, Neptune conjunction, which is exactly quincunx his Uranus; while my first husband's North Node is exactly sesquiquadrate his Uranus, East Point conjunction.

Though Neptune is associated with the reflections of my 7th harmonic that are in both my second, and first, husband's chart, Neptune is not in a 7th harmonic aspect in my chart. However, my Saturn (which is in three 7th harmonic aspects) is in my twelfth house, and my North Node (which is in one) is in Pisces, describing my second husband's Pisces Sun and my first husband's Pisces Ascendant and East Point. Also, my Pluto (which is in three 7th harmonic aspects) is exactly semisquare my Neptune, which is exactly square my Midheaven, while Pluto is exactly sesquiquadrate my Midheaven. Not only is Neptune tightly linked to my 7th harmonic aspects, but the 8th and 4th harmonic aspects by which it is linked add the principles of transformation and maternalism to the principle of partnership and marriage.

Continuing with observations on the first 12 harmonics: the 5th harmonic aspects are descriptive of the children, and the 10th harmonic aspects are descriptive of the father, or the mother if she is the 10th house parent. The children of the native are often like the parents of the native. The angular separation of the 5th harmonic is $^1/_2$ the angular separation of the 10th, giving a similar vibration. 72° (the basic separation of the 5th harmonic) +108° (the multiple separation of the 10th harmonic)

= 180° or $\frac{1}{2}$ 360°. 36° (the basic separation of the 10th harmonic) + 144° (the multiple separation of the 5th harmonic) = 180° or $\frac{1}{2}$ 360°. As a result, a planet making a 5th harmonic aspect to the Midheaven (MC) will make a 10th harmonic aspect to the Imum Coeli (IC), and a planet making a 5th harmonic aspect to the IC will make a 10th harmonic aspect to the MC. There is, therefore, a connection of the 5th harmonic to the houses of both the mother and the father, through the intermediacy of its sub-harmonic the 10th.

The 9th harmonic aspects are descriptive of in-laws. More importantly however, the 9th harmonic's association with completion especially helps you to understand discrepancies in charts. For example, my second husband has a Pisces Sun and no earth in his chart, and yet he is very organized and structured in his career. Before becoming aware of the 9th harmonic, I agreed with other astrologers who said he was "over-compensating." Now, knowing that his Saturn in the third house is 159°57'10" ($^4/_9$) from his Midheaven, I realize that he finds completion (9th harmonic) in the mental (third house) structuring (Saturn) of his career (Midheaven). Also, this completion is related to his foundation, his base, since in the fraction ($^4/_9$) completion (9) is referring to the foundation (4). As for the separation, the principle is work, in relation to nebulousness (music), in regard to the career. Work would have a coloration of the self, the theatre and completion; and music, a coloration of the theatre and partnership. The principles of the positions reiterate the principle of the separation. The principle of the position of Saturn at 02° Scorpio 07'5.88" is money combined with other people's money, in relation to partnership, in regard to the theatre. The principle of the position of the Midheaven at 22° Taurus 09'55.8" is the foundation combined with money, in relation to completion, in regard to the career. The foundation would have a double coloration of money; and the career, a double coloration of the theatre.

The Saturn-Midheaven aspect can also refer to my husband's personal life, if the Midheaven is thought of as the purpose in life, rather than as the career. Saturn could then be the responsibility that he feels toward me (3rd house—I am a double Gemini), which gives him a feeling of completion (9th harmonic). This completion still refers to the foundation. The principle of the separation would be service, in relation to nebulousness (idealism), in regard to the goal. Service would have a coloration of the self, children and completion; and idealism, a coloration of children and marriage. The principle of the position of Saturn might be love combined with power, in relation to marriage, in regard to children. The principle of the position of the Midheaven might be the foundation combined with love, in relation to completion, in regard to responsibility. The foundation would have a double coloration of love; and responsibility, a double coloration of children.

Description of Relationships

As for interaspects, the difference in the harmonics, as well as the difference in the angular separations, show the difference in relationships. Though I am not proposing Sun sign astrology, you can tell a great deal just looking at the Suns and the degrees between them. The Sun can be thought of as the ego of the respective people. Considering the first 16 harmonics, there are the following examples.

The birthdays of my mother and father are just four days apart (different years), resulting in a 03° difference between the angular separations of their Suns in reference to my Sun. My father's Sun is 160°57'23" from my Sun, with that separation in the 9th harmonic, and the degrees equaling 7. With my father I always felt a sense of completion (9th harmonic). That sense of completion was derived from our partnership (7), which had a coloration of the self and work, and the power of the void. He gave me art lessons, and I critiqued his plays and poetry. My mother's Sun is 157°06'14" from my Sun, with that separation in the 16th harmonic, and the degrees equaling 4. With my mother there was a partnership (16th harmonic), with a coloration of the self and service. She looked to me for guidance from the time I was seven years old. Our partnership was derived from that nurturing (4), which was mainly on my part. The coloration was of the self, the child and partnership.

My second husband's Sun is 85°31'49.4" from my Sun, with the degrees equaling 4. (The separation is not in any of the first 16 harmonics.) I've always thought my second husband's relationship to me is very much like mine was to my mother, but with the nurturing (4) mutual now. Both the separation between my Sun and my mother's, and the separation between my Sun and my second husband's, have a 5 in them. In my mother's case, I ascribed the child to 5, which is appropriate in my husband's case too since we have children. Also, when my mother was alive she was in show business (5), and my husband is in it, and I was, and am, involved with it through them. My son's Sun is 166°42'13" from my Sun, with that separation in the 13th harmonic, and the degrees equaling 4. Again the emphasis is on nurturing, but with a different quality because of the different numbers which make up the separation. There is a double Virgo quality to the nurturing— I worked with him to help him overcome his dyslexia. (The meaning of the harmonic is derived from the meaning of the separation.)

As for my first husband's Sun, it is 44°42'30.2" from my Sun, with that separation in the 8th harmonic, and the degrees equaling 8—a double emphasis on life, death and regeneration. The harmonic between my mother's Sun and mine is the 16th—a sub-harmonic of the 8th. My first husband's relationship to me was not like mine to my mother; however, there was the hard quality of the 2 series with both of them, in contrast to the soft quality of the 3 series that there was with my father. My daughter's Sun is 62°20'54.2" from my Sun, with the degrees equaling 8. Though the principle is still Scorpionic, there is not the Scorpionic reference of the 8th harmonic. Also, with my first husband there is a double emphasis on nurturing (he is a Cancerian), while with my daughter there is an emphasis on service and values. As an aside, it is interesting that my Sun (02° Gemini) is 62° from the Aries Point (00° Aries), and my daughter's Sun (04° Leo) is 62° from my Sun. Thus, the relationship of my Sun to the Aries Point (a point of connection to the outside world) is the same as the relationship of my Sun to my daughter's Sun. The relationship of my ego to the outside world, therefore, is reflective of the relationship of my ego to my daughter's ego.

Harmonic Complexes and
Grand Harmonic Complexes

The individual aspects and interaspects having been considered, it is now time to consider what I call Harmonic Complexes and Grand Harmonic Complexes. Harmonic Complexes consist of aspects (or interaspects) in a harmonic combined with aspects (or interaspects) in the same harmonic. Harmonics of a sub-harmonic are included, i.e., the 3rd harmonic in the 9th, because they are akin. $^1/_3$ is the lowest common denominator of $^3/_9$ and augments the flow of the 9th harmonic. Grand Harmonic Complexes consist of aspects (or interaspects) in the same harmonic that, when combined, divide 360° in three parts, and proceeding in the same direction, each part is less than 180°.(A is in X harmonic aspect to B, which is in X harmonic aspect to C, which is in X harmonic aspect to A. The three parts may be further subdivided.) Though aspects (or interaspects) in one harmonic combined with aspects (or interaspects) in other harmonics are significant, Harmonic Complexes are even more significant because they establish a harmonic theme. As for Grand Harmonic Complexes, they, like their prototype, the Grand Trine, connect one planet or point to another in continuous 360° circles. When there is a Grand Harmonic Complex in a chart, that harmonic is particularly important for the person or event which that chart represents.

For instance, my natal Jupiter is 152°47'48" ($^3/_7$) from my natal Saturn, which is 155°21'25" ($^3/_7$) from my natal Pluto, which is 51°50'45.6" ($^1/_7$) from my natal Jupiter, going around the 360° in a continuous circle.[31] (Jupiter at 13° Virgo 34'33"+154°17'8.5" = 17° Aquarius 51'42"; Saturn at 16° Aquarius 22'22" + 154°17'8.5" = 20° Cancer 39'30"; Pluto at 21° Cancer 43'48" + 51°25'42.8" = 13° Virgo 09'31.1"; note that the difference between where the planet should be with the addition of the harmonic, and where it is, is never more than from one degree to the next.) My natal Vertex at 12° Virgo 33'26.28" and my natal Part of Fortune at 18° Aquarius 13'59.88" are part of this Grand Harmonic Complex. The Vertex is 153°48'56" ($^3/_7$) from Saturn; the Part of Fortune is 153°29'48" ($^3/_7$) from Pluto; and Pluto is 50°49'37.9" ($^1/_7$) from the Vertex. The Vertex is not in a 7th harmonic aspect to the Part of Fortune, but they are pulled in by Jupiter, Saturn and Pluto.

Another Grand Harmonic Complex that I have is my natal Jupiter $^3/_7$ to my natal Saturn, which is $^2/_7$ to my natal Moon, which is $^2/_7$ to my natal Jupiter. (My Moon is 00° Gemini 21'6.48", and Saturn + 102°51'25" = 29° Taurus 13'47.4", and the Moon +102°51'25" = 13° Virgo 12'31".) My natal Chiron at 28° Taurus 59'51.72", as well as my Vertex and Part of Fortune, is part of this Grand Harmonic Complex. The Part of Fortune is not in a 7th harmonic aspect to Chiron (it is to my Sun and Moon), and Chiron is not in a 7th harmonic aspect to Jupiter, but they are pulled in by Saturn, the Moon and the Vertex.

The two Grand Harmonic Complexes can be combined into one, with the 360° divided in four parts then. The Moon is 51°22'41.8", and Chiron is 52°43'56.6" from Pluto, both in 7th harmonic aspect to it. Diagrams of the first, second and combined Grand Harmonic Complexes and the planetary pictures that are formed from them are as follows:

FIGURE XVI - Grand 7th Harmonic Complexes

I.

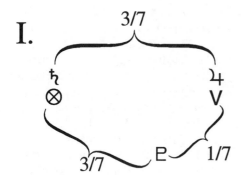

V♃ 7th H. ♄⊗ ⎫   ♄ ☍ ♇/V
♄⊗ 7th H. ♇ ⎬   ♄ ☍ ♃/♇
♇ 7th H. V♃ ⎭   ⊗ ☍ ♇/V
              ⊗ ☍ ♃/♇

II.

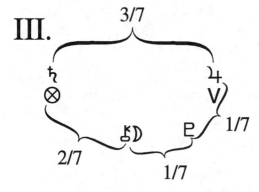

                ♊ ☍ ♄/V
V♃ 7th H. ♄⊗ ⎫ ☽ ☍ ♄/V
♄⊗ 7th H. ♊☽ ⎬ ♊ ☍ ♃/♄
♊☽ 7th H. V♃ ⎭ ☽ ☍ ♃/♄
                ☽ ☍ ⊗/V
                ☽ ☍ ♃/⊗

III.

* V♃ 7th H. ♄⊗ ⎫ ♇ ☌ V/♊
  ♄⊗ 7th H. ♊☽ ⎬ ♇ ☌ ♃/♊
  ♊☽ 7th H. ♇ ⎭ ♇ ☌ ☽/V
  ♇ 7th H. ♃   ♇ ☌ ☽/♃

* In addition to the planetary pictures in Complexes I and II

Though the combined Grand Harmonic Complex divides 360° in four parts, it is flowing like the first and second Grand Harmonic Complexes because its planets and/or points are still connected in continuous 360° circles. Note that the harmonics in each of the complexes add up to $^7/_7$ (I. $^3/_7 + ^3/_7 + ^1/_7 = ^7/_7$; II. $^3/_7 + ^2/_7 + ^2/_7 = ^7/_7$; III. $^3/_7 + ^2/_7 + ^1/_7 + ^1/_7 = ^7/_7$). The planetary pictures formed from the 7th harmonic relate to it.

The combined Grand Harmonic Complex suggests that for me partnership or marriage (7th harmonic) will be emotionally (the Moon) compelling (Pluto), as well as both expansive (Jupiter) and restrictive (Saturn). Moon-Pluto and Jupiter-Pluto will be particularly related to partnership or marriage because the fraction representing their separations is $^1/_7$—marriage in relation to itself. (As explained, the partner is described by the 7th harmonic too.) Chiron, the Vertex and the Part of Fortune are also in this Grand Harmonic Complex, adding the concepts of stepparenting, fate and fortune. The stepparenting is especially related to the emotionality; the fated quality, to the expansion; and the good fortune, to the restriction. (Of course, the houses, signs and degrees of these planets and points will make the delineation more explicit.)

There are harmonics into which these separations fit that are more exact than the 7th, but the 7th takes precedence. It takes precedence because it is one of the first 12 harmonics, and the orb is no more than from one degree to the next. As explained however, the more exact harmonic may give more specific information, even if the less exact harmonic is the prevailing harmonic.

PROGRESSIONS TO GRAND HARMONIC COMPLEXES

This combined Grand Harmonic Complex and my other Grand Harmonic Complexes that have Jupiter in them (there is a Grand 13th Harmonic of Jupiter, Midheaven and Uranus) may particularly relate to my second marriage, since my Solar Arc Ascendant at the time of that marriage was exactly opposite my Jupiter. A Grand 11th Harmonic Complex that has Neptune, the Ascendant and Uranus in it may particularly relate to my first marriage, since my Solar Arc Ascendant at the time of that marriage was exactly opposite my Neptune. This Grand 11th Harmonic Complex, though activated at that specific time, indicates in general that my hopes and wishes, as well as friends (11th harmonic) are erratic or innovative (Uranus) and nebulous or idealistic (Neptune). (Unusual astrology or unusual astrologers would fulfill the symbolism of a combined Uranus and Neptune.)

GRAND HARMONIC COMPLEXES IN MAGNIFIED CHARTS

Though we are now discussing harmonics as aspects in the radix chart, I must say that Grand Harmonic Complexes in the magnified chart are equally descriptive. For instance, in my 7th harmonic chart there is a Grand 9th Harmonic Complex with two name asteroids and a Uranian planet. The asteroid with my name at 25° Libra 16' is $^4/_9$ to the asteroid with the name of my second husband at 05° Aries 24', which is $^2/_9$ to Hades at 24° Gemini 37', which is $^3/_9$ (or $^1/_3$) to the asteroid with my name. Though $^1/_3$ is more specifically the 3rd harmonic, it is included because the fractions $^3/_9$ and $^1/_3$ are "equivalent." An interpretation that could be given of this Grand 9th

Harmonic Complex, imposed upon my 7th harmonic chart, is that I (my name asteroid) find completion (9th Harmonic Complex) in the marriage (7th harmonic) to my second husband (his name asteroid). Hades being included in this Grand 9th Harmonic Complex relates, I believe, to a karmic or past-life association. Also, each fraction is appropriate for the particular relationship, with the number of the denominator referring to the number of the numerator. $^4/_9$, the fraction between my name asteroid and my husband's, is completion in reference to maternalism or the home. Incidentally, my second husband's and my composite Ascendant is 24° Gemini 17', conjunct this Hades.

INTERASPECT GRAND HARMONIC COMPLEXES

To return to radix charts, aspects between them that form Grand Harmonic Complexes are particularly important. As an example, there is the Grand 9th Harmonic Complex between my second husband and myself. For simplicity's sake, I will just give the degrees, which is feasible with the 9th harmonic because its separation is an integer, and my orb is from one degree to the next. My husband's Sun at 07° Pisces is $^1/_9$ to his Venus and Chiron at 16° and 18° Aries, which are $^1/_9$ to my Mercury, Chiron at 27°, 28° Taurus, which are $^2/_9$ to his East Point, Cupido at 17° Leo and Neptune at 18° Leo, which are $^3/_9$ (or $^1/_3$) to his Jupiter, Dark Moon Lilith at 17°, 18° Sagittarius, which are $^2/_9$ to his Sun. (Dark Moon Lilith adds a seductive quality.) If Poseidon (a Super-Neptune) is included, his at 27° Virgo would be $^1/_9$ from his East Point, Cupido and Neptune and $^2/_9$ from his Jupiter. Though he has a Grand 9th Harmonic Complex without my intervention, my Mercury and Chiron do fit into his Grand 9th Harmonic Complex appropriately. Chiron relates to stepparents, and my Mercury rules my fifth house of children, as well as my fourth house, my Sun, Moon, Venus, Vulcanus, name asteroid, South Node, Neptune, Apollon, Mars, Vertex and Jupiter. With my Mercury, Chiron, which is apropos of his Venus, Chiron, I am bringing him completion through our marriage and the stepson it brought him.

INTERASPECT HARMONIC COMPLEXES

Even if the interaspects do not form a Grand Harmonic Complex, the aspects one person has in a particular harmonic which connect to another person's chart in that same harmonic (Harmonic Complexes) are significant. For instance, I recorded the 9th harmonic aspects in the chart of myself, of my second husband, of my first husband and of his second wife. I then looked to see the 9th harmonic interaspects between myself and my first and second husband that connected to our 9th harmonic aspects, and between my first husband and his second wife that connected to their 9th harmonic aspects. Though the descriptiveness of the asteroids and Uranian planets has been demonstrated, for simplicity's sake only the ten planets, Ascendant, Midheaven, and Nodes are being considered. The 9th harmonic was chosen for this comparison because the forming of 9th harmonic aspects between charts can help to integrate the respective individuals. Through their connections they may reach completion—one of the meanings of the 9th harmonic.

Linear diagrams of these interaspect 9th Harmonic Complexes, showing the different fractions between the planets and points have been drawn (see Figure XVII). I is the diagram of the interaspect 9th Harmonic Complexes between my second husband and myself; II is between my first husband and myself; III is between my first husband and his second wife. F stands for the female, and M, for the male, but the initials of the first names could be used instead. G.H.C. stands for Grand Harmonic Complex. Some planets and points are pulled into aspect by the contiguity of the numbers. The planetary pictures that are formed from the 9th harmonic combining of planets and points in two charts are recorded. My second husband's Moon equaling my Mars/Saturn midpoint by a conjunction is modified by the fact that the combination of the three planets forms a 9th Harmonic Complex. Though these diagrams are of the interaspect 9th Harmonic Complexes, the same format can be used to good advantage with other interaspect Harmonic Complexes, such as the 7th, 5th and 13th. In the case of the 9th, I have begun with Pisces because of its prominence, but Aries might be the best starting place in most cases. Tallies can be made of the aspects and interaspects, but the quantity, without the quality, is not discriminative.

Considering the ten planets, Ascendant, Midheaven and Nodes, I have three 9th harmonic aspects—Venus-Pluto, Mars-Ascendant and Saturn-Neptune. All three are connected to my second husband's chart by 9th harmonic interaspects (I). My Venus-Pluto at 11° Gemini-21° Cancer is linked to his chart by his North Node at 02° Virgo, conjunct my South Node at 03° Virgo. My Mars-Ascendant at 09° Virgo-20° Aquarius and my Saturn-Neptune at 16° Aquarius-07° Virgo are linked to his chart and to each other by his Moon at 28° Scorpio and his Mercury at 18° Aquarius. My second husband has nine 9th harmonic aspects, including two exact trines (Venus-Jupiter and Jupiter-Neptune) which form his only exact Grand Trine. (That Grand Trine is within the interaspect Grand Harmonic Complex already described on page 132.) With just the factors stated above, this is a Grand Trine of Venus, Jupiter and Neptune. His other 9th harmonic aspects are Sun-Venus, Sun-Jupiter, Sun-Neptune, Moon-Mercury, Saturn-Midheaven, Saturn-South Node and Midheaven-South Node. My planets and points connect 9th harmonically to all of these aspects. Venus-Jupiter, Jupiter-Neptune, Sun-Venus, Sun-Jupiter and Sun-Neptune are attached by 9th harmonic aspects to my Mercury, which is the ruler of practically everything in my chart. A Grand 9th Harmonic Complex is formed. My second husband's Moon-Mercury, as already outlined, is connected to my 9th harmonic aspects of Mars-Ascendant and Saturn-Neptune. His Saturn-Midheaven at 02° Scorpio-22° Taurus, Saturn-South Node at 02° Scorpio-02° Pisces and Midheaven-South Node at 22° Taurus-02° Pisces form a Grand 9th Harmonic Complex, which is linked to my chart by my North Node at 03° Pisces, which is exactly conjunct his South Node.

Considering the same factors, my first husband's chart[32] does not connect 9th harmonically to any of my three 9th harmonic aspects. He has seven 9th harmonic aspects, including two exact trines. The trines are Uranus-Pluto and Neptune-Midheaven. His other 9th harmonic aspects are Moon-Ascendant, Mercury-South

Figure XVII – Interaspect 9th Harmonic Complexes

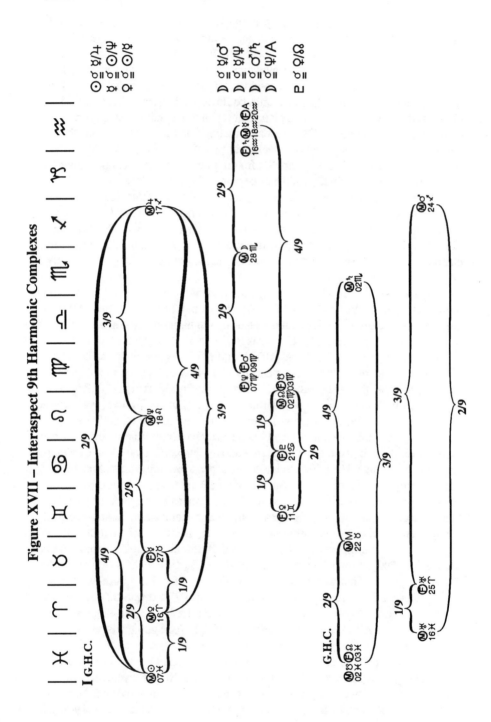

Figure XVII – Interaspect 9th Harmonic Complexes

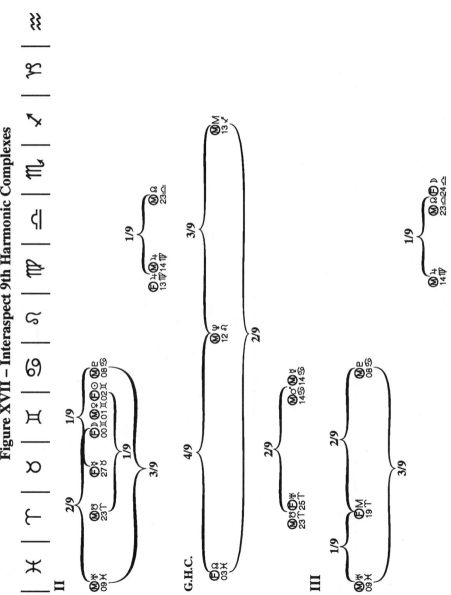

Figure XVII – Interaspect 9th Harmonic Complexes

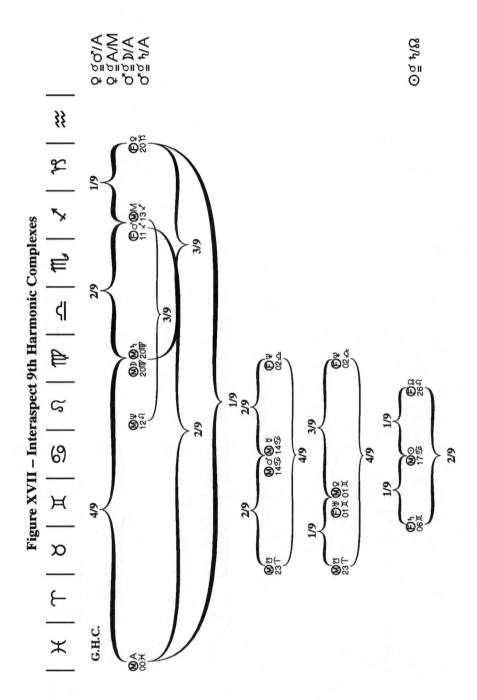

Node, Mars-South Node, Jupiter-North Node and Saturn-Ascendant. My planets and points connect 9th harmonically to five of his seven 9th harmonic aspects, including his only exact trines (II). His Uranus at 09° Pisces trine Pluto at 08° Cancer is attached to my Mercury at 27° Taurus (featured in a Grand 9th Harmonic Complex with my second husband) which, as mentioned, is the ruler of practically everything in my chart. My Moon at 00° Gemini, as well as Mercury, ties in with the trine. (Interestingly, my first husband has a Cancer Sun and a Virgo Moon.) His Neptune at 12° Leo trine the Midheaven at 13° Sagittarius is linked to my North Node at 03° Pisces, which converts his trine into a Grand 9th Harmonic Complex. (My North Node was featured in a Grand 9th Harmonic Complex with my second husband.) His Mercury-South Node and Mars-South Node, both at 14° Cancer-23° Aries, tie in with my Uranus at 25° Aries. His Jupiter-North Node at 14° Virgo-23° Libra is linked to my chart by my Jupiter at 13° Virgo, exactly conjunct his. His Moon-Ascendant and Saturn-Ascendant do not connect 9th harmonically to my chart.

All seven of my ex-husband's 9th harmonic aspects do connect 9th harmonically to his present wife's chart (III). His Moon-Ascendant at 20° Virgo-00° Pisces and Saturn-Ascendant at 20° Virgo-00° Pisces are linked to her Venus-Mars at 20° Capricorn-11° Sagittarius. Incidentally, she is a Capricorn, and so fulfills in a positive way the symbolism of his Moon conjunct Saturn in the seventh house. His Neptune trine Midheaven is also attached to her Mars at 11° Sagittarius, which converts his Neptune-Midheaven, Moon-Ascendant and Saturn-Ascendant into a Grand Harmonic Complex. (I only convert his Neptune-Midheaven into a Grand Harmonic Complex.) His Uranus trine Pluto is connected to her Midheaven at 19° Aries. His Mercury-South Node and Mars-South Node tie in with her Neptune at 02° Libra. His Jupiter-North Node is linked to her chart by her Moon at 24° Libra, exactly conjunct his North Node.

My ex-husband's present wife has five 9th harmonic aspects—Sun-Ascendant, Venus-Mars, Saturn-North Node, Uranus-Neptune and Pluto-South Node. Three of the five are connected to my ex-husband's chart by 9th harmonic aspects. Her Venus-Mars, as already outlined, is connected to his 9th harmonic aspects of Moon-Ascendant, Saturn-Ascendant and Neptune-Midheaven, forming a Grand Harmonic Complex. Her Uranus-Neptune is linked 9th harmonically to his South Node, with her Uranus at 01° Gemini exactly conjunct his Venus at 01° Gemini. This Harmonic Complex is tied in with the Harmonic Complex of his Mercury-South Node and Mars-South Node, which is connected to her Neptune. Her Saturn-North Node at 06° Gemini-26° Leo is attached to his Sun at 17° Cancer.

COMPARISON OF INTERASPECT HARMONIC COMPLEXES

Comparing the interaspect Harmonic Complexes between my present husband and myself with those between my ex-husband and myself, and with those between my ex-husband and his present wife, is enlightening. The harmonics are like electrical circuits, and one person's circuitry may help to complete another person's. In the cases of my present husband and myself and of my ex-husband and his present wife, the completion of each other's electrical circuits seems to be better accomplished than in the case of my ex-husband and myself. Though in any harmonic there can be completion of circuits, the 9th harmonic is especially related to completion. The 7th harmonic is related to marriage, but the 9th may be associated with longevity of the marriage because of this connection with completion. So far, my marriage to my second husband has lasted 35 years, while my first husband's marriage to his second wife has lasted $26^1/_2$ years. In comparison, my marriage to my first husband, in which I did not feel a sense of completion, lasted less than five years.

Of course, I am not proposing that all people who complete each other's electrical circuits will be married—even a little while. For a description of the relationship, it's important to note in what houses, signs and degrees the particular planets and points are, and what other exact aspects they make. (Naturally, the houses of the points will only be relevant if points other than the Ascendant and Midheaven are being considered.)

As for the houses of the 9th harmonic connections mentioned above, my present husband brings me his Sun (in three 9th harmonic interaspects) and South Node (in two 9th harmonic interaspects) from his seventh house, while I bring him my Neptune and Mars (each in two 9th harmonic interaspects) from my seventh. The only planet my ex-husband brings me from his seventh house is Jupiter (one interaspect), and the only planet I bring him from my seventh is Jupiter (one interaspect), and I believe the main purpose of our marriage was to produce our **Sagittarian** son. From my ex-husband's fifth house of children, his Mercury, Mars, and Pluto connect 9th harmonically to my planets. His Mercury, Mars and Pluto connect 9th harmonically to his present wife's planets too; and his Sun, also in the fifth house, connects to one of his present wife's 9th harmonic aspects. Her Mars in the fifth house, in 9th harmonic aspect to her Venus, connects 9th harmonically to three of his 9th harmonic aspects. They have five children—two boys (Mars) and three girls (Venus). My present husband and I have no planets in our fifth houses, so there is no possibility of connections from them. My ex-husband's present wife has no planets in her seventh house, so there is no possibility of connections from it. However, my ex-husband brings her the three planets that are in his seventh house—all three in 9th harmonic aspects in his chart, and connecting in 9th harmonic interaspects to her chart.

Tools

Having spoken about harmonic aspects and interaspects, and the Harmonic Complexes they may form, I shall now speak about the tools that can be used to see these harmonic aspects and interaspects. Of course, Graphic Harmonic Planet Sorts or angular separations within charts and angular separations between charts are offered on personal computer programs or can be ordered from computer services. Astro also has a harmonic dial option now. However, there are graphs and dials that can be made by hand.

Harmonic Graphs

Harmonic graphs are invaluable tools. The graphs are of particular value in studying families. The story of my experiments with these graphs follows.

5TH HARMONIC GRAPHS

In March of 1978, I heard Ken and Joan Negus speak on "Techniques of Comparison." In this lecture they mentioned making family pentagrams (five-pointed figures), based on the 5th harmonic. John Addey, thinking that the 5th harmonic has genetic significance, had done pentagrams of his family and of the royal family of England. To see what your family pentagram is, the Neguses said you should make a graph with 00° Aries through 11° Gemini on the first horizontal line; 12° Gemini through 23° Leo on the second horizontal line; and so on in sequence until the fifth and last line, which would have 18° Capricorn through 29° Pisces. (360° is being condensed into 72°.) They leave a space under each degree to put a planet or personal point and make a separate graph for each person. The 5th harmonic aspects and interaspects are shown by vertical conjunctions. The Neguses said to allow an orb of two degrees on either side of the exact degree.

When I did a graph of my immediate family, I put the five lines of degrees at the top of the page, and then put the planets and personal points of seven people underneath the five lines. The seven people are my father, my mother, myself, my first husband, our son, my second husband and our daughter. They were listed in this order from the top down on the right-hand side of the page. The ten planets, Ascendant, Midheaven and Nodes of each person were placed on the graph. The degree of each factor was written underneath each factor, i.e., 02°♊ underneath my Sun. My way, the aspects are shown by horizontal conjunctions at the same space or within two spaces on either side. The interaspects are still shown by vertical conjunctions, but, with the seven people on the same graph, their 5th harmonic interaspects are seen more easily. When there are quintiles, biquintiles or conjunctions between the factors of the different people, vertical lines are formed.

Including two degrees on either side of each degree (as the Neguses instructed), there are four vertical lines that have at least one of the ten planets or the Ascendant, Midheaven, North Node or South Node of each of the seven people. These lines are at the sequences of 11° Taurus-29° Aquarius, 13° Taurus-01° Pisces, 14° Taurus-02° Pisces and 27° Taurus-15° Pisces. Essentially, there are three prominent lines—11° Taurus-29° Aquarius, 13° Taurus-01° Pisces and 27° Taurus-15° Pisces—with the 13° and 14° Taurus lines overlapping. (The 11° and 13° Taurus lines also overlap, so 13° Taurus could be considered the center of the 11° and 14° Taurus sequences.) All five degrees of each sequence are filled, so there are three family pentagrams. For instance, the 27° Taurus-15° Pisces pentagram has 27° Taurus at one point, with my Mercury at 27° Taurus and my mother's Saturn at 28° Taurus; 09° Leo at the next point, with my father's Mars at 08° Leo; 21° Libra at the third point, with my first husband's North Node and our son's Neptune at 23° Libra; 03° Capricorn at the fourth, with my mother's Midheaven at 02° Capricorn and my daughter's Saturn at 01° Capricorn; and 15° Pisces at the fifth, with my second husband's Uranus at 16° Pisces.

Ken Negus, who is a professor, said that each student in his doctoral program has two or three points on his family pentagram, which is more than his children have. Pondering this statement, I thought the pentagram, then, is not just for the family. Ken is involved in a creative process with his students, and he is an authority figure to them (both 5th harmonic). (Saturn signifies the father as the authority figure, but the Sun has an association with authority figures in general, and with the king in particular. This particular association could relate to the pentagram's importance in the royal family.) To further investigate the question of whether the 5th harmonic has special significance in heredity, I decided to do a graph of the 9th harmonic as well.

9TH HARMONIC GRAPHS

The 9th harmonic graph was constructed in the same way as the 5th harmonic graph, only this time the first line is 00° Aries through 09° Taurus, and so on in sequence until the ninth and last line which has 20° Aquarius through 29° Pisces (see Figure XVIII). (360° is being condensed into 40°.) Including two degrees on either side of each degree, there are seven vertical lines that have at least one of the ten planets or the Ascendant, Midheaven, North Node or South Node of each of the seven people. These lines are at the sequences of 12° Aries-02° Pisces, 13° Aries-03° Pisces, 14° Aries-04° Pisces, 16° Aries-06° Pisces, 17° Aries-07° Pisces, 18° Aries-08° Pisces and 24° Aries-14° Pisces. Essentially, there are three prominent lines—13° Aries-03° Pisces, 17° Aries-07° Pisces and 24° Aries-14° Pisces—with the 12° and 14° Aries lines overlapping the 13° Aries line, and the 16° and 18° Aries lines overlapping the 17° Aries line. (The 13° and 17° Aries lines also overlap somewhat.)

COMPARISON OF 5TH AND 9TH HARMONIC GRAPHS

Comparing the 9th harmonic with the 5th harmonic, I noticed that there are coincidences between the three prominent lines of the 9th harmonic and the three prominent lines of the 5th harmonic. Regarding the prominent lines, there are the following coincidences. The second line of the 9th harmonic coincides at 17° Sagittarius with the first line of the 5th harmonic and at 27° Taurus with the third line of the 5th harmonic. The 9th harmonic third line coincides at 04° Libra with 05° Libra in the 5th harmonic first line, and at 14° Pisces with 15° Pisces in the 5th harmonic third line. The 9th harmonic first line coincides at 03° Pisces with 01° Pisces in the 5th harmonic second line. Also, the number of planets and personal points in the prominent lines of the 9th harmonic are almost double the number of planets and personal points in the prominent lines of the 5th harmonic. Since in the graphs, 40° (the 9th harmonic separation) is "folded back" on itself almost double the number of times that 72° (the 5th harmonic separation) is "folded back" on itself, this result is to be expected. However, since the result is as expected, it indicates that the connections between the members of my immediate family are as highlighted in the 9th harmonic, as they are in the 5th harmonic. And, there is a family nonagon where all nine degrees of the sequence are filled. This is the 24° Aries-14° Pisces nonagon which has 24° Aries at one point, with my Uranus at 25° Aries and my first husband's South Node at 23° Aries; 04° Gemini at the next point, with my Sun at 02° Gemini; 14° Cancer at the third point, with my first husband's Mercury and Mars at 14° Cancer; 24° Leo at the fourth, with my son's Pluto at 23° Leo and my daughter's Midheaven at 26° Leo; 04° Libra at the fifth, with my daughter's North

Figure XVIII — 9th Harmonic Graph

00♈ 01♈ 02♈ 03♈ 04♈ 05♈ 06♈ 07♈ 08♈ 09♈ 10♈ 11♈ 12♈ 13♈ 14♈ 15♈ 16♈ 17♈ 18♈ 19♈ 20♈ 21♈ 22♈ 23♈ 24♈ 25♈ 26♈ 27♈ 28♈ 29♈ 00♉ 01♉ 02♉ 03♉ 04♉ 05♉ 06♉ 07♉ 08♉ 09♉

10♉ 11♉ 12♉ 13♉ 14♉ 15♉ 16♉ 17♉ 18♉ 19♉ 20♉ 21♉ 22♉ 23♉ 24♉ 25♉ 26♉ 27♉ 28♉ 29♉ 00♊ 01♊ 02♊ 03♊ 04♊ 05♊ 06♊ 07♊ 08♊ 09♊ 10♊ 11♊ 12♊ 13♊ 14♊ 15♊ 16♊ 17♊ 18♊ 19♊

20♊ 21♊ 22♊ 23♊ 24♊ 25♊ 26♊ 27♊ 28♊ 29♊ 00♋ 01♋ 02♋ 03♋ 04♋ 05♋ 06♋ 07♋ 08♋ 09♋ 10♋ 11♋ 12♋ 13♋ 14♋ 15♋ 16♋ 17♋ 18♋ 19♋ 20♋ 21♋ 22♋ 23♋ 24♋ 25♋ 26♋ 27♋ 28♋ 29♋

00♌ 01♌ 02♌ 03♌ 04♌ 05♌ 06♌ 07♌ 08♌ 09♌ 10♌ 11♌ 12♌ 13♌ 14♌ 15♌ 16♌ 17♌ 18♌ 19♌ 20♌ 21♌ 22♌ 23♌ 24♌ 25♌ 26♌ 27♌ 28♌ 29♌ 00♍ 01♍ 02♍ 03♍ 04♍ 05♍ 06♍ 07♍ 08♍ 09♍

10♍ 11♍ 12♍ 13♍ 14♍ 15♍ 16♍ 17♍ 18♍ 19♍ 20♍ 21♍ 22♍ 23♍ 24♍ 25♍ 26♍ 27♍ 28♍ 29♍ 00♎ 01♎ 02♎ 03♎ 04♎ 05♎ 06♎ 07♎ 08♎ 09♎ 10♎ 11♎ 12♎ 13♎ 14♎ 15♎ 16♎ 17♎ 18♎ 19♎

20♎ 21♎ 22♎ 23♎ 24♎ 25♎ 26♎ 27♎ 28♎ 29♎ 00♏ 01♏ 02♏ 03♏ 04♏ 05♏ 06♏ 07♏ 08♏ 09♏ 10♏ 11♏ 12♏ 13♏ 14♏ 15♏ 16♏ 17♏ 18♏ 19♏ 20♏ 21♏ 22♏ 23♏ 24♏ 25♏ 26♏ 27♏ 28♏ 29♏

00♐ 01♐ 02♐ 03♐ 04♐ 05♐ 06♐ 07♐ 08♐ 09♐ 10♐ 11♐ 12♐ 13♐ 14♐ 15♐ 16♐ 17♐ 18♐ 19♐ 20♐ 21♐ 22♐ 23♐ 24♐ 25♐ 26♐ 27♐ 28♐ 29♐ 00♑ 01♑ 02♑ 03♑ 04♑ 05♑ 06♑ 07♑ 08♑ 09♑

10♑ 11♑ 12♑ 13♑ 14♑ 15♑ 16♑ 17♑ 18♑ 19♑ 20♑ 21♑ 22♑ 23♑ 24♑ 25♑ 26♑ 27♑ 28♑ 29♑ 00♒ 01♒ 02♒ 03♒ 04♒ 05♒ 06♒ 07♒ 08♒ 09♒ 10♒ 11♒ 12♒ 13♒ 14♒ 15♒ 16♒ 17♒ 18♒ 19♒

20♒ 21♒ 22♒ 23♒ 24♒ 25♒ 26♒ 27♒ 28♒ 29♒ 00♓ 01♓ 02♓ 03♓ 04♓ 05♓ 06♓ 07♓ 08♓ 09♓ 10♓ 11♓ 12♓ 13♓ 14♓ 15♓ 16♓ 17♓ 18♓ 19♓ 20♓ 21♓ 22♓ 23♓ 24♓ 25♓ 26♓ 27♓ 28♓ 29♓

FATHER	♆ ♀ ♅ 23♊03♐04♐ · ♂ M 08♌ 29♎ · ♃ 03♏ · ♄ 15♐ · ☋ 08♋ · ☉ ☽ 21♐ 22♐ · ♇ 14♊ · A ☿ ☊ 06♑ 07♑ 08♑
MOTHER	A☽ 05♈ · ☿ ☊ ♇ 08♐09♈29♊ · ♂ 12♐ · ♄ 28♉ · ♅ 01♒ · ☉ ♀ ♃ 25♐05♒26♐ · ☋ 09♎ · M 02♑ · ♆ 25♋
MYSELF	A 20♒ · ♃ 13♍ · M 07♐ · ☊ 03♓ · ☿ 27♉ · ☽ 00♊ · ☉ 02♊ · ♅ 25♈ · ♀ ♇ 11♊21♋ · ☋ 03♍ · ♄ ♆ 16♒ 07♍ · ♂ 09♍
1ST HUSBAND	☊ ♃ 23♎14♍ · ♄☽ A 20♍00♓ · ♆ M 12♌ 13♐ · ♇ ♅ 08♋ 09♓ · ♀ 01♊ · ☋ ♂☿ 23♈14♋ · ☉ 17♋
SON	☿ 00♐ · ♃ ♆ ♄ 12♉23♎ 24♎ · M 11♈ · ☋ ☉ ♀ 14♌ 15♐ 26♑ · ♇ 23♌ · ♅ 17♋ · ☽ 29♌ · ♂ 12♒ · ☊ 14♒ · A 27♋
2ND HUSBAND	M ♄ ☋ 22♉02♏02♓ · ♀ ☉ ♃ ♆ 16♈07♓17♐18♌ · ♇ 10♋ · ♂ 24♐ · ♅ 16♓ · A 28♌ · ☊ 02♍ · ☽ ☿ 28♏18♒
DAUGHTER	♀ ☉ 13♍ 04♌ · ☋ ☽ 06♈ 17♉ · ♆ ♅ 04♏ 15♌ · ☿ 17♌ · ☊ M A 06♎26♌16♏ · ♄ ♃ ♇ 01♑22♏02♍ · ♂ 05♍

Node at 06° Libra; 14° Scorpio at the sixth, with my daughter's Ascendant at 16° Scorpio; 24° Sagittarius at the seventh, with my father's Moon at 22° Sagittarius, my mother's Sun and Jupiter at 25° and 26° Sagittarius and my second husband's Mars at 24° Sagittarius; 04° Aquarius at the eighth, with my mother's Venus at 05° Aquarius; and 14° Pisces at the ninth, with my second husband's Uranus at 16° Pisces.

COMPARISONS TO 7TH HARMONIC GRAPHS

Then I constructed a 7th harmonic graph, with the first line 00° Aries through 20° Taurus, and the second line 21° Taurus through 12° Cancer, etc. There is an irregularity in this graph because the second, fourth and sixth horizontal lines of the degrees must have an extra degree to compensate for the fact that the angular separation of the 7th harmonic is not a whole number. Including two degrees on either side of each degree, there are eight vertical lines that have at least one of the ten planets or the Ascendant, Midheaven, North Node or South Node of each of the seven people. Again there are essentially three vertical lines—05° Aries-14° Aquarius, 09° Aries-18° Aquarius and 19° Taurus-28° Pisces—with the other lines overlapping. Two of these three prominent lines of the seventh harmonic coincide with prominent lines of both the 5th harmonic and the 9th harmonic. The 7th harmonic third line coincides at 15° Sagittarius with 17° Sagittarius in the 5th harmonic first line, 17° Sagittarius in the 9th harmonic second line and 13° Sagittarius in the 9th harmonic first line. Also, the 7th harmonic first line coincides at 26° Taurus with 27° Taurus in the 5th harmonic third line and 27° Taurus in the 9th harmonic second line. And, there are two family heptagons formed from the first and second prominent lines of the seventh harmonic.

It seems as if the 5th harmonic does not have a special significance in heredity. The 9th and 7th appear to be equally highlighted in the family. In fact, each harmonic may be hereditarily significant. Each may indicate degrees that are prominent for you and the people who are close to you—degrees that are prominent in terms of the meaning of the particular harmonic. The 5th harmonic would show this prominence in terms of creativity and children; the 9th, in terms of completion and inlaws; the 7th, in terms of partnership and the partner.

DEGREE AREAS

Having come to this assumption, I returned to an investigation of the harmonic graphic procedure itself. An orb of two degrees on either side of the exact degree is one degree more on either side than I usually allow. With such an orb other harmonics are encompassed. (With my orb some are, but not as many.) However, in making a study of the interrelationships in a particular harmonic of a number of people, a certain leeway may be defensible. One person is sometimes the link between two others. For instance, in the 9th harmonic my South Node at 03° Virgo is the link between my mother's Midheaven at 02° Capricorn and my father's Pluto at 14° Gemini. Also, looked at in a different way, what we may be seeing here is degree areas, rather than degrees, being highlighted in particular harmonics.

As an example, in the 9th harmonic graph of my immediate family there are clusters of personal points in certain areas. In seven consecutive vertical lines, 07°

Aries-13° Aries, there are five Midheavens out of seven. In seven different consecutive lines, 21° Aries-27° Aries, there are four Suns out of seven. In five other consecutive lines, 06° Taurus-00° Aries, there are three Ascendants out of seven. Oddly, the seven lines with the densest cluster of Midheavens is separated by seven lines from the seven lines with the densest cluster of Suns, which is separated by eight lines from the five lines with the densest cluster of Ascendants, which is separated by six lines from the seven lines with the densest cluster of Midheavens. In the 40° of the 9th harmonic separation, for my immediate family there is approximately a 06½° on and off pulse regarding the three personal points of Midheaven, Sun and Ascendant. As for the Moons, the densest area is in six consecutive lives where there are three Moons out of seven. These six lines are 05° Aries-10° Aries, overlapping the densest area of the Midheavens at 07° Aries-13° Aries.

To further examine this concept of degree areas, I decided to add Suns of my progenitors. The Sun was chosen because for most of my progenitors I did not have timed charts. In those cases where I had already rectified the charts, the rectified Sun was used. (The charts were rectified according to personality and events.) In the other cases the Sun at noon was used.

The Suns of ten ancestors were added. The charts of my mother's mother and father had already been rectified. I could not trace my maternal lineage to the prior generation because the family Bible I was to inherit had been discarded through the negligence of the attorney for the estate. Fortunately, that was not the case on my father's side where the family Bibles supplied the dates of birth of my father's maternal grandmother and grandfather and paternal grandmother and grandfather, as well as his mother, father, sister and maternal aunt. The charts of my father's grandparents and maternal aunt were cast for noon. The charts of my father's mother and sister had been rectified. As for the birth time of my father's father, it had been noted. The most probable explanation I can give for such an unusual occurrence in 19th century America is that my father's paternal grandfather, who was a doctor, may have been present at his son's delivery and, concerned with accurate observations, may have recorded the time.

Regarding the birth times of the seven people in my immediate family, there was a comparable unusual occurrence concerning an exact time being recorded. My mother was born at home, and her mother was awake at the delivery and heard the 12 o'clock whistle blow just as she gave birth. (In 1912 such accuracy was still unusual.) As mentioned, my mother was also awake at my delivery and noted the time, which was the same as that recorded on my birth certificate. I, in turn, was awake at the deliveries of my two children and noted the times, which were the same as those recorded on their birth certificates. As for the birth time of my second husband, it had been given to me by his mother. The time was on the hour, and I had rectified the chart, making it 7 minutes and 18 seconds earlier, which changed the Ascendant only one degree. I had also rectified the charts of my father and first husband, and their charts, along with the chart of my second husband, have proven quite reliable.

Considering the Suns of my ten ancestors, three Suns out of ten are in the 21° Aries-27° Aries lines—the lines which have four out of the seven Suns of my immediate family. However, if the 28° Aries line is included, two more Suns are in the cluster. These are the Suns of my father's mother and maternal grandmother. My father's maternal aunt is in the 29° Aries line, but just by 2 minutes and 59 seconds of arc. Her chart was cast for noon, so her Sun may easily be in the 28° Aries line also. The other three people in this cluster are my father's sister at the 23° Aries line, my father's maternal grandfather at the 21° Aries line and my father's paternal grandfather at the 25° Aries line.

In my immediate family, my father has his Sun in the 21° Aries line. Noticing that it is my father's sister, mother, maternal aunt, maternal grandmother, maternal grandfather and paternal grandfather whose Suns are in this cluster, I thought that this "genetic factor" may have come down from my father (particularly the maternal side of his family). Though my Sun (22° Aries line) and my mother's Sun (25° Aries line) are in this cluster, I hypothesized that my mother's family would not have their Suns there. It had already been observed that my mother's mother and father do not. Not having the birth dates of previous generations, I then looked at all the charts (eight) of relatives on my mother's side in her generation and mine that are in my possession. There are my mother's two sisters, two brothers and the two sisters' four children. The two sisters' four children have birth certificate times, and the two sisters have observed times. As for the two brothers, the degrees of their Suns are prescribed by the family tradition that my maternal grandmother's five children had all been born between midnight and noon. None of these eight additional Suns are in the cluster of 21° Aries-29° Aries.

My collateral theory was that there would be a cluster that is characteristic of my mother's family. The Suns of my mother's father and mother are in the lines 12° Aries and 14° Aries, respectively. If four more lines are included to form a cluster from 12° Aries to 18° Aries, four out of the eight added Suns are in that cluster. The Suns are those of my mother's two sisters, and two of their children (in the lines 13° Aries, 18° Aries, and 12° Aries, 15° Aries). In fact, the Sun of one of the two children is the same as the Sun of his mother's father (who is my mother's father as well)— 22° Virgo in the 12° Aries line. (Interestingly, the relationship of the mother to her son is the same as her relationship to her father.) Each of my mother's two sisters has two children, and in each case one of the two has the Sun in this cluster. Perhaps, one child received this genetic factor, and the other is carrying it. To check this possibility, I looked at the next generation. (Of course, in this generation all the times are from birth certificates.) Each of the two children who do not have their Suns in this cluster has two children, and in each case one of the two has her Sun in this area. For one of these children, one line (11° Aries) has to be added, but if you take that child's Sun, her grandmother's and her great-grandmother's, in other words, the lineal descent, only four lines (11° Aries-14° Aries) of the cluster are required to comprise the Suns.

After the relatives on my mother's side, two cousins from my father's side (the children of my father's sister), with birth certificate times, were added. Then, a subsequent husband of my maternal grandmother, without a birth time, was included. Their Suns fit appropriately into the emerging pattern too.

Strangely enough, the center of the cluster which holds my father's family's Suns is about the 24° Aries-14° Pisces sequence, one of the three vertical lines that was shown as prominent in the 9th harmonic with the Ascendant, Midheaven, Nodes and all the planets. Similarly, the center of the cluster which holds my mother's family's Suns is the 15° Aries-05° Pisces sequence, at the middle of the other two vertical lines that were shown as prominent in the 9th harmonic with the Ascendant, Midheaven, Nodes and all the planets. The original prominence was based only on a nucleus of seven. As more family members were added, their Suns lined up mainly in accordance with their side of the family.

For the additional investigation, I had made another 9th harmonic graph but had not written the 9th harmonic degree sequences on it, since it could be placed beneath the degree sequences of the original 9th harmonic graph. To designate my Sun, the Sun symbol (☉) was used. To designate the Suns of the other people, letters were used: H = husband—for the first, a small 1 was added at the top of the H (H^1) and for the second, a small 2 (H^2); S^1 = son from the first marriage; D^2 = daughter from the second marriage; F = father; M = mother; A = aunt and U = uncle—for the second-born aunt and second-born uncle a small 2 was added at the top of the A and U; C = cousin—for the children and grandchildren of the second-born aunt a small 2 was added at the top of the C; GM = grandmother; GF = grandfather; GA = grandaunt. The letters for my mother and her family were done in red, while the letters for my father and his maternal family were done in blue, and those for his paternal family were done in green. The clusters were therefore easily seen. For myself, blue was used because, before knowing that I would be in my father's blue maternal famly cluster, I identified more with that part of my family than I did with the other parts. My children were done in blue too, and my husbands, in pencil. My Sun was placed about half-way down the page. On the same horizontal line were the symbols for the people of my generation—my husbands and my cousins. On the line beneath were the symbols for the people of the next generation—my children and my cousins' children. On the line above were those for the people of the previous generation—my mother, father, aunts and uncles. On the line above that were my grandparents and grandaunt. On the line above that were my great-grandparents. These five lines include the thirty-two people that have already been mentioned.

At this point, I decided to add five more lines above these five lines, since there was birth information going back to 1664 on the family of my father's paternal grandmother. I listed the generations on the right-hand side of the graph, starting from the top with the first generation and ending with the tenth generation (my children's), with room for future generations below. The first generation was

written $\underset{6Gs}{\overset{1st}{GEN.}}$, with the 6 Gs standing for the six grands that have to be put before grandmother and grandfather (GM and GF on the graph) in that generation. Unfortunately, the record is only of the direct male line. In four generations there is only one birth date per generation, and in one generation there are two birth dates (the wife's birth date is given). So sparse a distribution is not sufficient to see if there is a pattern.

Returning to the more recent generations, I looked at the Suns of some in-laws without birth times. In the past generations we were looking at in-laws too—my mother's family are in-laws to my father's family, and my father's mother's family are in-laws to my father's father's family—and the 9th harmonic is very much related to in-laws.

As a result of these inquiries, I have the following views. People who marry into the family tend to fit into the family clusters. They also introduce new clusters from their families. For a cluster, the child may inherit one gene from his father and one from his mother. If both the mother and father are in the same cluster, there would be a greater chance the child would be there too. However, there is always the possibility that the child will be a throwback to one or more of his grandparents and will manifest one of the cluster genes not manifested in the charts of his parents. As an example, my daughter's Sun is not near my Sun or her father's Sun, but it is in a line which is either the line, or next to the line, of her paternal grandmother's Sun. Their Suns are in a third cluster, which had emerged. This cluster, which is neither the one of my mother's family nor the one of my father's maternal family, is the one in which the Sun of my father's father (my paternal grandfather) falls.

FAMILY PENTAGRAMS, NONAGONS, AND HEPTAGONS

At this time, I decided that the charts (Ascendant, Midheaven, Nodes and all the planets) of my maternal and paternal grandparents should be considered in relation to the prominent lines that had been established from the charts of the seven people in my immediate family. As explained, for my paternal grandfather I had a timed chart, and for the other three, I had previously rectified charts. Diagrams with the degrees in the three prominent sequences of the 5th harmonic, of the 9th harmonic and of the 7th harmonic were drawn (see Figure XIX). What was discovered is that my grandparents, for the most part, have positions on these degrees of the family pentagrams, nonagons and heptagons, even though my grandparents hadn't been included in their original construction.

Addey states that when one point of a family pentagram has been empty for a couple of generations, there is a tendency for succeeding generations to marry people who will fill in this neglected point. My husbands satisfy Addey's statement, but they were part of the construction of my family pentagrams. However, the addition of my grandparents indicates that these pentagrams had significance in the family even before my husbands entered it. Interestingly, in the number I sequence of the 5th harmonic, the 29° Aquarius point of the pentagram had been empty for the two previous generations when I married my first husband, and his Ascendant at 00° Pisces filled in the empty point. (This point had been filled in the generation preceding my grandparents', since at 29° Aquarius my father's paternal grandfather has his Uranus.) In the number III sequence of the 5th harmonic, the 15° Pisces point of the pentagram had been empty for the two previous generations when I married my second husband, and his Uranus at 16° Pisces filled in the empty point. (This

Figure XIXa – Three Prominent Sequences

5th Harmonic

	I					II					III				
	11♉	23♋	05♎	17♐	29♒	13♉	25♋	07♎	19♐	01♓	27♉	09♌	21♎	03♑	15♓
1. Maternal Grandmother	M 10♉											♀ 07♌	♅ 22♎		
2. Maternal Grandfather		♃ 24♋	☽ 04♎	A 17♐			♃ 24♋	M♀ 08♎	A 17♐					♄ 03♑	
3. Paternal Grandmother	♃ 11♉			M 15♐		♃ 11♉			♄ 20♐	A 03♓				☿ 02♑	
4. Paternal Grandfather						♇ 14♉		A 09♎							
5. Father				♄ 15♐					☉ 21♐			♂ 08♌			
6. Mother		♆ 25♋					♆ 25♋	☋ 09♎			♄ 28♉			M 02♑	
7. Self		♇ 21♋								☊ 03♓	☿ 27♉				
8. 1st Husband					A 00♓					A 00♓			☊ 23♎		
9. Son	♃ 12♉			☉ 15♐		♃ 12♉	A 27♋						♆ 23♎		
10. 2nd Husband				♃ 17♐					♃ 17♐	☋ 02♓					♅ 16♓
11. Daughter			☊ 06♎					☊ 06♎						♄ 01♑	

7th Harmonic

	I							II							III						
	05♈	26♉	18♋	09♍	01♏	22♐	14♒	09♈	00♊	22♋	13♍	05♏	26♐	18♒	19♉	10♋	02♍	23♎	15♐	06♒	28♓
1. Maternal Grandmother						☋ 23♐												♅ 22♎			
2. Maternal Grandfather										♃ 24♋			☊ 26♐		♇ 19♉				A 17♐		
3. Paternal Grandmother			☽ ♅ 19♋20♋			♄ 20♐	♀ 16♒			♅ 20♋			☉ 28♐	♀ 16♒					M 15♐		
4. Paternal Grandfather													☿ 28♐			♅ M 10♋11♋				♀ 05♒	☽ 00♈
5. Father					M♃ 29♎03♏	☉ ☽ 21♐22♐						♃ 03♏				☋ 08♋			♄ 15♐		
6. Mother	A☽ 05♈	♄ 28♉						☊ 09♈	♄ 28♉				☉ ♃ 25♐26♐							♀ 05♒	
7. Self		☿ 27♉		♆ ♂ 07♍09♍			♄ 16♒		☽ ☉ 00♊02♊	♇ 21♋	♃ 13♍			♄ A 16♒20♒			☋ 03♍				
8. 1st Husband			☉ 17♋						♀ 01♊		♃ 14♍					♇ 08♋		☊ 23♎	M 13♐		
9. Son			♅ 17♋				♂ ☊ 12♒14♒	M 11♈										♆ ♄ 23♎24♎	☉ 15♐		
10. 2nd Husband					♄ 02♏	♂ 24♐							♂ 24♐	☿ 18♒		♇ 10♋	☊ 02♍				
11. Daughter	☋ 06♈										♀ 13♍	♆ 04♏			☽ 17♉		♇ 02♍				

Figure XIXb – Three Prominent Sequences

9th Harmonic

	I									II									III								
	13♈	23♉	03♋	13♌	23♍	03♏	13♐	23♑	03♓	17♈	27♉	07♋	17♌	27♍	07♏	17♐	27♑	07♓	24♈	04♊	14♋	24♌	04♎	14♏	24♐	04♒	14♓
1. Maternal Grandmother			☉ 04♋										A 19♌							♆ 05♊					☋ 23♐		
2. Maternal Grandfather					☉ 22♍									☿ 26♍		A 17♐			♆ 23♈				☽ 04♎		☋ 26♐		
3. Paternal Grandmother							M 15♐		A 03♓	♆ 16♈						M 15♐	☋ 28♑										
4. Paternal Grandfather	♆ 12♈								♃ 05♓									♃ ☋ 05♓ 06♓								♀ 05♒	
5. Father						♃ 03♏	♄ 15♐					☋ 08♋				♄ 15♐									☽ 22♐		
6. Mother							♂ 12♐				♄ 28♉														☉ ♃ 25♐ 26♐	♀ 05♒	
7. Self									☊ 03♓		☿ 27♉								♅ 25♈	☉ 02♊							
8. 1st Husband				♆ 12♌			M 13♐					♇ 08♋						♅ 09♓	☋ 23♈		♂☿ 14♋						
9. Son	M 11♈			☋ 14♌			☉ 15♐									☉ 15♐	♀ 26♑					♇ 23♌					
10. 2nd Husband		M 22♉				♄ 02♏			☋ 02♓	♀ 16♈			♆ 18♌			♃ 17♐		☉ 07♓							♂ 24♐		A 16♓
11. Daughter				♅ 15♌		♆ 04♏							♅ ☿ 15♌ 17♌									M 26♌	☊ 06♎	A 16♏			

point had been filled in the generation preceding my grandparents', since my father's maternal grandfather has his North Node at 14° Pisces.) My second husband's Uranus filling in a point on our family pentagram is appropriate because my child (5th harmonic) is his stepson (Uranus). Also, from my second husband's Uranus in Pisces in the seventh house there is an exact biquintile to my son's Neptune in the fourth house and an exact quintile to my Mercury, the ruler of my fourth and fifth houses. Note that the planet Uranus and the sign Pisces figure in the earlier generation placements—Uranus at 29° Aquarius and North Node at 14° Pisces. It is my first husband's 00° Pisces Ascendant that is conjunct the first placement, but my second marriage can not be considered separately from my first, since my child connects the two.

The family nonagons and heptagons operate similarly to the family pentagrams. For instance, in the number III sequence of the 9th harmonic the 14° Cancer point of the nonagon had been empty for at least the two previous generations when I married my first husband, and his Mercury and Mars at 14° Cancer filled in the empty point. (He also brought me my son, whose Pluto at 23° Leo filled in the 24° Leo point that had been empty for at least the three previous generations.) In that same sequence the 14° Pisces point of the nonagon had been empty for at least the two previous generations when I married my second husband, and his Uranus at 16° Pisces filled in the empty point. (He also brought me my daughter, whose Midheaven at 26° Leo filled in the 24° Leo point and whose Ascendant at 16° Scorpio filled in the 14° Scorpio point—points that had been empty for at least the three previous generations.) My second husband's Uranus filling in a point on our family nonagon is appropriate because completion (9th harmonic) was achieved through his marrying me (his Uranus in the seventh house, $^1/_9$ from my Uranus—the ruler of my Ascendant) and bringing me our daughter (her Midheaven and Ascendant). My husband's Uranus is $^4/_9$ from our daughter's Midheaven and North Node and $^3/_9$ (or $^1/_3$) from her Ascendant, forming an interaspect Grand Harmonic Complex. My Uranus is $^3/_9$ (or $^1/_3$) from our daughter's Midheaven and $^4/_9$ from her North Node and Ascendant, also forming an interaspect Grand Harmonic Complex. We are completing our daughter's 9th harmonic electrical circuit, and she is completing ours. What could be more appropriate with two Uranuses involved!

Naturally, not only is there a tendency to marry someone who will fill in the most neglected points, but there is a tendency to marry someone who will fill again those points that have been most filled before. For example, in this same 9th harmonic sequence, my second husband's Mars at 24° Sagittarius reiterates my mother's Sun and Jupiter at 25° and 26° Sagittarius, my father's Moon at 22° Sagittarius, my maternal grandfather's South Node at 26° Sagittarius and my maternal grandmother's South Node at 23° Sagittarius. And, of course, just as with the neglected points, what is being brought, as well as what it is being brought to, is meaningful. My husband's Mars is being brought to my family's and my positions in the area of his Mars. My maternal grandparents' South Nodes being together (and the results thereof) led to my mother's Sun and Jupiter being in that area, which led to her choosing my father with his Moon there, which led to my choosing a man with his Mars there. It is not that the planets cause these events, but rather that they are reflections of what we and our families already are.

REPEATED FAMILY THEMES

These diagrams are a wonderful device for seeing repeated family themes. For instance, in the number III sequence of the 5th harmonic, it can be seen that my mother's Midheaven (hers is an exactly timed chart) is exactly conjunct her father's Saturn. In the number I sequence of the 5th harmonic, the number I and II sequences of the 9th harmonic and the number III sequence of the 7th harmonic, it can be seen that my father's Saturn is exactly conjunct his mother's Midheaven. (This factor did not figure in the rectification of my grandmother's chart because, as fate would have it, at that time I thought my father's birth year was one year earlier than it actually was.) My mother was separated from her father at a very young age, and my father separated himself from his mother when he was a young man, both possible expressions of the Saturn of one conjunct the Midheaven of the other. When my mother's mother and father were divorced, he went to another state, and my mother never saw him again. At the first opportunity my father left home and lived in Paris for many years, pursuing his studies and career as a artist. He visited his parents several times but left each time, until on one visit he met my mother and never returned to Paris again. Though on one level the separation of my father from his mother is not comparable to the separation of my mother from her father—my mother was much younger at the time of her separation—on another level it is. Some of the correspondence during the years my father was in Paris is in my possession. My grandmother absolutely doted on my father, and the separation was (as was the separation of my mother from her father) extremely painful. In my parents' relationship, in some ways, my father was repeating his relationship with his mother while my mother was repeating her relationship with her father. Though my father never returned to Paris, my mother and father separated when I was three and a half years old. Interestingly, the degree of my father's Saturn and his mother's Midheaven—15° Sagittarius—is the same degree as my son's Sun, and my son lives in California and is, therefore, separated from me.

The symbolism of the degrees highlights these family themes. In *The Degrees of the Zodiac Symbolized* mentioned previously, the symbol for 15° Sagittarius, which is called a degree of Direction, is *An arrow in mid-air*. In true Sagittarian fashion, my father and my son took flight. The symbol for 17° Sagittarius (my mother's father's Ascendant), which is called a degree of Abandonment, is *A man afloat upon a raft*. The abandonment of the family by my mother's father was to keep himself afloat. My second husband brings his Jupiter to this degree. His Jupiter in the fourth is exactly square his Uranus in the seventh and rules his fifth house and his Jupiter and Mars. (The stepchild he gained from his marriage is a Sagittarian male.) My husband brings the expansiveness and benevolence of his Jupiter to the "abandonment" that began with the persona of my maternal grandfather. The word "began" is used only in the context of this limited study. I'm sure it all began long before my grandfather.

One final observation on these diagrams is concerning my father and myself. My father was born just after an eclipse, with 01° between his Sun and Moon, while I was born just before a lunation, with 02° between my Sun and Moon. When the Sun and Moon are close, the chance of their being together in one of the family pentagrams, nonagons or heptagons is, of course, greater. In the 5th harmonic (#II), only my father's Sun is picked up. In the 9th harmonic, there are his Moon (#III) and his Jupiter (#I), which is the ruler of his Sun and Moon. In the 7th harmonic, his Sun, Moon and Jupiter (#I) and Jupiter (#II) are all included. In the 5th harmonic (#III), my Mercury, which is the ruler of my Sun and Moon and practically everything else in my chart, is picked up. In the 9th harmonic, there are my Mercury (#II) and my Sun (#III). In the 7th harmonic, my Mercury (#I) and my Sun and Moon (#II) are all included. My interpretation would be that for both of us the archetypes of man and woman (Sun and Moon) are most fulfilled in partnership (7th harmonic). We found this partnership together—his Moon is $^3/_7$ from my Mercury, and my Moon is $^3/_7$ from his Jupiter. (Though the graphs are used as guides to the aspects and degree areas, the exact aspects should be calculated.) This partnership was an intellectual one (Mercury and Jupiter, which represent us as well—a Gemini and a Sagittarian). Also, the fraction is partnership, in reference to communication. But the partnership was tinged with emotion (our Moons). His Moon is $^4/_9$ from my Sun, and his Sun is $^4/_9$ from my Sun and Moon—completion (9th harmonic) was found in our relationship. The fraction is completion, in reference to emotion. But, most importantly, both of his luminaries and both of mine are involved. So great is the expansiveness of our interaspects that from the time we rediscovered each other when I was twelve and a half years old until he died ten years later, we could sit in his one-room apartment for hours on end and feel as if we were on cloud nine.

Of course, these investigations are just preliminary and suggestive. I have only studied my family. Other people should study theirs. Their reward will be insights into themselves and the ancestors from whence they came.

Harmonic Dials

Having spoken about harmonic graphs, I shall now proceed to harmonic dials. Though metal, cardboard or plastic dials with disks can be bought (Astro has a plastic dial and disk option), paper ones can be made by hand. What must be made are various harmonic paper dials and a 6-inch paper disk to fit on top of them. A thumbtack to fit upside down through the middle of the disk and the selected dial is needed. The disk would be a 360° version having twelve divisions, with the MC-IC line and the Ascendant-Descendant line being emphasized, and the MC-IC line being the pointer. The dials would have 360° divided by the harmonic number, i.e., the 4th harmonic dial would have $^{360}/_4$, or 90°, spread over the 360° circle. (Or, thought of another way, 360° is condensed in 90°.) Hatch marks are drawn on the dial to make the appropriate number of divisions, i.e., the 4th harmonic dial would have 90 divisions. A protractor, or disk with 360 divisions, is helpful in the making of the dials. The number of the harmonic (in this case, 4) is the number of divisions (on the protractor, or disk with 360 divisions) that fits between each hatch mark on the dial. The hatch marks are drawn beyond the 6-inch disk, so that when the 6-inch disk is placed over the dial, the hatch marks can be seen. The radix planets, personal points, asteroids and Uranian planets are placed in their appropriate positions in relation to the hatch marks. The disk with 360 divisions also helps in the placement of the figures.

4TH, 5TH, 6TH, 7TH, 9TH, 11TH AND 13TH HARMONIC DIALS

The making of the 4th, 5th, 6th, 7th, 9th, 11th and 13th harmonic dials will be demonstrated. On the 5th, 7th, 9th, 11th and 13th harmonic dials, the Descendant (D), Imum Coeli (I), Antivertex (XX) and South Node (☋) are included because on these dials these points are in different positions than the Ascendant (A), Medium Coeli or Midheaven (M), Vertex (V), and North Node (☊). On the 4th and 6th harmonic dials, these extra points are not included because on these dials these points are not in different positions than their complementary points.

The 4th harmonic dial would have 90 divisions ($^{360}/_4$), with Aries, Cancer, Libra and Capricorn positions from the Midheaven counterclockwise for 30°. Next there would be Taurus, Leo, Scorpio and Aquarius positions for 30°, until the last 30° where there would be Gemini, Virgo, Sagittarius and Pisces positions. The three sections consist of cardinal, fixed and mutable signs.

The 5th harmonic dial would have 72 divisions ($^{360}/_5$), with Aries positions starting from the Midheaven and proceeding counterclockwise. Virgo positions would begin 06° from the Midheaven and proceed counterclockwise. Aquarius positions would begin 06° later. Cancer positions would begin at the Ascendant. The order in this quadrant is Cancer, Sagittarius, Taurus; in the following quadrant, Libra (at the IC point), Pisces, Leo; and in the last quadrant, Capricorn (at the Descendant point), Gemini, Scorpio, and so back to Aries. Unlike the positions on the 4th harmonic dial, the positions on the 5th harmonic dial do not necessarily correlate to the positions in the zodiac. For instance, on the 5th harmonic dial my Uranus at 25° Aries 33' is $01^1/_2$° into the Sagittarius section because you continue counting past the Aries section.

The 6th harmonic dial would have 60 divisions ($^{360}/_6$), with Aries, Gemini, Leo, Libra, Sagittarius and Aquarius positions from the Midheaven counterclockwise for 30° until the IC where there are Taurus, Cancer, Virgo, Scorpio, Capricorn and Pisces positions for 30° until the Midheaven. The two sections consist of positive and negative signs.

The 7th harmonic dial would have 52 divisions, even though $^{360}/_7 = 51°25'42.8"$. The Aries positions would start at the Midheaven and proceed counterclockwise for $04^1/_3$°. The Scorpio positions would begin at that point and proceed for $04^1/_3$° more ($^2/_3$°, 03°, $^2/_3$°). The Gemini positions would come next ($^1/_3$°, 04°). Then, the Capricorn positions ($04^1/_3$°); Leo positions ($^2/_3$°, 03°, $^2/_3$°); Pisces positions ($^1/_3$°, 04°); Libra positions ($04^1/_3$°); Taurus positions ($^2/_3$°, 03°, $^2/_3$°); Sagittarius positions ($^1/_3$°, 04°); Cancer positions ($04^1/_3$°); Aquarius positions ($^2/_3$°, 03°, $^2/_3$°); Virgo positions ($^1/_3$°, 04°), and so back to Aries. The positions on the 7th harmonic dial do not necessarily correlate to the positions in the zodiac. For instance, my Uranus at

25° Aries 33' is ¹/₂° into the last degree of the Pisces section. Also, there is some fudging because 52° is an integral approximation of the fractional 51°25'42.8" separation.

The 9th harmonic dial (see Figure XX) [33] would have 40 divisions ($^{360}/_9$), with Aries, Leo and Sagittarius positions from the Midheaven counterclockwise for 10° until the Ascendant where there are Cancer, Scorpio and Pisces positions for 10°. At the IC there are Gemini, Libra and Aquarius positions for 10° until the Descendant where there are Taurus, Virgo and Capricorn positions for 10° until the Midheaven. The positions on the 9th harmonic dial do not necessarily correlate to the positions in the zodiac. For instance, my Uranus at 25° Aries 33' is ¹/₂° into the sixth degree of the Gemini, Libra, Aquarius section. The four sections consist of fire, water, air and earth signs.

Figure XX – 9th Harmonic Dial

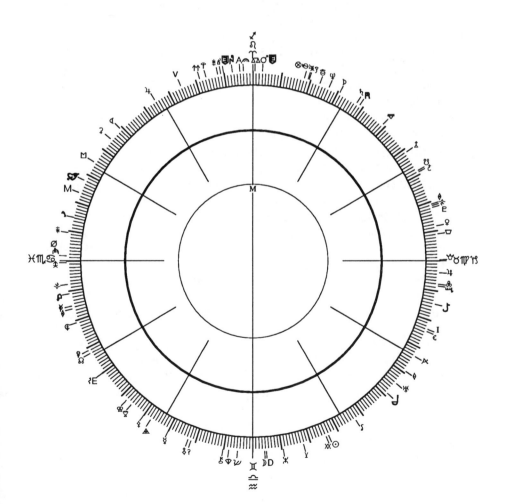

The 11th harmonic dial would have 33 divisions, even though $^{360}/_{11}$ = 32°43'38.1". The Aries positions would start at the Midheaven and proceed counterclockwise for 02$^3/_4$°. The Pisces positions would begin at that point and proceed for 02$^3/_4$° more ($^1/_4$°, 02°, $^1/_2$°). The Aquarius positions would come next ($^1/_2$°, 02°, $^1/_4$°). Then the Capricorn positions ($^3/_4$°, 02°); Sagittarius positions (02$^3/_4$°); Scorpio positions ($^1/_4$°, 02°, $^1/_2$°); Libra positions ($^1/_2$°, 02°, $^1/_4$°); Virgo positions ($^3/_4$°, 02°); Leo positions (02$^3/_4$°); Cancer positions ($^1/_4$°, 02°, $^1/_2$°); Gemini positions ($^1/_2$°, 02°, $^1/_4$°); Taurus positions ($^3/_4$°, 02°), and so back to Aries. The positions on the 11th harmonic dial do not necessarily correlate to the positions in the zodiac. For instance, my Uranus at 25° Aries 33' is $^1/_2$° into the first degree of the Cancer section. Also, there is some fudging because 33° is an integral approximation of the fractional 32°43'38.1" separation.

The 13th harmonic dial would have 28 divisions, even though $^{360}/_{13}$ = 27°41'32.3". The Aries positions would start at the Midheaven and proceed counterclockwise for 02$^1/_3$°. The Taurus positions would begin at that point and proceed for 02$^1/_3$° more ($^2/_3$°, 01°, $^2/_3$°). The Gemini positions would come next ($^1/_3$°,02°). Then the Cancer positions (02$^1/_3$°); Leo positions ($^2/_3$°, 01°, $^2/_3$°); Virgo positions ($^1/_3$°, 02°); Libra positions (02$^1/_3$°); Scorpio positions ($^2/_3$°, 01°, $^2/_3$°); Sagittarius positions ($^1/_3$°, 02°); Capricorn positions (02$^1/_3$°); Aquarius positions ($^2/_3$°, 01°, $^2/_3$°); Pisces positions ($^1/_3$°, 02°), and so back to Aries. The positions on the 13th harmonic dial do not necessarily correlate to the positions in the zodiac. For instance, my Uranus at 25° Aries 33' would be $^1/_2$° into the last degree of the Aquarius section. Also, there is some fudging because 28° is an integral approximation of the fractional 27°41'32.3" separation.

INCLUSION OF LOWER AND HIGHER HARMONICS

The harmonic dials described—4th, 5th, 6th, 7th, 9th, 11th and 13th—give you most of the lower harmonics and some of the higher ones as well. The conjunctions on the 4th harmonic dial show the bodies and points that are in that harmonic. The 4th harmonic includes the 1st and 2nd harmonic at the conjunctions and shows the 8th harmonic at the opposition, and the 16th, at the squares. (In other words, some of the bodies and points at a conjunction in the 4th harmonic could be from the 1st or 2nd harmonic, and the bodies and points at the opposition are those that will be included at the conjunction in the 8th harmonic, and the bodies and points at the squares are those that will be included at the conjunction in the 16th harmonic.) The other dials follow suit: considering the harmonic numbers, the harmonics that are divisible in the harmonic are included at the conjunctions; the harmonic at the opposition is double the harmonic at the conjunction; and the harmonic at the squares is double the harmonic at the opposition. The sequence for the other dials is as follows: 5th harmonic dial, 1st harmonic included—10th harmonic at opposition, 20th at squares; 6th harmonic dial, 1st, 2nd and 3rd included—12th at opposition, 24th at squares; 7th harmonic dial, 1st included—14th at opposition, 28th at squares; 9th harmonic dial, 1st and 3rd included—18th at opposition, 36th at squares; 11th harmonic dial, 1st included—22nd at opposition, 44th at squares; 13th harmonic dial, 1st included—26th at opposition, 52nd at squares. With these seven harmonic dials, the only one of the first 16 harmonics that isn't shown is the 15th harmonic.

ADVANTAGES OF HARMONIC DIALS

The harmonic dials have certain advantages over the harmonic graphs. One advantage is that the sub-harmonics can be seen at the opposition and squares. When considering a body or personal point, you would point the MC of the MC-IC line on the disk toward the body or personal point on the dial. The opposition will be at the IC of the MC-IC line, and the squares will be at the Ascendant-Descendant line. The division in which the body or point in question falls, and the adjacent divisions, I usually regard as being within orb. This orb is the same as my "within a degree" orb, when the harmonic has an integral separation (1st, 2nd, 3rd, 4th, 5th, 6th, 8th, 9th, 10th, 12th, 15th, etc.). This orb is very similar to my "within a degree" orb, when the harmonic has a fractional separation (7th, 11th, 13th, 14th, 16th, etc.). Of course, in the 13th harmonic, for instance, this orb encompasses $3/_{28}$ or $1/_9$ of the zodiac, and when the oppositions and squares on the dial are included this orb encompasses almost $1/_2$. Since the closest conjunctions on the dial are the most powerful, always work from the center of exactitude out. In the same way that aspects from one degree to the next in the magnified harmonic charts show what is especially highlighted in a particular harmonic, the conjunctions that are most exact (less than from one degree to the next) on the dials show what is especially highlighted in that harmonic. As for including the oppositions and squares, although they represent the sub-harmonics (which have a similar vibration to the harmonic), the oppositions and squares should be differentiated from each other and from the conjunctions. Although the sub-harmonics and the harmonic are combined on the dial, the different meanings of the sub-harmonics and the harmonic must be remembered.

A benefit derived from this first advantage is that on the 4th harmonic dial you can see the planetary pictures. The bodies and points that are equidistant from each other on the dial will form planetary pictures with each other—the body or point in the middle will be conjunct, opposite, square, semisquare or sesquiquadrate the midpoint of the other two. The planetary pictures are not necessarily shown on harmonic dials other than the 4th because the concept of planetary pictures is derived from the 4th harmonic, which includes the 1st (the conjunction) and the 2nd (the opposition) at the conjunctions and has the 8th (the semisquare and sesquiquadrate) at the oppositions. On the other harmonic dials, these bodies and points at the conjunctions may form planetary pictures, but the original chart will have to be checked to see if those pictures are formed. (For these other harmonics, I just take direct planetary pictures—conjunctions and oppositions to the midpoint.) To give an example, Pluto, the Moon and Jupiter are conjunct on my 7th harmonic dial. Pluto, which is conjunct the midpoint of the Moon and Jupiter ($1/_7$ from each), forms a planetary picture. The Moon, which is not conjunct, opposite, square, semisquare or sesquiquadrate the midpoint of Jupiter and Pluto, does not form a planetary picture; however, the Moon is 77°18' ($3/_{14}$) from their midpoint, equivalent to a semisquare or sesquiquadrate ($3/_8$) in the 4th harmonic.

On these other harmonic dials, those bodies and points that are equidistant at the conjunctions, whether they form planetary pictures or not, are connected according to the meaning of that particular harmonic and its sub-harmonics. Perhaps, these pictures could be called *harmonic pictures,* a phrase I've coined to distinguish them from planetary pictures. These harmonic pictures illustrate the fact that aspects other than the conjunction, opposition, square, semisquare and sesquiquadrate to a midpoint are descriptive. Just as the conjunction to a midpoint has an Arian quality; the opposition, a Taurean one; the square, a Cancerian; and the semi-square and sesquiquadrate, a Scorpionic quality, the other aspects have their harmonic correlations. The trine to a midpoint has a Geminian quality; the quintile and multiple, a Leonine quality; the sextile, a Virgoan one; the septile and multiples, a Libran one; the novile and multiples, a Sagittarian; the decile and multiple, a Capricornian; the undecile, an Aquarian; and the semisextile and multiple, a Piscean quality.

For instance, the Sun/Moon midpoint relates to the combined archetypes of conscious and unconscious, man and woman (husband and wife or father and mother). Consequently, a square to the Sun/Moon midpoint will describe these combined archetypes in terms of the 4th harmonic concerns—emotion, more nurturing parent and the foundation; a trine, in terms of the 3rd harmonic concerns—communication, siblings and "the lower mind"; a quintile or biquintile, in terms of the 5th harmonic concerns—creativity, children and romance; etc. See the first and second column of Table IV, Harmonic References, for other harmonics and other concerns. Of course, there are always individual references because of the zodiacal correlations in the individual chart, i.e., the 3rd harmonic correlates to 3, the third house, Gemini and Mercury. (The placement of the midpoint and factor aspecting it is also relevant.)

Another advantage of the harmonic dials is that there is more room on the dials for additional factors, such as the Uranian planets and asteroids. For the most part, my research on asteroids was conducted separately from my research on harmonic aspects. The asteroids Ceres, Pallas, Juno and Vesta had been included in the magnified harmonic charts. Later, the other asteroids which I was studying were added to these charts, but, as mentioned, the magnified chart is not the best device for seeing harmonic aspects. When the dials were constructed, the harmonic aspects of all these added asteroids were easily seen. The ideas which I had formulated about the meanings of the harmonics in my separate harmonic research, and the meanings of the asteroids in my separate asteroid research, were confirmed in this combination on the dials of both my harmonic and asteroid research. (The next chapter deals with that asteroid research.)

A third advantage of the harmonic dials is that you can solar arc any body or point by moving the pointer the number of degrees and minutes of the Solar Arc (the angular separation between the progressed and natal Sun). Of course, with the dial you can not have exactitude to the minute, but having seen the aspects visually, you can calculate them, if you wish, to the second. A comparison of two different Solar Arcs of the same body or point appropriate to a particular event is interesting.

For example, moving the pointer from my Descendant on my 7th harmonic dial 17°53'20" (the Solar Arc at the time of my first marriage) brings it to the conjunction of Neptune and Apollon. Neptune and Apollon are not in any 7th Harmonic Complex, Grand or otherwise, or even in a 7th harmonic aspect (considering the bodies and points outlined). They are conjunct in my natal chart, and their distance from the Descendant is approximately this Solar Arc. Thus, in all my harmonics at the time of my first marriage my solar-arced Descendant came to the conjunction of Neptune and Apollon, but the addition of other bodies and points in these other harmonics would modify the interpretation. One of the meanings of the combination of Neptune and Apollon, as given in *Rules for Planetary Pictures,* is "Deception on a large scale. Embezzlements. Dissolution on a large scale." [34] Though I believe that there can be positive expressions of Neptune-Apollon such as "Occult science," another meaning given by the author, in the case of my first marriage the negative expressions seem to apply. Moving the pointer from my Descendant on my 7th harmonic dial 23°13'38.6" (the Solar Arc at the time of my second marriage) brings it to the conjunction of Pluto, the Moon, Jupiter and the Part of Fortune, setting off my Grand 7th Harmonic Complex. See diagram III on page 130 and its interpreta- tion concerning compulsion, emotionality, expansiveness and good fortune on page 131. Chiron, the Vertex and Saturn are also in this 7th Harmonic Complex, and, though my solar-arced Descendant had progressed more than a degree beyond them by the time of the marriage, the effect of the Vertex and Saturn was still being counted with my "from one degree to the next" orb. In all my harmonics at the time of my second marriage, my solar-arced Descendant came to my Jupiter because their aspect was a conjunction. (The solar-arced Descendant was 13° Virgo 41'22", and my natal Jupiter is 13° Virgo 34'33.96".)

On the dial, harmonics can be read in combination with their sub-harmonics, if their different meanings are taken into account. Considering the 7th harmonic in combination with its sub-harmonics, the oppositions and squares to my solar-arced Descendant at the time of my first and second marriages are also related to the marriages. However, the oppositions (the 14th harmonic) will be more related to children in the marriage, with a coloration of the self and maternalism; and the squares (the 28th harmonic) will be more related to goals in the marriage, with a coloration of relationship and sex. (Instead, the oppositions could be related to romance in the marriage, with a coloration of the self and the home, while the squares could be related to the career in the marriage, with a coloration of one's own money and the partner's money.)

Though you can add the Solar Arc to all the bodies and points, when investigating marriages those bodies and points associated with the marriages should be especially noted. The asteroid with the name of my first husband is appropriate for my first marriage, and the asteroid with the name of my second husband is appropriate for my second marriage. Also, those bodies and points can be solar-arced in each harmonic and looked at in terms of that harmonic. Even when a solar-arced body or point comes to the same conjunction throughout the harmonics (as is the case with my solar-arced Descendant coming to my Neptune-Apollon at my first marriage, and to my Jupiter, at my second), the addition or subtraction of other bodies and points at the conjunction in the different harmonics is revealing.

At the time of other events, the Solar Arc of other bodies and points associated with those events would be emphasized. For instance, the Solar Arc of the fifth and eighth house cusp (I use Placidian houses) at the times of the birth of my children is descriptive. The Solar Arc of the asteroid with the name of my son is appropriate for his birth, and the Solar Arc of the asteroid with the name of my daughter is appropriate for her birth. The 5th and 8th harmonic would be the most related to the birth of children—the 5th because of its association with children, and the 8th because of its association with reproduction.

A fourth advantage of the harmonic dials is that you can take any event chart and look at it in relation to the harmonic dials to see which bodies and points in which harmonic aspects were activated by that event. (That event can, of course, be the birth of another person.) For example, in the transit chart of my second marriage, Kronos (which is associated with things above average and with the State— marriage is by the State) is at 29° Taurus 12' conjunct my natal Chiron at 28° Taurus 59' and my natal Moon at 00° Gemini 21'. My Chiron and Moon are in my Grand 7th Harmonic Complex, including Pluto, Vertex-Jupiter and Saturn-Part of Fortune—the same Grand 7th Harmonic Complex that was set off by my solar-arced Descendant at that time. (Note diagram III on page 130 and its interpretation on page 131.) Looking at the 7th harmonic dial, you can see that while the solar-arced Descendant was activating the Pluto, Moon, Jupiter, Part of Fortune sector of the Complex, the transiting Kronos was activating the Chiron, Saturn, Vertex sector. The transiting Kronos coming to my Chiron-Moon at the time of my second marriage occurs in every harmonic because it is a conjunction. Transiting Mars at 14° Virgo 26', conjunct my natal Jupiter, is activating my Grand 7th Harmonic Complex too. Because this aspect is a conjunction it occurs in every harmonic, along with the solar-arced Descendant. (On the dial the solar-arced Descendant is between transiting Kronos and transiting Mars.) As with the Solar Arc, the transits should be looked at in relation to each harmonic in terms of the meaning of that harmonic. The oppositions and squares on the dial will be relevant, but each according to its individual harmonic meaning.

Name Asteroid Experiment with Harmonic Dials

Having spoken of the advantages of the harmonic dials, I shall mention one of the experiments I have done with them. The MC of the MC-IC line on the disk was pointed toward the name asteroids of people on each harmonic dial to see how those people are involved with the meaning of that harmonic. In my harmonics, an asteroid with a name other than my name will show how that person is involved with the meaning of that harmonic in relation to me.

My first and second husband were among those whose name asteroids were examined. A comparison of the asteroid with the name of my first husband to the asteroid with the name of my second husband follows. Only those asteroids referred to thus far (six personal name asteroids and five other asteroids, which will be discussed more fully in the next chapter) are included. The addition of still other asteroids discussed in the next chapter tells more of the story, but this examination is sufficient to demonstrate a procedure that can be used to compare two or more people harmonically.

A graph was drawn, with the number of each harmonic on the left-hand side, and going from left to right two lines for each harmonic, with the top line for my first husband and the bottom line for my second (see Figure XXI). There are three divisions for the conjunctions, followed by three divisions for the oppositions, followed by three divisions for the squares to the right of the name asteroid, which are followed by three divisions for the squares to the left of the asteroid. The key to the glyphs of the asteroids and unknown planets (Uranian, etc.) is above the graph. (The asteroid chapter gives the names of the personal name asteroids and explains their correspondence to the names of the people.)

The MC of the MC-IC line of the disk was focused on the asteroid with the name of the particular husband on the harmonic dial. That asteroid was written on the graph in the middle division of the three divisions for the conjunctions. All bodies and points in the division with the name asteroid on the dial were written on the graph in their respective order, as were all bodies and points in the previous division and in the subsequent division. As with the conjunctions, the respective order of the bodies and points at the opposition and at the squares on the dial is followed on the graph. In the conjunctions on the graph, the number that is above each body or point (other than the name asteroid) gives the numerator of the harmonic fraction between the body or point and the name asteroid. For instance, in the 5th harmonic on the top line the glyph of the asteroid with the name of my first husband () is conjunct the glyph of Venus (♀) with a 1 above it, showing that Venus is quintile ($^1/_5$) the name asteroid; on the bottom line the glyph of the asteroid with the name of my second husband (⚸) is conjunct the glyph of the Midheaven (M) with a 2 above it, showing that the Midheaven is biquintile ($^2/_5$) the name asteroid. A sign at the left or right top of a division on the graph indicates that that division on the dial begins (left) or ends (right) with that zodiacal sign. If there are several signs on the dial division (such as cardinal, fixed or mutable signs for the 4th harmonic), the first sign (♈, ♉, or ♊) is listed on the graph division.

The bodies or points that are at the angles of the dial (the MC-IC line and the Ascendant-Descendant line, which is square to it) are outstanding. For instance, on my 7th harmonic dial, the asteroid with the name of my first husband is in the division before the MC, and the asteroid with the name of my second husband is in the division after the MC. The asteroids are on either side of the Aries Point, which is always at the MC of the dial. Outstanding for me in partnership will be someone with the name of my first husband and someone with the name of my second husband. My former husband's name asteroid being just before the Aries Point indicates some closure in our relationship, while my present husband's name asteroid being just after indicates a new beginning. In the division before the IC (♎) are the East Point and Uranus, with no bodies or points in the division after the IC. The two name asteroids being combined with the East Point and Uranus in the 14th

Figure XXI - Harmonic Dial Graph
Key to the Glyphs

🄴 First Husband & Son's Name Asteroid		⚵ Ceres	♃ Zeus
〔 Second Husband's Name Asteroid		⚴ Pallas	♈ Kronos
Ɲ My Name Asteroid		⚵ Juno	♅ Apollon
⚶ Asteroid with Name Equivalent to Mine		⚶ Vesta	♇ Admetos
♈ Daughter's Name Asteroid and		⚷ Chiron	⚸ Vulcanus
My Middle Name Asteroid		⚵ Cupido	⚹ Poseidon
🄴 Asteroid with Name Similar to		⚵ Hades	⊖ Transpluto
First Husband's, Son's & Daughter's			

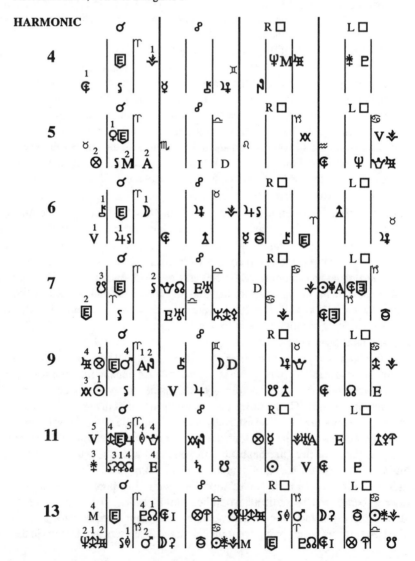

harmonic means that romance and children in the partnerships will be sudden and unusual. In the division before the Ascendant point (♑) are Hades and the asteroid with the name similar to my first husband's, my son's and my daughter's, with no bodies or points in the division after the Ascendant point. My two husbands' name asteroids being combined with Hades and this asteroid with a name similar to my children's in the 28th harmonic means that purpose in the partnerships relates to my children. Hades is another name for Pluto and so is associated with its concerns, among which are death and regeneration. In the division after the Descendant point (♋) is Vesta, with no bodies or points in the division before the Descendant point. The incorporation of Vesta at the 28th harmonic means that purpose in the partnerships relates to vested interests. Also, my natal Vesta is in the fifth house at 00° Cancer and so relates, for me, to children (fifth house) and the desire to fill the maternal void (00° Cancer). (The shading of the individual numbers of the harmonics would be interpreted.)

Having illustrated the importance of the angles of the dial, I shall compare my husbands' name asteroids throughout my harmonic dials, using the Harmonic Dial Graph. The bodies and points in the center division are listed first, since their aspects are the most exact. The inclusion of the adjacent divisions, particularly on the higher harmonic dials, pulls in many bodies and points. On these higher harmonic dials one could choose to use only the center division. However, since the name asteroids are treated equally, the more inclusive orb is valid in terms of the comparison. Each harmonic will be considered separately from its sub-harmonics, even though on the dial the sub-harmonics include the harmonics. There will be some comments on the combination of the harmonics with their sub-harmonics. The meanings given for the harmonics, bodies and points are just some possibilities. Others would be applicable.

4TH HARMONIC DIAL
In my 4th harmonic the asteroid with the name of my first husband is in aspect to Vesta ($^1/_4$—nurturing in reference to itself). As mentioned, my Vesta is in the fifth house and so has much to do with children. This husband's name asteroid is just before the Aries point (♈), and Vesta, just after—closure for one and a new beginning for the other. The asteroid with the name of my second husband is in aspect to Hades ($^1/_4$), and Hades has a Plutonian, as well as a karmic or past-life connotation.

At the opposition, or 8th harmonic (sex, regeneration, and the partner's values), with my first husband there is nothing, and with my second, there are Chiron, Mercury and Cupido. Mercury is duality, and this is my second marriage. Also, my Mercury rules my Sun, Moon, Venus, fourth and fifth house cusps, and South Node, Vertex and planets in my seventh house. Chiron is the foster parent, or stepparent, and Cupido is marriage and family. Cupido is just before the mutable section (♊) and so is at the end of the fixed, emphasizing the boundary between these two modes.

At the squares (or 16th harmonic), with my first husband there are Neptune, the Midheaven, Apollon, Juno and Pluto. The 16th harmonic corresponds to marriage but has a coloration of the self and service. Juno and Pluto joined can be a compulsive marriage; with Neptune, the Midheaven and Apollon added, there can be much idealism or deception. At the squares, with my second husband there is the asteroid with my name. When the harmonic (4th) is combined with its sub-harmonic (16th), our name asteroids are combined in this 16th harmonic that corresponds to a marriage wherein the self is dedicated to service.

5TH HARMONIC DIAL

In my 5th harmonic the asteroid with the name of my first husband is in aspect to Venus ($^1/_5$—creativity, which includes children, in reference to itself), and our son (whose name is the same as his father's) is very Venusian, with his Venus exactly opposite his Ascendant. This name asteroid is still before the Aries Point (♈), but now with Venus as well. The asteroid with the name of my second husband is in aspect to the Midheaven, Part of Fortune and Ascendant (all $^2/_5$—creativity in reference to love, or the daughter). Our daughter is the product of the creativity of our relationship. Purpose (Midheaven), Fortune (the Part of) and persona (Ascendant) are connected with this creativity. The Part of Fortune is at the beginning of the Taurus section (♉), reiterating the emphasis on love or the daughter (money and values too).

At the opposition, or 10th harmonic (career, purpose and paternalism), with my first husband there is nothing, and with my second, there are the IC and Descendant—points of the home or foundation, and the partner.

At the squares (20th harmonic), with my first husband there are the Antivertex, the Vertex and Vesta. The 20th harmonic corresponds to money and relationship, with the power of the void. The Antivertex and Vertex have an air of fatedness, and Vesta is vested interests, which refers to this husband's making money from investments. Vesta for me also refers to children. The Antivertex is at the beginning of the Capricorn section (♑), and the Vertex and Vesta are at the beginning of the Cancer section (♋), emphasizing these two signs of career and home, father and mother. At the squares, with my second husband there are Neptune, Hades, our daughter's name asteroid (which is also my middle name asteroid) and Apollon. Neptune, Hades and Apollon refer to my second husband's making money from the music business, primarily now from the musical theatre. Neptune relates to music; Hades, to jazz; and Apollon, to business, but also to music and theatre since Apollo was the patron of music and the god of the sun. Our daughter (her name asteroid in a sub-harmonic of the harmonic of children and entertainment) is also involved in show business. Hades is at the beginning of the Aquarius section (♒), emphasizing innovation in the jazz.

6TH HARMONIC DIAL

In my 6th harmonic the asteroid with the name of my first husband is in aspect to Chiron and the Moon ($^1/_6$—work in reference to itself), and his work when he was married to me was as a teacher, another meaning of Chiron. Also, my Moon is at 00° Gemini, and he was involved with lower education (Gemini). His name asteroid is still before the Aries Point (♈), with the Moon after it. The asteroid with the name of my second husband is in aspect to Jupiter and the Vertex ($^1/_6$), and he has governing positions in his work. My Jupiter is at 13° Virgo, and the governing positions are involved with the employment of others (Virgo).

At the opposition, or 12th harmonic (nebulousness and idealism), with my first husband there are Cupido and Vesta—marriage and vested interests. There was idealism, but in the end both the marriage and the vested interests dissolved. Cupido is at the end of the positive section, and Vesta is at the beginning of the negative (♉), emphasizing the boundary between these polarities. At the opposition, with my second husband there are Vulcanus and Hades, and in this case the nebulousness of the 12th harmonic may relate to music. Hades in relation to my present husband has already been associated with music because of its aspect to Neptune in my 20th harmonic, and Vulcanus is associated with power.

At the squares (24th harmonic), with my first husband there are Jupiter, my second husband's name asteroid and Vulcanus. The 24th harmonic corresponds to service but has a coloration of values and nurturing. Also, 24 was the age at which I married my second husband, an expansive (Jupiter) powerful (Vulcanus) person and brought him into contact with my first husband and my son of the same name. At the squares, with my second husband there are Chiron, Mercury, Transpluto, my first husband's name asteroid and Cupido. At these squares, the previous message of the contact between my first husband/son and second husband is repeated, with the additional information that this contact will be accomplished through marriage (Cupido) in which my second husband will be a stepfather (Chiron). (Chiron was interpreted in the 6th harmonic as the teacher, but the 24th harmonic has the coloration of values and nurturing, calling to mind the stepfather.) Transpluto adds the force of a Super-Pluto, and Mercury may refer to duality or to me—a double Gemini. The Chiron, Mercury and Cupido are from my 8th harmonic, but now with the addition of Transpluto and the asteroid of my first husband/son. (The asteroid of my first husband/son first combines with the asteroid of my second husband in my 7th harmonic.) Of course, Jupiter and the Vertex are included from my 6th harmonic; Hades, originally from my fourth; and Vulcanus, from my 12th. What was foreshadowed in previous harmonics all comes together in my 24th, with my marriage to my present husband at the age of 24. As always, the asteroid of my former husband is just before the Aries Point (♈). Cupido is just before the negative section (♉) and so is at the end of the positive, emphasizing the boundary between these two polarities.

7TH HARMONIC DIAL

In my 7th harmonic the asteroid with the name of my former husband is in aspect to the South Node ($^3/_7$—partnership in reference to communication) and in aspect to the asteroid with the name of my present husband ($^2/_7$—partnership in reference to values). The asteroid with the name of my present husband is only in aspect to the asteroid with the name of my former husband ($^2/_7$). As explained, my first husband's asteroid is just before the Aries Point (♈), and my second husband's asteroid is just after. This is the only harmonic dial on the graph where these two name asteroids are conjunct. (The 24th harmonic is not on a separate harmonic dial.) It was through my marriages (my 7th harmonic) that my first husband/son and second husband were bound in close association (South Node). (The analysis on pages 159 and 161 of bodies and points at the angles of my 7th harmonic dial [7th, 14th and 28th harmonics] is somewhat different because that analysis only deals with the division immediately before and after the angles.)

At the opposition (14th harmonic), with my first husband there are the East Point, Uranus, my daughter's first name/my middle name asteroid, and the North Node. The 14th harmonic corresponds to romance and children but has a coloration of the self and maternalism. The East Point, Uranus and the North Node being combined could mean that the self (East Point) will be involved in sudden and unusual (Uranus) close connections (North Node). The name asteroid would further personalize this combination. At the opposition, with my second husband there are the East Point, Uranus, Poseidon, Zeus and Pallas. The elimination of the name asteroid and the North Node and the addition of Poseidon, Zeus and Pallas may relate to the continuance of the second marriage. The self (East Point) will still be involved with the sudden and unusual (Uranus), but the personal close connections (name asteroid and North Node) will not. Poseidon is a Super-Neptune, usually expressing the nebulousness and idealism of Neptune in a more positive manner, and Zeus is associated with creativity and procreation. Most importantly, Pallas adds a perceptive, judicial quality. With both my former and present husband, the East Point and Uranus are just before the Libra section (♎), which is the end of the Pisces section, emphasizing the boundary between these two signs (nebulousness vs. partnership).

At the squares (28th harmonic), with my first husband there are Hades, the asteroid with a name similar to his (as well as to my son's and daughter's), the Sun, Admetos, the Ascendant, the Descendant and Vesta. The 28th harmonic corresponds to paternalism and limitation but has a coloration of one's own and the partner's values and money. This combination with my ex-husband may refer to the stoppage (Admetos) of our marriage (Ascendant-Descendant), and his separation from his son (Sun). (Admetos can be ending or never-ending. Of course, analysing after the fact helps.) The bringing together of my first husband's/son's name asteroid with my second husband's, my daughter's, and this asteroid with a name similar to my first husband's/son's and daughter's on my 7th harmonic dial describes the fact that through the visitation rights of my ex-husband, he and my present husband and son from my first marriage and daughter from my second marriage were all connected. As for Hades, it can refer to something already "used," which a child from a previous marriage is. Vesta being involved in my 28th harmonic is also appropriate because there was always a problem concerning child-support money. At the squares, with my second husband there are Vesta, Hades, the similar name asteroid and Transpluto. The deletion of the Sun, Admetos and the Ascendant may be helpful to our relationship. The addition of Transpluto may not be helpful in its obsessiveness but may be in its transformative powers. With both my former and present husband, Hades and the similar name asteroid are just before the Capricorn section (♑), which is the end of the Gemini section, emphasizing the boundary between these two signs (duality vs. limitation). Also, Vesta is at the beginning of the Cancer section (♋), emphasizing nurturing.

9TH HARMONIC DIAL

In my 9th harmonic the asteroid with the name of my first husband is in aspect to Mars and Apollon ($^4/_9$—completion in reference to maternalism), and not only is he a very Martian person, but what completion (9th harmonic) he brought me was through our son (Mars). My first husband's asteroid is also in aspect to the Part of Fortune and Ascendant ($^1/_9$—completion in reference to itself). Another aspect from his name asteroid is to the asteroid with my name ($^2/_9$—completion in reference to values), and one of the main issues between us was the difference in our values. The Part of Fortune, Ascendant, and my name asteroid being connected with my first husband's reflects the fact that my completion (my name asteroid in the 9th harmonic) has been through our son (his name asteroid is the same as his father's). My Fortune (the Part of) and persona (Ascendant) are involved in this completion. My ex-husband's name asteroid and the Mars are before the Aries Point (♈), and the Ascendant and my name asteroid are after it. Through our divorce, not only was there closure with the anger of this husband, but there was a new beginning for myself. The asteroid with the name of my second husband is in aspect to the Sun ($^1/_9$) and in aspect to the Antivertex ($^3/_9$—completion in reference to communication—or $^1/_3$—communication in reference to itself). Again, there is an allusion to completion through children—this time with the general symbol for children, the Sun. Also, this husband (his name asteroid) brought me a Leo (Sun) daughter. The Antivertex adds a fated quality.

At the opposition (18th harmonic), with my first husband there are Chiron, the Moon and the Descendant. The 18th harmonic corresponds to completion but has a coloration of the self and regeneration. Also, 18 was the age at which I married my first husband, which is indicated by the Descendant (marriage partner) and Moon (he is a Cancerian). The Chiron may relate to the fact that my former husband was a teacher, as was Chiron. Chiron was also a centaur, combining the lower and higher nature of man. The Moon and Descendant are at the beginning of the air section (♊), emphasizing this element. At the opposition, with my second husband there are Jupiter and the Vertex, mirroring a fated (Vertex) expansiveness and completion (Jupiter) with him.

At the squares (36th harmonic), with my first husband there are Cupido, my daughter's first name/my middle name asteroid, Zeus and Vesta. The 36th harmonic corresponds to completion but has a coloration of communication and service. Again, completion is through marriage and family (Cupido) and procreation and creativity (Zeus). Added to the need for completion through communication and service is the dedication of the Vestal Virgins (Vesta). Cupido is at the end of the air section, and my daughter's first name/my middle name asteroid is at the beginning of the earth section (♉), emphasizing the boundary between these two elements. Zeus and Vesta are at the beginning of the water section (♋), emphasizing this element. At the squares, with my second husband there are the South Node,

Vulcanus, the North Node, Hades and the East Point. In reference to him, completion, with a coloration of communication and service, is through the power (Vulcanus) of the self (East Point) vis-a-vis close relationships (the Nodes) that have a karmic or past-life connotation (Hades).

11TH HARMONIC DIAL

In my 11th harmonic the asteroid with the name of my first husband is in aspect to Jupiter and the Vertex ($^5/_{11}$—hopes and wishes in reference to children). My first husband's asteroid is also in aspect to Zeus, the asteroid with a name equivalent to mine, and my middle name asteroid ($^4/_{11}$—hopes and wishes in reference to maternalism). My middle-name asteroid is also my daughter's first-name asteroid, but with its exact conjunction to an asteroid with a name equivalent to my first name, the reference seems to be to me. This combination with my former husband relates to our hopes and wishes being fulfilled by the fated (Vertex) procreation (Zeus) of our son (the name asteroid of my first husband/son and two name asteroids of mine). Jupiter and Zeus (the Greek equivalent of Jupiter) may be particularly descriptive of our son, since he is a Sagittarian. However, since this husband is very expansive regarding 11th harmonic concerns such as nonconformity, the Jupiter and Zeus are also descriptive of him. Zeus, the husband/son name asteroid, and Jupiter are just before the Aries Point (Υ), and my two name asteroids are just after. The asteroid with the name of my second husband is in aspect to Ceres and Juno ($^3/_{11}$—hopes and wishes in reference to communication or a Gemini). My second husband's asteroid is also in aspect to Venus ($^1/_{11}$—hopes and wishes in reference to "itself"—in other words, the basic 11th harmonic) and in aspect to the North Node and East Point ($^4/_{11}$—hopes and wishes in reference to maternalism). This combination with my present husband relates to our hopes and wishes being fulfilled by his marriage (Juno) to me, a double Gemini and the mother (Ceres) of his stepchild (11th harmonic). Love (Venus), close connections (North Node) and the self (East Point) are involved in this fulfillment.

At the opposition (22nd harmonic), with my first husband there are the Antivertex and my name asteroid. The 22nd harmonic corresponds to maternalism but has a double coloration of love, values or money. The combination of our name asteroids and the Antivertex in a harmonic corresponding to maternalism indicates a fated connection between us in this regard. At the opposition, with my second husband there are Saturn and the South Node. In relation to maternalism (22nd harmonic), there is between us a strong sense of responsibility (Saturn) regarding close connections from the past (South Node).

At the squares (44th harmonic), with my first husband there are Mercury, the Part of Fortune, Vesta, Uranus, the Ascendant, the East Point, Vulcanus, Pallas and Kronos. The 44th harmonic corresponds to transformation but has a double coloration of the endings of all matters. This combination of bodies and points may relate to our final transformation through divorce (Uranus). In the case of my present husband's name asteroid in my 14th harmonic, I considered the addition of Pallas, accompanied by Poseidon and Zeus, as bringing a perceptive, judicial quality to Uranus and the East Point; but in the case of my former husband's name asteroid in my 44th harmonic, I am considering the addition of Pallas, accompanied by Vulcanus and Kronos, as bringing to Uranus and the East Point the judicial decree (see Uranian Planet Key Words). Mercury, the Part of Fortune, Vesta and the Ascendant being included is appropriate because Mercury relates to documents (the divorce papers), Vesta relates to vested interests (with which divorce papers deal), and the Part of Fortune is fortunate, while the Ascendant is half of the marriage axis. At the squares, with my second husband there are the Sun, Vertex, Pluto and Hades, indicating that our final transformation is through children (Sun) and regeneration (Pluto). This transformation would be fated (Vertex) and karmic (Hades).

13TH HARMONIC DIAL

In my 13th harmonic the asteroid with the name of my first husband is in aspect to the Midheaven and Pluto ($^4/_{13}$—the final outcome in reference to maternalism) and in aspect to the North Node ($^1/_{13}$—the final outcome in reference to itself). Transformation (Pluto) regarding paternalism (Midheaven) in close relationships (North Node) was the final outcome. In this final outcome the self and communication (13th harmonic) were very much involved. My first husband's name asteroid is just before the Aries Point (Υ), and Pluto and the North Node are just after. The asteroid with the name of my second husband is in aspect to the asteroid with a name equivalent to mine, and Zeus ($^1/_{13}$—the final outcome in reference to itself) and in aspect to Neptune, Apollon and Mars ($^2/_{13}$—the final outcome in reference to values). This combination of the asteroid with the name of my second husband and the asteroid with a name equivalent to mine indicates that in the final outcome we will most likely be together. Creativity (Zeus), idealistic (Neptune) and radiant (Apollon) energy (Mars) conspire toward this end. My present husband's name asteroid and mine are at the end of the Sagittarius section, and Mars is at the beginning of the Capricorn section ($\VS$), emphasizing the boundary between these two signs—expansion vs. contraction.

At the opposition (26th harmonic), with my first husband there are the Part of Fortune, Kronos, Hades, the IC and the South Node. The 26th harmonic corresponds to transformation but has a coloration of values and service. Fortune (the Part of), authority (Kronos), past lives (Hades), the foundation (IC) and close connections from the past (South Node) all played their part in this transformation. The Part of Fortune and Kronos are at the end of the Virgo section, and the South Node is at the beginning of the Libra section ($\Libra$), emphasizing the boundary between these two signs—service vs. partnership. At the opposition, with my second husband there are Transpluto, the Moon, Ceres, the Sun, Juno and Vesta. Transpluto is a Super-Pluto and so relates to reproduction; both the Moon and Ceres are symbols of nurturing; the Sun, of children; Juno, of marriage; and Vesta, of vested interests (to me a vested interest in children, since my Vesta is in the fifth house). 26 was my age at the birth of the daughter of this husband and myself, and that birth certainly resulted in a transformation in our relationship. Transpluto is at the end of the Gemini section, and the Sun, Juno and Vesta are at the beginning of the Cancer section ($\Cancer$), emphasizing the boundary between these two signs—duality vs. nurturing.

At the squares (52nd harmonic), with my first husband there are the asteroid with the name of my second husband, the asteroid with a name equivalent to mine, Neptune, Zeus, Apollon, Mars, Transpluto, the Moon, Ceres, the Sun, Juno and Vesta. At the squares, with my second husband there are the asteroid with the name of my first husband/son, the Midheaven, Pluto, the North Node, the Part of Fortune, Kronos, Hades, the IC and the South Node. Considering each harmonic separately as we have been doing, my 52nd harmonic with my former husband is the same as my 13th and 26th harmonic with my present husband, while my 52nd harmonic with my present husband is the same as my 13th and 26th harmonic with my former husband. This duplication occurs, even if you only consider the center division of the graph. (See the Harmonic Dial Graph.) You can look at the interpretations of the bodies and points and the boundaries between the signs for my 13th and 26th harmonic and apply them to my 52nd. The 52nd harmonic corresponds to marriage but has a coloration of children and values. It is a sub-harmonic of the harmonic of the final outcome. Could these combinations be saying that marriage related to children and values with my first husband will be, in the final outcome, marriage related to children and values with my second husband? It could possibly be the reverse, but when you put the pointer on my former husband's name asteroid, at my 52nd harmonic the asteroid with the name of my present husband is conjunct the asteroid with the name equivalent to mine, and Juno (a symbol for marriage) completes the picture. As mentioned, the two marriages are interrelated because of the bringing of the son from the first marriage into the second. Of course, since my son's name is the same as his father's, these combinations are also saying that my son, in the final outcome, will be included in the marriage of my second husband and myself.

CONCLUSION

The comparison of my husbands' name asteroids on seven harmonic dials (4-13) having been completed, a few comments are in order. As mentioned, you might choose to use only the center division on the higher harmonic dials, since their harmonics encompass more bodies and points. However, the influence of the bodies and points in the adjoining divisions, though not as intense, is still felt. In the higher harmonics there is an overlapping of harmonics. The dial is showing a more generalized view of the combination of harmonics—now for a more particular one. The relationship between these two name asteroids—the relationship out of which this comparison has come—should be explored.

The asteroid with the name of my first husband is 103°57'29" from the asteroid with the name of my second husband. The principle of the angular separation could be analyzed, but what is the harmonic into which this separation fits? The two name asteroids are in 7th harmonic aspect to each other ($^2/_7$—marriage in reference to values) and are conjunct on the 7th harmonic dial, but 01°06'04" from exactitude. They are in even closer aspect in the 52nd harmonic ($^{15}/_{52}$—marriage [with a coloration of children and values] in reference to service [with a coloration of the self and children]) only 00°06'43" from exactitude. (They are square on the 13th harmonic dial.) The harmonic that is most exact is the 142nd ($^{41}/_{142}$—marriage [with a coloration of the self, maternalism and values] in reference to children [with a coloration of the self and maternalism]) only 00°00'52" from exactitude.

Since these name asteroids are not in an angular separation where every minute has its own basic harmonic, the angular separation of these name asteroids relates to both specific and general harmonics. While the 142nd harmonic, being most exact, is most specific; the 7th, being one of the first 12 harmonics, takes precedence. The 52nd is another variation on the same theme. All three harmonics are relevant.

Though harmonics should be examined separately, their commingling can not be disregarded. With harmonics there are many voices in counterpoint. There are reverberations. New notes are sounded, while the old ones are still resounding—which brings us to music.

Harmonics in Music

At an NCGR banquet in May of 1982 I heard Neil Michelsen speak about the translation of his astrological chart into music by Gerald Jay Markoe, a composer and astrologer. The idea of a connection between astrology and music had long intrigued me, so I ordered the musical translation of the birth chart of my husband, myself and our daughter and of the composite chart of my husband and myself. Gerald said that for the purposes of research he would translate each birth chart into three versions—one version played on a koto (13-string Japanese harp), and two versions on a piano, with one of the two limited to only two octaves. He also agreed to add the four asteroids Ceres, Pallas, Juno and Vesta in the second half of the third version, though he had never used asteroids and was afraid they would obscure the music. It was decided that the nine musical natal charts on cassette would be played for my husband, myself and our daughter to see if we could identify whose chart was being played and if we preferred one version to another.

MUSICAL EXPERIMENT

On May 31, 1982 at 04:20 P.M. EDT in Forest Hills, New York, the experiment was begun. My husband, our daughter and I were each handed a large piece of paper on which to write our reactions to each version and our judgment as to whose chart was being played. Secrecy was necessary, so no one would be influenced by the judgment of the others. The charts in the koto version were played first. To give an example of reactions, on my sheet for the first musical chart in this first version I wrote, "some notes dissonant—some very high—oriental sounding—some very low" and my husband's name; for the second musical chart I wrote, "happier sounding—more light-hearted—funny high notes—even higher notes—some dissonance" and my daughter's name; for the third musical chart I wrote, "heavier sounding—more intense" and my own name. The charts in the full keyboard piano version were played next, and again we wrote our reactions and judgments. The charts in the two-octave piano version were played last, and they had three parts— the musical chart without asteroids, with asteroids alone, and with planets and asteroids combined. This time we wrote our reactions, not only to the three musical charts, but to the three parts of each chart and our judgments.

We all felt that the koto version of the charts was most descriptive. The piano rounds off the notes to the well-tempered scale, while the koto gives the exact notes. We all thought that in the two-octave piano version the third part, with the planets and asteroids combined, was the most interesting. Gerald agreed as well that his fear the asteroids would obscure the music was unfounded.

Just before we began the experiment, Gerald had told us that in his experience a person likes his own music best. While the first two charts in the koto version were being played, I started to wonder if this experiment was worthwhile. The music was pleasant but left me cold. These were the charts which I identified as my husband's and my daughter's. When the third chart was played, I thought, "Now this is music," and knew it was mine. I was able to distinguish my chart, my husband's, and my daughter's in all three versions. On the other hand, my husband confused his chart with mine in all three versions. He liked his music best every time but said to himself, "It's so beautiful, it must be Nona's." For instance, on his sheet for the first musical chart in this first version he wrote, "tonal—peace—Nona—Eternal." The chart was his, but his Sun is in the seventh house, so he gave his identity to me. He did discern our daughter's chart in the two-octave piano version. Our daughter recognized her own chart in the koto version, which is the most distinctive. Not only did she like her music best, but from the first note she knew it was hers. She said it was like music she used to improvise on the piano—highs and lows, frenetic and peaceful—and she recognized it on a deep level. She also correctly identified me in the piano version, and her father in the two-octave piano version.

After the nine natal charts had been played and their identities revealed, the composite chart of my husband and myself was played. We all agreed that it sounded more harmonious than the individual charts of my husband and myself. The expression "we could make such beautiful music together" may be more literal than has been thought.

CORRELATIONS BETWEEN MUSICAL AND ASTROLOGICAL HARMONICS

After our experiment was completed, Gerald gave me the sheet music of the charts and explained the following correlations between the musical, and the astrological, harmonics. A vibrating string on a guitar, koto or other stringed instrument is comparable to the 360° of the chart. If you lightly touch the middle of the string, the 2nd harmonic, which is the loudest, is produced. If you touch the string at a point $1/3$ of its length, the 3rd harmonic, which is the next loudest, is produced. As the harmonic number becomes higher, the sound becomes progressively softer, with the exception of the 11th and 13th harmonic, which are much softer than expected. Above the 16th harmonic, the human ear can not hear the harmonics. In addition to some harmonics being softer than others, some are more dissonant than others. The 7th harmonic has some dissonance and some consonance. The 11th and 13th harmonic are dissonant. But as Gerald stated, music and a chart without some dissonance would be boring.

He discussed the angular separations between the Ascendant and the planets, Midheaven and North Node in the three birth charts. He said that those bodies and points whose angular separations from the Ascendant are close to a lower harmonic would be expressed, while those that are not, would be blocked. (Your Ascendant is what you show to the world.) For example, the angular separation between my Ascendant and my Sun is 102°07'6.6", which is close to the 7th harmonic, while the angular separation between my Ascendant and my Moon is 99°53'22.2", which is not close to one of the lower harmonics. As a result, my Sun would be expressed, but my Moon would be a blocked and dissonant spot which could hardly be heard. Gerald attributed a number from 1-10 to the angular separations between the Ascendant and the planets, Midheaven and North Node in the three birth charts. The attribution of strength or expression was based on the particular harmonic and the closeness of the angular separation to it. Points from 7-10 were considered strong, and points from 1-4 were considered weak, with 5 and 6, average.

When our scores were compared, for the most part the expression of my present husband's planets and points and the expression of mine were complementary. My Sun, Mercury, Mars and Saturn are expressed strongly, while his are not. (In fact, his Mars and Saturn have some of his lowest scores.) His Moon and Uranus are expressed strongly, while mine are not. (In fact, my Uranus has my lowest score, and Gerald characterized my Moon as a "blocked spot.") For both of us, Pluto, the Midheaven and North Node are expressed strongly.

Wondering if the free-flowing or blocked expression of a quality might be relevant to the choice of a partner, I looked at my former husband's chart. Like my present husband and unlike me, his Moon and Uranus are expressed strongly, while his Sun is not. Again, those planets which are most blocked in me—the Moon and Uranus—would have been freely expressed by my partner; and the Sun, which is blocked in him, would have been freely expressed by me. Unlike my present husband and me, his Venus, Jupiter and Neptune are expressed strongly, and his Pluto, Midheaven and North Node are not. His free expression of Venus, Jupiter and Neptune and my blocked expression of Jupiter and average expression of Venus and Neptune are complementary. Of course, his free expression of Neptune might have contributed to deception. The fact that my Pluto, Midheaven and North Node are expressed freely could have compensated for the fact that my ex-husband's are not. However I think my present husband's and my mutual expression of Pluto, Midheaven and North Node contributes to the longevity of our partnership—there is compulsive (Pluto) purpose (Midheaven) in our close relationships (Node). Finally, unlike my present husband, but like me, the Mercury, Mars and Saturn of my ex-husband are expressed strongly. This free expression of Mercury, Mars and Saturn on both our parts is quite descriptive because we argued a lot (Mercury, Mars), which resulted in our separation (Saturn).

Harmonic musical translation of charts is at its inception. More experiments should be conducted to see if people can discriminate between charts. Feedback as to the reasons for their choices should accompany those choices, since, as demonstrated in the case of my husband and daughter, the score is not the only relevant factor. Gerald's hypothesis that if the angular separation between a body or point and the Ascendant is in one of the lower harmonics, the quality of that body or point is strongly expressed must be tested further. An objective system of attributing strength or expression to the angular separations should be devised for this purpose. (Of course, the decision as to whether the factor is strongly expressed in the life is subjective.) In hopes of finding such a system, Gerald suggested that the Astrodynes[35] for the three charts that we had been analyzing be checked to see if there were an equivalence between his quantifying of power and theirs. The Astrodynes were ordered, but there wasn't an equivalence, since their evaluation of aspect power is based not only on closeness of aspect, but on sign and house placement. Also, the Astrodynes only include some of the harmonic aspects. If an objective system were devised, more than Gerald's hypothesis, which just relates to the Ascendant, could be tested. Some people, who do not express the energy of a particular planet through their Ascendants, may through their Midheavens, Suns, Moons, etc. This possibility could be tested too. My other thought that the strength of the expression may effect the choice of a partner would also have to be examined further.

For a number of years Astro offered Gerald Markoe's Astromusical Charts on cassette. The possible versions were piano, koto, or synthesizer interfaced with a computer. In addition to angular separations from the Ascendant to the planets, Midheaven and North Node, there were geocentric distances from the Earth to the planets. There could also be angular separations from any one of the planets, Midheaven or North Node to all the other factors. (Asteroids could be added too.) Options included a personal astrology chart to music, the astrology charts to music of ten famous and infamous people and the musical correlations of planets, houses, signs and aspects.

My minor investigation, which has been of the literal translation of harmonics in aspects into harmonics in music, has led me to believe that there should be a major investigation of this translation. Certainly, these options afford an opportunity for such an investigation, and the musical analysis of charts, individually and synastrically, could prove to be extremely helpful in astrological interpretation.

Harmonic Distributions

Finally, though my harmonic research has been on magnification, and harmonic aspects (whether in music or not), rather than on harmonic distributions characteristic of particular groups, I do have some thoughts on the latter.

A tendency for there to be a 4th harmonic distribution of planets characteristic of prominent professionals has been shown in Michel and Francoise Gauquelin's collection of prominent writers, athletes, actors and scientists. It occurred to me that this 4th harmonic tendency could relate to the Moon's connection with the public. The Gauquelins gathered their collection from reference books, so their professionals have to be prominent. To be prominent one must be connected with the public, i.e., one is known by the public. As has been stated, the square (4th harmonic) is associated with the fourth house, Cancer and the Moon, and the Moon is associated with the public. The Gauquelins' more recent research indicates that these planetary distributions are reflective of the personality traits, rather than the professions, of their prominent people. Whether the distributions are reflective of the personality traits or the professions, the prominence remains and, hence, the association with the Moon.

As for John Addey's study of 972 nonagenarians, I have the following thoughts. Addey considered the aspects of the Sun to Saturn and found a characteristic distribution of "3 x 36 or the 108th harmonic, three waves in each 10°, in other words, the Indian Navamsa measure of $3^1/_3°$."[36] (The Indian use of $3^1/_3°$, which is one-ninth of 30°, is equivalent to the Western use of 40°, which is one-ninth of 360°.) The same distribution occurs with the Sun to Mars, Jupiter and Uranus—the only other planets Addey investigated in his study. He accounts for this distribution by writing, "The number nine (the Navamsa measure being one-ninth part of a sign) is distinctively connected with the completion of a cycle."[37] Though this explanation may be valid, I also think the explanation is that the experimental group, nonagenarians, had all "achieved their 90th year";[38] and the number 9 is "connected" with 90, since 90 is 9, with the addition of the void and its power. In this case, 9 stands for 90, as it were. Though the meaning of a number is significant, I have found the *association* of numbers is significant in itself.

Addey also writes of the Venus-Saturn separation in relation to marriage. His study of 116 jockeys whose dates of birth and marriage are given in *The Directory of the Turf* (1970 edition) is cited. He states that "There are points where the Venus-Saturn relationship is strongly associated with marriage, for example, when Venus is separating by about $04^1/_2°$ from, or applying by 07° to, a conventional Saturn aspect...."[39] The conventional aspects he refers to are the twelve 30° aspects—conjunction, semisextile, sextile, square, etc., and they are from natal Saturn to progressed Venus.

Though these separations are not necessarily applicable to people from different samples, I looked to see where my progressed Venus had been in relation to my natal Saturn at my two marriages. At the time of my first marriage my progressed Venus was at 04° Cancer 07'14.16", 137°44'51" from my natal Saturn at 16° Aquarius 22'22.44". Venus was not separating by about $04^1/_2°$ from, or applying by 07° to, a conventional Saturn aspect. It was separating from a sesquiquadrate to Saturn by about $02^3/_4°$. However, more importantly, it was separating from a 21st harmonic aspect to Saturn ($^8/_{21}$, which had been exact at 03° Cancer 30'56.4") and was applying to a 13th harmonic aspect to Saturn ($^5/_{13}$, which would be exact at 04° Cancer 50'3.44"). $^8/_{21}$ is communication in reference to reproduction. $^5/_{13}$ is maternalism in reference to children. These harmonics take precedence in the hierarchy of the harmonics, but the meaning of the closest harmonic is more specific (see pages 110-11). The closest harmonic (seconds from exactitude) at the time of marriage was the 115th ($^{44}/_{115}$), which is the harmonic for the separation 137°44'21". $^{44}/_{115}$ is marriage (7) in reference to reproduction (8). At the time of my second marriage my progressed Venus was at 10° Cancer 57'58.9", 144°35'36" from my natal Saturn. Venus was not separating by about $04^1/_2°$ from, or applying by 07° to, a conventional Saturn aspect. It was applying to a quincunx to Saturn by about $05^1/_2°$. However, more importantly, it was separating from a 5th harmonic aspect to Saturn ($^2/_5$, which had been exact at 10° Cancer 22'22.44"). $^2/_5$ is children in reference to love or values. This harmonic takes precedence in the hierarchy of the harmonics, but the meaning of the closest harmonic is more specific. The closest harmonic (seconds from exactitude) at the time of marriage was the 122nd ($^{49}/_{122}$), which is the harmonic for the separation 144°35'25". $^{49}/_{122}$ is children (5) in reference to maternalism (4). Colorations would be given by the individual numbers. Additional information would be given by an analysis of the separations and positions of the planets.

Even without further elucidation, these closer harmonics are more descriptive of the marriages than $04^1/_2$° separations from, or 07° applications to, conventional aspects or any aspects. I also think closer harmonics, though maybe not the same ones as I observed, are what Addey was observing. Addey does say, "it is much more likely that a 6° rhythm for Venus progressed, something like a five-year cycle, would suit the case better."[40] Interestingly, there are 06°50'44.74" between my progressed Venus at my first marriage and my progressed Venus at my second marriage.

Conclusion

In conclusion, having studied harmonic magnification, as well as harmonic aspects both in and out of music (with some thoughts on harmonic distributions), I must say astrology is more complex than we imagined. There are circles within circles. With traditional astrology, we may just have heard part of the Music of the Spheres—the fundamental tone. Through harmonics we may be able to hear the overtones—the higher frequencies—which in many cases may be the dominant ones.

CHAPTER THREE

Asteroids

An asteroid, to quote *The Random House College Dictionary* is:

> *n.* **1.** *Astron.* any of the thousands of small bodies of from 480 miles to less than one mile in diameter that revolve around the sun in orbits lying mostly between those of Mars and Jupiter. **2.** *Zool.* an asteroidean; starfish.—*adj.* **3.** starlike. [< Gk *asteroeid(és)* starry, starlike. See ASTER-, OID)

(The largest diameter is now more than 480 miles.)

To quote this same source, a planet is:

> *n.* **1.** *Astron.* **a.** any of the nine large heavenly bodies revolving about the sun and shining by reflected light... **b.** a similar body revolving about a star other than the sun. **c.** (formerly) a celestial body moving in the sky, as distinguished from a fixed star, formerly applied also to the sun and moon. **2.** *Astrol.* a heavenly body regarded as exerting an influence on mankind. [ME *planete* < ML *planete,* pl. (taken as sing.) of LL *planetae* < Gk *planetai,* lit. wanderers]

Though the definitions of asteroids and planets are similar, there are differences. In contrast to only nine planets, there are thousands of asteroids. Asteroids are smaller and no astrological influence is attributed to them. As for the last difference, after studying them for over twenty years, I can affirm that this omission is erroneous. While I don't consider that the asteroids affect our behavior, any more than do the planets, they do reflect it and us. The fact that they are small is irrelevant because the power of a symbol is not in its size, but in its meaning. Anyone who has felt the "power" of Pluto, the second smallest of the planets, will have to agree. Finally, asteroids, though smaller, are more than just small planets, or planetoids.

The derivation of their name is from "star," rather than "wanderer." Stars are self-luminous. They shine by their own light, not reflected light. This distinction between asteroids and planets is not literally true, but it appears to be symbolically true since the asteroids' meanings have greater clarity.

It is appropriate that the asteroids should be the subject of Chapter 3 (3rd house, Gemini, Mercury, trine). Gemini is the sign of the twins, and the asteroids and planets are two similar but separate entities. The main distinction between the asteroids and planets, I feel, is that the asteroids do not rule one of the twelve houses and signs. The position of Ceres (the largest of the asteroids), in the asteroid belt between Mars and Jupiter, is where a planet would be expected according to Bode's Law of Planetary Distances. The gravitational pull of Jupiter could have prevented a planet from forming. Another theory is that the asteroids may have been formed from the collision of two planets. Whatever their origin, the asteroids communicate a multitude of significant information, and the third house is the house of communication. The astronomers who discover the asteroids have the privilege of naming them. Most of these astronomers, unlike most of the astronomer-astrologers who named the planets, are not astrologers, and yet the names they have chosen are ideal. The names of the planets are of gods and goddesses who have many meanings and myths, while the names of the asteroids are often of people, places or minor deities who only have one meaning or myth. Each asteroid has a specific message to deliver, and Mercury was the messenger of the gods. As for the trine, it flows like the element mercury (quicksilver), and when the asteroids are added their meanings flow like quicksilver into the spaces between the planetary key words, transforming those words into sentences.

Originally, I had planned this chapter on asteroids as the sixth and last chapter, since they seemed so climactic. (The seventh chapter was added later.) But, as I was finishing my second chapter, ACS Publications asked me to write a booklet on asteroids for their *All About Astrology* series. When told that I was going to write a chapter on asteroids for my book, the publisher said to proceed, and then ACS would see if the chapter could fit the format of the series as well. (It did, and part of that chapter was adapted and published at the end of 1987 as *Personal Name Asteroids.*) Upon finishing my second chapter, I began my chapter on the asteroids, which fate had decreed would be the third. (It was not feasible to write the sixth chapter without having written the third, fourth and fifth first, and ACS wanted the asteroid booklet as soon as possible.)

The number 6 associations (6th house, Virgo, Mercury, sextile) would have been relevant. There is still the Mercury correspondence; Virgo is associated with detail and analysis; and, though I do not attribute rulership to the asteroids, Ceres and Vesta do seem associated with Virgo. On the other hand, Pallas and Juno seem associated with Libra, and some of the other asteroids, with other signs. The sixth house, sixth sign and sextile are the house, sign, and aspect of work, health and service. The third house, third sign and trine are the house, sign, and aspect of communication, near travel and relatives. Upon reflection, the latter correspondences, combined with the correspondence to the planet Mercury, the messenger of the gods, seem more relevant.

Asteroid Studies

In July of 1972 I first heard about asteroids when Eleanor Bach spoke on the symbolism of the planets and of the asteroids Ceres, Pallas, Juno and Vesta. Ms. Bach's book *Ephemerides of the Asteroids, Ceres, Pallas, Juno, Vesta* had not been published as yet, but she had the ephemerides with her. Though loath to add anything to the charts, I put these asteroids in my chart and in the charts of the people I know best. Discovering these asteroids were worth investigating further, I began adding them to all my charts, joined a study group that met at Eleanor Bach's house every week or so, and later read Zipporah Dobyns' accounts of her observational research.

In March 1976, I began a project on lunations which is written about in detail in Chapter 4. Ceres, Pallas, Juno and Vesta were then put not only into personal charts, but into the New and Full Moon Charts which I calculated every month. With all succeeding asteroids, as their ephemerides were received the asteroids were added to that month's and every subsequent month's charts. This procedure enabled me to handle the additional information in a structured and consistent manner. Predictions were written before the lunation, and then as the month proceeded what happened, and under what transits it happened, was recorded. In this way the accuracy of the predictions could be checked. This project continued until January 1984. Since its completion, I have continued to keep a journal to help in my investigations.

CONFIGURATIONS

In my investigations I do consider both T-Squares and Cosmic Squares (as well as other major configurations), though when hundreds of asteroids are included, T-Squares become Cosmic Squares. A T-Square, compared to a Cosmic Square, is a different combination of factors and aspects. Therefore, the combination of the numerical principles of the particular factors with the numerical principles of the particular aspects is different. (In a T-Square, Factor A would be square Factors B and C, with the zodiacal correspondences of 4 [square]. In a Cosmic Square, Factor A would be opposition Factor D and square Factors B and C, with the zodiacal correspondences of 2 [opposition] and 4 [square].)

ORB

In my research with all of the asteroids, the orb, unless otherwise specified, is from one degree to the next. For example, with aspects in the 30° sequence, a body or point at 15° would aspect one at 14°, 15° or 16°; with semisquares or sesquiquadrates, a body or point at 05° of the cardinal signs, for instance, would aspect one at 19°, 20° or 21° of the fixed. Aspects with this orb are designated as exact. Other orbs were tried but were found less discriminating.

ACCURACY IN CALCULATIONS

The positions of asteroids, other than the first four, are listed in the ephemerides only at ten-day intervals. During the interval when an asteroid changes direction, interpolation is especially difficult. All the asteroids that I use are now in my computer program. In the past, asteroids which I had calculated myself were marked

"St.D." (stationary direct) or "St.R" (stationary retrograde) during these intervals, indicating that the minutes were probably not correct.

The size of the asteroids subjects them to much perturbation. However, when their positions are calculated by a computer into which corrections for the perturbations have been entered, these positions can be remarkably accurate. Astro computes the asteroids to an accuracy within a few seconds of arc, except for those asteroids whose orbit takes them inside the orbit of the Earth. The positions of those asteroids are somewhat less accurate.

Twenty asteroids which Astro offers for individual charts are Ceres, Pallas, Juno, Vesta, Chiron, Amor, Dembowska, Diana, Dudu, Eros, Frigga, Hidalgo, Icarus, Lilith, Pandora, Pittsburghia, Psyche, Sappho, Toro and Urania. Though originally calculating the positions of these twenty asteroids myself, I later reordered most of my charts so as to obtain this greater accuracy. (In my charts, these twenty asteroids are calculated geometrically—see Chapter 2.)

RELEVANCE OF MYTHOLOGY

The mythology of the deities whose names were given to some of the asteroids is relevant. What I have discovered is that the particular mythology, whether Greek, Roman, Egyptian, etc., is relevant to the expression of the asteroid in the chart.

The origin and derivation of a myth is also relevant. One myth may be based on other myths, and there are asteroids named for equivalent deities. As an example, Roman mythology is very much a compilation of other mythologies, such as Greek and Egyptian. Ceres, Minerva, Juno and Vesta are the Roman equivalents of the Greek goddesses Demeter, Pallas Athene, Hera and Hestia. Pallas and Athene (or Athena) are both names of the Greek goddess Pallas Athene. Neith is an Egyptian goddess, identified with Pallas Athene by the Greeks. There are ten asteroids that were named for these nine goddesses. (There is an asteroid Pallas and an asteroid Athene.)

Roman mythology, though very much influenced by Greek mythology, is not as poetic, or as involved with the creation of archetypes for human experience, as Greek mythology. The Romans, compared to the Greeks, were more interested in mythology's practical applications. They had a catalog of the deities, their protective powers and the rites necessary to obtain this protection. The Roman gods were intended for the preservation of the State, or the family, which was considered a part of the State.[1] This different quality is relevant to the manifestation of an asteroid or planet named for a Roman god or goddess.

On the other hand, Roman mythology has been the intermediary between Greek mythology and Western civilization. The planets are known to us mainly by Roman names—Mercury (Hermes), Venus (Aphrodite), Mars (Ares), Jupiter (Zeus), Saturn (Cronus), Uranus (the same), Neptune (Poseidon) and Pluto (the same)—so Greek myths told with Roman names are part of our cultural heritage. The myths concerning the Greek gods and goddesses will be applicable to the equivalent gods and goddesses in Roman mythology. However, those myths will not be as relevant if they are no longer integral to the particular Roman god or goddess. New myths or associations may have been devised instead.

As for Egyptian mythology, though some of its gods and goddesses are similar to the Greek and Roman, Western civilization is not as familiar with the Egyptian myths. Egyptian mythology has a formal quality. There is an involvement with death and the attainment of eternal life. In the mythology, as in the life of Egypt, the family is very important. The chief family in its pantheon is Isis, Osiris and their son, Horus. The formal quality of Egyptian mythology is reflected in the asteroids named for its deities.

Since the particular mythology, whether Greek, Roman, Egyptian, etc., is relevant to the expression of the asteroid in the chart, it is important to distinguish between the expression of a myth in one culture and its expression in another.

To understand the differences between the four asteroids Ceres (1), Pallas (2), Juno (3), Vesta (4) and four asteroids associated with them, it was necessary for me to order the 100-year custom ephemerides[2] of the associated four. They are Demeter (1108), Athene (881), Hera (103) and Hestia (46). (Demeter, Hera and Hestia are Greek equivalents, and Athene is an additional name.)

SEQUENCE OF ASTEROIDS

The numbers (1 for Ceres) relate to the order of discovery, and, like other numbers, they correlate to the natural zodiac (1, 1st house, Aries, Mars, conjunction). Though the synopses of the asteroids were made without consideration of their numbers, their numbers reflect, in terms of the asteroids' order, some attribute of each asteroid. For instance, there is a certain directness about Ceres, balance about Pallas, sociability about Juno, and protectiveness about Vesta that reflects their respective 1,2,3, and 4 sequence.

The numbers of the associated four, and of the other asteroids, are equally appropriate. The numbers above 12 are reduced to a number from 1-12, but the coloration of individual numbers within the original number is retained. The sequence of the numbers within the number is significant. The first and last number are the most important, with the first being more prominent. If there are numbers in-between, they are encompassed by the initial and final number. For example, Demeter's number (1108) is reduced to 10, which correlates to the 10th house, Capricorn, Saturn, decile, but it retains the coloration of its individual numbers. Considering its sequence, 1108 begins with the assertiveness of the 1, but ends with the death and regeneration of the 8. Within that beginning and end are the initiative of the 1 and the void of 0.

RELEVANCE OF DISCOVERY DATA

The discovery date and place and the discoverer are relevant. The relevance of dates has already been discussed in Chapter 1, and the relevance of names will be discussed later in this chapter. Also, knowing the date and place enables you to examine the transits, and they are descriptive of the asteroid discovered.

My sources for the discovery data are *Tables of Minor Planets* by Frederick Pilcher and Jean Meeus, *Minor Planet Circulars* and conversations with Dr. Brian Marsden, director of the Minor Planet Center. According to Dr. Marsden, until 1925 astronomers tended to use LMT, and to consider the day as beginning at noon so that the date would not have to be changed at midnight. At the beginning of 1925, GMT or UT was substituted for LMT to standardize the time and place. Astronomical photography had been introduced in 1891, and the date and time the photographic plate is taken is now considered the date and time of discovery. If the time is given, the chart can be cast using UT and the coordinates for the place of discovery. If there is no time for the discovery, I cast the chart for midnight (00:00 hours LMT or ST) of the discovery date and place. Though the midnight chart is not as descriptive as the timed chart and astronomers before 1925 considered noon as the beginning of the day, the midnight chart is an archetypal chart for the official date of discovery and the asteroids discovered thereon.

For the most part I did not have the discovery date and place and discoverer until after researching the asteroid, so these facts were merely a reaffirmation of what had already been realized.

Synopses of Four Pairs of Asteroids

What follows is a synopsis of the meanings of Ceres and Demeter, Pallas and Athene, Juno and Hera, and Vesta and Hestia, based on my investigations. Many of the meanings of the equivalent asteroids are shared, but there are differences as well. The mythology of each goddess is given because, as mentioned, it is relevant. With these asteroids, and the ones synopsized subsequently, the discovery date and place and the discoverer are listed, since they are pertinent.

As for the orbits of the asteroids, I've found them indicative. They are analyzed individually when those orbits are other than between Mars and Jupiter. Most of the asteroids, including these eight, orbit between Mars and Jupiter. My conclusion is that this containment surrounds them with the self-assertiveness of Mars and the expansiveness of Jupiter.

The designers of the glyphs and their motivations, if known, are given. Astro markets a Macintosh font with over 100 astrological symbols, including 41 asteroid glyphs, many of which I designed either with other people or by myself. The glyphs for the first four asteroids discovered are Ceres (?), Pallas (♀), Juno (⚳) and Vesta (⚶). They were designed, or at least adopted, by astronomers and appear to be a sickle, spear, sceptre and sacred flame, respectively. (The last glyph was adapted by Eleanor Bach from the astronomers' glyph, which was a square box with a flame on top.) I designed the glyphs for the later four by turning the glyphs for the first four upside down. Thus, the glyph for Demeter is ⅔; for Athene, ⅗; for Hera, ⚹; for Hestia, ⚴; showing the association between the first four and the later four. In the Appendices, there is a list of the asteroids with glyphs.

CERES AND DEMETER

Ceres (1) was the first asteroid discovered. Its discovery date is January 1, 1801, the same day as Ireland was united with Great Britain; its discovery place is Palermo, Sicily; and its discoverer is Giuseppe Piazzi. The discovery date of Demeter (1108) is May 31, 1929; its discovery place is Heidelberg; and its discoverer is K. Reinmuth.

Ceres was the Roman goddess of the grain and Earth Mother. Originally an Italic deity, she became a practical Roman expression of the Greek goddess

Demeter. Demeter, whose origin is Indo-European, was also goddess of the grain and Earth Mother, but with more emphasis on her role as Earth Mother—with Ceres there was more emphasis on her role as goddess of the grain. The *Cerealia* on April 19 was Ceres' chief festival.

Demeter was the daughter of Cronus (Saturn) and Rhea, and the sister of Zeus (Jupiter), Hera (Juno), Hestia (Vesta), Poseidon (Neptune) and Pluto.[3] She was the mother of Kore, or Persephone (Proserpina or Proserpine) by Zeus. Her primary myth is concerning the loss of her daughter.

Kore had been kidnapped by Pluto, and Demeter looked for her everywhere, carrying two torches—from whence the expression "carrying the torch" for someone. As she traveled through Arcadia, Poseidon changed himself into a horse to seduce her against her will. By Poseidon she was the mother of Arion—a horse who could speak and who had the right feet of a man—and of Despoena (the mistress)— a daughter whose name must not be spoken. During her search, she was governess of the son of the king of Eleusis. (Eleusis is where the Eleusinian Mysteries of Demeter were later celebrated.) She attempted to make the boy immortal by placing him in the fire, but his mother intervened. There is an association of Demeter in this case with governing, and with nurturance for a higher purpose. Persephone (her name had been changed from Kore in the underworld) was finally returned to her mother so that Demeter would end her "strike" (she refused to let the crops grow until her daughter was returned). However, Persephone had eaten the seed of a pomegranate given to her by Pluto (she accepted his seed). Since in effect the marriage had been consummated, she was required to spend four months of every year with Pluto. The myth is an explanation of the seasons—of death and rebirth.

The iconography of Demeter consists of a crown of ears of corn, a sceptre, a torch, stalks of wheat, ears of corn, a basket of fruit, a piglet and a serpent. She is sometimes depicted wearing a black gown. Her flower is the poppy, the flower of sleep and death. These emblems are also associated with Ceres because she was identified with Demeter by the Romans.

Interestingly, Ireland, which was united with Great Britain on the same day as Ceres was discovered, is a Ceres-type country—agricultural and still mourning the subsequent separation of Southern and Northern Ireland. (The chart of the Union of Ireland and Great Britain at 00:00 hours is almost exactly the same as the 00:00 hours discovery chart of Ceres.)

Demeter and Ceres in the chart are symbols of nurturance, either received or given by the native. The Moon is too, but the Moon is more changeable and erratic in its expression—not as devoted to a higher purpose. (The grandmother, nurse or governess can be signified by these asteroids.) As an extrapolation from their nurturance of the grain and of the child, Demeter and Ceres also represent productivity or work. Ceres, whose role as goddess of the grain is more emphasized, gives a more specific expression of the particular productivity or work. This asteroid can also literally refer to grain or cereal, the latter word being derived from Ceres.

In the chart (at least in our Greco-Roman culture), Demeter, Ceres and the Moon are the primary indicators of the mother. Demeter is related to the mother as an abstract concept of fertility, while Ceres is descriptive of a specific manifestation of that concept. Of course, some mothers can be more a Demeter-type—more the Earth Mother than the goddess of the grain.

The myth of Demeter and Persephone is germane as well to Ceres. Either Ceres or Demeter, if appropriately posited and aspected, can symbolize the abduction or loss of a child or of someone nurtured or nurturing. However, Demeter is an archetypal expression of that loss, and Ceres, a more literal expression. To elucidate, the person with Demeter highlighted will feel the loss on a deep psychological level, even if it does not occur on a mundane level. Naturally, if both Demeter and Ceres are highlighted, there will be an even greater emphasis on this myth.

The midpoint of Ceres and Demeter is the place at which the meanings of both asteroids are combined. Its house, sign, numerical position and planetary pictures (conjunctions, oppositions, squares, semisquares and sesquiquadrates to the midpoint) will describe that combination.

PALLAS AND ATHENE

The discovery date of Pallas (2) is March 28, 1802; its discovery place is Bremen; and its discoverer is Heinrich Wilhelm Matthias Olbers. The discovery date of Athene (881) is July 22, 1917; its discovery place is Heidelberg; and its discoverer is Max Wolf, who introduced astronomical photography.

Pallas Athena, or Pallas Athene, one of the twelve Olympians, was the Greek goddess of wisdom, prudent warfare and arts and crafts. Her origin is Mycenaean. She was the favorite child of Zeus who sprang "fully armed" from his head. Metis, the Titaness, was her mother, but when Zeus was told by an oracle that Metis would bear him first a daughter, and then a son who would usurp his position, he swallowed her—hence, Pallas Athena's unusual birth.

Ares, referring to this brain child, said to Zeus, "All the other gods who live on Olympus obey thee and each of us submits to thy will. But she, thou never curbest neither by word nor deed; she does as she pleases."[4] From the beginning Athena defied Zeus. Hephaestus (Vulcan) asked for her hand before he struck the blow to release her from Zeus' head. Zeus agreed, but she refused to honor his promise. It seems Pallas Athena, who was also a tamer of horses, which are associated with Sagittarius ruled by Jupiter (Zeus), was the only one who could tame Zeus.

As for Ares, she was often in conflict with him. She was a warrior, but a warrior of principle, in contrast to Ares who loved the battle for its own sake. The olive tree, whose branch is an emblem of peace, was her creation. When the Judgment of Paris resulted in the Trojan War, she fought on the side of the Greeks. Pallas Athena was a protectress of the heroes, who helped Hercules in his labors, guided Perseus in his adventures and assisted Odysseus in completing his odyssey. She gave aid to the heroes not because of attraction to them but because of admiration for them. She was chaste, which was rare on Mount Olympus.

Her association with pattern perception is derived from her patronage of architects, sculptors, spinners and weavers. She invented the potter's wheel, the bridle, chariot, ship, plow, ox-yoke, flute and science of numbers. She was also the defender of law and order, the protectress of clans, and the guardian of cities, particularly Athens.

The iconography of Pallas Athena consists of a helmet, her aegis (breastplate with the head of Medusa), shield and spear. Sometimes in her guise as the goddess of useful arts, she is depicted instead with the distaff. The olive tree, serpent, sea-eagle, cock, and owl are sacred to her. The eagle is the bird of power; the cock, the bird of assertiveness; and the owl, the bird of wisdom. "She personifies the clear upper air...."[5]

Both Pallas and Athene in the chart are indicators of assertiveness for the sake of a principle. They represent the ability to perceive the entire picture, in contrast to Mercury which represents the ability to reason and communicate. (Interestingly, the introduction of astronomical photography by Athene's discoverer has increased our perception of the entire astronomical picture.) There is also a reference to the law. The favored child of an intellectual, or literally Sagittarian, parent can be denoted by them too.

Another expression of Pallas in the chart relates to the fact that synonyms or homonyms of a name are akin to that name. Palace is not the same spelling as Pallas, but it has the same sound, and so Pallas can be a symbol for palace. For instance, my husband's first job as a musical contractor on Broadway was at the Palace Theatre, and that story is told in the position (house, sign, numerical) and exact aspects of his Pallas. Admittedly, sounds will be different in different languages and at different times. An association with palaces, other than phonetic, is that Pallas Athena "was probably the goddess who guarded Mycenaean castles in old days."[6]

In *The Columbia Encyclopedia* under Athena, or Pallas Athena, there is the following explanation of how Pallas was added to Athena's name: "It was said that because she accidentally killed PALLAS she set the name Pallas before her own." In some myths the one whom Athena has killed is not her playmate Pallas, but the giant Pallas who had tried to molest her. In either case Pallas has incorporated what she has killed. Could it be that what she has incorporated is a darker side of herself and that by taking its name she has succeeded in integrating the *shadow?* Asteroids, planets or points that are exactly conjunct Pallas seem to be particularly integrated with it, especially if Pallas is before them. Of course, the name Pallas refers not only to the goddess who placed that name before her own, but to the playmate or giant who was killed.

The asteroid Pallas and the asteroid Athene are both related to wisdom, prudent warfare and arts and crafts. However, only Pallas relates to the integration of the enemy, or shadow, in the process of practising these functions. If there is an exact aspect between Athene and Pallas, that aspect may show how Athene can be integrated with Pallas, i.e., a sextile, through work, a square, through nurturing, a trine, through communication, etc.

The midpoint of Pallas and Athene is the place at which the meanings of both asteroids are combined. Its house, sign, numerical position and planetary pictures will describe that combination.

JUNO AND HERA

The discovery date of Juno (3) is September 1, 1804; its discovery place is Lilienthal (near Bremen, Germany); and its discoverer is Karl Harding. The discovery date of Hera (103) is September 7, 1868; its discovery place is Ann-Arbor, Michigan; and its discoverer is James Craig Watson.

Juno was the Roman goddess of marriage and childbirth. The month of June, the most popular marriage month, was named after her. She was much revered. Every woman had her Juno, just as every man had his Genius. As the protectress of women, she was honored on March 1 at the *Matronalia*. As one of the three most important deities, she was worshiped with Jupiter and Minerva (Pallas Athena) on Capitoline Hill. As Juno Moneta she was associated with finances after a mint was established in a temple dedicated to her. She was originally a separate Italic deity who became a practical Roman expression of the archetypal Greek goddess Hera. In this expression, however, her functions were much wider than those of her Greek equivalent. She was not just protectress of women, but protectress of the State.

As for Hera, her origin is Aegean. One of the twelve Olympians, she was the daughter of Cronus and Rhea, and the sister of Zeus, Demeter, Hestia, Poseidon and Pluto. She was the wife of Zeus and the mother of Ares, Hebe, Ilithyia and Hephaestus (Vulcan). In the contest among Hera, Pallas Athena and Aphrodite, Paris chose Aphrodite as the fairest. For his reward Aphrodite gave him Helen, the most beautiful woman in the world, thus precipitating the Trojan War. Hera, naturally, fought on the side of the Greeks.

Hera, the Greek goddess of marriage and childbirth, is best known for her constancy as the wife of Zeus, whose infidelities were legendary. She had power in her own right as queen of the sky but felt powerless in relation to her husband. She could not stop his unfaithfulness, though she did persecute those with whom he was unfaithful. She, like Juno, is associated with the adornment of women. She symbolizes an ability to renew oneself, as each year she renewed her virginity by bathing in the spring Canathus at Nauplia. Despite his infidelities, Zeus said of her, " 'Never has love for goddess or mortal woman so flooded my senses and filled my heart!' "[7]

The iconography of Hera consists of a crown, veil, sceptre, flower and pomegranate. The white lily is supposed to have sprung from her milk. The cuckoo, crow, peacock and cow are sacred to her. The iconography of Juno consists of a crown, veil, sceptre, flower, patera (goblet or bowl) and thunderbolt. Sometimes, like Pallas Athena, she is depicted with a shield, spear and serpent. The goose, raven and peacock are sacred to her.

It has been suggested that Juno in the chart is associated with anger at powerlessness because Juno is the smallest asteroid. This suggestion is not well-founded. For one, though Juno is the smallest of the first four asteroids, it is not anywhere near the smallest of the asteroids. The next five discovered after the first four are all smaller than it is, and others are even smaller than that. The anger sometimes associated with the asteroid Juno mirrors the anger Hera felt at being powerless in relation to Zeus. In fact, I have found the asteroid Hera more reflective of that anger than the asteroid Juno. However, neither Hera nor Juno are experienced by everyone as anger at powerlessness.

Both Hera and Juno in the chart are metaphors for marriage or the married woman. One marriage might be a Hera-type, and another, a Juno-type. Juno relates to a marriage in which there is greater equality. The placements (house, sign, numerical) and exact aspects of Hera and Juno will give you clues as to which marriage is which. The relationship (including angular separations and midpoints) between Juno and Jupiter and between Hera and Jupiter in the chart is also revealing. In addition, the relationship between Hera and the Uranian planet Zeus and between Juno and Zeus describes the interplay of their respective functions. (Jupiter's function would be comparable to Juno's; Zeus' would be comparable to Hera's, with the exception that the Uranian planets have an esoteric, Uranian quality. See Uranian Planet Key Words in the Appendices.) Though the stories of the conflicts between Hera and Zeus are germane to Juno and Jupiter, they are "once removed." In Roman mythology it is the power shared between Juno and Jupiter, rather than the conflict between them, which is emphasized.

Juno and Hera in the chart are also related to the concerns of women, among which is their adornment. These asteroids can be expressed as involvement with women's fashions.

The midpoint of Juno and Hera is the place at which the meanings of both asteroids are combined. Its house, sign, numerical position and planetary pictures will describe that combination.

VESTA AND HESTIA
The discovery date of Vesta (4) is March 29, 1807; its discovery place is Bremen; and its discoverer is Heinrich Wilhelm Matthias Olbers. The discovery date of Hestia (46) is August 16, 1857; its discovery place is Oxford; and its discoverer is Norman Robert Pogson.

Vesta was the Roman goddess of fire, both domestic and ceremonial. She is a practical Roman equivalent of the Greek goddess Hestia, whose origin is Indo-European. Hestia, one of the twelve Olympians, later gave her place on Mount Olympus to Dionysus (Bacchus.) She was the oldest child of Cronus and Rhea and the sister of Zeus, Demeter, Hera, Poseidon and Pluto. As the oldest, she was most venerated. She is the Greek archetype of the sister; as Demeter is of the mother; Pallas Athena, of the daughter; and Hera, of the wife. Hestia was sought in marriage by Poseidon and Apollo, but she vowed to remain a virgin. Though Hestia, like Vesta, was the goddess of the hearth, both private and public, it was the Romans who originated the cult of the Vestal Virgins.

The Vestal Virgins protected the sacred flame of the State. If the flame ever went out, they could only relight it with sacred fire, such as that of the sun. They were chosen from patrician families when they were from six to ten years of age and served for thirty years. They took vows of chastity and if they broke these vows, they were buried alive. The Vestals were consulted on matters of state. After their service they could marry but most preferred to retain the prerogatives of their position, which were like those of a princess. Vesta's chief festival, the *Vestalia*, was celebrated June 9.

Hestia and Vesta have very little iconography. Vesta is always depicted wearing a veil. Their temples were circular. Fire, both of the hearth and altar, is sacred to them.

Hestia is a variation of Hester meaning star, and the Sun is a star, from whose fire the sacred flame of the Vestal Virgins could be relit. According to *Name Your Baby*, Vesta means "she who dwells or lingers."

Hestia and Vesta in the chart relate to the home and hearth. These asteroids can reflect experiences with the home, such as moving to another one or visiting one that has significance for you; and with the hearth, such as the pilot light going out on the stove. There are literal references to fireplaces (where our original hearths were), such as moving to or visiting a dwelling with one. There is protectiveness toward the home that can be manifested literally as locks and keys, which are meant to provide security. The conservatism expressed in conserving the flame is transformed into conserving the traditions of the family and country. With Vesta, in contrast to Hestia, there is the fear that you will be "buried alive" if you should fail in this conservation. Vesta in the chart represents extreme commitment to duty. That commitment is often to one's career, but, if Vesta is appropriately posited, it may be to one's marriage or one's children.

Also, Vesta is vested interests—the interests which are supposed to give us financial security. Hestia is related to vested interests too. As Eleanor Bach has observed, the Mafia, which is a combination of vested interests and protectiveness toward the "family," is a distortion of the Vesta principles. Other words that begin like Vesta, such as vest, vestee, vestiary and vestibule, as she says, are associated with Vesta. Being sent away to boarding school at a young age is another expression of Vesta that I have noted. It mirrors the fact that at a young age the Vestal Virgins were taken from their homes.

The midpoint of Vesta and Hestia is the place at which the meanings of both asteroids are combined. Its house, sign, numerical position and planetary pictures will describe that combination.

Another Synopsis

Having completed my synopses of these four pairs of asteroids, outlining their similarities and differences, let me continue with my experiences concerning the asteroids and with my synopsis of the meanings of one of them.

CHIRON

Some astronomers have recently suggested that Chiron is a comet; however it is still listed as an asteroid in the *Ephemerides of Minor Planets* for 1992. The official discovery date and time of Chiron (2060) is October 18, 1977 at 09:08:30 UT (02:08:30 AM PDT). The photographic plate, on which Chiron was later found, was taken on this day at this time at Palomar Mountain, California. Charles Kowal found Chiron on this plate November 1, 1977, circa 10 AM PST, in Pasadena, California. Both charts are descriptive of the asteroid Chiron. Look at the later chart (Astronomer-

Discovery Chiron), not only as an individual chart, but as a chart in relation to the earlier chart (Photo-Discovery Chiron). (Note asteroids whose names are the same as, or similar to, the names of the discoverer and of the discovery places.)

Sometime around December 1978 when the *Ephemeris of Chiron* was published by Phenomena Publications, I became aware that there was another asteroid to study and decided to put it as well in my charts. The *CAO Times* had also published an *Ephemeris of Chiron*. Its glyph, which a CAO General Convention had voted to accept, was designed by an artist who does not want to be identified. I use its glyph (⚷), rather than the glyph of Phenomenon Publications (⚷), because a K over an ellipse seems more appropriate, and ⚷ is too similar to the glyph for the Uranian planet Hades (♇).

Chiron figured in Greek mythology as the wise and benevolent centaur. He was the son of Cronus and the ocean-nymph Philyra, husband of the Naiad Claricles and father of Thea. Most of his life he lived in the cave where he was born. His teachers were Artemis and Apollo, the goddess of the moon and the god of the sun, and he in turn was teacher and foster parent to the heroes. He taught them riding, hunting, philosophy, ethics, music, astrology and medicine. Heracles (Hercules) accidentally wounded him, according to some accounts in his knee, and to others in his left heel or ankle. In constant pain, he gave up his immortality to die in place of Prometheus, who was eternally tortured because he had stolen fire from the gods as a gift to man.

The fact that Chiron was a centaur—half-man and half-horse—gives him an association with Sagittarius, whose glyph is a centaur. In addition, Zeus (Jupiter, ruler of Sagittarius) was Chiron's half-brother. (Pluto and Poseidon were also his half-brothers, while Demeter, Hera and Hestia were his half-sisters.) Another connection is that when Chiron died Zeus placed him in the heavens, supposedly as the constellation Sagittarius. Erminie Lantero points out in her book, *The Continuing Discovery of Chiron*, that though the constellation of Chiron is really Centaurus, since that of Sagittarius was believed to represent Chiron, this is a valid association. Chiron's being a teacher, involved with both the physical and mental, is Sagittarian as well. His being a centaur (Sagittarian glyph) reflects the dichotomy of man's nature, but Chiron himself is never depicted as having a struggle between his lower and higher nature.

The orbit of an asteroid is relevant to the meaning of an asteroid, as are the other associations with it. The orbit of most of the asteroids is between Mars and Jupiter. This containment surrounds most of the asteroids with the self-assertiveness of Mars and the expansiveness of Jupiter. The orbit of these asteroids in the asteroid belt is not in the orbit of any planet. The orbit of Chiron is between Jupiter and Uranus. This containment surrounds Chiron with the expansiveness of Jupiter and the humanitarianism of Uranus. Chiron's orbit is in the orbits of Saturn and Uranus and crosses the orbit of Saturn. Being in those orbits relates Chiron to the qualities of Saturn and Uranus. (This combination could refer to the unusual teacher, foster parent or stepparent.)

It is an interesting correlation that the asteroid named for Chiron, who was the son of Saturn (Cronus) and grandson of Uranus, should have its orbit in the orbits of the planets Saturn and Uranus. Also, two of the three possible sites for the wound sustained by Chiron are the knee, ruled by Saturn, and the ankle, ruled by Uranus. Zane Stein has suggested that Chiron is a link between the conservatism of Saturn and the radicalism of Uranus—a true independent.

Chiron in the chart is the indicator of the wounded healer, who can be literally the foster parent, stepparent, custodian, teacher or doctor. Figuratively, Chiron can be the person who sacrifices himself for someone else. This asteroid is important in close relationships because we are often healers and teachers to, or are healed and taught by, those people to whom we are closest—parents, partners, lovers and close friends. Of course, those people are the ones whom we can wound and who can wound us. The position (house, sign, numerical) and exact aspects of Chiron indicate who is the healer to you or to whom you are the healer or how you can be the healer to yourself. Secondarily, in determinations such as this, noting what the aspected planets rule is helpful.

As a specialized literal indication, Chiron may symbolize someone who is disabled, particularly in regard to his legs. (Note the position and exact aspects of the asteroid.) Chiron, wounded in the knee, ankle or heel, was a centaur with the lower body and legs of a horse. To the wounded, a wheelchair, prosthesis or brace supplies the "horsepower" of the lower body and legs of the centaur.

The asteroid Chiron is also related to a seeking after knowledge and truth. Chiron is reputed to be the one who saw the stars as integrated into constellations and who named them accordingly. What a magnificent expression of the desire to find meaning in the universe. He finally experienced the ultimate knowledge—that of death—which he accepted willingly. When Chiron is activating the chart there may be experiences with death, as well as with sickness, education and the guardianship of people or money.

The person with Chiron prominent in his or her chart is usually "different" from his or her peers, as Chiron was different from the other gods and the other centaurs. The price of being different is frequently pain, through which that person may gain compassion for the pain of others—ergo, the wounded healer. And that compassion may be expressed through healing, teaching or stewardship. However, if compassion is not gained, the principles of Chiron, like all principles, can be distorted.

Synopses of Ten *CAO Times* Asteroids

The next milestone in my asteroid research occurred when I heard J. Lee Lehman, an astrologer and Ph.D. biologist, lecture in February of 1981. She spoke of the ten asteroids Sappho (80), Hidalgo (944), Eros (433), Lilith (1181), Icarus (1566), Pandora (55), Toro (1685), Amor (1221), Psyche (16) and Urania (30). Dr. Lehman, from positions in right ascension and declination supplied by Dr. Brian Marsden, calculated the ephemerides, which either had been or were being published by the *CAO Times*. I purchased those that had already been published (the first five) and the others as they were published.

What follows are synopses of the meanings of these ten asteroids, based on my observational research. In this research the insights of Dr. Lehman have been extremely helpful. When the names of the asteroids are based on mythological characters, those myths are considered. When the names are not, whatever associations there are are considered. In both cases these associations include facts about the places of discovery and the discoverers. What I've realized is that the associations, whether they are or are not mythological, are relevant.

SAPPHO

The asteroid Sappho (80) was discovered May 3, 1864, in Madras by Norman Robert Pogson. Another source gives May 2 for the discovery, which is probably the day in England while May 3 is the day in India. A time adjustment for Europe seems likely, since not only had most asteroids been discovered in Europe but Pogson had discovered asteroids in Oxford before going to Madras. Madras, a city in South East India, is a cultural center with a fine university.

Sappho was a Greek poetess who lived in the seventh and sixth centuries B.C. She taught young women poetry, music and dance. Her poems for the most part are passionate love lyrics. Papyrus rolls and vellum codices of their texts were found buried in Egypt. In complete form, we only have *Hymn to Aphrodite* and *Ode to a Beautiful Girl*. She was a lesbian (that word was derived from the place of her birth, Lesbos), but she was married at one time and had a daughter, Klëis. Her mother's name was also Klëis, and her father's name was probably Scamandronymous. As an aristocrat, Sappho was exiled twice. There is a legend that she committed suicide for love by jumping from a cliff. Though this story is probably untrue, it has meaning in our culture because it has become part of our culture. Sappho's Leap, at Cape Ducato on Leucas, is known as the spot from which Sappho jumped into the sea.

Dr. Lehman said that the asteroid Sappho refers to sex and that its transits are a timer of sexual relationships. I was skeptical of these statements and thought that Sappho's sexual significance would be limited to lesbian relationships. To my surprise I found that Sappho does relate to sex in heterosexual and male homosexual relationships as well and is a timer of the first sexual encounter in the particular relationship. Look at Sappho's transiting house, sign, numerical position and exact aspects in regard to the natal chart. The progressed chart in regard to the natal chart is also descriptive of that sexual relationship.

Sappho's poetry is full of longing. Perhaps, that longing is more relevant than whether the longing is woman for woman, man for woman, woman for man or man for man. What comes to mind is the story in Plato's *Symposium* of the origin of love. According to this story, we were originally pairs—some, two females, some, two males, and some, half male and half female. Then Zeus split us in two, and ever since each of us has been looking for his other half. In sex, as in love, we are often seeking to be interlocked with another. Without love, the interlocking usually isn't very binding. The design of a glyph, I have found, as well as the choice of a name, is appropriate. The glyph of the asteroid Sappho (♀♀), which Dr. Lehman chose, is two Venus symbols interlocked. Fittingly, the Greek Aphrodite of Sappho's *Hymn to Aphrodite* is equivalent to the Roman Venus. (The difference between Aphrodite and Venus is that, as in Greek compared to Roman mythology in general, Aphrodite is more archetypal than Venus.)

Of course, the asteroid Sappho does refer to lesbians too, though because of its other references, it may not be statistically more prominent in their charts. The two Venus symbols interlocked resemble a woman's sexual organs—the ovaries, uterus and vagina. What Lee Lehman chose as Sappho's glyph has been used by lesbian activists as a symbol since the early 1960s. Also, sapphism is another word for lesbianism. However, upon looking in *The Random House College Dictionary,* I found not only the expected definition for lesbian, but "**3.** (cap.) erotic: so called from the reputed character of the ancient inhabitants of Lesbos and the tone of their poetry." Sappho was a Lesbian, as well as a lesbian, and it may be the eroticism associated with the former that enables the asteroid to describe sexuality in general.

Despite the asteroid's reference to sex, Sappho in the chart has other meanings than sex. Lee Lehman has made this observation too. (Not every part of the associations of an asteroid or planet needs to be reflected in every case.) I have seen connections to education, particularly where women are together, as were the women at Sappho's school. (Interestingly, the city where Sappho was discovered is a cultural center with a fine university.) Poetry is associated with this asteroid. Also, Sappho can be a symbol for duality. The two interlocked Venus symbols of its glyph can be a "metaphor" for two women, identical twins, the sign of the twins and double signs, i.e., two out of the three factors, Sun, Moon and Ascendant, are in the same sign.

EROS

The asteroid Eros (433) was discovered August 13, 1898, in Berlin by Gustav Witt. At that time and for a long time after, it was the only known body, besides the Moon, to come so close to the Earth. (See Amor for a discussion of the orbit of Eros.)

Eros was the Greek god of love, whom the Romans identified with Cupid (Amor). Originally Eros was considered the son of Erebus and the Night and was supposed to bring harmony to chaos. Later he was considered the son of Aphrodite and Ares (sometimes Hermes or Zeus was thought to be his father). Eros, the constant companion of his mother, shot his arrows at god and man alike, causing them to fall in love—often an unrequited love. Wounding himself by accident, Eros fell in love with Psyche. Though she promised never to try to see his face, she broke her vow and had to go through many trials before they were reunited and married on Mount Olympus. Associated with the god of love are the rose, the hare, the cock and the goat.

The glyph of Eros (♋), designed by Al Morrison, is a heart pierced by an arrow, symbolizing the heart-piercing quality of this asteroid. A state of compulsion is the result of this piercing. Dr. Lehman's key phrase for Eros is smitten love, which is most apt. However, I don't find, as she does, that when the Eros of one person makes an exact aspect to a planet of another person, the Eros person is necessarily the smitten one. This state of affairs is more likely when the aspect is an exact conjunction—perhaps in this case Eros wounds himself with his own arrow.

Smitten love usually involves the eyes. We speak of "love at first sight" and of someone "shooting a glance" at someone else. The piercing arrow has taken the form of a piercing look. Eros seems particularly strong when the Sun is involved, which may be because the arrows were shot into the heart, and the Sun rules the heart. Also, the Sun rules one of the eyes, and the eyes shoot and receive the piercing glances.

Though the asteroid Eros is often related to an unrequited love, it can be related to a reciprocal love. The love of Eros and Psyche, who were finally united forever in a marriage on Mount Olympus, was mutual. Psyche had to go through many trials because she didn't trust Eros. Eros had to forgive Psyche for not trusting him and help her in her trials. To me those trials are symbolic of the process of transforming that first pang of love into a true and lasting love. In that process the relationship between erotic love (Eros) and the soul (Psyche) is tested, and trust is required. That relationship is described by the angular separations and exact aspects between Eros and Psyche, both in the chart and between charts.

I have also seen the asteroid Eros refer to sharp pains, operations and the piercing of a bullet (the gun and bullet are the present-day equivalent of the bow and arrow). People or shows with the name Hart, which sounds like heart into which the arrows were shot, are signified by the asteroid too. Probably, Eros has particular relevance to New York because as Al Morrison points out in the *Ephemeris of Eros* the "I love New York" promotion features a red heart with "love" inscribed on it.

AMOR

The asteroid Amor (1221) was discovered March 12, 1932, in Uccle by E. Delporte. The glyph of Amor ($\heartsuit$), designed by Tee A. Corinne, has a vulval shape.

Amor was the Roman god of love, who was also known as Cupid. He was identified with Eros, the Greek god of love. There are similarities, but there are differences too. Each accompanied his mother and shot his arrows at god and man alike, causing them to fall in love, and the story of Psyche is told of both Eros and Cupid (Amor). However, Amor, unlike Eros, was never a primordial force who brought harmony to chaos. Amor was considered the son of Venus and Mercury, while Eros was usually considered the son of Aphrodite (Venus) and Ares (Mars). Eros and Amor were originally depicted as beautiful youths with wings, but Amor or Cupid was later depicted as a naked child with or without wings. In this guise he is often a decoration for architecture and Valentine Cards—the latter expressing the sentiment of love.

The astronomical comparison of Amor to Eros is also enlightening. The orbit of both Amor and Eros is between the Earth and Jupiter. This containment surrounds them with the earthiness of the Earth and the expansiveness of Jupiter. The orbit of Amor and Eros is in the orbit of Mars, relating them both to the self-assertiveness of that planet. However when they cross the orbit of Mars, Amor, compared to Eros, goes closer to both the Earth and Jupiter, emphasizing for Amor, more than for Eros, the earthiness and the expansiveness.

The English translation of the Latin word Amor is love, and that is what the asteroid Amor symbolizes. It isn't the sexuality or eroticism of Sappho or the erotic love of Eros, but just unadorned love (the naked Cupid). It isn't the love of Venus either, which is based on affinity and harmony. It is the caring and concern that you might feel for a child or close friend, as well as for a lover or partner. If with a lover or partner there are not only Sappho and Eros contacts, but Amor contacts, another dimension is added to the attraction. With that dimension, the pleasure or happiness of that other person may be more important to you than your own.

Certainly, which planets, points or asteroids are in contact with Amor, and what interaspects are forming those contacts, is significant. The effect is very personal and powerful if the personal points or your name asteroids are involved. (The name asteroids are the next milestone.) Interaspects, like aspects (and angular separations), will have the meanings of the associated number, house, sign, planet (and aspect), as explained in Chapter 1. The relationship between love (Amor) and the soul (Psyche) is described by the angular separations and exact aspects and interaspects of Amor and Psyche. The difference between Eros in relation to Psyche, and Amor in relation to Psyche, is made clear when the lineage of Eros and Amor is considered. Eros reflects the fact that Aphrodite (Venus) and Ares (Mars) were his parents, while Amor reflects the fact that Venus and Mercury were his. (The former combination is more passionate, while the latter is more contemplative.)

PSYCHE

The asteroid Psyche (16) was discovered March 17, 1852, in Naples by A. de Gasparis. Naples is the city in Southern Italy which is overshadowed by Mount Vesuvius.

Psyche was the mortal who was loved in Greek mythology by Eros and in Roman mythology by Amor (Cupid). The story, which was told in *The Golden Ass* or *Metamorphoses* by the second century Latin writer Lucius Apuleius, is as follows. Psyche, the daughter of a king, was so beautiful Venus became jealous of her. Venus sent her son to punish Psyche, but he wounded himself with his own arrow and fell in love with her instead. He came to her only at night and made her promise she would never try to see him. Suspecting that he was a monster, she lit a lamp, at which point he awakened and left her because she had not trusted him. Psyche, searching for Cupid everywhere, arrived at the temple of Ceres. There, after Psyche had sorted the sheaves and ears of corn and barley, Ceres advised her to go to Venus to ask her forgiveness. She did, and Venus set her a series of almost impossible tasks. The first was to separate grains in the storehouse of her temple. Psyche, overwhelmed by the task, did nothing, but Cupid sent ants to do it for her. The second was to bring back golden fleeces, which she did with the advice of the river god. The third was to gather water from the source of the Styx. In this third task she was assisted by an eagle. Venus then told her to descend to Hades and return with some of Proserpina's beauty in a box. In this last endeavor she was helped by the tower she meant to throw herself from, thinking that was the only way to descend to Hades. The tower informed her of a cave through which she could descend and warned her of the dangers with which she would be beset. Though told not to open the box, she opened it to take some of the beauty because she wanted to appear more beautiful to her husband. Only sleep was in the box, and it overcame her. Cupid put the sleep back in the box, reviving Psyche, and she completed her final test. She was then made immortal, united with the god of love and had a daughter with him named Pleasure.

In Greek mythology in the 5th-4th centuries BC, Psyche had become the soul symbolized by the butterfly and then the personification of the soul. In the story, Psyche's trials involve becoming nurturing and productive (separating the grains and bringing back the golden fleeces and the water) and finally facing death (descending to Hades for the beauty of the Queen of Hades). Perhaps, Psyche's being united with the god of love is a sign of their finally being soulmates.

The asteroid Psyche relates to the struggle to achieve a true and lasting love. Trust is often a factor. (To live beneath the shadow of Mount Vesuvius requires trust too.) I have seen transiting Psyche active at the time of the beginning and the end of relationships. In meeting, marriage, composite and relationship charts, Psyche, as well as Eros and Amor, should be noted to see how the couple is playing out this myth of Psyche and the god of love.

Psyche also refers to the soul or spirit, and psychic sensitivity. People with this asteroid strong in their charts tend to be intuitive. The glyph of Psyche (Ψ), designed by Al Morrison in the shape of the Greek letter Psi, resembles Neptune's trident; however, Psyche's psychism is clearer, less nebulous than Neptune's. This asteroid is active at the beginning and the end of psychoanalysis. Also, I have seen transiting Psyche (and Chiron) active at the time a college student switched her major to psychology and at the time she switched her major from psychology.

LILITH

The asteroid Lilith (1181) was discovered February 11, 1927, in Algiers by B. Jekhovsky. He named the asteroid in honor of Mme. L. Boulanger, but she is not listed in the reference books consulted thus far, so I do not have any information about her. Algiers, the capital of Algeria, is known for the Casbah. France captured Algiers in 1830, but in 1962, after many revolts in the city, Algiers won independence.

Lilith, or Lilis, was the first wife of Adam in Jewish mythology. She refused to accept the authority of Adam and left Paradise, where he soon was given Eve, made from his own rib. Lilith haunts the night and is antagonistic toward the newborn. She is symbolic of the mother who is both loved and feared. Her origin is probably Assyria where she was Lilitu, the storm demon.

The glyph of Lilith (⚸), designed by Tee A. Corinne, is a diagrammatic hand. Dr. Lehman in the *Ephemeris of Lilith* writes that this glyph "can represent either a greeting or the signal to stop. Lilith thus represents a choice between alternatives...." The alternatives may be two different people. I have noticed, as Lee Lehman has, that the asteroid Lilith relates to making a choice after the dark night of the soul—a reaching closure.

The asteroid Lilith is also associated with the issue of equality between the sexes. (See Pandora for the contrasting principle.) There is sometimes an antagonism toward the newborn because children can be a threat to independence and freedom, and hence equality. This antagonism may be felt by the man, rather than by the woman.

Lilith has an alluring quality, but the allure will quickly dissipate if there is not equality between the alluring and the allured. (Storms may ensue.) If there is equality, the attraction can be positive. (The meanings of Lilith evoke the allure of the Casbah, combined with the autonomy of Algiers.) The Dark Moon Lilith (Ø), which is supposedly the Earth's unseen moon, is not the same as the asteroid Lilith. The Dark Moon Lilith has the seductive quality of a siren and represents hidden fascinations. The allure of the asteroid Lilith is not that of a siren, and though it is subtle, it is not totally hidden. Despite my having seen the asteroid Lilith prominent with people in show business, the Dark Moon is even more prominent, probably because of the Moon's connection with the reflected image and with the public. The Dark Moon does not reflect visibly, but it seems to reflect on an invisible, perhaps subconscious level.

Lilith sounds like lily. There is an asteroid named Lilium, which is the genus of the flower lily, so that asteroid might be more relevant to the lily. However, the asteroid Lilith and the Dark Moon Lilith are relevant. They would be associated with France, whose monarchal emblem is the fleur-de-lys or lis (lily). They would also be associated with Egypt, whose emblem is the lotus, one of whose definitions is water lily. The Egyptian lotus (in contrast to the American and Indian lotus) and the water lily are of the same genus. In *A to Z Horoscope Maker and Delineator* by Llewellyn George, "lilies" and "water lily" are listed as words related to the Moon. The Dark Moon Lilith is even called a Moon. Just as the Dark Moon, in comparison to the asteroid, is more connected to people in show business, I feel it is more connected to these nations. Curiously, show business and sovereignty have a lot in common. The entertainers of today have taken the place, for the most part, of the monarchs of yesterday.

PANDORA

The asteroid Pandora (55) was discovered September 10, 1858, at Dudley Observatory in Albany, New York by G. Searle. The glyph of Pandora (⊐), designed by Lee Lehman, represents a box.

Pandora in Greek mythology was the first woman, whom Zeus told Hephaestus (Vulcan) to create as a punishment to mankind. Athena breathed life into her. All the Gods gave her gifts, hence her name which means "The all-gifted one." She was sent to the Titan Epimetheus, the brother of Prometheus, as his bride. Her dowry was a box, which was never to be opened. Out of curiosity Pandora opened it, and all of the evils of the world escaped, leaving only hope still in the box. Pandora is the Greek equivalent of Eve, who supposedly brought evil to the world by eating, and tempting Adam to eat, the fruit of the tree of the knowledge of good and evil.

My research concurs with Dr. Lehman's statement that there is a cascade effect with the asteroid Pandora. One action or event leads to a whole series of unexpected actions or events. Uranus on the contrary relates to one sudden, unexpected happening. The cascade effect is like all the evils proceeding from the one action of opening Pandora's box. However, the effect need not be evil. The process of change that occurs may be all to the good.

The asteroid Pandora is highlighted in synastry. An exact interaspect of the Sun or Moon to Pandora is particularly powerful. (After all, just as Eve was the mother of us all according to the Bible, Pandora was, according to Greek mythology.) Another interaspect which is very interesting is Lilith to Pandora. As Dr. Lehman points out, though alluring at first, frequently it doesn't last very long. Changes result, especially in the Lilith person, whom the Pandora person has shaken up. When the dust settles, the Lilith person usually feels better about the Pandora person than the Pandora person feels about the Lilith person. The relationship, though brief, is very significant.

Perhaps, the reason for the Lilith-Pandora dilemma is that there is a conflict between their principles. Lilith was the first wife of Adam, and Pandora is the equivalent of Eve, his second wife. Eve, with the exception of tempting Adam with the apple, seems to have been quite docile, while Lilith would not accept Adam's authority. Also, Pandora brings its cascade effect to the feelings of anger at inequality that Lilith represents.

HIDALGO

The asteroid Hidalgo (944) was discovered October 31, 1920, in Bergedorf (near Hamburg, Germany) by Walter Baade. According to *The Columbia Encyclopedia*, this astronomer "presented evidence for the existence of two different stellar populations of older and newer stars."

Hidalgo in *The Random House College Dictionary* is defined as "**1.** a man of the lower nobility in Spain. **2.** a man of landed property or special prestige in Spanish America." Another definition of Hidalgo is "a state in central Mexico," and Hidalgo y Costilla, Miguel is "1753-1811, Mexican priest, patriot, and revolutionist." The asteroid was named for this Mexican champion of liberty.

Encyclopedias yield further detail about the state and the man. The state's main industry is mining. Silver, gold, copper, lead, iron, mercury and sulfur are produced. The main crop is maguey (amaryllis), from which the national drink is extracted. (The amaryllis family and the lily family are related. There is an asteroid named Amaryllis.) Hidalgo was originally occupied by the Toltec, then the Chichimec and finally the Aztec Indians. It was conquered by the Spanish in 1530 and became a separate state in 1869. Miguel Hidalgo y Costilla was born May 8, 1753, at Corralejos (near Guanajuato), Mexico. (The chart of a famous namesake is relevant.) He was a Creole who used only the last name of his father. As a priest in the town of Dolores, he tried to help the Mexican Indians by introducing olive groves, vineyards, a porcelain factory and the silk industry. When Napoleon invaded Spain in 1808, Hidalgo became involved with a group to support Spain against France. Shortly, however, the group began to support the independence of Mexico from Spain. Successful at first, Hidalgo was finally defeated, stripped of his holy orders by the Inquisition and shot as a rebel.

The glyph of Hidalgo (⸘) was designed by Zane Stein to represent the eccentricity of the asteroid's orbit between Mars and Saturn. (Its eccentricity is even greater than that of Pluto and Chiron.) This containment surrounds Hidalgo with the self-assertiveness of Mars and the status-seeking of Saturn. Hidalgo's orbit is in the orbits of Jupiter and Saturn and crosses the orbit of Jupiter. Being in those orbits relates Hidalgo to both the expansiveness of Jupiter and the limitation of Saturn.

Lee Lehman said that the asteroid Hidalgo refers to self-assertion, and my studies corroborate her statement. But it is not just a Mars-like self-assertiveness.

The person with Hidalgo strong in his chart seems to feel he or she has to try harder. This person may feel disenfranchised because of being illegitimate, a minority or in another way distinct from others. The self-assertiveness of the Mars and the need for prestige of the Saturn is magnified by the Jupiter in-between. Could it be that implicit within Hidalgo's definition as "the lower nobility" is the desire to become the higher nobility? (Interestingly, its discoverer "presented evidence for the existence of two different stellar populations of older and newer stars.")

Despite this desire to become the higher nobility, the Hidalgo self-assertion is often for something outside the self. The Hidalgo person is a rebel, but usually a rebel with a cause. Both machismo and nationalism are operative words, and there is no thought of the risks involved.

Literally, Hidalgo may represent Spanish or Spanish-American factors. Also, Hidalgo can represent someone with the name of Don, since the Hidalgo is the lowest rank of nobility entitled to be addressed as Don. Another meaning of don is a head, fellow or tutor of a college, so Hidalgo can relate to a teacher. On a more metaphorical level, Dôn was the mother of Gwydion in Celtic mythology, so Hidalgo can refer to the mother of someone similarly named. For instance, with Hidalgo exactly conjunct my East Point, I am the mother of Gwynn.

ICARUS
The asteroid Icarus (1566) was discovered June 27, 1949, in Palomar Mountain, California by Walter Baade. The glyph of Icarus (▽) was designed by Lee Lehman.

Icarus in Greek mythology (based on Cretan legends) was the son of Daedalus, an Athenian master craftsman, and Naucrate, a Cretan slave. Daedalus, having murdered his nephew, a rival craftsman, had sought asylum in Crete. There he constructed the labyrinth in which the Minotaur, half-man and half-bull, was kept. The Minotaur was the progeny of Pasiphaë and a white bull sent to the king of Crete by Poseidon. Daedalus had helped Pasiphaë satisfy her passion for the bull by building a wooden cow that she could enter. When Minos, the king of Crete and husband of Pasiphaë, discovered the complicity of Daedalus, he had Daedalus and Icarus imprisoned in the labyrinth themselves. Pasiphaë freed them, and Daedalus made wings from feathers and wax so that he and his son could escape from Crete. He warned his son, but Icarus, in his delight at being free, flew too close to the sun, the wax melted, and he fell into the sea and drowned.

The orbit of Icarus is between the Sun and Jupiter. This containment surrounds Icarus with the irradiation of the Sun and the expansiveness of Jupiter. Icarus' orbit is in and crosses the orbits of Mercury, Venus, the Earth and Mars. Being in those orbits gives Icarus a smattering of the restlessness of Mercury, the sensuousness of Venus, the earthiness of the Earth and the self-assertiveness of Mars. Icarus goes closer to the Sun than any other known body, except comets. However, this preeminence may soon be usurped. While doing research at the Hayden Planetarium, I learned of an asteroid, coming out of the constellation Gemini from the Geminid Meteor Shower, which goes closer still. This asteroid has not been named or even numbered yet and is temporarily called 1983 *T. B.* (According to the designation system used since 1925, 1983 is the year of discovery; *T* stands for the period of the year; and *B* stands for the second asteroid that was reported discovered during that period.)

The asteroid Icarus represents flying too close to the sun. Zane Stein's scenario in the *Ephemeris of Icarus* concurs with my observations. Often a feeling of restriction will be felt, succeeded by the escape from that restriction. The relief at the escape will often result in an exhilaration that allows no restraint. The lack of restraint may be followed by a fall. The glyph, which looks like a wing with a line through it, represents the consequent cancellation of flight. The position (house, sign, numerical) and exact aspects of Icarus will show where a person will take risks. People with exact interaspects of Icarus and a planet, asteroid or personal point will take more risks together than they would separately.

The astrologer and Ph.D. psychologist Zipporah Dobyns has found, as I have, that Icarus has a Leo association. A person with Icarus prominent in his or her chart may be involved with creative self-expression, love affairs or other Leonine concerns. There can be precocity, followed by a sudden termination of the premature activity. However, unlike the mythological Icarus, the Icarian person may fly again, perhaps the next time taking a different course. The creative and performing arts and politics seem particularly related to Icarus because of the frequent rise and fall of those who practise them. There is also a literal soaring quality to some forms of dance (athletics too).

And, Icarus can literally refer to flying. When my daughter went para-sailing, transiting Mars was exactly conjunct her natal Icarus, and the parachute is pulled by a motorboat (Mars). When my son went hot-air ballooning, the transiting Moon was exactly conjunct his natal Icarus (a balloon is a rounded enclosure, and the Moon rules rounded enclosures). Of course, the position and exact aspects of Icarus describe circumstances of the flight other than the type of aircraft involved, and Icarus relates to more traditional flying as well.

Another association to Icarus is assassinations—some politically motivated, and some not, like the assassination of John Lennon. In rereading the story of Daedalus and Icarus, I realized that Icarus was really the victim. True, in his natural joy at being released from prison he flew too close to the sun, but he never would have been imprisoned if it hadn't been for his father's actions. His father had assassinated his nephew and then conspired against the king. Icarus was punished, not for what he had done, but for who he was.

As an example of how the asteroids of a person, just like the Ascendant, Sun, Moon and other planets, can become recognizable, there is the following. Diana Rosenberg, a fellow researcher on the asteroids, and I were speaking on the phone after John DeLorean was arrested for selling heroin to save his car company. I had just read an article about him with a picture of his car, the DeLorean, and said Icarus should be strong in his chart and involved with his Sun because his car is very much involved with his ego and looks like it has wings. Diana found his chart in *The Gauguelin Book of American Charts*, and when his Icarus was calculated it turned out to be at 14° Capricorn 06', exactly conjunct his Sun at 15° Capricorn 54', both in the tenth house. Icarus is also exactly square his Ascendant at 13° Aries 46'.[8]

Subsequently, the jury, feeling that DeLorean had been victimized by entrapment, acquitted him. One of the stories in the August 17, 1984 *New York Post* concerning his acquittal was titled "The rise and fall of a boy wonder."

TORO

The asteroid Toro (1685) was discovered July 17, 1948, at Lick Observatory in Mount Hamilton, California by C. A. Wirtanen. The glyph of Toro (♀), designed by Joelle K. D. Mahoney, resembles the head of a bull.

Toro is defined in *The Random House College Dictionary* as *Spanish.* a bull, *Bos taurus africanus (ibericus)*, bred esp. for combat in the bull ring." The Minoans, Greeks and Romans practised a form of bullfighting, but it was probably the Moors who brought bullfighting to Spain. The Moors originally inhabited North West Africa—perhaps accounting for the classification *Bos taurus africanus*. Though these bulls are bred for their strength and their aggressiveness, the goal of the bullfight is their domination. The bullfight is a drama of life and death, in which the bull, who may maim or kill in the process, is usually killed himself at the end.

The *Encyclopædia Britannica* states that Toro is an ancient fortified town in Spain, and the Cortes of 1371, 1442 and 1505 "made Toro and its code of laws celebrated." Cortes is "a Spanish term literally signifying the 'courts,' and applied to the states, or assembly of the states, of the kingdom."

The orbit of Toro, which is very erratic, is between Venus and Jupiter. This containment surrounds Toro with the stick-to-it-iveness of Venus and the expansiveness of Jupiter. Toro's orbit is in and crosses the orbits of the Earth and Mars. Being in those orbits relates Toro to the earthiness of the Earth and the self-assertiveness of Mars. Other than the Moon, Toro is the body that comes closest to the Earth.

Lee Lehman said that Toro amplifies whatever it contacts, and my research confirms this statement. The houses, signs and exact aspects with which Toro is involved are amplified. Its glyph, which resembles the head of a bull, also resembles a dish antenna, which picks up television signals from communication satellites. The resemblance of the glyph to this apparatus may indicate that the amplification associated with Toro echoes this conduction of signals down to Earth. There is already an association of the Earth with Toro because, as stated, aside from the Moon, Toro comes closer to the Earth than any other body.

The asteroid Toro also reflects the definition of Toro. The strength and power of the fortified town, where government would be amplified by an assembly of the states, is signified by this asteroid. The great tenacity and bullheadedness, which the bull exhibits in the ring, is similarly signified. The person with Toro prominent in his or her chart may be aggressive, or there may be aggression toward him or her. The position and exact aspects of the asteroid will tell you where and how. There is an association with Spain and the other countries in which bullfighting is popular, as well as with Africa (the word africanus is part of Toro's classification). As for the finale of the bullfight, part of the goal of life is the acceptance of death. Man, unlike the bull, may die many times metaphorically, before reaching this goal.

URANIA

The asteroid Urania (30) was discovered July 22, 1854, in London by J. R. Hind. Greenwich is a metropolitan borough of London, and it is from there that geographic longitude is measured.

In Greek mythology Urania, one of the nine daughters of Zeus and the Titaness Mnemosyne (Memory), was the Muse of Astronomy and Celestial Forces. Through Apollo, the Leader of the Muses, she and her sisters were involved with the musical arts, often entertaining the gods. Also, the Muses had rulership over springs and streams, practised healing and prophecy, and brought inspiration to those whom they blessed with their favor. By Apollo, according to some myths, Urania was the mother of the poet Linus, who was supposed to have invented melody and rhythm.

There are asteroids named for all nine Muses. In addition to Urania (30), there are Klio (84), the Muse of History; Euterpe (27), the Muse of Music; Thalia (23), the Muse of Comedy; Melpomene (18), the Muse of Tragedy; Terpsichore (81), the Muse of Choral Dance and Song; Erato (62), the Muse of Lyric and Amorous Poetry; Polyhymnia (33), the Muse of Hymn and Religious Dance (she later became the Muse of Mimic Art); and Kalliope (22), the Muse of Heroic or Epic Poetry. (Urania is usually in the eighth position between Polyhymnia and Kalliope.) Before the tradition of nine Muses, there were considered to be three. Melete (56), the Muse of Meditation, was one of the three original Greek Muses. Musa (600) is Latin for Muse.

Urania's attributes are the globe and compass or dividers, and she is usually depicted seated. The Muses are crowned with violets, but sometimes Urania wears a crown of stars. Urania means "Heavenly," according to *Name Your Baby*. The glyph of Urania (⋉) is the compass, Urania's attribute which is a tool of measurement. John Addey chose this glyph, with the angle of the dividers set at exactly 30°, as it was on 3000 year-old Greek amphorae. Al Morrison executed the design, according to Addey's instructions.

The asteroid Urania is related to astronomy and astrology. Its position (house, sign, numerical) and exact aspects describe the form that these sciences will take. For example, an astrologer who has written an astrological book that has been published has Urania in the ninth house at 19° Aries in the following exact aspects— semisextile the Midheaven, square Mercury and semisquare Jupiter. The positions and rulerships of the two planets, as well as the other exact aspects of the three factors, tell more of the story.

Urania is also prominent in the charts of other scientists and of musicians. Other scientists and musicians are involved with measurement—the latter in the form of measures and meters. There is the Muse of Music, Euterpe, but she "favored rather the wild and simple melodies of primitive people than the more finished art of music and was associated more with Dionysus than with Apollo."[9]

It has been stated that astrologers (probably other scientists and musicians too) who are not inspired do not have Urania prominent in their charts. However, I have not been able to verify this statement since Urania has been prominent in every chart of an astrologer that I have seen. Perhaps, all the astrologers whose charts I have are inspired. Or, since the differences are descriptive, perhaps in the charts of uninspired astrologers, Urania is still prominent but indicates this lack of inspiration. Naturally, to know who is inspired and who is not may be impossible, and maybe the very act of seeking meaning in the universe, as astrologers do, is inspirational. In support of this hypothesis, I have seen Urania highlighted in the charts of people who are not astrologers, astronomers, other scientists or musicians, but who are seeking to decipher the meaning and order of the universe.

There is an association of Urania with Uranus. The asteroid might be a feminine expression of the planet. Urania is as scientific and inventive as Uranus but doesn't seem to be as erratic and revolutionary. However, looking for meaning in a mainly materialistic society is revolutionary in itself.

Personal Name Asteroids

And now for the next milestone—on April 4, 1981 at 03:00 PM there was a meeting at my house of the New York Research Committee of the National Council for Geocosmic Research. (Actually, the meeting did not officially begin until shortly after the lunation at 03:19 PM.) I was the research chairman at that time. At this meeting Martin Adelman, a data processing consultant, suggested that we conduct a study on personal, or common, name asteroids. He felt that in studying them, rather than asteroids named after mythological characters, we would be eliminating variables. The association would be to a specific person with the name of the asteroid, rather than to the general mythology of the god or goddess.

Out of this meeting a subcommittee of five people, Martin Adelman, J. Lee Lehman, Diana Rosenberg, Michael Shapiro and myself, evolved. We met to list on 3 x 5 cards the over 2000 asteroids already named at that time. Once the asteroids were on index cards, we could alphabetize them and choose those asteroids which we wanted to research. We decided that asteroids with the names either of subcommittee members or of their close relatives should be chosen. Since this was an initial study, we felt it should be conducted on the people we knew best and for whom we had accurate data.

The asteroids Martina (981), Julia (89), Diana (78) and Michel (1348) were chosen because they were the asteroids whose names were closest to the names of the subcommittee members. (Lee's first name is Julie.) When we chose I was the only member who did not have an asteroid the same as, or similar to, his or her name. The asteroids Jeanne (1281) and Sy (1714), the names of my mother and husband, and Elsa (182) and Patricia (436), the names of Martin's mother and ex-wife, were chosen as the asteroids with the names of close relatives.

The names of the asteroids Diana, Jeanne, Elsa and Patricia are exactly the same as the given names of the people we were hypothesizing they represented. Martina is a feminized version; Julia is a different spelling; Michel, a different language; and Sy, a nickname for Seymour—the given name of my husband. Using these eight asteroids, we could research not only whether the asteroid with the name of a person, but whether the asteroid with the closest approximation to the name of a person, is relevant to the so-named person. The asteroid with the closest approximation was only considered when there was no asteroid with the exact name.

HYPOTHESIS

The hypothesis that was formulated by Martin Adelman is as follows: "A. If an individual has in actuality proven to be of great significance to a native, and B. there is an asteroid with the name of that individual, then C. that asteroid ought to be placed prominently in the native's horoscope, according to generally accepted astrological principles—conjunct or opposition within 10° an appropriate personal planet or personal point, i.e., the Moon is generally associated with the mother, or there may be a particular association according to the particular meanings of the charts of the individual and the native." (Naturally, this statement would apply to an asteroid with the native's own name.) Martin's hypothesis was considered, though there was disagreement concerning his limitation of the aspects to two and his use of a 10° orb.

PREDICTIONS

Right ascensions and declinations for the eight asteroids were ordered from Dr. Brian Marsden. Dr. Lehman was to calculate the ephemerides from these positions. Before these positions were received, I asked that each person on the subcommittee predict where his or her name asteroid and/or the name asteroids of significant individuals would be situated in his or her chart and in the charts of significant individuals. For instance for Martin, there was Martina in Martin's chart, in his ex-wife's chart, in his mother's chart and in his father's chart; there was Patricia, the name of Martin's ex-wife, in her chart and in Martin's chart; there was Elsa, the name of Martin's mother, in her chart, in Martin's chart, and in Martin's father's chart. (Later there were other placements, such as Martina and Patricia in their three children's charts, but for Martin these are the positions with which we began.)

By making predictions the subcommittee had the opportunity to take into account "the particular meanings of the charts." One of the members, Michael, chose not to make any predictions, and the other members only made predictions in those cases where they were inclined to do so. In our predictions, Lee, Diana and I added other aspects, and Lee and I decreased the orb to 02° (somewhat larger than my usual orb). What we were investigating in this part of the experiment was not so much the significance of the name asteroids, as the ability of astrologers to accurately predict the positions of factors which had not even been studied as yet.

Regarding the 32 original positions (9 for Martin, etc.), there were 16 predictions (3 for Martin, etc.). Out of 16 predictions, 5 were correct and 11 were incorrect. Decidedly, some judgment was required to determine whether a prediction was correct or not. For example, Lee said in her prediction concerning the asteroid Julia in her own chart that it was "maybe in the twelfth house or conjunct, opposition or square Ceres or Saturn within 02°." She thought your own name asteroid would show how you view your name, and when she had first begun to talk, she had objected to being called Julie. (She was named after her maternal grandmother Julia but was called Julie.) She subsequently used her middle name, which is Lee. I judged her prediction correct because her Julia turned out to be in her twelfth house. Though there is no conjunction, opposition or square within 02° from her Julia to her Ceres or Saturn, her prediction had specified one or the other, not both. The one that there is is certainly descriptive of her reaction to her name—she wanted it dissolved.

It was observed that limiting the aspects to just the conjunction and opposition did not allow for the diversity in relationships and that the 10° orb was too diffuse. For a second part of the experiment, I added to the conjunction and opposition, the semisextile, semisquare, sextile, square, trine, sesquiquadrate and quincunx from one degree to the next. (All aspects have meaning, but these are the ones that I have found most powerful.) The addition of these aspects increased the possibility of contact, but the decrease in the size of the orb decreased the possibility. The advantage of the addition was an increase in the likelihood of descriptiveness, since, as stated, a different and specific meaning is attributed to each aspect, as well as each separation.

Having judged the accuracy of predictions based on "the particular meanings of the charts," in this second part of the experiment I judged what would be the accuracy of predictions based on general meanings, using the nine aspects and orb mentioned. To explain, a prediction based on general meanings is that your name asteroid will be in your first house or closely aspecting your Ascendant, East Point, Sun, Moon or ruler of your Ascendant. These expectations were fulfilled in some cases, but in others, such as the case of Lee, they were not. Out of 32 original positions, 11 were "correct" and 21 were "incorrect."

PERSONAL REPRESENTATION

Though the results of predictions, both "particular" and "general," were not impressive, part of the hypothesis, "there may be a particular association according to the particular meanings of the charts," was invariably confirmed. That association was always in accordance with astrological principles, but it was not always in accordance with general rules. Each case was individual, but in each case the asteroid with the name of a person proved to be representative of that person, even if the name were a feminized version, a different spelling, a different language or a nickname.

To give an example, Michel in Michael's chart is at 04° Leo 27' in the eleventh house, close to Uranus at 02° Leo 11'. When Michael discovered this placement he felt the shock of recognition, since he said what he'd always wanted most was to be different. Michael by this placement is represented as being Cancerian (04°), Leonine (Leo) and Aquarian (eleventh house), with the Aquarian quality emphasized by the proximity of Uranus. Considering those aspects specified above, there are the following aspects that are exact. Michel is semisquare Michael's Ascendant at 20° Virgo 28', Midheaven at 19° Gemini 02' and South Node at 18° Gemini 28' (at the midpoint between the Ascendant and Midheaven in the eleventh house). These three personal points, denoting the persona, prestige, and close relationships, are connected to the Michel by an aspect of transformative power. Michel is sextile Mars at 05° Libra 03' in the first house, so with this aspect of work and service there are two metaphors for the self (Mars and first house). Another personal point connection is from the Vertex in the sixth house at 03° Pisces 58' (Finger of God with Mars). This exact quincunx to both Michel and Uranus ties them together, although they are two degrees apart. Michael's work (sixth house) has been as an artist (Pisces and quincunx). I had asked that every asteroid available to us, such as Ceres, Pallas, Juno, Vesta, Chiron, the other name asteroids, and whichever of the ten asteroids had already been published by the *CAO Times*, be added to the charts. Excluding the other name asteroids for now, the only aspect to Michel with this addition is a trine from Hidalgo in the third house at 03° Sagittarius 59'. Hidalgo refers to self-assertion, and it is in a degree and house of communication and a sign of philosophy. It is exactly connected to Michel and to Uranus in an aspect of communication. As mentioned, what Michael wanted most was to be different (Uranus, eleventh house). In expressing this difference, he asserted himself in communication (03°, third house, trine) of his philosophy (Sagittarius).

The general rules are upheld in that Michel is exactly semisquare Michael's Ascendant, but more importantly Michel in its placement and exact aspects describes the particular associations that Michael has in relationship to himself.

Another example is of the asteroid Diana in Diana's chart. The asteroid is at 12° Pisces 51' in the ninth house, in an exact trine to the Ascendant at 12° Cancer 16'. Diana had predicted that her Diana would be "conjunct the Ascendant or conjunct the ruler of the Ascendant or trine the Ascendant." She felt in harmony with her name. Further research did indicate that an exact trine of your name asteroid to your Ascendant equates to a feeling of harmony regarding your name (unless there are aspects which countermand this harmony). Diana by her name asteroid placement is represented as being doubly Piscean (degree and sign), combined with Sagittarian (ninth house). The asteroid Diana is also exactly square Vesta at 12° Gemini 55' in the twelfth house, sextile Eros and the seventh house cusp at 12° Capricorn 10' and 12° Capricorn 16', and quincunx Urania at 13° Libra 01'℞. Diana is extremely committed to duty (Vesta), regarding the home and nurturing (Cancer Ascendant), the partner (Eros and seventh house cusp) and astrology (Urania).

Analysis of the degree and aspect equivalencies will give further detail. To illustrate an analysis of degree equivalency, 12° is the degree of all of these factors, except Urania. 12° equates to Neptune. Diana's Neptune is at 07° Virgo 47' in the third house, rules her Midheaven, Icarus, North Node, Diana, Ceres and Mercury and is in an exact semisextile with her Moon at 06° Libra 40'—reinforcing my exposition.

The fact that there is an exact aspect of Diana's name asteroid to Urania is interesting. Lee also has an exact aspect to Urania from her name asteroid. Though she had rejected her first name in favor of her middle name, she had to deal with her first name again in this astrological study (Urania) of the personal name asteroids. Her Julia is semisquare an exact conjunction of Jupiter and Urania in Gemini in her tenth house. The semisquare is the aspect of transformation, and she transformed her name. Also, she has been involved with writing (Gemini) and publishing (Jupiter) treatises on astrology (Urania), including the *Ephemeris of Diana*. The publishing of that ephemeris was an outgrowth of this study, and Lee's Jupiter rules her Sagittarian Diana, which is exactly conjunct her fifth house cusp of creativity. Martin's name asteroid, though not fulfilling the expectations of contact with the first house or personal points, is also exactly aspecting his Urania. This time the aspect is a square. We found that the name asteroid is very much related to the person's identity. When the person's identity is very much related to being an astrologer, there is usually an exact aspect from the Urania either to the name asteroid or to the Ascendant, Sun, Moon or Midheaven. (The public identity is more related to the Midheaven.)

The examples I have given have been of the native's name asteroid in the native's own chart, but the native's name asteroid in a significant individual's chart proved to be as descriptive. For instance, Diana's husband's asteroid Diana is at 05° Capricorn 25' in the third house, exactly conjunct his Venus at 04° Capricorn 46'. To Diana's husband she represented a loving (Venus) relative (third house) with whom he shared the responsibilities (Capricorn) of their children (05°). Though they eventually separated, that characterization is still appropriate. His Diana is also exactly trine his North Node at 06° Virgo 16' in the eleventh house and Kronos at 04° Taurus 09'ᴙ in the seventh house (Grand Trine); quincunx Zeus at 04° Leo 07'ᴙ in the tenth house; square Admetos at 04° Aries 33'ᴙ in the sixth house, sesquiquadrate Cupido, Neptune at 19° Leo 20'ᴙ, 20° Leo 20'ᴙ in the tenth house (Fist of God);[10] and semisquare Toro at 19° Scorpio 13' in the second house. (The Uranian planets Kronos, Zeus, Admetos and Cupido are included in this delineation. We used Uranian planets in the common name asteroid study, but until now for simplicity's sake I have not mentioned them.)

Close relations (Node), authority (Kronos), procreation (Zeus), stoppage (Admetos), marriage (Cupido), idealism or deception (Neptune) and amplification (Toro) are connected to the Diana through various aspects defined by their numerical associations. The Admetos square may have contributed to Diana and her husband's breakup but may also have contributed to the longevity of their emotional attachment, which continued even after the breakup. Their marriage lasted thirty-five years and was only terminated by his death. As explained, the stoppage of Admetos can relate to ending, or to a perpetual "going around in circles" which is never ending—at least "till death us do part."

INTERASPECTS, SEPARATIONS AND MIDPOINTS

Interaspects are also representative. Diana's Diana at 12° Pisces 51' is exactly conjunct her husband's Uranus at 13° Pisces 41' in the fifth house, square his Sun at 12° Sagittarius 55' in the second house, trine his Pluto at 11° Cancer 51'ᴙ in the ninth house, semisextile his Urania at 11° Aquarius 31' and Ceres at 13° Aquarius 54' in the fourth house, and sesquiquadrate his Saturn at 28° Libra 43' in the first house and Pandora at 28° Cancer 48'ᴙ in the tenth house. (The Saturn and Pandora form two interlocking Fists of God with the Diana, Uranus and Sun.) Her husband's Diana at 05° Capricorn 25' is exactly square Diana's Moon at 06° Libra 40' in the fourth house, and opposite her Pandora at 06° Cancer 45' in the twelfth house (T-Square). Note the Pandora involvement in both cases.

Without going into all of the exact previously prescribed aspects, let me just add some examples regarding the asteroid Diana in the charts of Diana's children. Diana's daughter's Diana is in her tenth house at 19° Aquarius 03'ᴙ, sextile her

Saturn at 20° Sagittarius 29'. Diana's son's Diana is in his fourth house at 12° Sagittarius 15', conjunct his Saturn at 12° Sagittarius 59' and quincunx his Moon at 13° Cancer 54'. These positions, appropriate for "the mother," form appropriate interaspects. Diana's daughter's Diana is sextile Diana's Sun at 19° Aries 19', and Diana's son's Diana is square Diana's Diana at 12° Pisces 51', as well as conjunct his father's Sun at 12° Sagittarius 55'.

Though only the 30° aspects, semisquares and sesquiquadrates have been mentioned, all the aspects—all the angular separations—are meaningful. The separations between name asteroids in one chart and name asteroids in another are descriptive of the relationship between the so-named people. Separations between name asteroids within a single chart are descriptive of what that relationship means to the one whose chart it is. Midpoints of name asteroids in charts and between charts are points of interaction between the people who are identified by the names. (If the midpoint is of name asteroids for the same person, i.e., the first and second name, it will be a point at which factors descriptive of that person are combined.)

ANALYSIS OF A FAMILY

As part of our research, Martin analyzed the asteroids Patricia and Martina in twenty-eight charts. These included the natal charts of Martin, Patricia, their three children and Martin's father, whom Martin believes may have been a prototype for his ex-wife. There was also a "conception chart" of Martin, based on the theory that conception occurs when the transiting Moon conjuncts the natal Ascendant nine months before birth. Interestingly, the transiting Moon was exactly conjunct the transiting Patricia. Also, there were two-person relationship charts of Martin with Patricia, Martin with each of their three children, Patricia with each of their three children and each child with each other child. There were three-person relationship charts of Martin with Patricia and one child, Martin with Patricia and another child, Martin with each possible combination of two of their children, Patricia with two of their children and the three children together. In addition, there were four-person relationship charts of Martin and their three children, Patricia and their three children and Martin, Patricia and two of their children. Finally, there was a five-person relationship chart of Martin, Patricia and their three children.

Martin presented his analysis to the group, and the way in which the asteroids Patricia and Martina figured in these charts was very descriptive. Though the asteroids were reflective of the present relationships, Martin said they were also reflective of past-life relationships with his ex-wife and three children, as told to him by a psychic.

PAST LIVES

As asteroids, both personal and otherwise, were added to my own and other charts, I too discovered that they described, not only the present life, but also details of past lives that had been told to me either by a psychic or by psychic flashes that I had had myself. When names are part of those revelations, the asteroids with those names are appropriately placed. Sometimes, conjunctions, midpoints, or other configurations of those placements will indicate connections between names in past and present lives.

Some people will object that we do not know if there are past lives. They may say that the psyche was just picking up the positions of the asteroids, even though some of these asteroids had not been discovered at the time of the psychic readings or of the psychic flashes. However, I believe that the planets, as well as the asteroids. tell both the present and the past. The reason that the past lives become more evident with the addition of the asteroids is that the asteroids are more specific.

RELATIONSHIP AND COMPOSITE CHARTS

In Martin's relationship charts, the metamorphosis that occurred with the addition or subtraction of the time and place of each person mirrored the literal addition or subtraction of that person. A relationship chart is a chart calculated for the midpoint in time and space (average latitude, average longitude) between two or more charts. Until then I had only used composite charts, which consist of the midpoints between the factors in two or more charts. With composites the midpoint of two or more Midheavens is calculated, and then the other house cusps are derived from this composite Midheaven, using a Table of Houses for the location of the relationship. The midpoints of two or more Suns, Moons, etc., are then calculated.

Having always found the composite chart very descriptive of the relationship, I had never felt the need to calculate the relationship chart. However, Martin's presentation was so revealing, I proceeded to do relationship charts, in addition to composite charts. What I discovered was that while the composite chart describes the relationship, the relationship chart describes what happens in the relationship. For example, the composite Sun of my present husband and myself is in Aries, while our relationship Sun is in Libra (equaling our natal Sun/Moon midpoints). Though within our relationship there is a great deal of independence (Aries), we did marry and do have a true partnership (Libra).

It is particularly enlightening when there is a name asteroid for each person in a relationship. I already had the ephemeris for the Sy asteroid. Fortunately, in the fall of 1981, asteroid 2382, which had been discovered April 13, 1977, at Perth Observatory in Bickley, Australia, was named Nonie in honor of the daughter of Peter Jekabsons, a member of the astronometric team. Nonie is a nickname for Nona.

When there is a name asteroid for each person in a relationship, usually you can tell which planets, asteroids and personal points in the relationship and composite charts refer to each person by noting the exact aspects to each name asteroid. In the case of my relationship chart with my husband, Sy, this discrimination between name asteroids is more difficult because the Nonie and the Sy are exactly conjunct at 12° Cancer 59' and 13° Cancer 06'. However, this exact conjunction is descriptive of what happens in the relationship—we act in concert regarding the home and nurturing.

PROGRESSIONS AND TRANSITS

Having asked the members of the subcommittee to put the asteroids with names of significant individuals into the natal charts of relevant individuals, I then asked them to progress these asteroids to the time of significant events in the lives of these individuals, and to look at the transits at that time as well. After they did, it was evident that progressions and transits of and to the name asteroids are descriptive of the events at that time.

For instance, when my husband Sy and I met, the transiting Sy at 25° Gemini 54' in the tenth house was exactly conjunct Urania (24° Gemini 18'), our composite Ascendant (24° Gemini 17'), our composite Sun/Moon midpoint (24° Gemini 38'), as well as Sy's 25° Gemini progressed Midheaven and my 25° Gemini progressed Sun. The transiting Sy was also square Jupiter (24° Virgo 30'), trine the Part of Fortune (24° Libra 26'), sextile Admetos (25° Aries 39') and semisquare Nonie, the asteroid with my name (11° Leo 01'). In relation to Sy's natal chart, transiting Sy was in his tenth house, opposition his Mars (24° Sagittarius 22')—ruler of his ninth house and Venus—and sesquiquadrate his Icarus (10° Aquarius 36'). In relation to my natal chart, transiting Sy was in my fourth house, square my Sappho (25° Virgo 18') and my Icarus (25° Pisces 07')—T-Square—sextile my Uranus (25° Aries 33')—ruler of my chart, of Saturn and of my Part of Fortune—semisquare my Kronos (11° Taurus 39') and Zeus (10° Leo 05'), Klotho (11° Leo 36') and sesquiquadrate my Psyche (09° Scorpio 28'℞)—Fist of God with Icarus. Without analyzing all the enumerated aspects, let me just say that Urania means "Heavenly"; Psyche is active at the beginning of love relationships; there were to be "things above average" (Kronos) and procreation (Zeus); Klotho is the asteroid with a name equivalent to mine; and Sy and I both took great risks (Icarus) in that we married one month and twenty-nine days after we met.

At the time we married, transiting Sy was at 17° Cancer 06' in the fifth house, exactly semisquare transiting Nonie at 01° Virgo 04' in the seventh house. Our name asteroids had continued in the semisquare aspect they formed at our meeting, but now they equaled our natal Sun/Moon (husband/wife) midpoints, which equal each other by a sesquiquadrate. The transiting Klotho was at 17° Capricorn 48'℞, also equaling our natal Sun/Moon midpoints. My husband's natal Sun/Moon midpoint is 17° Capricorn 49', while mine is 01° Gemini 27'. His North Node (02° Virgo 09') is exactly conjunct my South Node (03° Virgo 16'), equaling our Sun/Moon midpoints. His Venus (16° Aries 25'), Juno (16° Libra 20'℞), name asteroid of our daughter (17° Libra 29'℞) and name asteroid of my son (01° Pisces 06'), as well as my Sun (02° Gemini 34') and Eros (17° Capricorn 13'℞) also equal these midpoints, making this connection the most powerful between our charts.

As regards our secondary progressed name asteroids without going into all the prescribed aspects, at the time of our meeting and marriage Sy's progressed Sy was exactly semisquare my progressed Nonie. (At the time of the marriage progressed Sy was 14° Taurus 59' and progressed Nonie was 28° Gemini 43'.) The semisquare of the meeting and marriage charts was reiterated. The semisquare is a Pluto aspect, and the relationship was very Plutonian—powerful, obsessive and transformative.

By solar arc progressions (which I find more karmic than secondary progressions), at the time of my meeting and marrying my husband Sy, my solar-arced Nonie was exactly conjunct my natal Sy. My natal Sy is in the fifth house at 13° Cancer 37', and at our meeting my solar-arced Nonie came to 13° Cancer 49' and at our marriage it came to 13° Cancer 58'. (Solar-arced Nonie was also exactly conjunct our relationship Nonie and Sy.) My natal Sy is exactly sextile my Vertex and Jupiter in the seventh house. My solar-arced Nonie came along and activated the natal potential of Sy for me. In like manner at the time of our meeting and marriage, Sy's solar-arced Sy came along and activated the natal potential of Nonie for him. His solar-arced Sy was exactly conjunct his natal Klotho, which is exactly conjunct his natal Nonie, both in the tenth house. (Klotho is the asteroid with a name equivalent to Nona because Klotho was the Greek Fate who is equivalent to the Roman Fate Nona.) The solar-arced Sy was also exactly conjunct my natal fourth house cusp and exactly square Sy's natal Sun in the seventh house.

To return to event charts, the name asteroids of lesser characters at the events will be appropriately posited in the charts too. For instance, my mother, Jeanne, was at the wedding of my present husband, Sy, and myself. Transiting Jeanne was at 07° Sagittarius 39' in the ninth house, exactly conjunct Saturn at 07° Sagittarius 58' and my natal Midheaven at 07° Sagittarius 41'. I believe my mother is represented by my tenth house (Saturn, Midheaven) and she was a Sagittarian (Sagittarius, ninth house). Also, an event chart has within it the end result of the event, so name asteroids of characters who will figure in future events, which are the outcome of this one, will be appropriately posited. At the wedding of my ex-husband and myself, my transiting name asteroid at 02° Cancer 41'℞ was exactly square his transiting name asteroid at 02° Aries 44', and exactly trine the transiting name asteroid of my present husband at 03° Pisces 07' (exactly conjunct his natal South Node and my natal North Node, at his natal Sun/Moon midpoint, which equals mine).

NEW NAMES

A significant event in the life of an individual is the assumption of a new name, and that event is mirrored in the name asteroids. My present husband first used the name Sy to introduce himself to some acquaintances on the golf course. His family knew him as Seymour, while his friends and business acquaintances knew him as "Red," which made golf acquaintances the best ones on whom to try out the new name. He felt that Sy, a nickname for Seymour, sounded preferable to Seymour (too old-fashioned) or Red (too childish). However, it wasn't until he went away to play in an orchestra at a resort a year later that he decided to introduce himself as Sy to everyone he met. A couple of days later he met me, and a couple of months later we were married. He said that at the time he decided to use the name Sy, he felt more ready for responsibility. His natal Sy is at 03° Taurus 24', exactly conjunct Kronos at 04° Taurus 07', opposition Saturn at 02° Scorpio 07'℞ and Eros at 03° Scorpio 37', square Zeus at 03° Leo 02'℞ (T-Square) and semisextile Nonie at 04° Gemini 19', conjunct Klotho at 05° Gemini 24'. On his part it was love at first sight (Eros) when he (Sy) met me (Nonie, Klotho) and became the responsible (Saturn) head of the family (Kronos) to me and my procreation (Zeus), a Sagittarian (Zeus) son.

It seems as well that the discovery or naming of a new asteroid is a significant event for the individual who has the same, or a similar, name. Martin told the subcommittee that when the asteroid Martinez was named, he went through a Pluto-type change. The change was a Pluto type because it was a total transformation that was at first very internal. He said that the change was accentuated by the fact that while Martina is a feminine name, Martinez is a masculine name.

INITIAL COMPUTER RUN

Also, the subcommittee discovered that the charts for the beginning and for the end of an asteroid's initial computer run are descriptive of the meaning of the asteroid being run. The calculation of a 100-year ephemeris, which was the result of each computer run, sometimes spanned four days. (The zodiacal positions had to be translated from right ascensions and declinations.) After the completion of those runs, Lee Lehman calculated, and the subcommittee studied, the charts of those "events." Though the timing of the beginning and the end was not elected, the relevance of their charts was apparent. Then, in the fall of 1982 Astro added an option of a 100-year custom ephemeris for any asteroid. Up to four asteroids can be run concurrently. The time of the calculation is listed at the top of each page, and I realized that the charts for the beginning and for the end of these computer runs, which span sixteen minutes, are meaningful too. These charts are descriptive in terms of the meaning of the asteroid or asteroids being run, in relation to the person for whom they are being run.

As an example, one Astro ephemeris is of my two name asteroids and my son's two name asteroids. In the chart for the beginning of this run there is the following emphasis on us, as well as on the Fates to which Nonie and Klotho refer. One of my son's name asteroids is 18° Virgo in the fifth house, exactly conjunct the fifth cusp (the child), quincunx the Midheaven and Moon (the parents), semisextile the Part of Fortune (Fortune means Fate), semisquare the Vertex (a "fated" quality), and opposite my name asteroid Nonie. Nonie is 18° Pisces in the eleventh house, exactly conjunct the eleventh cusp (the astrologer, and I have an Aquarius Ascendant). My name asteroid also forms exact aspects to the Midheaven, Moon, Part of Fortune and Vertex. Klotho, my other name asteroid, is 20° Scorpio ℞ in the sixth house, exactly square the Moon and my natal Ascendant, opposite the East Point (T-Square), semisextile the Part of Fortune and semisquare the Sun (the child, and it sounds like son). My son's other name asteroid is 27° Sagittarius in the seventh house, exactly square Venus, sextile Pluto and semisquare Jupiter. (Pluto can be reproduction, and my son has a Sagittarius Sun, with Venus exactly opposite his Ascendant. Also, my son's name is the same as his father's, so the seventh house placement is appropriate for his father who was my first husband.)

STATIONS

Noting the stations of the asteroids is another procedure which I have found helpful. Eleanor Bach introduced the concept that the degree in which a planet or asteroid has a station remains sensitive in the nature of that body at least until its next station. Transits to these degrees are called "hidden aspects." In the October 1983 issue of her *Planet Watch*, she suggested looking at "the last station of planets before birth, and those that occur after birth…" (The stations after birth would be in the progressed chart.) Trying this suggestion with the planets and asteroids, I found that if the planet or asteroid was direct at birth, not only was the direct station before birth particularly important, but also the retrograde station before and after birth. On the other hand, if the planet or asteroid was retrograde at birth, not only was the retrograde station before birth particularly important, but also the direct station before and after birth. The stations are cycles like the lunations or harmonics, and what a station is coming from and going toward is implicit in what it is. Even if these stations will never occur in the progressed chart during the person's life, they are enlightening. In reference to the natal chart, conjunctions are the most important, and if a natal planet or asteroid is exactly conjunct one of its own three adjacent stations, that body is especially emphasized. Revealing too are exact aspects and interaspects of the stations, especially those of the name asteroids.

For instance, the last retrograde station of my husband's name asteroid before his birth is 02° Taurus (conjunct his 03° Taurus natal position), square the last retrograde station of our daughter's name asteroid before her birth at 03° Aquarius. This 03° Aquarius station is opposite both the last retrograde station of her brother's (my son's) name asteroid before his birth at 04° Leo (conjunct his 04° Leo natal position) and the last retrograde station of Klotho before my birth at 04° Leo. These 04° Leo stations are conjunct the first retrograde station of Nonie after my birth at 05° Leo. The stations form appropriate aspects and interaspects to the natal charts. My husband's 02° Taurus station is semisextile my 02° Gemini Sun; and our daughter's 03° Aquarius station is trine my 02° Gemini Sun and opposite her 04° Leo Sun; while my 04° and 05° Leo stations are conjunct our daughter's 04° Leo Sun, and, of course, my son's 04° Leo name asteroid. The last retrograde station (02° Taurus) of Sy before my husband's birth is also semisextile the last direct station of Nonie before his birth at 01° Gemini, which is conjunct my 00° Gemini Moon and my 02° Gemini Sun. (Relevant composite and relationship charts are exactly aspected too.)

Though the three stations bracketing the birth are particularly important, the interconnectedness of the stations is to be noted at other times too. For instance, my name asteroid Nonie was stationary direct at 25° Virgo at the end of May 1981; my son's name asteroid was stationary direct at 26° Pisces in mid-November of 1983; Nonie was stationary direct at 25° Gemini at the end of February 1984; my son's other name asteroid was stationary direct at 25° Sagittarius in mid-August 1984. The second direct station of my name asteroid is in a new cycle, but a cycle that aspects the first one. These exact aspects of the stations mirror my relationship with my son during this period. At issue, to give an example, were criticality (Virgo), delusion (Pisces), communication (Gemini) and philosophy (Sagittarius), usually during near and distant travel (Gemini and Sagittarius). The stations, which also form exact appropriate aspects to pertinent natal, composite and relationship charts, were exactly and appropriately aspected at times when the stations' concerns were accentuated.

RETROGRADATION

A station, whether it is direct or retrograde, emphasizes a planet or asteroid. As for retrogradation, this backward motion, even if not at the time of a station, emphasizes the body in the nature of a retrospection. In the natal chart, if it is your name asteroid that is retrograde, there may be some difficulty or delay in the expression of your identity; if it is someone else's, there may be in the expression of his or her identity in regard to you.

EXPANSION OF THE STUDY

As our research continued, we expanded the study to include all those people with names of the initial eight asteroids who are listed in *The American Book of Charts* and *Profiles of Women* by Lois M. Rodden and *2001: The Penfield Collection* by Marc Penfield. (Diana Rosenberg prepared this part of the research.) We found it more difficult dealing with people only known publicly, since the common name asteroid is so personally descriptive. However, when we were aware of some fact integral to the person, we perceived how appropriate the position of the name asteroid was.

Michel Gauquelin has his Midheaven at 00° Taurus 59' and his Jupiter at 03° Taurus 16'℞, according to *The American Book of Charts* (A Data, which is the most accurate). When we added his Michel it was at 27° Libra 41' in the third house. The opposition from his Michel to his Midheaven and Jupiter is not exact, but the asteroid forms an exact within a degree symmetrical pattern with them (planetary picture) which is very powerful. Gauquelin is most known for his research with prominent (Jupiter) professionals (Midheaven), and he worked with his wife, Francoise (Michel in Libra). Though this research is a public expression of his Michel, I have met Gauquelin and observed that this "prominent professionalism" is expressed personally as well. As the Gauquelins have concluded from their research: character traits are the basis of prominence in a profession.

For another part of our research, Martin ordered his natal positions of 300 asteroids from Dr. Brian Marsden. The asteroids that Martin chose were those with names that had relevance to his life. He chose first, middle and family names of people that were important to him, the names of places he'd lived or visited, subjects he'd liked or loathed. Not only were those asteroids in appropriate positions, but they were activated when these people, places or entities came into his life. Asteroids with his middle and family name were descriptive of him, as well as of pertinent family members, i.e., an asteroid with his middle name, which was derived from the name of his maternal grandmother, was conjunct Ceres. Asteroids whose names were related in his life were often together in stelliums. Rather than the multiplicity of asteroids confusing the issues, it made these issues more evident.

As we added asteroids to our charts, we found the same phenomenon. Though we began with only eight name asteroids, other asteroids, including name ones, were later ordered from Astro. Then, Zipporah Dobyns and Mark Pottenger gave me my natal positions for 368 asteroids. Mark had written a program which lists the positions in geocentric and heliocentric longitude, grouping them in different categories, such as "fates," "work and finance" and "personal names." The program also lists the longitudes in zodiacal order. Though these asteroids were not hand-picked by me, many of their positions were relevant to my life and showed the same pattern of appropriateness and activation as Martin's had shown. Listings of other people's natal asteroid positions were also provided to me. When I got my own computer, which has a hard disk drive, I was able to run the positions of 392 asteroids—later 452, and then 464.[11] (I now have Mark's program for 942 asteroids, but my book does not deal with this latest acquisition.) Mark's program provides not only their natal and progressed (secondary and solar-arced) positions, but their harmonic positions as well. My initial impression that the asteroids particularize the generalities of the planets has been repeatedly confirmed.

CONCLUSIONS REGARDING PERSONAL REPRESENTATION

Martin said our experiments rule out the idea that forces are coming from the asteroids or planets. What we are dealing with here is not name energy, but name specificity. The names are symbols, and sometimes they are puns or plays on words. The more I've worked with the asteroids, the more I've agreed with his statement.

My conclusions are that an asteroid with your name or the name of someone close to you is posited in natal, progressed, transit, relocation, return, harmonic, composite and relationship charts in such a way that it is descriptive of your relationship to yourself, if it is your name; or to that other person, if it is his or her name. The asteroid whose name is the closest will be descriptive, even if the name is not exact. An asteroid whose name is close will have relevance, even though the asteroid whose name is closest will be most specific. Of course, as new asteroids are discovered and named, what is the closest name may change.

As for the comparative relevance of names, the first name is most descriptive of the person, while the middle name, unless it is taken as the first, is subsidiary. Middle names are often derived from family names, and, if so, this association is shown. The family name is most general and describes the individual's associations to that family.

RELEVANCE OF MEANING

Another discovery we made is that the meaning and derivation of the name is also relevant, and the name is in your life in principle, even if not in person. The asteroid's position in your chart, therefore, will show not only your relationship to a person with that name, but also your relationship to the principle of that name.

To explain, as part of our experiments we had consulted *Name Your Baby* by Lareina Rule in regard to the names of the asteroids we were studying. When the names were biblical, we consulted the *Metaphysical Bible Dictionary* as well, which is based on the teaching of Charles Fillmore. Unexpectedly, we found that the meanings and derivations were as important as the myths we were eliminating by studying asteroids with common, rather than mythological, names. For instance, Martina means "martial, warlike one," Martina is a feminine name, and where it is posited there is a "feminine" Mars-like quality. (Now I can add that Michael Shapiro's Martina is exactly sesquiquadrate his name asteroid, connecting Martina's quality, as well as people named Martina, to Michael's identity by an aspect of transformative power.) The fact that the derivation of the name is Latin gives it Roman connotations. Those connotations are ones of practicality and fortitude. Also, we found that insight into the meaning of a name is given by the lives of well-known people with that name. (For most of the names, Lareina Rule lists well-known namesakes.) Martina Navratilova, the tennis champion, is the most famous exponent of the exact name. There is no asteroid Martin, so Martina is the closest approximation to the first name of Martin Luther, the priest who founded the Protestant Reformation, and of Martin Luther King, Jr., the civil-rights leader who had a dream. These famous people illustrate an aggressiveness that is not just dedicated to conquering, as Mars' aggressiveness was.

Relevance of Heliocentric Nodes

Another unexpected discovery we made was that the heliocentric nodes of the asteroids are significant. Diana had been studying the heliocentric planetary nodes, and she suggested we inquire as to their asteroidal counterpart. A listing of the positions of the heliocentric ascending nodes in absolute longitude was found in the *Ephemerides of Minor Planets*. (The descending nodes are exactly opposite.) We had used this book as the source for our indexing of the asteroids but had not been aware of the nodal locations among all the other elements. After accessing these positions, what we realized was that the salient quality already attributed to an asteroid was suggested in its heliocentric ascending nodal position. For example, this position for Sappho, to which sexuality had been attributed, was 08° Scorpio 23'2.83". (The principle of the degree can be combined with the sign, in relation to the minute, in regard to the second.) This was the location listed in the 1982 *Ephemerides of Minor Planets*. Though the location will be somewhat different in different years, I feel this position is especially meaningful because to my knowledge this time was the first that a group of astrologers was tuning into this position.

"The nodes of any orbiting body are the two locations where the plane of that body intersects the plane of the Earth's orbit, also known as the ecliptic. The ascending planetary node is analogous to the Moon's North Node." (As employed here, planetary node refers as well to the node of a minor planet, or asteroid.) This quotation is from the "Overview of the Nodes," written by Diana Rosenberg and J. Lee Lehman for the *Asteroid Names & Nodes* that we decided to publish after discovering the significance of the heliocentric nodes of the asteroids.

Heliocentric nodes are from the vantage point of the Sun, in contrast to geocentric nodes which are from the vantage point of the Earth. Some people have objected to the use of heliocentric nodes because we are using geocentric positions of planets and asteroids. However, heliocentric nodes (like heliocentric positions of planets and asteroids) can be combined with geocentric positions of planets and asteroids to give some overview of the mundane by assuming a vantage point outside it.

CONJUNCTIONS TO HELIOCENTRIC NODES

A planet, asteroid or point whose longitudinal position is conjunct an ascending heliocentric node will have a coloration of the asteroid or planet whose node it is, i.e., a planet (including a Uranian planet), asteroid or point conjunct the node of Ceres (20° Gemini 03') will be associated with the qualities and myth of Ceres. (Conjunct would be at 19°-21° Gemini.) I discovered that the node of a name asteroid is descriptive of the way a person or place with that name interfaces with the world. The principle of the name would interface with the world in that way also. (The node of an asteroid with the name of an entity other than a person or place would describe how that entity, or its principle, interfaces with the world too.) The sign and numerical position of the node, combined with its house and exact aspects (particularly conjunctions and oppositions) in the natal chart, would be considered. The descending node, which is exactly opposite the ascending node, is related to the ascending node as opposite houses or signs are related.

An asteroid whose ascending node is in either the same degree or the degree before or after the ascending node of a name asteroid is associated with the person or place with that name. An asteroid whose ascending node is opposite either that same degree or the degree before or after (in other words, conjunct the descending node) is more associated with "the other," than with that person or place. (The opposition is the aspect of relationship.) Naturally, those ascending nodes most exactly conjunct or opposite each other are the most tied together. (Exact aspects other than the conjunction and opposition connect the nodes, but in terms of the meanings of those aspects, rather than in terms of the self or of the other.) Examples of conjunctions to both ends of the nodal axis follow.

Using the 1984 *Ephemerides of Minor Planets*, the first in which the name Nonie appears for asteroid 2382, the ascending node of said asteroid is 05° Sagittarius 44'. One of the ascending nodes conjunct this node is that of Sabrina at 06° Sagittarius 35'. The meaning of Sabrina, as given in *Name Your Baby*, is "From the boundary line," and the name was made famous by the play *Sabrina Fair* and film *Sabrina*. The meaning of Nona (of which Nonie is an English nickname), as given in this same book, is "Ninth child." However, Nona is also one of the three Roman Fates—the one who weaves the thread of life. As the weaver, Nona is very involved with boundaries, and the Nonas I have known of, or known, including myself, have been also.

Nonie's descending node at 05° Gemini 44' is conjunct the ascending node of Preiska (04° Gemini 06'), Preziosa (05° Gemini 04'), Edisona (04° Gemini 12'), Vala (05° Gemini 15'), Kalliope (05° Gemini 59') and Harding (04° Gemini 35'). My second husband's last name is Press, which is similar to Preiska and Preziosa, and he is a musician—Kalliope is a musical instrument, as well as the Greek Muse of Heroic poetry. Edison means "Son of Edward," and my first husband's name is Edward, and he is the son of Edward, and our son is named Edward, so he is the son of Edward too. There is also the association with Thomas Edison, and my first husband and son are inventive. Vala means "Chosen one," and both husbands are Jewish. As for Harding, with my second husband I lived for eleven years on a street named Horace Harding and stayed one vacation on a street named Harding. Just recently, exploring this vacation area, I realized it must have been this same street named Harding on which my first husband and I spent our honeymoon. The vacation and honeymoon hotels were not chosen by us, and each hotel was chosen by a different person, so there was no intentional choice involved. Of course, this proximity of nodes was not known at those times, and the asteroid Nonie had not even been discovered as yet.

There are eleven other ascending nodes conjunct the descending node of Nonie. The names of these asteroids are relevant to me in regard to the other, but in ways that are more personal and so less obvious. Naturally, I am not suggesting that everybody named Nona, or Nonie, will marry someone named Press. Besides there being other ascending nodes, there are other associations with Preiska and Preziosa. Other associations might be the printing press, the president or a pressing quality, and the associations don't have to relate to a husband, Also, these words appear to be foreign, and there may be meanings in their foreign language, or languages, of which I am not aware.

FINDING MEANINGS

To find meanings I looked in the aforementioned *Name Your Baby,* dictionaries, encyclopedias and books of mythology. To find for whom or what the recently named asteroids were named, the best source is the *Minor Planet Circulars/Minor Planets and Comets.* Dictionaries, encyclopedias, etc., will tell you the etymological and mythological derivations of Nonie, but the *Circulars* will tell you that the so-named asteroid was named in honor of the daughter of a man involved in the discovery, which is also meaningful.

There are difficulties in finding the meanings. They are not only different in different languages, but meanings change over time, which makes finding them still more difficult. The positions of the nodes are changing too, so what is together at one time is not at another. This changing is particularly true as regards the relationship between the nodes of the planets, which are moving forwards, and the nodes of the asteroids, most of which are moving backwards. However, these different combinations at different times may be what the nodes are about. Our interface with the world changes.

MOTION OF THE NODES

We had erroneously believed at first that the nodes of the asteroids, like those of the planets, move forwards through the ecliptic at a rate of approximately one degree per century. Instead, when the nodal movement of the asteroids is forward, it is usually less than that of the planets. The difference between the heliocentric nodes on January 1, 1900 and on January 1, 2000 is -00°01' for Ceres; +00°22' for Pallas; -00°24' for Juno; +00°35' for Vesta; and +00°30' for Chiron.[12] This nodal movement of both the planets and asteroids is due to the precession of the equinoxes. Perhaps, the dissimilarity between the nodal movement of the planets and asteroids is due to the asteroids' greater perturbation.

In the *Ephemerides of Minor Planets,* a fixed equinox is used. However, in the *Ephemerides* for 1992 a conversion from the ecliptic and equinox of 1950 to the ecliptic and equinox of 2000 was made, increasing the position of the nodes by almost forty-two minutes.

Lists of the Asteroids

Lists of the asteroids, in the alphabetical order of their names and in the zodiacal order of their nodes, are in the Appendices. The heliocentric ascending nodes of the planets have been inserted in these lists. Degrees, minutes and seconds are given for the nodes, and the seconds are not rounded off to the closer second. The lists are based on *Ephemerides of Minor Planets* for epoch 1990, November 5.0 ET, with the ecliptic and equinox of 1950. (These are the latest ephemerides on disk. Some additional asteroids have been included.) November 5, 1990 is not the day of observation. The positions of the nodes are projected from previous observations, and November 5.0 ET is the epoch or instant of time used as a reference for 1990. The positions of the nodes, which are the osculating (true) nodes, may be somewhat different on different days of the year, but the position given for the year is significant.

The alphabetical listing will enable you to find out if there is an asteroid with a name important to you, and the zodiacal listing will enable you to see the juxtaposition of nodes. You can discover what exact aspects the node of an asteroid with a name important to you forms in your chart. You can see the colorations that are brought to planets, asteroids or points when their longitudinal positions are conjunct the ascending nodes of asteroids or planets. Though preliminary examination of juxtapositions could be visual, you will need to record the names and nodes of the pertinent asteroids and then investigate the meanings of the names and record those meanings. (Record the descending, as well as the ascending, node of a pertinent asteroid. As explained, an opposition to an ascending node will be a conjunction to its descending node.) Different meanings or derivations will be relevant to different people represented by the name asteroids or to different charts in which the longitudinal positions are located.

Another way in which the lists can be utilized is to note names that are highlighted in the news, and then see if there is an asteroid with that name. (Note the name of the article writer too.) Since the fall of 1981, I have checked the news and lists. The meanings of the names tell you what principles are being activated at the time. The positions of the nodes tell you how the people, places, or products, with these names are interfacing with the world and why at certain times certain names are activated. At those times there are appropriate aspects to the nodes of the asteroids with these names. Check the names of the asteroids whose nodes are conjunct the nodes of these name asteroids. The nominal principles of the former asteroids are combining with those of the latter asteroids.

Of course, if you have the transiting longitudinal positions of the asteroids, those positions will also give you information as to why certain names are activated at a particular time. The stations both before and after the activation are significant. Look at the transiting astrological factors in reference to your own chart at the time the news comes into your consciousness. The observer becomes part of the observed.

Heliocentric, Geocentric, Etc.

I've used geocentric transiting positions with the lists, but perhaps heliocentric would be informative too. As I see it, the heliocentric positions are from the "point of view" of the Sun. In fact, having explored the Solar System View Option on my computer program, I believe that (like the Sun-centric positions) the Earth-centric, the Mercury-centric, the Ceres-centric, etc., are from the "point of view" of the particular body. In other words, the positions are in terms of the principles of that body. The view from the Sun is in terms of the principles of the Sun; from the Earth, in terms of the principles of the Earth; from Mercury, in terms of the principles of

Mercury, etc. For instance, the view from the Sun is in terms of creativity, fame and regality; from the Earth, in terms of our mundane concerns; from Mercury, in terms of mentality, communication and mutability; from Venus, in terms of harmony, love, and beneficence; from Mars, in terms of initiative, passion and aggression; from Jupiter, in terms of expansion, judgment and benevolence; from Saturn, in terms of limitation, responsibility and discipline; from Uranus, in terms of nonconformity, liberation and originality; from Neptune, in terms of spirituality, empathy and dissolution; from Pluto, in terms of transformation, power and regeneration; from Ceres, in terms of nurturing, loss and productivity. (The views from outside the earth encompass larger principles, rather than specific concerns.)

Personal associations in the geocentric chart are relevant, i.e., my Sun is the ruler of my Descendant, indicating that the Sun for me throughout the different reference points has particular association with partnership. This partnership association pertains as well to the view from the Sun (heliocentric chart). Exact conjunctions from the other reference positions to the geocentric chart, and between the other reference positions, should be noted. Exact conjunctions between one person's positions and another's are descriptive. Exact aspects within a particular reference, i.e., as seen from the Sun, show how the principles of that body (the Sun) are integrated.

The Moon is always conjunct the Earth, with them both opposite the Earth position of the body from whose view the positions are cast. The view of the body from the Sun is always opposite the view of the Sun from the body. Also, the further from the Earth the body is, the closer the other bodies are to each other. However, I think there is something to be learned from looking at our mundane concerns from different vantage points in our solar system.

Lost and Rediscovered Asteroids

Some of the asteroids that have been discovered have subsequently been lost. There are ten asteroids listed as lost in the 1982 *Ephemerides of Minor Planets.* In the 1987 *Ephemerides of Minor Planets,* only six asteroids are listed as lost—four have been found and no new ones have been added to that category. Those still lost were Nolli (473), Albert (719), Hapag (724), Mildred (878), Ingrid (1026) and Mally (1179). Those found were Hamiltonia (452), Nicolaia (843), Detre (1538) and Adalberta (330).

I have speculated that the loss and rediscovery of an asteroid, just like its discovery, is relevant to someone or something with the name of that asteroid. If that entity were in existence during the period, or at the time, the asteroid was lost, or at the time it was rediscovered, that status or change in status would be reflected in that entity's existence. The loss or rediscovery would be reflected in his, her or its interface with the world, as shown by the position of the node of the asteroid. (Though while the asteroid is lost, the position of the node is not exact, it is listed.)

A person with one of these names who comes to mind is Ingrid Bergman. She was born August 28 or 29, 1915,[13] in Stockholm, Sweden, so she would have been seven years old when the asteroid Ingrid was discovered August 13, 1923 and probably seven or eight years old when it was lost. ("Year of last observations" is listed as 1923.[14]) What might have occurred at those times to reflect these events I don't know. However, the birth of her son two years before her marriage to his father, Roberto Rossellini, certainly reflects the listed 14° Cancer 32'2.4" position of the node of Ingrid. The Cancer sign gives the association with motherhood; the Leo numbers 14 and 32 give the association with a child. The interface of Ingrid Bergman with the world, which was very shocked by her "love child," is shown by this nodal position. Her interface through her work as an actress is also shown— Cancer relates to the reflection or image, and Leo relates to show business. Also, this node is exactly conjunct her natal Saturn at 13° Cancer on either day, again accentuating parenthood and career.

The principles embodied in the nodal position would be the same if the asteroid were not lost, but the loss places an emphasis upon them. The entity with the name of the lost asteroid is somewhat different, as was Ingrid as a mother and as an actress. She died in 1982, without the asteroid bearing her first name ever being rediscovered.

Another person with one of these names is Albert Einstein. He was born March 14, 1879,[15] in Ulm, Germany, so he would have been thirty-two years old when the asteroid Albert was discovered October 3, 1911 and probably thirty-two years old when it was lost. ("Year of last observations" is listed as 1911.[16]) Whether the discovery and loss were reflected in his personal life, I do not know, but they seem to be reflected in his public life. According to *The Columbia Encyclopedia,* in 1910 he resigned an adjunct professorship at the University of Zurich to accept a full professorship at the German University, Prague, and in 1912 "he accepted the chair of theoretical physics at the Federal Institute of Technology, Zurich." Also, this encyclopedia states that in 1911 Einstein "asserted the equivalence of gravitation and inertia," and 1911 is the midpoint between the founding of his special theory of relativity (1905) and his general theory (1916). The listed position of the node of Albert is 06° Libra 05'34.8", and what Einstein was trying to achieve in his work (06°), which culminated in his unified field theory, was a harmony (Libra) between the microcosm and the macrocosm. The house in which this node falls in his chart is the fourth—the foundation or base (unified field theory). Additionally, this node is exactly quincunx his eleventh house natal Neptune (given as 07° Taurus 52'), the ruler of his Midheaven and Sun in the tenth house. Not only is Neptune involved, but the quincunx is a Neptunian aspect, and Einstein's work was very nebulous, both literally and figuratively. Albert Einstein died in 1955, without the asteroid bearing his first name ever being rediscovered. (There is an asteroid 2001 named Einstein.)

A list of the ten asteroids, their dates of discovery, years of loss and rediscovery (if possible), their approximate nodal positions and their actual nodal positions (if the asteroids have been rediscovered), follows. The actual nodal position is from the ephemeris in which the asteroid was first listed as rediscovered. Note that only the node of Adalberta is far from where it was supposed to be. The reason for this exception is that the designation Adalberta was assigned to the object A910 *CB,* discovered in 1910 by Max Wolf.

Table X - Loss and Rediscovery — Asteroids

#	Name	Date of Discovery	Year Loss	Year Redis.	Approximate Node	Actual Node
330	Adalberta	Mar. 18, 1892 (1910)	1892	1980	29°♓ 34'48.0"	16°♌ 39'15.52"
452	Hamiltonia	Dec. 06, 1899	1976	1978	03°♋ 19'15.6"	02°♋ 14'41.06"
473	Nolli	Feb. 13, 1901	1901		04°♓ 08'52.8"	
719	Albert	Oct. 03, 1911	1911		06°♎ 05'34.8"	
724	Hapag	Oct. 21, 1911	1911		24°♎ 57'36.0"	
843	Nicolaia	Sep. 30, 1916	1916	1981	04°♈ 32'31.2"	03°♈ 49'38.64"
878	Mildred	Sep. 06, 1916			22°♍ 41'49.2"	
1026	Ingrid	Aug. 13, 1923	1923		14°♋ 32'02.4"	
1179	Mally	Mar. 19, 1931			07°♈ 34'12.0"	
1538	Detre	Sep. 08, 1940	1976	1981	13°♓ 31'25.2"	12°♓ 51'02.63"

Though the year of rediscovery is given on the list, the year of official change of status when the rediscovery is listed in the ephemeris is important too. As regards the four asteroids that have been rediscovered, that year is 1983 for Hamiltonia, Nicolaia and Detre, and 1984 for Adalberta. There is at least a two-year interval between rediscovery (discovery also) and listing. My choice of years of loss and rediscovery is based on information provided by the ephemerides.

In the 1983 ephemeris it is stated that Nicolaia was found in May 1981 by H. Schuster, using the orbit obtained by L. Schmadel. Schmadel and L. Kohoutek had remeasured the plates of 1916, which was the "Year of last observations" until the 1981 "Oppositions used for improvement." The names of the astronomers involved in the rediscovery, as well as the discovery, would be relevant. Interestingly, in 1983 the node of Schuster (2018) was 05° Libra 40'18.77" and the node of Schmadel (2234) was 05° Aries 53'20.33", exactly conjunct the approximate descending and ascending nodes of Nicolaia. (The approximate position is probably the position at the time of the loss.)

In the same ephemeris, on the same page, it is stated that Hamiltonia was "considered to be lost since 1976."[17] (This year would be the year of the official designation. The asteroid's position had been in question earlier, since in the 1982 ephemeris 1973 is written with a question mark under "Year of last observations.") The year of rediscovery is not given, but 1978 is the last year listed under "Oppositions used for improvement."[18] The last year listed is probably the year of rediscovery because the observations of that year are apparently the ones that change the status from lost to found.

Also in the ephemeris of 1983, there is the information that Detre was considered to be lost since 1976, and 1981 is the last year under "Oppositions used for improvement." In the ephemeris of 1984, for Adalberta under this heading, 1980 is given as the last year, and 1910 is given as the first.[19] Previously, 1892 had been the year given under "Year of last observations," but that was before the object A910 *CB,* discovered in 1910, had become Adalberta. C. Bardwell determined the orbit of this asteroid, discovered by M. Wolf.[20]

An entity with one of the names of these rediscovered asteroids is the play *Nicholas Nickleby,* the first and last name of which sounds like Nicolaia. (The title is actually *The Life and Adventures of Nicholas Nickleby,* but the show is usually called just by the main character's name.) The asteroid was rediscovered in May of 1981, and the play opened on Broadway that fall. The cover story of the October 5, 1981 issue of *Time* was devoted to the show, and "Dickens' Nicholas Nickleby" and "Broadway Blockbuster" were emblazoned across the cover. The actual position of the node of Nicolaia was 03° Aries 49'38.64" (1983 ephemeris), and "Blockbuster" does have an Arian quality. Also, *Nicholas Nickleby* was aggressively active (Aries) in its communication (03°)—not only was audience participation elicited, but the eight and a half-hour length of the show was a magnificent assault. The drama was shown as a four-part mini-series on television in January of 1983, the year of the asteroid's official change of status. The book *Nicholas Nickleby* by Charles Dickens had been published in 1839, and the Royal Shakespeare Company's production first opened in London in June 1980. However, the production's opening on Broadway was a resurgence of *Nicholas Nickleby,* not unlike the rediscovery of the asteroid Nicolaia.

The meanings and derivations of the names of the ten asteroids would provide insight. Not only the entities with the names, but the principles of the names, might be affected by the discovery, loss and rediscovery of the asteroids.

Some of the names do not sound like names, at least not in English. Nevertheless, Adalberta has Ada and Bert in it and is a German variation of Albert; Hamiltonia has Hamilton in it; and Detre sounds somewhat like Deirdre. As for Nolli, Mally and Hapag, according to *The Random House College Dictionary,* noli means "not" in Latin; mal means "bad," "wrongful" or "ill" (mal with a capital letter means "Malachi" or "Malayan"); and hap means "a person's luck or lot" or "a covering, esp. one of fabric for warmth." (These meanings of hap make me think of the Fate who measures the thread of life [the lot] and the Fate who spins or weaves it.) Hap with a capital letter means Apis, which is defined, *"Egyptian Religion.* a sacred bull, worshiped at Memphis," thought to be an incarnation of Osiris or Ptah. Looking in *The Columbia Encyclopedia* under Egypt to see if there were an event that occurred there in 1911, the year of the discovery of Hapag, I found that Lord Kitchener became British consul general in Egypt in 1911. He had conquered the Sudan, which had become the Anglo-Egyptian Sudan.

Continuing Research

Much research needs to be done on the hypothesis that there is a synchronicity between the loss or rediscovery of an asteroid and the happenings concerning an entity or principle with its name. The currently lost and recently rediscovered asteroids (as of 1987) have been outlined, so that perhaps other astrologers will choose to pursue this research. The asteroids and their nodes should also be researched more fully, and it was to open up this study to the astrological community that the subcommittee, known as the Asteroid Committee, published *Ephemeris of Diana* and *Asteroid Names & Nodes* in November 1981.

For the publishing of the ephemeris, a grant, which I supplemented, was given by the National Council for Geocosmic Research. The expense of publishing *Asteroid Names & Nodes* was assumed by J. Lee Lehman. An interesting synchronicity is that in 1981—the year of the committee's asteroid study and publishing—Atari introduced a new video game called "Asteroids." Another interesting synchronicity is that in the fall of 1981—the season of the committee's publishing—asteroid 2382 was named Nonie.

After the publishing of these pamphlets, Martin Adelman, Michael Shapiro and Lee Lehman were no longer active on the Asteroid Committee. Diana Rosenberg and I continued on the committee, studying the eight asteroids for which we already had ephemerides and ordering new asteroid ephemerides from Astro. Though the committee had the complete support of the national board, the then-president of the local board was diametrically opposed to the personal name asteroid research. As a result, November 2, 1982, I resigned as research chairman of the New York Chapter of NCGR. Even after my resignation, Diana and I persisted in our research, studying the asteroids and designing glyphs for them. Lee remained a friend to the research, continuing her own, and furnishing Diana and myself such information as a computerized alphabetical and zodiacal listing of the asteroid names and nodes for 1985.

CUSTOM EPHEMERIDES

The first asteroids for which I ordered custom ephemerides were Nonie (2382), Klotho (97), Eduarda (340) and Edwin (1046). Nonie was ordered because it is the pet name, or nickname for Nona, which is my name and the name of the Roman Fate who wove the thread of life. Klotho (another spelling is Clotho) was ordered because Klotho is the equivalent in Greek mythology of the Roman Nona. I wanted to research if Nonie, being my name in sound, as well as in fact (there have been people who have called me Nonie), and Klotho, being my name only in translation, would manifest on different levels. Also, would the fact that Nonie is a pet name affect its quality? Eduarda and Edwin were ordered because they are both close approximations to Edward, the name of my son and first husband. I wanted to research the question of whether when there are two asteroids with similar names, some approximately-named people will be described by one asteroid, and some, by the other.

What I discovered is that both Nonie and Klotho relate to me, since my name is Nona. For instance, my second husband's Nonie is at 04° Gemini 19', and his Klotho is at 05° Gemini 24' (see page 000), both conjunct the descending node of Nonie. However, these asteroids also relate to destiny, but Klotho refers to destiny on a deeper or more primal level. The fact that Nonie is a pet name does give it a lighter quality. As for Eduarda and Edwin, I think it is possible for one Edward to be more an Eduarda, and another, to be more an Edwin. On the other hand, an Edward may act as an Eduarda in one area, or at one time, of his life, and as an Edwin, in, or at, another. (See the meanings of Eduarda and Edwin for the differences.) The midpoint of similar or equivalent name asteroids is the place at which both asteroids are brought together. The midpoint of Eduarda and Edwin will describe a person named Edward, particularly if he is called Ed, Eddie or Eddy, which are all nicknames for both Edward and Edwin. Or the midpoint of Eduarda and Edwin can represent the point of interaction between two separate people with these names. Also combined are the meanings of both asteroids.

Subsequent to ordering these asteroids, I realized that the second syllable of Edwin sounds like my father's first name, Wynn, and that Edwin is the asteroid with the personal name closest to his. My father's given name is his mother's maiden name. My middle name, Gwynn, is a variation on my father's name, and my daughter was given my middle name as her first name. I then realized that not only was "Gwynn" derived from "Wynn," but the only asteroid other than Edwin with a name close to Gwynn was Gunnie, which doesn't sound as close. (Interestingly, from further research I discovered that Edwin was a king who was given sanctuary at Gwynedd.)

Later, Guinevere (2483), which sounds more like Gwynn than Edwin (Guinevere's first syllable is pronounced Gwynn), was listed in the 1985 ephemeris. In the 1984 ephemeris the asteroid that was to be named Guinevere had been given the provisional designation 1928 *QB*, which means it was the second asteroid *(B)* discovered between August 16th and 31st *(Q)* in 1928. Apparently, its orbit had not been sufficiently observed for the asteroid to receive even a provisional designation until 1984. The asteroid Guinevere, whose custom ephemeris I ordered, was even more descriptive of my daughter than Edwin and did relate to me secondarily (middle name). Nevertheless, Edwin is descriptive, since it was the closest known publicly until 1985. In addition, Edwin still has the *personal* name closest to my father's name and to his mother's maiden name.

An asteroid which is named after the place of its discovery, Winchester, Massachusetts, is Winchester (747). It's first syllable sounds like my father's name, and I've found that the first syllable is the most significant. Winchester is the asteroid which I now consider my father's name asteroid; however, the asteroid Edwin is relevant to my father. Illustrating that, for me, these asteroids are connected, my Edwin is exactly inconjunct my Winchester.

If a person, place or entity is important in your life, often different asteroids that represent that person, place or entity will be connected. One way that connections can be evidenced is through aspects. If a name is important to you, an asteroid with one variation of that name and an asteroid with another variation of that name may be in an exact aspect.

Importance can be shown by prominence. Edwin is particularly prominent in my chart, being at 21° Aquarius 00', exactly conjunct my Ascendant at 20° Aquarius 27' and exactly trine my Nonie at 20° Gemini 45' in the fourth house. I identified with my father, believe he is represented by the fourth house, rather than the tenth, and communication (trine) was the hallmark of our relationship. As for my paternal grandmother, she was a substitute mother to me, I called her nana, grandmother in Italian is nonna (Nonie in the fourth), and I was her favorite grandchild (flowing aspect). Also, the fourth house relates to ancestry, and Wynn is an ancestral name that comes from this grandmother. Guinevere (my middle name is Gwynn) at 20° Scorpio 01'℞ is connected to my Edwin, Ascendant and Nonie as well. (Strangely, my research revealed an obscure saint named Nonna, who was a nun at Ty Gwyn, and whose sister was Gwen [both place and person like Gwynn], mother of Cybi [like Sy, my husband].)

Diana and I shared the first four custom ephemerides, and then we ordered four more. These ephemerides were of Lachesis (120), Atropos (273), Peter (1716) and Roberta (335). Lachesis and Atropos, together with Klotho, were the three Fates in Greek mythology. The asteroids Klotho, Lachesis and Atropos, which are not personal names, became part of the personal name asteroid study so that they could be compared to the asteroid Nonie. Peter was ordered because it is the name of Diana's son, and Roberta, because Diana and I have known quite a few Roberts.

DISCOVERY CHARTS

Before analyzing these and other asteroids, let me just insert some observations on discovery charts. As mentioned, the chart for the discovery of an asteroid is descriptive of the asteroid discovered. Since 1925, the time of the exposure of the photographic plate has been recorded. If the astronomer does not indicate otherwise, his first plate with the asteroid is considered to be the one on which the asteroid was found. The Photo-Discovery Chart cast for this time (UT with the discovery place coordinates) is particularly descriptive. (Mark Pottenger has provided the users of his asteroid program with a list of the discovery data for 452 asteroids. The UT of the photo discoveries of those asteroids discovered since 1925 is included, along with the coordinates of their discovery places.)

Another realization is that the Photo-Discovery Chart relates to people and other entities that have the same name as the discovered asteroid. The asteroids with different names in that chart show the relationship of those different people or entities to the discovered entity. (Compare the natal chart of the same or different named entity to the Photo-Discovery Chart of the asteroid.) As for the Astronomer-Discovery Chart (when the astronomer sees the photographic plate), it is also descriptive of the asteroid and associated entities, but in terms now of the seen rather than the unseen. The astronomer has now entered the picture.

If there is no time of the discovery, cast the chart for midnight (00:00 hours LMT or ST) of the discovery date. What I have found is that the midnight chart is an archetypal chart that describes the inner nature of everything highlighted that day. Noon charts appear to describe the outer nature. Among everything highlighted that day would be asteroids discovered and people born. The midnight, rather than the noon, chart seems particularly related to asteroids discovered, perhaps because asteroids were discovered by astronomers, and are discovered by astronomical photography, during the midnight hours.

Synopses of Asteroids in the Personal Name Study

My synopses of the meanings of eighteen asteroids follow. Much more research needs to be done on these asteroids and on the others that I have studied, but the procedure that I have found most fruitful is demonstrated by these and my other synopses. The first nine of the eighteen asteroids are the eight in the original study conducted by the committee, plus Artemis in comparison to Diana. Fourteen of the eighteen are personal name asteroids. With the personal name asteroids, the meaning of the name (including the origin, nicknames, variations and famous namesakes) listed in *Name Your Baby* by Lareina Rule is given first.

DIANA AND ARTEMIS

> **DIANA**—Latin: Diana. "Goddess; divine one." Diana was the Roman moon goddess and deity of the hunt. Notable namesakes include actresses Diana Wynyard, Diana Lynn, Diana Dors, Deanna Durbin, Diane Varsi.
> English nicknames: **Di, Dian, Dee**.
> English variations: **Deana, Deanna, Dianna, Dyana, Dyane**.
> Foreign variations: **Diane** (French).

The asteroid Diana (78) was discovered March 15, 1863, in Düsseldorf by C. T. R. Luther. The asteroid committee decided, at Diana Rosenberg's suggestion, to use as the glyph a D shaped like a bow. This decision was made because we wanted to retain the first letter of the name, as well as suggest Diana's role as goddess of the hunt. The glyph of Diana (Ð) was designed by Michael Shapiro, the member of the committee who is a graphic artist.

Though the committee did not study the asteroid Artemis, I have studied it myself with the help of the computer program designed by Mark Pottenger for 464 asteroids, which include Artemis as well as Diana. Artemis (105) was discovered September 16, 1868, in Ann-Arbor, Michigan by James Craig Watson. My glyph for Artemis, ∂, is the reverse of the glyph for Diana, showing the association between these two asteroids.

In Roman mythology Diana was later identified with the Greek Artemis. The similarities and differences between the goddesses Diana and Artemis should be explored.

Artemis, one of the twelve Olympians, was associated with the moon and the chase. She was the daughter of Zeus and Leto and the twin sister of Apollo, who was associated with the sun. Artemis was born first and helped in the delivery of her brother. She asked Zeus to grant her eternal virginity, bows and arrows, all the mountains of the world, and ocean and river nymphs to be her companions and servants. He granted her wishes and appointed her goddess of roads and harbors. She was also patroness of childbirth and the bringer of sudden, but peaceful, death to women. Like Apollo, she was involved with healing and the protection of animals. She joined him, the Muses and Graces at Delphi in song and dance. She had fond feelings for Orion, her hunting companion, whom she killed unintentionally at the instigation of Apollo. The myth most associated with her is that of Actaeon. When he accidentally saw her bathing, Artemis changed him into a stag and set his dogs upon him. The place in which she was particularly revered was Arcadia, and the laurel, fir tree, bear, dog, hind and boar are sacred to her. Her iconography consists of a bow and quiver, javelin, torch, crescent, and attendant animal.

The Roman Diana was goddess of the moon and of the chase. She was identified with the characteristics and myths of Artemis but was a practical Roman expression of them. As explained, the Romans were more interested in the protective powers, than in the archetypal qualities, of their gods and goddesses. Diana was worshiped at her temple on the Aventine in Rome. Her festival was on August 13. Because she was identified with Artemis, their emblems and iconography are the same.

The origin of Artemis was Eastern, and that of Diana was Italic. Both Artemis and Diana in their earlier forms were goddesses of fertility, i.e., the many-breasted Artemis or Diana of Ephesus, although in their later forms they were protectresses of chastity. Perhaps this dichotomy is integral to the meaning of Artemis and Diana. Perhaps the myth of Actaeon is expressive of this dichotomy. Though all the gods and goddesses punished the infractions of mortals, there was usually more cause than in the case of Actaeon. He inadvertently happened upon the goddess while he was hunting, so his seeing her "unapparelled"[21] was not intentional. Her overweening pride was the cause of her excessive punishment of him, but her inclusion of two variant principles may have been the cause of her overweening pride. To be worshiped as the archetype of both fertility and chastity is heady stuff. The other virgin goddesses, Pallas Athena and Hestia (Vesta), were not faced with such a quandary.

A difference between Artemis and Diana is illustrated by the fact that there was an unusual procedure for the selection of priests at the temple of Diana in a grove on the outskirts of Rome (see *The Golden Bough* by Sir James Frazer). The priest was an escaped slave who had earned his office by killing his predecessor in single combat. He in turn was subject to supplantation by another escaped slave who would kill him in single combat. The associations to the worship of Diana are ones of violence and subservience. The ritual involved two men fighting to the death for the right to serve her, and each either was or had been enslaved. (Frazer believed that the priest was the mate of Diana and that he was a king, slain to make way for the new king.)

Diana in the chart refers to someone with the name of Diana, or its nicknames or variations. A big difference between Diana and Artemis is that so few people are named Artemis, it is not even listed in *Name Your Baby*.

The asteroid Diana is also an indicator of the desire for respect and adoration. Its placements (house, sign, numerical) and exact aspects will describe on what one prides oneself. Diana signifies a person who will expect to be worshiped unequivocally. The person with this name may not have such expectations if the placement and exact aspects of Diana indicate otherwise. However, for the so-named person, such worship will be an issue. The fact that the sound of the English word "die" is in the name of Diana is not without significance. This question of respect and adoration is a matter of life and death.

The asteroids Diana and Artemis are Lunar symbols, representing the "liberated" woman, mother, home or Cancerian male. There is an association with the public—Diana and Artemis were associated with the moon. (Show business is a popular expression.) There is also an association with twinning—Artemis was the twin of Apollo. (Note exact aspects and interaspects of Diana and Artemis with the asteroid Apollo or the Uranian planet Apollon.) The adoration the Diana (Artemis) person craves may be given by the public or by a person with whom he or she has or feels a twinship. The Diana (Artemis) person is an exemplification of female independence—Diana and Artemis were deities of the hunt and hunting was still within the province of the male. However, an independent state is difficult to achieve when there is a need for unequivocal worship.

The iconography and other associations of the goddesses Artemis and Diana are manifest in the asteroids Artemis and Diana. For instance, Artemis was particularly revered in Arcadia, Greece. As a result, I anticipated that a woman who has an important position in the school system in Arcadia, California, would have Artemis and Diana prominent in her chart in relation to work. Her Artemis is exactly quincunx Ceres, which can relate to productivity, and semisextile Athene, whom the Grecian Arcadians claimed was born in Arcadia. Diana is in an exact T-Square with Vesta (vested interests) in the third house of lower education, and this woman makes her living from lower education. She also lived for a long time on Crescent Drive, and the crescent is part of the iconography of these moon goddesses. Also, the Roman Vesta and Greek Hestia, goddesses of the hearth, are related to the home, as is the Moon.

Artemis and Diana manifest similarly in the chart, except each has the different emphasis of its particular mythology. Though Artemis craves adoration, that adoration is not as associated with domination. Artemis is more involved with self-rulership, and Diana is more involved with rulership of others. Artemis is the freedom-loving stalker of the woods, while Diana is more at home in the forum. The midpoint of Diana and Artemis is the place at which the meanings of both asteroids are combined. Its house, sign, numerical position and planetary pictures will describe that combination.

MARTINA

MARTINA—Latin: Martina. "Martial, warlike one." A name from planet
Mars, which the ancients called the god of war.
English nicknames: **Marta, Martie, Marty, Tina**.
Foreign variation: **Martine** (French).

The asteroid Martina (981) was discovered September 23, 1917, in Simeïs, Crimea, USSR by S. Belyavsky. Diana Rosenberg and I chose a glyph which had been designed by Michael Shapiro. The glyph of Martina (⇈)—an M shaped like two arrows—was chosen to suggest the association with Mars, as well as to retain the first letter of the name.

As mentioned, the lives of Martina Navratilova, Martin Luther and Martin Luther King, Jr. give insight into the meaning of the asteroid. Martina Navratilova is a tennis champion, whose energy and aggressiveness helped her not only to become a champion, but to defect from Czechoslovakia. Martin Luther and Martin Luther King, Jr. were two religious leaders who used their energy and aggressiveness to fight for religious and civil rights.

Saint Martina, Saint Martin and Saint Martin I are other examples. Saint Martina, about whom there is little information, was a virgin martyr, whose feast day is January 30. To quote *The Columbia Encyclopedia* regarding Saint Martin, "the son of a soldier, he gave his military cloak to a beggar, became a convert, and refused to fight Christians." Born in the fourth century, in Pannonia, Hungary, he is patron saint of France, and his feast day is November 11 (Martinmas). Regarding Saint Martin I, he was a pope born in the seventh century, in Todi, Umbria, who was exiled to the Crimea (where Martina was discovered). He was proclaimed a martyr after his death, and in 1969 his feast day of November 12 was changed to April 13.

Martina in the chart refers to someone with the name of Martina or Martin, or one of the nicknames or variations for those names. There is an asteroid named Tina, so though the asteroid Martina would relate to people with the name Tina, the asteroid Tina would be more relevant. On the other hand, there is no asteroid named Martin, so Martina would be the asteroid most applicable to people named Martin or its nicknames or variations. Martin, the masculine equivalent of Martina, has the same meaning as Martina. In addition, places such as St. Martin, San Martin and Martinique would be indicated by, as well as express the qualities of, the asteroid Martina. There would be a reference to France too, since Saint Martin is patron saint of France.

The asteroid Martina is also an indicator of a feminine Mars-like quality. The placements (house, sign, numerical) and exact aspects of Martina will show where and how one is Mars-like in a feminine way. According to *The Random House College Dictionary,* one of the meanings of feminine is gentle, and synonyms for gentle are peaceful, soothing, humane, lenient and merciful. The Martian energy or aggressiveness is expressed in a feminine manner. A negative expression is aggressiveness that is repressed or dissipated, so that it results in passive-aggressive behavior. A positive expression is aggressiveness that is devoted not only to conquest, but to a higher purpose. The Martina person may even become a martyr to fulfill that purpose.

MICHEL

MICHAEL—Hebrew: Mikhael. "Who is like God," A spiritual and orderly one who practiced absolute truth. Honoring the archangel St. Michael. Michael Arlen, writer; Mickey Mantle, baseball star; Mickey Rooney, actor; Mike Todd, motion picture producer.
English nicknames: **Mike, Mickie, Micky.**
English variation: **Mitchell.**
Foreign variations: **Michel** (French), **Michele** (Italian), **Miguel** (Spanish), **Mikael** (Swedish), **Micheil** (Scotch), **Mischa** (Slavic).

The asteroid Michel (1348) was discovered March 23, 1933, in Uccle by S. Arend. Diana Rosenberg and I designed the glyph, which is based on a sketch by Michael Shapiro. The glyph of Michel (ꟽ)—a closed M—was designed to keep the first letter of the name and to give the impression of wings. The archangel Michael would have had wings, and to even attempt to practice absolute truth is very "winged," i.e., "elevated or lofty."

Michel in the chart refers to someone with the name of Michael, or its nicknames or variations, of which Michel is a French variation. There are asteroids named Mitchella and Michelle, so though the asteroid Michel would be relevant to people with those names, it would not be most specific. Michelle is a feminine form of Michel.

The asteroid Michel is also an indicator of the practice of absolute truth. The placements (house, sign, numerical) and exact aspects of Michel show one's relationship to this practice. Naturally, not everyone with the name Michael or its variations will be absolutely honest, but, for that person, honesty will be an issue.

Michel in the chart is associated with chivalry as well. Knighthood in Great Britain is conferred "In the name of God, of St. Michael, and St. George. . . ."[22] St. Michael, who was the guardian angel or "prince" of Israel, understood the "word" of God and fought against evil with a sword. Another association is with the administration of the law. The feast of St. Michael is September 29, and that was the day the civil magistrates were chosen. Also, St. Michael is depicted weighing souls, not only indicating "iconographical links with ancient Egyptian paintings . . .,"[23] but suggesting the scales of justice.

JEANNE

> **JEAN**—French: Jeanne. "God is gracious." See **Jane**. St. Jeanne D'Arc (Joan of Arc), 15th-century French heroine; Jean Simmons, actress.
>
> **JANE**—Hebrew: Y-hohhanan. "God is gracious." A feminine form of John. Jane Austin, English novelist; Jane Addams, social worker; actresses Jane Russell, Jane Powell, Jane Wyman, Jane Fonda, Jan Sterling, Jayne Mansfield.
> English nicknames: **Janie, Janey, Jeanie, Jeaney, Jennie, Jenny, Netta, Zaneta.**
> English variations: **Jan, Janet, Janette, Janice, Janina, Janna, Jayne, Jean, Jeanne, Jennette, Joan, Joanne.**
> Foreign variations: **Jeanne, Jeannette** (French), **Johanna** (German), **Gianina, Giovanna** (Italian), **Juana, Juanita** (Spanish), **Sinead, Shena, Sheena**(Irish), **Sine, Seonaid** (Scotch).

The asteroid Jeanne (1281) was discovered August 25, 1933, in Uccle by S. Arend. Diana Rosenberg and I chose a glyph which had been designed by Michael Shapiro. The glyph of Jeanne (꩜)—a J shaped like a ladle—was chosen to retain the first letter of, and to suggest the graciousness associated with, the name Jeanne.

Jeanne in the chart refers to someone with the name of Jean, or its nicknames or variations, of which Jeanne is a French variation. There are asteroids named Jenny, Janice, Janina and Johanna, so though the asteroid Jeanne would be relevant to people with those names, it would not be most specific. There is no asteroid named John, so Jeanne would be applicable to people named John. However, there are asteroids named Jean-Jacques and Jonathan Murray, so if the person were known as Jack, the former might be more applicable, and if known as Jonathan, the latter might be. The most famous namesakes of John are Saint John, "whom Jesus loved," Saint John the Baptist, who was beheaded, King John of England, who approved the Magna Carta, and John Kennedy, the United States President who was assassinated.

The asteroid Jeanne is also an indicator of the graciousness of God. Or the Jeanne person herself or himself may exhibit graciousness. The placements (house, sign, numerical) and exact aspects of Jeanne will describe where and how such benevolence could be expected. That benevolence might be expressed through another person who could be identified by the name asteroid which represents that person. Chart comparison and composite and relationship charts are also helpful in determining where and how another person might express that benevolence.

Jeanne in the chart is associated as well with the qualities of Jeanne D'Arc. (Jeanne d'Arc was born January 15, 1412 N.S., at local sunset, in Domrémy, France.) Those qualities are heroism, determination and faith, and a person with Jeanne appropriately positioned will exhibit those qualities. Perhaps it is those qualities which call forth that graciousness of God or result in that graciousness of the Jeanne person.

JULIA

> **JULIA**—Latin: Julia. "Youthful one." The feminine form of Julius. Julia Ward Howe, poet, social worker (1819-1910); Juliana, Queen of the Netherlands; Julia Peterkin, writer; actresses Julia Marlowe, Julie Harris, Julie London.
>
> English nicknames: **Julie, Jill, Juli, Gillie.**
>
> English variations: **Juliet, Julietta, Juliette, Juliana, Julina, Juline, Joletta.**
>
> Foreign variations: **Giulia, Giulietta** (Italian), **Julie, Juliette** (French), **Julia, Julieta** (Spanish), **Julie** (German), **Sile** (Irish), **Sileas** (Scotch).

The asteroid Julia (89) was discovered August 6, 1866, in Marseille by E. Stéphan. The glyph of Julia (⨎)—a J with a curl at the top—was designed by Diana Rosenberg and myself. The J is to retain the first letter of the name, and the curl is to suggest "Youthful one."

The Julian gens was one of the most distinguished Roman patrician clans, and Julius Caesar and his daughter Julia are two of its prime examples. Julia was married to Pompey, the Roman general and statesman. While she lived, she kept peace between her father and husband, but after her death they became enemies. Pompey was subsequently assassinated in Egypt. Julius Caesar was, of course, the Roman statesman and general who was assassinated by political opponents thought to be his friends.

Julia in the chart refers to someone with the name of Julia or Julius, or one of the nicknames or variations for those names. There are asteroids named Julietta and Juliana, so though the asteroid Julia would be relevant to people with those names, it would not be most specific.

The asteroid Julia is also an indicator of a youthful quality. Not only is "Youthful one" its meaning, but it is relevant to Juliet because Juliet is an English variation of Julia. Shakespeare's Juliet, just thirteen years old, is the exemplification of the youthful maiden. However, for love she gives up the vitality ("power to live or grow") which is the essence of youth. With Julia there is a similar emphasis on giving up all for love.

Another association of Julia is to rulership and, sometimes, to assassination. Julius Caesar and his son-in-law Pompey were assassinated, and the former, through Shakespeare's *Julius Caesar*, is *known* for his assassination. Interestingly, Juliet, though not assassinated, kills herself by stabbing, as Caesar was killed. Also, while Julia, Caesar's daughter, kept peace between her father and husband until her death, it was the death of Juliet and Romeo which reconciled their feuding families.

PATRICIA

> **PATRICIA**—Latin: Patricius. "Noble one." The feminine form of Patrick.
> St. Patricia, 7th century, is one of the patrons of Naples, Italy. Patrice Munsel, opera singer; Patricia McCormick, champion diver; Patty Berg, champion golfer; actresses Patrice Wymore, Patti Page.
> English nicknames: **Pat, Patti, Pattie, Patsy, Patty**.
> Foreign variations: **Patrice** (French), **Patrizia** (Italian).

The asteroid Patricia (436) was discovered September 13, 1898, in Heidelberg by Max Wolf and A. Schwassmann. The glyph of Patricia (♃)—a curved P—was designed by Diana Rosenberg and myself. The glyph is intended to give a graceful effect and to keep the first letter of the name.

Patricia in the chart refers to someone with the name of Patricia, or its nicknames or variations. There is an asteroid named Patrice, so though the asteroid Patricia would relate to people with the name Patrice, the asteroid Patrice would be more relevant. Patrice is also a French variation for Patrick. Though there is an asteroid Patrick Gene, for some Patricks, the different language, and for others, the feminized version, might be more appropriate. An asteroid has just been named Patsy, and that asteroid would be most applicable to someone who is called by that nickname.

The asteroid Patricia is also an indicator of nobility, whether of class or mind or spirit. Originally in Ancient Rome the patricians were the only ones entitled to hold public office. They, as members of the privileged class, were the protectors or patrons of the disenfranchised. The word patrician comes from the Latin and means "of the fathers." Those people with Patricia appropriately positioned will be paternalistic, as well as patrician *(noblesse oblige)*. There is an association to Naples, since Saint Patricia was one of the patrons of Naples.

Also, the asteroid Patricia sometimes has the connotations of a patsy. To quote *The Random House College Dictionary,* a patsy is *"Slang.* **1.** a person upon whom the blame for something falls. **2.** a person who is easily deceived, persuaded, etc." (Most likely, the asteroid Patsy would have this connotation as well.) Sometimes in being a protector or patron, one can become a patsy.

ELSA

ELSA—Old German: Elsa, "Noble one." See **Elizabeth**. Elsa, bride of Lohengrin in German legends; Elsa Maxwell, writer, lecturer; Elsa Lanchester, actress.

ELIZABETH—Hebrew: Elisheba. "Consecrated to God; oath of God." St. Elizabeth, mother of John the Baptist; Elizabeth I and II, English queens; Elizabeth Barrett Browning, English poet; Elizabeth Rudel Smith, Treasurer of the U.S.; actresses Elizabeth Taylor, Bette Davis, Betta St. John, Betty Grable, Betty Hutton.
English nicknames: **Bess, Bessie, Bessy, Beth, Betsey, Betsy, Bett, Betta, Bette, Bettina, Betty, Elsa, Else, Elsie, Libby, Lisa, Lise, Liza, Lizzie, Lizzy.**
English variations: **Elisabeth, Elisa, Elise, Elissa, Eliza, Elyse, Lisbeth, Lizabeth.**
Foreign variations: **Elisabeth, Elise, Lisette, Babette** (French), **Elisabetta, Elisa** (Italian), **Elisabeth Elsa, Else** (German, Dutch, Danish), **Isabel, Belita, Elisa, Ysabel** (Spanish), **Elisabet** (Swedish), **Eilis** (Irish), **Ealasaid, Elspeth** (Scotch).

The asteroid Elsa (182) was discovered February 7, 1878, in Pola, Istrie, Austria (now Pula, Yugoslavia) by Johann Palisa. The glyph of Elsa (∈)—a rounded E— was designed by Diana Rosenberg and myself. The glyph is intended to suggest an ornamental or Elizabethan quality and to retain the first letter of the name.

In medieval German legend Elsa was a princess of Brabant to whom King Arthur sent Lohengrin, a knight of the Holy Grail. Lohengrin saved her from marriage to an undesired suitor and married her himself on the condition that she not ask his identity. She did repeatedly, and he finally revealed himself and so was required to leave her for the castle of the Grail. The story is recounted in a German epic poem c.1285-1290, supposedly by Wolfram von Eschenbach. The opera *Lohengrin* (1848) by Wagner is based on this poem.

Elsa in the chart refers to someone with the name of Elsa, or its nicknames or variations. Elsa itself is an English nickname for Elizabeth, so there would be relevance to someone named Elizabeth, but in the sense of a nickname—a name that is more familiar or informal. However, there is an asteroid named Elisabetha, in addition to asteroids named Elisa, Bettina and Isabella, so though the asteroid Elsa would relate to people with those names, it would not be most relevant.

The asteroid Elsa, like the asteroid Patricia, is an indicator of nobility, but Patricia has the association with the Roman senatorial aristocracy (patricians), and Elsa, with consecration to God (Elizabeth). Elsa has the added association to Arthurian legend, in which her story is very much like that of Psyche and Eros or Amor (Cupid) in Greek or Roman mythology. The similarity is that Elsa, like Psyche, could not accept her beloved on faith alone; the difference is that Psyche and Cupid were reunited, while Elsa and Lohengrin were not.

Martin Adelman, one of the original members of the asteroid committee, found, and my observations confirm his, that the asteroid Elsa also has a "this or else that" quality—in other words, a quality of vacillation. (Interestingly, even Elsa's place of discovery has changed names and hands.) Queen Elizabeth I is a famous namesake. Her personal and public life exemplify that vacillation, as well as the noble dedication to a higher purpose ("consecrated to God"), which is often associated with the Elsa person.

SY

> **SEYMOUR**—Old French: St. Maur. "From the town of St. Maur, Normandy, France." Seymour Berkson, publisher (1905-1959); Seymour Harris, noted educator.

The asteroid Sy (1714) was discovered July 25, 1951, in Algiers by L. Boyer. The glyph of Sy (𝄢)—a curved S with an extra arabesque—was designed by Diana Rosenberg and myself. The glyph is intended to imply a flowing quality and to retain the first letter of the name.

Saint Maurus, or Saint Maur, from whom the name Seymour is derived, was a nobleman's son who in the sixth century became a monk under the supervision of Saint Benedict. When commanded by Saint Benedict to save a boy from drowning, Saint Maurus is reputed to have done so, obliviously walking on water. The French Benedictine Congregation of Saint-Maur (1621-1818), which bears his name, is known for its learning. His feast day, which had originally been January 15, was changed to October 5.

Sy in the chart refers to someone with the name of Seymour, or its nicknames or variations. Sy is a nickname for that name and so has a more familiar or informal quality. However, there is no asteroid with that name, so Sy would be the asteroid most applicable to someone named Seymour. Another reference is to places named Seymour or St. Maur or to Normandy, since the town of St. Maur is there. In English history the family name of Seymour is prominent. Jane Seymour was the third queen of Henry VIII and mother of Edward VI. Thomas and Edward Seymour, her brothers, were influential nobles at the court, until they were beheaded. William Seymour was an English nobleman, imprisoned for marrying Arabella Stuart, a cousin of James I.

The asteroid Sy also relates to sadness, singers, musicians and actors. Sy sounds like "sigh"; sadness is often expressed through a sigh; and singing, playing a wind or brass instrument, and acting require a breathing which is like a sigh.

An additional expression of the Sy quality is the saving of people, as Saint Maurus saved the boy from drowning. There is a song called "Suddenly Seymour," which was characterized in the *New York Post* of June 23, 1984 as "the song of self-realization through another person." That characterization captures the savior quality of Sy.

EDUARDA

> **EDWARD**—Old English: Eadward. "Prosperous guardian." A trusted warden of other people's property. Edward I, II, III, IV, V, VI, VII, VIII, kings of England; Edward Teach, 18th-century English pirate; Eddie Cantor, comedian.
>
> English nicknames: **Ed, Eddie, Eddy, Ned, Ted, Teddy**.
>
> Foreign variations: **Eduardo** (Italian, Spanish, Portuguese), **Edouard** (French), **Eduard** (German, Dutch), **Edvard** (Swedish, Danish).

The asteroid Eduarda (340) was discovered September 25, 1892, in Heidelberg by Max Wolf. The glyph of Eduarda (⨲)—an E within a shield—was designed by Diana Rosenberg and myself. The E is to retain the first letter of the name, and the shield is to suggest the guardian.

Edward has been a very popular name for kings of England. One of these kings, Edward the Confessor, founded Westminster Abbey, which is where the kings and queens of England are coronated and buried. His death in 1066 led to the Norman Conquest. He was canonized, and either he, or Saint George, is considered the patron saint of England.

Eduarda in the chart refers to someone with the name of Edward, or its nicknames or variations. Eduarda is a feminization of the Italian, Spanish and Portuguese variation Eduardo. Places named Edward or variations thereof, are referred to by Eduarda as well. Companies, such as Con Ed, are signified too. There is an asteroid Edisona (742), but Con Ed is how the company is popularly known.

The asteroid Eduarda is also an indicator of guardianship. A softer quality is brought to this indicator by the Romance language variation and the feminization of its name. The feminine quality is naturally not restricted to women but is archetypal (see Martina for definition of feminine). As for the guardianship, it might be assumed by a ruler or a protector or a steward of someone else's property, finances or person. Eduarda can indicate the foster parent, stepparent or custodian. In this regard, there is a similarity to Chiron, which is also indicative of these roles. However, a difference is that Chiron's connotation as the wounded healer is not relevant to Eduarda.

The Eduarda guardianship is usually prosperous or fortunate. Westminster Abbey, founded by Edward the Confessor, is an example of such guardianship. Nevertheless, all principles can be inverted. Edward Teach, listed as one of the namesakes, was known as Blackbeard, who as a pirate appropriated, rather than protected, people's property.

Another Eduarda association is to heraldry. The shield can be not only a piece of armor, but an escutcheon on which to identify oneself and one's family. Genealogy is an allied association.

EDWIN

> **EDWIN**—Old English: Eadwine. "Prosperous friend." Sir Edwin Arnold, 19th-century English poet; Edwin Stanton, U.S. Secretary of War; Edwin Booth, famous American actor; Edwin Arlington Robinson, American poet.
> English nicknames: **Ed, Eddie, Eddy**.
> Foreign variation: **Eduino** (Italian, Spanish).

The asteroid Edwin (1046) was discovered December 1, 1924, at Yerkes Observatory in Williams Bay, Wisconsin by G. Van Biesbroeck. The glyph of Edwin (⧢) —a reversed E within a shield—was designed by Diana Rosenberg and myself. The similarity between the glyph of Edwin and that of Eduarda is meant to suggest the similarity between the two asteroids.

Like the king of England Edward the Confessor, Edwin was a king who is considered a saint. He lived in exile in Gwynedd, Wales, and in East Anglia because Ethelfrith, king of Northumbria, kept him from the throne of Deira. (Edward lived in exile in Ely and Normandy because Sweyn and Cnut, kings of Denmark, usurped the throne of England.) Eventually, Edwin killed Ethelfrith and became king of Northumbria himself. His first wife was Cwenburg of Mercia, and his second was Ethelburga of Kent. The latter was instrumental in his conversion to Christianity, and he in turn was instrumental in the conversion of many of his subjects. (Edward's wife, Edith, was very religious too, and in fact she and Edward reportedly lived as brother and sister.) Edwin built the church on whose site York Minister now stands, as Edward built the church on whose site Westminster Abbey now stands. Edwin was killed at Hatfield Chase by Penda of Mercia. Though he lived in the 7th century, the ruins of Edwin's palace were not discovered until 1957. His feast day is October 12, while Edward's is October 13.

Edwin in the chart refers to someone with the name of Edwin or Edwina (there is no asteroid named Edwina), or their nicknames or variations. The English variation given for Edwina is Edina. Ed, Eddie, and Eddy are English nicknames for both Edward and Edwin. As mentioned, I believe it is possible for one Edward to be represented by the asteroid Eduarda, and another, by the asteroid Edwin. The representation may be different at different times or in different areas of the life. If both asteroids are representative of the native, where he is a "prosperous guardian," he will be symbolized by Eduarda, and where he is a "prosperous friend," he will be symbolized by Edwin. However, I believe an Edwin (probably an Edwina too) will be represented by the asteroid Edwin, since this is the exact name, not an approximation. Eduarda would be relevant but not most specific.

The asteroid Edwin is also an indicator of a prosperous or fortunate friend. Edwin is derived from the Old English name Eadwine; and Edward, from the Old English name Eadward. Both are compounds containing the word ead, meaning rich or happy (prosperous). The difference is that Eadwine contains the word wine, meaning friend, and Eadward contains the word ward, meaning guardian. As for Edwin, the modern version of Eadwine, it has the word win in it, and an Edwin person strives to win. As for Eduarda, the feminized Romance language variation of Edward, it is softer sounding than Edwin, and an Eduarda person has a softer quality than an Edwin person. (Naturally, with appropriate prominence of these asteroids in your chart, you, or someone else in your life, can be shown to be an Eduarda or Edwin person without being called by either of those names.)

The city of Edinburgh is another association of the asteroid Edwin. Edina, which is an English variation of Edwina, means "From the city of Edinburgh," as well as "Prosperous friend." Lareina Rule writes that Edina is a "Poetical name for the capital city of Scotland."

Edwin, like Eduarda, is associated with heraldry and genealogy. The glyph of Eduarda was designed as an E within a shield because of the name's definition as prosperous guardian. The definition of Edwin does not have the word guardian in it, but the shield was retained to show the similarity between Eduarda and Edwin (three of Edward's nicknames are also Edwin's, etc.). It seems the design of a glyph is not arbitrary but is in accordance with the principles of the object for which it is designed. Though not expected, the association to heraldry/genealogy was observed again.

GUINEVERE

> GUINEVERE—Old Welsh: Gwenhwyvar. "White wave, white phantom."
> The wife of King Arthur in English legends. See **Gwendolyn, Genevieve.**
> English variations: **Gaynor, Guenna, Gwenore, Jennifer, Genevieve, Vanora.**
> Foreign variation: **Ginevra** (Italian).
>
> GWENDOLYN—Old Welsh: Gwendolyn. "White-browed one." Gwendolyn was the wife of Merlin the magician in old Welsh legends. See **Guinevere.**
> English nicknames: **Gwen, Gwennie, Gwenda, Guenna.**
>
> GENEVIEVE—Old German: Geno-wefa. "White wave," See **Guinevere.**
> St. Genevièvre, A.D. 420-519, patron of Paris; Genevieve Tobin, actress.

The asteroid Guinevere (2483) was discovered August 17, 1928, in Heidelberg by Max Wolf. The glyph of Guinevere (♉)—a cursive G shaped like a crown—was designed by my daughter and myself. (With her first, and my middle, name being Gwynn, our collaboration was inevitable.) We wished to retain the first letter of the name and to suggest Guinevere's role as queen. A filigreed crown seemed most appropriate for this romantic figure.

The origin of Arthurian legend is in Welsh poetry. Its references were combined subsequently with other British legends and transported to France, Italy and Western Europe via the Bretons and Normans. In the Middle Ages these stories came to express ideals of romance and chivalry. Two of the most famous expressions of these ideals are *Morte d' Arthur* by Sir Thomas Malory, completed in 1485, and *Idylls of the King* by Alfred, Lord Tennyson, appearing between 1859 and 1888. Our modern-day examples are *Camelot*, the musical (opening on Broadway in 1960), and the film (1967).

The existence of King Arthur is supported by historical fact. He was a prince of South Wales who became King of Britain about 510. After victory over the Saxons, he reigned peacefully until his nephew Modred revolted against him. They both were killed in 542.[24] It is the embellishment of these facts which became the legends, of which the following is part.

Guinevere, the wife of King Arthur, was the daughter of King Laodegan of Carmalide. Arthur loved her, and she fell in love with him without knowing who he was, so their marriage was not just a dynastic one. They lived in Camelot, which was probably Winchester,[25] the capital of Medieval England. The Knights of the Round Table gathered there. Sir Launcelot du Lac, the noblest and most chivalrous of these knights, fell in love with Guinevere. She, returning his love, betrayed Arthur. When Arthur discovered her betrayal, she was to be burned to death, but Launcelot rescued her and took her to his castle. Arthur was reconciled to Guinevere at the pope's behest, and Launcelot returned to his own country, Bayonne (France). After a year Arthur followed and attacked Launcelot. While Arthur was gone his nephew (or illegitimate son) Modred, claiming Arthur was dead, had himself crowned king and planned to marry Guinevere. She escaped to the Tower of London (only possible if the tradition is true that Julius Caesar, rather than William the Conqueror, founded it). Arthur returned from France, fought Modred, and they killed each other. When Guinevere heard that Arthur was dead, she entered a nunnery and became an abbess. Launcelot found her, but he became a monk when Guinevere, feeling guilt for what they had done, said he should never see her again.

The orbit of Guinevere, like that of most of the asteroids, is between Mars and Jupiter. This containment surrounds Guinevere with the self-assertiveness of Mars and the expansiveness of Jupiter. However, this orbit, unlike that of most of the asteroids, enters the orbit of Jupiter. Being there relates Guinevere to the qualities of that planet. Guinevere, in Arthurian legends, is the wife of King Arthur, and he is a Jupiterian figure—a ruler who is both noble and philosophical. By the end of the story she can be similarly described.

Guinevere in the chart refers to someone with the name of Guinevere, or its nicknames or variations. Although in the Lareina Rule book, Gwynn is not mentioned as a variation, it does relate because it has the same sound and derivation as the first syllable of Guinevere. There are asteroids named Genevieve and Ginevra, so though the asteroid Guinevere would be relevant to people with those names, it would not be most specific.

The asteroid Guinevere is also an indicator of a person who might have as a marital partner someone of prominence and who would expect nobility, idealism and chivalry from that partner, prominent or not. As a result of these expectations, which are difficult to meet, the Guinevere person could become involved in a romantic relationship, in addition to the marital one. If this relationship were to become illicit the Guinevere person would feel she/he had not lived up to her/his own ideals. The asteroids Arthur (2597) and Lancelot (2041) give further insight into how this myth is being played out. Literally, Guinevere can represent royalty. This asteroid is appropriately configured in the charts of the royal families of Great Britain, as well as of other countries.

Despite this royal association, there is an association with the Round Table and its democratic ideals—at a round table there is no head of the table. There is a reference to Great Britain, or to Camelot as the exemplification of an ideal place. This latter association leads to an association with the Kennedys, and particularly with Jacqueline Kennedy who especially related to *Camelot.* There is a dispute about her time, which is variously given as 02:30 PM EST, 02:30 PM EDT or 03:02 PM EDT. The 02:30 PM EDT is most probable because EDT was in effect and time to the minute is unlikely on July 28, 1929, at Southhampton, New York. That day and place, whatever Jacqueline's birth time, her Guinevere was at 08° Taurus (probably in the sixth house), exactly semisextile her Jupiter at 09° Gemini (probably in the seventh house) and exactly sesquiquadrate her Saturn at 24° Sagittarius ℞ (probably in the second house). Taurus is the sign of the partner's death, 8 is the number of death, and Jupiter and Saturn bring both expansiveness and restrictiveness—her Jupiter through a Neptunian aspect and her Saturn through a Plutonian one.

The name Guinevere means "white wave, white phantom." White reflects "nearly all the rays of sunlight or a similar light"; a wave is "a disturbance on the surface of a liquid body"; a phantom is "an apparition or specter."[26] There is a quality of fantasy and illusion (wave) surrounding the asteroid Guinevere, and even apparitions or spectors may sometimes be seen or sensed under its influence. However, the visions are usually not chimerical, appearing as they do under an almost all-reflecting light.

To illustrate how the principles of the nodes interface with the world at a particular time, there is the following example of entertainment and rulership. Extrapolating from the retrograde movement of Guinevere's heliocentric ascending node between 1984 (the first listing) and 1991, its rate of movement is -00°00'43.44" per year. Extrapolating from the retrograde movement of Winchester's heliocentric ascending node between 1982 (my first accurate ephemerides) and 1991, its rate of movement is -00°00'52.46" per year. Considering precession of the equinoxes, Neptune's heliocentric ascending node moves at a rate of +00°00'39.6654" per year. However, the fixed equinox is the frame of reference used here for the asteroids and so should be for the planets. The first year that the asteroid ephemerides list the nodes of the planets is 1987. Extrapolating from the retrograde movement of Neptune's heliocentric ascending node between the 1987 and 1991 listings, its rate of movement is -00°01'0.49" per year. In 1960, the year the musical *Camelot* opened, the node of Winchester, which was probably Camelot, was 10° Leo 01', separating from a conjunction with the node of Neptune at 11° Leo 43' and from a trine with the node of Guinevere at 11° Sagittarius 58'. By 1967, the year the movie

Camelot appeared, the node of Winchester at 09° Leo 55' was no longer exactly conjunct the node of Neptune (11° Leo 36') or trine the node of Guinevere (11° Sagittarius 53'). In 1963, when the Kennedys' brief reign had ended, the node of Winchester at 09° Leo 59' had just moved into another degree, making that conjunction and trine no longer exact. For a time, Neptune and Guinevere were both aligned with Winchester. During that time, the artistic illusion of Neptune was brought to Guinevere and Winchester—Guinevere, which already had a fantastical quality, and Winchester, which gained that quality through its immortalization as Camelot. According to the song, "In short, there's simply not a more congenial spot for happ'ly ever aftering than here in Camelot!"

NONIE

> NONA—Latin: Nona. "Ninth child."
> English nickname: **Nonie**.

The asteroid Nonie (2382) was discovered April 13, 1977, at Perth Observatory in Bickley, Australia by the observatory. (Perth Observatory does not credit individuals.) The asteroid was named in honor of the daughter of Peter Jekabsons, a member of the astronometric team. The glyph of Nonie (♇)—an N with a circle at the top—was designed by Diana Rosenberg and myself. The N is to retain the first letter of the name, and the circle, together with the final vertical line of the N, is to suggest a 9.

Nona was one of the three Roman Parcae, who are the practical Roman equivalent of the Greek Moerae or Fates. The Greek Fates were Klotho, Lachesis and Atropos; the Roman were Nona, Decuma and Morta. Nona, like Klotho, spun or wove the thread of life, while Decuma measured it, and Morta cut it. They had the gift of prophecy. The Parcae developed from the Roman birth-goddess, Parca, and were present at every birth, decreeing the fate of the child. They were also present at every marriage and death. According to some accounts, the power of the Fates was greater than that of Zeus (Jupiter).

Nonie in the chart refers to someone with the name of Nona, or its nicknames or variations. Nonie is an English nickname for Nona and so has a lighter quality than the name from which it is derived. Nonie is also a nickname or pet name for Nora. Nora is an Irish abbreviated form of Honora and is related to Leonora, which is related to Lenore, which is probably a form of Eleanor, which is an old form of Helen. There are asteroids named Nora, Honoria, Leonora, Eleonora and Helena (and the meanings of these names are different from those of Nonie), so for a person with one of those names, the respective asteroid would be most relevant. All the same, there would be an association of the asteroid Nonie to these so-named people.

The asteroid Nonie is also an indicator of destiny. Nona, as well as being the Roman Fate who wove the thread of life, means ninth, and the number nine refers to completion or destiny. However, fate seems to be referred to on a deeper or more primal level by Klotho. Greek mythology is more archetypal than Roman, and Nonie not only was named after the daughter of one of its "discoverers" but does have the lighter quality of a nickname. Despite this lighter quality, Nonie, which has as its first syllable the word no, is sometimes related to denial or negation.

There is the already indicated connection with the grandparents. In Italian the familiar form for grandparents is nonni; for grandmother, nonna; and for grandfather, nonno. I have noticed that when grandparents have been prominent in the life, the Nonie is appropriately prominent. The word nun originates from the Latin nonna too, and often the Nonie person does exhibit a nun-like devotion.

Another association of Nonie is to noon. The definition of noon in *The Random House College Dictionary* is "**1.** midday. **2.** twelve o'clock in the daytime. **3.** The highest, brightest, or finest point or part. **4.** *Chiefly Literary,* midnight. [ME *none,* OE *non* < L *nona* ninth hour. See NONE²]." The nones was originally the canonical hour or service fixed for 3 PM (the ninth hour of the day), but the time of that service was changed to shortly after noon, thus giving noon its name. Many important events, such as coronations and the swearing in of United States' presidents, are scheduled for high noon. Interestingly, my mother (whose only offspring she named Nona) was born at noon, exactly when the noon whistle blew, while my paternal grandfather was born at midnight—"Chiefly Literary." (I too was born at midnight—12:14 AM EST.)

KLOTHO

The asteroid Klotho (97) was discovered February 17, 1868, in Marseille by E. W. L. Tempel. The glyph of Klotho (⚵)—a K within a spindle—was designed by Diana Rosenberg and myself. The K is to retain the first letter of the name, and the spindle is to suggest the Spinner, which is what Klotho was.

In *The Random House College Dictionary* Clotho is defined as "*Class. Myth.* the Fate who spins the thread of life. Cf. **Atropos, Lachesis.** [< L < Gk *Klotho,* lit., the Spinner = *Kloth(ein)* (to) spin + -*O* suffix used in making names of women]." Also, Klotho or Clotho sounds like cloth, which is "a fabric formed by weaving, felting, etc...."

Klotho, one of the three Greek Fates or Moerae, is considered either a daughter of Night and Darkness or a daughter of Zeus and the Titaness Themis. The function of the Fates was to assure that destiny was fulfilled. Those who tried to escape its decrees were faced with Nemesis, the goddess of divine retribution. Klotho's attribute is a spindle.

Klotho in the chart is an indicator of destiny. Compared to Nonie, Klotho refers to destiny on a more archetypal level. Just as Greek mythology is further removed from our Western civilization than Roman mythology, Klotho's description of one's destiny is further removed from our everyday mundane life than Nonie's description. Klotho is what is at the root of Nonie and might not be perceived by the casual observer. The root may be from a past life. (The other asteroids named for Greek goddesses are also a prior reference to the asteroids named for equivalent Roman goddesses.)

To give a brief example, a man, with Nonie in Gemini in the third house and Klotho in Scorpio in the eighth house, is a writer whose writing has as its base the motivation to probe deeply and to gain power. The exact aspects, as well as the number symbolism, would give further information (his Klotho is exactly conjunct Chiron, and there is the desire to be a teacher, healer or steward of other people). Naturally, the same dynamic would apply to functions other than work.

Klotho is the fabric of your life and may literally refer to designers of cloth or clothes, i.e., textile or fashion designers. Nonie, being the Roman equivalent of Klotho, has relevance to such designers too. Lachesis and Atropos, being involved with the spinning process, have some, but a lesser, relevance.

LACHESIS

The asteroid Lachesis (120) was discovered April 10, 1872, in Marseille by A. L. N. Borrelly. The glyph of Lachesis (⚲)—an L within a spindle—was designed by Diana Rosenberg and myself. The L is to retain the first letter of the name, and the spindle is to suggest the association with Klotho—the Spinner. Also, all three Fates were sometimes referred to as spinners.

In *The Random House College Dictionary* Lachesis is defined as *"Class. Myth.* the Fate who determines the length of the thread of life. Cf. **Atropos, Clotho.** [< L < Gk, personification of *láchesis* destiny = *lache(în)* (to) happen by lot + *-sis* -SIS]."

Lachesis, another of the three Greek Fates or Moerae, has disputed parentage too—sometimes, Night and Darkness, sometimes Zeus and Themis. Though the function of the Fates was to enforce destiny, "Lachesis was chance, the element of luck that a man had the right to expect.[27] Like the other Fates, she had the gift of prophecy. Her attribute is a scroll.

Lachesis in the chart is an indicator of destiny—but destiny which has a fortuitous quality. The placements (house, sign, numerical) and exact aspects of this asteroid will describe your lot in life. There is often an element of luck involved, and these placements and aspects will show where and how that luck might be expected.

This asteroid can also literally refer to lotteries. Lotteries are not just "million dollar ones." Prospective jurors for a particular case are chosen by lots—frequently, so are draftees. Even Fortune Cookies, which are a form of lots, are related to Lachesis.

ATROPOS

The asteroid Atropos (273) was discovered March 8, 1888, in Vienna by Johann Palisa. The glyph of Atropos (⚲)—an A within a spindle—was designed by Diana Rosenberg and myself. The A is to retain the first letter of the name, and the spindle is to suggest the association with Klotho—the Spinner. Also, all three Fates were sometimes referred to as spinners.

In *The Random House College Dictionary* Atropos is defined as *"Class. Myth.* the Fate who cuts the thread of life. Cf. **Clotho, Lachesis.** [< Gk: lit., not turning, hence, inflexible. See A-[6], -TROPE]."

Atropos, the last of the three Greek Fates or Moerae, is variously reported too as the offspring of Night and Darkness or of Zeus and Themis. She was sometimes described as spinning the past, while Klotho was described as spinning the present, and Lachesis, the future. "Atropos was inescapable fate, against which there was no appeal.[28] It seems the power of the Fates was greater than that of the gods. Atropos' attribute is a scale or scissors.

Atropos in the chart is an indicator of destiny—but destiny which has an inflexible quality. Those matters about which you are inflexible will be shown by Atropos. With this asteroid exactly aspecting the angles related to marriage, such as the Ascendant and the Descendant or the East and West Point, marriage is a matter of life and death. Divorce, though it may occur, will not be an easily-chosen option.

This asteroid is also an indicator of death—that fate which is inescapable. At the November 15, 1982 Lunation, Atropos was at 16° Aries 19'℞, exactly quincunx Lachesis at 16° Scorpio 18'. (As shall be explained in the next chapter, the lunation sets the stage for the month.) In the *New York Times* of November 17, 1982, there was an article stating that on November 16 anthropologists reported "the largest group of complete skeletons surviving from ancient Roman times had been unearthed at Herculaneum." Atropos was still in an exact quincunx to Lachesis, as well as an exact trine to the ascending node of the asteroid Herculina at 17° Cancer 25'.[29] The trine is the aspect of communication; Herculaneum is where the find was made; Lachesis represents the luck that making such a find requires; the quincunx suggests the previous concealment of the skeletons; Atropos pertains to death, and its retrograde motion symbolizes the reference to the past. (Atropos was close to its direct station, which was to occur at the beginning of December.) In addition, the Uranian planet Kronos, which means "everything above average," having been at 16° Gemini 17'℞ at the lunation, was in an exact Finger of God with Atropos and Lachesis.

Another relevant story in the newspapers November 17 was concerning the return to Britain the previous day of 64 persons who had died in the Falklands War. Due to public protest, the bodies, which had been buried in the Falklands, were exhumed—shades of the unearthing at Herculaneum—so that they could be buried in their native land. The trine to the node of Herculina could also be referring to the herculean quality of these two happenings. As for the node's position at 17° Cancer 25', it indicates an interface with the world, which is involved with death (1 + 7 = 8) and the homeland (Cancer).

When the Fates form planetary pictures, or exact aspects, with each other, the meanings of the Fates are combined. The fabric of life, the lot in life and the end of life are closely connected. Also, there is an asteroid Moira (638), that indicates a combination of the three meanings. Moira is the singular of Moirai or Moerae. The glyph which I designed is an M within a spindle (⚹).

PETER

PETER—Latin: Petrus. "Rock or stone." Honors St. Peter, acclaimed as the first Pope of the Catholic Church. Peter the Great, Russian Emperor; Pierre Curie, French chemist; Peter O'Toole, Peter Ustinov, actors.
English nicknames: **Pete, Petie, Petey**.
Foreign variations: **Pietro, Pedro, Pero, Piero** (Italian), **Pedro** (Spanish), **Peadair** (Scotch), **Pierre** (French), **Petrus** (German), **Peadar** (Irish), **Pieter** (Dutch).

The asteroid Peter (1716) was discovered April 4, 1934, in Heidelberg by K. Reinmuth. The glyph of Peter ()—a P with the loop shaped like the pope's miter and a cross on the descender—was designed by Diana Rosenberg and myself. The glyph is meant to retain the first letter of the name and to suggest the pope.

Saint Peter was the disciple who, though he denied Christ three times, became the leader and spokesman of the apostles. Christ called him the rock on which he would build his church. Peter was the first bishop of Rome, and the pope, who is his successor, is the head of the Roman Catholic Church. He is believed to have been crucified head-downwards in Rome. His feast day with Saint Paul is June 29. His principle attribute is two crossed keys because Christ gave him the keys of heaven.

Peter in the chart refers to someone with the name of Peter or its feminine equivalent Petra, or one of the nicknames or variations for those names. (Petra means rock too.) There are asteroids named Pierre and Pierretta, so though the asteroid Peter would be relevant to people with those names, it would not be most specific. Places named Peter, or variations thereof, are referred to as well by this asteroid.

The asteroid Peter also describes your "rock" or foundation. Where and how the asteroid is placed in the chart will show what that foundation is. On the other hand, Peter can relate literally to rock. I have observed appropriate aspects to and from Peter when a couple had their lawn landscaped with rock formations, and when a boy dug a grave for his cat and hit rock. In this latter case there was an ephemeris of the boy's name asteroid, and his transiting name asteroid was exactly semisextile transiting Pluto (death and underground—digging), which was exactly sextile transiting Peter (rock). Of course, the literal rocks have a metaphorical significance as well—the boy, having had his pet for many years, lost part of his foundation when the pet died, and the couple, having had recent fluctuations in their marriage, may have been trying symbolically to put it on a more solid foundation.

There is also an association of this asteroid with the pope and the Vatican. For instance, when I went with a woman friend to the Vatican Show at the Metropolitan Museum, transiting Peter had returned to the same degree as my natal Peter and was exactly semisquare transiting Venus. My friend, with no knowledge of the aspects, had invited me to accompany her at the particular day and time. Though I had no knowledge of the aspects either, once at the exhibition I felt an unexpected rapport with the subject matter and sensed there was an intense activation of my natal Peter. Returning home, I checked the ephemerides and discovered, in addition to the above, that my friend's Peter was exactly quincunx mine and exactly trine the most powerful contact between our charts—her Ascendant exactly conjunct my Moon. As for the opening of the show at the Metropolitan Museum February 26, 1983, it had closely coincided with transiting Peter's direct station at 23° Gemini.

Another reference of Peter is to British Royalty, who have been coronated on the Stone of Scone since 1296. In that year it was captured by Edward I from the Scots, whose kings had always been ordained upon it. I wonder if there aren't references also to places known for their rocks, such as Stonehenge. When I visited it with my husband and two children in the summer of 1983, there were appropriate aspects involving our natal and progressed positions, as well as the transiting position, of this asteroid.

A final association that I have made is to the male sexual organ. This association would be derived from the slang expression for that part of the anatomy. (The asteroid Pecker relates to slang for that same part, but whereas Peter is also the stone or foundation, Pecker is also pecking or picking at something or someone.) The usual procedure of looking at the placements (house, sign, numerical) and exact aspects in the chart will give you an idea of what that organ represents to the person whose chart it is.

ROBERTA

> **ROBERTA**—Old English: Hroth-beorht. "Shining with fame." Roberta La
> Rue, noted hydrologist; Roberta Peters, operatic singer.
> English nicknames: **Bobbie, Bobby, Bertie.**
> English variations: **Robina, Robinia, Robinette, Bobbette.**
> Foreign variations: **Robine** (French), **Ruperta** (German).

The asteroid Roberta (335) was discovered September 1, 1892, in Heidelberg by A. Staus. The glyph of Roberta (℞)—an R with a dot in the middle of an elongated loop—was designed by Diana Rosenberg and myself. The glyph which resembles the Eye of Horus, was designed to retain the first letter of the name and to represent the sun and its shining.

Roberta in the chart refers to someone with the name of Roberta or Robert, or one of the nicknames or variations for those names. Lareina Rule lists as a famous namesake for Robert, "Robert the Bruce, king of Scotland (1306-1329), who preserved his country's independence." A famous association with Roberta is Jerome Kern's musical comedy *Roberta* (1933) about the love affair between a Russian princess and an American football star. Its most famous song is "Smoke Gets in Your Eyes."

The asteroid Roberta is also an indicator of one's reputation—where one is "shining with fame." A man who has Roberta at 10° Virgo 36' in his second house, exactly conjunct his third house cusp, is a quality assurance process engineer. He is known for his analytical ability (Virgo), regarding evaluative thinking (second house, conjunct third cusp). The exact aspects give more information, i.e., his Roberta is exactly quincunx his Midheaven, Part of Fortune conjunction, reiterating the connection to his career indicated by the 10° of the Roberta.

There is an association of the asteroid Roberta with robbery, kidnapping (a form of robbery) or usurpation. This association would be derived from the name's first syllable, which is rob. The person with a prominent Roberta, may be the robbed, rather than the robber. Patricia Hearst, having appropriate aspects natally and at the time of her kidnapping, is an example of both. After being robbed of her freedom, she became a robber herself.[30] Nonetheless, the robbery may not always be literal.

As mentioned, the ascending node of an asteroid will give insight into its quality, and during most of this century both the ascending node of Roberta and the fixed star Regulus have been at 28° Leo. Regulus in the heart of the Lion constellation is the "Royal Star," and some of the power and honor, associated with Regulus, is associated with Roberta. However, when there is a solar connection (Leo), there is always the possibility of eclipse. It is fitting that *Roberta* should be about an American football star and a Russian princess. Stars, theatrical or athletic, are the royalty of today. As for the possibility of eclipse, our famous stars, football or otherwise, are always under the threat of obscuration, and the expatriate Russian princess had been deposed.

General Observations on Name Asteroids

Having completed synopses of the meanings of the eighteen asteroids in the personal name asteroid study, I would like to make some general observations on name asteroids.

Often, people with the same name who are important in your life will be similar. For instance, with my Roberta at 26° Cancer 08' in the sixth house, exactly sextile my Mercury at 27° Taurus 01' in the third house, the important Roberts in my life have been writers. As an example, the Robert to whom I was engaged between my first and second marriages was a writer, and the Robert who gave me my first astrological reading subsequently became a well-known writer on astrology.

Another observation is that asteroids whose names approximate a person's name will often combine in the chart of that person or in the chart of a "significant other." The degree of inexactness in the name of the asteroid often correlates to the degree of inexactness in this combination.

Using Mark Pottenger's program for 392 asteroids, there is the following example. A woman, Nanette, who has no exact name asteroid, has the asteroids Nancy in the first house at 17° Libra 06', Anna in the seventh house at 16° Aries 08', Roxane in the tenth house at 19° Cancer 40' and Antwerpia in the fourth house at 12° Capricorn 27'ℝ. In *Name Your Baby*, under both Nanette and Nancy it says "See **Anne**." As mentioned, I've found the beginning the most important part of a name. Appropriately, Nancy, whose first syllable is the same as the first syllable of Nanette, is in the first house. Also appropriately, Anna, which has the same meaning, is in Aries exactly opposite. Roxane, whose meaning is different but whose second syllable has the same meaning as Nanette, is inexactly square both Nancy and Anna. Antwerpia, which is a Belgium city but which begins with the sound of Anne, is also inexactly square these two asteroids. The midpoint of Roxane and Antwerpia focuses these inexact squares. It is in the first house at 16° Libra 03', exactly conjunct Nancy, the asteroid whose name is closest to the name Nanette.

Roxane and Antwerpia would refer, respectively, to the so-named person and city; and with their placement in the tenth and fourth house and in Cancer and Capricorn, they would relate to the parents. Anna in Aries in the seventh house would evidence an identification with the partner, already indicated by this woman's Libra Ascendant and Aries Descendant. However, these three asteroids as well as Nancy reiterate sounds and meanings associated with this woman's name, and in their combination highlight that name.

Synopses of 10 More Asteroids

These general observations completed, I shall conclude my synopses with ten more asteroids from various sources. The first three are Astraea (5), Hebe (6) and Iris (7). Their custom ephemerides were ordered from Astro. The next three are Bacchus (2063), Apollo (1862) and America (916). Their ephemerides were published by the *CAO Times,* with the positions for Bacchus and America being calculated by Dr. J. Lee Lehman, and those for Apollo, by Daniel Green. The calculations of Lee Lehman were based on positions in right ascension and declination supplied by Dr. Brian Marsden. These three ephemerides were published after the original ten published by the *CAO Times.* (The meanings of those ten asteroids have already been synopsized.) The last asteroids to be discussed are Dudu (564), Dembowska (349), Pittsburghia (484) and Frigga (77). Their ephemerides are in a book written by Batya Stark and Mark Pottenger and published by ACS Publications. Synopses of the meanings of these ten asteroids, based on my investigations, follow.

ASTRAEA

The asteroid Astraea (5) was discovered December 8, 1845, in Driesen, Prussia by K. L. Hencke. The glyphs for the fifth through ninth asteroids were found by Al Morrison in the 1853 edition of the *Nautical Almanac.* He writes that the astronomer-royal had adopted glyphs for the first eight asteroids and subsequently discarded those adopted for the last four. (Either the ninth glyph was included but had not been adopted, or there were nine glyphs adopted.) As mentioned, the glyphs given in the synopses of the first four asteroids are those of the astronomers', or at least adaptations thereof. The glyphs I use for asteroids 8 and 9 are also those adopted by the astronomer-royal. The glyph for Flora (8) is ⚘ and for Metis (9) is ⚚. A glyph of a flower is appropriate for the Roman goddess of flowers, and two intersecting orbs with a star above them is appropriate for the first wife of Zeus. Metis did share her wisdom with her husband from inside him after he swallowed her. The two orbs probably represent the heads of Zeus and Metis intertwined. The astronomer-royal's glyph for Astraea (⚓) is a sailing ship's anchor. Not knowing that there had been a glyph designed for Astraea already, I designed one myself. My glyph (⚖) is scales, which is an attribute of Astraea, the goddess of justice. Though there is a similarity in the stability of the anchor and the balance of the scales, the earlier glyph has that complexity associated with the Victorian period in which it was designed.

Astraea in Greek mythology was identified with Dike, the goddess of justice and daughter of Zeus and the Titaness Themis. There are asteroids named Dike (99), Themis (24) and Justitia (269), but there are differences between the mythological associations of Astraea and those of these goddesses. Dike was one of the three Horae, the Greek and Roman goddesses of the seasons, who were daughters of Zeus (Jupiter) and Themis. The three are Eunomia (order), Dice or Dike (justice), and Eirene or Irene (peace). Their relationship to ethics, however, was not as emphasized as their relationship to the seasons. (There are asteroids named Eunomia [15] and Irene [14] too.) Themis, their mother, was the Greek personification of law, and

Justitia was the Roman personification of justice. Though Dike, Themis and Justitia, like Astraea, are related to justice, Astraea has an added Virgo association. During the Bronze Age, after the Golden and Silver, because of man's wickedness, Astraea left the earth to become the constellation Virgo. Astraia (Astraea) means the Starry Maid. She is portrayed not only with the scales but with a crown of stars.

Astraea in the chart is an indicator of justice and law. I have seen Astraea appropriately activated at the time people married, had jury duty, were subpoenaed, went to arbitration or grievance or became aware of justice or injustice in general. A justice or lawyer can literally be represented. Additionally, a Virgoan quality is associated with this asteroid. In other words, its quality is analytical, dualistic, and service-oriented, and Astraea may sometimes designate the Virgoan person—the Starry Maid. As the Starry Maid, Astraea brings a shining star-like connotation to that Virgoan quality or person. That shining is sometimes expressed as prominence, sometimes as magnanimity.

An example of a natal position of Astraea that involved justice, legalities, and the dualistic Virgoan quality, combined with prominence of the people and events concerned, is the following. A woman, whose natal Astraea is at 19° Libra 06' in the seventh house, knowingly entered into two bigamous marriages. This position placed an emphasis on the legalities of marriage; bigamy is dualistic; and she expected that "justice" would be done in the end. Justice was particularly a factor because the woman herself was the product of a bigamous marriage, unknowingly entered into by her mother. Her father (19°), incidentally a Virgo, was the bigamist. Subconsciously, the daughter may have been repeating the *primary experience,* hoping it would be set right this time. In the second marriage it was. The second husband eventually found his first wife, obtained a divorce and married the second wife legally. Of course, not everyone with this position would have such experiences. The aspects give more information. The Astraea is exactly sextile Athene (law) at 20° Sagittarius 37' in the ninth house and quincunx Hades (second-hand) at 19° Pisces 21' in the twelfth house and Amor (love) at 19° Taurus 45'℞ in the second house, forming two interlocking Yods. There is also a square to Transpluto (Super-Pluto) at 18° Cancer 44'℞ in the fourth house and a semisquare to the Dark Moon Lilith (hidden fascinations) at 03° Virgo 07' in the sixth house.[31]

HEBE

The asteroid Hebe (6) was discovered July 1, 1847, in Driesen, Prussia by K. L. Hencke. As mentioned, the glyph for Hebe was given in the 1853 edition of the *Nautical Almanac*. This glyph (♈), adopted and then discarded by the astronomer-royal, and my glyph (♈), designed without my knowing there was already one, are both cups. The similarity between the glyphs is expected, since Hebe was the cupbearer to the gods. The difference is that the earlier cup is more elongated and has a cross as a stem, while mine is more rounded and has a circular base.

The following is the listing given in *Name Your Baby*:

> HEBE—Greek: Hebe. "Youth." Hebe, daughter of Zeus in Greek myths, was the goddess of youth.

No nicknames, variations or famous namesakes are stated. Hebe is not included in the personal name asteroid study because I do not have any charts of people named Hebe. However, judging from my experience with the other personal name asteroids, if I did, the positions of Hebe would be descriptive of people with that name.

Hebe, the daughter of Zeus and Hera, was the Greek goddess of youth, who herself was eternally youthful. She was the dutiful daughter of powerful parents and became the wife of Heracles (Hercules), the personification of strength and courage. They were married when Heracles died and was deified. By him she was the mother of Alexiares and Anicetus. Her most important role was cupbearer to the gods, bringing them nectar and ambrosia. However, after a fall in which she was indecently exposed, the beautiful youth Ganymede replaced her in this duty.

Hebe in the chart is an indicator of youthfulness and of a mate who is herculean. It is related to marriage, symbolizing the youthful bride of the heroic groom. There is an asteroid Herculina (532).

It is also an indicator of where and how one wants to bring something immortal to the universe. Ambrosia and nectar, the food and drink brought to the gods by Hebe, mean "not mortal" and "life-giving," respectively. That something immortal may be in the creative or performing arts, or it may be through our children, which are often our gift to posterity and our attempt to achieve immortality ourselves. That something may even be brought through death. A woman, whose Hebe is at 02° Scorpio 10'℞ in the first house, helped her husband to achieve a peaceful death (Scorpio is the sign of death, and 2 is the number of the spouse's death). This help was not euthanasic, but psychological and emotional. He died at home with his family surrounding him, and his wife holding him and telling him she was strong enough to let him go now.

Another reference of Hebe is to the fall which she suffered. Though the Hebe person desires to serve, she may be removed from her duties because, sometimes through no fault of her own, she has been indecently exposed. (Although for simplicity, only the feminine pronoun has been employed, this experience is not limited to the female.)

There is also a reference to the Jewish people, derived from the fact that Hebe is short for Hebrew. This word has been used disparagingly, but no disparagement is meant by my association. It seems the universe, to make its references, takes those words it has at hand, whether they be puns or plays on words or slang expressions. As an example, October 1, 1984 at 09:00 PM EDT the nine-part series *Heritage: Civilization and the Jews* began on Channel 13. Somewhere between November 6 when the position of Hebe in the ephemeris is 13° Cancer 27.8' and November 16 when it is 13° Cancer 31.6'℞, Hebe made its retrograde station, exactly conjunct the United States Sun at either 12° or 13° Cancer, depending on which chart you use for July 4, 1776. This station occurred about the time of the middle of this series, and 13° and Cancer relate to one's heritage, and Hebe was going towards a direct station at 28° Gemini. 28° equals 10, the Saturn number, and Saturn has a lot to do with civilization, and, of course, Gemini is communication.

Finally, Hebe is activated when cups are featured, such as when they are bought or won. Interestingly, there is a great deal of emphasis on cups, and the ceremonial drinking of wine from them, in both the Jewish and Christian religions. There is in the celebration of marriages too, even when they are not religious.

Ganymede, the beautiful youth who replaced Hebe, was also cupbearer to the gods, but he particularly served Zeus (Jupiter). The asteroid Ganymed (1036) represents a beautiful youth and can relate to homosexuality, which Ganymede later typified. This asteroid is also an indicator of service to a Jupiterian person—older, successful person or one with the ninth house, Sagittarius or Jupiter prominent.

IRIS

The asteroid Iris (7) was discovered August 13, 1847, in London by J. R. Hind. The glyph for Iris (⊕), adopted and later discarded by the astronomer-royal, is a star inside a bell jar. A bell jar is associated with scientific experiments, and so with the gaining of information. My glyph (⌒) is a rainbow, which is associated with Iris, the goddess of the rainbow. While the glyph given in the 1853 edition of the *Nautical Almanac* reflects the Victorian period of its composition, my glyph reflects the Modernistic period of its composition. Periods aside, in the small size required on a chart, a star inside a bell jar would be hard to discern.

The following is the listing given in *Name Your Baby*:

> **IRIS**—Greek: Iris. "The rainbow, the iris flower." Iris was the messenger of
> the Greek gods, also representing the rainbow.

No nicknames, variations or famous namesakes are stated. Though Iris is a much more prevalent name than Hebe, I do not have any charts of people named Iris. As a result, Iris is not included in the personal name asteroid study. As with Hebe, my past experience with the personal name asteroids persuades me that the positions of Iris would be descriptive of people with that name.

Iris, the golden-winged daughter of Thaumas and the ocean-nymph Electra, was the Greek personification of the rainbow. Her sisters were the Harpies, whose lives she induced the winged twins Zetes and Calais to spare. Good-natured in regard to both the gods and mortals, she delivered the messages of the gods, particularly those of Hera. Hermes (Mercury) was also known as the messenger of the gods, but particularly of Zeus. Both Hermes and Iris are depicted wearing winged sandals and carrying the caduceus (herald's staff).

Iris in the chart is an indicator of the messenger. There are associations to the rainbow, which, according to *The Random House College Dictionary*, is "1. a bow or arc of prismatic colors appearing in the heavens opposite the sun and caused by the refraction and reflection of the sun's rays in drops of rain." There is Sun and Moon symbolism here, with the rainbow (Iris) being a reflection (Moon) of the sun's rays (Sun) in water (Moon). The Sun and Moon rule the eyes, and the iris is the colored part of the eye which contracts or expands to keep out or let in the light. The eyes see and send messages to the brain. The rainbow connection of Iris brings messages from the gods in the form of free associations. And, Iris is related to the arts, which bring messages from the gods, often in "living color." A girl, whose Lachesis (the measurer of the thread of life) is exactly conjunct her Iris, measures video tape time for television.

Iris also has a "Somewhere Over the Rainbow" quality—a feeling that somewhere there is an ideal place, if only we could find it. This feeling is not necessarily a problem, unless we escape into a world of dreams and give up striving for the ideal in the real world. An appropriate way to combine the real and the ideal is through the arts. Judy Garland, with whom the song "Over the Rainbow" will always be associated, has Iris at 05° Cancer 52' in her twelfth house, exactly square to the minute her North Node at 05° Libra 52' and her South at 05° Aries 52' in her fourth and tenth house, respectively.[32] The 05° correlates to show business; the twelfth house, to the illusion of film; the sign of Cancer, to the emotional quality that suffused her singing; and the square with the Nodes, to the close emotional relationship she established with her audience. The fourth and tenth houses of the Nodes describe the conflict between the home and the career or outside world. Dorothy (Judy) in *The Wizard of Oz* was transported to the land of Oz, but she kept wanting to get back home to Kansas. The interpretation of Iris in terms of Judy Garland's public life can be extended to include her personal life. From this perspective, 05° would refer to love affairs and children, and I'm sure she brought that "Somewhere Over the Rainbow" quality to them too.

Like all the asteroids, Iris can make literal references. Not only can it refer to the iris of the eye, but it can refer to the rainbow and to the trade name Iris. There were descriptive aspects to my Iris and from transiting Iris when I bought a beaded bag that looked like the rainbow; when I slept for a week on sheets with a rainbow design; when I went to a party at the Rainbow Room; and when I had to resume wearing an old nightgown because a new one was stolen from my wash. Looking at the old nightgown for washing instructions, I discovered its trade name was Iris.

The trade names (and other connotations) of the products you buy, of the places in which you buy them, of the products you use and of the places to which you go, should be noted. The cost of the products and the telephone numbers and addresses of the places are important too. For the numbers, use the astrological correlations. (Considering cost, the astrological correlation of the dollar number is in relation to that of the cent number—in so far as the symbolism of cost is concerned.) Sometimes there are asteroids with the names you have noted. If not, use these names to free-associate. Literal references are synchronous with metaphorical ones, and one of the greatest advantages of the asteroids is that the knowledge of them helps to make clear this synchronicity.

Another example of a literal reference, which is also metaphorical, is Iris' reference to the iris flower. When a woman bought irises to decorate her new office, there were descriptive aspects to her Iris and from transiting Iris. Articles about the iris or other flowers appear in newspapers and magazines under suitable placements and aspects of the equivalent asteroids. The asteroid Lilith (and the Dark Moon Lilith) equate to the lily. There is also an association of the asteroid Iris with the lily, and hence with the lotus, and so on a metaphorical level with France and Egypt. In

The Random House College Dictionary under fleur-de-lis there is "**3**. the iris flower or plant," under lily there is "**4**. fleur-de-lis, esp. as the symbol of France" and under lotus there is "**4**. any of several water lilies...." In *The Columbia Encyclopedia* under lotus, the blue or white Egyptian lotus is characterized as "sacred from remote times and the national emblem of Egypt." (The lotus is an attribute of the Egyptian Solar deity Horus, son of Isis and Osiris.)

BACCHUS

The asteroid Bacchus (2063) was discovered April 24, 1977, in Palomar Mountain, California by Charles Kowal. (This is the official date and place of the discovery, though Bacchus, like Chiron, was probably "discovered" by Kowal a few days later in his office in Pasadena.) The glyph of Bacchus (Ψ), based on a suggestion from Lee Lehman and Zane Stein, was designed by Al Morrison. The glyph represents a glass, which is appropriate for the god of wine.

Bacchus, whose name is probably Lydian in origin, was the Roman god of wine, who in Greek mythology is known as Dionysus. Dionysus, whose worship probably originated in Phrygia, was the Greek god of wine, but also of fertility, joyous life and hospitality. The Greeks identified him with the Egyptian Osiris.

Dionysus, the only god to have a mortal parent, was the son of Zeus and Semele. At the instigation of Hera, Semele had asked that Zeus appear to her as a god. When he did, she was burned to death, and Zeus placed their unborn child in his thigh. In time Dionysus was delivered from Zeus' thigh and so was called "Twice born." Another instance of his being born again occurred when he was brought back to life by his grandmother Rhea after being torn to pieces by the Titans. (There is a similar story in Orphic legend.) Born in Thebes, Greece, he spend his childhood on the mountains, taken care of by the nymphs of Nysa and educated by Silenus and the Muses. The making of wine from the grape was discovered by Dionysus when he was grown. He traveled throughout the world bringing his gift, which in moderation brought joy, and in excess, madness. He had been mad himself until he consulted the oracle at Dodona. Dionysus was also a prophet. In his travels he fell in love with and married Ariadne who had been deserted by Theseus. When he took the place of Hestia as one of the twelve Olympians, he rescued his mother from Hades, renaming her Thyone and bringing her to Olympus. In Orphic legends Dionysus is identified with Zagreus, the Cretan god who originally was equivalent to Zeus. According to these legends he was the son of Zeus and Demeter, or Kore, and took part in the Eleusinian Mysteries of death and rebirth. The myths and legends of Dionysus are relevant to Bacchus.

Though the worship of Bacchus and Dionysus was orgiastic, the wine and dancing were used to create an ecstatic frenzy, and that frenzy could be religious or creative. Later there was reform in their worship. They became patrons of the arts. Tragedy and comedy originated in the literary contests at the festivals of the Greek god.

Bacchus, as well as Dionysus, is usually depicted as an almost effeminate youth, wearing a wreath of ivy or vine leaves and an animal skin. Their attributes are the goblet, or grapes, and the thyrsus. Sacred to them are the vine, laurel, ivy, rose, asphodel, lion, panther, tiger, lynx, dolphin, goat and ox.

The orbit of Bacchus is between Mercury and Mars. This containment surrounds Bacchus with the mental activity of Mercury and the dynamic energy of Mars. Bacchus' orbit is in the orbits of Venus, the Earth and Mars and crosses the orbits of Venus and the Earth. Being in those orbits gives Bacchus a smattering of the sensuousness of Venus, the earthiness of the Earth and the self-assertiveness of Mars. Due to its strange orbit, as Lee Lehman explains in her ephemeris of this asteroid, Bacchus spends less time in the first half of the zodiac and more in the second. She postulates that Bacchus' expression is probably different when it is traversing the zodiac quickly than when it is traversing it slowly. In the cases I have studied, it seems as if the Bacchus energy is more easily synthesized when the asteroid is moving quickly. However, since Bacchus spends less time moving quickly, there are fewer examples of that phenomenon. More cases would have to be studied to see if speed is a factor, and, certainly, even if it is, it is just one factor.

Bacchus in the chart is an indicator of joyous abandonment. What that is will be shown by the position and exact aspects of Bacchus. Like Lee Lehman, I found this abandonment may express itself as enraptured love, religious fervor or drunkenness, and the drunkenness may be caused by alcohol, sugar or drugs. A positive expression of this asteroid can be in the joy that one person brings to another. The synastry between them will reveal the source of this joy.

Bacchus is also a signifier of the arts, particularly the theatrical ones. The forms of tragedy and comedy were developed at the festivals of Dionysus (Bacchus). A brother and sister, whose father was a writer of tragedies and comedies, both have Bacchus in the tenth house. Their father's comedies were mainly burlesques, which are like the satyr plays at the festivals. Both were involved with the theatre in their own careers. The sister, who was a singer as well as an actress, has Apollo in the twelfth house, exactly semisextile Bacchus. Apollo was a musician god, and at the Pythian Games, which were in his honor, the main feature was the musical contests, with flute players, cithara (lyre) players and singers. On the other hand, a brother and sister, whose mother is a manic-depressive, both have Bacchus in the fourth house. Manic-depression may be symbolized by the combination of comedy and tragedy (one satyr play combined with three tragedies) at the festivals or by the frenzy of the Dionysia and the Bacchanalia.

With Bacchus, as with the Bacchanalia, there is the possibility of excess. The person under the influence of Bacchus tends not to protect him or her self. But, as Bacchus was born again, the Bacchus person may be too. Bacchus was half-mortal, but finally he ascended to Mount Olympus as a god.

A literal reference of Bacchus, the Roman god of wine, is wine. The purchasing or receiving of a bottle of wine, and the first sip of a new bottle, are good occurences to time. Cast a chart of the event and look at that chart in relation to the charts of the people involved—the purchaser, or the giver and receiver or the drinker, of the wine. The label on the bottle lists a wealth of information, such as the name of the wine, the bottler, importer, places of production and importation, the year and the trademark. Consider the asteroids that represent these factors. Also, there are asteroids other than Bacchus, such as Vinifera, which relate to wine; Venus and Neptune do too; but as always the whole chart is descriptive. Consider the circumstances surrounding the purchasing, the receiving and the drinking. The circumstances would include the names of the people involved, their appearance and their conversations. As always, there is a subtext which sometimes is more important than the text.

A literal reference of Bacchus in the news is the following. The October 29, 1984 *Newsweek* has an article titled "Busting the Beer Bust" on pages 96-97. (I note the pages of articles for their numerological equivalence to the houses, signs, etc.) The article speaks of an organization called Bacchus (Boost Alcohol Consciousness Concerning the Health of University Students). I usually cast the chart of a magazine or newspaper article for midnight ST or LMT on the date of the publication. There were appropriate exact aspects of the transiting factors, such as Venus and Uranus being conjunct at 10° and 11° Sagittarius—10°, limitation; 11°, change; and Sagittarius, higher education. More specifically, Bacchus, sesquiquadrate the midnight Midheaven, was at 25° Virgo, and 25° equals the public while Virgo is the sign of health. Even more specifically, the asteroid Beer was at 03° Scorpio 41', conjunct Pluto (transformation) at 02° Scorpio 13'! There were also appropriate exact aspects to the heliocentric nodes. For instance, Venus and Uranus were trine (communication aspect), Bacchus was semisquare (transformation aspect), and the Midheaven and IC at 11° Taurus 11' and 11° Scorpio 11' were square (nurturing aspect) the ascending node of Neptune at 11° Leo 37'. Mercury and Saturn, conjunct at 17° Scorpio, were conjunct the descending node of Mercury at 18° Scorpio 09' and semisquare (transformation aspect) the ascending node of the asteroid Beer at 01° Libra 47'. A long-term aspect was Pluto at 02° Scorpio, conjunct the descending node of Bacchus at 02° Scorpio 42'; a short-term aspect was Beer at 03° Scorpio 41', conjunct this descending node of Bacchus. The conjunction is the 1st house, Aries, Mars aspect—in other words, it relates to the self. (Though Beer was named for an astronomer, the literal definition of beer, an alcoholic beverage made from cereal, is being used. On a metaphoric level, this asteroid has an asociation with Ceres, from whose name cereal is derived, and with being—bear—which is a variation of beer. Beer can be the *being*; the *bearer*—mother or mother figure; and what we *bear*— our children or our work.)

Newsweek usually comes out a week before the date on the cover, and the transits on that day are also important. (In addition, I note the transits occurring when I read the news because they are important in relation to my chart. The experimenter is in the experiment.) It would be helpful if we had a chart for the beginning of the organization Bacchus, as well as one for the beginning of *Newsweek*. Even without these specific applications, it's apparent that what, and when, news comes into public consciousness is described figuratively in the heavens.

APOLLO

The asteroid Apollo (1862) was discovered April 24, 1932, in Heidelberg by K. Reinmuth. Lost shortly after discovery, Apollo was rediscovered March 28, 1973, at Harvard by McCrosky and Shao, using an ephemeris calculated by Dr. Brian Marsden.

The glyph of Apollo (☉), as received in a dream, was designed by Al Morrison. It is, to quote him, "the chariot in which the Sun rides daily," which is appropriate for the god of the sun.

Apollo was the Greek god of light, healing, prophecy, music, poetry, dance, fine arts, philosophy and science. Though a healer, he was the bringer of sudden death. He was also protector of flocks and herds and patron of sailors and of the founding of colonies. The origin of Apollo was probably both Asiatic and Dorian. In Roman mythology, in typical practical fashion, he became primarily the god of healing.

One of the twelve Olympians, Apollo was the son of Zeus and Leto and twin brother of Artemis (Diana) who assisted in his delivery. Hera's jealousy had caused Leto to be in labor for nine days and nights. Apollo slew Python, the guardian of the oracle at what was to be Delphi. As a penance he was exiled to Tempe for a number of years. He had many loves, some unrequited. The nymph Daphne escaped him when she was changed into a laurel tree. He changed the beloved, but heartbroken youth Cyparissus into a cypress. Coronis, while carrying Apollo's child, married Ischys. Apollo killed her but saved their son from the flames of the funeral pyre. The son was Asclepius, the healer raised by Chiron. When Asclepius was killed by Zeus with a thunderbolt fashioned by the Cyclopes, Apollo killed the Cyclopes. As a result Zeus made him serve Admetus, king of Pherae. After this servitude Apollo became moderate and controlled and no longer defied Zeus. As the Leader of the Muses, the music and dances he led them in were calm, rather than frenzied.

The worship of Apollo was very different from that of Bacchus and Dionysus, particulary before their worship had been reformed. Instead of orgiastic frenzy, there was formalized purification. Apollo's most famous oracles were at Delphi and Tempe, and they were infallible. At Delphi there was a theatre and stadium in which literary, musical and athletic contests were held. Dionysus, whose tomb was also there, prophesied in the winter when Apollo was away in "a land of perpetual light and happiness far to the North."[33] This was the land of the Hyperboreans, and they were virtuous, as well as happy.

Apollo is usually depicted as an athletic youth, either nude or with a chlamys (short woolen mantle) over his shoulder. His attributes are a bow and arrows, shepherd's crook, lyre and oracular tripod. Sacred to him are the laurel, palm tree, wolf, snake, mouse, grasshopper, swan, raven and hawk.

The orbit of Apollo is between Mercury and Jupiter. This containment surrounds Apollo with the mental activity of Mercury and the expansiveness of Jupiter. Apollo's orbit is in and crosses the orbits of Venus, the Earth and Mars. Being in those orbits gives Apollo a smattering of the sensuousness of Venus, the earthiness of the Earth and the self-assertiveness of Mars. Apollo was the first Earthcrosser discovered and so gave its name to the family of asteroids which cross the orbit of our planet. This Apollo Family includes, of those asteroids treated here, Icarus, Toro, Bacchus and Apollo. Only those asteroids which cross the orbit of the Earth can collide with the Earth, giving them potentially an "impacting" nature. They are thought to be cometary nuclei.

Apollo in the chart is an indicator of a radiant quality. This asteroid relates to Sun-like factors, such as prominence, the creative and performing arts, and children, the son in particular. It can literally symbolize the sun, though there is an asteroid Helio (895). For instance, when the mini-series "The Sun Also Rises" was first shown on television (beginning at 09:00 PM EST, December 9, 1984), transiting Apollo was at 29° Leo 12', just about to make its retrograde station at that degree exactly conjunct the fixed star Regulus in the "Heart of the Lion." The mini-series was based on the book of the same name by Ernest Hemingway. Transiting Apollo was also exactly semisextile Hemingway's Sun at 28° Cancer 32', trine his North Node at 29° Sagittarius 16' and semisquare his Venus at 13° Cancer 08'. His Sun is ruler of his twelfth house, Apollo and Mercury, and his Venus is ruler of his second and third and an interception in his ninth. (Hemingway's birth information is classified as A data in Lois M. Rodden's *The American Book of Charts*.)

Apollo has great power and intensity. When this asteroid is in exact aspect to the Sun, or in other ways shows an association with it, the Sun-like quality of the asteroid is emphasized. The associations are shown by Apollo placements in the fifth house, or in Leo, or in 05° or a number of degrees that adds up to 5. When Apollo is in exact aspect to the Moon, the reflector of the sun, the Sun-like quality of this asteroid is emphasized, but in a reflective way. This reflectivity can be expressed by Apollo placements in the fourth house, or in Cancer, or in 04° or a number of degrees that adds up to 4. When Apollo is in exact aspect to the Nodes, the points at which the Moon crosses the apparent path of the Sun, the Sun-like quality of this asteroid is emphasized in close ties. Also, exact interaspects of Apollo with the Sun, Moon or Nodes would bring this radiant quality in its different manifestations to the particular relationship. Exact aspects and interaspects with other planets, points, etc., would have their own distinct message to bring. As for the midpoint of Apollo and the asteroid Helio, meaning sun, it is the place at which the solar meanings of both asteroids are combined.

There would be the possibility of extreme fieriness, burn-out or eclipse, with Apollo representing the god of the sun. However, this asteroid usually has an apollonian nature, which is to quote *The Random House Dictionary of the English Language,* "2. (l.c.) serene, calm, or well-balanced; poised and disciplined." (The Dionysian nature is characterized as "2. recklessly uninhibited; unrestrained; undisciplined; frenzied; orgiastic," while the bacchic is "2. (l.c.) riotously or jovially intoxicated.")

Another reference of Apollo is to healing, prophecy, philosophy and science. Twins, whether literal or figurative, are also signified by Apollo and his twin Diana or Artemis. There can be a feeling of twinship between two people with exact interaspects of Apollo in one chart and appropriate personal points, planets, asteroids (such as Diana and Artemis), or Uranian planets in the other. The Uranian planet Apollon is associated with Apollonian concerns too, but with an unusual (Uranian) and hidden quality. The duality that is associated with Apollon is derived from Apollo's being a twin. The midpoint of Apollo and Apollon is an important point highlighting their concerns.

AMERICA

The asteroid America (916) was discovered August 7, 1915, in Simeïs, Crimea, USSR by G. Neujmin. It was named for America, which had been named in honor of Amerigo Vespucci. Amerigo, who was an explorer of coastal South America for Spain and Portugal, was born March 9, 1451, in Florence, Italy. The glyph of America (⛰) was designed by Al Morrison. It is taken from the Great Seal of the United States of America, which eighteen people had suggested he use. The glyph is the top-part of the pyramid with the eye of Providence within it.

America, though used primarily to refer to the United States of America, is actually the entire Western Hemisphere, which includes North, South and Central America. The United States of America is identified with the Declaration of Independence, adopted July 4, 1776, in Philadelphia.[34] This document is a magnificent expression of the right of the people to resort to revolution if the natural rights of mankind are not upheld. The United States is probably the greatest industrial nation in the world. It has extraordinary natural resources, which make it capable of being self-sufficient. But, it is known for being the "melting pot" of many different nations. Though the United States has not always been able to live up to the idealism of its beginning, it is that idealism (symbolized by the Statue of Liberty) which is most associated with America.

America in the chart is an indicator of the Western Hemisphere, primarily the United States. The placements (house, sign, numerical) and exact aspects of America show what one has been known for in America. What one has been known for, in other words, one's "contribution" to America, does not have to be a matter of fame and fortune. For example, my father was an artist, involved with the theatre, and though not eminently successful, he always made a living as an artist. In his chart, America is at 22° Virgo 17' in the eighth house, exactly square his Sun and Moon at 21° Sagittarius 37' and 22° Sagittarius 37' in the twelfth house and his Neptune at 23° Gemini 25'℞ in the sixth house, forming an exact T-Square. Neptune correlates to art; the Moon, to reflection or image; and the Sun, to the theatre. The Sun rules his eighth house, Apollo, Mars, Vertex and Apollon, while the Moon rules his seventh house, South Node, Transpluto, Zeus and Cupido. Apollo and Apollon, as well as the Sun, relate to the theatre, and his art was mainly for the theatre. Cupido is both art and the family, and he was also known for his family, which was prominent in theatrical and literary circles. Zeus is not only creation, but procreation, and as with most of us who have progeny they were his biggest contribution.

Another reference of America is to the hope for a perfect society. As mentioned, its glyph of a pyramid is taken from the Great Seal of the United States. In *the asteroid America* Nora Safran writes in reference to the founding fathers and their choice of a pyramid that it "symbolized the Egyptian concept of 'maet': truth and justice, as they hoped it would be embodied in a perfect society." (As an extrapolation from the founding father's choice, the asteroid America relates to Egypt.)

Literal references of America occurred when a man joined the American Golf Club; when the next day he spoke to ASCAP (the American Society of Composers, Authors and Publishers), after receiving a notice from them; and when the following day, as power of attorney for his aunt, he received money from three bank accounts that had escheated to the state (the United States of America). Not only were there fitting aspects at the time, but a month before, his name asteroid and the asteroid America had both made a retrograde station, exactly conjunct each other.

As another example of literal references, if a person's being or not being American is emphasized, it will be shown by the placements and exact aspects of America. An emphasis might be, in the first case, that one's forebears "came over on the Mayflower," or one marries such a person; in the second case, that in America one is or marries a foreigner.

DUDU

The asteroid Dudu (564) was discovered May 9, 1905, in Heidelberg by P. Götz. The glyph of Dudu (♋), designed by Batya Stark, is three blobs of matter. The glyph is intended to suggest doo doo, which is spelled differently, but sounds the same.

Though *The Asteroid Ephemeris: Dudu, Dembowska, Pittsburgh, Frigga* by Batya Stark and Mark Pottenger was written tongue in cheek, the choice of glyphs and many of the interpretations are appropriate. The reason is that the authors were using associations, similarities in sound or meaning and plays on words. What I discovered in studying the asteroids discussed in this chapter is that associations, similarities in sound or meaning and plays on words are relevant to the meanings of the asteroids. On the other hand, the cookbook interpretations the authors give to satirize many astrologers' absolutist statements are not to be taken literally. What is to be taken literally are the ephemeris, which is accurate, and an "Afterword" by Zipporah Dobyns, which is based on her astrological observations of the four asteroids.

There is a character named Dudu, pointed out to me by Diana Rosenberg, in Lord Byron's *Don Juan*, the sixth and seventh cantos. Dudu is one of the odalisques (concubines) in the harem where Don Juan, disguised as a woman, spends the night. He is put in her bed, but she believes he is a woman, and there is only friendship between them. When the Sultana, who loves Don Juan, hears that he has spent the night with Dudu, she orders her attendant to dispose of them. Not only is Dudu innocent, but she is described as "shy," "serious," "serene," and "kind."

In *Asteroid World: Summer 1987*, Seraphita Sebastian writes that Dudu is a female name in Nietzsche's *Thus Spake Zarathustra*. Interestingly, Nietzsche's Dudu is very similar to Byron's Dudu. Both are unemancipated Middle Eastern women. Though not an odalisque, Nietzsche's Dudu is a dancing girl, also submissive to men.

As another notation of Dudu, Seraphita lists the Sumerian scribe Dudu (2189-2169 BC), whose name is inscribed on a statue dedicated to Ningirsu, the god of fields and irrigation.

Don Juan, Thus Spake Zarathustra and the Sumerian statue are classical sources which are part of our culture. They express particular associations of the name Dudu and, therefore, particular associations of the asteroid Dudu.

As for linguistic similarities, in German, "du" means you. It is the familiar form of the second person singular. This form is intended to be used when addressing relatives, close friends and children. The repetition of the word du to form the name Dudu is like the repetition of sounds to form words in baby talk. The prime examples of those words are Mama and Papa. Dudu in *Don Juan* does have a family (familiar) quality. Dudu in *Thus Spake Zarathustra* bespeaks Nietzsche's concept that the role of women is to be the mother of the Superman.

Dudu in the chart is an indicator of doo doo. I have seen this asteroid activated and activating when a woman was given a summons for leaving dog droppings on the sidewalk, at times of discussions about incontinence and feces specimens and at periods of rectal bleeding. As in *Don Juan*, Dudu may symbolize someone who, through no fault of her or his own, is given "the dirty end of the stick." This asteroid, activated and activating at times of cleaning out refuse, can symbolize something or someone discarded. Dudu is such a person, but she aids in Don Juan's escape, escaping with him. Eliminating what is no longer needed allows for what is.

Dudu can indicate duty—as the other side of the same coin—"do your duty" is a double entendre. Dû in French is defined as "due, duty, owing." Du in German has already been defined as the familiar (family) form of you. Combining these two meanings, Dudu in the chart is integral to you (you 2x), in relation to the family and your *duty* to it. The placement (house, sign, numerical) and exact aspects of Dudu will signify what *you* believe are your duties, particularly in regard to those close to you.

Reflecting Byron's literary depiction of Dudu, this asteroid can refer to a concubine or secondary wife, which is what an odalisque is. A concubine would be "a woman who cohabits with a man to whom she is not married," and a secondary wife would be a wife in a bigamous or polygamous marriage. In this specialized expression, duty is an issue, particularly to the family. When a marriage contract has not been entered into, as in the first case, or has been abrogated, as in the second, what are the duties of the couple? In the bigamous marriage the triangularity of the glyph is certainly fitting.

Another specialized reference of Dudu, apropos of the Sumerian scribe with that name, is to the scribe or the inscriber. Astrologers, particularly those who have a strong sense of duty, fit into this category. Scribes recorded astrological observations, as well as the religious and secular *duties* or laws, the contracts and the letters of divorce. Apropos of Nietzsche's Dudu, there can also be an allusion to the dancer. Dance was originally a *sacred communication* with the gods. The particular manifestation is shown by the placement (house, sign, numerical) and exact aspects of Dudu. For instance, a woman who has her Dudu in the tenth house at 16° Virgo

13', exactly sextile Mercury in the ninth house, reads and critiques scripts (modern-day scribe), and a woman who has her Dudu in the fifth house at 11° Leo 43'℞, exactly conjunct the ascending node of Neptune, was a dancer. Of course, these placements and exact aspects also manifest in relation to duty to the family.

DEMBOWSKA

The asteroid Dembowska (349) was discovered December 9, 1892, in Nice by A. Charlois. The glyph of Dembowska (?), designed by Batya Stark, is a question mark. The glyph is intended to suggest the fact that there seem to be no clues from the name as to the meaning of this asteroid.

Apparently, Dembowska is a surname. Mark Pottenger gives Ercole Dembowski (1821-1881) on his list of discovery data as the probable person for whom the asteroid was named. Mark writes that Dembowski "established a private observatory at Naples, later transferred to Milan. His careful measures of double stars marked an important stage in this branch of astronomy." My analysis of this asteroid, which was made without knowledge of this prominent namesake, is in keeping with these facts concerning his life.

Dembowska in the chart is an indicator of something unknown. It is interesting that the choice of a question mark for the glyph was made humorously, and yet the choice is very apt. I have seen Dembowska activated and activating when questions were asked and when answers were received. The answers may sometimes be results of tests or applications. The questions might be in the form of an interrogation. Natally the asteroid shows those concerns about which there is a question mark. It can be important in synastry when there is a "question" about the relationship. The "keyword" given for Dembowska in *The Asteroid Ephemeris: Dudu, Dembowska, Pittsburgh, Frigga* is **It Seemed Like a Good Idea at the Time**. Though intended as a jest, this phrase does suggest the "questionable" quality of this asteroid.

There is also a question of power, or a quest for power, associated with Dembowska. Perhaps, that association relates to the fact that within the name is the word "bow," meaning "to bend the knee or body or incline the head, as in submission, salutation, or acknowledgment." With Dembowska, submission, or, at least, acknowledgment, is an issue. As for *question* and *quest*, both are derived from the Latin verb *quaerere*, meaning to ask or to seek, and the Dembowska person is a questioner and a quester.

PITTSBURGHIA

The asteroid Pittsburghia (484) was discovered April 29, 1902, in Heidelberg by Max Wolf. The glyph of Pittsburghia (♄), designed by Batya Stark, is a smokestack. The glyph is intended to represent the industrial pollution which, despite the city's recent urban redevelopment program, is still popularly associated with Pittsburgh.

Pittsburgh is a city in Pennsylvania which is situated where the Allegheny ("stream of the Cave People") and the Monongahela ("high banks falling down") come together to form the Ohio ("white with frothing water") River. "The rivers crown Pittsburgh as the nation's largest inland port."[35] The land where the two rivers join is called the Golden Triangle. Because Pittsburgh has built 500 bridges over these rivers, the city is referred to as "City of Bridges." John Augustus Roebling, the pioneer of suspension bridges and designer of the Brooklyn Bridge, designed the Allegheny Bridge. Pittsburgh is known for industry involved with steel, coal, oil, gas, electrical equipment, glass and railroads, which has earned it the titles of "Steel City" and "Smokey City." More recently, it has been known for the Steelers, its football team which has won four Super Bowls.

Originally founded on the site of Shannopin, an Indian town, Pittsburgh was a fur-trading post. In the French and Indian Wars it was disputed by the French and British, with the British capturing Fort Duquesne, built by the French, and renaming it Fort Pitt after the English statesman William Pitt. November 27, 1758, John Forbes, the British general, announced this new name and the name derived from it, Pittsborough—the settlement around the fort. The spelling of borough with an "h" was from his native Scotland, and the retention of the "h" has been insisted on by Pittsburghers ever since. The first charter is dated April 22, 1794, [36] and in 1816 Pittsburgh became a city. This city has been enhanced by benefactors, such as Andrew Carnegie who donated Carnegie Institute. In the late 1940s ordinances were passed which have transformed Pittsburgh. It is now as exceptionally clean as its natural setting is exceptionally beautiful. A part of Fort Pitt and its site is preserved in Point State Park at the apex of the Golden Triangle, the epitome of that natural setting.

Not only Pittsburgh, but William Pitt, for whom Pittsburgh was named, would be a relevant association of the asteroid Pittsburghia. There are parallels between the two associations. William Pitt, the son of Robert Pitt and Harriet Villiers, was born November 15, 1708, Golden square, Westminster, England. Gold is emphasized in both the Golden square of Pitt's birthplace and the Golden Triangle of Pittsburgh's site. Thomas Pitt, William's grandfather, sold the Pitt diamond to the duke of Orleans, and it now belongs to the French government. George Villiers, 1st duke of Buckingham, immortalized in *The Three Musketeers,* was the receiver of the French queen's diamond necklace. It seems both the Pitt and Villiers family have an association with France, involving diamonds. Diamonds, like coal for which Pittsburgh is known, are made of carbon. Both diamonds and coal are mined, and the **pit** figures in their excavation. Also, in Pitt's family the connection of the British and French parallels their connection in Fort Pitt's construction by the French and naming by the British. Britain was helped in its defeat of France in North America by the policies of William Pitt. He was a member of Parliament under kings George II and III. Shortly after being created 1st earl of Chatham in 1766, he went into seclusion for a couple of years, with a mental affliction, either physical or psychological. Though Pitt did not favor American independence, he admired the independent spirit of the colonies and tried to effect a compromise with them. He was a brilliant orator, who was known for his own honesty and independence. He was the father of William Pitt, who was also a member of Parliament, and became Prime Minister, under King George III.

The definitions of the name of the person for whom Pittsburgh was named should also be considered. *Name Your Baby* lists William as "Old German:

Willihelm. 'Resolute protector,' " and Pitt as "Old English: Pyt. 'From the hollow or pit,' or Old German: Bittan. 'Desire; Longing.' " Will is an English nickname, and William the Conqueror and William Shakespeare are famous namesakes of William.

Pittsburghia in the chart is an indicator of Pittsburgh. For instance, May 24, 1983, the day of my Solar Return, I went to Pittsburgh, never having been to that city before. My husband was there for the opening of the show *Sophisticated Ladies,* which he was contracting, and I joined him to celebrate my birthday. In my Solar Return, Pittsburghia turned out to be at 20° Gemini 57', in the third house (near travel), exactly conjunct my natal Nonie (my name asteroid) at 20° Gemini 45'. Both were in a Finger of God configuration with Solar Return Klotho (Fate and an equivalent name for Nona) at 20° Capricorn 30'℞ and my natal seventh-house cusp at 20° Leo 27' (my husband was the cause of my going to Pittsburgh). An interesting synchronicity, which I realized at the opening of the show that night, was that its title song was published the year of my birth, which is what we were celebrating. A synchronous celebration that night was the 100th birthday of the Brooklyn Bridge in New York designed by Roebling, the designer of the Allegheny Bridge in Pittsburgh. My birthday was my 50th, so the Brooklyn Bridge's birthday was double mine, putting the Brooklyn Bridge and me in a *harmonic* relationship to each other.

Pittsburghia is also an indicator of matters associated with Pittsburgh. In general, those matters would concern power; in particular, they would concern the natural resources, products and history of Pittsburgh. Before putting Pittsburghia into my chart, I thought it should relate to my maternal grandfather because he invented an oil cracking system, and he inherited the proceeds from the Lackawanna Railroad which his mother had owned and run, and Pittsburgh is known for oil and railroads. (Texas is better known for oil, but there is no asteroid named Texas.) My Pittsburghia, at 11° Capricorn 04'℞ in my eleventh house, is in an exact Grand Trine with my Vertex at 12° Virgo 33' and Jupiter at 13° Virgo 34' in my seventh house and my Kronos at 11° Taurus 39' in my second house. I had already chosen my seventh house as the house of my maternal grandfather. Jupiter is expansive, the Vertex adds a fated emphasis, and Kronos is the head of the family. Unfortunately, I was not able to put Pittsburghia into my grandfather's chart, since he was born outside the range of the asteroid's ephemeris. However, when this asteroid was put into the charts of other family members, it appropriately related to this relative, as well as to the concerns of Pittsburgh. As an example of a reflection of the history of Pittsburgh, I think its name asteroid may refer to a combination of France and Britain, i.e., in the news or in one's family background. (Pittsburgh derived its name from the fort built by the French and named by the British.)

Other references of Pittsburghia are to matters associated with William Pitt, for whom the fort was named. There were combinations of France and Britain in his background and life. He was a "resolute protector" of the empire and his family. He used his strong "will" to achieve what he wished—his "desires" and "longings." On the other hand, for a couple of years he went into seclusion. He seems to have had a deeper and darker side, like the **pits** of Pittsburgh. The position (house, sign, numerical) and exact aspects of Pittsburghia indicate where there is great power and will to fulfill longings, only sometimes they are unfulfillable. There may be a deeper, darker side. Of course, delving into the **underworld** can excavate a great wealth of insight and understanding.

The power that is associated with Pittsburghia can be transformative as Pittsburgh was transformed into a city with little pollution from a city where you had to drive with your headlights on at high noon. February 28, 1985, it was announced in the *New York Post* that "Pittsburgh is the best place to live in America... according to new research." Usually I cast a chart of a newspaper article for midnight ST or LMT on the date of the newspaper. Pittsburghia was at 03° Sagittarius, exactly opposite Hades and Chiron at 02° and 03° Gemini, sextile Jupiter at 04° Aquarius, semisextile Neptune at 03° Capricorn and Pluto, Vesta at 04° Scorpio (Pluto ℞) and sesquiquadrate America at 17° Aries and Venus, Mars at 19° Aries. Pittsburgh had been a Hades-town. Now Pittsburghia was also aspected by Jupiter (expansion), Neptune (idealization), Pluto (transformation), Vesta (home), Venus (beauty), Mars (self-assertiveness), America ("best place to live in") and Chiron. Chiron is the educator, and the research and its announcement were educating the newspaper-reading public. (Pittsburghia was exactly aspecting the Sun at 02° Taurus, Neptune and Mars at 02° and 04° Scorpio ℞, Kronos at 04° Aquarius, Jupiter at 03° Capricorn ℞ and Zeus at 19° Aries in the chart of the first charter. Pittsburghia was also exactly aspecting the Sun, Kronos at 04° Sagittarius, Pallas at 04° Taurus ℞, Venus at 18° Libra and Apollon at 18° Aries ℞ in the chart of William Pitt.)

As an example of a literal reference to one of Pittsburgh's nicknames—Steel City—a woman with natal Pittsburghia exactly conjunct her Ascendant and Moon married a man whose middle name was Steelman. (He used that name as his first.) She was a powerful person herself, but a planet or asteroid exactly conjunct the Ascendant is reflected in the partner since the Descendant is exactly opposite. Also, this partner came from Philadelphia, for which there is no asteroid. Perhaps, at this time, the asteroid for Pittsburgh can stand for this other prominent Pennsylvanian city. (The asteroid Philippina is also appropriate for Philadelphia because both begin with the same syllable and have the same derivation.)

Another observation of how astrology works on both a symbolic and literal level simultaneously is that the asteroids can represent objects that look like their glyphs. For instance, based on the exact aspects involving Pittsburghia and on the appearance of its glyph, I correctly anticipated that the instrument to be used in cryosurgery would be cylindrical and that there would be smoke or steam arising from the procedure. This representativeness may be true of the planets, but for the most part their glyphs are more abstract than those for the asteroids.

FRIGGA

The asteroid Frigga (77) was discovered November 12, 1862, in Clinton, New York by C.H.F. Peters. The glyph of Frigga (🖕), designed by Batya Stark, is a hand with the middle finger raised. The glyph is intended to represent the hand gesture whose meaning sounds very much like Frigga.

Frigga was the Norse mother goddess of the sky and conjugal love. She was the wife of Odin, the principal god who ruled by magic and was the lord of the runes. He was also the god of song, poetry and intelligence, who had given up one eye for knowledge, and the god of war, who at Valhalla entertained the heroes who had fallen in battle. Frigga, the principal goddess, was pictured as wise, like Odin. They were the parents of Balder, a god of the light, who was killed despite Frigga's efforts first to protect him and then to have him brought back from the dead. They were also considered to be the parents of "seven sons who founded the seven Saxon kingdoms in England."[37] As to the marriage of Frigga and Odin, it was not one of fidelity for either of them. In Roman mythology Frigga was identified with Venus, and Odin, with Mercury. In German mythology Frigga and Odin were known as Frija and Woden, and Frija's day became Friday, while Woden's day became Wednesday. The meaning of Frija is "well-beloved" or "spouse."

There are other asteroids that are named for gods and goddesses of Teutonic (Norse or Germanic) mythology. They are Wodan (2155), another spelling for Woden; Thora (299), a feminine name for the Norse god Thor who was identified with Jupiter; Donar (2176), the Germanic equivalent of Thor; Ulla (909), a feminine name for the Norse god Ull who was the stepson of Thor; Nerthus (601), the Germanic personification of the maternal earth; Iduna (176), the Norse goddess of youth-sustaining apples; Hel (949), the Norse goddess of the underworld; Freia (76), the Norse goddess of love, marriage and fertility, often confused with Frigga; Walküre (877), the Germanic spelling for Valkyries, the Norse warrior maidens; and Brunhild (123) and Waltraut (890), Germanic Valkyries.

Regarding Walküre, Brunhild and Waltraut, I've found that they represent "warrior maidens" who serve both as messengers and nurturers. They have the electrical (Uranus) quality of the Aurora Borealis which, according to legend, is the light from the maidens' armor. (Differences are that with Walküre the emphasis is on a group working together, while with Brunhild and Waltraut the emphasis is on individuals working in a group. Brunhild has the added connotations of her passionate relationship with the hero Siegfried.)

A distinction has been made between Greek and Roman mythology, and a distinction between them and Teutonic mythology should be made. Some of the Teutonic myths are similar to the Greek and Roman, but with a quality of their own. That quality is for the most part warlike. The Valkyries, who chose which warriors would die, engaged in the fighting. Valhalla was the place, fashioned of spears and shields, where they brought the dead heros not only to feast, but to indulge in war games. The wives of the gods, except for Frigga, are hardly mentioned. Those goddesses who were revered are depicted as militaristic themselves. Even Frigga bested Odin at times. Also, in Teutonic mythology the gods were not immortal; they were rather just supermen who were destroyed at the "Twilight of the Gods," only to be replaced by new supermen. The harshness of the Teutonic mythology may reflect the harshness of the Northern climate.

Within the Teutonic, there is a difference between the Norse and the Germanic mythologies. In Germany there was an acceptance of the priest king, reflected in the greater aggrandizement of the intellectually powerful Woden (Odin). The Angles and the Saxons believed that their kings were descended from Woden. In Scandinavia there was an acceptance of many independent chieftains, reflected in the greater aggrandizement of the physically powerful Thor (Donar). It was in Scandinavia that the legends were recorded, chiefly in the *Eddas*.[38]

Frigga is described as majestic. She wears long white robes that can become dark like the sky. A batch of keys hangs from her waist.

Frigga in the chart is an indicator of marriage or the married woman. Hera and Juno are also, and, as explained, one marriage or married woman might be a Hera-type, and another, a Juno-type. Another might be a Frigga-type, reflecting the mythology of that goddess. (One area of a marriage might be indicated by one of the asteroids, and another area, by a different one.) Frigga is depicted as wiser and more independent than Hera and Juno. In regard to her independence, the Norse goddess sometimes chose to protect different warriors than Odin did, and, unlike the classical goddesses, she was not a model of faithfulness. The myth of Frigga's loss of her son, which is similar to Demeter's or Ceres' loss of her daughter, does not have an equivalent in the myths of Hera or Juno. Also, Frigga would have the martial connotations of Teutonic mythology. Freia (Freya) for which I designed the glyph, ᛩᛃ, to show the connection to Frigga, is an indicator of marriage or the married woman, but a more peaceable indicator than Frigga. Freia was the wife of Odur, the sunshine, and she as one of the benefic Vanir is associated with sunshine too. (Frigga belonged to the Aesir, the first race of gods, who fought against the second race, the Vanir.)

Another expression of a Frigga-type marriage that I have observed is marriage to a person who is German or of German extraction. Possibly, this reference would apply to people of other Teutonic backgrounds, such as Scandinavian or Anglo-Saxon. However, it may not because the people of those backgrounds seem less affected in the present day by the militarism which is the salient characteristic of Teutonic mythology.

As with the other asteroids named for married couples in the various mythologies, the relationship (including angular separations and midpoints) between Frigga and Wodan in the chart is revealing. Frigga and Wodan would have the militancy of Teutonic mythology; Hera and Zeus, the poetic quality of Greek mythology; Juno and Jupiter, the practicality of Roman mythology; and Isis and Osiris, the formal quality of Egyptian mythology. (Unlike the other couples, Isis and Osiris are associated with the lights—the female and male principles.) The midpoint of each pair is a point of integration of their individual principles. (Isis and Osiris are always close together, at least in this century, so there is a greater chance of their being conjunct or, at any rate, in the same house or sign.)

Finally, the asteroid Frigga is an indicator of the slang expression which sounds like its name. The asteroid can refer to the act which this expression represents or to the conquest which some people consider this act to be.

Dynamics

The dynamics of the meanings and of the different mythologies observed in this study of forty-seven asteroids should be of assistance in the study of the others.

LITERAL AND METAPHORICAL

And the study of the meanings and of the different mythologies helps us to understand how our lives are lived simultaneously on literal and metaphorical levels. The following conversation, with a woman whose chart and life situation were familiar to me, illustrates that simultaneity.

When I spoke to her of the significance of purchases, she challenged me to explain the meaning of the purchase of her *boots*. I asked her their name and when she had bought them. She said they were Peter Kaiser boots, bought the previous afternoon. My response was, "Peter means stone—foundation, which your home is for you. You moved back to your apartment less than two days, in other words one day, before your purchase. One day relates to the self. Natally, you have Peter exactly conjunct Diana, the goddess of the moon, emphasizing the home again. As for Kaiser, it is the German emperor or king, and you would feel very regal and important in the boots." She affirmed that those were her exact feelings, even before knowing the boots were Peter Kaiser. Discovering the boots were black, I told her, "They would have a Saturnine or Plutonian quality." I then inquired as to where she'd bought them, and she said Footworks. My reaction was, "That name has a Pisces and Virgo quality. The Lunar Eclipse coming February 20 (in fourteen days) is exactly conjunct your Pluto in Virgo in the tenth house. The Sun would be opposite in your fourth house, with both the Sun and Moon exactly square your East Point. You are going through disruption (eclipse), in relation to the hidden (Pisces) and to service (Virgo) in your home (fourth house), career (tenth house) and self (East Point). Pluto rules your Ascendant and is about to make a retrograde station, exactly conjunct your Ascendant. There is transformation (Pluto), in relation to your persona (Ascendant)."

A chart of the purchase time, compared to the chart of this woman, would reveal even more detail, but even without the event chart, much was revealed. This analysis of the woman's purchase, in relation to her chart, helped her to understand the psychological implications of her moving back to her apartment. Buying these boots in this store was the literal expression of a metaphorical meaning.

MYTHIC ROLE PLAYING

And the study of the myths, and the factors which symbolize them, helps us to understand how our lives parallel the myths. At an NCGR Conference at the end of May 1987, astrologer-author Rob Hand said that astrology "describes mythic energy patterns"; that people are playing roles in the myths, but you can't tell which roles they are playing. What I have found is that you usually can tell, if you have the asteroids with the names of the characters in the myths and the names of the people playing out those myths.

For instance, regarding the Demeter (Ceres) - Persephone (Proserpina) myth, my asteroid program gives me the four asteroids with those names. It also gives me the asteroids with the names of my daughter, myself, my mother and my maternal grandmother. They are Guinevere, Nonie, Jeanne and Margarita, respectively. (My glyph for Persephone is ♇; for Proserpina, ♇; and for Margarita, ♏. The other glyphs have already been given.)

My daughter's Ceres is at 16° Scorpio 48', exactly conjunct her Ascendant at 16° Scorpio 12' and opposite her Moon at 17° Taurus 42'. Exactly conjunct her Moon is my Proserpina at 16° Taurus 34'. Exactly square this opposition, forming a Cosmic Square, is her Uranus-Mercury at 15° Leo 56'-17° Leo 56'℞ and my Saturn at 16° Aquarius 22'. (The square is the maternal aspect.) Obviously, the myth of the loss of the daughter is very important in our relationship. Our synastry indicates that she is playing the role of Ceres and that I am playing the role of Proserpina. In our relationship chart, the exact conjunction of Proserpina at 29° Taurus 50' and Nonie (my name asteroid) at 29° Taurus 58' reaffirms this indication. These asteroids are exactly conjunct my natal Chiron-Moon at 28° Taurus 59'-00° Gemini 21'.

Conversely, my Ceres is 05° Aries 35', exactly conjunct my mother's Ascendant at 05° Aries 17' and Moon at 05° Aries 33'. In this case, I seem to be playing the Ceres-role, particularly since that asteroid is in my first house, in Aries, exactly semisquare (obsession aspect) my Ascendant and semisextile (self-sacrifice aspect) my East Point. My mother seems to be playing the Proserpina role from my perspective, with my Proserpina at 16° Taurus 34' exactly sextile (service aspect) my Jeanne (my mother's name asteroid) at 15° Pisces 08'. (Note the Roman mythological emphasis—Ceres and Prosperpina.) Again, this myth is shown to be very important. At a very young age I did become the mother to my mother. She, along with her four sisters and brothers, had been taken from her Cancerian mother. This "abduction" was the end result of my grandmother's separation from her husband, my mother's stepfather, who was an attorney. In my relationship chart with my mother, Margarita (my grandmother's name asteroid) is 21° Scorpio 22', exactly conjunct my mother's natal Nonie at 22° Scorpio 29' and my natal Guinevere (my daughter's name asteroid) at 20° Scorpio 01'℞. My mother is bringing her asteroid with her daughter's name and I am bringing my asteroid with my daughter's name, to our relationship asteroid with her mother's/my grandmother's name. Perhaps, the grandchild and the great-grandchild are a gift to the progenitor who lost her children. (My grandmother's Ceres is 20° Scorpio 22'℞.)

The fulfillment of the myths takes place over many generations. Of course, there are other parts in this myth—Pluto played his part in the abduction of the daughter. And, naturally, at different times and in different places we play different roles. Nevertheless, the benefit of understanding the playing out is incalculable.

ASTEROID LISTINGS

The asteroid listings, both zodiacal and categorical, have been very helpful in my study of asteroids. The listings in my computer program now include ten planets, the Nodes (the Mean South Node), Antivertex, East Point, Ascendant, Midheaven, eight Uranian planets and Transpluto. I add the true South Node, Vertex, Part of Fortune, intermediate cusps, Dark Moon Lilith and Halley's Comet to my zodiacal listings. The result is a linear chart that can be compared to other linear charts—

natal, progressed, harmonic charts and Solar, Lunar, planet and asteroid return charts. The asteroids may also be added to circular charts. The twenty-three categorical listings can be used to explore a particular question. Whatever the question, all or some of the asteroids under the relevant category, such as relations, first names, business, or fates, can be considered.

Categories you've formed yourself might be studied. For instance, a French category I've formed includes Paris (3317), named for the Trojan warrior, but representing the capital of France as well; Lutetia (21), Lutetia Parisiorum was the ancient name of Paris; Riviera (1426), named for the southeast Mediterranean coast of France; Gallia (148), an ancient region including France; Martina (981), Saint Martin is a patron saint of France; Carol (2214), feminine of Charles, the name of many rulers of France, i.e., Charlemagne and Charles de Gaulle; Lois (2210), feminine of Louis, the name of many kings of France; Lilith (1181), with a sound like lily (fleur-de-lis), the monarchal emblem of France; and Iris (7), one of the definitions of fleur-de-lis.

A COMPUTER-LIKE LANGUAGE

The linear chart, I've realized, can be read as sentences in a computer-like language. Those sentences would include exact conjunctions and their combination in major configurations with other exact conjunctions. Intuition helps in the reading of that language because it is a mixture of literal and abstract symbols. The words in the sentences may literally represent the meanings of the factors, or the words may be abstracted from those meanings. There may be past-life references.

With my natal chart as an illustration, there are the following exact conjunctions to my Ascendant. My Ascendant (20° Aquarius 27') is conjunct Margarita (20° Aquarius 28'), McAuliffe (20° Aquarius 49'), Edwin (21° Aquarius 00'), Gagarin (21° Aquarius 41'), Martina (21° Aquarius 49') and Asia (21° Aquarius 57'). Margaret, of which Margarita is an English and Spanish variation, means "a pearl," and a pearl is formed around an irritating foreign object. My maternal grandmother was named Margaret. McAuliffe and Gagarin were both astronauts—McAuliffe, the teacher-astronaut who was killed when the Challenger exploded January 28, 1986, and Gagarin, the first human orbital space traveler. Edwin means "prosperous friend" and is like my first husband's and son's name. Martina means Mars-like in a feminine way, and Mars is known as the red planet. Asia is the continent which includes China and Japan, whose people have black hair and slanting eyes. The Ascendant can refer to the appearance, as well as the persona, and not only do I have slanting eyes, but my natural hair color is *black* with *red* highlights.

These conjunctions are in an exact Grand Trine with Penelope (19° Gemini 26'), Sapientia (20° Gemini 20'), Iris (20° Gemini 22'), Nonie (20° Gemini 45'), Circe (20° Gemini 49') and Alice (19° Libra 29'ʀ), Nemo (20° Libra 33'ʀ), Juno (21° Libra 12'ʀ), Transylvania (21° Libra 47'ʀ). At the Gemini point of the Grand Trine, Penelope means weaver, and she was the faithful wife of Odysseus. Sapient means wise or sage. Iris was the messenger, and goddess of the rainbow. Nonie is a nickname for my name and for the Roman Fate who spins and weaves the thread of life. Circe was the enchantress with whom Odysseus had three sons. At the Libra point of the Grand Trine, Alice means "truthful one" and is associated with Wonderland. Nemo is named for the Jules Verne character who was a "builder of advanced technology."[39] Juno was the Roman goddess of marriage, and Transylvania is a region in *Central* Romania but has the name Sy in the *middle* of it. Romania is spelled like Romany which means Gypsy, and the derivation of "Gypsy" is "Egyptian." A psychic said that my husband Sy and I shared a past life in Egypt, so there would be a reference to Sy in the asteroid's association, as well as in its name. (Another association of the asteroid is the Transylvanian *vampire* Count Dracula, also evoking an *other life*!)

The exact conjunctions in the Grand Trine could be read as "The persona and appearance (Ascendant) are like that of 'a pearl' (Margarita), a prospective space traveler-teacher (McAuliffe), a 'prosperous friend' (Edwin), a first venturer in space (Gagarin), and a peacefully assertive person (Martina), having slanting eyes and black hair with red highlights (Asia and Martina). That persona/appearance is connected communicatively (trine) to the faithful wife (Penelope) and the 'wise' (Sapientia) messenger (Iris), which is my identity and fate (Nonie) and the kind of 'enchantress' (Circe) I am. Both that persona/appearance and identity are connected communicatively (trine) to the truthful (Alice), advanced (Nemo) marriage partner (Juno), Sy, from a past life in Egypt (Transylvania)."

As more factors are added to the linear chart, the sentences become more explicit. As these factors are combined in different configurations, the meanings of the particular configurations encompass the meanings of the factors.

SIMILARITIES BETWEEN ASTEROIDS
Though in my synopses I have focused on the differences between the asteroids, it is also important to notice when there is an emphasis on asteroids which are similar in meaning, sound or mythology. Like other factors in astrology, the asteroids establish themes by repetition.

For instance, appropriately, my first name asteroid Nonie (20° Gemini 45') and my middle name asteroid Guinevere (20° Scorpio 01') exactly aspect my Ascendant at 20° Aquarius 27'. (My middle name asteroid is my daughter's first name asteroid.) However, not only is Nonie exactly trine and Guinevere exactly square my Ascendant, but there are other asteroids, with similar meanings, sounds or mythologies, showing connections to my persona (exactly aspecting my Ascendant or posited in my first house). By scanning my natal asteroid zodiacal listing it can be seen that my Adeona (20° Pisces 47'), which is similar in sound to Nona, is in my first house, semisextile my Ascendant; my Moira (19° Cancer 58'), which is similar in mythological meaning to Nona, is quincunx my Ascendant. Moira is the singular of Moirai, the Greek Fates, and Nona is one of the Roman Fates. Moira is also an Irish form of Mary, Martha and Agnes. I don't have the position of my Agnes, but my Martha (21° Scorpio 19'ℝ) is square my Ascendant, and my Mary (00° Aries 18') is in my first house. (The Aries sign reinforces this natural Aries house.) My Maria (19° Taurus 40'), which is a variation of Mary, is square my Ascendant. My Margarita (20° Aquarius 28'), which shares with Mary the variation Miriam, is in my first house, conjunct my Ascendant within a minute. My Martina (21° Aquarius

49'), which shares several nicknames with Martha, is in my first house, conjunct my Ascendant. An exact T-Square is formed by my Martha, Maria, Ascendant, Margarita and Martina. My Rita (06° Pisces 45'), which is a nickname for Margarita, is in my first house, incidentally, square my Midheaven at 07° Sagittarius 41'.

In analyzing a general emphasis, the individual meanings of those factors contributing to that emphasis still have to be considered. As mentioned, Margaret, of which Margarita is a variation, means a pearl and my grandmother's name was Margaret. Also, Margaret is the patron saint of Scotland.

My grandmother was of Scottish descent, and the definition of pearl fits her. Considering all my relatives, the persona of my grandmother was the most like mine. Margarita (there is no asteroid Margaret) shows my identification with my grandmother Margaret most specifically. On the other hand, the other asteroids whose names begin with Mar reiterate this identification, though not so specifically. All the asteroids cited are related to my name asteroid Nonie, emphasizing the identification even more.

The asteroids whose names begin with Mar may also be reinforcing the meaning of the asteroid Martina, which is exactly conjunct my Ascendant. Only Martina has a name derived from the planet Mars, but it seems the relationship in my chart between Martina and these other asteroids is emphasizing the fact that my persona is Mars-like in a feminine way. (Martina and the other names are all feminine.) My grandmother Margaret's persona had a feminine Mars-like quality too. (The asteroids in the first house and in Aries are associated with Mars also.)

This brief analysis has not fully dealt with the significance of these asteroidal connections. In the search for that significance, the meanings, derivations and connections of the other mentioned asteroids would have to be considered as well. The gist, however, is that similarities, as well as differences, must be observed as we learn to use the many new symbols that have come into our ken.

Genetic Equation

Thus far, over 3000 asteroids have been discovered, named, and are available to us for study. Though there are astrologers who object that we can never study all the asteroids, now that we know the asteroids give significant information, our voyage of discovery, like that of the astronomers, must proceed.

According to some Russian astronomers there are an estimated 100,000 asteroids in all.[40] Why should the heavens provide us with such a multitude of astrological factors? According to the cover story (November 6, 1983) of the *New York Times Magazine,* "Keeping Up with the Genetic Revolution," there are an estimated 100,000 genes. While reading that article, I thought of the analogy between genes and asteroids. Both give very specific information, and there are many of them—even to the extent of the same estimation. With the multitudes that we contain, the planets alone are unable to describe the individuality of ourselves and of our lives. Perhaps, we can never know it all, but, perhaps, that many genes and that many asteroids are needed to tell the entire story.

CHAPTER FOUR

Lunations

Asteroids may be needed to tell the entire story, but lunations shed light on that story. And, of course, lunations had to be the subject of Chapter 4 (4th house, Cancer, Moon, square), since a lunation is a New Moon. Also, the cycle of the Moon is divided into *four* quarters—the New Moon, the First Quarter, the Full and the Last Quarter Moon.

Emphasis of the Lunation

In March 1976, I first learned about lunations while attending a lecture given by Sophia Mason. Sophia had rediscovered the significance of lunations, which at one time had been used by astrologers for predictive purposes. She had found that the lunation, the monthly conjunction of the Sun and Moon, explains why some transits have an impact and others do not. She said that the Sun and Moon conjunction activates the concerns of the natal house in which it falls. Also, the aspects of the lunation to the natal chart will show what is emphasized that month.

Her procedure was to draw each month's lunation around the natal chart and to copy the degree and sign of the New Moon and planets from the ephemeris. She suggested using acetate and a felt pen for the lunation positions, so that each month's lunation could subsequently be erased, and the new one substituted. The orb she allowed was 05° from the Sun and Moon of the lunation to the natal positions; 10° from the Sun and Moon of the lunation to the other lunation positions; and 01° from the other lunation positions to the natal positions. Then the events that were promised by the New Moon she timed by the transits of the Sun and Moon to the natal chart during that month. The transits of those natal and lunation planets that had been aspected by the Sun and Moon conjunction were also used by her as a timer. Change of house or sign was important. (In her book *Lunations and*

Predictions, which I later read, she writes of putting the lunation around the progressed chart and following the same procedure.)

The Full Moon, the monthly opposition of the Sun and Moon, she considered to either trigger or reinforce or contravene the promise of the New Moon. The Full Moon might have a promise of its own.

The Solar and Lunar Eclipses, being specialized instances of the New and Full Moons, were treated like them, only considered to have more impact. (The Solar Eclipse occurs when the New Moon is near the Node of the Moon, and the Lunar Eclipse occurs when the Full Moon is near the Node of the Moon.)

Lunation Project

What appealed to me most in Sophia's presentation was her statement that you should write down what you think is going to happen and then write what did happen. I took her at her word, and thus began a project which lasted from March 1976 to January 1984—almost eight years. My study of lunations continued after that time, but my predictions were no longer formally recorded.

When beginning the project, I first drew up the previous lunation of February 29, 1976, writing what had happened and under what transits those events had occurred. Subsequently, my predictions were written before the lunation. Usually listed was the date on which the prediction had been made. If, as occurred a few times during the almost eight years, I was unable to make my prediction until after the lunation, the date of that "prediction" was always chronicled. In my predictions I noted the transits under which, rather than the dates on which, events would occur. As a rule, ephemerides were not consulted to see when those aspects were due because I wanted to avoid self-fulfilling prophecies. The predictions were written in ink. On an average, my prediction is one-half to three-quarters of a page, while my account of what happened is four and a half pages. The last year of the project I wrote about what happened every day, rather than just about what happened on the days when there were references to the lunation. In this way I had a control. The days when there weren't references were controls for the days when there were. In other words, in regard to their relevance to the lunation, events on non-referential days could be compared to events on referential days.

MY PROCEDURE

My procedure was to draw each month's lunation around my natal chart. Sometimes the lunation was drawn around the natal charts of other people as well. Acetate was not used because the biggest advantage of this experiment was that it provided a permanent record of the lunation charts, of the predictions regarding them, and of the accuracy of those predictions, for future reference. At first, per Sophia's instructions, just the degree and sign of the New Moon and planets were listed, but before too long for more precision the minutes were included. After experimenting with various orbs, the orb allowed was from one degree to the next, whether to the natal or to the lunation positions and whether from the lunation Sun and Moon or from the other lunation positions. Planetary pictures were noted. Besides the planets, there were the first four asteroids, Ceres, Pallas, Juno and Vesta. In a year the Uranian planets were added. Shortly thereafter, though Sophia did not include them, the angles of the lunation chart were inserted in the ring with the lunation positions. The angles would be of a person's place of residence. (In my case the place of both my residence and my birth is New York City.) If the person were to be in another place at the time of the lunation, or if I wanted to see the person in relation to another place at the time of the lunation, the angles of that place were inserted also. Then, the Full Moon chart with its angles began to be drawn around this New Moon chart, which was around the natal chart. Subsequently, as additional asteroids were put in personal charts they were added to future New and Full Moon charts. Dark Moon Lilith, Halley's Comet and, finally, Transpluto were inserted too.

If the New or Full Moon were a Solar or Lunar Eclipse, the same procedure was followed, only the effect was considered to last longer. The effect lasts at least until the next eclipse period, which is approximately six months later. As Sophia said, an eclipse has more impact.

The positions of the planets for the New and Full Moons and the Solar and Lunar Eclipses were taken from *Mundane Data,* published by the American Federation of Astrologers. The charts in these booklets are set up for Washington, DC, but the angles were easily changed to those of another place by taking the difference between the sidereal time of Washington, DC, and the sidereal time of the other place; adding it to, or subtracting it from, the sidereal time of the chart; and looking in the Table of Houses at the latitude of the new locality. Beginning in 1983, both a Solar Eclipse chart and a New Moon chart, or a Lunar Eclipse chart and a Full Moon chart, were given for an eclipse. The eclipse chart is for the time of the peak of the eclipse, while the New or Full Moon chart is for the time of the exact conjunction or opposition of the Sun and Moon. From 1983-1985, the difference between the times of the eclipse charts and the times of the New or Full Moon charts is as little as three minutes and as much as fifteen minutes. (In *1986 Mundane Data,* there is obviously an error because the difference between the times is an average of ten hours, longer than the length of any of the eclipses.)

MY CONCLUSIONS

After following the procedure outlined above for nearly eight years, I believe that the lunations are significant and do elucidate why some transits have more of an impact than others. The lunation gives you a "fix" for the month, according to the natal house in which the Sun-Moon conjunction falls and the exact aspects it and the other lunation bodies and points make to the natal chart. Then, as I see it, the transiting bodies (especially the fast-moving ones) and points "carry the message" of the New Moon to the lunation, natal, and transiting bodies and points. Conjunctions particularly are to be noted, and change of house or sign is important. The Full Moon shows the outcome of the New Moon. The transiting entities that act as timers were not found to be limited to the Sun, Moon and those natal and lunation planets that had been aspected by the Sun and Moon conjunction.

Princess Grace

As an example of my conclusions, see Figure XXII. This figure represents the natal chart of Grace Kelly, with the lunation (New Moon) of August 19, 1982 and the Full Moon of September 3, 1982 set for Monaco, Monaco, around the natal chart. The natal chart is from Lois Rodden's *Profiles of Women*. The time of the New Moon in Monaco was 04:45:27 AM – 1D; the time of the Full Moon, 02:28:53 PM – 1D. These times are of the geometric conjunction and opposition of the Sun and Moon (see pages 19-20).

Movie star Grace Patricia Kelly became Princess Grace of Monaco when she married Prince Rainier III on April 18, 1956. September 13, 1982 at 10:30 AM – 1D, near La Turbie, France, as Grace was returning to Monaco, her car went out of control on a mountain road at a bend called Devil's Curve. She suffered head injuries when her car plunged 75 feet. September 14, 1982 at 10:30 PM – 1D, fifteen minutes after being removed from her life-support system, she died.

Though after the fact, rather than before, my reading follows the format employed each month for my predictions. Mentioned first are the concerns of the natal house activated by the Sun-Moon conjunction, and that conjunction's exact aspects to the natal and lunation chart. (The 30° aspects and the semisquares and sesquiquadrates were always mentioned.) The asteroids include the ones I was using in my lunation study, as well as some others from my 392-asteroid program. The glyphs of the asteroids, Uranian planets, Transpluto, Dark Moon Lilith and Halley's Comet are given so that their placement on Figure XXII can be seen. In addition, there is a listing of asteroids with glyphs in the Appendices. When no glyph has been designed for an asteroid, its name has been written.

THE LUNATION AND ITS ASPECTS

The lunation, at 25° Leo 48'41.04" in Grace's tenth house of restriction and status, was exactly conjunct Julia—♃ (24° Leo 56'), King (26° Leo 33') and her Rhea (24° Leo 52'). The lunation was also semisextile Selene (26° Virgo 51') and her Julia (25° Virgo 11'); sextile Pluto (24° Libra 41') and the Uranian planet Poseidon—♆ (24° Libra 56'); square her Mars (25° Scorpio 38'); trine Juno—⚵ (24° Sagittarius 16'), Isis (24° Sagittarius 18'), Neptune (24° Sagittarius 21'ʀ), Guinevere—♈ (24° Sagittarius 33'ʀ), and Fortuna (25° Aries 15'); quincunx Crescentia—☾ (24° Capricorn 31'ʀ), Martina—♈ (25° Capricorn 49'ʀ), her Lilith—⚸ (26° Capricorn 50'), and her Pallas—⚴ (24° Pisces 03'ʀ); sesquiquadrate Michel—♍ (11° Aries 07'ʀ), Skuld (09° Capricorn 11') and her Icarus—▽ (09° Capricorn 19'); and semisquare the Uranian planet Apollon—♈ (09° Libra 06'), Hebe—♀ (09° Libra 38'), Lachesis—φ (11° Libra 30'), Europa (11° Cancer 06') and the Uranian planet Vulcanus—⚴ (11° Cancer 22').

The placement of the lunation in Grace's tenth house is consistent with the emphasis on her restriction and on her status that occurred this month of her accident and death. Also, Saturn, and so the tenth house, is associated with Father Time, who is sometimes called the Grim Reaper. The conjunction of the lunation to Julia, which means "Youthful one," relates to the fact that Grace was only 52 years old when she

Figure XXIIa – Lunation around Natal Chart of Princess Grace

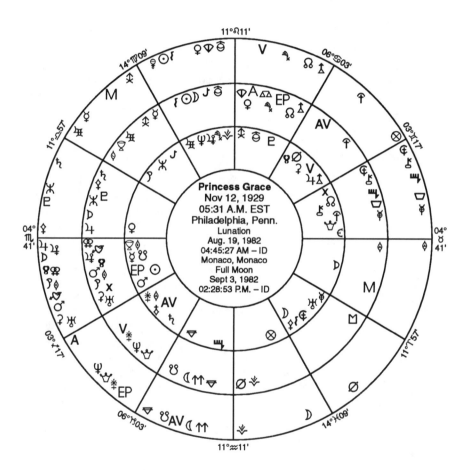

Figure XXIIb – Lunation around Natal Chart of Princess Grace

Inner Ring

⚶ 05♏54
⚴ 06♏42
☿ 10♏42
☋ 12♏10
Nemesis 15♏41
EP 16♏07
☉ 19♏34
♂ 25♏38
Gaea 02♐05
⚵ 10♐29
⚴ 11♐15
⚳ 11♐28
AV 14♐42
♄ 28♐06
▽ 09♑19
ɰ 26♑50
Lucifer 03♓40
⊗ 06♓58
☽ 21♓50
⚸ 24♓03℞
Isis 01♈24
{ 03♈02℞
⚳ 06♈51℞
♅ 07♈56℞
♆ 08♈15℞
☽ 21♈18℞
€ 04♉49℞
♆ 06♉18℞
♇ 08♉41℞
⚷ 11♉37℞
☊ 12♉10
X 02♊37℞
♆ 12♊25℞
♃ 14♊05℞
V 14♊42
? 16♊41℞
∅ 17♊09
☋ 00♋21℞
Fortuna 17♋48
♇ 19♋31℞
⊖ 27♋21℞
⚵ 09♌05℞
⚶ 13♌03
⚴ 13♌31℞
Rhea 24♌52
♃ 27♌31
♆ 03♍25
♄ 07♍28
♪ 25♍11
♅ 00♎29
♄ 01♎21
Carolina 17♎21
♀ 28♎51

Middle Ring

♀ 04♏54
♂ 05♏38
♃ 07♏36
☋ 08♏03
♂ 09♏15
⚴ 09♏30
♄ 11♏17
Siva 15♏18
Thule 15♏20
X 16♏18
? 19♏56
♅ 00♐37
V 20♐14
⚵ 24♐16
Isis 24♐18
♆ 24♐21℞
♆ 24♐33℞
Gaea 01♑27
Skuld 09♑11
☋ 12♑40
☾ 24♑31℞
♈ 25♑49℞
▽ 27♑14℞
∅ 11♒59
⚶ 15♒24℞
M 11♈07℞
M 17♈13
Fortuna 25♈15
⚴ 01♉34
♆ 10♉19℞
▽ 11♉24
ɰ 11♉29
⚷ 27♉37
⚳ 02♊11
♇ 16♊38℞
AV 20♊14
Europa 11♋06
♆ 11♋22
☊ 12♋40
EP 14♋37
⚴ 16♋54
♎ 18♋40
Lutetia 19♋44
A 03♌16
♀ 05♌41
♆ 10♌05
⊖ 18♌57
♪ 24♌56
☉☽ 25♌48
King 26♌33
{ 04♍46
Anubis 11♍21
☿ 17♍21
⚵ 20♍05
Selene 26♍51
♄ 09♎06
⚶ 09♎38
⚴ 11♎30
♄ 18♎27
Lucifer 21♎31
⚸ 22♎31
♇ 24♎41
♅ 24♎56
☽ 04♏07
♃ 04♏14

Outer Ring

♃ 06♏33
♃ 07♏49
☽ 09♏25
♀ 10♏17
☋ 12♏40
⚴ 13♏08
♄ 15♏06
♂ 15♏07
Thule 17♏56
♂ 18♏59
Siva 19♏01
? 24♏07
♅ 00♐50
A 06♐43
♆ 24♐16℞
♆ 24♐38
⚵ 24♐57
EP 27♐10
Isis 27♐37
Gaea 02♑42
▽ 08♑27℞
Skuld 10♑57
☋ 11♑43
A 20♑10
☾ 23♑25℞
♈ 24♑36℞
⚶ 12♒23℞
☽ 10♓40
∅ 29♓25
Rhea 12♈16℞
Fortuna 26♈18
⚴ 01♉48℞
♆ 10♉16℞
▽ 13♉40
ɰ 14♉30
⚷ 27♉43℞
⚳ 02♊13℞
⊗ 06♊43
♇ 16♊42
♆ 11♋31
☊ 11♋43
Europa 16♋47
⚴ 17♋41
V 20♋10
⊖ 19♌07
♆ 22♌24
♀ 24♌36
{ 10♍38
☉ 10♍40
♀ 11♍39
⚵ 20♍21
M 26♍38
☿ 07♎31
♄ 09♎18
♄ 19♎56
♅ 25♎04
♇ 25♎07
Lucifer 27♎13
⚸ 28♎21

died. The conjunction to King relates to the fact that she was royalty. (It also relates to Martin Luther King, Jr. The asteroid was named for him, and he also met a violent death.) The lunation and both asteroids were conjunct her Rhea, the great mother goddess, which Grace represented.

This multiple conjunction was in a Finger of God configuration with Pluto, Poseidon, in Grace's twelfth house and her Pallas in her fifth house. Grace's perception (Pallas) was affected when she had a cerebral hemorrhage, either while driving her car, causing the accident, or as a result of the accident. Pluto refers to death, and Poseidon, which is a Super-Neptune, to the mysteriousness and oddness (Poseidon is a Uranian planet) of the accident. Julia, the lunation, King, and her Rhea were square Grace's Mars at 25° Scorpio 38' in her first house, fitting the diagnosis of a cerebral hemorrhage. Also, Mars is ruler of her sixth house, relating that planet to her health.

Another Finger of God configuration, connected to the first one, was Julia, the lunation, King, and Grace's Rhea quincunx Crescentia, Martina, and her Lilith in her third house, and her Pallas in her fifth house. The Finger of God, or Yod, being a combination of a sextile and two quincunxes, is a combination of work or physical health with nebulousness or mental health. Martina is like a feminine Mars, emphasizing the head again. Crescentia, though a German legendary heroine, sounds like Crescent and so has an association to the Crescent Moon. Grace was a Lunar figure—mother of her country, as well as of her three children. The Crescent Moon is either the first or the last quarter. In this case the symbolism of the last quarter seems more fitting. Lilith is related to "reaching closure." There is also an association with France—the fleur-de-lys (lily) is the monarchal symbol of France. (Martina also refers to France since Saint Martin is a patron saint of France.) Grace's accident occurred in France, and she died in Monaco, which has French connotations. Monaco, an independent principality, would be ceded to France if Prince Rainier did not have an heir; and Rainier is a descendant of the French Goyon-Matignon family which took the name Grimaldi when the Grimaldi male line died out.

The semisextile of Julia, the lunation, King, and Grace's Rhea to Selene, and her Julia in her eleventh house, repeats the Lunar symbolism, since Selene was the ancient Greek goddess of the moon, worshiped at the New and Full Moon. The involvement of Grace's Julia reiterates the symbolism of "Youthful one," already evoked by the lunation Julia.

The Grand Trine of Julia, the lunation, King, and Grace's Rhea to Juno, Isis, Neptune and Guinevere in her second house, and Fortuna in her sixth house, relates to the short journey (Geminian major configuration) that resulted in Grace's accident and to the mass media communication (Geminian major configuration) that resulted from that accident and Grace's subsequent death. Grace was a famous wife (Juno), Lunar figure (Isis), who was an actress and whose Moon was in Pisces (Neptune). She was also a Guinevere figure, being a princess and being married to a prince. Fortuna was the Roman goddess of Fortune, one of whose attributes is the wheel. Interestingly, had Grace or her daughter Stephanie been able to turn the wheel of the car away from the cliff, the accident would have been avoided. Though

Fortuna is usually associated with good fortune, we do not always know what is good fortune and what is not. What seems unfortunate for Grace may be fortunate. Through this fateful turn of events, her family gained greater responsibility and understanding which, for a devoted mother and wife, is most fortuitous.

Another major configuration was a Fist of God (like a Finger of God but with more punch). Julia, the lunation, King, and Grace's Rhea were sesquiquadrate Michel, Skuld, and Grace's Icarus. The Fist of God, being a combination of a square and two sesquiquadrates, is a combination of the foundation or the ending with transformation or death. Michel was in Grace's fifth house, exactly conjunct her sixth, and Grace, rather than the chauffeur, was performing a service (sixth) for her daughter (fifth) in driving her back to the palace. Michel is associated with chivalry, and Grace was showing the courage and generosity of a Chevalier, only in a car rather than on a horse. Skuld fell in Grace's third house of short journeys, exactly conjunct Grace's Icarus in that same house. Skuld was one of the Scandinavian Fates—the dwarf who was the Fate of the future. Icarus represents "flying too close to the sun." The flying is followed by a fall. Witnesses described Grace's car as flying off the road before falling 75 feet.

The semisquare of Julia, the lunation, King, and Grace's Rhea to the Uranian planet Apollon, Hebe, Lachesis, Europa and the Uranian planet Vulcanus repeats some of the same symbolism. Apollon is associated with Apollo, the Greek and Roman god of the sun, but has the esoteric and eccentric quality of the Uranian planets. Hebe was the goddess of youth who had a fall. Natally Grace's Hebe is exactly conjunct her Ascendant, so she was a Hebe-type figure in regard to her persona. Lachesis was one of the Greek Fates—like Skuld, the one who determines the future. Apollon, Hebe and Lachesis were in Grace's eleventh house, with Lachesis exactly conjunct her twelfth. Europa is a personification of Europe, and Vulcanus is related to fated happenings. Europa and Vulcanus fell in Grace's ninth house of foreign countries, and the foreign country of Monaco in Europe was most affected by her death. (Though Monaco was her adopted country, it is still foreign in terms of her natal chart cast for Philadelphia.) Other countries in Europe, as well as the United States, sent their rulers or their rulers' representatives to her funeral which took place one day after the subsequent New Moon. (Though each lunation is studied as a separate entity, subsequent ones refer to previous ones, and previous ones allude to subsequent ones.)

PLANETARY PICTURES
After recording the natal house position and exact aspects of the lunation, I would record planetary pictures, consistently listing the lunation bodies and points which equaled the natal Sun/Moon, Venus/Mars and Mars/Saturn midpoints. In Grace's case, her natal Mars/Saturn midpoint is in her second house at 11° Sagittarius 52'. Lunation Anubis (11° Virgo 21') equaled this midpoint by a square; lunation Fortuna (25° Aries 15'), by a sesquiquadrate; and lunation Martina, Icarus (25° Capricorn 49'ʀ, 27° Capricorn 14'ʀ), by a semisquare. The Mars/Saturn midpoint can describe the limitation (Saturn) of energy (Mars). The ultimate limitation of

energy is death. Fortuna, Martina and Icarus have already been defined. Anubis was the Egyptian god of death.

What natal bodies and points equal the natal midpoints is always an important consideration. The natal chart shows what a body, point or midpoint means to the native. In Grace's case, her natal Juno (10° Sagittarius 29'), Atropos—♀ (11° Sagittarius 15'), Athene—⚳ (11° Sagittarius 28') equal her natal Mars/Saturn midpoint by a conjunction; her natal Vulcanus (12° Gemini 25'℞), by an opposition; her natal Lilith (26° Capricorn 50'), by a semisquare; and her natal Transpluto—⊖ (27° Cancer 21'℞), by a sesquiquadrate. Juno refers to the married woman; Atropos, to the cutting of the thread of life; Athene, to perception. Vulcanus is a Uranian planet related to fated happenings. Lilith is associated with "reaching closure" and with France; and Transpluto is a Super-Pluto. (Lunation Juno and Vulcanus and Grace's natal Lilith were exactly aspected by the lunation.)

OTHER LUNATION FACTORS AND THEIR ASPECTS

Next, exact aspects of other lunation factors and the configurations that they formed would be discussed. At this lunation there was a multiple factor aspect of Diana—☽ (04° Scorpio 07'), Jupiter (04° Scorpio 14'), Sappho—⚵ (04° Scorpio 54') and Eros—⚘ (05° Scorpio 38'), square Venus (05° Leo 41'). There was also a multiple factor major configuration, which in New York City included the Ascendant-Descendant axis. This configuration was a Cosmic Square of Mars (09° Scorpio 15'), Klotho—♀ (09° Scorpio 30'), Descendant (10° Scorpio 11'), Patricia—⚶ (11° Scorpio 17') opposite the Ascendant (10° Taurus 11'), the Uranian planet Admetos—♀ (10° Taurus 19'℞), Pandora—⛢ (11° Taurus 24'), Lilith (11° Taurus 29'), square Amor—♡ (10° Leo 05'), opposite Dark Moon Lilith—∅ (11° Aquarius 59'). In my prediction I wrote about this aspect and configuration, though Klotho, whose ephemeris I did not receive until the following month, was not mentioned. Not having previously seen in the six and a half years of my study two such multi-factor configurations so closely conjunct in a lunation chart, I figured "something major should occur."

The involvement of the lunation Ascendant (10° Taurus 11') with the multiple factor configuration was in New York City, rather than in Monaco. (With me and others in New York, events occurred that fit the symbolism of this configuration.)

In Monaco there was an involvement of the lunation Ascendant (03° Leo 16') with the multiple factor aspect. Lunation Venus at 05° Leo was pulled into an exact conjunction with the lunation Ascendant by the stellium at 04°-05° Scorpio. To the Monegasques, their princess was the embodiment of beauty and charm (Venus).

The multiple factor aspect and the lunation Ascendant in Monaco were also exactly tied in with Grace's natal Ascendant (04° Scorpio 41'), Hebe (05° Scorpio 54'), Klotho (06° Scorpio 42') and her Descendant (04° Taurus 41'), Elsa—∈(04° Taurus 49'℞) and Guinevere (06° Taurus 18'℞). This emphasis in Monaco on Grace's chart relates to the fact that her accident and death highlighted that month's Monacan persona, in relation to Grace's youthful (Hebe), fateful (Klotho) persona and her fated (Klotho) fall (Hebe). The conjunction of lunation Diana, Jupiter,

Sappho, Eros to Grace's Ascendant, Hebe, Klotho brings the principles of the former to the principles of the latter. Diana, like Artemis, was goddess of the moon and brought "sudden, but peaceful, death to women." (Shortly after her accident, Grace went into an irreversible coma.) Jupiter was king of the gods and relates to the greatest expansion or completion. (Death is one form of completion.) Sappho was the Greek poetess reputed to have fallen from a cliff to her death. (Grace fell from a cliff to hers.) Eros was god of love who pierced the heart with his arrows. I have seen Eros refer to sharp pains, and such pain would have been produced by the cerebral hemorrhage Grace suffered. (The orbit of Eros is in the orbit of Mars.) Lunation Eros was 05° Scorpio 38', which relates to the heart (05°) combined with transformation (Scorpio), in relation to suddenness (38'). Blood is pumped by the heart; a cerebral hemorrhage would transform the flow; and apparently the transformation was sudden. That month's Monacan persona was also highlighted in relation to Grace's husband (Descendant). Rainier is described by the Elsa and Guinevere conjunct his wife's Descendant. (Grace is too because close conjunctions to the Descendant reflect upon the Ascendant.) He is a "Noble one," and he had to make the "this or else that" (Elsa) decision whether or not to remove Grace from her life-support system. Regarding Guinevere, Rainier is a romantic royal figure who lost his mate, as Guinevere lost Arthur.

The multiple factor configuration was exactly tied in with Grace's natal Mercury (10° Scorpio 42'), South Node (12° Scorpio 10'), Chiron—⚷ (11° Taurus 37'ᴙ), North Node (12° Taurus 10'), Uranian planet Zeus—⚹(09° Leo 05'ᴙ), Midheaven (11° Leo 11') and IC (11° Aquarius 11').

Her Mercury (ruler of her eighth and eleventh house) and her South Node are in her first house. Mercury and the South Node in the first is descriptive of Grace— as an actress and princess, she was a communicator. Lunation Mars, Klotho, Patricia being conjunct her Mercury, South Node brought the excessive energy of the Mars to Grace and to her short journey with close connections (Mercury, South Node). Such excessive energy can result in an accident. Lunation Klotho adds a fated quality; lunation Patricia, a patrician quality. Also, Grace's middle name was Patricia, making this configuration more specifically relevant to her. (In fact, Patricia is the asteroid most relevant to her because there is no asteroid named Grace or one of that name's variations.) Her Chiron and North Node are in her seventh house. Her husband, as custodian of Monaco's citizens, is a Chiron figure. The Nodes across the first and seventh emphasize the importance of close connections, with the South Node sometimes sweeping away the concerns of its house and sign. On her short trip (Mercury), Grace (first house placement) was unexpectedly (eleventh house rulership) swept away (South Node) to her death (eighth house rulership). Lunation Admetos, Pandora, Lilith being conjunct her Chiron, North Node brought the stoppage of the Admetos, the cascade effect of the Pandora, and the "choice between alternatives" of the Lilith to her husband.

Her Zeus is in her ninth house, close to her Midheaven. Such fiery status is appropriate for Grace's career as movie star and sovereign. Zeus, Midheaven is also descriptive of her accident. It was in a foreign country (ninth house), and the engine of her car caught on fire (Zeus) when the car fell from a great height (Midheaven), leading to her end of life (the Zeus, Midheaven is opposite her I.C.). Her Zeus, Midheaven, and IC are on the heliocentric nodes of Neptune, lending a coloration of illusion and nebulousness to her fiery status. Such a conjuncture is appropriate for the illusion of a movie star and sovereign and for the nebulousness of her accident. Lunation Amor being conjunct Grace's Zeus and Midheaven brought the love of Amor to her fiery status with the coloration of illusion and nebulousness. The whole world mourned her tragic accident and death. Lunation Dark Moon Lilith being conjunct Grace's IC brought the hidden fascination of the Dark Moon to her end of life (IC). Grace was a Dark Moon Lilith figure herself, with her natal Dark Moon (17° Gemini 09') exactly quincunx her East Point (16° Scorpio 07'). The whole world was fascinated by the mystery of this famous luminary's death. Also, in her accident, she literally "blacked out" (Dark Moon).

GRACE'S ACCIDENT
As stated earlier in this chapter, the transiting bodies and points carry the message of the lunation to the lunation, natal, and transiting bodies and points. September 13, 1982 at 10:30 AM (the time of Grace's accident) in La Turbie, France (the nearest town), transiting Mars was at 25° Scorpio 28', conjunct Grace's Mars at 25° Scorpio 38'. Grace was having a Mars Return, but every two years she had a Mars Return, without having a fatal accident. This time transiting Mars was carrying the message of the lunation major configuration of Mars, Klotho, Patricia opposite Admetos, Pandora, Lilith, square Amor opposite Dark Moon Lilith. One of the messages of this Cosmic Square, in combination with Grace's chart, concerned the car accident and subsequent death of this patrician woman (Patricia). (As for transiting Patricia, it had come to Grace Patricia's natal East Point—the self.) Transiting Mars was also square the lunation at 25° Leo 48' and so bringing the message of lunation Mars (through the Lunar aspect of the square) to the lunation itself. The principles of the lunation and of its relationship to Grace's natal chart would then be activated. Those principles in combination with Grace's chart concerned the fated accident, restriction and death of this Lunar figure. (See pages 272, 275-76.)

Aspects of transiting Mars to other transiting bodies and points would also be significant. For instance, transiting Mars was conjunct the transiting asteroid Nemausa. Zipporah Dobyns writes in her *Asteroid-World: Winter 1987,* "Nemausa sometimes seems to be a key to a central issue in a chart." She told me that this association may be related to the fact that Nemausa has such a regular orbit the asteroid is a key to calculations of the celestial equator. Having found that Nemausa is a key to a central issue, I have used as this asteroid's glyph an X, as in "X marks the spot." The sign, house, degree and exact aspects of Nemausa would describe that central issue. Transiting Nemausa was at 25° Scorpio 54' in the first house of both Grace's chart and the accident chart. The conjunction of Nemausa to Mars marks Mars as involved in this central issue of the chart. Transiting Nemausa and Mars were exactly trine the transiting Moon at 25° Cancer 03', connecting this energy to a Lunar figure. Though flowing, the trine is not necessarily a favorable aspect. "To go with the flow," whether of a person or a car, can be very unfavorable.

The transiting Moon, in turn, was carrying the message of the lunation to the lunation (25° Leo 48') in the form of the Neptunian semisextile. The transiting Moon had brought that message from the tenth house of restriction to the ninth house of expansion. Other lunation bodies and points aspected by the lunation also received that lunation message from the transiting Moon. For example, lunation Pluto and Poseidon, which had been aspected by the lunation in the form of the Virgoan sextile, were now aspected by the transiting Moon in the form of the Lunar square. (Transiting Pluto and Poseidon were as well.)

The transiting Sun was carrying the message of the lunation to lunation and transiting Zeus, to transiting Anubis and to the lunation Vertex. The transiting Sun was 20° Virgo 13'; transiting Zeus, 20° Virgo 32'; transiting Anubis, 20° Virgo 41'. They were conjunct lunation Zeus at 20° Virgo 05' and square the lunation Vertex at 20° Sagittarius 14' (fiery fatefulness). Anubis had its own message, brought from Grace's natal Mars/Saturn midpoint (see pages 276-77). The transiting Sun and Anubis had brought their messages from the tenth house of restriction to the eleventh house of disruption.

Transiting Venus, which had come from the lunation multiple factor square, was now at 06° Virgo 45', exactly semisextile lunation Venus at 05° Leo 41'. Transiting Venus had brought its message from the ninth house to the tenth. This lunation square had already highlighted Grace's natal Ascendant, Hebe, Klotho at 04°-06° Scorpio, and her Descendant, Elsa, Guinevere at 04°-06° Taurus. In La Turbie, France, where the accident occurred, the transiting Midheaven was 04° Leo 34', exactly conjunct the lunation Ascendant in Monaco (03° Leo 16') and lunation Venus (05° Leo 41'). (The transiting Midheaven in Monaco was only one minute different.)

The transiting Midheaven had come from a lunation T-Square. The lunation Midheaven in Monaco had been 17° Aries 13' exactly opposite the IC (17° Libra 13'), Saturn (18° Libra 27'), square Halley's Comet—♄ (16° Cancer 54'), Astraea— ♎ (18° Cancer 40'), Lutetia (19° Cancer 44'), Grace's Fortuna (17° Cancer 48') and her Pluto (19° Cancer 31'℟). This message of the lunation Midheaven T-Square in Monaco had been carried by the transiting Midheaven to the lunation Ascendant, Venus multiple factor square in Monaco. Venus rules the IC, Saturn conjunction in Libra. Saturn can be limitation; Comets are powerful activators, with Halley's particularly related to prediction; Astraea is the "Starry Maid"; Lutetia, an ancient name for Paris, and so related to France; Fortuna is Fortune, and Pluto can be death.

At some time during each day since the lunation, the transiting Midheaven would have brought its lunation message to the lunation Ascendant in Monaco. However, the other appropriate aspects to lunation, natal and transiting bodies and points would not have occurred at the same time. It is a matter of accretion.

Another appropriate aspect at the time of the accident was the exact conjunction of the transiting East Point (09° Scorpio 18') to transiting Jupiter (08° Scorpio 14'). Most astrologers would consider this conjunction most auspicious. However, both transiting Jupiter and the East Point were exactly conjunct lunation Mars, Klotho, Patricia, activating the by now well-known lunation Cosmic Square. Transiting

Jupiter had come from the lunation multiple factor square. I had written in my prediction, "when the planets in the square aspect the planets in the Cosmic Square, there should be an activation of the principles involved—perhaps the stoppage or the going around in circles of the Admetos." ("Planets" was meant to include other bodies and personal points.)

GRACE'S DEATH

September 14, 1982 at 10:30 PM in Monaco, Monaco, Princess Grace died. Transiting Jupiter at 08° Scorpio 30' was still exactly conjunct lunation Mars, Klotho, Patricia. Other exact aspects were transiting East Point now at 10° Taurus 47', conjunct lunation and transiting Admetos and lunation Pandora, Lilith; transiting Vesta at 11° Aquarius 10'℞, conjunct lunation Dark Moon Lilith; and transiting Carolina at 10° Leo 36', conjunct lunation Amor. The lunation Cosmic Square had been activated again, and there had been "an activation of the principles involved"—the stoppage of the Admetos can represent death. As outlined before, this lunation Cosmic Square was exactly tied in with Grace's natal Mercury, South Node, Chiron, North Node, Zeus, Midheaven and IC. The transiting asteroid Carolina, with its exact conjunction to Grace's Zeus, Midheaven, represents Caroline, Grace's older daughter, who would then be replacing Grace as "first lady" of Monaco. Transiting Venus at 08° Virgo 36', North Node at 10° Cancer 49', South Node at 10° Capricorn 49', and eighth house cusp, Guinevere, Juno at 25° Sagittarius 03', 25° Sagittarius 11', 26° Sagittarius 15', were also exactly aspecting the lunation Cosmic Square.

The transiting Midheaven at the time of death was 05° Aquarius 59', tying in exactly with the lunation square of Monacan Ascendant, Venus, square Diana, Jupiter, Sappho, Eros. As outlined before, this lunation square tied in exactly with Grace's natal Ascendant, Hebe, Klotho, opposite Descendant, Elsa, Guinevere. The transiting Midheaven had come from Grace's sixth house of physical health to her fourth of the end of life. The transiting Sun at 21° Virgo 41' was exactly sesquiquadrate the transiting Midheaven and formed 8th harmonic aspects (semisquares and sesquiquadrates) to the lunation square and Grace's natal opposition. (At the time of the accident the transiting Sun had also formed 8th harmonic aspects to the transiting Midheaven, lunation square and Grace's natal opposition.)

The transiting Ascendant was 01° Gemini 20', exactly conjunct lunation and transiting Hades—♇ (02° Gemini 11', 02° Gemini 11'℞), which were conjunct Grace's natal Nemausa and eighth house cusp (02° Gemini 37'℞, 03° Gemini 17'). Hades is another name for Pluto and for the underworld. A central issue (Nemausa), already evidenced in Grace's natal chart, is death (eighth cusp), perhaps on a short trip (Gemini). Opposite the transiting Ascendant and Uranian planet Hades was transiting Uranus at 01° Sagittarius 08', conjunct Grace's natal Gaea and second house cusp (02° Sagittarius 05', 03° Sagittarius 17'). Uranus, ruler of Grace's natal fourth house, describes the suddenness of the end of her life. Gaea is the personification of the earth, to which Grace was metaphorically returning. The transiting Ascendant was also exactly semisextile lunation and transiting Atropos (01° Taurus 34', 00° Taurus 44'℞). Atropos cuts the thread of life. Both Hades and Atropos had made their retrograde stations between the New Moon and Grace's death. (Hades had returned to the exact minute of its lunation position.) Their stations had placed even more emphasis on Hades and Atropos. The transiting Ascendant, Hades was exactly sesquiquadrate lunation Saturn (18° Libra 27'), Grace's natal Carolina (17° Libra 21') and transiting Mercury (16° Libra 28'), ruler of the first and fifth cusp of the death chart. The involvement again of Carolina with Saturnine symbolism points again to Grace's status in Monaco passing to Princess Caroline. The lunation T-Square, with Saturn opposite the Monacan Midheaven, square Halley's Comet, Astraea, Lutetia, Grace's Fortuna and her Pluto, was activated. Transiting Halley's Comet at 18° Cancer 06' was tying in with the lunation T-Square still and the transiting Ascendant, Hades. As for transiting Saturn at 21° Libra 09', it had come to lunation Lucifer, Pallas (21° Libra 31', 22° Libra 31').

The position of the asteroid Lucifer was put into Grace's natal chart, as well as into the New Moon, Full Moon, accident, and death charts, because her accident had occurred at a bend called Devil's Curve. (Though Lucifer literally means light-bringing, it is another name for the Devil.) Her perception (Pallas) had been affected at this curve. (At the time of the accident, Saturn was 20° Libra 59'.) Grace's natal Lucifer is 03° Pisces 40' in her fourth house, opposition her Neptune at 03° Virgo 25' in her tenth house, exactly square her Nemausa, eighth house cusp and her Gaea, second house cusp.

The transiting Moon at the time of death was 16° Leo 35', exactly square lunation Siva (15° Scorpio 18'), Thule (15° Scorpio 20'), Nemausa (16° Scorpio 18'). This lunation stellium had been conjunct Grace's natal Nemesis (15° Scorpio 41'), East Point (16° Scorpio 07'). Siva was the Hindu god known as "the Destroyer"; Thule is "the limit of any journey"; Nemausa, as explained, "a key to a central issue." Nemesis was a Greek goddess, sometimes of divine retribution, and sometimes of fertility—similar to Artemis. Nemesis is identified with Leda, mother of Helen by Zeus.[1] With her natal Nemesis exactly conjunct her East Point, Grace was a Nemesis figure.

As for transiting aspects to the lunation itself, transiting Nemesis at 24° Cancer 47' was exactly semisextile the lunation at 25° Leo 48'; transiting Martina (24° Capricorn 42') was quincunx; transiting Poseidon, Pluto (25° Libra 11', 25° Libra 29'), sextile; transiting Fortuna, Part of Fortune (25° Aries 50'℞, 26° Aries 15'), trine. These transiting bodies and points were in a Cosmic Square. Transiting Mars, Nemausa (26° Scorpio 28', 26° Scorpio 31') were still square the lunation, as they had been at the time of the accident. Transiting Neptune, Guinevere, Juno (24° Sagittarius 17', 25° Sagittarius 11', 26° Sagittarius 15') were still trine the lunation as they had been at the time of the lunation and accident, only now the transiting eighth house cusp was added (25° Sagittarius 03'). The transiting Nodes (10° Cancer 49', 10° Capricorn 49'), Apollon (09° Libra 27') and Rhea (10° Aries 27'℞) formed 8th harmonic aspects to the lunation. The transiting North Node square Rhea, with both sesquiquadrate Mars, Nemausa, were in a Fist of God. Rhea had already been highlighted in terms of Grace, since her natal Rhea had been conjuncted by the lunation. Rhea represents Grace who, as an actress and princess, was the great mother goddess.

THE FULL MOON

The Full Moon chart, which is drawn around the New Moon chart, is a transit to the New Moon chart. That transit shows the culmination or outcome of that New Moon. Grace's accident did not occur until September 13, and her death did not occur until September 14. However, this final outcome in relation to her natal chart was foreshadowed in the Full Moon on September 3.

The message of the New Moon at 25° Leo 48'41.04" in Grace's tenth house of restriction and status had been brought to the Full Moon at 10° Pisces 40'54.48" in Grace's fourth house of the home and the end of life. The degree combined with the sign, in relation to the minute, in regard to the second, gives insight. 25° Leo 48'41" can be the regal (Leo) wife (25°), in relation to confinement (48'), in regard to the life force (41"). 10° Pisces 40'54" can be the dissolution (Pisces) of structure (10°), in relation to the ending (40'), in regard to a prominent person—"king of the gods" (54").

At the Full Moon, transiting Venus was at 24° Leo 36', exactly conjunct the lunation at 25° Leo 48'. Venus had come from the ninth house to the tenth. I had written in my prediction, "When Venus comes to the lunation at the Full Moon, the square will be reactivated in terms of the concerns of the lunation." (Always note conjunctions of the transiting Sun, Moon, Mercury and Venus to the lunation Sun-Moon, Mercury and Venus.) Transiting Venus had brought its message, which emphasized Monaco's and Grace's persona, to the concerns of the lunation. These concerns, in relation to Grace, included restriction and status, violence, and mysterious transformation or death. (See pages 272, 275-76.)

The positions of the asteroids Hygiea and Aesculapia were put into Grace's natal chart, as well as into the New Moon, Full Moon, accident, and death charts, because health and healing are significant in the case of an accident and death. Hygiea was the Greek goddess of health, and Aesculapius was the Roman god of medicine and healing. The glyph I designed for Hygiea (ƒ) is a snake, since that goddess is often depicted feeding one. The glyph I designed for Aesculapia (♀) is two snakes intertwined, since the symbol of the physician is the caduceus, which has two intertwined snakes. Snakes, which shed their skins, are associated with healing. I've found Hygiea more related to health, and Aesculapia more related to the healer. (Makhaon, which was later added to my asteroid program, is more related to surgery.)

The transiting Sun at the Full Moon was 10° Virgo 40'54", exactly conjunct the transiting asteroids Hygiea (10° Virgo 38') and Toro—♀ (11° Virgo 39'), all in Grace's tenth house. Toro amplifies what it contacts. At this culmination of the lunation, transiting Hygiea, Sun, and Toro had brought their lunation messages to lunation Anubis (11° Virgo 21'), the Egyptian god of death. Transiting Hygiea, Sun, and Toro were activating the lunation Cosmic Square of Mars, Klotho, Patricia opposite Admetos, Pandora, Lilith, square Amor, opposite Dark Moon Lilith, and that major configuration's exact conjunctions to Grace's natal Mercury, South Node, opposite Chiron, North Node, square Zeus, Midheaven, opposite IC. Transiting

Hygiea, Sun, Toro and lunation Anubis were exactly sextile, trine, semisextile and quincunx the respective legs of these lunation and natal Cosmic Squares.

The transiting asteroid Aesculapia was at 12° Scorpio 40' in Grace's first house, exactly conjunct the Mars, Klotho, Patricia of the lunation Cosmic Square and the Mercury, South Node of Grace's natal Cosmic Square. There was a transiting Yod of Sappho (10° Scorpio 17'), Aesculapia, sextile Hygiea, Sun, Toro, quincunx Rhea (12° Aries 16'℞). Sappho had come from the lunation multiple factor aspect of Diana, Jupiter, Sappho, Eros (conjunct Grace's Ascendant, Hebe, Klotho, opposite her Descendant, Elsa, Guinevere) square the Monacan Ascendant, Venus, carrying that lunation square's message. (See pages 277-78.)

There was a transiting Grand Trine of Hygiea, Sun, Toro, trine Skuld (10° Capricorn 57'), South Node (11° Capricorn 43'), trine Admetos (10° Taurus 16'℞). After Grace's accident, her heart was kept beating by a life-support system. The life-support system amplified (Toro) her heart (Sun) and health (Hygiea) through its flowing (Grand Trine) fated (Skuld) connection (South Node). When the connection to her life-support system was shut off, there was a flowing of the amplified heart and health into a fated connection with death (Admetos).

LISTINGS

All the relevant positions of bodies and points in Grace's natal chart, as well as in the New Moon, Full Moon, accident and death charts, have not been mentioned. The purpose has been to demonstrate my methodology, not to delineate all of the positions and their aspects. Figures XXIII and XXIV are two zodiacal listings—one of Princess Grace's natal chart and the other of the lunation on August 19, 1982, in Monaco, Monaco. The listings are of 468 asteroids in the option *Many Interesting Asteroids.* (When the delineations were written, my listing was of 392 asteroids, with an additional six calculated by myself. The six asteroids are ones I had been using in August 1982 that were not included in the 392 asteroids.) The reader can use these listings to find other relevant positions and make his or her own delineations.

DISTINCTIONS OF MYTHOLOGY

For the most part in my above explications, distinctions between the different mythologies were not made. Though similarities in meanings, sound or mythology have been emphasized instead, distinctions are pertinent. In writing about aspects to the lunation, I mentioned the general Lunar emphasis and didn't distinguish between the particular Lunar emphases. There was the Lunar emphasis of the New Moon itself; of the ancient Greek goddess of the moon, Selene; of the heroine in German legend whose name sounds like Crescent, Crescentia; and of the Egyptian goddess of the moon, Isis. Isis, in contrast to these other Lunar symbols, has the formal quality of Egyptian mythology. This quality of composure and tranquillity is evidenced by the asteroid Isis in both Grace's natal chart and the lunation chart. To use Grace's natal chart as an illustration, Grace has Isis at 01° Aries 24' in the fifth house. The 01° and sign of Aries relate Isis to Grace's "apparent self," while the fifth house relates Isis to the sphere of regality. Grace's Isis is exactly opposite

Figure XXIII
Asteroid Listing for Princess Grace
Philadelphia, Penn. Nov 12, 1929 5h 31m 0s Zone 5.0

No.	Name	Position	No.	Name	Position	No.	Name	Position	No.	Name	Position
42	ISIS	1♈23.2	2212	HEPHAISTOS	14♏53.7R	2682	SOROMUNDI	19♍25.1	3350	SCOBEE	25♍11.4
1281	JEANNE	1♈30.9R	1	CERES	16♏42.8R	3361	ORPHEUS	21♍52.3	335	ROBERTA	25♍19.7
3152	JONES	2♍05.4R	620	DRAKONIA	17♏46.9R	577	RHEA	24♍52.1	2351	O'HIGGINS	25♍36.0
10	HYGIEA	3♈02.4R	876	SCOTT	19♏47.9R	2146	STENTOR	26♍13.0	3052	HERZEN	26♍40.2
3317	PARIS	3♈33.8R	2741	VALDIVIA	21♏58.8R	2065	SPICER	26♍16.7	1258	SICILIA	27♍38.4
2375	KINGEL	3♈50.9R	12	VICTORIA	22♏34.8R	3072	VILNIUS	27♍04.4	1924	HORUS	28♍18.1
287	NEPHTHYS	4♈50.1R	1288	SANTA	23♏38.4R	1143	ODYSSEUS	27♍41.1	953	PAINLEVA	28♍39.5
1284	LATVIA	6♈39.9R	2250	STALINGRAD	26♏50.8R	2976	AETOLIA	27♍58.6	1714	SY	29♍21.6
532	HERCULINA	11♈28.9R	2815	SOMA	27♏51.7R	1342	LAUTARO	28♍53.5	3009	COVENTRY	29♍43.1
798	RUTH	11♈50.1R	1058	GRUBBA	28♏55.2R	21	LUTETIA	29♍14.6	1589	FANATICA	0♎29.5
3050	CARRERA	12♍57.6R	1027	AESCULAPIA	0♐21.8R	2001	EINSTEIN	29♍23.6	2632	GUIZHOU	0♎43.8
1345	POTOMAC	14♈37.6R	3031	HOUSTON	0♐01.9R	2579	SPARTACUS	1♎11.1	241	GERMANIA	1♎11.6
151	ABUNDANTIA	15♍56.3R	340	EDUARDA	1♐58.5R	2382	NONIE	2♍01.5	787	MOSKVA	1♎14.2
78	DIANA	21♈19.6R	790	PRETORIA	2♐15.2R	498	TOKIO	2♍01.5	436	PATRICIA	1♎21.6
1242	ZAMBESIA	22♈38.9R	2631	ZHEJIANG	2♐15.2R	2340	HATHOR	3♍36.9	434	HUNGARIA	1♎26.8
1431	ARACHNE	22♈28.1R	2632	WASSERMAN	5♐30.2R	1563	NOEL	3♍39.9	119	ALTHAEA	1♎40.2
3362	KHUFU	24♈30.1R	2979	MURMANSK	8♐48.2R	2878	PARAMEDES	5♍31.4	313	CHALDAEA	1♎50.3
145	HERRICK	25♈01.4R	541	DEBORAH	9♐00.1R	2456	EURYDIKE	6♍46.3	2239	PARACELSUS	3♎51.3
1145	ADEONA	26♍36.3R	780	ARMENIA	11♐32.0R	75	WLADILENA	7♍14.6	905	UNIVERSITAS	3♎58.4
1812	GILGAMESH	26♈47.1R	24	THEMIS	11♐55.3R	1180	VIENNA	7♍30.0	1475	YALTA	4♎04.4
3338	RICHTER	27♍03.1R	2297	DAGHESTAN	12♐53.0R	397	VIENNA	7♍33.5	212	MEDEA	4♎42.6
2531	CAMBRIDGE	29♍23.3R	140	SIWA	15♏55.3R	1879	BROEDERSTROOM	8♍29.1	14	IRENE	5♎59.4
3449	ABELL	1♉51.3R	1464	ARMISTICIA	15♏37.6R	201	PENELOPE	8♍41.7	1322	COPPERNICUS	6♎51.6
203	POMPEJA	4♊55.1R	1285	JULIETTA	17♏48.5R	679	PAX	9♍00.4	469	ARGENTINA	6♎52.1
251	SOPHIA	4♉49.0R	19	FORTUNA	18♏33.1R	3092	HERODOTUS	9♍43.3	2835	RYOMA	7♎06.9
182	ELSA	4♉41.9R	1140	CRIMEA	19♏13.5R	228	AGATHE	10♍07.2	1685	TORO	7♎18.4
40	HARMONIA	5♊58.4R	1193	AFRICA	20♐08.4R	445	EDNA	11♍19.3	77	FRIGGA	8♎47.7
288	GLAUKE	5♉58.4R	2768	GORKY	20♐09.6R	1864	DAEDALUS	11♍11.6	1602	INDIANA	9♎47.3
2483	GUINEVERE	9♉19.3R	1197	RHODESIA	21♐57.8R	2059	BAGHUIVARI	12♍45.7	34	CIRCE	10♎27.0
1457	ANKARA	8♊33.5R	3095	OMARKHAYYAM	22♐15.3R	2270	YAZHI	13♍21.3	93	MINERVA	10♎27.0
896	SPHINX	9♉22.8R	444	GYPTIS	23♐26.0R	580	SELENE	15♍55.6	1516	HENRY	10♎52.6
156	XANTHIPPE	10♊55.3R	904	ROCKEFELLIA	24♐38.3R	1862	APOLLO	16♍05.5	849	ARA	12♎52.4
3147	SAMANTHA	10♊33.3R	26	PROSERPINA	25♐58.7R	2214	CAROL	17♍19.5	3288	SELEUCUS	16♎52.6
2060	CHIRON	11♊37.7R	2244	TESLA	26♐55.2R	3320	NAMBA	17♍19.6	235	CAROLINA	17♎23.1
2344	XIZANG	12♉45.5R	2597	ARTHUR	27♐15.3R	2284	SAN-JUAN	17♍21.7	257	SILESIA	17♎38.1
1799	XUKRAINA	14♊41.4R	2598	TADJIKISTAN	27♐35.7R	3199	NEFERTITI	18♍27.3	2736	OPS	17♎43.9
2104	TORONTO	15♉06.9R	981	MARTINA	28♐18.1R	1367	NONGOMA	18♍31.9	1866	SISYPHUS	19♎46.7
3302	HAETHON	17♊51.2R	1294	ANTWERPIA	0♑09.8R	697	GALILEA	18♍24.9	323	BRUCIA	20♎14.9
302	POMONA	17♉53.1R	2657	BASHKIRIA	0♑53.1R	2709	SAGAN	19♍55.9	1716	PETER	20♎36.4
2031	BAM	18♊32.4R	170	MARIA	2♑27.0R	464	MEGAIRA	20♍13.0	2678	HISPANIA	20♎39.0
2114	KASSANDRA	19♉53.9R	1282	UTOPIA	2♑33.2R	1718	NAMIBIA	21♍11.5	804	BONESTELL	20♎46.9
2046	LENINGRAD	25♉04.4R	1496	TURKU	3♑44.9R	631	PHILIPPINA	22♍06.3	3129	FLAVIA	21♎11.6
271	PENTHESILEA	25♉08.3R	1991	MIDAS	3♑57.6R	1773	RUMPELSTILZ	21♍18.6	1896	BEER	21♎26.7
564	DUDU	0♊58.2R	886	WASHINGTONIA	5♑17.9R	3218	DELPHINE	22♍28.2	2588	PANDORA	21♎35.0
2056	NANCY	0♊37.9R	3063	MAKHAON	5♑54.7R	1198	ATLANTIS	22♍28.2	55	SAPPHO	21♎38.2
244	SITA	2♊22.4R	2053	NUKI	8♑32.7R	2860	PASACENTENNIUM	22♍44.9	80	PEKING	22♎09.0
51	NEMAUSA	3♉37.9R	2193	JACKSON	9♑00.2R	1561	ESTONIA	22♍54.1	2045	JILIN	23♎23.3
408	FAMA	3♉22.4R	2193	SIBERIA	9♑22.4R	3012	MINSK	23♍25.4	2398	ALICE	24♎09.0
1138	ATTICA	4♊41.4R	1312	VASSAR	10♑47.4R	3351	SMITH	23♍28.2	291	TAPIO	24♎26.9
100	HEKATE	4♉41.4R	179	KLYTAEMNESTRA	13♑03.0R	1771	MAKOVER	23♍54.2	1705	HAMBURGA	24♎48.1
829	ACADEMIA	8♊49.2R	4	VESTA	13♑08.5R	2228	SOYUZ-APOLLO	24♍02.1	449	DARWIN	25♎36.6
672	ASTARTE	8♊49.2R	1036	GANYMED	15♑07.4R	793	ARIZONA	24♍24.8	1991	HATSHEPSUT	26♎04.5
1046	EDWIN	9♍05.4R	3043	SAN-DIEGO	15♑48.6R	511	DAVIDA	24♍24.6	2436	SMILEY	26♎35.7
216	KLEOPATRA	13♊15.2R	8	FLORA	17♑05.6R	1554	YUGOSLAVIA	24♍28.6	1613	SAPIENTIA	26♎42.8
307	NIKE	14♊15.6R	2152	HANNIBAL	17♑11.4R	2698	AZERBAJDZHAN	24♍38.4	275	CHEKHOV	27♎31.4
1112	POLONIA	14♊22.0R	2148	EPEIOS	18♑11.4R	477	ITALIA	24♍51.6	1814	BACH	27♎48.7
1139	ATAMI	14♊23.5R	7	IRIS	18♑59.8R	89	JULIA	25♍11.4	2610	TUVA	28♎40.3
3354	MCNAIR								349	DEMBOWSKA	29♎55.3
									576	EMANUELA	0♏18.8

Figure XXIV
Asteroid Listing for Lunation
Monaco, Monaco   Aug 18, 1982   4h 45m 27s   Zone -1.0

No.	Name	Long.
1879	BROEDERSTROOM	0♏18.9R
266	ALINE	1♈21.6R
300	GERALDINA	2♈41.6R
2768	GORKY	3♍29.9R
2193	JACKSON	3♏59.3R
2383	BRADLEY	4♏38.8R
2309	MR-SPOCK	5♏45.0R
2169	TAIWAN	6♏29.3R
3043	SAN-DIEGO	9♊20.6R
1388	APHRODITE	9♈57.4R
1348	MICHEL	11♏07.7R
1813	IMHOTEP	11♏28.9R
1516	HENRY	13♏21.1R
577	RHEA	13♏21.1R
12	VICTORIA	16♏00.8
2055	METIS	16♏58.8
2035	DVORAK	18♏30.0R
852	WLADILENA	19♏44.2
1132	HOLLANDIA	20♏55.3
43	ARIADNE	23♏39.3
2001	EINSTEIN	23♏39.8
212	MEDEA	23♏55.4
1625	THE-NORC	25♏11.8R
19	FORTUNA	25♏15.7
92	UNDINA	26♏07.0
1772	GAGARIN	0♐28.3
1	HOUSTON	0♐57.7
1011	LAODAMIA	1♐35.0
273	ATROPOS	2♐53.1
849	ARA	4♐34.4
453	TEA	9♐01.5
1197	RHODESIA	9♐01.5
1457	ANKARA	9♐11.5
55	PANDORA	11♐24.3
257	SILESIA	11♐32.6
1181	LILITH	11♐32.6
1932	HOOVERIA	15♐21.9
1278	KENYA	15♐58.6
3224	IRKUTSK	16♐04.7
620	DRAKONIA	17♐00.7
484	PITTSBURGHIA	17♐36.9
3356	RESNIK	17♐56.6
1896	BEER	18♐11.0
1613	SMILEY	19♐56.0
1712	ANGOLA	20♐09.0
2178	KAZAKHSTANIA	20♐16.4
1475	YALTA	20♐16.9
1188	GOTHLANDIA	22♐38.8
2303	RETSINA	22♐58.8
877	WALKURE	23♐07.0
3354	MCNAIR	24♐29.5
46	HESTIA	27♐09.0
3320	NAMBA	27♐37.3
2060	CHIRON	28♐29.0
2835	RYOMA	29♐01.2
2212	HEPHAISTOS	29♐06.6
1314	PAULA	0♑12
572	ASTARTE	2♑25.9
327	COLUMBIA	0♓16.1

Long.	Name	No.
1♉39.1	RITA	1180
1♍44.2	PARSIFAL	2095
1♏46.0	MINERVA	93
2♏14.3	IRENE	14
5♊11.4	URANIA	30
6♍26.6	ROBERTA	335
6♏26.5	ARTEMIS	105
7♏52.4	ATTILA	1489
8♊18.2	PHAETHON	3200
8♏34.0	INDIANA	1602
8♏54.0	DEMBOWSKA	349
10♏27.9	RUTH	798
11♏51.9	HORUS	1924
13♏01.5	NANCY	2056
14♏01.5	GREENWICH	2830
19♏17.5	TRANSVAALIA	2715
19♏34.8	ATLANTIS	1198
20♏12.3	RA-SHALOM	2100
21♏41.4	VATICANA	416
23♏16.7	VILNIUS	3072
25♏51.1	NONGOMA	1367
26♊18.8	PETER	1716
25♏53.1	KASSANDRA	114
29♏29.9	ADEONA	145
2♐46.6	ALTHAEA	119
4♐09.7	OHIO	439
5♐24.9	MARIA	170
5♐44.9	ARABIA	1157
5♐52.9	CAMBRIDGE	2531
3♐04.8	TUVA	2610
3♐27.8	ELSA	182
3♐28.9	HEBEI	2505
3♐40.2	BEN-MAYER	2863
4♐55.4	GALLIA	148
4♐55.4	FREIA	76
5♐52.1	HELSINKI	1495
6♐52.0	PASACENTENNIUM	2860
6♐54.0	APOLLO	1862
7♐55.3	SPICER	2065
8♐40.0	DUPONTA	1338
8♐08.1	UGANDA	1279
10♐11.5	ASTRONOMIA	1154
10♐12.3	ETHIOPIA	1432
12♐14.4	GILGAMESH	1812
12♐14.4	EUROPA	52
13♐28.8	POLONIA	1294
13♐57.4	ANTWERPIA	759
13♐57.9	VINIFERA	697
14♐07.7	GALILEA	638
14♐33.2	MOIRA	866
14♐39.7	CALTECH	
14♐33.2	FATME	
14♐30.1	NEMESIS	128
17♐20.0	CROATIA	589
17♐41.1	ROXANE	317
17♐40.6	ASTRAEA	5
18♒58.9	JUEWA	139
19♒44.5	LUTETIA	21
19♒48.8	PANNONIA	1444

Long.	No.	Name	Long.
21♋04.8	2597	ARTHUR	25♋38.3
21♏17.3	101	HELENA	25♋38.7
21♏20.0	2305	SPARTACUS	26♋57.8
21♋50.1	3351	KING	26♋37.2
23♏24.2	2700	SMITH	27♋57.4
23♏27.3		BAIKONUR	28♋11.5
24♋04.2	382	DODONA	28♋17.0
24♋05.2	3353	JARVIS	28♋39.8
25♋26.5	1284	LATVIA	29♋28.7
26♋00.6	2273	YARILO	0♌05.7
27♋01.8	389	INDUSTRIA	0♌18.7
27♋22.0	201	PENELOPE	0♌26.4
28♏55.2	2575	BULGARIA	2♌28.0
28♏58.1	1685	TORO	2♌28.9
9♋44.8	916	AMERICA	2♌53.3
0♌20.6	1046	EDWIN	2♌59.8
0♌33.5	1981	MIDAS	3♍10.8
0♌58.4	2566	KIRGHIZIA	3♍26.8
1♌02.6	1363	HERBERTA	3♍45.7
1♌10.7	449	HAMBURGA	4♍14.7
1♌53.0	2632	GUIZHOU	4♍18.4
1♌58.4	1814	BACH	4♍45.7
2♌35.1	1285	JULIETTA	4♍46.3
2♌49.4	3317	PARIS	4♍54.1
4♋03.0	10	HYGIEA	5♍44.5
4♌25.6	75	EURYDIKE	6♍23.8
4♌28.3	1543	BOURGEOIS	7♍44.5
5♋08.5	8	FLORA	8♍00.1
5♌04.4	258	TYCHE	8♍00.7
5♌09.7	291	ALICE	8♍02.7
6♌52.4	1322	COPPERNICUS	8♍38.3
7♋36.0	26	PROSERPINA	8♍40.0
8♋12.5	3350	SCOBEE	9♍16.7
8♌28.5	34	CIRCE	9♍47.3
10♋05.3	86	SEMELE	10♍00.0
11♌07.3	905	UNIVERSITAS	10♍42.9
11♋49.2	1912	ANUBIS	11♍21.7
11♌55.4	2244	TESLA	12♍18.2
11♌58.6	2567	ELBA	12♍50.6
12♋40.6	2617	TUCSON	12♍56.4
13♋13.8	984	JIANGXI	14♍09.6
13♋33.4	904	ROCKEFELLIA	15♍07.9
14♋08.6	2293	GUERNICA	15♍11.5
14♌52.0	1431	ITALIA	15♍48.5
18♋22.0	1589	LUANDA	16♍22.6
19♋40.8	228	FANATICA	17♍57.0
20♋13.1	1870	AGATHE	17♍59.6
20♋30.8	1870	GLAUKOS	17♍59.6
21♋55.1	727	NIPPONIA	18♍04.0
21♋58.4	2171	KIEV	18♍14.3
22♋00.5	787	MOSKVA	18♍25.6
22♋07.2	341	CALIFORNIA	18♍31.0
22♋18.3	1579	HERRICK	18♍02.3
22♋39.2	2250	STALINGRAD	19♍21.9
23♋00.2	1426	RIVIERA	19♍43.0
24♋29.0	2598	MERLIN	19♍50.0
24♋36.7	301	BAVARIA	20♍53.0
24♋56.7	407	ARACHNE	20♍58.9
25♋26.9	216	KLEOPATRA	22♍01.7

Figure XXIII
Asteroid Listing for Princess Grace
Philadelphia, Penn. Nov 12, 1929   5h 31m 0s   Zone 5.0

No.	Position	Name
2362	0♏48.3	MARK TWAIN
3352	1♏12.0	MCAULIFFE
1268	1♏56.4	LIBYA
1625	3♏49.0	THE-NORC
1763	4♏39.7	WILLIAMS
81	4♏39.9	TERPSICHORE
1980	5♏15.3	TEZCAILIPOCA
359	5♏54.1	GEORGIA
6	6♏01.4	HEBE
1640	6♏42.2	NEMO
97	7♏11.4	KLOTHO
52	7♏45.2	EUROPA
30	8♏31.4	URANIA
747	8♏37.7	WINCHESTER
1798	8♏39.0	WATTS
136	9♏25.1	AUSTRIA
5	11♏10.8	ASTRAEA
877	11♏33.3	WALKURE
2155	11♏38.3	WODAN
2174	11♏41.7	ASMODEUS
2041	11♏47.1	LANCELOT
224	12♏36.3	OCEANA
2101	13♏24.6	ADONIS
2161	13♏41.4	GRISSOM
638	13♏41.4	MOIRA
1224	13♏45.0	FANTASIA
2287	13♏58.3	KALMYKIA
2202	14♏10.7	PELE
2210	15♏32.4	LOIS
128	15♏41.8	NEMESIS
3124	18♏29.0	KANSAS
211	19♏00.3	ISOLDA
727	19♏56.8	NIPPONIA
715	20♏16.0	TRANSVAALIA
1703	20♏47.1	BARRY
2807	22♏03.8	KARL-MARX
3355	22♏44.8	ONIZUKA
101	23♏17.4	HELENA
453	23♏52.2	TEA
2668	24♏12.0	TATARIA
2117	24♏48.4	DANMARK
95	25♏52.2	ARETHUSA
327	26♏31.5	COLUMBIA
866	26♏36.3	FATME
3353	27♏08.4	JARVIS
50	27♏20.3	VIRGINIA
2169	27♏28.5	TAIWAN
105	27♏43.7	ARTEMIS
1914	27♏46.8	HARTBEESPOORTDAM
2584	27♏51.3	TURKMENIA
759	29♏36.1	VINIFERA
279	0♐49.8	THULE
439	2♐05.4	OHIO
1184	2♐06.4	GAEA
2273	2♐10.4	YARILO
2224	2♐23.5	TUCSON
2566		KIRGHIZIA

No.	Position	Name
890	3♐32.5	WALTRAUT
2335	3♐49.6	JAMES
148	5♐11.7	GALLIA
1915	5♐22.4	QUETZALCOATL
2791	6♐56.8	PARADISE
1816	7♐41.1	LIBERIA
1932	7♐44.1	JANSKY
1188	9♐00.3	GOTHLANDIA
433	9♐12.4	EROS
9	9♐45.6	METIS
86	10♐01.0	SEMELE
1338	10♐15.8	ALINE
266	10♐29.6	DUPONTA
3	10♐46.0	JUNO
2170	11♐13.3	BYELORUSSIA
3554	11♐14.8	AMUN
273	11♐28.9	ATROPOS
881	11♐47.6	ATHENE
2062	12♐09.6	ATEN
2100	12♐23.8	RA-SHALOM
1712	12♐57.3	ANGOLA
585	13♐12.5	BILKIS
2367	13♐31.5	PRAHA
103	13♐53.1	HERA
589	14♐16.2	CROATIA
1432	15♐04.7	ETHIOPIA
3224	16♐28.5	IRKUTSK
1680	17♐24.8	BOLIVIANA
1810	17♐25.3	EPIMETHEUS
465	17♐27.1	ALEKTO
1348	17♐30.5	MICHEL
2355	18♐26.5	NEI_MONGGOL
2365	18♐49.8	INTERKOSMOS
2200	18♐59.0	PASADENA
2473	19♐06.7	HEYERDAHL
616	19♐10.7	ELLY
443	19♐15.6	PHOTOGRAPHICA
1213	19♐22.8	ALGERIA
1912	19♐42.9	ANUBIS
1279	20♐30.1	UGANDA
2938	20♐37.8	HOPI
1221	20♐56.9	AMOR
1363	21♐04.2	HERBERTA
944	22♐00.5	HIDALGO
2700	22♐01.2	BAIKONUR
334	25♐32.6	CHICAGO
1170	26♐11.2	SIVA
895	26♐57.4	HELIO
76	27♐15.6	FREIA
2102	28♐47.1	TANTALUS
2315	29♐24.8	CZECHOSLOVAKIA

No.	Position	Name
916		AMERICA
92		UNDINA
2906		CALTECH
2462		NEHALENNIA
2567		ELBA
301		BAVARIA
99		DIKE
430		HYBRIS
43		ARIADNE
472		ROMA
2095		PARSIFAL
300		GERALDINA
2607		YAKUTIA
1566		ICARUS
1629		PECKER
293		BRASILIA
44		NYSA
797		MONTANA
1809		PROMETHEUS
2863		BEN_MAYER
2082		GALAHAD
2515		GANSU
1426		RIVIERA
2484		ANTARCTICA
2063		BACCHUS
123		BRUNHILD
149		MEDUSA
1154		ASTRONOMIA
71		NIOBE
2197		SHANGHAI
2505		HEBEI
46		HESTIA
314		PAULA
350		ORNAMENTA
2617		JIANGXI
2830		GREENWICH
2779		MARY
3097		TACITUS
1108		DEMETER
1940		WHIPPLE
2176		DONAR
2118		FLAGSTAFF
3053		DRESDEN
416		VATICANA
1011		LAODAMIA
1537		TRANSYLVANIA
1181		LILITH
67		ASIA
418		ALEMANNIA
2592		MARTHA
3133		HUNAN
2121		SENDAI
2309		MR-SPOCK
1923		OSIRIS
2410		MORRISON
371		BOHEMIA

No.	Position	Name
258	3♏29.5	TYCHE
671	3♏35.2	CARNEGIA
2720	4♏45.5	PYOTR_PERVYJ
2178	5♏01.7	KAZAKHSTANIA
1277	7♏17.1	DOLORES
770	7♏30.4	BALI
1489	7♏37.2	ATTILA
16	8♏46.3	PSYCHE
389	9♏44.4	INDUSTRIA
1388	10♏41.8	APHRODITE
474	10♏43.5	PRUDENTIA
265	11♏24.0	ANNA
2503	12♏08.8	LIAONING
1495	13♏13.7	HELSINKI
232	16♏26.6	RUSSIA
1772	17♏26.9	GAGARIN
484	18♏34.2	PITTSBURGHIA
1149	23♏16.5	VOLGA
317	23♏29.0	ROXANE
1444	25♏32.4	PANNONIA
139	26♏00.7	JUEWA
1966	26♏15.2	TRISTAN
2308	26♏24.5	RETSINA
2076	27♏17.2	HEILONGJIANG
399	27♏48.7	PERSEPHONE
1702	0♐18.5	KALAHARI
2054	1♐02.6	GAWAIN
1336	1♐09.5	ZEELANDIA
382	1♐23.6	DODONA
2230	2♐08.7	YUNNAN
2283	3♐16.2	BRADLEY
2055	3♐27.7	DVORAK
1930	3♐40.6	LUCIFER
1431	5♐09.9	GUERNICA
1430	5♐53.6	SOMALIA
1813	6♐27.0	IMHOTEP
2598	8♐15.0	MERLIN
432	11♐07.4	PYTHIA
1132	13♐01.4	HOLLANDIA
2171	14♐03.2	KIEV
1686	15♐05.8	DE-SITTER
120	16♐10.6	LACHESIS
932	16♐35.9	HOOVERIA
29	18♐19.9	AMPHITRITE
1159	18♐38.0	GRANADA
3198	19♐47.9	WALLONIA
1077	20♐00.5	TEUTONIA
2437	22♐15.3	AMNESTIA
1130	22♐44.2	SKULD
2	24♐04.1R	PALLAS
546	25♐40.0R	HERODIAS
310	25♐51.2R	MARGARITA
1870	25♐56.4R	GLAUKOS
466	26♐19.9R	TISIPHONE
1125	26♐23.3R	CHINA
1584	26♐56.9R	FUJI
1157	28♐54.9R	ARABIA

Figure XXIV
Asteroid Listing for Lunation
Monaco, Monaco Aug 18, 1982 4h 45m 27s Zone -1.0

1629	PECKER	22♍04.8	2	PALLAS	22♎32.1	3361	ORPHEUS	5♐52.8	32	POMONA	26♑25.8R
1193	AFRICA	22♍42.9	1866	SISYPHUS	22♎49.2	2102	TANTALUS	5♐57.7R	1566	ICARUS	27♑14.4R
2631	ZHEJIANG	23♍12.3	464	MEGAIRA	23♎37.3	631	PHILIPPINA	6♐37.3	2031	BAM	27♑58.8R
2117	DANMARK	24♍29.8	445	EDNA	24♎01.6	323	BRUCIA	7♐34.5	1312	VASSAR	0♒33.1R
532	HERCULINA	25♍12.2	671	CARNEGIA	24♎31.2	1940	WHIPPLE	7♐44.9	2807	KARL-MARX	2♒55.3R
2101	ADONIS	25♍28.9	790	PRETORIA	24♎33.8	1277	DOLORES	8♐02.1	770	BALI	3♒56.9R
310	MARGARITA	25♍57.6	1703	BARRY	29♎01.4	2398	JILIN	8♐18.1	1771	MAKOVER	4♒32.4R
580	SELENE	26♍51.1	2709	SAGAN	0♏21.1	203	POMPEJA	8♐59.7	399	PERSEPHONE	6♒29.7R
95	ARETHUSA	27♍14.8	1140	CRIMEA	0♏43.9	2365	INTERKOSMOS	11♐36.5	2118	FLAGSTAFF	7♒12.4R
16	PSYCHE	27♍50.3	1705	TAPIO	0♏59.2	1966	TRISTAN	14♐13.6	3052	HERZEN	7♒16.6R
2584	TURKMENIA	27♍51.6	1563	NOEL	1♏56.7	2741	VALDIVIA	14♐33.0	1702	KALAHARI	8♒12.0R
2473	HEYERDAHL	28♍10.2	3147	SAMANTHA	1♏57.4	1537	TRANSYLVANIA	16♐03.7	136	AUSTRIA	9♒15.9R
498	TOKIO	29♍12.3	1125	CHINA	2♏52.8	2510	SHANDONG	17♐15.4	2170	BYELORUSSIA	11♒34.0R
2351	O'HIGGINS	0♎19.0	334	CHICAGO	3♏24.2	2456	PALAMEDES	18♐10.8	1915	QUETZALCOATL	13♒03.3R
3012	MINSK	2♎33.5	78	DIANA	4♏07.2	780	ARMENIA	19♐15.8	2315	CZECHOSLOVAKIA	13♒14.2R
2046	LENINGRAD	3♎04.6	2297	DAGHESTAN	4♏20.3	1108	DEMETER	19♐36.2	232	RUSSIA	13♒37.7R
2059	BABOQUIVARI	4♎30.3	80	SAPPHO	4♏54.3	340	EDUARDA	22♐16.9	2791	PARADISE	15♒03.0R
2053	NUKI	4♎34.7	585	BILKIS	5♏30.6	2210	LOIS	22♐31.7	4	VESTA	15♒24.4R
2155	WODAN	5♎23.7	433	EROS	5♏38.2	123	BRUNHILD	23♐58.6	3199	NEFERTITI	16♒33.7R
40	HARMONIA	5♎26.2	1149	VOLGA	5♏59.1	3	JUNO	24♐16.6R	3352	MCAULIFFE	16♒56.9R
81	TERPSICHORE	5♎48.3	1810	EPIMETHEUS	6♏09.4	42	ISIS	24♐18.1	2041	LANCELOT	17♒07.4R
3198	WALLONIA	6♎32.0	287	NEPHTHYS	7♏23.9	2483	GUINEVERE	24♐33.9R	2462	NEHALENNIA	17♒51.3R
418	ALEMANNIA	6♎49.7	2174	ASMODEUS	7♏57.0	307	NIKE	26♐17.7R	156	XANTHIPPE	18♒31.4R
350	ORNAMENTA	6♎50.1	1027	AESCULAPIA	8♏03.1	3338	RICHTER	27♐18.8	224	OCEANA	19♒18.0R
763	CUPIDO	7♎03.4	97	KLOTHO	9♏31.0	2355	NEI_MONGGOL	28♐26.2	2200	PASADENA	19♒45.8R
408	FAMA	7♎32.5	436	PATRICIA	11♏17.4	2146	STENTOR	28♐47.2R	2230	YUNNAN	19♒56.9R
466	TISIPHONE	7♎41.9	2682	SOROMUNDI	11♏33.3	1923	OSIRIS	28♐53.2	797	MONTANA	20♒11.7R
804	HISPANIA	7♎49.7	288	GLAUKE	12♏11.6	2228	SOYUZ-APOLLO	29♐20.9R	2779	MARY	26♒48.6R
1584	FUJI	8♎03.1	1224	FANTASIA	12♏14.4	1282	UTOPIA	29♐36.4R	2410	MORRISON	28♒06.2R
144	VIBILIA	8♎15.2	793	ARIZONA	14♏01.1	2214	CAROL	0♑14.6	140	SIWA	29♒18.2R
564	DUDU	8♎41.2	1170	SIVA	15♏18.0	24	THEMIS	0♑34.6R	1541	ESTONIA	29♒31.7R
3554	AMUN	9♎33.8	279	THULE	15♏20.0	1184	GAEA	1♑28.9	1281	JEANNE	1♓02.3R
6	HEBE	9♎38.1	2239	PARACELSUS	16♏00.5	100	HEKATE	1♑29.3	67	ASIA	2♓49.3R
244	SITA	9♎51.2	51	NEMAUSA	16♏18.5	2367	PRAHA	4♑00.2R	679	PAX	3♓37.7R
3362	KHUFU	10♎55.1	616	ELLY	17♏21.6	2148	EPEIOS	5♑07.7R	895	HELIO	3♓42.1R
179	KLYTAEMNESTRA	10♎55.6	1	CERES	19♏56.7	3288	SELEUCUS	5♑39.8	2436	HATSHEPSUT	5♓01.7R
712	BOLIVIANA	11♎10.2	2720	PYOTR_PERVYJ	20♏08.0	1345	POTOMAC	5♑43.9R	2469	TADJIKISTAN	5♓58.3R
474	PRUDENTIA	11♎23.5	546	HERODIAS	20♏17.9	1430	SOMALIA	6♑43.1	2045	PEKING	8♓53.3R
3218	DELPHINE	11♎24.5	2979	MURMANSK	20♏54.6	430	HYBRIS	6♑46.3R	50	VIRGINIA	9♓04.3R
120	LACHESIS	11♎30.3	511	DAVIDA	21♏18.0	251	SOPHIA	7♑44.7R	469	ARGENTINA	9♓15.1R
2344	XIZANG	11♎45.6	1044	TEUTONIA	21♏29.6	576	EMANUELA	8♑12.6R	1336	ZEELANDIA	12♓15.1R
77	FRIGGA	12♎21.0	944	HIDALGO	21♏46.2	1130	SKULD	9♑11.7	265	ANNA	14♓04.3R
2698	AZERBAJDZHAN	12♎46.9	747	WINCHESTER	23♏20.7	1640	NEMO	9♑18.6	3355	ONIZUKA	16♓26.8R
371	BOHEMIA	13♎54.2	2335	JAMES	26♏33.6	1554	YUGOSLAVIA	9♑34.0R	1288	SANTA	16♓33.3R
7	IRIS	14♎40.1	2152	HANNIBAL	27♏45.0	472	ROMA	10♑46.7R	3039	YANGEL	17♓28.6R
886	WASHINGTONIA	15♎45.3	2736	OPS	29♏24.8	44	NYSA	11♑14.4R	2369	CHEKHOV	18♓54.1R
211	ISOLDA	15♎59.2	2202	PELE	29♏44.4	953	PAINLEVA	11♑48.9R	1763	WILLIAMS	19♓14.9R
2660	WASSERMAN	16♎06.0	1242	ZAMBESIA	0♐21.3	1143	ODYSSEUS	15♑15.1R	716	BERKELEY	20♓47.8R
2657	BASHKIRIA	18♎12.3	1798	WATTS	1♐31.8	3063	MAKHAON	16♑44.9R	29	AMPHITRITE	21♓30.2R
103	HERA	20♎08.1	293	BRASILIA	1♐59.5	3449	ABELL	17♑07.7R	2270	YAZHI	21♓50.9R
1139	ATAMI	20♎09.8	890	WALTRAUT	3♐02.2	2976	LAUTARO	18♑06.6R	434	HUNGARIA	23♓20.3R
3009	COVENTRY	20♎56.9	2362	MARK TWAIN	3♐51.1	313	CHALDAEA	20♑15.9R	1718	NAMIBIA	23♓50.9R
444	GYPTIS	20♎58.9	1258	SICILIA	4♐05.2	2670	CHUVASHIA	21♑08.0R	2815	SOMA	25♓54.0R
1930	LUCIFER	21♎31.7	3018	GODIVA	4♐08.5	660	CRESCENTIA	24♑31.9R	99	DIKE	28♓15.2R
1138	ATTICA	21♎44.0	151	ABUNDANTIA	4♐09.7	1914	HARTBEESPOORTDAM	24♑44.5R	3050	CARRERA	28♓17.4R
2668	TATARIA	22♎26.3	1142	AETOLIA	4♐33.3	829	ACADEMIA	25♑23.6R	2382	NONIE	28♓30.2R
397	VIENNA	22♎26.6	443	PHOTOGRAPHICA	5♐48.3	981	MARTINA	25♑49.5R	275	SAPIENTIA	28♓59.6R

her Patricia at 01° Libra 21'. Patricia is exactly semisquare, and Isis is exactly sesquiquadrate, her East Point at 16° Scorpio 07', tying these asteroids to her "self." Patricia is the name asteroid most relevant to Grace, and she was always known for a patrician and composed Lunar quality. (The funereal and familial involvements of Egyptian mythology are also appropriate.)

DISTINCTIONS OF TIME

The time a lunation occurs gives insight into its meaning too. The lunation (geometric conjunction) occurred in Monaco at 04:45:27 AM. That time can be the woman (04h), in relation to the "king of the gods" (45m), in regard to completion (27s). The Full Moon (geometric opposition), the culmination of the lunation, occurred in Monaco at 02:28:53 PM. That time can be the death of the partner (02h), in relation to government (28m), in regard to death (53s). These are both Daylight Saving Time, which is what is external. What is *behind* the 4 is a 3 (transportation), and what is *behind* the 2 is a 1 (accident).

OTHER CHARTS AND LOCATIONS

The lunation chart in Monaco was placed around the natal chart of Grace to show the former's relationship to the latter. However, the lunation chart is relevant to Monaco. That chart could be placed around the natal chart of Monaco or be looked at as a separate chart. For instance, the lunation chart as a separate chart set for Monaco has the lunation in the second house of the partner's death; Saturn at 18° Libra 27', exactly conjunct the IC at 17° Libra 13', in a T-Square; Mercury at 17° Virgo 21' in the third house, exactly conjunct the third house cusp at 16° Virgo 30', with Mercury ruling itself, the third house cusp and an eleventh house interception. This in a lunar month when the partner of Monaco's ruler died unexpectedly from an accident on a short trip.

Not only the lunation chart in Monaco is relevant. The lunation chart in Philadelphia is also—now in terms of the place where Grace was born. For instance, the lunation chart as a separate chart set for Philadelphia has the Ascendant at 07° Taurus 51', exactly opposite the Uranian planet Cupido (♃) at 07° Scorpio 36', Descendant (07° Scorpio 51'). Cupido is family, and most of Grace's family still lives in Philadelphia. This Ascendant-Descendant opposition is between the lunation square and the lunation Cosmic Square and pulls in Grace's Uranian planet Kronos (♈) at 08° Taurus 41'ʀ. Of course, Grace is one of Philadelphia's most prominent natives (Kronos). Interestingly, while the Ascendant-Descendant in Philadelphia is between the lunation square and the lunation Cosmic Square, the Ascendant-Descendant in Monaco contacts the lunation square, and the Ascendant-Descendant in New York contacts the lunation Cosmic Square. The lunation chart as a separate chart set for New York has the Ascendant at 10° Taurus 11', with Admetos exactly conjunct it. Though much has been written about Grace's accident and death, I don't believe they have been previously written about in terms of the lunation. I was born in New York and experienced this lunation in New York, and five years later in New York I'm writing about this lunation in regard to Grace's accident and death (Admetos).

SIGNS AND PORTENTS

My experience is that there are always signs, always portents, but for the most part we do not see them, at least not consciously. Perhaps they are sensed unconsciously. Films, plays and books, filled with creative choices fraught with meaning, are a prime source of these signs and portents. The film Grace was making when she met Prince Rainier was *To Catch a Thief*.[2] She played the part of Frances Stevens. Frances means "from France" and Steven means "crowned one," which is what Grace became through this meeting. In the movie, Frances Stevens is supposed to be driving on the same road on which Grace, coming "from France," later had her fatal accident. Cary Grant, her co-star in this film, was the only Hollywood star at her funeral. Within this film are intimations of Grace's marriage to follow in a year and her accident and death in 27 years.

Observations on Lunations

Having completed my analysis of the August 1982 lunation, in regard to Princess Grace's chart, I shall make some observations on lunations in general.

CONNECTING LINK

The lunation or eclipse is a connecting link between people. The lunation gives bearings or a "fix" for the month; the eclipse gives a fix until the next eclipse period. For a month, transits to the lunation are significant. For at least six months, transits to the eclipse are significant. Everyone is affected by that fix. Everyone is affected differently because of the different natal houses, bodies and points that are activated, but affected nevertheless. Also, the different expression of those houses, bodies and points in the natal chart affects their expression in the lunation chart, as well as in other event charts. Natal placements, rulerships and exact aspects are always relevant. Just as the lunation or eclipse chart gives a fix for the month or six months, the birth chart gives a fix for the lifetime.

As an example of an effect on people in general, there is the meeting of the MTA (Metropolitan Transportation Authority) in Manhattan on April 13, 1977. This was a meeting, concerning the curtailment of subway services, to which the public was invited. My husband and I, who had been active in an effort to lessen this curtailment, attended the meeting. Shortly after the meeting began at 08:30 AM EST, violence erupted. People, including white-haired elderly women, stormed the podium. The energy was very Martian, and though my husband and I did not take part in the violence, we were surrounded by it. There are no classic Mars aspects in the transiting chart, but there are between the transiting chart and the lunation chart. The lunation had occurred March 19, 1977 at 01:33:20 PM EST. Lunation Mars had been at 29° Aquarius 45'. At the beginning of the meeting (08:30 AM), the transiting Moon was 27° Aquarius 40', and the transiting Midheaven was 27° Aquarius 59'51.36". The transiting Moon and Midheaven were coming to this erratic (Aquarius and 29°) Martian energy, characteristic of this lunar month. (The Midheaven would be conjunct, from one degree to the next, seconds after 08:30 AM, and the meeting probably didn't start until then. I was not recording to the second in 1977.)

Of course, there are other ramifications of this lunation and this transiting chart. To mention a couple, the transiting Midheaven had come from its 23° Aries 18' position at the lunation, exactly conjunct Venus (24° Aries 17'℞) and the South Node (24° Aries 23'). At the meeting the transiting Sun at 23° Aries 30' and transiting South Node at 24° Aries 21' were exactly conjunct the lunation Midheaven, Venus and South Node. The lunation message of restriction and status (Midheaven), combined with values (Venus), and relationships (South Node) had been activated by this conjunction from the transiting Sun and South Node. This conjunction lasted all day, and everywhere we went that day the pridefulness of the Sun, South Node, merged with that lunation message. The sign of Aries added an aggressiveness, and the relationships were sometimes swept away (South Node).

In other cities the lunation Midheaven would not have been exactly conjunct Venus and the South Node, so the effect would not have been as strong. Also, there is the lunation in reference to the natal chart of Greater New York City to be considered.

The adoption of a new charter including the five boroughs occurred January 1, 1898 at 00:01 AM EST. The lunation Midheaven, Venus, South Node (23°-24° Aries) were exactly conjunct Greater NYC's Vertex (25° Aries 51') and square its Mercury (22° Capricorn 31'℞) and Part of Fortune (25° Capricorn 27'). In this natal chart, the exact conjunction of the Vertex to the Moon at 26° Aries 40' and the exact conjunction of the Part of Fortune to the North Node at 26° Capricorn 57' pull the Moon and Moon's North Node into this configuration. With the Antivertex and South Node included, there is a Cosmic Square across the first, seventh, tenth and fourth houses. Greater NYC's natal chart has strong Lunar symbolism, which the lunation was activating. New York City is known for its social services—for its taking care of its "children"—but when "mother" doesn't take care as the children think she should, there is great anger. (My Uranus at 25° Aries 33' is exactly conjunct NYC's Vertex, Moon in that Cosmic Square, connecting me to the protest. My husband's Vesta at 22° Capricorn 39' is exactly conjunct NYC's Mercury, connecting him too.)

Also, the lunation at 29° Pisces 02'49.92" fell in Greater NYC's sixth house of service, exactly square (Lunar aspect) the city's Mars - Venus conjunction (29° Sagittarius 16' - 29° Sagittarius 54') in its third house of transportation. The Venus and Mars rule the city's first and seventh house of the self and the other. As for lunation Mars at 29° Aquarius 45', it was exactly sextile Greater NYC's Mars-Venus conjunction in the transportation house. The sextile is service, and what was being disputed was the curtailment of transportation services.

LUNATIONS VS. ECLIPSES

Another factor contributing to the disruptiveness on April 13 is that the culmination of the March 19th lunation was the April 3rd Lunar Eclipse. The Solar and Lunar Eclipses have more impact than the New and Full Moons, and the effect of the eclipses lasts longer. Also, around the time of eclipses there seems to be a more electric, or erratic, quality.

As mentioned, for an eclipse there is both an eclipse chart for the time of the peak of the eclipse and a New or Full Moon chart for the time of the exact conjunction or opposition of the Sun and Moon. As an example, April 3, 1977 at 11:09:27 PM EST, the Full Moon occurred with the Moon at 14° Libra 17'0.6" and the Sun at 14° Aries 17'0.6". At 11:18:00 PM EST, the Lunar Eclipse occurred with the Moon at 14° Libra 22'14.88" and the Sun at 14° Aries 17'21.84".

With an eclipse, the light goes out. There is disruption of the continuity. When the light comes on again, things are different or are seen differently. My observations indicate that the peak of the eclipse shows what is disrupted (eclipsed). If it is a Solar Eclipse, the beginning of the disruption is shown; a Lunar Eclipse, the culmination. On the other hand, the New Moon shows the new beginning of that lunar month; the Full Moon, the culmination. If the New Moon occurs after the Solar Eclipse there may be a new beginning for what was eclipsed.

The times of the New or Full Moon chart and the eclipse chart would be compared in terms of their numerological correspondences. Similarly, you would consider the positions of the Sun and Moon, as well as of other bodies and points. The Ascendant, Midheaven, East Point, Part of Fortune, Vertex and intermediate cusps are especially noted, since they are the most different. Their exact aspects would be compared. For instance, the Ascendant of the April 3rd Full Moon chart is 11° Sagittarius 43', while the Ascendant of the April 3rd Lunar Eclipse chart is 13° Sagittarius 29'. The Full Moon Ascendant makes exact 8th harmonic aspects (semisquares and sesquiquadrates) to Greater New York City's Cosmic Square, while the Lunar Eclipse Ascendant does not. Such contact from the Full Moon chart, rather than from the Lunar Eclipse chart, augers a less disruptive culmination. The conclusion of our fight against the curtailment of subway services was conciliatory. There was curtailment, but much less than had been announced—a compromise which both sides considered successful.

THE MEDIA AS THE MEANS

The lunation is also shown as a connecting link between people via the media. For example, when there is a particular subject matter, style or setting in several episodes and movies shown on television around a particular time, this synchronicity can usually be traced to a transit to the lunation chart. The particular emphasis will be shown in the lunation chart, and then the transits will activate that emphasis. The activation will often extend over three days if the transiting body is one (such as the Sun, Mercury or Venus) which moves approximately a degree per day. Of course, an individual may "tune in" to a particular emphasis because of an activation of his or her own chart by the lunation and the transits to it. The emphasis would also be different in different places because of different points and intermediate cusps in those places at the lunation.

LUNATION CYCLE VIS-À-VIS RETROGRADATION CYCLE

Another observation concerning lunations is that there is an overlapping of the lunation cycle by the direct and retrograde cycle of the planets and asteroids. A planet or asteroid may be going towards its station, whether direct or retrograde, at the same time that it is carrying its message from the New Moon to the Full or from one New Moon to the next. At the MTA Meeting April 13, 1977, transiting Venus had returned to its February 17, 1977 lunation position, conjunct my Uranian planet Hades. (Venus had been direct at 13° Aries and was now retrograde at 12° Aries.) In my February 17th prediction, I had associated that transiting Venus-natal Hades conjunction with the projected closing of our subway station entrance, writing that "Venus is natally in my fourth, and I feel that the loss of this entrance would definitely affect my home and its desirability." Almost two months later when I was confronting that loss, that configuration was repeated. Also, at the March 19th lunation, Vesta (home and vested interests) had returned to its February 17th lunation position. (Vesta had been retrograde at 11° Cancer and was now direct at 12° Cancer.) The result of this overlapping of different cycles is that, though each lunation is considered as a separate entity, each lunation is not entirely discrete. One lunation may relate to another. Therefore, references to a previous lunation should be noted. Each lunation is a new beginning, but there are other cycles with their own beginnings and endings.

QUARTER MOONS

As for the Quarter Moons, I only observed them toward the end of my study after reading an article by Sophia Mason in the February 23, 1982 *American Federation of Astrologers Bulletin*. This article is called "Forecasting a 'Mini-Crisis' Period with Quarter Moons." Sophia says that when the Quarter Moon makes a square, opposition or conjunction to a natal planet within a degree, there will be a mini-crisis. My observations are that, even when in hard aspect to a natal planet within a degree, the Quarter Moon does not necessarily indicate a crisis. Like the New and Full Moon, the Quarter Moon activates what it exactly aspects, but that activation has to be seen within the context of the lunar cycle. The entire lunar cycle is important, but the fix for the month is still the New Moon, and all else must be considered in relation to it. The First Quarter Moon is the midpoint between the new beginning and the culmination; the Last Quarter Moon, the midpoint between the culmination and the next new beginning. The Quarter Moons are like signposts along the way in the trip from one new beginning to another.

A realization I came to while studying the Quarter Moons is that certain relationships between bodies and/or points will result in their being activated by the lunar cycle. Between the New Moon and Quarter Moon there are approximately 97°-98°; between the New Moon and Full Moon, approximately 194°-195° (or 166°-165° on the other side of 180°). The extra 07°, in addition to the 90° of the Quarter Moon square, is for the 07° in seven days that the transiting Sun has traveled. The extra 14°, in addition to the 180° of the Full Moon opposition, is for the 14° in fourteen days that the transiting Sun has traveled. (The lunation period is 29 days, 12 hours, 44 minutes and 3 seconds, so the degrees and days in my explanation are approximate.) Bodies and/or points which are connected by the separations of the lunar phases are in readiness to be activated by the lunar cycle. The lunar cycle, being involved with the cycle of the Moon in relation to the Sun, seems to be particularly associated with man-woman, husband-wife, father-mother, ego-emotion, conscious-unconscious, relations. Those bodies and points in such a potential "lunar complex" are particularly descriptive of a combination of the Sun and Moon symbolism.

PRENATAL LUNATIONS AND ECLIPSES

Though for the most part my study concerned current lunations and eclipses, I did do some work on prenatal lunations and eclipses. It has been said by some astrologers that the last lunation and eclipse preceding a person's birth are relevant to that person. My research supports that contention.

At first I drew the prenatal lunation or eclipse around the natal chart, as had been done with the current lunations and eclipses. My procedure now is to cast the chart for the prenatal lunation or eclipse in the place of the person's birth, and then to put the person's natal chart around that lunation or eclipse chart. Reasoning after the fact as to why I might have found this reversed procedure preferable, I realized that the natal charts of people (events too) are transits to the preceding lunation and eclipse chart. In the case of current lunations and eclipses, they are transits to the natal chart. (Of course, what is current to some people and events will be prenatal to others.)

The prenatal lunation and eclipse set up preconditions for a particular period. Just as the current lunation and eclipse are a connecting link between people living at the same time and place, the prenatal lunation and eclipse are a connecting link between people born around the same time and place. There are connections between such people even if they never meet. Outer planet and Uranian planet positions connect them, but also they are connected by their prenatal lunations and eclipses.

Of course, for the people born around the same time and place, those prenatal charts will have different relevance because of the different relationships between their natal charts and those prenatal charts. The name asteroids of the people born around the same time and place, both in the natal and the prenatal charts, and the personal points in the natal charts will especially highlight the difference.

The prenatal charts also show connections to people significant to the native. For instance, the Midheaven of my prenatal eclipse chart is exactly conjunct one of my natal name asteroids, and both Midheaven and asteroid equal my daughter's natal Sun/Moon midpoint by a semisquare. In addition the Saturn of my prenatal eclipse chart equals my daughter's Sun/Moon midpoint by an opposition. Another woman has this same chart as her prenatal eclipse, and its Descendant equals her son's Sun/Moon midpoint by a conjunction. In this prenatal eclipse chart, the Descendant is exactly sesquiquadrate the Moon. (The Sun, being seven minutes in advance of the Moon, is into the next degree and so out of orb.) A third woman also has this same chart as her prenatal eclipse; and its Ceres, Venus in the fourth house equal by a conjunction, and its Neptune, Gaea in the tenth house equal by an opposition, her daughter's Sun/Moon midpoint. Ceres is a Roman symbol, and Gaea is a Greek symbol, of motherhood. Individualizing these symbols of motherhood, in the daughter's natal chart the name asteroid of her mother equals the Sun/Moon midpoint by a semisquare. The Ceres, Venus conjunction is descriptive of the mother's chart, since she has a Taurus Sun.

This eclipse chart is especially related to parental concerns with its Moon exactly semisquare and sesquiquadrate the Ascendant-Descendant axis and Saturn exactly opposition and conjunct its Midheaven-IC axis. However, as mentioned, all lunation and eclipse charts are related to Sun-Moon symbolism. In my daughter's prenatal lunation chart, the IC equals my natal Sun/Moon midpoint by a conjunction, and her father's natal Sun/Moon midpoint by a sesquiquadrate. In my daughter's prenatal eclipse chart, the Sun and Moon equal my natal Sun/Moon midpoint by a semisquare, and her father's natal Sun/Moon midpoint by a square. In my husband's prenatal eclipse chart, one of my name asteroids equals by a conjunction; the Sun, Moon and Nodes equal by a square; and Juno equals by a semisquare, my natal Sun/Moon midpoint. In my husband's prenatal lunation chart, the East Point, Ascendant-Descendant are exactly square our composite Ascendant-Descendant, while the Midheaven-IC are exactly conjunct these composite points. Not every child and parent or husband and wife will have such connections, but the connections they have will be descriptive of their relationship.

The prenatal lunation and eclipse charts operate like the current ones. The transiting bodies and points carry the message of the lunation or eclipse to the event chart—the event, in relation to a person, being his or her birth. The Full Moon shows the outcome of the New Moon, and eclipses have more impact than lunations. As with current lunations and eclipses, the whole lunar cycle should be noted. The First Quarter Moon, Full Moon or Last Quarter Moon following the prenatal lunation or eclipse may come after the birth. Even if they all do, this lunar cycle is important in terms of the person with this prenatal lunation. Connections to significant people are shown. For instance, the Last Quarter Moon following my husband's prenatal eclipse, and his birth, is conjunct my Midheaven to the minute.

Lunations, eclipses and stations are similar. All three sensitize particular positions. These astronomical events are like exclamation points—both emphasize certain parts of the "text."

On page 210 I wrote about stations of the name asteroids of significant people in my life. If the natal name asteroid was exactly conjunct its station that fact was mentioned, since the asteroid was especially emphasized. The Ascendant of my prenatal eclipse chart ties in exactly with those stations and natal positions. The Sun-Moon and Venus of my prenatal lunation chart tie in exactly too. For example, the 03° Taurus position of my husband's name asteroid, Sy (which exactly conjuncts its last retrograde station before his birth), is exactly conjunct the 04° Taurus Descendant of my prenatal eclipse chart and the 04° Taurus Sun-Moon and Venus of my prenatal lunation chart.

Lunation charts, like other charts, describe past, as well as present, lives. As I wrote on pages 205-06, asteroids describe details of past lives revealed to me either by psychics or by psychic flashes I have had myself. When names are part of those revelations, the asteroids with those names are appropriately placed. Prenatal lunations and eclipses, looked at in reference to natal charts, highlight both past-life, and present-life, connections between the relevant people.

Accuracy of Predictions

In conclusion, the purpose of my lunation study was not to predict what was going to happen, but to test the value of lunations. However, in the process of testing the value of lunations, the accuracy of my predictions increased considerably. I did not keep a tally of the percentage of times my predictions were correct. It would have been difficult to do so because some of my predictions were specific and some were general. My predictions increased in accuracy as I discovered how the astrological symbolism was manifesting for the particular person at that time. There was also improvement as I decreased the orb, allowing only an orb from one degree to the next. As asteroids, Uranian planets, and other bodies were added, my predictions became more specific. When an ephemeris for an asteroid was received, the position of that asteroid was placed in that month's and every subsequent month's charts. Not only was the lunation study a means of testing the value of the lunations, but it was a means of testing the meanings of the asteroids. In time I was even able to predict under what aspects to the lunation, natal, or transit chart a letter or phone call would be received from a particular person. Sometimes I predicted a specific event which did not occur. In that case, usually the event occurred under the aspect I said it would, but the event was a different expression of the possibilities. Usually the actual event was an even more appropriate expression of the symbolism than I had imagined.

Some mundane predictions were made, but for the most part I limited myself to personal predictions. Though the lunation was sometimes drawn around the natal charts of people who were close to me, I could make accurate predictions concerning those people from the lunation drawn around my natal chart alone. The lunation in relation to third house symbolism referred to my brother and cousins; fifth house symbolism, to my children; seventh house symbolism, to my husband, etc. The third house symbolism, for example, might be in the form of my natal third house, of the sign Gemini, of natal or transiting Mercury or of the trine. The personal name asteroids added further discrimination. Naturally, the lunation still referred to me as well.

During the last year of the project when I used those days without references to the lunation as controls for those days with references, the significance of the lunations was further supported. Events on days with lunation references (aspects to the lunation, changes of houses, signs, etc.) had greater relevance to the lunation than events on days without such references.

The lunation study also confirmed what I had already been observing. The harmonious aspects (sextiles and trines) do not necessarily correspond to positive events or conditions. The inharmonious aspects (squares and oppositions) do not necessarily correspond to negative events or conditions. The transits to the lunation, the messages the transiting bodies and points are bringing from the lunation, the positions to which the messages are being brought, have to be considered. Also, the transiting Moon can be in the same exact aspect (from one degree to the next) for several hours but can change house or sign in that time. In a couple of hours it will certainly change its degree. In a few minutes the transiting angles, other axes and intermediate cusps will change their degrees. These changes reflect a different manifestation. Aspects, as well as signs, planets and numbers, correspond to the symbolism of the houses of the natural zodiac.

The improvement in the accuracy of my predictions, resulting from this study, could be attributed, at least in part, to the fact that I was observing manifestations and recording what I observed. The very process was enlightening. However, what I found in this study is that lunations and eclipses do highlight a particular period. Lunations and eclipses shed light on that period—not the bright light of the sun, but the reflective light of the moon. Perhaps, more can be seen in the dark of the night than in the light of the day. Even the Full Moon is seen only at night, and the lunation begins with the Dark of the Moon.

CHAPTER FIVE

Solar Returns

Chapter 5 (5th house, Leo, Sun, quintile) is naturally about Solar Returns. The Solar Return is based on the premise that the return of the Sun to the exact degree, minutes and seconds of its natal position is descriptive of the ensuing year. The following is what I have observed in the process of finding this premise to be true.

Relationship to the Natal Chart

The Solar Return can be read as a separate chart, but the relationship of the Solar Return to the natal chart is always important. To better see this relationship, the Solar Return can be put around the natal chart of the person whose return it is. The Solar Return can also be put around the natal charts of people who are significant in that person's life. The cusps of the Solar Return chart should be included as was done with the Ascendant or Midheaven Equal House Chart around the natal chart (see pages 48-49). The principles of the Solar Return houses are being brought to the principles of the natal houses. For example, the Solar Return under which my son left home had its Ascendant-Descendant across his natal fourth-tenth houses and its Midheaven-IC across his natal first-seventh houses. Since he was leaving home to make his own way in the world, how appropriate that not only principles of the self-the other should activate principles of home-career (mother-father), but also principles of career-home (father-mother) should activate principles of the self-the other.

The Solar Return will reflect appropriate natal planets, asteroids, and particularly personal points, of the native and of people who are important in the native's life that year. For instance, the year my second husband, Sy, and I were married, his Solar Return angles (Ascendant-Descendant, Midheaven-IC, Antivertex-Vertex and East Point-West Point) were exactly the same as his natal angles. The repetition of the natal angles in the Solar Return always marks a significant year, but in my husband's case the repetition is especially appropriate. Natally, my husband has his East Point at 17° Leo 18', his Uranian planet Cupido at 17° Leo 51'ᴙ, his Neptune at 18° Leo 30'ᴙ, with his West Point at 17° Aquarius 18' and his Mercury at 18° Aquarius 13'. The East Point is the actual self; Cupido means marriage; and Neptune rules his Sun in Pisces in the seventh house of marriage, to which his Sun had returned. The West Point is the actual other, and its conjunction to Mercury could represent me—a double Gemini. That year, my Solar Return Vertex was exactly conjunct my husband's natal Antivertex, both at 20° Cancer. With his Solar Return's repetition of his natal angles, my Solar Return Vertex was not only conjunct his natal Antivertex, but also his Solar Return Antivertex. His Solar Return Nonie at 22° Cancer was separated by only 01° plus minutes from his Solar Return Antivertex, his natal Antivertex and my Solar Return Vertex. The Vertex and Antivertex have a fated quality. In my case, the Vertex especially relates to marriage because natally it is in my seventh house, exactly conjunct my Jupiter. Reflecting my natal angles that year was my Solar Return Ascendant-Descendant's exact conjunction to my natal Midheaven-IC. Also, my Solar Return Sy (11° Gemini) was exactly conjunct my Solar Return Venus (12° Gemini) and my natal Venus (11° Gemini), opposite my Solar Return Saturn (11° Sagittarius) and square my natal Vertex, Jupiter (12°, 13° Virgo), forming a T-Square. I'd just had a Venus Return too, and Sy (name asteroid) was to become the loving (Venus) father (Saturn) to my son.

The year I married my first husband, my Solar Return Vertex was exactly conjunct his natal Midheaven, both at 13° Sagittarius, square my natal Vertex, Jupiter, at 12° and 13° Virgo, and square my Solar Return Eduarda and Part of Fortune at 14° Pisces and North Node at 15° Pisces (T-Square). Not only is my first husband's name Edward, but the son we were to conceive was to be named Edward. Interestingly, the angles of this Solar Return were exactly the natal angles of the son who was to be conceived under this Solar Return, and I believe the purpose of this marriage was the procreation of this son. My Solar Return Ascendant, and our son's natal Ascendant, both at 27° Cancer, were forming an exact Fist of God with my Solar Return Vertex, my first husband's natal Midheaven, our Sagittarian son's natal Vertex (all 13° Sagittarius) and my natal Antivertex (12° Pisces). My first husband's Solar Return East Point (10° Gemini) was exactly square his natal East Point (10° Pisces) and his Solar Return South Node and natal Nonie (both 11° Virgo). This T-Square was connected with the Fist of God involving my Solar Return Ascendant and our son's natal Ascendant. Reflecting my natal angles that year, my first husband's Solar Return Vertex-Antivertex was exactly square my natal Ascendant-Descendant; and his Solar Return Midheaven-IC was exactly square my natal Midheaven-IC. Another personal name asteroid activation was his Solar Return Klotho (the Greek Nona) being exactly conjunct within a minute his natal Edwin (our son's and his other name asteroid), both at 05° Libra. Exact 8th harmonic aspects to my first husband's Solar Return Vertex-Antivertex and my natal Ascendant-Descendant were formed by these name asteroids.

Though the Solar Return has been spoken of in terms of a person, instead the return can be of an event. That return describes the course of that event during the ensuing year.

Solar Returns can also be cast for relationship charts, which are the midpoint in time and space between two or more charts. The Solar Return of a relationship chart is descriptive of that relationship during that ensuing year. For instance, the Solar Return of my second husband's and my relationship chart for the year we were married had the Solar Return Midheaven-IC exactly conjunct my natal Midheaven-IC; the Solar Return Vertex-Antivertex exactly conjunct my natal Vertex-Antivertex; the Solar Return Ascendant-Descendant exactly conjunct his natal West Point-East Point; and the Solar Return East Point-West Point exactly conjunct our natal Lunar Nodes.

Relocation

Regarding relocation at the time of one's Solar Return for the purpose of having more favorable angles, I have the following thoughts. Where one is located at the time of the Solar Return is relevant, but where one is located subsequently is also relevant. As an example, unintentionally at the time of her 1974 Solar Return, my daughter was in Miami Beach, Florida. She returned to New York City, her place of residence and birth, after her Solar Return. That year she began her theatrical career, appearing Off-Off-Broadway as Hedvig, the central character, in Ibsen's *The Wild Duck*. Under this Solar Return, she also made her first commercial. The Solar Return for her relocation was descriptive of her theatrical activities, but the Solar Return for her place of residence and birth was also. See Figure XXV, her Solar Return for Miami Beach, Florida, and Figure XXVI, her Solar Return for Manhattan, New York, with her natal chart around each Solar Return. The natal chart is around the Solar Return charts, so the Solar Return angles can be more easily seen.

The time a return occurs gives insight into its meaning. (The date does too, but each year the month and day will be either the same or within one day of being the same.) In both Miami Beach and New York City the Solar Return occurred at 05:11:27 AM EDT—theatrical activities, in relation to sudden changes, in regard to expansion. The ST hour of 4 (the reflected image) is what is behind the DT hour of 5 (theatrical activities). In Miami Beach the Ascendant was 13° Cancer 51', while in New York City it was 26° Cancer 40'. Though in both Miami Beach and New York City the Moon was in the fifth house of theatre at 01° Sagittarius 08', in New York City her natal name asteroid, Guinevere (26° Capricorn 38'℞), was on the horizon, appropriate for her appearing in that city as a central character in a play. Solar Return Icarus at 27° Capricorn 15'℞ was also on that Descendant. Icarus has a Leo association, often precocious, and my daughter was only fifteen and a half years old when she became an actress. She had flown to Miami Beach before her Solar Return and had flown back after it (Icarus); and Hedvig, her character, is symbolized by the wild duck (Icarus). At the end, Hedvig dies when she shoots herself in the *heart*, which is like Icarus dying when he flies too close to the *sun*. (The name of the character played is important too, but I do not have an asteroid for Hedvig.)

Figure XXV – Natal Chart around Solar Return for Relocation

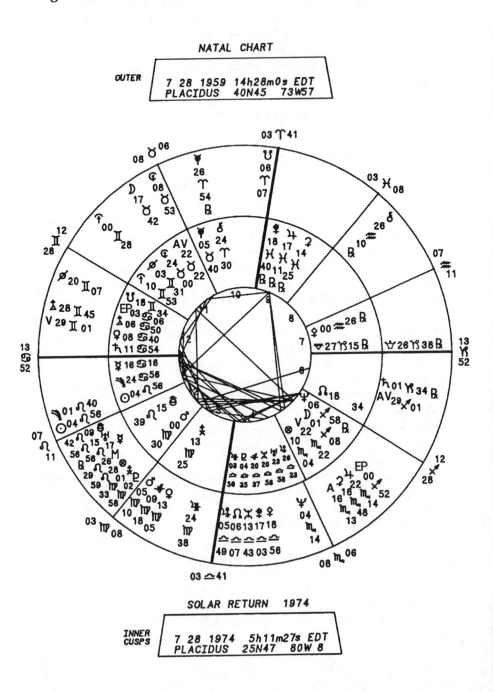

NATAL CHART

OUTER

7 28 1959 14h28m0s EDT
PLACIDUS 40N45 73W57

SOLAR RETURN   1974

INNER
CUSPS

7 28 1974 5h11m27s EDT
PLACIDUS 25N47 80W 8

Figure XXVI – Natal Chart around Solar Return for Birthplace

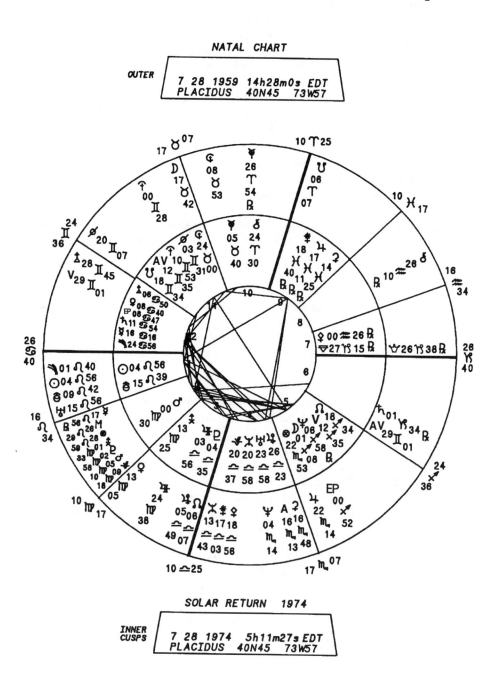

NATAL CHART

OUTER

7 28 1959   14h28m0s EDT
PLACIDUS   40N45   73W57

SOLAR RETURN   1974

INNER CUSPS

7 28 1974   5h11m27s EDT
PLACIDUS   40N45   73W57

Also in New York City, the Solar Return fifth house cusp at 17° Scorpio 06' was exactly conjunct my daughter's natal Ascendant at 16° Scorpio 12', opposite her natal Moon at 17° Taurus 42' and square her natal Mercury at 17° Leo 56'ᴙ. The Ascendant is related to acting because it is the persona; the Moon, because it is the reflected image; and Mercury, because it is communication. (Her age at this Solar Return was 15, which correlates to Mercury.) Another appropriate personal point conjunction in New York City was Solar Return Venus exactly conjunct the Solar Return East Point, both at 08° Cancer. It was in New York City that she played the part of the daughter (Venus).

Natal Jupiter was highlighted in both places. In Miami Beach, the Solar Return Vertex was at 22° Scorpio 22', exactly conjunct her natal Jupiter at 22° Scorpio 13'. The activation in Miami Beach of her Jupiter in the first house was fated (Vertex). In New York City, the Solar Return Part of Fortune was at 22° Scorpio 52', exactly conjunct her natal Jupiter at that degree. The activation in New York City of her Jupiter in the first house was fortunate (Part of Fortune). In Miami Beach, her Solar Return set the stage, while in New York City, her Solar Return placed her on that stage.

Furthermore, not only the Solar Returns for the location, residence, and birth are relevant. In fact, I believe Solar Returns for all places are relevant—in terms of the particular place. Even if at your Solar Return you are not at a particular place, were not born there and do not visit it during a Solar Year, that year is still described in terms of that place by your Solar Return in that place. As an example, under my daughter's 1974 Solar Return she signed a contract with a theatrical agency that had offices in Los Angeles, as well as in New York. She did not go to Los Angeles that year, but her Solar Return in Los Angeles describes that Los Angeles connection. In that chart, the *West* Point is even exactly conjunct the name asteroid of her *West* Coast Los Angeles agent!

In the same way, I've found that a natal chart relocated to a place, even when the person does not go to that place, describes the person in relation to that place. As an example, my relocated Ascendant in Los Angeles, California, and environs, is exactly square my Ceres at 05° Aries 35', and the Los Angeles area represents to me a place of separation from mother and mothering. My mother moved to Santa Ana in 1965 and died in Palm Springs in 1974. My son moved to Los Angeles in 1975 and is now residing in Irvine. The particular degree of the relocated Ascendant combined with the sign, in relation to the minutes, will give more detail. (My relocated Ascendant in Santa Ana is 04° Capricorn 46'; in Palm Springs, 06° Capricorn 00'; in Los Angeles, 04° Capricorn 13'; and in Irvine, 04° Capricorn 55'.)

Synchronicity of the Moment

As for timing the exact second of the Solar Return, what is happening at that exact moment is synchronous with the Solar Return, and so reflective of its meaning. For instance, at the time of my 1982 Solar Return I was at the movie *Dead Men Don't Wear Plaid*. The alarm on my calculator had been set to go off at the exact time of my Solar Return. In the film Steve Martin had just said that Veronica Lake never said No. He then asked her if she would do him a favor. She said No at the exact moment the alarm sounded. I realized that this Solar Year would relate to my saying No to something to which I never said No. (As it turned out, this Solar Year related to my saying No, and to my being told No.)

Steve Martin is not only the one who asked the question, but also the star and a co-writer of the film. Martina is the asteroid whose name is closest to the name Martin. That asteroid (05° Aquarius) was forming an exact T-Square with Klotho (06° Scorpio), the Greek Nona, and Dembowska (06° Taurus), the questioner, which Martin is in the film. Martina was emphasized in the world at that time because it was at the degree of its retrograde station which was to occur in a couple of weeks. Martina was emphasized in my Solar Return at that time because that asteroid was exactly semisquare the Solar Return Ascendant (21° Sagittarius). Also, Martina was sextile Atropos (06° Aries), and both were quincunx Eros (05° Virgo), forming an exact Finger of God. Interlocked with this exact Yod was another of Klotho sextile Eros, and both quincunx Atropos. On one level, Klotho is Nona. On another, Klotho is part of a symbolic translation of the movie's name—*Dead Men Don't Wear Plaid.* Atropos signifies Death or dead men; Klotho represents cloth; and Eros can mean "shot through." With Klotho exactly sextile (dualistic aspect) Eros in Virgo (dualistic sign), the meaning can be cloth shot through with many different threads, which plaid is.

Veronica Lake (for whom unfortunately I have no asteroids), said No to Steve Martin. The beginning of Nonie is No, and not only was the Solar Return Ascendant exactly opposition my natal Nonie (20° Gemini), but in the Solar Return chart there were five exact interlocking Fingers of God, and Solar Return Nonie (02° Pisces) was in three of them. Four of these Yods included the Vertex (03° Leo) and/or the Part of Fortune (03° Capricorn), and two included the Sun (02° Gemini). Nonie was also in an exact mutable T-Square with Uranus (02° Sagittarius) and the Sun, which interlocked with an exact Grand Trine in air of Mars, Pallas (01°, 02° Libra) and the Antivertex (03° Aquarius). (Not having the Nonie or Klotho and Atropos Ephemerides at that time, I was unaware of these configurations or of those mentioned in the paragraph above.) Nonie, as the nickname for Nona, relates to me; but as the Roman Fate equivalent to the Greek Fate Klotho, it also relates to cloth. With Nonie exactly square both the Sun (conjunct the cusp of and in the dualistic sixth house, in the dualistic Gemini sign) and the Uranus (to which the work "motley" is related[1]), the meaning can be plaid. Plaid is woven cloth; both the Fates Klotho and Nona were weavers; and motley is a combination of different colors, as in plaid.

Plaid is associated with the Scottish, and one of the expressions of this Solar Return was the following. The McComb Family Bible, which I was to inherit, had been discarded through the negligence of the lawyer for the estate. This Bible had belonged to my Scottish maternal grandfather, William McComb. (At the Solar Return, Klotho was exactly conjunct the Uranian planet Cupido, which means family.) There could be no adequate compensation for this loss, but I had sought redress through the probate court. (At the Solar Return, Pallas, which relates to law, was exactly conjunct Mars, and both were part of two of the Fingers of God with Nonie. Jupiter was part of another one of the Yods.) It was during this Solar Year that I learned from their lawyer that the bonding company would give no compensation for the loss of the family Bible of my Scottish forebears. Emphasizing the Scottish theme further, the last name of the bonding company's lawyer was Scottish, as was the last name of the Clerk of the Probate Court with whom I first filed my complaint, as was the first name of the lawyer for the estate.

Transits to the Solar Return

Transits to the Solar Return activate its potential. At the time the lawyer for the bonding company said No to me regarding compensation, the five interlocking Solar Return Fingers of God were aspected. The exact conjunctions were from the transiting Moon (01° Libra) to Solar Return Mars, Pallas (01°, 02° Libra); from the transiting South Node (04° Capricorn) to the Solar Return Part of Fortune (03° Capricorn); from the transiting Vertex (03° Scorpio) to Solar Return Jupiter (02° Scorpio); and from the transiting Antivertex (03° Taurus) to Solar Return Roberta (03° Taurus). (At the Solar Return, Roberta was with Nonie and Mars, Pallas, in one of the five interlocking Fingers of God.) Apropos of the Scottish theme, Roberta is associated with Robert the Bruce, King of Scotland, "who preserved his country's independence." The Solar Return Grand Trine of Mars, Pallas, the Antivertex and the Sun, and the Solar Return T-Square of the Sun, Uranus and Nonie, were therefore aspected as well. The transiting Moon was sesquiquadrate transiting Martina (16° Aquarius) and square my Vesta (00° Cancer), forming an exact Fist of God. (I was losing my "vested interests"—Vesta—in the family—Cancer.)

The Solar Return T-Square with Martina, Klotho and Dembowska and the two Solar Return interlocking Fingers of God with Martina, Atropos, Eros and Klotho were activated by the transiting Nodes and Uranus. In fact, the transiting North Node (04° Cancer) and Uranus (05° Sagittarius) formed two interlocking Fingers of God with Solar Return Martina and Dembowska. (The question was being answered.) The transiting North Node at 04° Cancer was a connecting link. Its 04° connected the 05° Aquarius and 05° Virgo of Solar Return Martina and Eros with the 03° Aquarius of the Antivertex in the Solar Return Grand Trine and with the 03° Leo of the Vertex, the 03° Capricorn of the Part of Fortune and the 03° Taurus of Roberta in the Solar Return interlocking Yods.

Progressions to the Solar Return

Progressions to the Solar Return also activate its potential. At the time the lawyer for the bonding company said No to me regarding compensation, the five interlocking Solar Return Fingers of God were aspected. Some exact aspects were my progressed Mars (03° Libra) conjunct Solar Return Mars, Pallas; my progressed ninth cusp (03° Capricorn) conjunct the Solar Return Part of Fortune; and my progressed Klotho (01° Virgo) opposite Solar Return Nonie. The Solar Return Grand Trine of Mars, Pallas, the Antivertex and the Sun, and the Solar Return T-Square of the Sun, Uranus and Nonie, were therefore aspected as well.

The Solar Return T-Square with Martina, Klotho and Dembowska, and the two Solar Return interlocking Fingers of God with Martina, Atropos, Eros and Klotho, were activated by progressed Nonie at 06° Cancer. Also, the progressed Antivertex at 19° Aries, progressed Sun at 19° Cancer and progressed Vertex at 19° Libra formed 8th harmonic aspects to Solar Return Eros.

The lawyer for the bonding company said No to my application for compensation, but I had said No to the negligence of the lawyer for the estate. Though I received no compensation, my objective was achieved because the lawyer for the estate was censured by the court.

Progressions of the Solar Return

The Solar Return itself can be progressed. The Solar Quotidian is a method of progression in which the angles advance approximately one degree per day. The Sun advances approximately one degree, and the Moon approximately twelve degrees, per year. During a year, the planets and asteroids also progress at the rate of their daily movement. Primarily, the progressed angles and Moon catalyze the solar return and natal positions. Though this type of progression is meaningful, I have discovered another type which is meaningful too. As I wrote regarding harmonic charts, an interval of space can equate to an interval of time. One degree of angular separation can equate to one month of time. Progressing both the bodies and points a degree per month shows when particular parts of the year's message will be catalyzed. And, as stated regarding harmonic charts, since the number is paramount, different periods of time are interchangeable. A number of degrees can represent a number of days or a number of weeks, as well as a number of months, within the year. When you see a repeated separation between bodies and/or points, you can figure that events, which are described by those bodies and/or points, will occur in that number of months, of weeks and of days.

As with all of astrology, the events may be a mixture of literal and figurative expressions. For instance, there may be a repeated three-degree separation between bodies and/or points which can describe your literally listening to the album "The Tempest" three days after your Solar Return. That repeated three-degree separation may describe as well your figuratively having a tempest in your life three months after your Solar Return.

Synchronicity in the Media

Also, there is synchronicity between your Solar Return and what is in the newspapers, or other media, on the day of your Solar Return. (The emphasis may be different in places whose newspapers and other media are different.) The Sunday sections of the newspaper, and some magazines, come out only once a week. If your Solar Return does not fall on the date of their publication, those weekly sections, and magazines, that come out within the week after your Solar Return are reflective of your Solar Return. Of course, the reflection of the Solar Return is always in relation to the natal chart.

Other Returns

There are returns other than the Solar that are significant. The Lunar Return is the return of the Moon to the exact degree, minutes and seconds of its natal position. Rather than the ensuing year, that return is descriptive of the ensuing month.

Another difference I've found is that the Solar Return has a Solar quality, while the Lunar Return has a Lunar quality. In other words, the Solar Return is related to the ego, conscious and self-expression, while the Lunar Return is related to the emotions, unconscious and family.

There are also planet, asteroid and true Lunar Node returns, and they are related to the concerns of the particular planet or asteroid or the Lunar Node. For example, Venus Returns are related to love and money; Juno Returns, to marriage; and the Lunar Node Returns, to close connections. Individual concerns of the planet, asteroid or Node, as well as of the Sun or Moon, are shown in the natal chart. The asteroids for which Astro calculates returns are Ceres, Pallas, Juno, Vesta and Chiron. (Returns of Halley's Comet [for this century], Transpluto, the Uranian planets and Dark Moon Lilith can be cast too.)

The return of the planet, asteroid or Lunar Node is descriptive of the period until the planet, asteroid or Lunar Node's next return. For example, the last Juno Return before a marriage is descriptive of that marriage. Returns of Neptune and Pluto are approximate because these planets are moving so slowly that several hours of time can equate to one second of arc. Returns of the Sun, Moon, planets and asteroids, even if they are outside the life span, still seem to have relevance to the native.

Activations of one return by another highlight certain periods. For instance, the Sun in a Lunar Return being exactly conjunct the Midheaven in that year's Solar Return would highlight that month.

DIFFERENCES BETWEEN GEOMETRIC AND APPARENT RETURNS

As mentioned in Chapter 2, the seconds difference between the geometric and the apparent positions of the planets and asteroids can make degrees differences in the angles of the planet or asteroid returns. With Solar, Lunar and Lunar Node Returns, there will be no differences between the angles of the geometric return and the angles of the apparent return. The reason is that the formula for calculating geometric positions is:

$$\text{geometric position} = \text{apparent position} + \left(\frac{8.32 \text{ minutes} \times \text{A.U. distance to Earth}}{1440} \right) \times \text{daily motion}$$

(A. U. means astronomical unit, which is the mean distance between the Earth and the Sun; 8.32 minutes is the time it takes light to travel 1 A. U.; and 1440 is the number of minutes in a day.) Since distance and daily motion are factors in this formula, if there are differences between the distance and/or daily motion at the time of birth and the distance and/or daily motion at the time of the return, there can be differences in the angles. The return Sun has the same distance and motion as the natal Sun. The return Moon does not necessarily have the same distance and motion as the natal Moon, but the Moon is so close to the Earth that the differences are negligible. The Lunar Node differences are similarly inconsequential. On the other hand, the distance and daily motion of the return planet or asteroid can be very different from those of the natal planet or asteroid, and the planets and asteroids are not so close to the Earth that these differences are negligible. Therefore, the angles of the geometric planet or asteroid return can be very different from the angles of the apparent planet or asteroid return. When there are differences, I find the geometric return more descriptive. (Similarly, the return of Halley's Comet, Transpluto, the Uranian planets and Dark Moon Lilith could be very different.)

Precession Corrected Tropical Returns

Though my research has primarily been on the tropical return without precession, I have done some investigation of the precession corrected tropical return. The precession corrected tropical return allows for the precession of the equinoxes, which move backwards at approximately 50" per year. As a result, the Sun in the Solar Return, the Moon in the Lunar Return, and the planet or asteroid in the planet or asteroid return moves forward in the zodiac approximately 50" per year. The precession corrected tropical return is the same as the sidereal return, only the latter is in the framework of the sidereal zodiac. The ayanamsa (the difference between the tropical and sidereal zodiac) is approximately 24° at this time. Consequently, the placements and aspects of the precession corrected tropical return and the sidereal return are the same, but the positions in the sidereal return are approximately 24° earlier in the zodiac.

After comparing precession corrected tropical Solar and Lunar Returns to non-precession corrected tropical Solar and Lunar Returns, I have come to the conclusion that precession corrected Solar and Lunar Returns also have validity. They appear to say the same thing as the non-precession corrected Solar and Lunar Returns, but more obscurely.

As an example, the year my mother died, my non-precession corrected Solar Return had Saturn (03° Cancer 37') exactly conjunct the Moon (03° Cancer 05') and square Pluto (04° Libra 11'ℝ). The conjunction is the aspect of the self; and the square, the aspect of the mother. With the Ascendant at 07° Capricorn 59', Saturn is the ruler of the chart. Saturn is also the signifier of separation and of the more authoritative parent. The Moon is the signifier of the more nurturing parent, as is the sign Cancer. Pluto can relate to death, and its degree (4) is the Lunar number. This Solar Return square was forming an exact T-Square with my natal Ceres (05° Aries 35'); and Ceres is that symbol of the mother which relates specifically to the separation of mother and daughter. My relocated Ascendant (06° Capricorn 00') in Palm Springs, where my mother died, was tying in exactly too—square my natal Ceres and conjunct my Solar Return Ascendant. On the other hand, with my precession corrected Solar Return, the Moon at 11° Cancer 49' was no longer exactly conjunct Saturn but had moved to the midpoint of Mars and Saturn (12° Cancer 11'). One reading of this planetary picture is death of the mother. This interpretation is the same as my interpretation of the exact T-Square, but this planetary picture is not as obvious as that major configuration.

There are other corresponding emphases. For instance, with the non-precession corrected return. the Antivertex was in the first house separated by 01° plus minutes from the second house cusp and by minutes from my natal Saturn. The second house is the house of the death of the other, and Saturn is the planet of the more authoritative parent, which I considered my mother to be. With the precession corrected return, Pluto (repeating the first-second house emphasis) was in the first house, exactly conjunct the second house cusp; Neptune (repeating the emphasis on natal Saturn symbolism) was exactly conjunct the IC and my natal Midheaven; the Ascendant (repeating the emphasis on the fated Vertex-Antivertex axis) was 11° Virgo 17', exactly conjunct my natal Vertex, Jupiter at 12° and 13° Virgo. (As for the Jupiter, my mother was a Sagittarian.)

These corresponding emphases illustrate the fact that the symbolism of the two returns is the same, but a comparison of the Ascendants illustrates again that the precession corrected Solar Return is less obvious. As with the planetary picture versus the T-Square, the precession corrected Solar Return's 11° Virgo 17' Ascendant does not describe, as obviously as does the non-precession corrected Solar Return's 07° Capricorn 59' Ascendant, a year of separation from one's mother.

Parallels between these two types of returns happen repeatedly—to the extent that I cannot consider the happening coincidental. My only explanation for this parallelism is that it may be a form of antiscion, or mirror image, which reflects our destiny twice.

Endings and New Beginnings

Another observation I've made regarding returns is that often, just before the new return, something happens which is an expression of the old return. It is as if the new theme could not be introduced before the old theme had been given a grand finale!

To close, returns of the Sun, as well as of the Moon, planets and asteroids, mark the new beginning of a cycle after the closure of the cycle's previous new beginning. What is happening at that moment is reflective of the meaning of that new beginning, in relation to the person or entity whose return it is. When there are differences between the geometric and the apparent returns, the geometric show the actual closures and new beginnings within those never-ending cycles.

CHAPTER SIX

Research

Chapter 6 is about research—statistical and clinical. This chapter begins with my article "The New York Suicide Study," which appeared in 1978 in the *Journal of Geocosmic Research,* Vol. 2, No. 2, published by the National Council for Geocosmic Research, Inc. That study is statistical. The article is followed by the presentation of research conducted after the article was ready for publication and by a discussion of research in general.

As mentioned, asteroids were to be the subject of Chapter 6, but when Chapter 2 was almost finished I was asked to write a booklet on asteroids for ACS Publications. Chapter 6 couldn't be written before Chapters 3, 4 and 5, so the asteroid chapter became the third; and this chapter, the sixth. That part of my third chapter that concerns the NCGR Personal Name Asteroid Study is the basis for my booklet, *Personal Name Asteroids,* which was published at the end of 1987. The subject of Chapter 6 (6th house, Virgo, Mercury, sextile) is appropriately research, since these astrological correlates symbolize this analytical process.

The New York Suicide Study

Since March 11, 1974, the New York Chapter of NCGR has been involved in an astrological study of suicide. Our overall hypothesis was that there would be some pattern discernible in the astrological charts of suicides that would be absent in those of a control group. Many different patterns were investigated. What follows is an account of the tests we have done so far.

GATHERING THE DATA

Suicide appeared to be a good subject for research because it is a specific timed act, and official certification seemed a clear-cut criterion for selecting our cases. Luann Russell, Joanna Shannon, and I gained access to the public records and copied off information on all the certified suicides that occurred in New York City during a five-year period from 1969 through 1973. There were 2,250 certified suicides during this period. We recorded the death data, such as time, place, and method of suicide, as well as the birth data, such as day and place. But we were only able to obtain birth times for those who were born in New York City after 1930. The reason is that we only had access to New York City records, and birth times were not recorded there until 1931. As a result, the timed births number only 311, about 14 percent of the total. However, we have the preliminary data for many suicides born outside New York City, and in the future may be able to gather the birth times in other cities, states, and countries.

COLLECTING A CONTROL GROUP

We also collected 311 controls born in the same years and boroughs of New York City as the suicides. We felt that it was necessary for the controls to be born in the same years as the suicides so that the two groups would have the same outer-planet configurations. Identical years also equalize inner-planet aberrations, such as Mars sometimes being in the same sign for six months. We chose controls from the same boroughs as the suicides so as to get a similar cross-section of New York City for both groups.

Before selecting the controls, we took the suicides (which had been gathered according to suicide year and borough) and rearranged them according to birth year and borough. We then arranged the years chronologically and proceeded through each year and borough selecting an equal number of controls as we had suicides.

The controls were selected using *Tables of Random Sampling Numbers* by M.G. Kendall and B. B. Smith (London: Cambridge University Press, 1939). Within each year and borough the birth certificates have five-digit serial numbers beginning with 00001. Taking the first five digits in the random-number tables, we looked for a birth certificate in the first year and borough that had a corresponding serial number. If the random number was higher than any serial number for that year and borough, we marked the random number "too high" and proceeded to the next random number. If the corresponding birth certificate had no time of birth on it, we marked the random number "no time" and moved on. In this way we could not be accused of arbitrarily discarding a number. We proceeded straight through the random-number tables without going back to the beginning for each year or borough.

The controls are unknown to us. I did check to see that we hadn't by chance accessed any of the New York City suicides from 1969 through 1973. We had not, but it is possible that some of the controls did commit suicide in other years in New York City, or in the same years in other places. This supposition is very unlikely, however, because the percentage of people who commit suicide is extremely small.

We could have chosen as controls people who were dead of causes other than suicide. But since the earliest timed births were in 1931 and the latest suicides were in 1973, our controls could be no older than 42, and most would have had to be younger. We decided that since death before 42 years of age is unusual, it would be preferable to have a control group of "average" people, randomly selected.

ANOTHER DATA SOURCE

Nevertheless, we did run tests on 52 suicides with 41 controls who had all died of causes other than suicide. This data was gathered in Michigan by Luci Titunik. We did not include these suicides and controls in our final study, however, because we wanted a homogeneous group. Also, the Michigan controls were not necessarily born in the same years as the Michigan suicides, and so were not a good control group as far as planetary configurations are concerned.

INITIAL ANALYSIS OF THE DATA

Birth charts with the ten traditional planets, four major asteroids, and eight Uranian planets were erected by Neil Michelsen's Astro Computing Services, using Placidus house cusps. In addition to erecting the charts, the computer produced summaries of: the traditional planets and the asteroids in signs, houses, elements, and qualities; the signs on Placidus house cusps; the houses in which the house rulers are located; the houses in which the rulers of the intercepted signs are located; the aspects (repeated several times, using various orbs), including the classic aspects (conjunction, semisextile, sextile, square, trine, inconjunct, and opposition) and lesser-used ones (semisquare, sesquisquare, quintile, and biquintile); 1°-orb midpoints, with hard aspects (conjunction, semisquare, square, sesquisquare, opposition) and soft aspects (semisextile, sextile, trine, inconjunct) to the midpoints.

The summary program we used belongs to Dr. Zipporah Dobyns, who uses soft as well as hard aspects to the midpoints. Though soft aspects to the midpoints may be meaningful, we eventually intend to summarize the hard and soft aspects separately. Also, at the time that we did our initial analyses, the Uranian planets were not included in the summaries because they were not yet on the computer disk and thus could not be machine-tabulated. They were, however, taken into account later (see below).

Additional computer programs were written by research analyst Milton Stark. One of these counted the signs on the house cusps and the traditional planets and asteroids in signs and houses. It then computed probability values based on the chi-square test to determine whether or not the distributions had significance.

Another of Stark's programs analyzed the 1st through the 12th harmonics, plus the 16th, 24th, and 48th harmonics, deriving probability values from the *t* test. Using the traditional planets and the asteroids, we tested the harmonics two planets at a time (angular separation), three at a time (planet-to-midpoint planetary pictures) and four at a time (midpoint-to-midpoint planetary pictures). We tried them without orbs and with 3° and 5° orbs. To give an example, when we ran the 4th harmonic two planets at a time without orbs, the computer tabulated the deviations (say, between the Sun and the Moon) from 0° to 45°. When we ran the 4th harmonic with a 3° orb, the deviations from 0° to 3° were tabulated, with the maximum deviation being 3°. For a more detailed examination of the data we had a program that showed the frequency distribution and gave the means. Using this program, we ran the 1st and 4th harmonics two and three planets at a time.

Milton Stark also designed a program which analyzed the degrees of the zodiac, counting the number of planets (including asteroids) and Placidus house cusps in each degree.

Yet another of his programs enumerated the t-squares, the t-squares connected with trines, and the t-squares connected with grand trines. We tested different orbs to see if *t* test and probability values demonstrated better results with one orb as opposed to another.

In addition we employed the UCLA Stepwise Discriminant Analysis program to ascertain which planetary pairs in which angular separations discriminated best between the suicides and the controls. An advantage of stepwise discriminant analysis is that it assigns weights to the factors analyzed, according to which factors discriminate best. We used various moduli (such as 15°, 45°, and 90°) of the angular separation between planetary pairs, with various orbs.[1]

There were hand counts as well. I counted traditional planets, asteroids, and Uranian planets conjunct the Placidus cusps within 2° to discover if there were more of these bodies conjuncting the cusps of the suicide charts. I calculated the number of bodies in each quadrant. I tabulated the medical birth information, such as the number of hours of labor, presentation (normal or abnormal), and Rh-factor difficulties. This information had been noted when we recorded the birth times in the belief that possibly, correlating with difficult transits at birth, the suicides would have had more difficult births than the controls.

RESULTS OF THE EARLY TESTS

We began our analysis when we had collected a full year of suicides. We started with 1973, for which there were 98 suicides with timed births. The 1973 controls had not been selected as yet, so we used theoretical frequencies for the first computer runs.

After the controls had been obtained, we found that a few factors that had seemed of consequence in the 1973 suicides without controls no longer were consequential. For example, according to the theoretical frequency we assumed, Neptune and Pluto appeared to be closer to the suicides' Ascendants than expected, but then Neptune and Pluto were also found to be closer than expected to the controls' Ascendants. Theoretical frequencies are not very reliable when used in astrological studies.

The next years to be completed were 1969 and 1970. We combined them to make a group of 110 suicides and 110 controls that could now be compared with the 98 suicides and 98 controls for 1973.

Some of the factors tested did not differentiate between the suicides and the controls in any year. These included the traditional planets and the asteroids in signs and houses, the signs on the Placidus house cusps, and the aspects. A decrease in the orb of the aspects did not increase their power to discriminate between the suicides and the controls. Neither did the planets in the quadrants differentiate between the two groups. And there was no difference in the medical birth information.

Other factors which were found to be significant for the 1973 group were not significant for the 1969-70 group. For example, the traditional planets and asteroids in harmonics and in the frequency distributions that were significant in 1973 were not significant in 1969-70. Frequently occurring planetary pictures and frequently tenanted degrees of the zodiac in the 1973 charts did not replicate in the 1969-70 charts. And the discriminant analysis program chose different pairs of planets in the 1969-70 group than it had in the 1973 group.

TESTING NEW HYPOTHESES

We continued with our tests. When results that seem significant in a subgroup of a sample do not replicate in another subgroup of the same sample, it usually means that the results are in fact not significant. But suppose there is some factor that differentiates the subgroups from each other. In the case of our study, the years when each subgroup committed suicide had temporary factors that differed. Eclipses, stations, and transits affect different degrees of the zodiac in different years. I hypothesized that different sorts of natal charts might become suicide-prone in different years.

ECLIPSES ON HEAVILY TENANTED DEGREES

I decided to investigate this hypothesis using eclipses, since they are believed by many astrologers to have a greater influence on events than other astrological factors. Taking the degrees occupied by the greatest number of planets and Placidus house cusps (as tabulated by the degree program), I compared these with the degrees in which eclipses occurred around the time of the suicides. I compared the prominent degrees of the 1973 suicides and controls with the 1972 and 1973 eclipse degrees, and the prominent degrees of the 1969-70 suicides and controls with the 1969 and 1970 eclipse degrees.

Though I used the 1972 eclipses for the 1973 group, I did not use the 1968 eclipses for the 1969-70 group. To do so would mean that three years of eclipses would have a chance to contact the prominent degrees of one group, while only two years of eclipses would have a chance to contact a similar number of prominent degrees of a group of similar size.

With regard to eclipses on heavily tenanted degrees, neither the 1973 group nor the 1969-70 group showed any essential difference between the suicides and controls.

I then reversed the procedure and counted the number of 1969-70 eclipses that hit the prominent degrees of the 1973 suicides. Again, there was no difference. This is particularly meaningful when you consider that there were nine eclipses in 1969 and 1970 and eleven in 1972 and 1973, thus giving the 1972 and 1973 eclipses a greater chance to contact the 1973 suicides' prominent degrees.

Most of the degrees which were tenanted by a higher-than-average number of planets were in Leo, Virgo, and Libra. But for most of the births Pluto was in Leo, and Neptune was in Virgo or Libra. This probably explains why the proportion of prominent degrees in these signs was so high for both the suicides and the controls.

AFFLICTIONS INVOLVING THE ASCENDANT

I also researched the supposition that suicides may have a sign on their Ascendants more frequently when there is a malefic in that sign, or when there are difficult aspects in the sign, or when the ruler is in 0° or 29° of a sign. This assumption proved valid in the 1973 group but not in the 1969-70 group.

TESTS ON THE ENTIRE GROUP

Eventually we completed collection of the 1971 and 1972 suicides and controls, and so had all five years. We combined the 1971-72 suicides as a third subgroup which we tested against the 1973 and 1969-70 subgroups. We then did summaries and computer runs on the 311 suicides and an equal number of controls. Again, no factors stood out significantly to distinguish the suicides from the controls. As for the prominent degrees, they changed again.

CARTER'S SUICIDE CRITERIA

We investigated C. E. O. Carter's statements concerning suicide. In *An Encyclopædia of Psychological Astrology,* 4th ed. (London: Theosophical Publishing House, 1954) Carter writes: "The mutable signs are the most frequent ascendants" (p. 172). Among the 311 suicides, there were 118 with cardinal Ascendants, 91 with fixed, and 102 with mutable. The differences are not that great, but there are more cardinal Ascendants than mutable.

I also counted the conjunctions, squares, and oppositions from Saturn and Uranus to the Sun and Moon, since Carter writes that there are "violent malefic afflictions to one or both of the luminaries…Saturn afflicts heavily….The principal afflictor in such cases, however, is Uranus" (p. 172). The difference between the number of these aspects in the suicide charts and the number in the control charts was not sufficient to be meaningful.

In addition, we examined the degrees that Carter says are suicide degrees (15° of the cardinal signs, 25° of the fixed, and 26° of the mutable). Tallying the traditional planets and Placidus cusps at these degrees, we found 64 placements in the suicide charts and 83 in the control charts at 15° of the cardinals. For 25° of the fixed signs, we counted 73 placements in the suicide charts and 94 in the controls. For 26° of the mutable signs, there were 95 placements in the suicide charts and 108 in the controls. In each case, there were more in the control charts than the suicide charts. When the computer counted the planets separately from the cusps, the controls still had a greater number of Carter's suicide degrees. When the Sun and Moon were counted separately from the planets and the Ascendant and Midheaven counted separately from the cusps, there was the same result.

Despite the fact that, since there are 360° in the zodiac, a larger number of cases than we have is needed to do an adequate study of the degrees, I believe our analysis is a good indication that Carter's degrees are not a valid indicator of suicide.

A VERNON CLARK-TYPE EXPERIMENT

Indeed, we did not find any factor that was a valid indicator of suicide. We began to think that possibly the problem was that the computer was counting separate entities. We decided to do an experiment with astrologers. If they could distinguish between the charts of suicides and controls and could tell us the combination of factors which prompted their decisions, perhaps we could program these combined factors.

Eighteen astrologers took part in the investigation. Each astrologer was given the birth charts of ten suicides paired with the birth charts of ten controls and asked to figure out which chart in each pair was the suicide. The astrologers first gave their answers without the death dates and times and then with them. We conducted the experiment a second time with a different set of ten suicides and controls. Sixteen astrologers analyzed the first set, thirteen did the second, and eleven did both sets.

Without the death dates and times, none of the astrologers performed significantly above chance. With the death dates and times, one astrologer did significantly above chance, but this could still have been chance, since only twenty cases had been done. We questioned the one astrologer who tested above chance, but we were unable to find any combination of factors that could be programmed and used to discriminate between the suicides and the controls.

URANIAN PLANETARY PICTURES

When the Uranian planets were put on the computer disk, they could then be tabulated, and I consulted two Uranian astrologers who gave me seventeen planetary pictures for suicide. Most of these pictures are listed in the Witte-

Niggemann *Rules for Planetary Pictures* (New York: Hans Niggemann, 1959) as formulas for suicide or violent death. A couple of them had been formulated by the astrologers from personal experience. Some were for specific types of suicide, although we had not yet separated the 311 suicides according to method. (Later we did separate those who jumped—the second largest single category— from those who killed themselves by other means; see below.)

Using the 8th harmonic (thus taking into account not only the conjunction, but also the 180°, 90°, 45°, and 135° aspects), we ran these seventeen pictures and also the personal points (Sun, Moon, Midheaven, Ascendant, Node, and 0° Aries) equaling these pictures within a 1° orb. As with the other harmonics we had run, the closer a picture was to being exact, the greater weight the *t* test gave it. We had previously used either no orb or a 3° or 5° orb. Possibly, with only a 1° orb it would have been better merely to tabulate whether or not each case had the picture, using a chi-square if necessary to determine if there were significance. This objection was later answered by another program (see below). However, the Uranian astrologers believed that the planetary pictures of the suicides would be more exact that those of the controls.

There were only two planetary pictures that were significant at at least the 0.05 level, and they were significant for the controls. One of these pictures, for example, was Mars + Hades – Neptune = Moon, and it was significant at the 0.0348 level. But the Sun, Midheaven, Ascendant, Node and 0° Aries equaling Mars + Hades – Neptune were not significant, so it was probably only by chance that this picture was at that level.

Subsequently, Milton Stark wrote a new Uranian program. It was based on the methods of one astrologer who, after taking part in the first and second experiments to distinguish suicides from controls, did both a third and a fourth set. Although the astrologer did not discriminate significantly on the first two sets, he did on the last two.

Following his method, the program listed 40 factors in a 22.5° sequence. These factors included 14 general planetary pictures for suicide, 7 specifically for jumping, and 19 "personal points" (including death pictures such as Mars + Saturn – Midheaven). The hypothesis was that the 21 suicide and jumping pictures would contact the 19 personal points more frequently in the suicide charts than in the control charts. The astrologer specified an 0.5° orb, except in those pictures and personal points where the Midheaven or Ascendant was involved, in which case an 0.75° orb was used. Each time a planetary picture hit a personal point it received a score of 1 (thus answering the possible objection to the previous Uranian program). No chi-square test was computed (it was not necessary); there was just a tally after each pair of charts (one suicide, one control). The program assessed 68 suicides (all the cases of jumping among the 311 suicides), since some of the pictures applied specifically to jumping. This was the first time in our analysis that we separated the suicides according to method.

The total for the suicides was 1,670 points, and for the controls, 1,631, making an average of 24.55 points for each of the 68 suicide charts and 23.98 for each of the control charts—which is a negligible difference. An astrologer using this system for the 68 cases would get 35 right and 29 wrong, and in 4 cases would be unable to discriminate. This is the most complex program we have used so far, since it tallies not just separate factors (such as angular separation or planets in houses) in all the charts, but tallies the relationship in individual charts of 40 factors to each other.

Only the two aforementioned programs included the Uranian planets. We did not summarize the houses and signs of the Uranian planets because the houses and signs of Neptune and Pluto in the charts of the suicides were not significantly different from those of the controls. Since the Ascendants of the suicides and controls were not that dissimilar, and the orbital periods of the Uranian planets are even longer than the periods of Neptune and Pluto, it is logical to assume that we would not have had a significant difference in the case of the Uranian planets, either.

OTHER RECENT INVESTIGATIONS

Recently Thomas Shanks of Astro Computing Services wrote a new series of programs which we tried with the suicides and controls. These programs analyzed 15 geocentric factors (10 traditional planets, Ascendant, Midheaven, Node, Vertex, and East Point) according to their distribution along the ecliptic. The programs also analyzed some of the factors according to declination and mundane position.

Several ecliptic analyses were done. One simply studied the distribution of the 15 factors by longitude in 10° segments. Another analyzed the angular separations between all possible pairs of the 15 factors in 10° and 2° segments. Still another analyzed the distribution of midpoints in 2° segments. We also analyzed the angular separations between the 10 planets and the geocentric nodes of the planets in 2° segments, both pairwise (a planet to its own node only) and using cross combinations (each factor to all nodes).

All the declination studies were done in 2° segments. We analyzed the distribution of the 10 planets in declination, and the angular separations and midpoints in declination of the Ascendant and Midheaven as well as of the 10 planets.

The studies of mundane position used Gauquelin's method of dividing each planet's diurnal and nocturnal arc into equal sectors using time rather than space. Gauquelin placed a planet in its sector by noting the rising and setting times of the planet for the day of birth, and then converting the time of birth into a proportion of the time interval between rising and setting (if the planet was above the horizon) or setting and rising (if the planet was below the horizon). (For a more complete account of the method, see the Appendix in Michel Gauquelin, *The Cosmic Clocks* [Chicago: Regnery, 1967], pp. 232-38.)

First we analyzed the distribution of the planets and Node in the sectors, using 36 and then 12 sectors. We then did a harmonic analysis of these distributions to see if there were peaks at regular intervals in the diurnal circles similar to the peaks John Addey found in planetary distributions along the ecliptic. For this analysis we used 180 Gauquelin-type sectors.

In none of these investigations did we find a factor which significantly discriminated the suicides from the controls and which was also replicated in all three subgroups of suicide data.

THE IMPORTANCE OF CONTROLS

Our conclusions are not impressive. Perhaps the most important of them is that without controls, research is risky. And they must be "good" controls, born in the same years and places as the experimental group, and randomly selected.

An example of the problems that can occur without controls is found in David Hamblyn's preliminary report on 125 suicides in England. I checked to see if the factors that Hamblyn had found above chance were above chance for our 1969-70 suicides. They were not, with the one exception of Saturn, Uranus, and Pluto being above the horizon. But these three planets occurred above the horizon equally above chance in the 1969-70 controls.

One explanation is that during the time the subjects were born the planets in question were predominantly in north declination. Planets in north declination in northern latitudes have diurnal arcs of more than 12 hours, which in any random sample would bias them toward being above the horizon. Another explanation is that in northern latitudes the signs Cancer through Sagittarius take longer than the other signs to cross the Ascendant. During the time the subjects were born, most Plutos were in Cancer and Leo and most Uranuses were in Taurus, Gemini, and Cancer, while most Saturns were in Aries through Virgo—thus placing these planets more frequently above the horizon when the signs of long ascension were rising. These circumstances are probably true of David Hamblyn's suicides as well.

Similarly, in the harmonic analysis of Gauquelin-type sectors, the only one of Thomas Shanks's programs that does not use controls, we found one factor significant for the suicides. (The harmonics for the suicides were compared with the ideal harmonic curves, rather than with the harmonics for the controls. The same procedure was followed with the controls.) Uranus turned out to be significant in the 1st harmonic at the 0.008 level. The peak direction was at 84.89 (counting clockwise from zero at the horizon), which would place it near the Midheaven. But, as we noted with the Hamblyn study, Uranus was in north declination during the births of the subjects, biasing it toward being above the horizon. In other words, when Uranus (during the period it is in Taurus, Gemini, and Cancer) is near the Midheaven, the signs of long ascension are rising, so during this period there will be more people born with Uranus near the Midheaven. The only other significant factor in this experiment was Pluto in the 1st harmonic at the 0.001 level, and that was significant for the controls. The peak direction was at 99.11, so the explanations involving declination and signs of long ascension apply in this case as well.

Still another example of what, if we hadn't had good controls, might have been a problem with the New York suicides, is the following. I found that the rulers of the houses were frequently in opposite houses, such as the ruler of the 10th in the

4th and the ruler of the 7th in the 1st. But during the birth period of the suicides, Neptune was in Virgo and Libra (signs of long ascension), opposite its own sign, Pisces. I also noticed that the rulers of houses were often nine houses away, such as the ruler of the 1st in the 9th and the ruler of the 2nd in the 10th. But during the birth period of the suicides Pluto was in Cancer and Leo, three houses from its own sign, Scorpio, or nine houses in the opposite direction.

One can calculate the expected frequencies of planets in signs and aspects by analyzing the ephemeris for the birth years of the experimental group, but how does one figure the expectancy of the house rulers in the houses? It was only because I saw that the same pattern was occurring with the controls that I knew this pattern was not characteristic of the suicides. And there may be other aberrations of which we have not yet thought.

FUTURE RESEARCH

As for planets in the Gauquelin sectors, though we did not find significance for the suicides as a group, if we separated them according to type of suicide it is conceivable that we might. This is suggested by Gauquelin's discovery that certain planets tend to be near the horizon or meridian according to profession and that they are even more significantly close to the horizon or meridian according to personality characteristics. Perhaps the method of suicide is also an expression of personality characteristics. We might expect the type of person who committed suicide by gunshot to be quite different from one who committed suicide by drugs, and hence find different planets near the horizon or meridian according to the method of suicide. We intend to investigate this premise in the future.

Still other investigations remain to be done on this data. We have not looked at the distance of the planets from the Earth, mundane aspects, or the heliocentric positions of the planets.

We have, however, done just about all the traditional investigations, and some of the untraditional ones. The results so far are not significant, and that, I believe *is* significant.

Biorhythms

Further research was conducted. Biorhythms were investigated, using the SPSS (Statistical Package for the Social Sciences). In this case, untimed births, as well as timed, were studied. The hypothesis was that suicide was more likely to occur on the native's critical days. The chi-square test was applied, and the results were not significant.

More Vernon Clark-Type Experiments

Two more Vernon Clark-type experiments were conducted. For Sets I and II, controls had been matched to suicides so that there would be some pairs born on the same day and some pairs with the same sign on the Ascendant. This method had been suggested by several astrologers but was criticized subsequently. As a result, in Sets III and IV the suicides and controls were matched randomly. This new methodology did not increase the significance. In the third experiment, nine astrologers took part; in the fourth, six. Twenty-nine astrologers in all participated in the four experiments. Each experiment had two parts. The first part, to see if the astrologers could discriminate between the suicides and controls with just the birth data, did not include the death data. In the second part of Experiments I and IV the death dates and times were given, while in the second part of Experiments II and III progressed and transit charts for the deaths were supplied by Astro. Sometimes an astrologer who did the first part did not do the second. There were thirty-one times that an astrologer who participated in the first part without death data participated in the second part with death data. Eleven of those times, the score of the astrologer was the same with the death data as without; eleven times, the score was better; and nine times, it was worse.

One objection to the two-part format is that the astrologers did have an "investment" in their first-part choices. Consequently, they usually changed no more than one or two answers, if they changed their answers at all.

More astrologers have tried subsequently to distinguish between the suicides and controls, but not under the controlled circumstances that prevailed during the original experiments. Many of the astrologers have been given all the information at the beginning—the death data, the method used and the sex of the suicide. The expected increase in accuracy of the responses did not occur.

Comparisons According to Suicide Method

At the end of my article, I wrote that the suicides should be separated according to method of suicide. In the 311 suicides with timed births, there were 44 cases of suicide by drugs; 0 cases, by gases (oven); 12, by other gases (mainly carbon monoxide); 6, by drowning; 57, by stabbing; 9, by gunshot; 68, by jumping; 8, by other means (mainly subway); and 96, by hanging. There were not enough cases of any one method, so the nine methods were combined in three general categories: passive, aggressive and passive-aggressive. The research committee decided that suicide by drugs, gases, other gases and drowning is passive; by stabbing, gunshot, jumping and other means (such as throwing oneself in front of a subway train) is aggressive; and by hanging is passive-aggressive. Hanging was categorized as passive-aggressive, since it seems more aggressive than the methods in the passive group and more passive than those in the aggressive group. There were then 62 cases in the passive category; 153 in the aggressive category; and 96 in the passive-aggressive category. Not only were the three groups considered separately, but the passive-aggressive group was combined with the passive group to form a category of 158 cases, and with the aggressive group to form a category of 249 cases.

Again we utilized the summary program of Dr. Zipporah Dobyns and the statistical programs written by Thomas Shanks. With Shanks's programs, one group was used as the control for the other. Not only the aggressive group, but the aggressive + passive-aggressive group, was a control for the passive group; and the passive + passive-aggressive group was a control for the aggressive group.

With planets in signs, and planets in houses using the Gauquelin Sector Analysis, there was no significance at the .05 level. In aspect testing, with a 02° orb there were some aspects that were significant at the .05 level. However, since there were just a few cases of each aspect—under five—it was decided that the Yates correction should be applied. The Yates correction is a statistical adjustment implemented when the number of cases is small. It was also decided that there would be computer runs with a 04° orb with Yates correction and computer runs with a 04° orb without Yates correction. It was hoped that with a larger orb, the Yates correction would no longer be necessary. We also ran the 311 suicides versus the 311 randomly selected controls, in the signs and houses (Gauquelin sectors) and with the 02° and the 04° orb, with and without the Yates correction.

Concerning passive versus aggressive groups with the 02° and 04° orb with Yates correction and the 04° orb without Yates correction, there was not a replication of the original 02° orb without Yates correction aspect runs. For instance, the aspects tested were conjunctions, sextiles, squares, trines and oppositions—the sextiles and trines being the soft aspects; and the other aspects, the hard. In the original runs, the passive group compared to the aggressive + passive-aggressive group had shown the greatest significance. Astrologers associate Mars, Jupiter and Uranus with aggressive methods of suicide. I had noticed that with the passive group, $^2/_3$ of the significant aspects involving Mars, Jupiter and Uranus were soft, while the remaining $^1/_3$ significant hard aspects with those planets were $^1/_2$ of the time "softened" or "blocked" by Saturn. It seemed as if passive suicides might have soft aspects with "hard" planets more frequently, and vice versa. This supposition was not upheld with the new runs. Some of the same aspects were significant, but many were not, and others with different characteristics were substituted. The original "pattern" was lost, and no new one appeared. The volatility of the significance was due in great part, I think, to the disparity of the numbers: 62 passive compared to 249 aggressive + passive-aggressive suicides.

Finally, the comparison of the groups of passive suicides to aggressive suicides showed no greater significance than the comparison of the suicides to the randomly selected controls. The fact that the comparison of subgroups known to be disparate showed no greater significance than the comparison of the experimental group to the randomly selected group supports the credibility of that randomly selected group. This final test answered the objections of some astrologers who had contended that the lack of significant findings outlined in my article was due to the "unknown quantity" of the randomly selected controls.

Unreproducible Evidence

Though no further statistical tests were conducted on the suicides, I do have further observations concerning them. During the suicide study I noticed that the highest number of certified suicides in 1973 occurred August 12. We managed to gain access to the 1973 data on murders, and the most murders occurred the weekend of August 11-12. (More suicides and murders occur on weekends, but even more occurred that weekend.) At that time, in addition to exact aspects between the planets, there were three exact conjunctions of Uranian planets with planets and points. When Milton Stark, our statistician, was told this fact he said that, since the orbital periods of the Uranian planets are so long, we would be unable to see if a replication of these conjunctions would coincide with a replication of these results. The admonishment to pursue more reproducible evidence was followed.

Coming to the conclusion of my book, I felt the necessity to reexamine the unreproducible evidence. A chart was cast for 00:00 hours EDT, August 12, 1973, in New York City with the eight Uranian planets, Transpluto, Dark Moon Lilith and Halley's Comet. Astro's *Many Interesting Asteroids* was also run. I have found the midnight chart (00:00 hours ST or LMT) an archetypal chart for the day. (The noon chart is also, but on a more external level.) However, in this case I used Daylight Saving Time because that was the time which defined the weekend. Considering this period as extending from 06:00 PM Friday to 06:00 AM Monday, 00:00 hours Sunday is the exact middle of the week-end.

There were the three exact Uranian planet conjunctions noted previously— Vulcanus at 06° Cancer 28' conjunct the South Node at 07° Cancer 08', Uranus at 19° Libra 51' conjunct Poseidon at 20° Libra 33', and Pluto at 02° Libra 39' conjunct Apollon at 03° Libra 28'. Vulcanus can add force to the "close connections" of the South Node; Poseidon, a Super-Neptunism to the unexpectedness of Uranus; and Apollon, duality to the "deadliness" of Pluto. Most murders are within the family circle, and many suicides (self-murders) are an act against partners or relatives. The signs of these conjunctions were Cancer and Libra, and the degree of the South Node was 7 (partnership), the degree of Uranus was 19 (more authoritative parent) and the degree of Apollon was 3 (relatives). The minutes are fitting too. (The positions of the Uranian planets have been calculated with the mentioned improvement and are geometric, as are the positions of the asteroids and other bodies.) The Uranian planets will remain many years in the same signs, but their degrees and minutes, and those of the planets, asteroids and points connected with them, will change from day to day, or even minute to minute. Which planets, asteroids and points are connected will change too.

Another appropriate Uranian planet position was Admetos at 05° Taurus 04' St.℞. I have marked Admetos St.℞ because it is within a minute of its retrograde station. The *Uranian Transneptune Ephemeris 1850-2050,* which has the improved calculations, lists the dates of the stations of the Uranian planets. Studying these stations, I have found that if a person is born, or an event occurs, when a Uranian planet is within a minute or two of arc of its station, the associations of that Uranian planet figure prominently in the life of the person or event. Of course, if the person is born, or the event occurs, within a day or two of the station, the associations of the Uranian planet will be even more emphasized. For several years, since the following station is within a day or two of the previous station, the Uranian planet will be stationary at the time of the Solar Return of the person or event.

Admetos, in an exact T-Square, was opposite the Part of Fortune (04° Scorpio 41') and Pallas (06° Scorpio 11'), square the Midheaven (04° Aquarius 11') and

Jupiter (05° Aquarius 35'ᴮ). Admetos can be death; the Part of Fortune is a combination of the Ascendant, Sun and Moon; Pallas relates to perception and to the law; and Jupiter is excess, which could be the greatest number of suicides and murders. Continuing the theme of the family circle, Admetos was exactly quincunx Neptune (04° Sagittarius 40'ᴮ), Ceres (05° Sagittarius 17') and Juno (06° Sagittarius 51').

Other appropriate positions and exact aspects are the following. Toro (19° Libra 28') was conjunct Uranus and Poseidon, adding its amplification to their message. Attila (03° Scorpio 50') was conjunct the Part of Fortune, adding the associations of Attila the Hun to the aforementioned T-Square. Vinefera (08° Gemini 25') was sesquiquadrate Nuki (22° Libra 50'), Anubis (23° Libra 32') and Klotho (24° Libra 21'). Vinefera is the European grapevine from which wine is made, and suicide and murder are often committed under the influence of alcohol. Nuki sounds like Nuke, a nuclear weapon; Anubis was the Egyptian god of death; and Klotho was the Greek Fate who spins the thread of life.

As for the Ascendant, which is always outstanding, it was at 26° Taurus 27', exactly conjunct Fanatica (27° Taurus 27') and Libya (27° Taurus 58'). Fanatica is fanatical, and Libya is part of Northern Africa, but begins with the word lib meaning liberation or freedom. Suicide or murder is an act of fanaticism, and the goal may be freedom—from oneself or another. Exactly conjunct Fanatica and Libya was Pandora at 28° Taurus 05', and Pandora opened the box out of which all the evils of the world escaped. The Ascendant was also exactly sextile Halley's Comet (26° Cancer 08'), and semisextile the Antivertex (26° Aries 23') on one side and Nemausa (25° Gemini 21'), Dark Moon Lilith (25° Gemini 23') and Siva (26° Gemini 01') on the other. Halley's Comet is a powerful activator; the Antivertex is a fated point; Nemausa is "a key to a central issue in a chart"; Dark Moon Lilith has a quality of concealment; and Siva was the Hindu god called "the Destroyer." The Ascendant was exactly trine the Moon (27° Capricorn 32') conjunct Icarus (28° Capricorn 26'ᴮ). The Moon and Icarus formed an exact Fist of God with Sappho (28° Gemini 23'), Hekate (28° Gemini 47') and Demeter (28° Leo 29'). The Moon is a symbol of the mother; Icarus drowned when he flew too close to the sun; Sappho is reputed to have committed suicide; Hekate was the underworld lunar goddess of multiple aspect (my glyph is ☽); and Demeter was the mother whose daughter was taken from her by Pluto.

These appropriate positions and aspects are just a sampling, but I think they convey the complexity of the pattern. This pattern may never replicate, but does it matter? This is one unique moment in time, carrying its message which will never be quite the same again.

Comments on Statistical Research

Having completed my presentation of research conducted after my article on the New York suicide study was written, I have some comments on statistical research in general.

A FUNNY THING HAPPENED
ON THE WAY TO THE COMPUTER

In 1981 I was asked by NCGR to give a talk on what I'd discovered since becoming NCGR Research Chairman of the New York Chapter in 1974. The talk I gave was entitled "A Funny Thing Happened on the Way to the Computer." It was about statistical research that the research committee had done, not only on suicides but also on airplane crashes and alcoholics; and about statistical research that others had done. It was about the fact that either there had been no significance, or the significance had not been replicated, or the demographic effects had not been taken into account, or the controls used were not good controls.

Michel and Francoise Gauquelin's research on thousands of prominent professionals was discussed. Even that study was problematical. They had found Saturn close to rising (twelfth house) or culmination (ninth house) for scientists; Mars, for sports champions; etc. At first, they used expected frequencies to determine significance. As mentioned in my article there can be problems with expected frequencies. Later, they used people in one profession as controls for people in another, as well as people in their hereditary study as controls for people in their prominent professionals study. These controls were not good controls because the distribution of births was different for the different groups. For example, within the prominent professionals study, the scientists were born earlier than the sports champions; and, in general, the people in the prominent professionals study were born earlier than the people in the hereditary study. Professor Marvin Zelen then suggested that the Gauquelins collect the birth times of all people born on the days, and in the towns, on, and in, which the prominent people were born to see if there really were a difference. The Gauquelins followed this suggestion for the sports champions in a few towns, + or – three days. Testing Mars (which had had the greatest significance) in the key sectors (rise and culmination), what had been highly significant became borderline: .0000001 became .05. There were 303 champions compared to 16,756 non-champions. Aberrations in small groups are eliminated in large ones. My problem with the 62 passive compared to the 249 aggressive + passive-aggressive suicides is similar, albeit on a smaller scale.

The Funny Thing that had Happened on the Way to and from the Computer was I began to think that perhaps you can't characterize any group astrologically—not suicides, scientists, homosexuals or married people.

Statistics deal with groups, with averages, with means. As astrologers, we deal with individuals. Clinical observations can be made. In individual charts we may use harmonics and asteroids. They are enlightening, whether or not they are proven statistically significant for groups of individuals.

Another problem with statistical studies is that astrology is a matter of accretions. There are not only natal and progressed charts, but Solar Returns, which focus on a year, and Lunar Returns and lunations, which focus on a month. There are various levels of meaning too—mundane and metaphorical. And, houses, signs and planets have many meanings. Asteroids are more specific, but most of the asteroids that have been discovered aren't used by astrologers.

Compounding these problems is the fact that there are planets and asteroids that can not be taken into account because they haven't been discovered yet.

What is learned from the negative results of the computer studies is that in dealing with individuals we have to be careful not to follow any rules or formulas. I had asked the astrologers in the Vernon Clark-type studies to tell me the reasons for their choices. Their choices were often based on rules or formulas, such as "he has a prominent Neptune," or "he has a Uranian formula for suicide," so "he must be the suicide." Such rigid characterizations might have been the cause of the negative results of these studies.

As for the as yet undiscovered planets and asteroids, we may not be able to discover them all. And even if we do, the only constant is change. With the planets, the asteroids, and the whole universe moving, the chances of the entire chart repeating are nil.

The answer to this dilemma is not to discontinue research—clinical or statistical. What is more marvelous than trying to discover the secrets of the universe, even if they're never completely revealed? Maybe if we had a large enough computer to put in all the data, we could see the patterns. Surely, in the "great computer in the sky," everything is significant. If only we had access to so much data and to such a marvelous computer!

INTERFERENCE WITH THE DATA

That was the conclusion of my talk, but more years have passed, and a coda must be added to that conclusion. A difficulty with the continuance of research, clinical or statistical, is that there is increased interference with the data.

MERCURY RETROGRADE

For instance, it is becoming more difficult to research whether mail gets through on a Mercury retrograde when many astrologers won't mail anything themselves and are telling the public, in magazines and on TV, not to mail anything either. The expectation of lost mail on a Mercury retrograde is often fulfilled. There are problems at the post office anyway, so if a person ignores the Mercury retrograde prohibition, mail may get lost. But how often does mail get lost when Mercury is not retrograde? I myself have observed no greater problems with mail, or communication in general, when Mercury is retrograde than when it is direct. My mail was found on a Mercury retrograde! It was mail that had been lost in the past.

Mercury, or another body, retrograde does have a different quality—a retrospective one. The position and exact aspects of Mercury, or the other retrograde body, affect that quality. When the body changes direction, there may be changes. But, to avoid during the retrograde period the activities that correlate to that body is not necessarily advantageous.

A retrograde gives emphasis, which often gives great power. For example, another prohibition is against the signing of contracts during the Mercury retrograde period. Astrologers say that a contract signed during this period will not last. My present husband and I were married, and so signed the marriage contract, while Mercury was retrograde, and our marriage has lasted over thirty years to date.

A study should be conducted comparing the longevity of marriages with Mercury retrograde and Mercury direct. However, this study should be conducted before more people about to marry are dissuaded from marrying on a Mercury retrograde and before more people already married on that retrograde are persuaded to fulfill the astrological prophecy.

VOID-OF-COURSE MOON

There should also be a study of the void-of-course Moon. The Moon is called void-of-course from the time it makes its last major aspect (conjunction, sextile, square, trine or opposition) until it enters the next sign. Some astrologers contend that during this period activities should be spiritual, rather than material. They say that activities begun, products bought, and decisions made during this period will be unproductive.

Events during a void-of-course Moon are cited—a particular appointment that wasn't kept or a particular purchase of a product that was defective. My observations are that *in general* appointments are often broken, and goods are frequently shoddy. The Moon is only void 10% of the time, but even allowing for that factor I haven't observed any more or worse problems during that period than during the non-void period.

To examine the void period, I have perused my date book after the fact to see what activities occurred during the void-of-course Moon. Not only were there scheduled appointments kept and undefective products bought, but there were profitable decisions made and advantageous projects begun. For instance, tax returns were prepared that were not audited, and agreements were reached that were not abrogated. Another mini-study was of openings in New York of musicals that my husband played in and/or contracted. (These shows were chosen because I attended their openings and so knew their times.) What was being investigated was whether the state of the Moon in this regard is a good indicator of the length of time between the opening and the closing of a show. The Moon's course being void or not void did not prove a good indicator. In fact, a show that had one of the longest runs—two years—opened on a void-of-course Moon.

The void-of-course Moon may have a different quality. The Moon, until its next sign ingress, may be carrying the message of that last major aspect. In testing this premise, I cast charts for the times of void-of-course Moons (their last major aspect) before the births of people and events born during the void period. I also cast charts for the times of Moon Ingresses before the births of people and events born during the non-void period. Then, as a counterpart to the chart of the void-of-course Moon before the birth of an entity during the void period, a chart was cast for the last aspect of the Moon before the birth of an entity during the non-void period. For natives born in non-void periods, at first "the last aspect of the Moon" was limited to the major aspects (conjunction, sextile, square, trine or opposition). Then, "the last aspect of the Moon" was expanded to include minor aspects (semisextile, semisquare, quincunx or sesquiquadrate). Next, additional aspect charts were cast. The aspects were limited to those enumerated above, but not to an aspect with the Moon or to the last aspect before the birth. Finally, as a counterpart to the chart of the Moon

Ingress before the birth of an entity during the non-void period, a chart was cast for the Moon Ingress before the birth of an entity during the void period.

The unexpected result of casting the Moon Ingresses and the various aspect charts as "controls" for the void-of-course Moon charts is the following observations. Charts of exact aspects, both major and minor, are notable, whether before a void-of-course Moon or not. The Moon Ingresses and aspect charts (including void-of-course Moon charts) appear to be like the prenatal lunation and eclipse charts, which set up preconditions for a particular period. These charts relate to a person or event born during that period. The Moon Ingress period would be from the ingress in one sign until the ingress in the next sign. The aspect period is not so discrete. Not just the chart of the last aspect before the birth is related to the native. The charts of exact aspects surrounding the birth are germane. Of course, the aspects tested are high in the hierarchy of aspects, as outlined on pages 110-11, and the aspects after the birth would occur in the progressed chart.

The bodies and points seem to be carrying the message of the ingress or the aspect. To curtail activities during the void-of-course Moon period may be to miss the message. The ingress or aspect charts are archetypal charts. The Moon Ingress chart is an archetypal chart of the Lunar concerns (emotion, woman, mother, wife, etc.), combined with the ingress sign. The aspect charts are archetypal charts of a particular combination of the concerns of the particular planets. For instance, a Moon-Mercury conjunction chart is descriptive of a union of the emotions and mind; a Moon sesquiquadrate Saturn chart is descriptive of an obsessive link (8th harmonic) between the emotions and restriction. (There are other possibilities, as there are other correlations of these planets and aspects.) The aspect charts relate to the native in terms of the aspect. The chart (ingress or aspect) connects appropriately to the natal chart of the person or event born in the particular period. Connections to significant people, or events, in the life of that person, or event, are also shown. Name asteroids and personal points highlight the connections.

FURTHER RESEARCH

These observations should be further tested. However, like much of astrology, they do not lend themselves to statistical testing. Each ingress and aspect chart is unique and must be viewed in relation to a unique natal chart.

This coda, with its exhortation to conduct more research, brings to an end my chapter on research.

CHAPTER 7

Conclusion

It is fitting that Chapter 7 (7th house, Libra, Venus, septile) should be the conclusion of my book. Though the number nine correlates to completion, we've gone halfway round the zodiac when we come to the seventh house. The second half of the zodiac is a complement to the first, as the seventh house is to the first house, as the other is to the self, as the reverse side is to the obverse side of the coin. The principles of the last six houses are a balance, from the other side of the same coin, to the principles of the first six houses. What we're dealing with in this final chapter is a balance, a harmonization, of all that has come before—and what could be more Libran.

Conclusions

Every moment has meaning—even to the hours, minutes and seconds by which that moment is designated. Every chart of a moment is meaningful. Astrology is not just beginnings and endings—it's everything in-between. I have cast charts of thoughts, dreams, statements, phone calls, correspondence sent and received, reading a line, hearing a song, naming a group, walking into a restaurant, buying a product, seeing not only people, but places, signs, pictures and a rainbow; and those charts are all descriptive of that individual moment. Charts have even been cast of buying the same item different times, and each chart is descriptive of that purchase in terms of the individual moment. *When* you cast a chart or input a computer program is no accident either, and the charts of those events are descriptive too.

   The Earth turns against the background of the planets, asteroids and stars, and we perceive the patterns of that turning when those patterns relate to our own. Collective charts, such as lunations, eclipses, stations, ingresses, equinoxes, and solstices, are descriptive of vibrations in the world at large. The media seem especially attuned to those general vibrations. We, as individuals, read those words, hear that song or in some way "tune in" at the moment when our individual vibrations connect with the general ones.

PREDETERMINATION

Every moment already has its meaning, so everything must be predetermined. The pattern is too complex to be decided here and now. No one is alone. The choices of one may impinge on the choices of others. The threads of our lives and fates are interwoven in the larger fabric. As astrological factors are added to the charts, we see this complex interwoven pattern specifically described.

Some astrologers believe that there is predetermination with world events and leaders, though not with commonplace life and people. But how do you draw the line between important and unimportant events and people? I've cast charts of so-called unimportant events and people and seen the same patterns as I've seen with the important ones. Also, I've checked the astrological correlates of the exact hour, minute and second of thousands of "unimportant" events, and they are appropriate. I've even gotten to know when my watch has picked up a second or two because the seconds are not as appropriate.

Predetermination doesn't mean our fate is imposed upon us. Our fate arises from our character and past actions. I don't think of this process as punishment, but as cause and effect, and the effect is not a simplistic reverse image of the cause.

We may evolve in this life, but that evolution, foreseen by the universe, is reflected in our progressions and transits. It is not that we have no choice, but rather that the universe knows our choice.

My belief doesn't mean we should just sit back and let things happen. The universe may know, but we don't know for sure. Within the confines of ethics, we should try to make happen what we think should happen, knowing it may not happen. It is a matter of passive assertiveness or assertive passivity. We are part of a will greater than our own. We should try to understand that will, knowing we may never understand it all.

But, if everything is fated, what does it mean to say that something is fated? The answer to this question, as I see it, is that some places have signposts. The Vertex-Antivertex axis, the Uranian planet Vulcanus, the asteroids named for the Fates, are signposts marking the place. But all places have coordinates, even if they're not marked. Observe the signposts, and the coordinates, and, whenever possible, divine the rest.

MESSAGES

The universe is sending us messages in the form of people we meet or know, products we buy or use, places we visit or pass, media to which we tune in, and other happenings. The entire ambience of a happening is part of its message. The ambience includes, for instance in a home or restaurant, the pictures on the walls, especially those under which we sit, the clothes we and those near us wear, the food we eat, the conversations we conduct or overhear. The messages are mirrored in the charts of the happenings. When we observe those people, products, places, media, and charts, we are made aware, if only on a subconscious level.

To give an example of the message of clothes, there are the clothes I was wearing when first meeting my husband. At that meeting, my outfit was matching white shorts and top, with red oriental calligraphy embroidered on the left side. (The left is the personal side.) I still have my outfit and so was able to note its trade name. (My husband's is long since discarded.) The trade name of my matching set is Junior House Milwaukee. My 464 asteroid listing has no asteroid related to Milwaukee. However, Milwaukee is a port city in Southeast Wisconsin on Lake Michigan, thus having reference to my family since my mother was born in Michigan and my grandmother lived many years in Michigan. As for Junior House, in our Meeting Chart, Hebe is in the seventh house at 06° Pisces 34', exactly trine Mercury, Julia, in the eleventh house at 06° Cancer 13', 06° Cancer 41'. Hebe was the Greek goddess of youth, Mercury, ruler of the chart, is another indicator of youth, and Julia means "Youthful one."

Apropos of the oriental calligraphy, Asia at 05° Cancer 04' is exactly conjunct Mercury, Julia, with all three sesquiquadrate my natal Ascendant at 20° Aquarius 27'. The asteroids in the Eastern Hemisphere category were extremely active, and Asia, Mercury, and Julia were exactly conjunct the heliocentric ascending node of China. (Though my husband no longer has his outfit, he's sure he was wearing chino pants, his casual "uniform" at the time. According to *The Random House College Dictionary,* chino may be derived from Chino-, a combining form of Chinese.) These positions relate to me personally as a double Gemini (Mercury) woman (Cancer), with Aquarius rising (eleventh house) and Asia exactly conjunct her Ascendant. These positions relate to the world in general, in so far as July 1, 1957 (the day of our meeting), the "**Southeast Asia Treaty organization** announced the appointment of Pote Sarasin, Thai ambassador to the U. S., as its 1st secretary-general." The appointment was of a secretary (Mercury), representing countries (Cancer) in an organization (11th house) of Southeast Asia. This event is one of three events listed for this date in the *1958 Britannica Book of the Year,* "Calendar of Events•1957." (Note Southeast for Asia and for Milwaukee.) My natal Margarita, the name asteroid of my grandmother who lived in Michigan, is also exactly conjunct my Asia and Ascendant. In the Meeting Chart, Margarita is at 04° Taurus 37', exactly aspecting the aforementioned positions. My husband's natal Nonie (04° Gemini 19') and Klotho (05° Gemini 24') (my name asteroids) are at the midpoint of transiting Margarita and Asia, Mercury, Julia, with both Nonie and Klotho exactly conjunct the heliocentric descending node of Nonie. In my 464 asteroid listing there are no asteroids that represent white and/or red, the colors of my outfit. The asteroid in my listing which has the closest association to red is Rhodesia, which sounds like Rhoda, an English variation of Rose. Rhodesia, at 05° Aries 55', is exactly square Asia, Mercury, and Julia.

As can be seen, the messages are not always straightforward. They are often cryptic, relying on associations, similarities in sound or meaning, and plays on words to make the point. Mark the names of the people, products and places with which you come in contact. Even if there are no planets or asteroids with those names, consult name books, dictionaries, encyclopedias, and books on mythology for the meanings and associations of those names. There may be individual associations too. Also, note trademarks (they are like glyphs) and numbers (they correlate to the houses, signs, etc.). Often a number will be repeated, showing emphasis. Sometimes there will be a numerical theme shown in the numbers of the positions, times, prices, addresses, etc. The sequence of events and of entities and the proximity of places are significant. When a part of the body is sick or injured, look to the governing planet and its correlations, i.e., for the knees, bones, teeth and skin, governed by Saturn, look to 10, tenth house, Capricorn, Saturn and the decile. The right side of the body relates to the social life; the left, to the personal. Take notice of accidents and mistakes—they call attention.

Particularly note happenings that occur at the same or similar times, and happenings that have the same or similar meanings. The books, magazines, newspapers and mail that we read, the television and movies we watch, and the radio broadcasts and records to which we listen are part of that synchronicity and synonymity. (Advertisements are included in that reading, watching and listening.) In an individual life, two or three synchronous or synonymous events, not hundreds as in statistics, are enough to see the pattern.

WEB OF EVENTS
Often, there is a web of events, with one event relating to the next, with both of those relating to the following, etc. Charts of transits, progressions, stations, lunations, eclipses and returns during that period will reflect the interconnectedness of those events. Sometimes there will be a reference back to an event that happened many years ago. Though every moment has meaning, some moments, at certain times, for particular people, will be especially emphasized. As different transit charts activate a factor, which is currently sensitized by slow-moving transits, progressions, stations, lunations, or other individual and collective charts, that factor may come into a person's consciousness repeatedly.

Events occur on different levels. For instance, my husband accidentally stuck a hatpin in his eye and, at my insistence, went to his opthalmologist. When the doctor said that my husband had cut the conjunctiva but hadn't perforated the globe of the eye, I remembered that two and a half days earlier the globe of our old kitchen light fixture had fallen and broken as I was discarding it in the incinerator room. The globe of the light was like the globe of the eye. I didn't even know that the eyeball was called a globe but had recorded the times of both incidents. When charts were cast, the charts were appropriately connected. As an example, the Midheaven of the Eye Cutting Chart was exactly trine the Ascendant of the Light Breaking Chart, and the Ascendant of the Eye Cutting Chart was exactly quincunx the East Point of the Light Breaking Chart. Both charts had the slow-moving transit of Uranus at 00° Capricorn, 02° from Saturn at 02° Capricorn. In the earlier chart, the East Point was 01° Leo 18' quincunx them, and the Moon was 00° Libra 41' square Uranus (00° Capricorn 01'). In the later chart, the Ascendant was 01° Pisces 54' sextile them, and the Moon was 02° Scorpio 02' sextile Saturn (02° Capricorn 30'). In both charts the Moon was strongly configured, and the Moon is one of the **lights**.

When the prior Full Moon Chart was cast, it was seen to have the Sun at 01° Sagittarius 35' and the Moon at 01° Gemini 35'. With the Moon's conjunction to my Moon at 00° Gemini 21' and my Sun at 02° Gemini 34', the Full Moon had already sensitized my Sun and Moon. The Full Moon had already sensitized my husband's Sun/Moon midpoint, with the Moon's sesquiquadrate, and the Sun's semisquare, to his Sun/Moon midpoint. Our interconnectedness is emphasized by our Sun/Moon midpoints equaling each other. Also, our Nodes had been activated by the Full Moon's square to my husband's North Node at 02° Virgo 09', conjunct my South Node at 03° Virgo 16', and to his South Node at 02° Pisces 09', conjunct my North Node at 03° Pisces 16'. The Nodes are close connections, which can be with others or within one's self. In the latter case, the Nodes can represent literal physical connections within the body.

My husband's right eye is the one that was pierced. According to astrological tradition, the Sun rules the right eye in men and the left eye in women. In the Eye Cutting Chart, the Sun was exactly conjunct the Midheaven. In the Light Breaking Chart, the Sun, ruler of the Leo Ascendant, was exactly conjunct the fifth house, ruled by the Sun in the natural zodiac.

Asteroids related to the Sun, or Moon, and health were particularly noted in the two event charts, the Full Moon Chart and my husband's natal chart. In both the Eye Cutting Chart and the Light Breaking Chart, the asteroid Horus (the Egyptian Solar Deity who lost an eye) was less than a degree from my husband's Horus. (My husband had just had a Horus Return.) In both charts the asteroid Sy (his name asteroid) was less than 02° from Horus, with Pallas (perception) in-between. On the wall of the doctor's new office, to which we'd never been, there was a picture of the Eye of Horus. Another asteroid which I expected to be prominent was Iris, which has Sun and Moon symbolism and which can literally refer to the iris of the eye. Appropriately, in the Eye Cutting Chart, it was exactly conjunct my husband's Leo Ascendant. Icarus, Neptune was in the eleventh house (the asteroid Icarus relates to the Sun, too), exactly square Mars in the first house and the asteroid Anna in the seventh house (T-Square). Ann is the name of a phone representative at the service center for our new Caloric stove who was on the phone with my husband when he pierced his eye. She is the one who told him to use a needle to unclog the five (Sun number) major holes of the burner. Instead, while Ann waited on the phone, he got an old hatpin of mine with a pearl top (Moon symbolism) and went into the kitchen to unclog the burner under her instruction. To place the receiver next to his ear, he used the hand holding the hatpin, and, in so doing, as Ann talked to him, stuck the hatpin in his eye.

Since what was being dealt with was a stove, I noted the asteroids Vesta and Hestia, goddesses of the hearth, and they were fittingly conjunct in an exact T-Square with the Sy, Pallas, Horus conjunction, and the Uranian planet Admetos. (Admetos represented the blockage of the burner.) My asteroid program has no asteroid named Caloric, but having found that an asteroid with a similar name will be relevant, I looked at the asteroid Caltech. It was at 01° Virgo 50', exactly conjunct the Eye Cutting Chart's Descendant at 01° Virgo 54' and my husband's North Node at 02° Virgo 09', conjunct my South Node. These positions had been activated by the Sun and Moon of the Full Moon Chart.

At the Full Moon, Jupiter at 00° Gemini 58'℞ had been exactly conjunct the Moon. Jupiter had come from a retrograde station two months before at 06° Gemini 07', exactly conjunct my IC, ruled by the **Moon** in the natural zodiac, and exactly square my husband's **Sun** (ruler of the right eye in men). The Uranian planet Hades had made its retrograde station around the same time at 08° Gemini, combining with Jupiter to bracket my IC at 07° Gemini 41', by a conjunction, and my husband's Sun at 07° Pisces 03', by a square. Hades can literally refer to debris, and the new stove was part of our total kitchen renovation, which produced a great deal of it. The Light Breaking and the Eye Cutting were related to that renovation, but the Jupiter conjunction to the Hades had symbolized the fortunate outcome of these accidents, as well as of the renovation.

SYNCHRONOUS HAPPENINGS

Close friends, and especially family, often experience similar events at similar times. My husband's brother and his wife in Florida had renovated their kitchen, without our knowing, at the same time we renovated ours. The Full Moon had been exactly square his 01° Virgo Sun and her 01° Pisces Sun. The kitchen is the heart (Sun) of the home (Moon). Four days after the Eye Cutting, our daughter decided to move from the apartment where she was living. The Full Moon had been exactly conjunct her 00° Gemini West Point and square her 02° Virgo Pluto (ruler of her Ascendant) in the tenth house. On that same day at 09:00 AM PST, a cousin of mine in California completed his dissertation on imaging—Sun and Moon symbolism again! The Full Moon had been exactly quincunx his 01° Capricorn East Point and trine his 00° Libra Poseidon and 01° Libra Midheaven. (Poseidon is a Uranian planet that represents light.) That same day at exactly 12:30 PM EST, our kitchen contractor arrived to complete the renovation of our kitchen.

It was not known, until after the fact, that the time between my cousin's event and mine was only a half-hour. The other synchronicities in the family weren't known till after the fact either. When you record the events in your own life, in the lives of those close to you, and in your family's lives (whether your family is close to you or not), you start to see how the web of events encompasses those lives too. Though a lunation will affect everybody, this particular one was especially relevant to my husband's and my close connections, with the Full Moon's exact square (Lunar aspect) to our exactly reversed Lunar Nodes.

Of course, someone who is not family or a close friend may be a close connection for a time. A case in point is our kitchen contractor, with whom for awhile we had more contact than we had with our family and close friends. We chose him out of seven contractors that we interviewed. After the contract was signed, I got his birth data and discovered that his East Point is exactly conjunct my IC and square my husband's Sun, and his IC is exactly conjunct my husband's North Node which is conjunct my South Node. Also, he was born the same year as (less than one month before) our daughter, and his outer planets make the same aspects as hers to our charts. His uncle, who is the owner of the company, and with whom we had no contact until after the contract was signed, turned out to be born the same year as my husband and the same day as my ex-husband. The same aspects are made to our charts by the owner's Sun, as are made by my ex-husband's Sun.

FAMILY ASSOCIATIONS IN THE NEWS

In the news, the presence of family names, places your family has lived or other associations to your family indicates that there is an emphasis on you and your family at that time. That emphasis will be illustrated in relevant charts by astrological factors with those names or associations.

To give an example, March 27, 1988, the front page of the *New York Times* announced that the Plaza Hotel had been sold to Donald Trump. The *Times* said that the sale had been disclosed the previous day. That previous day, a cousin of mine had been married, and the relatives from out of town were staying at the Plaza Hotel. The day of the front page article, the family was emphasized again by some of those Plaza-staying relatives meeting the New York relatives for brunch. The choice of hotel by the Plaza-staying relatives had been made because of proximity to the church and other mundane considerations. However, I had already privately associated this hotel with the family because the grandfather of my cousin had stayed on the Plaza at the Savoy Hotel, across from the original Plaza Hotel, on the night of his wedding to his first wife almost ninety years before. (The Savoy Hotel is no longer standing because it was replaced by the Savoy-Plaza Hotel, which has since been replaced by the General Motors Building.) That grandfather's second wife is the progenitor of my cousin and myself, but a previous or subsequent marriage is important in a family. (Actually, I am descended from his second wife and a previous husband.)

Relevant charts would be the chart of the newspaper article about the Plaza, cast for midnight EST on March 27, 1988, and the Marriage Chart of that grandfather and his first wife. (The time of the May 17, 1898 wedding is known because it is given in a letter written by him, along with a transcription of a newspaper article describing the wedding.) My asteroid program does not cover the year of the wedding but the name asteroids of the various people involved, past and present, were appropriately configured in the Newspaper-Plaza Chart. Also, the 14° Sagittarius Ascendant of the Marriage Chart was exactly conjunct the 15° Sagittarius Ascendant of the Newspaper-Plaza Chart and the asteroid Lutetia at that same degree. Lutetia Parisiorum is the ancient name of Paris, and the Plaza Hotel was modeled after a French chateau, and the bride was of French extraction. In the Newspaper-Plaza Chart, the Ascendant and Lutetia were exactly square the 15° Pisces Mercury in the third house, representing the news, as well as the public and the bride (Mercury is the ruler of the Descendant in both charts).

Of course there are other articles in that day's newspaper that are represented by other factors, and this article and those articles will relate to other people in different ways. Different factors will be important to different people.

The hotel where my stepgrandfather stayed on that wedding night, in **close proximity** to the Plaza, was evidently important to him, since he wrote about it to his daughter on an anniversary of that wedding. Evidently it was important to me because, as a result of my interest in the family history, a copy of the letter came into my possession after the death of this daughter. Evidently it was important to my cousin and her new husband because they had chosen, without foreknowledge, to be married on the day of the Plaza sale disclosure.

If a factor is important to a person in this life, or a past life, that importance will be indicated by the highlighting of that factor. One way a factor can be highlighted is through the media.

RELOCATED CUSPS

Usually on a chart cast by my computer, I will have relocated cusps listed. Those cusps will be drawn around the outside of the chart, showing the event which occurred in one place from the vantage point of another. For instance, if the chart is of a phone conversation, the relocated cusps will be at the location of the other person on the line.

In the aforementioned Marriage Chart and Newspaper-Plaza Chart, Paris, France, was chosen for the relocated cusps, before my knowing that Paris, Lutetia and other asteroids with French associations would be prominent. This location was chosen because of the bride's French ancestry. These relocated cusps and other angles were fitting. As an example, in Paris the Antivertex of the Marriage Chart was 22° Pisces 24' and the Antivertex of the Newspaper-Plaza Chart was 23° Pisces 49', exactly conjunct the North Node, Paris (23° Pisces 02', 24° Pisces 38') of the Newspaper-Plaza Chart. The Paris Antivertexes were also conjunct the Uranian planet Admetos at 21° Pisces 06', with the three combining to exactly square the Venus, Neptune, Pallas (20° Gemini 01', 21° Gemini 17', 23° Gemini 29') in the seventh house of the Marriage Chart. My stepgrandfather's bride died eleven and a half months after the marriage, of acute diffuse eclampsia—a toxemia (Neptune) of pregnancy—and kidney (Venus) failure, following the birth of twin (Gemini and 21°) daughters (Venus). As for Pallas, it sounds like palace, evoking the French chateau-style Plaza Hotel.

If I think an event relates to a past life, the relocated cusps for the place in which that life occurred will be drawn around the chart of the present event, showing the present event from the vantage point of the past place. Though past lives are speculative, I've found this technique helpful in the consideration of them.

PAST LIVES

Sometimes, the time at which a factor comes into your consciousness in this life may numerically and astrologically reflect the meaning of that factor for you in a past life.

Another observation concerning past lives is that at the anniversary of historical events there seem to be fitting progressions of people who may have lived through those historical events. This observation is unprovable, but such progressions might be a means of corroborating insights concerning past lives revealed to people by psychics or by psychic flashes they've had themselves.

As a final point regarding past lives, I believe that sometimes a person may be playing the part of someone from a past life, rather than literally being a reincarnation of that person. For instance, a person may represent a marriage partner from a past life but may not have literally been that partner. In that case, in the reexperiencing of unresolved encounters, an example of the prototype, rather than the prototype itself, would be sufficient. Events can take a similar but different form too.

HEREDITY

I've written about heredity before, particularly in Chapter 2, where harmonic studies involving my family are discussed. However, since the understanding of our antecedents and our descendants is so important in the understanding of ourselves, heredity will be discussed in more detail in this conclusion.

Similarities between the charts of parents and children are shown in different ways. To begin with the more obvious, sometimes at least one of the three personal points (Sun, Moon, Ascendant) of the child will be the same as one of the three personal points of one of the parents. For example, my daughter has her Ascendant in Scorpio and her father, my second husband, has his Moon in Scorpio. Also, she has her Sun in Leo, and he has his Ascendant in Leo. Rulerships should be noted too—both have their Sun rulers in Leo. Similarities can also be shown through house placements. Father and daughter have Neptune in the twelfth house—he 09°, and she 11° from the Ascendant. She has her Moon, and he has his Sun, in the seventh house. Though the placement of these luminaries appears to be the opposite, it is really very similar because the Moon represents the female principle and the Sun, the male. Then there are structural similarities. Our daughter's Moon in the seventh house is exactly opposite her Ascendant. Her father has his Moon in the fourth house, exactly square his Ascendant. The placement of the Moon (angular, with his in its natural house) and exact aspects of that body give them both an emphasis on the Moon.

This emphasis is in the chart of my mother as well. Her Moon is exactly conjunct her Ascendant. The Moon is emphasized, not only by its aspect, but by its being in the first house in Aries (the first house sign in the natural zodiac). Also, my mother's Sun and its ruler (Jupiter) are in her ninth house (Sagittarius' own house), with Jupiter exactly conjunct her Sun. My Sun and Moon and their ruler (Mercury) are in my third house (Gemini's own house), with Mercury 03° before my Moon, which is 02° before my Sun, placing the three in a symmetrical relationship. Though the ruler of my mother's Moon is not the same as, or in close proximity to, the ruler of her Sun, these rulers are in the same house.

My mother and I do not share signs or houses. In fact, the sign and house of my Sun are the exact opposite of hers. What we share is a similar structuring of our charts. While she is triple fire, I am triple air; while she is double Aries, I am double Gemini. We both have an emphasis on the natural zodiac and on the rulers of our Sun and Moon. This similar structuring is very descriptive of a quality I inherited from my mother. What we share is a tendency to be very much what we are.

This tendency did not come from my mother alone. My father has his Sun and Moon exactly conjunct in Sagittarius in the twelfth house. His Sun and Moon are not in close proximity to, or in the same house as, their ruler. He doesn't have an emphasis on the natural zodiac. However, there is a similar structuring of our charts too. While he was born just after an eclipse, I was born just before a lunation. While his Sun and Moon are double Sagittarius in regard to the sign and double Pisces in regard to the house, I am double Gemini in regard to the sign and house. His angularity is not as pronounced as my mother's, but he does have his Sun and Moon near an angle, as I do.

Interestingly, my degree of angularity is about half-way between theirs. His Moon is 13°, and his Sun 14°, from his Ascendant. My mother's Moon is 00° from her Ascendant, and her Sun is 07° from her Midheaven. My Moon is 07°, and my Sun 05°, from my IC. The average of the distance of my Sun and of my Moon from an angle is 06°13', which is about half-way between the average of those distances for my father (14°03') and the average for my mother (03°44'). Though my father's chart has been rectified, it was not rectified on this basis, and I have seen this phenomenon when none of the charts are rectified. The parent with a tighter orb and the parent with a looser orb often combine to form a child with an intermediate orb. Or two parents with the same factors in an inexact aspect may have a child with those factors in an exact aspect. When both parents exhibit a similar astrological format, then their child seems to have a greater likelihood of exhibiting that format.

Sometimes, the chart of a child will be a throwback to the chart of one of the grandparents or great-grandparents. My daughter's chart looks more like my mother's chart than it does like my chart or her father's chart. Perhaps, like recessive genes, some tendencies can be carried without being manifest. I may be carrying the astrological traits of my ancestors even when I am not exhibiting them in my chart. If I marry a man who is either exhibiting these same traits or carrying them because they were exhibited by his ancestors, probably the chances are greater these traits will be exhibited by our offspring.

My mother's mother and my husband's father have their Suns in Cancer, and my father's mother has her Moon in Cancer. The emphasis on the Moon that my mother and father exhibit may be an expression of the Cancerian personal points of their respective mothers; the emphasis I exhibit, an expression of those of my maternal and paternal grandmothers; the emphasis my daughter exhibits, those of her maternal great-grandmothers and her paternal grandfather; the emphasis my husband exhibits, the Cancerian personal point of his father. I may have chosen a man with this emphasis because he fits my familial profile. (Of course, my daughter, for instance, would be exhibiting the expressions of her maternal grandparents and mother and father as well.)

The angles represent the ancestors, so the angles are particularly related to heredity. When the mother is represented by the fourth house, and the father by the tenth, the seventh house is the house of the mother's mother and the father's father. The attribution is made according to whether the native perceives the ancestor as a maternal or paternal figure. (The mother could be perceived as a maternal figure, and the mother's mother as a paternal one.) In the case of my daughter, I am represented by her fourth house and her father by her tenth, and my mother and her father's father are represented by her seventh (fourth from the fourth and tenth from the tenth). On the seventh my daughter has her Moon, which describes my mother with the Moon exactly conjunct her Ascendant and describes her father's father with his Sun in Cancer. (Sometimes, descriptive planetary bodies, including asteroids, will cluster around the angle, rather than be posited in the angular house.)

Moving from the general to the particular, here is an example of how an asteroid can bring greater clarity to an understanding of one's own heredity.

There is an asteroid Odysseus (1143). Odysseus was the Greek hero of Homer's *Odyssey* who spent ten years trying to return home after the ten-year Trojan War. Odyssey (often l.c.) means, according to *The Random House College Dictionary*, "any long series of wanderings, esp. when filled with notable experiences, hardships, etc."

As mentioned, my father has his Sun and Moon in Sagittarius in the twelfth house. Such a placement can relate to a desire for travel, to a restlessness. However, when Odysseus is added to my father's chart, this asteroid is seen to be at 21° Sagittarius 00', exactly conjunct his Sun at 21° Sagittarius 37' and his Moon at 22° Sagittarius 37', equaling his Sun/Moon midpoint.

I've found that the asteroid Odysseus describes the wanderer. The wandering can be emotional instead of, or as well as, physical. There are setbacks while trying to get home again. Seeing the position of my father's Odysseus, I understood his wanderings, both literal and figurative, as they never could be understood from the planets alone.

My father as a young man had left America to go to Paris to pursue his studies and career as an artist. Neptune (23° Gemini 25'ᴙ) is exactly opposite his Odysseus, Sun, Moon conjunction; the asteroid America (22° Virgo 17'), exactly square (T-Square); his name asteroid (20° Scorpio 11'), exactly semisextile; and the asteroids Atlantis (22° Leo 37'ᴙ), Paris (23° Leo 57'ᴙ), exactly trine. I've found that Atlantis (⬦) refers to the Atlantic Ocean, as well as to the legendary island in the Atlantic Ocean. My father crossed the Atlantic to go to Paris, returning to America several times until on one visit he met my mother. When I was three and a half years old my parents separated. My father always wanted to return to Paris, but somehow he never could. There were always setbacks. I think Paris felt like home to him, but after we rediscovered each other when I was twelve and a half years old he realized that "home is where the heart is." (His asteroid with my name at 06° Scorpio 21' is exactly semisquare his Odysseus, Sun, Moon conjunction.) Mirroring Odysseus' ten-year patterns (war and wanderings), ten years later he died.

As for hereditary patterns, close family members have this asteroid in the following exact aspects. Like my father, I have Odysseus aspecting my Sun—in my case by an opposition. My first husband, who repeats the family Lunar emphasis by having his Sun in Cancer, has Odysseus sextile his Moon. The Moon is the ruler of his Sun, connecting his luminaries as my father's Sun, Moon conjunction connects his. In fact, he, like my father, has Odysseus at his Sun/Moon midpoint. Like my father, he also has this asteroid aspecting his name asteroid (semisquare). The son who resulted from my first marriage has Odysseus in his first house, representing himself (as well as his mother's father—tenth from the fourth). Odysseus is trine his Midheaven and sextile his IC, showing the relevance of this asteroid's symbolism to his father and mother, as well as to his career and home. He travels a great deal in his work and has Odysseus trine his Part of Fortune, like my mother's mother. Travel has been fortunate for them both. He has this asteroid semisextile his East Point, while I have it square mine. (The East Point, I believe, is how you are, while the Ascendant is how you act or react.) My second husband, who repeats the family Lunar emphasis by having his Moon in the fourth house square his Ascendant, has Odysseus sextile his Pluto. Pluto is the ruler of his Scorpio Moon and IC. Our daughter, who repeats the family Lunar emphasis by having her Moon opposition her Ascendant, has Odysseus quincunx her Venus. Venus is the ruler of her Taurus Moon. My mother has Odysseus sextile her Mars, which is the ruler of her Moon, Ascendant and East Point. The conjunction of her Moon and Ascendant repeats the family Lunar emphasis. Also, she has this asteroid semisquare her Jupiter. Jupiter is the ruler of her Sagittarian Sun, Jupiter and Mars, with the Mars connecting back to her Aries Moon, Ascendant and East Point through its rulership of them. Further highlighting this asteroid in the family, there is a conjunction of my mother's Odysseus (12° Aquarius 42'), my second husband's (11° Aquarius 20'), and our daughter's (12° Aquarius 56'ℝ). Finally, this asteroid of wandering is square my North Node from 03° Sagittarius 24'ℝ to 03° Pisces 16', and the Odysseus theme has been a prevailing one in my close connections. Some family members have been in show business, literally trouping about the country, but all have been trying figuratively to get home again. Some have succeeded in getting there, while others are still involved in their own personal odysseys.

The asteroid Odysseus has other meanings. It can refer to the mental and physical characteristics of Odysseus. He was very clever and had red hair, broad shoulders and short legs, with a scar on one leg. This asteroid can also signify multiple families such as Odysseus amassed. On his way home from Troy, he fathered three sons with Circe and twin sons with Calypso. Even after returning home and having a second son with his faithful wife, Penelope, Odysseus went to Thesprotia to sacrifice to Poseidon, married its queen and had another son with her. When she died he returned home again, which brings us back to the asteroid Odysseus as the significator of the wanderer, ever wending his way home.

Odysseus illustrates how the asteroids make the generalities of the planets and personal points specific. The positions of the asteroids, like those of the planets and personal points, are inherited. They tell the stories of our antecedents and our descendants.

SYNONYMITY IN FAMILIES

In those stories of our families, there are synchronous and synonymous events. Having previously written about synchronous events, I'll now treat synonymous ones.

As an example, semantic patterns stretch over many generations in families. Tracing the meanings and associations of the surnames that have come together through the marriages in a family will give insight into the family. Often the names are similar or complementary.

For instance, considering the similarities, my father's surname was Holcomb, and my mother's maiden name was McComb. My parents shared the "comb," pronounced koom, and they were very much alike. Comb, or combe means "valley." A valley implies hills or mountains, and the Holcombs and the McCombs were always devising ways to climb them. Comb (koom) sounds like "come to me," which brings to mind Dark Moon Lilith, which I've seen associated with show business and with the "siren song." (Show business has the allure of that song.) Both my parents, my paternal aunt, and my grandfather Holcomb were involved with show business. My grandfather McComb had inherited the proceeds from a railroad, and a train whistle is like a siren song. In addition, comb. is an abbreviation for combining to form a whole. On the other hand, comb (kom) is a toothed object, which is used to separate, or to remove what is undesirable. Comb can also mean "to search everywhere in." Comb as separator and searcher has a Virgoan quality. There is a strong strain of Virgo on both sides of the family. Also, *The Columbia Encyclopedia* says comb "refers to tools for…pressing home the weft…and for carding or combing fibers in preparation for spinning," and my parents named their daughter Nona, the Roman Fate who weaves and spins the thread of life. (As for "pressing home the weft," I married a Press.

Considering the complete surnames, there are both similarities and complementaries. The first syllable of Holcomb sounds like hole and whole. Hole is similar to valley, and whole is similar to comb. as an abbreviation for combining to form a whole. The second syllable repeats the message of the first. The Holcomb family did often get in a hole, financially or otherwise, but then there was a wholeness that got them out of it. As for McComb, it is a name broken in two parts. In Scottish, Mc or Mac means "son of," and Comb is a modification of the Gaelic Thómais, so McComb means "son of Comb," or "son of Thomas." (As for Thomas, my daughter married a man whose first name is Thomas.) Names with a prefix related to the father place a particular emphasis on the son, the lineage, the clan. The second syllable is not repeating the message of the first, but Thomas means "A twin," which is one of two similar parts. There has been a great deal of duality in the behavior of the McComb family. Astrologically, such "twinning" runs in both families with my being a double Gemini; my mother, a double Aries; and my father, a double Sagittarius. My grandfather McComb's Sun and Moon are in the same house, which is another form of duality.

As for unmitigated complementation in an earlier generation, my father's mother, who married a Holcomb, was the daughter of a woman whose maiden name was Obrist. Obrist is like bristle which is "a short, stiff hair of an animal." Bristles are used to make brushes, and what is more of a complement to a brush than a comb?

ASSOCIATIONS OF PLACES

Insight is also gained from tracing the meanings and associations of the places you and your family have lived. I've been helped in my research on my own family by the records of a relative who recorded the addresses, as well as the dates of birth, of many members of the family. If the names or purposes of places change, there still seem to be connections between what they were in the past, what they are in the present, and what they will be in the future.

For instance, where I lived as a girl you could see from my windows the Claremont Riding Academy next door. That academy became the ABC TV Studios. Horses bring to mind Jupiter, who, as *king* of the gods, could correlate to the show business of television studios. Mont means mountain, which is associated with high places. Clare or Clara means "Brilliant, bright, illustrious,"[1] and both brightness and television have to do with the reflection of light. A famous namesake for Clare is Clare Booth Luce, an American writer and diplomat. Another famous namesake is St. Clare. All of the above associations were made before my reading in *The Oxford Dictionary of Saints* that recently St. Clare "has been named patron of television."[2] As for ABC, it stands for American Broadcasting Company, and my natal asteroid America (26° Capricorn 19') is in an exact Grand Trine with my Mercury (27° Taurus 01') and my Hebe (25° Virgo 27'), Athene (27° Virgo 41'). Mercury refers to communication; Hebe, to the bringing of something immortal to the universe; and Athene, to perception. Mercury rules my Moon, Sun, Venus, Uranian planet Vulcanus, name asteroid Nonie, and my fourth and fifth cusps. Mercury also rules my Bacchus and Iris, and these asteroids are related to the arts. The Venus, Vulcanus, Iris and Nonie are in my fourth house. My home (fourth cusp, fourth house and Moon) was next to the ABC TV Studios (Bacchus, Sun and Iris), and twenty-five years after I left home my daughter (fifth cusp and Venus) became a contract player for nine months in a soap opera on ABC TV. (After completing my book, I discovered that my asteroid Klare is 25° Taurus 26'; my asteroid Clara, 26° Libra 02'ʀ, both tying in exactly with this Grand Trine; and my asteroid Clarissa is 08° Virgo 08', exactly square my fourth cusp at 07° Gemini 41'.)

Where I lived when a girl has a connection to where I lived when first born. At my birth my home was the Cambridge Hotel, two blocks from the Claremont Riding Academy, and Clare College is a college of Cambridge University. Another association with my first home is that Cambridge is like Cambria, the medieval name for Wales, and my ancestry on my father's maternal side is Welsh.

An example of the name of a place persisting after that name is changed concerns my first home. About fifty years after my parents and I left the Cambridge Hotel, I found its address on a microfilm of the 1933 Manhattan phone directory. Several days later I went to that address. The chart of my seeing the cooperative apartment building with no name, that had been the Cambridge Hotel, featured the asteroid Cambridge. The transiting Midheaven at 17° Capricorn 35' was exactly conjunct transiting Cambridge at 18° Capricorn 45'; square transiting Nonie at 19° Libra 37'. My parents' name asteroids were also featured. Among other things, the transiting midpoint of those asteroids at 21° Libra 52' equaled the transiting East Point at 20° Aries 38', as well as my natal IC at 07° Gemini 41' and my natal asteroid with my father's name at 22° Cancer 54'. My progressed chart repeated these emphases. My progressed midpoint of the name asteroids of my parents was at 07° Gemini 13', equaling the transiting midpoint of those name asteroids by a sesqui-quadrate. As a result, many of the same factors, including my IC and my asteroid with my father's name, equaled the progressed midpoint. My progressed chart duplicated the Cambridge emphasis with the Midheaven at 27° Capricorn 49' exactly conjunct Cambridge at 28° Capricorn 37'ʀ.

Not having the ephemeris of the Cambridge asteroid until a year later, I did not know its position. Not knowing where the Cambridge Hotel was until seeing it that day, I did not realize that it was on the same block as another building highlighted in my life. In that building an event occurred which paralleled events which had occurred while I lived at the Cambridge Hotel.

The aforementioned experiences are within this life, but there have been other experiences which relate to psychic flashes concerning past lives. At the moment when I've met the particular person, or seen the particular place, about which there will be, or has been, the psychic flash, the chart describes that past-life connection. Consequently, I suspect that if in a future life I were to pass the place once known as the Cambridge Hotel, and were to feel some sense of recognition, the asteroid Cambridge would again be highlighted.

Closure

And so, I've come to the end of this book which was begun thirteen years ago. As expressed at the beginning, the purpose of this book is to share the methods which have helped me catch a glimpse of what is hidden. Hopefully, my purpose has been achieved, though the messages which the universe is sending us are veiled. Those messages, which are often metaphorical rather than literal, are not always easily deciphered. We need to become aware of their subtext, if we are to understand them. Though they are within a particular time and place, I believe the messages cross the boundaries of this life, to reflect past times and places.

Notes

INTRODUCTION

1. A planet or point opposition another planet or point, with both square a third planet or point. See Table I on page 2 for the # of degrees in aspects.
2. The same, but more so, with another planet or point turning the T into a +.
3. Three planets or points trine each other.
4. The Nodes of the Moon are the points at which the Moon crosses the ecliptic (apparent path of the Sun); the Vertex is the intersection of the ecliptic with the prime vertical; and the East Point is the intersection of the horizon and prime vertical in the east. The mutable signs are Gemini, Virgo, Sagittarius and Pisces.
5. A chart that consists of the midpoints between the planets and points in the individual charts, i.e., the near midpoint between the Sun in chart A and the Sun in chart B is the Sun of their composite chart.

CHAPTER ONE

1. Zipporah Dobyns, an astrologer and Ph.D. psychologist, also equates the houses, signs and planets.
2. John Addey, *Harmonics in Astrology* (Green Bay, Wis.: Cambridge Circle, Ltd., 1977), p. 62.
3. The sesquiquadrate is a multiple of the semisquare.
4. The quincunx, or inconjunct, is a multiple of the semisextile.
5. Charubel, *The Degrees of the Zodiac Symbolized* (Chicago: The Aries Press, 1943), p. 50.
6. Esther V. Leinbach, *Degrees of the Zodiac* (Richmond, Va.: Macoy Publishing Co., 1973), p. XI.

7. This is the geometric position which is uncorrected for light-time. It is the true position and has the nutation (wobble of the Earth) correction. The apparent position, generally used by astrologers, is 02°34'31". See pages 19-21 for further explanation.

8. For a discussion of accuracy, see pages 18-24.

9. The East Point and West Point, and Antivertex and Vertex, are additional angles, and so, personal points. The East Point is the actual self, and the West Point, the actual other. The Antivertex is similar to the Vertex, but as Maritha Pottenger states in *The East Point and the Antivertex*, the Antivertex being on the eastern side of the chart is related more to the self, while the Vertex being on the western side is related more to the other.

10. The two parts of this equation, ♂ to ☿ and ☿ to ☉, might be analyzed separately as well.

11. The degree of my Sun (there are usually relevant contacts between the composite chart and the individual charts that comprise it).

12. Exponents of planetary pictures.

13. Reinhold Ebertin, *The Combination of Stellar Influences* (Württemberg: Ebertin-Verlag, 1972), p. 117.

14. An aspect is dexter when the faster moving planet is moving away from the slower planet; sinister, when it is moving toward the slower planet. This is not the same as an applying or a separating aspect: an aspect is applying when it is before exactitude; separating, when it is after exactitude.

CHAPTER TWO

1. Among them, *The American Ephemeris for the 20th Century, 1900 to 2000*, Neil F. Michelsen (San Diego, Calif.: Astro Computing Services, 1980), with seconds for the Sun and Moon (new edition, 1988).

2. To calculate geometric charts, the formula is :

$$\text{Geometric position} = \text{apparent position} + \left(\frac{8.32 \text{ minutes} \times \text{A.U. distance to Earth}}{1440}\right) \times \text{daily motion.}$$

3. Transpluto is a planet that astronomers have projected as a result of the perturbations of Neptune.

4. Dark Moon Lilith is a moon that some astrologers have projected.

5. The first asteroid discovered.

6. I rectified my second husband's birth time of 05:00 P.M. EST, given me by his mother, to 04:52:42 P.M. EST and consider it valid to use this rectified time in my research because there was no time on his birth certificate, the time given me was "rounded off," and the rectification was done long before his chart was used for my research.

7. Reinhold Ebertin, *The Combination of Stellar Influences* (Württemberg: Ebertin-Verlag, 1972), p. 154.

8. The Solar Arc is the difference between the position of the Sun in the progressed chart and the Sun in the radix chart. This arc is added to the positions of the planets and points in the radix chart.

9. John Addey, *Harmonics in Astrology* (Green Bay, Wis.: Cambridge Circle, Ltd., 1977), p. 116.

10. The relationship chart consists of the time and space midpoints, rather than the degree midpoints, between charts.

11. The Antivertex and Vertex are similar, but the Antivertex is related more to the self, while the Vertex is related more to the other. The Vertex and Antivertex are additional angles, formed from the intersection of the prime vertical and the ecliptic.

12. The East Point and West Point are additional angles, formed from the intersection of the prime vertical and the horizon.

13. A Uranian planet associated with fated happenings. There is a link with Vulcan, the Roman god of fire and metalworking — hence an association with power.

14. Poseidon is a Uranian planet which is a Super-Neptune.

15. Septile (51°25'42.8"), biseptile (102°51'25") or triseptile (154°17'8.5").

16. As mentioned before, Hades is a Uranian planet that may sometimes have a karmic or past-life context.

17. This conjunction would also be in the 7th Harmonic Midheaven Equal House Chart, from whose perspective one of Jupiter's references is the law.

18. In my Second Marriage Chart, this asteroid is at 15° Libra — only one degree away.

19. 7.8323925' is the number of minutes of arc, in proportion to 60 minutes of arc, that is equivalent to 4 days, 1 hour, 7 minutes and 18 seconds, in proportion to 31 days — the number of days within the next month. The number of minutes of arc is obtained as follows: $1 \cdot 7 \cdot 18/24 = .0467361$ (the hours, minutes and seconds divided by 24 hours); $4.0467361/31 = x/60' = 7.8323925'$ (this equation shows the 4 days and part of the 5th day in proportion to 31 days that is equivalent to X in proportion to 60 minutes of arc; 31 days is used because It is 6 months from the 26th of February (my husband's birthday) to the 26th of August, and 31 days from the 26th of August to the 26th of September.

20. 3 months, 6 days, 17 hours and 46 minutes from my birthday to the marriage equates to 03°13.045699'.

21. $342/365 = x/60' = 56.219178'$.

22. The increment is 24°16.231278', the degrees, minutes and seconds of arc which are equivalent to the time between my birth and my second marriage. Equations will be given subsequently.

23. By multiplication, a body in Cancer (my asteroid with his name) will progress faster than a body in Gemini (his asteroid with my name) because the increment each year is the zodiacal longitude of the natal position.

24. Geoffrey Dean, *Recent Advances in Natal Astrology* (Subiaco, W. Australia: Analogic, 1977), p. 329.

25. Llewellyn George, *A to Z Horoscope Maker and Delineator* (St. Paul, Minn.: Llewellyn Publications, 1973), p. 87.

26. Those asteroids are Amor, Dembowska, Diana, Dudu, Eros, Frigga, Hidalgo, Icarus, Lilith, Pandora, Pittsburghia, Psyche, Sappho, Toro and Urania.

27. Addey, *Harmonics*, p. 11.

28. James S. and Ruth E. Williamsen, *Astrologer's Guide to the Harmonics* (Green Bay, Wis.: Cambridge Circle, Ltd., 1977), p. ii.

29. Addey, *Harmonics*, pp. 130-1.

30. With the magnified harmonic charts there is no problem using a constant orb because the harmonic charts are essentially being compared to each other. The comparison of the harmonic charts yields a comparison of the principles and years to which the harmonics refer.

31. These 7th harmonic aspects were mentioned previously, but as separate aspects.

32. His chart is given in abbreviated form in Figure II.

33. A disk with 360 degrees (divisions) is between the dial and the 6-inch disk.

34. Hans Niggemann, *Rules For Planetary Pictures* (New York: Hans Niggemann, 1959), p. 207.

35. An astrological quantifying system devised by the Brotherhood of Light.

36. Addey, *Harmonics*, p. 79.

37. *Ibid.*

38. *Ibid.*, p. 74.

39. *Ibid.*, p. 159.

40. *Ibid.*

CHAPTER THREE

1. *New Larousse Encyclopedia of Mythology* (London: Hamlyn, 1968), pp. 199-200.

2. This option was added by Astro in September of 1982.

3. Another name for Pluto is Hades. As Hades, he was considered more mysterious and unyielding.

4. *New Larousse*, p. 108.

5. Catherine B. Avery, ed., *The New Century Classical Handbook* (New York: Appleton-Century-Crofts, Inc., 1962), p. 186.

6. H.J. Rose, *A Handbook of Greek Mythology* (New York: E.P. Dutton, 1959), p. 109.

7. *New Larousse*, p. 106.

8. The chart was recalculated by Astro so these positions are geometric and not rounded off to the closer minute.

9. Avery, pp. 472-3.

10. As mentioned previously, a Fist of God is like a Finger of God, only with more "punch."

11. Mark's positions deviate from the positions of Astro generally no more than + or – one minute of arc. The deviations are due to the fact that Astro calculates the positions geometrically for me and does not round them off to the closer minute.

12. These differences are based on Mark Pottenger's CCRS Program, which lists the heliocentric North Nodes (ascending) for January 1, 1900, as Ceres - 20° Gemini 40', Pallas - 22° Virgo 52', Juno - 20° Virgo 47', Vesta - 13° Cancer 33', and Chiron - 28° Libra 40'; and for January 1, 2000, as Ceres - 20° Gemini 39', Pallas - 23° Virgo 14', Juno - 20° Virgo 23', Vesta - 14° Cancer 08', and Chiron - 29° Libra 10'.

13. *Profiles of Women* by Lois M. Rodden gives August 28 at 03:00 P.M. MET, however, an update by Ms. Rodden in the April 20, 1985 *American Federation of Astrologers Bulletin* gives August 29 at 03:30 A.M. MET.

14. Institute of Theoretical Astronomy of the Academy of Science of USSR, *Ephemerides of Minor Planets for 1983* (Leningrad: Science, 1982), p. 269.

15. *The American Book of Charts* by Lois M. Rodden gives 11:30 A.M. LMT from a copy of the birth registration.

16. Institute of Theoretical Astronomy of the Academy of Science of USSR, *Ephemerides of Minor Planets for 1982*, p. 269.

17. *Ibid.*, p. 7.

18. *Ibid.*, p. 10.

19. Institute of Theoretical Astronomy of the Academy of Science of USSR, *Ephemerides of Minor Planets for 1984* (Leningrad: Science, 1983), p. 9.

20. *Ibid.*, p. 7.

21. Thomas Bulfinch, *Bulfinch's Mythology* (New York: The Modern Library, n.d.), p. 33.

22. *Ibid.*, p. 306.

23. David Hugh Farmer, *The Oxford Dictionary of Saints* (Oxford: Oxford University Press, 1983), p. 278.

24. Bulfinch, pp. 322-3.

25. *Ibid.*, p. 336.

26. *The Random House College Dictionary.*

27. *New Larousse*, p. 163.

28. *Ibid.*

29. The 1982 *Ephemerides of Minor Planets* gives the ascending node of Herculina (532) as 17° Cancer 25' 46.06" for August 19, 1982. This position would probably be within seconds of the November 16th position.

30. She was born February 20, 1954 at 06:01 P.M. PST in San Francisco, California, and her natal Roberta is 07° Capricorn 14'. Her kidnapping was on February 4, 1974 at 09:05 P.M. PST in Berkeley, California.

31. Transpluto might be at 18° Cancer 43' and Dark Moon Lilith at 03° Virgo 06' instead, since Astro does not give me the positions of these hypothetical bodies to the first decimal place.

32. The birth data is from *Profiles of Women* by Lois M. Rodden.

33. Avery, p. 128.

34. In the *NCGR Journal*, Vol. 4, No. 1, Michael Baigent makes a good historical case for accepting the 05:10 P.M. chart given by Ebenezer Sibly in the *New and Complete Illustration of the Occult Sciences*, published in 1790.

35. Andrea Kennet, *Beautiful Pittsburgh* (Beaverton, Ore.: Beautiful American Publishing Co., 1979), p. 9.
36. Carolyn R. Dodson, *Horoscopes of the U.S. States and Cities* (Tempe, Ariz.: American Federation of Astrologers, Inc., 1975), p. 140.
37. *Funk & Wagnalls Standard Dictionary of Folklore, Mythology, and Legend* (1972; rpt. New York: Harper & Row, Publishers, Inc., 1984), p. 426.
38. *New Larousse*, pp. 245-80.
39. *Minor Planet Circulars / Minor Planets and Comets*, April 8, 1982, p. 6831.
40. Zipporah Pottenger Dobyns, Intro., *The Asteroid Ephemeris* (Los Angeles, Calif.: TIA Publications, 1977), p. 13.

CHAPTER FOUR

1. *Encyclopaedia Britannica* (Chicago: Encyclopaedia Britannica, Inc., 1948), vol. 16, p. 211.
2. *Star*, October 5, 1982, p. 40.

CHAPTER FIVE

1. Llewellyn George, *A to Z Horoscope Maker and Delineator* (St. Paul, Minn.: Llewellyn Publications, 1973), p. 561.

CHAPTER SIX

1. Using a modulus of 90 is similar to using a 90° dial. To express a number "modulo 90" means to divide it by 90 and use only the remainder. Thus, a longitude of 227° (17° Scorpio) expressed modulo 90 or on a 90° dial would be 47° (227/90 = 2; remainder is 47). Similarly 227 modulo 15 = 2 (227/15 = 15; remainder is 2); and 227 modulo 45 = 2.—Ed.

CHAPTER SEVEN

1. La Reina Rule, *Name Your Baby* (New York: Bantam Books, Inc., 1966), p. 41.
2. David Hugh Farmer, *The Oxford Dictionary of Saints* (Oxford: Oxford University Press, 1983), p. 82.

Bibliography

Addey, John. *Harmonic Chart Tables*. Green Bay, Wis.: Cambridge Circle, Ltd., 1976.

The Asteroid Ephemeris. Los Angeles, Calif.: TIA Publications, 1977.

Asteroid Names & Nodes. New York: National Council for Geocosmic Research, Inc., 1981.

Attwater, Donald. *The Penguin Dictionary of Saints*, 2nd ed. Harmondsworth, England: Penguin Books, 1983.

Avery, Catherine B., ed. *The New Century Classical Handbook*. New York: Appleton-Century-Crofts, Inc., 1962.

Bach, Eleanor. *Ephemerides of the Asteroids: Ceres, Pallas, Juno, Vesta*. New York: Celestial Communications, Inc., 1973.

_____. *Planet Watch*, October, 1983.

Baigent, Michael. "Ebenezer Sibly and the Declaration of Independence." *NCGR Journal*, Vol. 4, No. 1: 44-46.

Britannica Book of the Year, 1958. n.p.: Encyclopaedia Britannica, Inc., 1958.

Brockett, Oscar G. *The Theatre: An Introduction*. New York: Holt, Rinehart and Winston, 1979.

Bulfinch, Thomas. *Bulfinch's Mythology*. New York: The Modern Library, n.d.

CAO Times (14 Ephemerides). New York, 1978-1983.

The Columbia Encyclopedia, 3rd ed. New York: Columbia University Press, 1968.

Corliss, Richard. "A Dickens of a Show." *Time*, October 5, 1981, pp. 76-79.

De Lee, Joseph B., M.D., and J.P. Greenhill, M.D. *Principles and Practice of Obstetrics*. Philadelphia: W.B. Saunders Co., 1947.

Dobyns, Zipporah. *Expanding Astrology's Universe*. San Diego, Calif.: ACS Publications, Inc., 1983.

_____. *Asteroid-World: Winter 1987*, p. 4; *Asteroid-World: Fall 1987*, pp. 3-6.

Don Juan. The Poetical Works of Lord Byron. New York: John W. Lovell Co., n.d.

Dunlap, David W. *On Broadway: a journey uptown over time.* New York: Rizzoli International Publications, Inc., 1990.

Encyclopaedia Britannica, 24 vols. Chicago: Encyclopaedia Britannica, Inc., 1948.

Ephemeris of Chiron. Toronto: Phenomena Publications, 1978.

Ephemeris of Diana. New York: National Council for Geocosmic Research, Inc., 1981.

Farmer, David Hugh. *The Oxford Dictionary of Saints.* Oxford: Oxford University Press, 1983.

Fields, Maxine. *Baby Names from Around the World.* New York: Pocket Books, 1985.

Funk & Wagnalls Standard Dictionary of Folklore, Mythology, and Legend. 1972; rpt. New York: Harper & Row, Publishers, Inc., 1984.

George, Llewellyn. *A to Z Horoscope Maker and Delineator.* St. Paul, Minn.: Llewellyn Publications, 1973.

Gottfried, Martin. *Broadway Musicals.* New York: Harry N. Abrams, Inc., 1979.

Grimble, Ian. *Scottish Clans & Tartans.* New York: Harmony Books, 1982.

Helbling, Robert E., and others. *First-Year German,* 2nd ed. New York: Holt, Rinehart and Winston, 1979.

Institute of Theoretical Astronomy of the Academy of Science of USSR. *Ephemerides of Minor Planets,* 1982-1987. Leningrad: Science, 1981-1986.

Johnson, Richard. "Death of a Legend." *New York Post,* Sept. 15, 1982, pp. 37-39.

Kennet, Andrea. *Beautiful Pittsburgh.* Beaverton, Ore.: Beautiful America Publishing Co., 1979.

Lantero, Erminie. *The Continuing Discovery of Chiron.* York Beach, Me.: Samuel Weiser, Inc., 1983.

"The Last Fairy Tale." *Newsweek,* Sept. 27, 1982, pp. 36-47.

Leerhsen, Charles, and others. "Busting the Beer Bust." *Newsweek,* October 29, 1984, pp. 96-97.

Lehman, J. Lee. *The Ultimate Asteroid Book.* West Chester, Penn.: Whitford Press, 1988.

March, Marion D. "Data Exchange." *American Federation of Astrologers Bulletin,* Vol. 47, No. 4: 111-14.

Mason, Sophia. "Forecasting a 'Mini-Crisis' Period with Quarter Moons." *American Federation of Astrologers Bulletin,* Vol. 44, No. 2: 53-59.

_____. *Lunations and Predictions.* Parma, Ohio: Aquarian-Cancerian Publications, 1977.

McAuliffe, Kathleen, and Sharon McAuliffe. "Keeping Up with the Genetic Revolution." *New York Times Magazine,* Nov. 6, 1983, pp. 40-44, 92-97.

Metaphysical Bible Dictionary, 2nd ed. Kansas City, Mo.: Unity School of
    Christianity, 1942.

Minor Planet Circulars / Minor Planets and Comets. Cambridge, Mass.: Minor
    Planet Center, Smithsonian Astrophysical Observatory.

Mundane Data. Tempe, Ariz.: American Federation of Astrologers, Inc.

National Enquirer, October 5, 1982; October 12, 1982.

New Larousse Encyclopedia of Mythology. London: Hamlyn, 1968.

New York Post, Nov. 17, 1982; June 23, 1984; August 17, 1984; Feb. 28, 1985.

New York Times, Nov. 17, 1982; March 27, 1988.

Nietzsche, Friedrich. *Thus Spake Zarathustra*. New York: Tudor Publishing Co.,
    1934.

Niggemann, Hans. *Rules for Planetary Pictures*. New York: Hans Niggemann,
    1959.

Nurnberg, Maxwell, and Morris Rosenblum. *Your Baby's Name*. New York:
    Agency Publishers, Inc., 1951.

Pilcher, Frederick, and Jean Meeus. *Tables of Minor Planets*. Jacksonville, Ill.,
    1973.

Rodden, Lois M. *The American Book of Charts*. San Diego, Calif.: Astro
    Computing Services, 1980.

————. *Profiles of Women*. n.p.: American Federation of Astrologers, Inc.,
    1979.

Rose, N.J. *A Handbook of Greek Mythology*. New York: E.P. Dutton, 1959.

Rule, La Reina. *Name Your Baby*. New York: Bantam Books, Inc., 1966.

Sebastian, Seraphita. "From the Asteroids' Hall of Fame," No. 2.

Asteroid-World: Summer 1987, pp. 1-3.

Silver, Nathan. *Lost New York*. n.p.: Houghton, Mifflin Co., 1967.

The Standard American Encyclopedia, 15 vols. Chicago: Standard American
    Corp., 1937.

Star, October 5, 1982.

Stark, Batya, and Mark Pottenger. *The Asteroid Ephemeris: Dudu, Dembowska,
    Pittsburgh, Frigga*. San Diego, Calif.: ACS Publications, Inc., 1982.

Vinocur, John. "For Princess's Family, the Parting is Forlorn." *New York Times*,
    Sept. 19, 1982, p. 16.

Withycombe, E.G. *The Oxford Dictionary of English Christian Names*. Oxford:
    Oxford University Press, 1977.

Appendices

Asteroids with Glyphs

Asteroid	Glyph	Asteroid	Glyph
Aesculapia	�	America	⚕
Amor	⍉	Apollo	⊖
Artemis	☽	Astraea	⚤
Athene	⚷	Atlantis	⫶⎕⫶
Atropos	⎊	Bacchus	Υ
Ceres	?	Chiron	⚷
Crescentia	☾	Dembowska	?
Demeter	♄	Diana	D
Dudu	☄	Eduarda	🄴
Edwin	🄴	Elsa	∈
Eros	☙	Flora	⚘
Freia	♅	Frigga	♒
Guinevere	♈	Hebe	⚱
Hekate	)(	Hera	✳
Hestia	⌃	Hidalgo	⟨
Hygiea	⚵	Icarus	▽
Iris	⌒	Jeanne	J
Julia	♑	Juno	✳
Klotho	⎉	Lachesis	⎊
Lilith	⚸	Margarita	M̩
Martina	⋔	Metis	♁
Michel	⋃	Moira	⚯
Nemausa	X	Nonie	N
Pallas	⚴	Pandora	▽
Patricia	♕	Persephone	℞
Peter	⚶	Pittsburghia	♂
Proserpina	℞	Psyche	⚿
Quetzalcoatl	Q	Sappho	⚹
Roberta	R	Tezcatlipoca	T
Sy	∫	Toro	♀
Urania	⋋	Vesta	⚶

Uranian Planet Key Words

In general, key words for the Uranian planets are "esoteric" and "extraordinary." The Uranian planets are esoteric because they are unknown, and extraordinary because they have the Uranian connotations of their name. The difference between the Uranian planets and the bodies with the same or similar names is that the Uranian planets have this hidden and unusual overlay.

Cupido ⚷ — Double Libra quality; Associations to the Roman god Cupid or Amor (Greek: Eros), such as marriage, family and other close relationships; Corporations; Organizations; Sociability; Harmony; Art.

Hades ⚸ — Scorpio quality, with a secondary Virgo quality adding fragmentation; Associations to the Greek god Hades or Pluto, such as the underworld, the hidden, debris and unpleasant things; Analysis, the breaking down into constituent parts; Antiquity, ancient or primitive cultures; Jazz; Astrology, a study from the distant past; Archeology, a study of the artifacts of past cultures; What has already been "used," such as previously married partners and adopted children or stepchildren; Recycling; Karmic or past-life references.

Zeus ⚹ — Sagittarian quality, with a secondary Leo quality adding creativity; Associations to the Greek god Zeus (Roman:Jupiter), such as leadership and controlled fire; The leadership can be in the political or theatrical arena; The controlled fire can take the form of thunderbolts, firearms, fire, rockets, railroads, machines, gas, oil, directed energy, creation and procreation.

Kronos ⚴ — Capricorn quality, with a secondary Cancer quality adding gentleness; Associations to the Greek god Kronos or Cronus (Roman:Saturn), such as head of the family, authority, state, ruler and everything above average; Independence.

Apollon ⚺ — Gemini quality, with a secondary Aquarius quality adding innovation; Associations to the Greek and Roman god Apollo, such as commerce, trade, science, art, music, duality and the Sun; The Sun association can be expressed as radiance and glory; Greatest success; Greatest expansion.

Admetos ⚳ — Taurus quality, with a secondary Pisces quality adding self-sacrifice; Associations to the legendary Greek king Admetus, whose wife, Alcestis, took his place when death came for him but was reunited with him when Heracles rescued her from the underworld; Death; Stoppage; Ending or never-ending; Earth; Geology; Roots; Stick-to-it-iveness; "Till death us do part"; Commitment; Adamancy; Going around in circles; Music, through the repetitiveness of practicing and playing and the serfdom of Apollo (god of music) to Admetus; Circulation; Containers, such as the TV set, computer monitor, elevator, and closet.

Vulcanus ⚶ — Double Aries quality; Associations to the Roman god Vulcan (Greek: Hephaestus), the lame god of volcanic fire and metalworking who worked underground and was married to Venus (Aphrodite), whom he caught in a net with Mars (Ares) when she betrayed him; Volcanism; Vulcanization, treatment of rubber to render it strong and pliant, as forging does iron and steel; Power; Force; Greatest strength; Fated happenings.

Poseidon ⚲ — Pisces quality, with a secondary Taurus quality adding a "down-to-earthness," often resulting in making money from Neptunian activities; Associations to the Greek god Poseidon (Roman:Neptune), such as spirit, esoterica, psychism, revelation, enlightenment, art, music, dance, theatre and seafaring; A Super-Neptune, more Neptunian than Neptune, but often signifying the positive expressions of Neptune; The light carrier; The spotlight.

APPENDIX THREE
Heliocentric Nodes
(in Alphabetical Order)

Heliocentric Nodes in Alphabetical Order
Epoch November 5, 1990   Equinox 1950.0   Planet nodes have number ####

# Name	Node	# Name	Node	# Name	Node
677 Aaltje	2♑43'41	3212 Agricola	19♋32'32	2508 Alupka	11♎07'43
2676 Aarhus	19♑09'34	645 Agrippina	0♈18'54	2353 Alva	24♈36'00
3277 Aaronson	24♊30'17	1800 Aguilar	3♌46'14	3581 Alvarez	7♏18'25
2366 Aaryn	7♒49'29	744 Aguntina	22♌13'23	1169 Alwine	14♐39'07
3654 AAS	20♎25'14	3192 A'Hearn	26♉28'08	650 Amalasuntha	4♏56'58
864 Aase	12♍40'14	3181 Ahnert	10♍38'31	284 Amalia	23♏24'09
2678 Aavasaksa	23♉37'40	2395 Aho	9♋01'43	113 Amalthea	3♌01'19
2722 Abalakin	13♌08'34	950 Ahrensa	1♎17'08	725 Amanda	8♊32'29
1581 Abanderada	14♋26'05	2826 Ahti	3♉21'37	1085 Amaryllis	19♌40'47
3480 Abante	8♎03'31	861 Aïda	24♋37'59	1035 Amata	1♈37'14
4263 Abashiri	27♑33'45	978 Aidamina	6♍08'50	1042 Amazone	22♉08'14
1390 Abastumani	28♈51'55	1918 Aiguillon	15♎06'05	1905 Ambartsumian	20♎58'08
3449 Abell	21♊03'36	1568 Aisleen	25♌46'25	2933 Amber	0♌59'14
2646 Abetti	22♓07'14	1404 Ajax	2♓16'01	193 Ambrosia	19♓37'04
2671 Abkhazia	17♏53'18	3067 Akhmatova	20♓04'56	986 Amelia	2♋34'00
456 Abnoba	18♏55'17	2153 Akiyama	17♉28'16	3471 Amelin	4♓39'39
151 Abundantia	8♉31'26	2067 Aksnes	0♍01'57	916 America	29♒25'28
829 Academia	22♓12'08	738 Alagasta	11♌53'01	516 Amherstia	28♒43'23
1150 Achaia	26♎08'28	1969 Alain	29♎04'17	3809 Amici	4♌23'50
588 Achilles	15♒52'23	2927 Alamosa	29♌58'31	367 Amicitia	23♊02'07
1821 Aconcagua	27♑00'21	4151 Alanhale	6♊32'20	871 Amneris	7♏32'18
523 Ada	20♐47'39	2500 Alascattalo	17♉34'10	2437 Amnestia	8♏31'56
330 Adalberta	16♌37'10	702 Alauda	19♑37'13	1221 Amor	20♍50'38
1996 Adams	0♈35'33	719 Albert	6♎05'34	2948 Amosov	28♎37'22
525 Adelaide	22♎56'50	1290 Albertine	7♒03'33	198 Ampella	28♐07'08
812 Adele	6♈52'12	2697 Albina	2♑28'57	29 Amphitrite	25♓55'40
647 Adelgunde	14♐24'55	1783 Albitskij	9♎10'24	3554 Amun	28♓01'21
276 Adelheid	0♏50'25	3174 Alcock	11♉54'59	1065 Amundsenia	29♒52'13
229 Adelinda	27♈54'17	2941 Alden	9♈56'27	3375 Amy	18♍40'36
145 Adeona	17♊03'56	1909 Alekhin	17♏03'33	980 Anacostia	15♑37'37
398 Admete	9♑38'19	2711 Aleksandrov	7♍27'17	2339 Anacreon	11♈36'50
608 Adolfine	23♑56'18	465 Alekto	0♒09'02	270 Anahita	13♐58'52
2101 Adonis	20♊34'32	418 Alemannia	8♐30'42	824 Anastasia	21♌10'50
268 Adorea	0♌29'25	259 Aletheia	27♊03'35	1173 Anchises	13♑12'08
239 Adrastea	0♎36'14	1194 Aletta	20♑54'05	2788 Andenne	14♈12'40
143 Adria	2♓41'28	3367 Alex	17♐54'58	2476 Andersen	22♊00'57
820 Adriana	28♋20'35	54 Alexandra	12♒51'52	2175 Andrea Doria	11♏43'33
1903 Adzhimushkaj	14♌59'36	1191 Alfaterna	14♉18'34	1296 Andrée	16♏29'19
91 Aegina	10♈22'40	1375 Alfreda	22♉15'57	2282 Andrés Bello	27♎16'35
96 Aegle	21♒37'59	1778 Alfvén	16♋36'41	3413 Andriana	6♒31'15
2401 Aehlita	20♉39'42	1213 Algeria	1♑30'23	175 Andromache	20♈50'59
159 Aemilia	13♌47'37	1394 Algoa	28♍24'52	2294 Andronikov	20♑46'12
1155 Aënna	8♉38'18	929 Algunde	20♍54'00	1172 Äneas	6♐46'37
396 Aeolia	9♐49'03	291 Alice	11♍08'22	3158 Anga	7♎11'28
369 Aëria	3♋57'12	1567 Alikoski	21♉12'54	1957 Angara	20♉28'25
2876 Aeschylus	2♈29'32	887 Alinda	20♋13'36	965 Angelica	10♉57'13
1027 Aesculapia	28♈57'44	266 Aline	25♏34'02	64 Angelina	9♒00'20
446 Aeternitas	11♉46'14	2526 Alisary	16♈34'39	3160 Angerhofer	10♒11'48
132 Aethra	18♐25'31	124 Alkeste	7♋44'15	1712 Angola	27♏32'31
1064 Aethusa	10♑08'37	82 Alkmene	25♈18'00	2162 Anhui	8♌09'32
1142 Aetolia	19♌02'06	3037 Alku	17♋28'16	791 Ani	9♌29'52
1187 Afra	26♒54'03	457 Alleghenia	9♐19'32	3358 Anikushin	26♑30'40
1193 Africa	19♑14'17	390 Alma	4♒48'37	1016 Anitra	8♈25'37
911 Agamemnon	7♓17'39	3045 Alois	5♋51'59	1457 Ankara	26♑03'23
2267 Agassiz	28♒07'29	925 Alphonsina	29♑14'43	265 Anna	4♓59'50
228 Agathe	12♒54'40	971 Alsatia	23♊16'58	2519 Annagerman	23♊23'22
2470 Agematsu	19♊11'55	1617 Alschmitt	4♍42'43	3055 Annapavlova	2♈53'29
1873 Agenor	17♎14'18	955 Alstede	21♓04'50	910 Anneliese	29♉38'48
47 Aglaja	2♈52'53	2232 Altaj	8♍05'50	3667 Anne-Marie	29♓38'48
641 Agnes	10♉39'07	119 Althaea	23♎15'57	3664 Anneres	20♐17'17
847 Agnia	0♑51'37	850 Altona	0♌59'21		
		4104 Alu	21♉34'56		

Heliocentric Nodes in Alphabetical Order
Epoch November 5, 1990   Equinox 1950.0   Planet nodes have number ####

2839 Annette 14♉07'15	959 Arne 29♉09'02	136 Austria 6♎01'30
817 Annika 5♌10'37	1100 Arnica 4♒00'47	2920 Automedon 20♏22'55
2572 Annschnell 19♎58'58	1018 Arnolda 29♓13'08	1465 Autonoma 16♍38'32
2404 Antarctica 20♋29'41	1304 Arosa 26♊56'02	2755 Avicenna 22♏20'12
2207 Antenor 8♍32'01	2958 Arpetito 27♑26'20	3994 Ayashi 21♉49'44
1943 Anteros 5♐45'26	2194 Arpola 16♉45'22	3290 Azabu 14♊53'33
129 Antigone 15♌51'08	404 Arsinoë 2♋05'03	1056 Azalea 13♋43'04
651 Antikleia 7♉51'25	1956 Artek 3♍33'42	2698 Azerbajdzhan 26♎13'45
1583 Antilochus 10♏39'19	105 Artemis 7♎52'29	1501 Baade 16♈31'42
1863 Antinous 16♓54'09	2597 Arthur 29♋53'25	3167 Babcock 17♈22'14
90 Antiope 10♊33'03	3961 Arthurcox 16♒06'39	2059 Baboquivari 20♎26'12
272 Antonia 7♉06'05	2023 Asaph 2♈49'21	2063 Bacchus 2♉40'40
1294 Antwerpia 20♊56'12	214 Aschera 11♓46'27	1814 Bach 19♈52'47
1912 Anubis 16♊00'53	3568 ASCII 27♉52'38	856 Backlunda 5♌01'16
3575 Anyuta 10♊50'17	2157 Ashbrook 19♊13'09	2940 Bacon 3♑37'08
2061 Anza 27♎20'28	3460 Ashkova 23♊17'28	333 Badenia 23♓44'46
4292 Aoba 21♒18'57	67 Asia 22♎21'06	2513 Baetslé 17♐14'37
2341 Aoluta 1♊08'43	1216 Askania 1♌09'15	3127 Bagration 23♑30'23
3810 Aoraki 3♐28'03	962 Aslög 25♌15'24	2358 Bahner 14♓26'54
4094 Aoshima 14♐20'22	2174 Asmodeus 29♐39'07	2776 Baikal 7♎11'51
3400 Aotearoa 13♐47'58	2848 ASP 8♓16'33	2700 Baikonur 21♍00'18
1388 Aphrodite 24♉05'22	409 Aspasia 1♐58'21	1280 Baillauda 23♑18'27
1862 Apollo 5♉18'42	958 Asplinda 13♓10'47	3115 Baily 18♐27'38
358 Apollonia 21♍54'57	246 Asporina 11♍55'29	1591 Baize 0♋05'00
3190 Aposhanskij 27♓56'32	4191 Assesse 21♏22'55	2549 Baker 15♎39'47
988 Appella 11♉50'35	1041 Asta 29♉59'47	3242 Bakhchisaraj 11♎07'12
1768 Appenzella 12♈05'24	2408 Astapovich 14♍16'49	3749 Balam 25♑15'30
1063 Aquilegia 4♋55'47	672 Astarte 13♓24'47	1491 Balduinus 13♒54'29
387 Aquitania 7♌54'04	1218 Aster 3♊25'30	770 Bali 14♉15'33
849 Ara 18♏05'32	658 Asteria 20♏48'13	2031 BAM 18♍48'05
841 Arabella 24♓17'16	233 Asterope 11♏43'17	324 Bamberga 27♒50'00
1157 Arabia 5♓43'10	5 Astraea 21♌07'49	1286 Banachiewicza
1087 Arabis 0♉06'06	1128 Astrid 29♉03'20	20♎26'35
407 Arachne 24♑14'16	1154 Astronomia 22♊37'01	1713 Bancilhon 0♊45'11
1005 Arago 19♓08'58	1871 Astyanax 25♌05'38	597 Bandusia 6♉12'26
973 Aralia 18♓06'41	152 Atala 9♌51'13	298 Baptistina 7♈46'14
1020 Arcadia 0♎22'24	36 Atalante 28♓14'22	2883 Barabashov 18♉06'22
1031 Arctica 8♏41'35	1139 Atami 2♏49'56	234 Barbara 24♌04'11
394 Arduina 6♊59'27	3546 Atanasoff 4♓47'37	1860 Barbarossa 12♌26'44
1502 Arenda 24♎10'34	111 Ate 5♒22'44	945 Barcelona 17♒48'44
737 Arequipa 4♎27'35	2062 Aten 18♐01'38	1615 Bardwell 2♍47'13
197 Arete 21♊24'45	3307 Athabasca 22♐44'15	2730 Barks 4♈32'08
95 Arethusa 3♐01'17	515 Athalia 1♌18'05	819 Barnardiana 2♓44'52
1551 Argelander 16♋54'00	230 Athamantis 29♏21'04	3693 Barringer 28♍18'46
469 Argentina 4♓06'52	730 Athanasia 4♋41'38	1703 Barry 21♋50'03
43 Ariadne 24♐21'43	881 Athene 6♑56'11	4204 Barsig 12♏18'18
1225 Ariane 11♈56'48	161 Athor 18♈12'13	2279 Barto 19♍32'51
1395 Aribeda 4♐58'23	1827 Atkinson 10♏27'56	4132 Bartók 22♍37'00
3496 Arieso 9♌22'08	1198 Atlantis 19♐24'23	3485 Barucci 15♒06'12
3523 Arina 25♉13'59	810 Atossa 2♍12'53	2657 Bashkiria 20♉01'14
2135 Aristaeus 10♎45'37	273 Atropos 8♍36'20	2033 Basilea 21♒17'19
3999 Aristarchus 26♑35'46	1138 Attica 13♑34'13	3991 Basilevsky 12♑20'33
2319 Aristides 22♋21'36	1489 Attila 4♍39'41	2434 Bateson 26♈55'18
2934 Aristophanes 22♎28'02	254 Augusta 28♈01'59	441 Bathilde 13♐19'45
793 Arizona 5♉41'23	1480 Aunus 3♊14'14	592 Bathseba 17♍54'38
1717 Arlon 10♓02'12	1488 Aura 24♓08'54	2702 Batrakov 6♐07'22
3376 Armandhammer	700 Auravictrix 6♋25'05	3931 Batten 27♒50'51
9♐37'35	419 Aurelia 19♏02'08	172 Baucis 1♓36'03
780 Armenia 24♌35'56	1231 Auricula 11♓36'28	1553 Bauersfelda 20♋34'03
514 Armida 28♐36'11	94 Aurora 2♈30'03	3683 Baumann 12♋13'15
1464 Armisticia 26♊36'04	63 Ausonia 7♓30'13	813 Baumeia 21♉30'40
774 Armor 9♐46'58	2236 Australia 7♈46'10	2306 Bauschinger 26♏32'16

Heliocentric Nodes In Alphabetical Order
Epoch November 5, 1990   Equinox 1950.0   Planet nodes have number ####

No. Name	Node	No. Name	Node	No. Name	Node
301 Bavaria	22♌03'25	1611 Beyer	27♏14'15	1215 Boyer	3♌15'25
3161 Beadell	21♓07'26	1963 Bezovec	16♋27'34	1342 Brabantia	12♒32'09
656 Beagle	3♎49'11	218 Bianca	20♍18'21	3430 Bradfield	13♉06'24
3314 Beals	29♓00'03	1146 Biarmia	4♏22'19	2383 Bradley	13♈59'19
1043 Beate	9♍02'04	3246 Bidstrup	17♎11'06	3488 Brahic	21♌36'19
3087 Beatrice Tinsley		585 Bilkis	29♍45'29	1818 Brahms	9♐03'45
	8♓19'15	4175 Billbaum	13♍11'20	640 Brambilla	24♏37'08
83 Beatrix	27♈13'56	2029 Binomi	7♑39'31	1168 Brandia	8♏11'37
2925 Beatty	6♏43'34	2873 Binzel	10♋33'05	3503 Brandt	6♎47'34
1349 Bechuana	6♏47'15	3924 Birch	1♓24'07	606 Brangäne	18♒14'36
3522 Becker	21♎18'37	960 Birgit	8♐44'41	293 Brasilia	1♊10'17
3737 Beckman	18♑06'35	2744 Birgitta	15♒16'47	3372 Bratijchuk	18♈54'08
1896 Beer	1♎41'56	2477 Biryukov	27♎53'09	1411 Brauna	14♑28'08
4026 Beet	17♌05'01	2633 Bishop	2♊02'38	4242 Brecher	0♉04'25
1815 Beethoven	20♋48'55	2038 Bistro	13♊05'00	786 Bredichina	29♊29'03
943 Begonia	23♋42'10	4289 Biwako	15♊29'15	3918 Brel	10♍13'06
1651 Behrens	6♎59'10	2145 Blaauw	24♐15'19	1609 Brenda	15♋03'25
1474 Beira	23♒24'34	4069 Blakee	25♏14'21	3824 Brendalee	29♒13'56
1052 Belgica	9♋11'30	2320 Blarney	28♋37'35	761 Brendelia	23♈35'13
2808 Belgrano	14♒20'29	2445 Blazhko	25♊41'43	1211 Bressole	9♌34'15
3747 Belinskij	8♉19'03	3318 Blixen	18♋48'35	3232 Brest	12♎02'02
178 Belisana	20♉48'04	2540 Blok	3♎00'40	4192 Breysacher	3♏34'38
1074 Beljawskya	7♉44'50	2507 Bobone	9♌46'10	2683 Brian	12♓09'11
695 Bella	5♑27'34	2637 Bobrovnikoff	25♓41'23	4029 Bridges	4♏15'50
1808 Bellerophon	13♈04'04	1487 Boda	7♐09'30	4209 Briggs	29♒58'31
3659 Bellingshausen		998 Bodea	1♒21'38	450 Brigitta	14♈08'28
	9♎24'21	3459 Bodil	8♋11'07	655 Briseïs	9♌44'18
28 Bellona	23♌59'51	371 Bohemia	13♑12'58	1071 Brita	22♉16'22
2626 Belnika	25♓35'35	720 Bohlinia	5♑31'03	1219 Britta	12♉08'15
1004 Belopolskya	3♍19'14	1141 Bohmia	15♋09'08	4079 Britten	14♊35'15
3498 Belton	13♏07'56	3948 Bohr	10♎14'22	521 Brixia	29♊29'20
2368 Beltrovata	17♑10'29	1635 Bohrmann	4♋06'45	1879 Broederstroom	
2030 Belyaev	19♍20'51	1654 Bojeva	25♈04'51		9♐28'32
734 Benda	2♈54'27	1983 Bok	23♈15'19	1315 Bronislawa	26♍03'27
1846 Bengt	18♈39'06	2338 Bokhan	22♋18'03	3385 Bronnina	17♎12'30
1784 Benguella	4♋51'25	3205 Boksenberg	29♋52'28	2773 Brooks	10♋48'25
976 Benjamina	4♐59'06	712 Boliviana	20♏30'19	3309 Brorfelde	29♈15'19
863 Benkoela	26♋34'30	2601 Bologna	18♑02'47	1746 Brouwer	21♒53'27
2863 Ben Mayer	0♌19'57	1441 Bolyai	13♐50'39	1643 Brown	18♑06'43
4093 Bennett	20♐09'38	2622 Bolzano	14♌24'10	3259 Brownlee	2♐15'23
1517 Beograd	3♊38'33	767 Bondia	19♊44'14	4203 Brucato	10♓53'41
776 Berbericia	19♊32'29	3129 Bonestell	0♌36'03	2430 Bruce Helin	15♉26'55
4184 Berdyayev	28♈05'30	361 Bononia	18♈36'17	455 Bruchsalia	16♊08'28
2998 Berendeya	6♍58'10	1477 Bonsdorffia	20♒28'28	323 Brucia	6♋56'13
653 Berenike	12♌44'40	1916 Boreas	10♓13'47	3955 Bruckner	23♈33'02
3093 Bergholz	8♑20'27	3859 Börngen	5♋44'56	290 Bruna	10♈02'27
716 Berkeley	25♌45'48	3075 Bornmann	4♓05'21	123 Brunhild	7♒29'33
3604 Berkhuijsen	19♈33'37	2706 Borovský	20♉34'40	2499 Brunk	11♎47'22
1313 Berna	28♑06'52	1539 Borrelly	22♌33'18	1570 Brunonia	9♎42'11
629 Bernardina	27♊10'11	1354 Botha	28♈16'24	901 Brunsia	24♐47'33
3038 Bernes	21♓15'49	741 Botolphia	10♋21'32	1811 Bruwer	17♍51'35
3467 Bernheim	14♋57'25	2337 Boubin	7♉03'02	2689 Bruxelles	10♎10'44
2034 Bernoulli	18♈38'44	1543 Bourgeois	17♑48'20	2488 Bryan	1♊59'51
422 Berolina	8♈40'09	3435 Boury	20♍21'38	3209 Buchwald	7♌47'41
3684 Berry	4♋35'51	859 Bouzaréah	5♉37'48	908 Buda	25♊09'13
154 Bertha	6♉34'48	2246 Bowell	5♏17'24	2524 Budovicium	8♑07'46
420 Bertholda	3♐50'42	3363 Bowen	2♎50'41	338 Budrosa	17♑13'11
1729 Beryl	8♈41'08	1639 Bower	23♒56'12	3469 Bulgakov	9♏06'41
1552 Bessel	9♈51'19	2996 Bowman	4♓05'13	2575 Bulgaria	21♒33'30
937 Bethgea	3♐18'00	3681 Boyan	12♌31'58	3890 Bunin	19♐10'46
250 Bettina	23♈59'08	2563 Boyarchuk	24♋15'15	2283 Bunke	16♎22'06
1580 Betulia	1♊41'56	2611 Boyce	11♊59'55	3447 Burckhalter	0♈10'08

Heliocentric Nodes in Alphabetical Order

Epoch November 5, 1990   Equinox 1950.0   Planet nodes have number ####

Number	Name	Position	Number	Name	Position	Number	Name	Position
3583	Burdett	3♉02'20	1240	Centenaria	23♒27'33	637	Chrysothemis	25♓14'12
384	Burdigala	17♉34'40	513	Centesima	4♎21'54	3094	Chukokkala	22♍04'04
374	Burgundia	8♏44'24	2198	Ceplecha	12♏44'56	2509	Chukotka	13♓19'19
834	Burnhamia	3♎12'03	807	Ceraskia	11♌57'29	2627	Churyumov	19♋11'27
2708	Burns	21♋38'10	1865	Cerberus	2♏22'16	2670	Chuvashia	14♑35'39
2593	Buryatia	3♊50'22	1	Ceres	20♊01'04	1275	Cimbria	8♎04'25
3254	Bus	13♉35'51	2252	CERGA	28♓02'47	1307	Cimmeria	23♏25'36
2490	Bussolini	2♏08'21	1571	Cesco	22♑33'47	1373	Cincinnati	26♑56'17
199	Byblis	28♊51'44	2089	Cetacea	12♋15'38	2298	Cindijon	18♎13'25
2170	Byelorussia	15♐30'55	1333	Cevenola	24♋40'28	3138	Ciney	14♏49'50
3505	Byrd	2♒13'53	1622	Chacornac	3♈59'09	34	Circe	4♎05'39
3306	Byron	2♏56'17	2981	Chagall	7♎28'19	2420	Čiurlionis	25♎11'49
2997	Cabrera	24♓45'52	4103	Chahine	22♈45'24	642	Clara	6♈49'40
297	Caecilia	1♓37'05	1671	Chaika	27♍18'58	302	Clarissa	7♈22'03
952	Caia	18♈09'20	1246	Chaka	20♑13'57	311	Claudia	20♊43'53
2926	Caldeira	10♏31'25	313	Chaldaea	26♍18'05	2461	Clavel	25♋57'25
341	California	28♈42'23	2562	Chaliapin	9♓42'23	1101	Clematis	21♎38'42
2542	Calpurnia	25♌55'52	2040	Chalonge	9♉29'18	1919	Clemence	26♓27'41
2906	Caltech	24♊03'44	3414	Champollion	24♈35'09	252	Clementina	21♎54'00
1245	Calvinia	1♍26'51	1958	Chandra	14♓32'00	4276	Clifford	16♊23'21
2531	Cambridge	14♋00'56	2051	Chang	4♏57'16	3034	Climenhaga	10♈11'55
957	Camelia	22♏28'31	3315	Chant	26♌29'37	1982	Cline	12♉05'04
2980	Cameron	22♍00'05	1707	Chantal	5♈42'52	3185	Clintford	10♊52'23
107	Camilla	23♍27'30	3906	Chao	28♌44'09	935	Clivia	16♈04'14
377	Campania	29♎43'02	3623	Chaplin	27♋54'06	661	Cloelia	5♓38'42
1077	Campanula	15♓51'42	2409	Chapman	20♌17'17	282	Clorinde	24♌28'14
2751	Campbell	5♐50'32	627	Charis	22♌09'15	2939	Coconino	19♓40'34
3327	Campins	9♊17'39	1510	Charlois	1♓06'37	237	Coelestina	23♊56'27
3015	Candy	7♉56'14	543	Charlotte	24♑51'37	1764	Cogshall	1♍50'52
1120	Cannonia	8♍10'42	388	Charybdis	24♓14'17	972	Cohnia	12♊16'24
740	Cantabia	25♋43'50	2984	Chaucer	21♊19'45	3495	Colchagua	3♌07'43
3563	Canterbury	27♐32'06	1804	Chebotarev	25♒14'21	1135	Colchis	20♓28'46
1931	Čapek	2♎07'05	2010	Chebyshev	8♈53'20	1973	Colocolo	3♎05'30
479	Caprera	15♌55'10	2369	Chekhov	17♉38'41	327	Columbia	24♓33'36
1391	Carelia	13♋17'04	2963	Chen Jiageng		489	Comacina	16♍45'36
491	Carina	25♍02'24			17♉20'42	1655	Comas Solá	20♋53'04
1470	Carla	28♓52'40	4207	Chernova	21♐01'46	3521	Comrie	28♉28'11
4121	Carlin	16♉19'02	2325	Chernykh	19♌42'25	58	Concordia	10♍50'36
2858	Carlosporter	8♌06'50	2783	Chernyshevskij		1528	Conrada	18♌51'56
1769	Carlostorres	18♒51'31			17♒35'20	315	Constantia	11♍10'08
360	Carlova	12♌08'24	2701	Cherson	14♈01'53	3061	Cook	7♋37'27
3294	Carlvesely	6♈44'58	568	Cheruskia	9♐29'24	2618	Coonabarabran	
558	Carmen	23♌28'16	334	Chicago	10♌07'37			11♑23'09
671	Carnegia	0♈16'33	2221	Chilton	5♈40'56	815	Coppelia	26♉48'47
2214	Carol	8♎35'07	623	Chimaera	7♏49'40	1322	Coppernicus	12♐43'58
235	Carolina	5♊49'20	1633	Chimay	24♋41'38	504	Cora	14♋19'03
1852	Carpenter	5♋15'33	1125	China	6♋47'53	2442	Corbett	10♎08'58
3837	Carr	23♏20'35	1787	Chiny	6♍50'29	2758	Cordelia	5♓18'34
4171	Carrasco	4♎43'13	2060	Chiron	28♎39'15	365	Corduba	4♎54'24
3050	Carrera	29♏32'00	2977	Chivilikhin	20♍06'38	425	Cornelia	0♊55'19
1683	Castafiore	26♒25'41	3113	Chizhevskij	5♎31'12	1232	Cortusa	22♐05'39
1116	Catriona	26♓25'09	2692	Chkalov	25♏52'18	1442	Corvina	10♏45'40
1344	Caubeta	29♉39'20	402	Chloë	9♌07'56	915	Cosette	8♈53'35
1974	Caupolican	17♍59'44	410	Chloris	6♋43'55	2129	Cosicosi	28♉03'28
505	Cava	0♋34'00	938	Chlosinde	28♌40'12	644	Cosima	19♋28'25
3305	Ceadams	1♉44'48	3784	Chopin	4♋14'38	2026	Cottrell	10♒59'12
2363	Cebriones	1♏12'04	1015	Christa	0♌40'33	2190	Coubertin	21♐52'38
4058	Cecilgreen	1♊27'29	2695	Christabel	2♉43'28	3009	Coventry	8♈06'51
1252	Celestia	20♌27'22	628	Christine	21♌37'28	1898	Cowell	13♍08'32
3857	Cellino	18♍33'58	1698	Christophe	26♉58'30	1476	Cox	0♓06'25
4169	Celsius	26♓38'34	2834	Christy Carol	28♈12'45	1725	CrAO	28♋54'17
186	Celuta	14♈16'16	202	Chryseïs	16♌37'36	486	Cremona	3♋47'28

Heliocentric Nodes in Alphabetical Order

Epoch November 5, 1990   Equinox 1950.0   Planet nodes have number ####

Name	Position	Name	Position	Name	Position
660 Crescentia	6♍39'20	4279 De Gasparis	25♐13'50	1789 Dobrovolsky	11♋39'26
1140 Crimea	11♊49'10	1867 Deiphobus	12♑58'17	382 Dodona	13♒04'29
2757 Crisser	9♈41'21	4060 Deipylos	17♍36'15	2451 Dollfus	1♓38'07
589 Croatia	27♍34'56	1244 Deira	6♑38'34	1277 Dolores	6♐58'32
1220 Crocus	23♋07'08	3798 De Jager	13♒57'31	2784 Domeyko	17♋39'40
1899 Crommelin	21♉43'02	1555 Dejan	18♒07'07	3450 Dommanget	11♊17'19
3531 Cruikshank	12♎30'54	157 Dejanira	1♊36'11	2176 Donar	29♊44'59
2731 Cucula	0♍59'26	184 Dejopeja	2♉02'33	3085 Donna	0♑30'56
2334 Cuffey	0♌33'10	3002 Delasalle	24♋57'17	1398 Donnera	26♑41'26
2226 Cunitza	12♉40'54	395 Delia	19♐05'59	3552 Don Quixote	20♓04'11
1754 Cunningham	12♍39'25	560 Delila	15♋03'16	668 Dora	4♏08'50
4183 Cuno	25♑14'02	3058 Delmary	27♎23'10	4076 Dörffel	16♓38'01
763 Cupido	19♑28'29	1988 Delores	15♋55'52	48 Doris	3♎21'37
1917 Cuyo	7♎49'04	3218 Delphine	2♎54'35	3802 Dornburg	18♌43'58
403 Cyane	4♐15'51	1274 Delportia	26♒41'54	339 Dorothea	23♍23'07
65 Cybele	5♍22'53	2954 Delsemme	13♍58'33	3416 Dorrit	19♈27'23
1106 Cydonia	27♒53'41	1848 Delvaux	1♓43'34	3194 Dorsey	4♊15'11
133 Cyrene	18♒38'24	3390 Demanet	12♈27'31	3453 Dostoevsky	0♒26'08
2315 Czechoslovakia	29♈57'23	349 Dembowska	2♉09'10	2684 Douglas	0♍44'38
1864 Daedalus	6♈07'57	1108 Demeter	24♏02'58	620 Drakonia	29♓43'55
2297 Daghestan	20♌09'52	1926 Demiddelaer	3♋14'18	263 Dresda	6♏11'27
1669 Dagmar	18♈37'00	4218 Demottoni	29♎10'04	3053 Dresden	6♈22'12
3256 Daguerre	24♍03'26	1335 Demoulina	22♍06'39	3273 Drukar	15♉59'41
1511 Daléra	21♊25'17	667 Denise	2♍44'03	3804 Drunina	21♈29'09
2919 Dali	11♍58'59	2134 Dennispalm	11♈19'29	1621 Druzhba	1♎25'06
3384 Daliya	19♌09'33	2400 Derevskaya	21♍38'33	1167 Dubiago	14♏22'09
4226 Damiaan	2♏27'10	1806 Derice	0♑37'17	2312 Duboshin	1♊33'58
61 Danaë	3♓22'38	3647 Dermott	5♌49'39	400 Ducrosa	26♒47'31
3415 Danby	13♐43'40	1339 Désagneauxa		3270 Dudley	26♌28'23
4021 Dancey	19♉10'04		20♑47'26	564 Dudu	10♊24'48
3120 Dangrania	10♏24'33	3268 De Sanctis	11♏17'06	1961 Dufour	29♈17'42
2068 Dangreen	5♋38'44	1588 Descamisada	8♋30'14	2772 Dugan	10♌12'36
2589 Daniel	28♌34'52	666 Desdemona	5♏05'23	571 Dulcinea	2♈43'17
1594 Danjon	9♊03'24	344 Desiderata	17♉58'48	1962 Dunant	15♈22'47
2117 Danmark	29♉19'47	1686 De Sitter	6♈15'21	3718 Dunbar	11♊16'32
2999 Dante	14♊31'52	1538 Detre	12♓46'48	2753 Duncan	14♓16'28
1381 Danubia	21♓32'16	3561 Devine	27♋32'28	3368 Duncombe	3♈50'21
1419 Danzig	3♏06'52	337 Devosa	24♓58'33	3123 Dunham	2♌38'44
41 Daphne	27♍40'47	1328 Devota	13♏17'31	3291 Dunlap	0♍51'31
2645 Daphne Plane		3892 Dezsö	9♍01'42	1338 Duponta	25♒11'20
	19♓19'06	2109 Dhotel	11♍51'41	3104 Dürer	11♍48'08
		78 Diana	3♓08'30	2231 Durrell	12♓10'19
1991 Darwin	28♒00'43	2389 Dibaj	3♓35'35	2055 Dvořák	10♓07'59
3321 Dasha	12♍21'20	3841 Dicicco	15♉40'38	2591 Dworetsky	26♓08'54
3146 Dato	2♋56'36	209 Dido	0♈19'46	2048 Dwornik	7♍06'05
1270 Datura	7♋26'13	1706 Dieckvoss	9♑15'27	200 Dynamene	24♒11'17
511 Davida	17♋19'15	2922 Dikan'ka	7♎28'44	1241 Dysona	21♒52'49
2725 David Bender	1♊33'13	99 Dike	11♉13'18	3082 Dzhalil	27♋16'25
4205 David Hughes	6♑00'01	3247 Di Martino	15♉13'17	2756 Dzhangar	20♓09'07
1037 Davidweilla	20♎12'16	2371 Dimitrov	24♏51'07	3170 Dzhanibekov	26♈42'20
3638 Davis	18♋52'51	2765 Dinant	17♓47'01	3687 Dzus	14♏43'55
3605 Davy	12♑08'40	1437 Diomedes	15♒07'29	1205 Ebella	22♈41'32
3126 Davydov	26♎07'13	106 Dione	1♊59'31	60 Echo	11♎23'50
1618 Dawn	12♋33'18	3671 Dionysius	21♊47'28	1750 Eckert	3♑15'33
1829 Dawson	22♑59'35	423 Diotima	9♏09'55	413 Edburga	13♋56'37
2359 Debehogne	25♎33'33	1805 Dirikis	18♏37'34	673 Edda	16♏33'13
3411 Debetencourt	8♊54'14	1319 Disa	16♐15'27	2761 Eddington	0♉53'10
541 Deborah	27♐33'35	4017 Disneya	1♉59'12	742 Edisona	4♊09'57
2551 Decabrina	10♈40'47	3535 Ditte	22♐08'11	517 Edith	4♑23'04
3610 Decampos	25♋31'17	3022 Dobermann	0♎19'06	1341 Edmée	17♋11'56
2852 Declercq	19♋44'15	3119 Dobronravin	20♋26'28	1761 Edmondson	16♊36'19
1295 Deflotte	4♎39'55	3013 Dobrovoleva	6♈49'31	445 Edna	22♑41'25

Heliocentric Nodes in Alphabetical Order
Epoch November 5, 1990   Equinox 1950.0   Planet nodes have number ####

340 Eduarda 26♈48'48	4044 Erikhøg 4♋13'53	3433 Fehrenbach 6♓29'01
2440 Educatio 16♏47'55	2167 Erin 12♐29'34	3658 Feldman 19♒58'35
1046 Edwin 10♈27'07	462 Eriphyla 14♋56'16	294 Felicia 15♌44'13
2754 Efimov 4♑48'34	705 Erminia 2♈29'58	109 Felicitas 2♈49'16
2269 Efremiana 6♊26'28	406 Erna 15♒44'10	1664 Felix 13♉48'26
13 Egeria 12♉44'23	698 Ernestina 10♉32'17	1453 Fennia 6♈32'13
2113 Ehrdni 22♈52'56	433 Eros 3♒44'21	1048 Feodosia 22♉25'16
2274 Ehrsson 18♓00'07	889 Erynia 12♌22'04	1745 Ferguson 18♊25'36
3617 Eicher 1♎05'45	1509 Esclangona 12♑58'21	2496 Fernandus 12♍44'08
442 Eichsfeldia 14♌26'45	1421 Esperanto 12♉38'53	72 Feronia 27♎31'15
2001 Einstein 26♓32'20	2253 Espinette 23♌29'45	4122 Ferrari 22♐10'39
694 Ekard 20♏06'20	622 Esther 21♌50'47	3308 Ferreri 21♍49'48
4116 Elachi 4♎32'34	1541 Estonia 1♈06'13	2286 Fesenkov 29♉07'19
2567 Elba 22♌18'08	2032 Ethel 29♈47'37	524 Fidelio 26♒26'16
858 El Djezaïr 6♊50'39	331 Etheridgea 21♈45'34	37 Fides 7♈08'54
130 Elektra 25♌16'28	1432 Ethiopia 2♌54'33	380 Fiducia 4♋49'36
354 Eleonora 20♌02'30	1119 Euboea 26♉58'39	2314 Field 3♉36'12
567 Eleutheria 28♉01'26	181 Eucharis 23♌31'29	1099 Figneria 23♈00'16
618 Elfriede 20♋41'36	217 Eudora 12♍31'10	2892 Filipenko 26♒27'18
1329 Eliane 11♌42'20	4063 Euforbo 22♋50'50	1616 Filipoff 17♉59'52
2650 Elinor 1♓57'26	45 Eugenia 27♌21'10	795 Fini 17♈00'35
956 Elisa 12♎17'08	743 Eugenisis 18♏46'20	1794 Finsen 11♏10'46
412 Elisabetha 16♋06'22	247 Eukrate 29♓51'15	4231 Fireman 20♐37'22
435 Ella 22♈46'15	495 Eulalia 6♎03'30	3342 Fivesparks 24♌06'16
2735 Ellen 14♓02'13	2002 Euler 28♍14'42	2118 Flagstaff 1♓06'41
3775 Ellenbeth 0♉15'42	185 Eunike 3♍25'35	1021 Flammario 25♋21'42
3711 Ellensburg 12♒25'59	15 Eunomia 22♑53'36	2588 Flavia 2♐14'31
2311 El Leoncito 6♏46'05	630 Euphemia 15♋12'37	1736 Floirac 9♍19'40
2196 Ellicott 1♏57'40	31 Euphrosyne 0♉37'21	4220 Flood 10♏58'19
3193 Elliot 11♈22'37	3655 Eupraksia 7♓52'02	8 Flora 20♋28'42
616 Elly 25♓48'04	2930 Euripides 29♓05'29	321 Florentina 10♉00'55
2493 Elmer 25♎39'41	52 Europa 8♌36'43	1689 Floris–Jan 3♌05'49
59 Elpis 19♍42'44	4007 Euryalos 6♈04'33	2302 Florya 7♒17'40
182 Elsa 16♋48'34	527 Euryanthe 0♌15'20	2994 Flynn 27♋52'10
3936 Elst 0♐11'27	3548 Eurybates 12♉52'15	2181 Fogelin 16♈53'05
2217 Eltigen 7♌33'29	75 Eurydike 28♓58'30	3223 Forsius 17♍56'19
277 Elvira 21♏13'01	195 Eurykleia 6♈41'32	1054 Forsytia 25♊45'11
1234 Elyna 4♒21'30	79 Eurynome 26♎18'31	19 Fortuna 0♏55'30
576 Emanuela 29♑21'09	27 Euterpe 4♋21'31	2789 Foshan 2♐15'02
481 Emita 6♊30'59	164 Eva 16♊37'01	2762 Fowler 3♒37'54
283 Emma 3♒54'42	3032 Evans 28♊07'01	3625 Fracastoro 12♏34'47
4282 Endate 25♒18'44	2130 Evdokiya 19♓37'24	1105 Fragaria 26♋50'17
342 Endymion 22♏12'17	503 Evelyn 8♊39'43	2133 Franceswright
4217 Engelhardt 24♓58'50	2656 Evenkia 5♋32'10	18♊11'21
2819 Ensor 17♈59'10	2664 Everhart 17♍20'05	1212 Francette 29♌05'28
4272 Entsuji 4♎02'46	1569 Evita 9♋13'01	2050 Francis 12♊02'35
221 Eos 21♌37'09	1576 Fabiola 16♍55'52	2824 Franke 12♒21'43
2148 Epeios 25♍53'52	1649 Fabre 25♌15'56	982 Franklina 28♑55'56
1810 Epimetheus 13♐40'37	1593 Fagnes 29♋34'55	1925 Franklin–Adams
3838 Epona 25♏07'06	751 Faïna 18♊21'09	23♋14'40
2928 Epstein 10♒21'40	408 Fama 28♑05'14	2845 Franklinken 23♌55'28
802 Epyaxa 7♈21'25	3478 Fanale 6♌01'46	862 Franzia 29♑47'32
62 Erato 5♌14'41	1589 Fanatica 0♋01'26	520 Franziska 4♉08'59
3251 Eratosthenes 21♌52'31	821 Fanny 29♎25'28	3917 Franz Schubert
3674 Erbisbühl 26♑43'40	1224 Fantasia 17♓45'07	16♌39'03
3114 Ercilla 26♍18'58	3248 Farinella 12♈07'13	309 Fraternitas 26♓05'42
894 Erda 10♎23'24	866 Fatme 0♋53'22	1093 Freda 25♉07'33
1254 Erfordia 17♑46'55	2583 Fatyanov 16♉41'46	678 Fredegundis 11♑16'30
1402 Eri 26♐43'36	1418 Fayeta 24♓40'36	76 Freia 24♎00'04
718 Erida 8♉06'51	2533 Fechtig 21♎34'57	3506 French 12♓45'35
163 Erigone 9♍46'49	3195 Fedchenko 5♑00'59	3369 Freuchen 27♐25'47
636 Erika 4♉35'46	1984 Fedynskij 5♎35'21	1561 Fricke 21♏53'32

Heliocentric Nodes in Alphabetical Order
Epoch November 5, 1990   Equinox 1950.0   Planet nodes have number ####

#	Name	Coord	#	Name	Coord	#	Name	Coord
3491	Fridolin	11♍00'28	2872	Gentelec	1♐05'57	1188	Gothlandia	4♈59'26
722	Frieda	15♉17'37	485	Genua	13♎15'15	1049	Gotho	12♓49'51
3642	Frieden	11♌01'32	1620	Geographos	6♓41'25	2621	Goto	5♋40'18
538	Friederike	20♌58'00	376	Geometria	1♒37'56	2278	Götz	23♉05'59
3651	Friedman	11♊11'04	3854	George	7♈51'50	3253	Gradie	29♉45'13
77	Frigga	0♈53'26	359	Georgia	5♈52'16	3202	Graff	24♎56'33
709	Fringilla	24♒03'36	3700	Geowilliams	18♍50'31	4247	Grahamsmith	4♌04'54
1253	Frisia	9♉32'59	300	Geraldina	12♉36'49	2666	Gramme	20♎33'11
854	Frostia	10♎22'10	1433	Geramtina	21♍16'21	1159	Granada	17♓23'46
2345	Fučik	3♒42'50	1227	Geranium	2♈04'25	1451	Grano	24♍47'19
1584	Fuji	4♒54'49	1337	Gerarda	9♍56'26	3154	Grant	12♋17'35
2184	Fujian	16♐23'16	2126	Gerasimovich	27♒21'06	1661	Granule	21♐16'54
3915	Fukushima	23♍07'55	122	Gerda	28♏06'29	424	Gratia	8♋53'42
3486	Fulchignoni	16♉45'55	663	Gerlinde	22♏29'30	3148	Grechko	0♈59'17
609	Fulvia	14♍59'32	241	Germania	0♑34'05	3387	Greenberg	6♏31'40
355	Gabriella	21♓39'13	2327	Gershberg	24♍28'05	2830	Greenwich	18♉30'55
2206	Gabrova	3♊27'37	686	Gersuind	3♐09'01	2527	Gregory	5♎58'11
1665	Gaby	1♋09'10	1382	Gerti	22♌43'17	984	Gretia	14♒01'08
2638	Gadolin	5♐22'46	710	Gertrud	19♌43'41	3280	Grétry	17♒00'43
1184	Gaea	25♓28'11	1672	Gezelle	0♎18'40	2837	Griboedov	1♊35'24
3545	Gaffey	1♊00'50	3371	Giacconi	23♑17'06	2049	Grietje	19♎32'27
1772	Gagarin	28♊03'46	1756	Giacobini	20♑52'35	2786	Grinevia	8♈51'22
1358	Gaika	21♈19'45	2937	Gibbs	25♐23'00	1362	Griqua	0♌47'55
1835	Gajdariya	26♑39'09	2742	Gibson	2♌25'51	493	Griseldis	27♓17'22
2082	Galahad	29♊56'28	1741	Giclas	25♌14'49	2161	Grissom	6♌13'30
1250	Galanthus	21♑27'32	1812	Gilgamesh	28♍26'32	1674	Groeneveld	5♋33'05
74	Galatea	17♎00'36	2537	Gilmore	4♓44'26	1058	Grubba	11♏24'06
427	Galene	27♋26'03	613	Ginevra	24♓31'35	496	Gryphia	27♌10'08
697	Galilea	15♈16'22	2658	Gingerich	5♏17'04	1993	Guacolda	7♍57'28
3576	Galina	20♈08'50	1599	Giomus	13♌10'09	2185	Guangdong	0♊25'33
4080	Galinskij	11♏43'51	352	Gisela	6♐49'14	2655	Guangxi	27♊54'58
3595	Gallagher	22♏40'42	492	Gismonda	16♉23'09	3048	Guangzhou	3♏58'42
2097	Galle	18♒58'32	3909	Gladys	8♏14'35	2544	Gubarev	5♒13'37
148	Gallia	24♌44'08	1687	Glarona	3♋13'33	2595	Gudiachvili	28♌11'03
1992	Galvarino	2♎25'18	857	Glasenappia	22♊30'08	328	Gudrun	22♓04'42
2317	Galya	6♎58'06	288	Glauke	0♌01'38	799	Gudula	14♍19'43
2515	Gansu	25♉38'32	1870	Glaukos	25♍41'42	2105	Gudy	3♑06'53
1036	Ganymed	5♏35'05	1823	Gliese	9♒37'45	2293	Guernica	23♈26'03
3076	Garber	15♎03'11	2205	Glinka	17♏30'41	2483	Guinevere	11♐37'48
2587	Gardner	27♊20'13	3267	Glo	20♋05'55	1960	Guisan	22♈02'02
1435	Garlena	9♎14'40	316	Goberta	3♌35'44	2632	Guizhou	18♈19'49
180	Garumna	12♒05'32	3018	Godiva	18♏04'25	891	Gunhild	15♋31'19
2388	Gase	23♒57'59	3047	Goethe	17♒14'52	983	Gunila	10♐26'10
951	Gaspra	12♐39'25	1728	Goethe Link	0♐21'03	657	Gunlöd	27♊28'37
1001	Gaussia	19♐08'31	1722	Goffin	17♍48'27	961	Gunnie	26♈24'03
2504	Gaviola	9♈43'58	2361	Gogol	12♉38'07	1944	Gunter	2♏02'04
2054	Gawain	23♑07'47	3101	Goldberger	4♍21'53	2012	Guo Shou-Jing	
764	Gedania	19♐02'49	1614	Goldschmidt	12♍07'02			6♑47'09
1267	Geertruida	24♈24'22	1226	Golia	17♈02'56	777	Gutemberga	14♑02'51
1272	Gefion	21♒10'01	2466	Golson	9♍18'17	3697	Guyhurst	21♓08'03
1777	Gehrels	4♓26'15	1891	Gondola	21♒32'00	806	Gyldenia	14♉31'47
2571	Geisei	6♊33'33	1562	Gondolatsch	9♌01'37	444	Gyptis	15♎18'04
1047	Geisha	17♊52'30	1177	Gonnessia	11♐53'33	4066	Haapavesi	0♐51'34
4261	Gekko	25♐20'52	4239	Goodman	24♑22'52	2151	Hadwiger	27♈39'46
1199	Geldonia	25♏40'36	1894	Goodricke	19♏58'41	1894	Haffner	17♐53'16
1073	Gellivara	9♉06'24	305	Gordonia	28♎42'35	682	Hagar	10♎36'34
1385	Gelria	24♋43'01	681	Gorgo	27♍33'03	1971	Hagihara	0♒00'25
3143	Genecampbell		2768	Gorky	22♉50'02	3676	Hahn	28♓33'16
		19♊48'10	2723	Gorshkov	2♏40'18	368	Haidea	17♏02'47
1237	Geneviève	27♑33'33	3640	Gostin	18♑47'02	3024	Hainan	27♈47'54
2093	Genichesk	4♍25'20	1346	Gotha	15♏53'48	1995	Hajek	16♉43'34
680	Genoveva	9♉44'21	1710	Gothard	26♓13'07	1483	Hakoila	11♊48'53

Heliocentric Nodes in Alphabetical Order
Epoch November 5, 1990   Equinox 1950.0   Planet nodes have number ####

1098 Hakone	28♒43'42	2521 Heidi	10♑56'35	2220 Hicks	4♋36'23
518 Halawe	23♎47'11	1732 Heike	5♍25'44	944 Hidalgo	20♈59'48
1024 Hale	28♉35'59	2380 Heilongjiang	24♒10'53	3025 Higson	23♑04'50
3299 Hall	11♐17'42	2016 Heinemann	16♈52'25	996 Hilaritas	17♓39'14
1308 Halleria	23♓51'43	4290 Heisei	3♐58'35	153 Hilda	17♏47'19
2688 Halley	5♋16'42	2379 Heiskanen	0♍38'08	684 Hildburg	6♓05'13
2640 Hällström	4♈01'41	100 Hekate	7♌07'13	898 Hildegard	1♐40'07
1460 Haltia	13♊57'31	2245 Hekatostos	24♊49'04	928 Hildrun	9♌22'47
449 Hamburga	25♊32'30	624 Hektor	12♋05'16	1642 Hill	8♓51'56
2535 Hämeenlinna	22♍18'24	949 Hel	20♒59'57	1897 Hind	3♊01'47
452 Hamiltonia	2♋13'00	699 Hela	2♐15'04	4000 Hipparchus	18♒17'41
2733 Hamina	1♌02'38	101 Helena	12♓55'05	426 Hippo	11♒09'36
723 Hammonia	13♍03'37	1872 Helenos	8♎30'48	692 Hippodamia	3♊02'29
2166 Handahl	13♍31'19	1845 Helewalda	22♌19'08	1999 Hirayama	27♌55'35
3826 Handel	0♏45'20	2290 Helffrich	5♍37'16	2356 Hirons	8♉38'29
2299 Hanko	23♍52'47	522 Helga	26♋53'22	1612 Hirose	19♒06'50
1668 Hanna	10♍39'13	1075 Helina	10♋34'30	2247 Hiroshima	6♈51'30
2152 Hannibal	10♐44'56	895 Helio	24♐10'45	3172 Hirst	22♊56'02
2573 Hannu Olavi	23♉48'42	967 Helionape	21♊59'04	706 Hirundo	25♒08'57
480 Hansa	26♏51'57	1370 Hella	5♒35'36	804 Hispania	17♓18'11
1118 Hanskya	18♒43'15	1273 Helma	26♑17'33	2746 Hissao	26♍44'25
724 Hapag	23♎45'11	1495 Helsinki	12♈45'05	3225 Hoag	8♎18'20
3549 Hapke	14♑10'02	801 Helwerthia	5♎38'40	2888 Hodgson	21♓00'01
578 Happelia	29♈17'52	2085 Henan	27♋48'28	1662 Hoffmann	0♓35'39
2003 Harding	4♊31'38	2005 Hencke	20♋54'50	1726 Hoffmeister	20♏53'09
1372 Haremari	27♒12'11	3077 Henderson	26♑58'45	788 Hohensteina	27♍48'35
2582 Harimaya–Bashi		225 Henrietta	16♎43'57	3720 Hokkaido	18♈54'35
	26♉03'55	826 Henrika	20♏05'24	3033 Holbaek	16♍23'37
3842 Harlansmith	15♓01'59	1516 Henry	5♌48'13	872 Holda	14♎27'24
40 Harmonia	3♋47'07	1365 Henyey	18♋06'47	1132 Hollandia	29♈48'52
1744 Harriet	27♈03'12	2212 Hephaistos	27♈46'08	4084 Hollis	27♊25'00
3216 Harrington	17♋40'43	103 Hera	15♌43'24	3573 Holmberg	28♐20'20
2929 Harris	22♌21'02	3696 Herald	12♒20'35	378 Holmia	22♏18'20
4149 Harrison	4♍33'25	880 Herba	23♐09'23	3590 Holst	8♌11'26
1914 Hartbeespoortdam		1363 Herberta	4♏37'47	1699 Honkasalo	3♑10'47
	0♌12'11	532 Herculina	17♋23'46	236 Honoria	5♎35'27
3341 Hartmann	22♌12'37	458 Hercynia	14♌23'28	932 Hooveria	14♈46'31
1531 Hartmut	8♑41'40	1885 Herero	25♒56'49	2938 Hopi	18♋40'07
736 Harvard	15♌27'23	1652 Hergé	11♐17'43	1985 Hopmann	5♒14'08
4278 Harvey	26♌02'51	1751 Herget	0♐02'20	3499 Hoppe	28♌09'42
2853 Harvill	23♎53'28	3234 Hergiani	16♊39'07	4294 Horatius	9♈26'43
3227 Hasegawa	3♍54'46	923 Herluga	17♎13'22	2435 Horemheb	12♍06'19
2734 Hašek	6♉54'24	346 Hermentaria	1♋47'23	805 Hormuthia	15♍55'42
4051 Hatanaka	15♑31'29	685 Hermia	24♏55'53	3744 Horn–d'Arturo	
2340 Hathor	0♏59'12	121 Hermione	14♊05'24		17♏44'06
2436 Hatshepsut	23♏44'39	546 Herodias	21♐30'30	3078 Horrocks	2♉44'41
2870 Haupt	25♊34'07	3092 Herodotus	8♈41'09	2913 Horta	29♈57'26
362 Havnia	26♈51'12	1579 Herrick	4♎14'32	1924 Horus	19♓51'01
3452 Hawke	28♉23'40	2000 Herschel	21♑36'16	3828 Hoshino	11♏41'13
1824 Haworth	14♈46'35	206 Hersilia	24♌46'29	2909 Hoshi–No-Ie	25♊20'00
3125 Hay	13♌56'05	135 Hertha	13♋25'13	3814 Hoshi-no-mura	
3941 Haydn	4♎59'15	1693 Hertzsprung	9♊43'55		21♌37'12
3846 Hazel	13♏29'12	3316 Herzberg	20♎10'33	2550 Houssay	8♍02'11
3023 Heard	20♏09'31	3052 Herzen	28♏09'19	3031 Houston	17♒21'49
6 Hebe	18♌20'55	1952 Hesburgh	18♊11'44	2534 Houzeau	17♍43'02
2505 Hebei	28♉52'36	69 Hesperia	5♋13'51	3888 Hoyt	25♍09'17
1650 Heckmann	19♎23'04	2844 Hess	7♌18'04	2069 Hubble	17♏01'25
108 Hecuba	20♓09'11	46 Hestia	0♎37'39	2547 Hubei	18♓02'09
207 Hedda	28♈48'24	4133 Heureka	24♒14'14	260 Huberta	15♍30'03
1251 Hedera	20♌22'19	2473 Heyerdahl	5♎12'53	379 Huenna	21♍44'57
476 Hedwig	15♑54'48	3069 Heyrovský	7♏03'54	2635 Huggins	6♑26'43
325 Heidelberga	14♓46'58	2441 Hibbs	19♌38'34	1878 Hughes	7♎28'00

Heliocentric Nodes in Alphabetical Order
Epoch November 5, 1990   Equinox 1950.0   Planet nodes have number ####

Entry	Value	Entry	Value	Entry	Value
2106 Hugo	1♍34'15	561 Ingwelde	9♍58'33	1558 Järnefelt	20♋34'43
4285 Hulkower	4♍41'27	1479 Inkeri	17♈54'50	1110 Jaroslawa	1♐26'38
2070 Humason	0♈49'22	848 Inna	27≏31'12	3353 Jarvis	5♐02'48
2592 Hunan	24≏02'06	3497 Innanen	11♍42'18	2964 Jaschek	0♓29'00
434 Hungaria	24♍46'59	1658 Innes	5♋09'47	1461 Jean–Jacques	
1452 Hunnia	20♈55'40	173 Ino	28♌01'01		14♋34'57
3730 Hurban	5♒07'08	704 Interamnia	10♑21'11	1281 Jeanne	29≏36'36
3434 Hurless	28Ⅱ03'30	2365 Interkosmos	12♑25'42	2763 Jeans	8♒18'57
3939 Huruhata	2♉06'24	85 Io	22≏51'01	3526 Jeffbell	12♉14'12
3425 Hurukawa	21♑18'54	2450 Ioannisiani	26♋54'30	1934 Jeffers	26Ⅱ10'24
1840 Hus	10♉11'56	509 Iolanda	7♏25'58	3188 Jekabsons	6♓02'23
3203 Huth	18♉07'35	112 Iphigenia	23♒16'27	1606 Jekhovsky	10≏15'17
2801 Huygens	3♉56'14	2115 Irakli	1♐10'54	526 Jena	17♌23'49
1678 Hveen	21♓11'53	794 Irenaea	9♍53'18	607 Jenny	14♋54'06
430 Hybris	9♐10'24	14 Irene	26Ⅱ12'20	1719 Jens	23♒14'07
10 Hygiea	13♑02'33	3224 Irkutsk	17♏37'15	3245 Jensch	18♓27'58
1842 Hynek	3♍01'43	177 Irma	17♓17'08	1414 Jérôme	23♌24'45
238 Hypatia	3≏35'18	1178 Irmela	19♍44'39	549 Jessonda	21♑13'44
1309 Hyperborea	25≏38'03	591 Irmgard	3♒53'13	544 Jetta	27♑51'53
587 Hypsipyle	24♒05'52	773 Irmintraud	22♒06'52	2617 Jiangxi	13Ⅱ38'23
98 Ianthe	23♓39'23	2585 Irpedina	16♌08'54	2080 Jihlava	23♈25'46
3436 Ibadinov	8≏04'39	1485 Isa	27♑32'49	2398 Jilin	27Ⅱ43'18
2423 Ibarruri	24♐44'08	210 Isabella	2♉22'14	2143 Jimarnold	16♈58'57
1566 Icarus	27Ⅱ29'41	364 Isara	15♋07'03	2874 Jim Young	18Ⅱ45'08
286 Iclea	28♌43'19	939 Isberga	26♒40'25	3088 Jinxiuzhonghua	
243 Ida	23♒51'30	1271 Isergina	7♌12'29		20♍55'43
1403 Idelsonia	6♍45'01	4095 Ishizuchisan	15♐29'24	2316 Jo–Ann	28♌18'42
2759 Idomeneus	20♍32'24	42 Isis	24Ⅱ06'15	4083 Jody	23♌07'42
963 Iduberga	2Ⅱ02'06	1409 Isko	27♍16'12	726 Joëlla	2♐08'33
176 Iduna	20≏23'16	190 Ismene	25♍23'07	1524 Joensuu	17Ⅱ28'58
3562 Ignatius	2♋27'01	1947 Iso–Heikkilä	1♋04'44	127 Johanna	0♉55'22
1684 Iguassú	15♋17'55	211 Isolda	23♐25'00	3726 Johnadams	15♋01'15
2820 Iisalmi	6♏15'22	1374 Isora	2♒12'14	3882 Johncox	15≏11'29
4037 Ikeya	13♈12'02	183 Istria	21♑38'54	899 Jokaste	12♐18'27
2828 Iku–Turso	14Ⅱ00'44	1735 ITA	8♈56'07	836 Jole	19♈19'45
3668 Ilfpetrov	13≏32'55	477 Italia	10♈09'42	2392 Jonathan Murray	
3622 Ilinsky	14♐09'16	918 Itha	0♓14'29		20♌48'10
2968 Iliya	3♑59'27	1151 Ithaka	14♏57'39	3152 Jones	1♒02'06
3750 Ilizarov	7♈41'56	1596 Itzigsohn	8♐52'42	1423 Jose	28♉18'30
1160 Illyria	3♈17'09	497 Iva	6♈10'09	649 Josefa	26Ⅱ44'07
2107 Ilmari	10♏58'49	1627 Ivar	12♌37'37	303 Josephina	13♓40'46
385 Ilmatar	14♓45'17	3634 Iwan	11♓12'16	921 Jovita	24≏42'44
1182 Ilona	5♓55'43	1546 Izsák	10≏48'31	652 Jubilatrix	25Ⅱ46'19
249 Ilse	4♓21'23	4157 Izu	6Ⅱ38'57	948 Jucunda	27♓06'03
919 Ilsebill	19♏35'06	3418 Izvekov	24Ⅱ15'30	664 Judith	24♍38'27
979 Ilsewa	21♏22'21	1942 Jablunka	15♓54'06	139 Juewa	1♈32'05
1520 Imatra	13♐06'27	2079 Jacchia	22♓41'41	2136 Jugta	28♌38'05
926 Imhilde	18♉59'19	2625 Jack London	8♌17'46	1248 Jugurtha	19Ⅱ01'58
1813 Imhotep	4♉48'32	2193 Jackson	6♉24'03	2487 Juhani	17♓13'47
2373 Immo	26♌10'01	1017 Jacqueline	28♋35'58	89 Julia	11♒02'24
1320 Impala	11Ⅱ37'04	1893 Jakoba	4Ⅱ14'14	816 Juliana	7♌29'27
1200 Imperatrix	24≏57'30	2335 James	19♈29'02	2704 Julian Loewe	27≏02'21
1165 Imprinetta	23≏17'08	2634 James Bradley		1285 Julietta	17♒51'34
3056 INAG	11♈06'22		13♌49'19	3766 Junepatterson	8♌34'58
1325 Inanda	13♈55'46	2073 Janáček	24Ⅱ41'00	3 Juno	19♍50'44
1532 Inari	0♓27'57	2028 Janequeo	2♐23'47	#### Jupiter	10♋02'47
3849 Incidentia	25♈42'48	2324 Janice	20♒23'05	3537 Jürgen	13♉48'16
1602 Indiana	14Ⅱ43'07	383 Janina	2♋46'57	269 Justitia	6♍15'03
389 Industria	11♑58'43	3301 Jansje	16♌32'05	2799 Justus	12♑36'03
2494 Inge	13♑08'20	1932 Jansky	8≏29'00	1183 Jutta	14♈46'20
391 Ingeborg	2♏28'07	1843 Jarmila	26♐35'42	2818 Juvenalis	0Ⅱ30'09
1026 Ingrid	14♋11'04			605 Juvisia	12♓25'06

Heliocentric Nodes in Alphabetical Order

Epoch November 5, 1990   Equinox 1950.0   Planet nodes have number ####

1500 Jyväskylä	19♈28'27	3754 Kathleen	20♋10'58	97 Klotho	9♍29'52
4227 Kaali	12♌38'32	2612 Kathryn	12♌25'37	583 Klotilde	17♐29'55
2257 Kaarina	23♏53'38	1113 Katja	24♒10'30	1040 Klumpkea	9♑43'11
2760 Kacha	22♓20'21	2961 Katsurahama	10♏35'56	104 Klymene	11♉43'33
2015 Kachuevskaya		1900 Katyusha	11♑27'34	179 Klytaemnestra	
	14♓05'53	4251 Kavasch	24♋49'07		11♐54'27
1874 Kacivelia	9♍23'29	1976 Kaverin	0♋28'38	73 Klytia	6♈43'42
3412 Kafka	7♒13'27	2949 Kaverznev	12♍43'32	3900 Kneževic	7♓53'35
4256 Kagamigawa	12♊04'27	2564 Kayala	3♍02'12	1384 Kniertje	2♍42'56
4284 Kaho	17♌08'24	2178 Kazakhstania	10♈58'46	1311 Knopfia	4♐51'18
1587 Kahrstedt	27♓25'03	4110 Keats	14♎05'40	1324 Knysna	3♒56'41
1694 Kaiser	13♈05'01	2261 Keeler	12♋18'32	3500 Kobayashi	14♒16'37
3880 Kaiserman	5♑58'51	2186 Keldysh	15♑12'38	1164 Kobolda	6♍27'02
1519 Kajaani	15♈22'41	2140 Kemerovo	4♑34'44	1233 Kobresia	20♑52'23
2894 Kakhovka	25♊50'35	1508 Kemi	14♈12'00	3432 Kobuchizawa	11♈35'21
3597 Kakkuri	26♊26'19	2932 Kempchinsky	19♍09'27	2427 Kobzar	17♏18'07
1702 Kalahari	13♋38'03	3675 Kemstach	10♓05'41	2087 Kochera	5♋12'37
3086 Kalbaugh	0♒13'50	3714 Kenrussell	29♈08'02	2396 Kochi	8♍09'30
4138 Kalchas	27♎16'00	1278 Kenya	29♊59'02	1850 Kohoutek	8♊31'03
1454 Kalevala	22♓09'04	1134 Kepler	5♈49'49	3370 Kohsai	24♌10'15
2699 Kalinin	3♊48'14	2216 Kerch	5♍19'06	1522 Kokkola	0♊08'55
2840 Kallavesi	28♉40'37	842 Kerstin	5♈36'03	3373 Koktebelia	26♍47'50
2805 Kalle	18♉53'31	2291 Kevo	19♍08'56	191 Kolga	9♍05'08
22 Kalliope	5♊47'44	1540 Kevola	22♊18'16	1929 Kollaa	5♋04'06
204 Kallisto	24♎43'24	1357 Khama	23♊22'17	2467 Kollontai	8♒45'39
2332 Kalm	1♊06'39	3068 Khanina	21♈06'03	3219 Komaki	19♑36'50
2287 Kalmykia	2♋52'23	2147 Kharadze	24♌28'43	1836 Komarov	2♑34'54
53 Kalypso	23♌23'25	3504 Kholshevnikov		1861 Komenský	23♈31'19
1387 Kama	22♎43'21		28♋21'47	1406 Komppa	2♒49'59
4254 Kamél	21♎37'58	3362 Khufu	1♍59'51	1283 Komsomolia	7♍17'57
2428 Kamenyar	8♈13'39	3751 Kiang	1♑24'14	3084 Kondratyuk	5♎28'37
1948 Kampala	22♈59'16	2077 Kiangsu	9♊01'45	3815 König	16♎53'24
2248 Kanda	3♉29'46	3319 Kibi	1♑00'23	1445 Konkolya	29♊09'22
2662 Kandinsky	8♓58'31	3779 Kieffer	28♉46'01	1890 Konoshenkova	
4265 Kani	6♌48'27	1759 Kienle	8♍25'17		9♊56'24
3124 Kansas	10♍36'06	1788 Kiess	11♍22'44	3347 Konstantin	13♎21'39
3437 Kapitsa	4♉13'50	2171 Kiev	11♋38'09	2008 Konstitutsiya	15♈07'12
1987 Kaplan	13♒48'26	470 Kilia	22♍46'34	2628 Kopal	26♎33'43
818 Kapteynia	10♊33'33	3142 Kilopi	20♏31'47	1631 Kopff	16♈29'03
3719 Karamzin	22♑09'15	2305 King	25♋00'56	3968 Koptelov	11♒40'06
3800 Karayusuf	4♋54'54	2947 Kippenhahn	13♑32'34	1505 Koranna	7♐57'38
1959 Karbyshev	14♑38'08	1780 Kippes	21♑01'04	2163 Korczak	22♋51'23
1682 Karel	25♒19'41	1156 Kira	0♋43'15	940 Kordula	9♊01'50
2651 Karen	6♌31'03	2566 Kirghizia	21♉09'32	2988 Korhonen	10♋29'24
1676 Kariba	24♉10'40	216 Kirik	0♓11'50	1855 Korolev	10♎33'53
832 Karin	14♐16'11	2609 Kiril-Metodi	3♒26'59	158 Koronis	8♑07'15
4264 Karljosephine	4♎25'35	1578 Kirkwood	13♊40'01	2966 Korsunia	16♉08'33
2807 Karl Marx	28♈16'36	4208 Kiselev	27♌17'20	1697 Koskenniemi	1♓13'21
2125 Karl-Ontjes	15♒27'27	2271 Kiso	16♌09'29	2072 Kosmodemyanskaya	
3811 Karma	8♓29'49	3785 Kitami	1♍23'01		25♈51'19
2288 Karolinum	15♊49'15	2679 Kittisvaara	27♎46'01	3134 Kostinsky	16♐36'58
3758 Karttunen	20♊27'47	2322 Kitt Peak	14♎17'38	2726 Kotelnikov	25♓32'22
781 Kartvelia	17♌58'05	4181 Kivi	1♍35'25	2737 Kotka	9♓23'43
1316 Kasan	27♏43'49	1825 Klare	18♑26'57	3914 Kotogahama	21♒12'46
1828 Kashirina	4♎21'43	1723 Klemola	29♌33'52	1799 Koussevitzky	6♍22'39
114 Kassandra	13♍50'06	216 Kleopatra	5♏08'31	867 Kovacia	16♉27'06
646 Kastalia	2♒28'12	2199 Klet	26♌30'12	1859 Kovalevskaya	
3982 Kastel	11♐28'49	3903 Kliment Ohridski			12♓52'46
3608 Kataev	18♊10'31		11♓52'00	3383 Koyama	18♌47'22
1817 Katanga	28♊18'51	84 Klio	27♒10'13	3040 Kozai	22♌54'55
2156 Kate	16♈43'51	3166 Klondike	11♊32'54	2536 Kozyrev	4♑51'56
320 Katharina	9♏48'09	3520 Klopsteg	2♌15'52	3036 Krat	23♈55'02

Heliocentric Nodes in Alphabetical Order
Epoch November 5, 1990   Equinox 1950.0   Planet nodes have number ####

# Name	Node	# Name	Node	# Name	Node
1849 Kresák	20♉14'54	507 Laodica	23♑51'14	2004 Lexell	4♈07'34
548 Kressida	18♋00'59	2912 Lapalma	17♋44'24	954 Li	12♍59'26
800 Kressmannia	24♒42'03	1008 La Paz	20♈12'58	2503 Liaoning	11♈25'41
488 Kreusa	24♊32'25	3215 Lapko	6♊48'03	771 Libera	7♏40'02
242 Kriemhild	26♎47'42	1029 La Plata	29♈44'41	125 Liberatrix	18♍46'01
2887 Krinov	28♋35'33	2397 Lappajärvi	25♌22'24	1816 Liberia	2♍50'30
3233 Krišbarons	17♓13'48	1504 Lappeenranta	4♋23'39	264 Libussa	19♉20'32
3455 Kristensen	18♍19'40	1819 Laputa	1♌59'43	1268 Libya	21♓15'00
4038 Kristina	3♓52'53	1895 Larink	15♊12'15	1951 Lick	10♌07'58
2796 Kron	8♍13'18	1162 Larissa	9♉33'56	1107 Lictoria	20♋27'30
2447 Kronstadt	26♌23'17	3690 Larson	24♏47'09	3322 Lidiya	10♐14'11
2296 Kugultinov	11♉52'24	2187 La Silla	16♌59'42	3454 Lieske	13♎13'03
1776 Kuiper	26♍28'12	2636 Lassell	8♋30'53	356 Liguria	24♋50'06
1954 Kukarkin	8♑11'14	639 Latona	9♑51'10	2877 Likhachev	20♊37'13
2159 Kukkamäki	20♓53'24	1284 Latvia	2♒34'26	213 Lilaea	1♌39'36
2794 Kulik	0♓13'44	3135 Lauer	4♒25'46	2346 Lilio	4♐26'03
1774 Kulikov	24♍56'15	1597 Laugier	8♍25'48	1181 Lilith	20♐25'00
2497 Kulikovskij	6♒33'52	467 Laura	22♒13'28	1092 Lilium	7♒30'40
3019 Kulin	13♋52'40	162 Laurentia	5♋59'07	3222 Liller	0♍51'11
3569 Kumon	11♍25'21	1938 Lausanna	21♍13'25	756 Lilliana	27♎34'42
553 Kundry	11♊57'57	2976 Lautaro	27♎09'50	2952 Lilliputia	22♒56'05
936 Kunigunde	1♊47'56	1401 Lavonne	7♑09'05	1003 Lilofee	18♌57'47
2280 Kunikov	16♋04'15	2354 Lavrov	25♍41'05	1383 Limburgia	11♎03'28
1503 Kuopio	16♍31'03	3660 Lazarev	24♐29'43	1490 Limpopo	13♐58'00
2352 Kurchatov	22♏04'02	2342 Lebedev	13♎16'29	468 Lina	21♈18'15
2349 Kurchenko	12♌47'47	3439 Lebofsky	7♈28'05	3153 Lincoln	10♉09'26
3073 Kursk	23♎39'19	38 Leda	25♑26'55	2686 Linda Susan	15♏37'39
4096 Kushiro	18♈32'48	2444 Lederle	15♑49'13	1448 Lindbladia	14♉37'58
1559 Kustaanheimo		3155 Lee	28♈05'58	1407 Lindelöf	29♐01'43
	27♒42'33	2766 Leeuwenhoek	0♓08'29	828 Lindemannia	1♈41'54
1289 Kutaïssi	12♎49'20	1261 Legia	6♊56'41	3204 Lindgren	18♋22'10
2492 Kutuzov	21♈01'02	691 Lehigh	27♊55'37	3474 Linsley	19♍09'18
3049 Kuzbass	4♋35'52	2548 Leloir	29♑16'34	1469 Linzia	8♎34'51
2233 Kuznetsov	6♐47'58	1565 Lemaître	20♐54'31	974 Lioba	26♊13'09
3331 Kvistaberg	17♍54'22	789 Lena	22♍21'55	846 Lipperta	21♈27'18
4127 Kyogoku	3♍31'52	3817 Lencarter	1♍13'16	2641 Lipschutz	27♈18'15
669 Kypria	20♍24'17	3796 Lene	29♐16'45	414 Liriope	20♋48'03
570 Kythera	14♏57'08	2046 Leningrad	14♊15'10	3910 Liszt	2♈30'23
336 Lacadiera	24♏37'15	4147 Lennon	18♑16'49	2577 Litva	2♎03'23
120 Lachesis	10♓59'10	969 Leocadia	17♋52'49	3006 Livadia	8♉06'53
208 Lacrimosa	4♈12'11	3572 Leogoldberg	22♏26'21	1062 Ljuba	11♓20'29
1851 Lacroute	24♈25'20	319 Leona	6♎12'06	1858 Lobachevskij	1♑48'18
2832 Lada	12♍23'00	3000 Leonardo	20♎36'09	1066 Lobelia	14♓46'40
2574 Ladoga	21♈58'53	1378 Leonce	13♉07'02	1937 Locarno	18♊39'11
39 Laetitia	6♍43'46	2782 Leonidas	10♈19'55	3377 Lodewijk	5♏54'22
2875 Lagerkvist	10♓01'43	728 Leonisis	22♊14'14	2501 Lohja	10♈47'51
1006 Lagrangea	27♑40'17	696 Leonora	28♑59'29	1820 Lohmann	24♌42'09
1412 Lagrula	5♊41'15	3793 Leonteus	19♎49'22	2210 Lois	3♌04'14
1498 Lahti	24♐46'50	844 Leontina	18♓33'09	463 Lola	6♉07'05
822 Lalage	29♎31'21	893 Leopoldina	24♌38'01	117 Lomia	18♓31'35
187 Lamberta	21♈21'12	2795 Lepage	2♏56'07	1379 Lomonosowa	19♍20'31
2861 Lambrecht	8♎14'19	2222 Lermontov	4♋37'46	2243 Lönnrot	22♈04'27
248 Lameia	6♐31'37	2616 Lesya	26♌15'09	1755 Lorbach	6♍48'45
393 Lampetia	2♏42'00	1264 Letaba	24♏41'47	1287 Lorcia	22♎11'47
1767 Lampland	11♎53'28	68 Leto	13♉52'16	165 Loreley	2♒20'47
2041 Lancelot	13♌37'25	35 Leukothea	23♓18'37	1939 Loretta	10♉06'42
2142 Landau	4♍51'06	1361 Leuschneria	14♍35'32	1114 Lorraine	15♎22'52
3132 Landgraf	23♋08'21	1997 Leverrier	22♓46'10	1326 Losaka	11♋27'47
2381 Landi	0♍02'44	2076 Levin	28♒31'21	2673 Lossignol	11♊20'10
683 Lanzia	19♐33'55	2810 Lev Tolstoj	12♎49'00	429 Lotis	9♏40'09
3240 Laocoon	25♑31'06	3673 Levy	12♈56'02	3489 Lottie	17♈47'12
1011 Laodamia	12♌08'02	4125 Lew Allen	5♑31'15	3897 Louhi	8♎37'49

Heliocentric Nodes in Alphabetical Order
Epoch November 5, 1990   Equinox 1950.0   Planet nodes have number ####

2556 Louise	3214 Makarenko 10♋09'54	3131 Mason–Dixon
6♌01'47	3063 Makhaon 17♑10'57	14♉34'20
868 Lova 25♋34'18	2139 Makharadze 16♐18'30	20 Massalia 26♎01'46
2750 Loviisa 15♉19'35	3196 Maklaj 12♈58'15	1904 Massevitch 16♋05'56
4091 Lowe 19♉27'37	1771 Makover 25♊56'52	760 Massinga 1♓34'42
1886 Lowell 21♊58'28	2568 Maksutov 27♊07'26	4293 Masumi 28♉03'30
3589 Loyola 20♋55'11	754 Malabar 29♍43'23	2685 Masursky 4♏48'58
1431 Luanda 27♋22'26	3479 Malaparte 16♎17'49	2680 Mateo 2♈35'15
2318 Lubarsky 2♍48'11	3057 Mälaren 14♊54'44	454 Mathesis 1♉58'07
2900 Luboš Perek 17♈30'41	1415 Malautra 28♒48'09	1592 Mathieu 15♋56'57
1292 Luce 1♑15'41	1179 Mally 6♈33'46	253 Mathilde 29♍13'05
1935 Lucerna 19♎42'13	1527 Malmquista 15♈43'50	1513 Mátra 15♌44'09
222 Lucia 19♊58'00	1072 Malva 6♋32'06	2586 Matson 16♍04'56
1176 Lucidor 1♑57'54	749 Malzovia 19♋21'55	883 Matterania 15♑08'55
1892 Lucienne 15♒13'12	3349 Manas 28♉13'23	2714 Matti 13♌44'18
1930 Lucifer 18♒13'00	758 Mancunia 15♋46'26	765 Mattiaca 26♒25'17
146 Lucina 23♊41'51	3461 Mandelshtam 27♉28'46	2295 Matusovskij 13♒28'12
281 Lucretia 0♉55'55	739 Mandeville 16♌15'48	1748 Mauderli 5♌35'57
1158 Luda 14♓23'23	3698 Manning 12♌22'07	3281 Maupertuis 18♓07'45
675 Ludmilla 22♐59'52	2219 Mannucci 12♊18'12	745 Mauritia 5♌38'59
292 Ludovica 13♉06'05	870 Manto 0♌23'12	3780 Maury 23♌16'43
1936 Lugano 25♐01'01	3186 Manuilova 19♍30'10	1607 Mavis 2♌27'50
1133 Lugduna 27♉51'13	565 Marbachia 15♏38'03	1217 Maximiliana 27♌55'44
599 Luisa 14♉18'00	1730 Marceline 21♍15'38	3977 Maxine 7♏51'24
141 Lumen 18♒24'30	1300 Marcelle 22♊38'33	348 May 29♊49'13
775 Lumière 27♑34'24	1332 Marconia 13♈42'41	2931 Mayakovsky 24♈58'24
2600 Lumme 5♋18'46	2173 Maresjev 24♍29'07	2131 Mayall 5♒28'21
2446 Lunacharsky 21♈50'36	310 Margarita 19♍14'46	3870 Mayré 21♎36'21
1067 Lunaria 19♑30'32	735 Marghanna 12♉43'50	1690 Mayrhofer 20♏17'03
809 Lundia 4♍06'17	1175 Margo 26♏50'12	3352 McAuliffe 16♋54'05
1334 Lundmarka 13♌03'10	2561 Margolin 15♍39'22	4148 McCartney 25♒14'52
3208 Lunn 16♌33'06	1434 Margot 2♍20'23	3777 McCauley 16♉05'49
3210 Lupishko 8♌03'01	1410 Margret 20♏50'12	3527 McCord 8♏46'19
713 Luscinia 8♏50'41	170 Maria 0♒53'20	1880 McCrosky 26♋34'30
21 Lutetia 20♊25'13	602 Marianna 1♓52'33	2007 McCuskey 16♈40'31
1303 Luthera 11♊44'51	2144 Marietta 18♌11'22	991 McDonalda 3♊44'35
2713 Luxembourg 9♓26'17	1486 Marilyn 2♓59'52	1853 McElroy 28♑29'24
1964 Luyten 28♏15'03	1202 Marina 20♉06'18	3066 McFadden 25♍09'53
2321 Luznice 15♉33'58	506 Marion 12♒40'59	2891 McGetchin 24♋44'01
2164 Lyalya 25♋34'57	912 Maritima 4♉12'44	2024 McLaughlin 8♊52'27
110 Lydia 26♉39'06	2180 Marjaleena 23♏06'09	1955 McMath 17♐54'28
1028 Lydina 3♊52'55	4253 Märker 14♓42'06	2289 McMillan 9♎24'42
917 Lyka 13♓04'06	2362 Mark Twain 8♈36'07	2417 McVittie 24♊18'29
2452 Lyot 2♈48'03	1010 Marlene 8♋33'00	4050 Mebailey 25♌43'11
897 Lysistrata 17♐26'58	746 Marlu 1♈28'07	873 Mechthild 29♌58'29
3108 Lyubov 11♍33'33	1174 Marmara 0♈39'54	212 Medea 13♒11'30
2204 Lyyli 10♍31'19	711 Marmulla 26♓43'29	149 Medusa 9♍05'14
1353 Maartje 1♏47'51	#### Mars 19♉03'05	2213 Meeus 6♌29'50
510 Mabella 22♎32'02	1877 Marsden 22♐29'18	464 Megaira 12♋09'38
2543 Machado 10♉30'42	2604 Marshak 2♌33'26	3774 Megumi 21♑47'01
3879 Machar 21♒38'43	3250 Martebo 24♎01'33	1968 Mehltretter 11♊12'42
2569 Madeline 16♊05'51	4061 Martelli 23♈49'45	688 Melanie 20♍35'56
318 Magdalena 11♍07'58	205 Martha 1♏30'34	3235 Melchior 17♋52'45
4055 Magellan 14♍18'18	981 Martina 15♉43'53	56 Melete 13♎07'57
2696 Magion 5♎52'05	2075 Martinez 21♋44'22	137 Meliboea 21♎52'08
2094 Magnitka 11♑31'38	1582 Martir 3♋33'35	676 Melitta 0♍02'59
1060 Magnolia 10♏45'41	2376 Martynov 1♊47'38	869 Mellena 4♍48'30
3677 Magnusson 25♎33'03	2779 Mary 19♊50'51	2237 Melnikov 28♋01'23
1459 Magnya 11♉03'12	1841 Masaryk 15♉05'40	18 Melpomene 0♍01'19
1355 Magoeba 14♏41'29	1467 Mashona 26♒20'15	373 Melusina 3♈29'38
3274 Maillen 27♈40'30	4126 Mashu 11♋36'34	
66 Maja 7♈22'56		
1321 Majuba 17♒39'01		

Heliocentric Nodes in Alphabetical Order

Epoch November 5, 1990   Equinox 1950.0   Planet nodes have number ####

2895 Memnon 13♌21'30	594 Mireille 4♍33'31	3220 Murayama 26♈15'56
1247 Memoria 11♍33'30	102 Miriam 0♏38'37	2982 Muriel 12♉41'10
2769 Mendeleev 11♋56'44	1610 Mirnaya 29♓17'50	2979 Murmansk 28♌28'47
3954 Mendelssohn 11♍08'42	3624 Mironov 5♈35'44	941 Murray 22♉11'09
1647 Menelaus 29♏43'01	569 Misa 1♒32'01	600 Musa 19♌00'30
4068 Menestheus 27♍16'35	3111 Misuzu 5♋01'33	3249 Musashino 15♊54'18
3740 Menge 24♓17'27	1088 Mitaka 24♉03'18	966 Muschi 12♊07'09
188 Menippe 0♐56'58	2924 Mitake–Mura 20♋28'46	1059 Mussorgskia 20♎04'58
1078 Mentha 3♋25'59	3289 Mitani 15♉59'21	2385 Mustel 2♍45'47
1967 Menzel 27♉22'09	1455 Mitchella 7♌54'19	381 Myrrha 4♌56'05
3553 Mera 21♏58'04	2262 Mitidika 0♈09'39	1758 Naantali 23♋21'57
536 Merapi 29♉07'04	2460 Mitlincoln 25♍39'07	4106 Nada 14♉32'48
1136 Mercedes 29♎03'25	4027 Mitton 13♎21'09	2394 Nadeev 7♌07'03
#### Mercury 17♉41'10	3262 Miune 12♊54'09	2071 Nadezhda 1♒46'09
3596 Meriones 25♓58'34	3555 Miyasaka 26♈17'31	1906 Naef 24♓23'42
2598 Merlin 17♎33'05	2090 Mizuho 9♓40'40	845 Naëma 12♉54'25
1051 Merope 0♎48'11	57 Mnemosyne 18♋44'50	2935 Naerum 15♌19'38
1299 Mertona 15♍16'19	733 Mocia 10♓51'41	4219 Nakamura 20♌06'49
808 Merxia 0♎49'32	3344 Modena 17♊33'42	3431 Nakano 12♒13'39
545 Messalina 4♓01'15	370 Modestia 20♑33'21	1327 Namaqua 27♉40'36
1949 Messina 24♐48'06	2764 Moeller 13♑21'19	3320 Namba 7♏55'10
1050 Meta 11♓54'37	766 Moguntia 7♏50'25	1718 Namibia 22♎38'04
792 Metcalfia 25♐02'16	2528 Mohler 12♍19'19	3374 Namur 15♊02'14
9 Metis 8♊28'32	638 Moira 13♋06'02	4222 Nancita 26♎35'49
2486 Metsähovi 29♓31'07	3080 Moisseiev 17♉53'07	2056 Nancy 15♏18'01
1727 Mette 12♌29'11	2419 Moldavia 17♍31'38	3607 Naniwa 1♈22'02
3016 Meuse 8♌30'54	3046 Molière 8♋16'32	2078 Nanking 16♉55'01
1574 Meyer 6♐14'00	1428 Mombasa 25♍29'38	1203 Nanna 14♏31'54
1739 Meyermann 22♎55'02	428 Monachia 17♈10'56	559 Nanon 21♋40'12
2229 Mezzarco 1♑47'41	833 Monica 22♓48'47	853 Nansenia 2♎25'18
2911 Miahelena 28♌52'40	2780 Monnig 4♑32'39	1876 Napolitania 3♒56'42
1348 Michel 27♊22'58	535 Montague 24♊18'23	3448 Narbut 14♉51'34
1045 Michela 27♐22'57	797 Montana 27♍58'07	3619 Nash 10♍53'51
3001 Michelangelo 27♑15'52	782 Montefiore 20♊01'32	1534 Näsi 2♊07'18
1376 Michelle 12♍58'53	947 Monterosa 18♉03'30	534 Nassovia 3♋51'56
2348 Michkovitch 6♎04'14	2602 Moore 7♍43'56	1086 Nata 12♒54'44
1981 Midas 26♓30'41	2110 Moore–Sitterly 19♌56'09	448 Natalie 7♉03'11
1753 Mieke 28♉09'44	1257 Móra 3♏21'52	1121 Natascha 27♍32'38
2715 Mielikki 20♎22'42	3106 Morabito 1♌37'27	811 Nauheima 10♌35'58
3165 Mikawa 28♊16'54	1901 Moravia 4♋25'04	192 Nausikaa 12♓55'41
1910 Mikhailov 20♎44'53	2277 Moreau 14♋58'00	3688 Navajo 19♈22'17
1526 Mikkeli 6♓36'53	3180 Morgan 23♓46'53	1634 Ndola 0♋18'32
1549 Mikko 24♊51'35	1210 Morosovia 16♋34'33	903 Nealley 9♍17'51
3381 Mikkola 17♐47'15	3783 Morris 3♊12'28	1223 Neckar 10♉37'25
2969 Mikula 1♎04'35	2410 Morrison 6♌04'36	3592 Nedbal 20♈10'12
3231 Mila 24♒07'30	787 Moskva 3♎40'24	3343 Nedzel 13♉08'55
1605 Milankovitch 23♍26'03	2915 Moskvina 22♓19'54	2790 Needham 20♉22'37
3699 Milbourn 4♋42'19	993 Moultona 3♏57'14	3199 Nefertiti 9♓25'54
878 Mildred 22♍41'49	2590 Mourão 13♏14'43	2462 Nehalennia 9♋20'06
4119 Miles 25♋14'45	1034 Mozartia 4♒09'52	2355 Nei Monggol 23♉32'04
1630 Milet 24♉17'53	2986 Mrinalini 21♉36'07	1122 Neith 2♊58'36
1826 Miller 3♑59'46	1832 Mrkos 3♒02'26	2907 Nekrasov 22♍18'12
2659 Millis 6♍48'30	2309 Mr. Spock 7♍06'35	1547 Nele 21♑02'05
2904 Millman 19♊18'07	2116 Mtskheta 20♍23'45	3538 Nelsonia 20♍02'39
2663 Miltiades 28♈07'01	3396 Muazzez 8♉02'31	51 Nemausa 25♍34'03
1127 Mimi 8♌23'04	2946 Muchachos 21♒37'27	128 Nemesis 16♊03'18
3840 Mimistrobell 11♉52'31	4031 Mueller 25♓20'33	1640 Nemo 25♓01'41
1079 Mimosa 29♒14'09	1608 Mündleria 4♍31'57	289 Nenetta 1♎44'32
93 Minerva 3♈56'00	1472 Muonio 14♉46'30	2260 Neoptolemus 25♊55'22
1458 Mineura 1♎13'22	3295 Murakami 17♍57'43	431 Nephele 27♋01'14
1670 Minnaert 28♉55'24		287 Nephthys 21♌52'51
3012 Minsk 24♓59'03		2869 Nepryadva 26♓53'58

Heliocentric Nodes in Alphabetical Order
Epoch November 5, 1990   Equinox 1950.0   Planet nodes have number ####

#### Neptune 11♌12'41	1696 Nurmela 20♈36'09	3361 Orpheus 9♎08'20
1318 Nerina 27♓48'58	150 Nuwa 25♎51'55	2329 Orthos 18♍51'02
601 Nerthus 19♍25'12	1356 Nyanza 9♊34'54	551 Ortrud 6♈07'34
1875 Neruda 13♎28'36	875 Nymphe 15♎48'20	2043 Ortutay 21♒42'53
3071 Nesterov 13♌58'31	44 Nysa 11♌02'42	3593 Osip 3♑27'48
659 Nestor 20♓24'26	3083 OAFA 16♓04'53	1923 Osiris 22♓32'46
3175 Netto 27♎44'24	3275 Oberndorfer 14♉56'33	1837 Osita 10♑31'35
2183 Neufang 27♊54'40	3128 Obruchev 11♋58'07	750 Oskar 9♊28'43
1129 Neujmina 29♐14'30	224 Oceana 22♓38'01	1369 Ostanina 0♎44'38
4216 Neunkirchen 22♎16'11	475 Ocllo 4♉37'05	343 Ostara 8♉18'42
2898 Neuvo 26♋14'34	598 Octavia 1♋40'42	2525 O'Steen 26♊35'57
1603 Neva 9♌45'08	1144 Oda 6♍57'31	1207 Ostenia 19♈56'53
1679 Nevanlinna 27♍03'51	2606 Odessa 17♎03'44	3169 Ostro 5♋50'38
2955 Newburn 2♉02'43	2775 Odishaw 11♋49'55	2681 Ostrovskij 6♊45'29
855 Newcombia 16♈52'08	1143 Odysseus 10♏35'26	1529 Oterma 10♋22'35
2086 Newell 14♌41'30	215 Oenone 24♈40'37	1126 Otero 0♈38'47
662 Newtonia 13♌27'00	1259 Ogyalla 14♊40'37	913 Otila 4♑30'37
2390 Nežárka 25♒21'23	2351 O'Higgins 2♓45'00	670 Ottegebe 24♍18'03
1831 Nicholson 12♊11'23	439 Ohio 21♎31'34	994 Otthild 2♈00'48
843 Nicolaia 3♈39'48	3626 Ohsaki 12♑40'33	401 Ottilia 5♉59'35
1343 Nicole 10♉49'07	2960 Ohtaki 10♌20'22	2962 Otto 23♉55'16
1720 Niels 7♌19'52	3843 OISCA 28♐53'25	2108 Otto Schmidt 27♒26'49
3117 Niepce 3♋01'11	3379 Oishi 26♌21'13	2227 Otto Struve 28♍27'41
2880 Nihondaira 9♉16'21	3565 Ojima 2♋04'20	1512 Oulu 9♈52'16
2972 Niilo 23♎50'36	1701 Okavango 0♊58'04	1473 Ounas 6♏11'43
307 Nike 10♋47'05	2084 Okayama 28♌39'05	1396 Outeniqua 29♓07'27
1185 Nikko 11♊29'43	4042 Okhotsk 8♍59'52	2800 Ovidius 12♋31'49
2386 Nikonov 4♈46'39	3149 Okudzhava 7♎50'06	2648 Owa 9♑30'18
779 Nina 13♑29'34	2454 Olaus Magnus 7♐12'34	3464 Owensby 24♒13'16
2539 Ningxia 12♎50'09	1002 Olbersia 13♓28'32	1740 Paavo Nurmi 25♑34'21
357 Ninina 17♌50'34	2897 Ole Römer 17♉54'07	363 Padua 4♊29'56
2421 Nininger 17♊28'37	2438 Oleshko 21♉50'42	1061 Paeonia 1♋15'21
71 Niobe 15♒46'01	304 Olga 8♍41'55	1032 Pafuri 15♊55'29
727 Nipponia 12♌35'26	2177 Oliver 22♉02'20	2859 Paganini 14♍50'17
2124 Nissen 16♉50'27	835 Olivia 9♒44'54	1535 Päijänne 26♐03'18
3770 Nizami 14♓58'41	2201 Oljato 16♊23'20	1889 Pakhmutova 25♉29'46
1298 Nocturna 29♑32'03	3287 Olmstead 3♏08'22	1921 Pala 22♉34'00
1563 Noël 23♉13'20	2310 Olshaniya 3♌57'27	1834 Palach 27♐57'01
703 Noëmi 3♏17'58	582 Olympia 5♍18'18	2066 Palala 26♋44'23
1068 Nofretete 18♒45'38	1022 Olympiada 21♋35'02	2456 Palamedes 26♒51'12
3008 Nojiri 18♍17'10	3095 Omarkhayyam	415 Palatia 6♌52'50
473 Nolli 1♓53'59	22♑59'55	49 Pales 15♑33'35
1367 Nongoma 0♑23'03	3637 O'Meara 27♎34'26	914 Palisana 15♐20'26
2382 Nonie 5♐41'48	3355 Onizuka 20♌24'33	2 Pallas 22♍36'47
4022 Nonna 8♑01'55	1389 Onnie 24♍12'42	372 Palma 26♒49'10
783 Nora 21♌42'34	2330 Ontake 20♌22'27	1548 Palomaa 26♋36'18
1463 Nordenmarkia 0♓57'13	2649 Oongaq 5♐00'49	1598 Paloque 27♑35'03
2464 Nordenskiöld 7♈58'49	1691 Oort 23♍48'14	2885 Palva 18♓48'50
555 Norma 10♌20'42	1738 Oosterhoff 13♋42'50	1243 Pamela 5♐32'33
1256 Normannia 27♏50'32	171 Ophelia 10♋07'41	539 Pamina 4♑26'22
3670 Northcott 16♋45'20	2099 Öpik 8♏22'45	2878 Panacea 18♒02'00
3869 Norton 8♐45'26	255 Oppavia 13♈20'16	2674 Pandarus 29♍12'26
3162 Nostalgia 8♌24'13	1492 Oppolzer 17♌19'03	55 Pandora 10♍09'26
2857 NOT 29♌29'00	2736 Ops 15♐06'25	2378 Pannekoek 0♎58'36
626 Notburga 11♓18'15	1195 Orangia 10♑51'04	1444 Pannonia 2♒48'34
3157 Novikov 12♉12'42	1080 Orchis 1♈34'07	70 Panopaea 17♉32'38
2495 Noviomagum 19♎11'54	2406 Orelskaya 12♈06'27	2973 Paola 6♓29'37
2520 Novorossijsk 6♈23'22	701 Oriola 3♐46'21	3176 Paolicchi 22♉58'23
2053 Nuki 12♎50'00	2188 Orlenok 20♌03'49	471 Papagena 23♊51'00
1206 Numerowia 24♒13'54	2724 Orlov 3♍13'03	2480 Papanov 4♉44'49
1368 Numidia 17♈51'31	2517 Orma 12♊03'32	2239 Paracelsus 20♈09'09
2502 Nummela 14♈22'34	350 Ornamenta 29♊54'46	

Heliocentric Nodes in Alphabetical Order
Epoch November 5, 1990   Equinox 1950.0   Planet nodes have number

2791 Paradise 5♓34'54	975 Perseverantia 8♉26'06	2613 Plzeň 7♑23'50
1779 Paraná 13♐55'38	3953 Perth 8♌38'44	1908 Pobeda 14♈11'38
1857 Parchomenko	4250 Perun 29♉50'05	3441 Pochaina 23♋10'07
25♏36'47	3005 Pervictoralex 27♍07'16	3311 Podobed 6♍52'40
2484 Parenago 24♎05'06	1716 Peter 3♐17'48	946 Poësia 9♊17'38
347 Pariana 25♊19'57	482 Petrina 28♍59'55	1830 Pogson 26♌59'44
3317 Paris 15♌17'50	3244 Petronius 1♋51'15	3606 Pohjola 10♐11'02
2095 Parsifal 2♓11'29	830 Petropolitana 11♓20'18	2021 Poincaré 4♍33'24
4087 Pärt 24♈17'17	3831 Pettengill 0♍50'48	3348 Pokryshkin 5♎22'21
11 Parthenope 5♌03'36	968 Petunia 28♎40'20	142 Polana 20♑40'07
2331 Parvulesco 15♐10'45	174 Phaedra 27♒21'48	1708 Pólit 12♎29'26
888 Parysatis 3♌46'11	322 Phaeo 12♐17'02	1112 Polonia 2♒53'35
2860 Pasacentennium	3200 Phaethon 24♐55'02	2006 Polonskaya 0♈33'00
4♓04'57	296 Phaëtusa 1♌08'17	2983 Poltava 7♐36'17
2200 Pasadena 15♓04'42	2357 Phereclos 28♍43'43	33 Polyhymnia 8♈13'30
3855 Pasasymphonia	274 Philagoria 2♋24'44	3709 Polypoites 6♎29'17
15♋34'51	280 Philia 9♈51'08	595 Polyxena 24♈05'45
3508 Pasternak 4♈34'11	977 Philippa 15♊32'59	308 Polyxo 1♎22'48
451 Patientia 29♊00'07	631 Philippina 14♏22'42	2771 Polzunov 27♎19'14
2727 Paton 21♎57'38	1869 Philoctetes 13♉38'35	32 Pomona 9♏56'41
1347 Patria 18♏56'32	196 Philomela 12♊06'02	203 Pompeja 17♓34'29
1978 Patrice 23♉56'39	227 Philosophia 27♒29'43	1305 Pongola 2♊40'30
436 Patricia 21♓01'48	25 Phocaea 3♏38'37	2792 Ponomarev 16♈16'12
2748 Patrick Gene 20♓06'43	443 Photographica	3074 Popov 18♓20'15
617 Patroclus 13♉44'55	24♍59'39	3896 Pordenone 22♏33'12
1601 Patry 14♊15'55	1291 Phryne 5♏21'50	1499 Pori 29♏21'57
1791 Patsayev 18♎40'58	189 Phthia 23♎11'18	2570 Porphyro 24♒03'44
3310 Patsy 11♑22'01	556 Phyllis 15♑37'11	1636 Porter 17♍54'48
2511 Patterson 25♊07'15	614 Pia 6♏51'50	2333 Porthan 9♉49'06
3525 Paul 10♑03'37	3772 Piaf 11♋05'02	757 Portlandia 22♈01'37
1314 Paula 24♐13'56	1000 Piazzia 23♒21'50	3933 Portugal 13♉44'35
278 Paulina 1♊38'53	4221 Picasso 7♎30'59	1757 Porvoo 9♉04'26
537 Pauly 0♌08'14	1366 Piccolo 24♈00'24	1131 Porzia 10♋19'27
1007 Pawlowia 7♒04'13	803 Picka 10♐55'33	1572 Posnania 5♈34'09
1152 Pawona 1♓37'57	784 Pickeringia 14♈31'46	1484 Postrema 12♊39'28
679 Pax 22♋09'35	1523 Pieksämäki 27♒20'33	1345 Potomac 16♌59'41
2039 Payne–Gaposchkin	1536 Pielinen 15♎10'23	4281 Pounds 7♎27'09
5♋32'55	2816 Pien 3♋33'15	3760 Poutanen 23♋31'24
3612 Peale 17♑07'19	1392 Pierre 27♓52'56	2367 Praha 10♎22'30
3304 Pearce 20♒05'44	312 Pierretta 6♈16'30	3164 Prast 4♊22'39
1629 Pecker 12♌15'39	3713 Pieters 18♋57'49	547 Praxedis 12♎53'42
3312 Pedersen 4♏26'20	3759 Piironen 22♑32'09	1238 Predappia 21♉30'00
2893 Peiroos 18♋05'40	1975 Pikelner 19♍55'06	3792 Preston 2♊51'53
118 Peitho 17♉10'20	1990 Pilcher 13♎08'07	790 Pretoria 11♐33'12
2045 Peking 10♈48'05	2694 Pino Torinese 9♐27'39	529 Preziosa 5♊00'17
1190 Pelagia 26♈01'55	648 Pippa 21♑35'50	884 Priamus 1♒00'20
2202 Pele 19♍42'46	3228 Pire 20♑17'18	1359 Prieska 3♊57'43
1667 Pels 20♊26'01	2506 Pirogov 14♍29'46	970 Primula 11♒16'23
1429 Pemba 17♉26'40	1082 Pirola 27♉28'58	508 Princetonia 14♉15'11
201 Penelope 6♏34'11	2672 Písek 8♌30'26	2653 Principia 14♎06'36
271 Penthesilea 5♓30'20	484 Pittsburghia 6♌59'24	2137 Priscilla 19♒46'58
3189 Penza 27♍21'55	1069 Planckia 22♌05'15	997 Priska 6♐56'55
1102 Pepita 6♏19'11	2639 Planman 18♊51'46	1192 Prisma 0♈55'33
554 Peraga 25♑07'19	2905 Plaskett 9♈34'50	902 Probitas 22♓34'11
1680 Per Brahe 23♊06'33	3620 Platonov 2♑15'13	194 Prokne 8♍59'13
2817 Perec 14♐24'04	2179 Platzeck 14♈54'45	3159 Prokof'ev 12♏41'34
2951 Perepadin 24♈52'27	1986 Plaut 26♌09'18	1809 Prometheus 9♋14'52
2482 Perkin 12♋44'29	2172 Plavsk 24♊09'27	26 Proserpina 15♉29'27
4043 Perolof 3♒10'39	3226 Plinius 8♋36'22	2372 Proskurin 7♋51'19
2422 Perovskaya 9♏31'40	3860 Plovdiv 19♑18'09	3540 Protesilaos 25♈44'42
1515 Perrotin 18♉58'43	#### Pluto 19♋33'00	147 Protogeneia 8♐30'59
399 Persephone 16♓16'27		474 Prudentia 11♍18'52

Heliocentric Nodes in Alphabetical Order
Epoch November 5, 1990   Equinox 1950.0   Planet nodes have number ####

261 Prymno	6♋14'25	906 Repsolda	9♉57'27	4071 Rostovdon	27♐12'06
3059 Pryor	0♎59'16	2254 Requiem	7♓43'49	615 Roswitha	13♈22'47
16 Psyche	29♌51'39	1081 Reseda	0♉27'40	874 Rotraut	10♎30'44
4001 Ptolemaeus	10♌15'29	1371 Resi	4♎54'14	1413 Roucarie	28♍38'47
2841 Puijo	1♋09'58	3356 Resnik	17♋52'18	2978 Roudebush	18♓33'55
762 Pulcova	5♒35'03	2303 Retsina	15♎02'33	1518 Rovaniemi	27♈21'32
1209 Pumma	29♊22'13	1096 Reunerta	20♊57'37	317 Roxane	0♍53'01
1659 Punkaharju	8♓08'54	528 Rezia	19♉44'27	1638 Ruanda	20♎14'06
3359 Purcari	24♈27'01	577 Rhea	28♒25'15	2457 Rublyov	20♌15'19
4040 Purcell	25♉27'50	907 Rhoda	12♉49'44	4286 Rubtsov	14♌19'07
2208 Pushkin	19♊05'42	1197 Rhodesia	15♐29'47	2474 Ruby	27♏34'10
3577 Putilin	10♑10'37	437 Rhodia	23♐06'21	3574 Rudaux	14♏45'17
2557 Putnam	7♎44'34	166 Rhodope	8♌47'26	1907 Rudneva	1♍41'28
2192 Pyatigoriya	21♎23'22	879 Ricarda	29♐47'50	4107 Rufino	28♐37'52
2122 Pyatiletka	15♋01'12	1230 Riceia	20♎16'35	4101 Ruikou	8♓42'57
2720 Pyotr Pervyj	23♋02'49	3972 Richard	12♍45'25	1773 Rumpelstilz	14♊17'43
632 Pyrrha	26♓43'15	4129 Richelen	5♐22'33	2899 Runrun Shaw	19♈18'38
432 Pythia	28♊23'50	1214 Richilde	15♑36'54	353 Ruperto–Carola	
2255 Qinghai	10♉44'26	3338 Richter	5♌41'17		12♋22'01
1297 Quadea	25♑48'00	3692 Rickman	9♏13'40	1953 Rupertwildt	14♊05'05
1239 Queteleta	12♊46'42	1514 Ricouxa	25♌22'53	1443 Ruppina	24♍40'01
1915 Quetzálcoatl	12♍22'07	4025 Ridley	26♌53'25	3756 Ruscannon	15♏31'54
755 Quintilla	26♍52'37	1025 Riema	12♍49'57	3516 Rusheva	11♍27'35
1786 Raahe	16♈09'02	1796 Riga	6♌50'01	1762 Russell	10♍21'46
1624 Rabe	13♌18'20	1883 Rimito	11♊24'20	232 Russia	2♍10'01
674 Rachele	28♉09'28	2654 Ristenpart	26♎27'12	1171 Rusthawelia	2♌31'59
1420 Radcliffe	20♐46'33	2690 Ristiina	15♌53'56	798 Ruth	4♏04'25
2833 Radishchev	6♓32'28	1180 Rita	27♊57'57	1249 Rutherfordia	18♐34'31
1644 Rafita	0♑25'47	1426 Riviera	4♓38'14	3285 Ruth Wolfe	5♐42'28
1839 Ragazza	20♉42'49	1145 Robelmonte	16♓19'30	2518 Rutllant	25♎10'07
1450 Raimonda	14♊28'27	1377 Roberbauxa	12♏44'47	1427 Ruvuma	18♊11'50
1137 Raïssa	18♊02'33	335 Roberta	27♌58'04	1856 Růžena	5♎25'21
4108 Rakos	14♎49'10	3428 Roberts	20♏46'17	4258 Ryazanov	2♊03'13
3332 Raksha	18♊26'33	2328 Robeson	1♎43'55	2835 Ryoma	5♈09'59
4130 Ramanujan	24♍58'02	3819 Robinson	15♉59'36	4163 Saaremaa	8♌46'21
3928 Randa	28♐42'40	4153 Roburnham	5♊41'16	1115 Sabauda	12♊08'00
1530 Rantaseppä	15♑28'36	904 Rockefellia	17♎43'04	665 Sabine	28♑22'55
708 Raphaela	24♓53'05	2529 Rockwell Kent		2264 Sabrina	5♐59'38
1148 Rarahu	25♌04'56		26♎57'36	2822 Sacajawea	3♋00'21
4113 Rascana	8♌17'35	2703 Rodari	19♌00'51	1626 Sadeya	9♑03'21
2100 Ra–Shalom	20♍16'17	3873 Roddy	9♐31'04	1364 Safara	3♓46'41
927 Ratisbona	7♈56'17	1557 Roehla	25♓02'46	3615 Safronov	15♌14'58
1882 Rauma	20♎53'53	1657 Roemera	14♋59'03	1163 Saga	7♌40'54
3985 Raybatson	23♊37'37	920 Rogeria	12♎30'57	2709 Sagan	0♐38'03
3007 Reaves	8♊27'16	2058 Róka	5♋05'36	2605 Sahade	21♍40'49
572 Rebekka	14♎07'44	3736 Rokoske	24♌56'25	2088 Sahlia	29♓17'15
573 Recha	12♓36'39	1269 Rollandia	14♌18'18	1533 Saimaa	1♍32'29
3365 Recogne	9♎15'26	472 Roma	6♌52'34	2578 Saint–Exupéry	
2884 Reddish	11♉03'24	2516 Roman	2♌55'48		25♉28'43
3778 Regge	9♓23'49	942 Romilda	11♊00'14	2615 Saito	22♒42'13
285 Regina	10♒49'37	4024 Ronan	24♉04'46	1979 Sakharov	22♎14'38
574 Reginhild	6♓26'23	2285 Ron Helin	7♍22'46	1166 Sakuntala	16♋16'58
1117 Reginita	26♌41'06	3293 Rontaylor	9♈15'38	2918 Salazar	15♌16'56
1111 Reinmuthia	12♌15'04	223 Rosa	17♉50'40	1456 Saldanha	14♑15'30
1577 Reiss	3♌09'15	314 Rosalia	20♍04'32	1715 Salli	8♉29'14
3871 Reiz	3♑31'59	900 Rosalinde	2♎05'20	562 Salome	10♊31'54
2552 Remek	13♓02'23	540 Rosamunde	21♎42'22	1436 Salonta	20♐17'46
575 Renate	19♓20'48	2057 Rosemary	14♈51'45	1083 Salvia	20♊24'42
1416 Renauxa	22♓35'18	985 Rosina	20♑03'43	3147 Samantha	5♏45'46
1792 Reni	12♊31'37	1646 Rosseland	29♋37'35	4016 Sambre	13♋23'44
1204 Renzia	7♈14'32	1350 Rosselia	19♌14'26	2624 Samitchell	11♍32'53
2468 Repin	6♏02'12	1440 Rostia	16♉31'38	2091 Sampo	24♋20'22

Heliocentric Nodes in Alphabetical Order
Epoch November 5, 1990   Equinox 1950.0   Planet nodes have number ####

3029 Sanders 13♒15'36	837 Schwarzschilda 19♎35'57	3182 Shimanto 7♐59'39
3043 San Diego 20♓33'31	989 Schwassmannia 3♐03'04	2879 Shimizu 29♌00'08
1760 Sandra 22♏13'23	1265 Schweikarda 14♒08'07	2908 Shimoyama 23♏07'46
1711 Sandrine 14♌41'34	3350 Scobee 23♓18'54	2530 Shipka 18♎35'11
2284 San Juan 25♌25'25	876 Scott 0♍51'54	3867 Shiretoko 19♊28'46
2745 San Martin 17♌19'47	3594 Scotti 10♊48'11	2849 Shklovskij 13♉42'58
1288 Santa 28♑42'29	155 Scylla 10♉36'23	1833 Shmakova 7♍54'03
4158 Santini 4♈48'03	1306 Scythia 4♑04'15	2074 Shoemaker 26♎42'48
275 Sapientia 13♌44'40	1482 Sebastiana 10♊51'10	2448 Sholokhov 10♌45'47
80 Sappho 8♏20'34	2785 Sedov 4♓12'38	3946 Shor 25♒37'19
3473 Sapporo 9♌09'37	892 Seeligeria 25♍28'32	2669 Shostakovich 22♑20'52
533 Sara 0♎01'58	3217 Seidelmann 13♒03'13	2777 Shukshin 6♉31'43
2987 Sarabhai 17♍04'31	2292 Seili 22♍01'18	1977 Shura 2♋00'20
3065 Sarahill 2♒46'47	2364 Seillier 12♉26'53	4196 Shuya 18♍11'43
1012 Sarema 12♊44'57	1521 Seinäjoki 12♈13'09	1405 Sibelius 11♒39'46
796 Sarita 2♉49'04	1913 Sekanina 28♊28'54	1094 Siberia 28♌39'04
1920 Sarmiento 3♊31'20	3426 Seki 5♈07'41	168 Sibylla 26♎30'02
2223 Sarpedon 10♏26'07	580 Selene 8♋59'03	2215 Sichuan 10♊48'49
3680 Sasha 25♈38'29	3288 Seleucus 8♏07'35	1258 Sicilia 29♑30'19
461 Saskia 6♍57'49	500 Selinur 19♑47'59	2343 Siding Spring 7♏44'46
3292 Sather 6♉28'45	86 Semele 26♊42'25	579 Sidonia 22♊27'36
2402 Satpaev 7♓17'59	2475 Semenov 29♎49'10	1632 Sieböhme 19♎32'38
#### Saturn 23♋06'43	584 Semiramis 11♑50'05	386 Siegena 16♍28'42
3598 Saucier 11♍05'00	2182 Semirot 21♉09'32	2560 Sigma 28♌03'54
1494 Savo 14♋33'16	1014 Semphyra 11♐36'18	552 Sigelinde 27♐09'09
1525 Savonlinna 9♑02'53	3133 Sendai 6♉43'31	459 Signe 29♈08'33
2917 Sawyer Hogg 18♓24'56	2608 Seneca 18♍55'00	1493 Sigrid 0♓17'04
3534 Sax 6♐47'05	550 Senta 0♑15'48	502 Sigune 12♌28'57
2081 Sázava 6♊04'05	483 Seppina 23♍51'16	3631 Sigyn 0♍47'05
1228 Scabiosa 7♒40'27	1103 Sequoia 27♐07'56	3201 Sijthoff 19♋02'20
2812 Scaltriti 7♊44'07	838 Seraphina 29♏56'55	3943 Silbermann 6♈33'13
460 Scania 24♎55'38	2225 Serkowski 27♊51'55	257 Silesia 4♉28'01
3333 Schaber 20♏47'55	2691 Sersic 19♒28'18	1733 Silke 8♍53'03
1742 Schaifers 1♍49'28	3392 Setouchi 26♐21'41	1446 Sillanpää 17♈06'57
1542 Schalén 1♏53'10	2121 Sevastopol 25♌13'50	1317 Silvretta 6♈51'44
1797 Schaumasse 29♈16'28	1737 Severny 27♒07'50	748 Simeïsa 25♐12'24
2485 Scheffler 7♋52'03	2263 Shaanxi 24♉04'57	2141 Simferopol 1♑36'39
643 Scheherezade 12♐06'17	1648 Shajna 10♌00'16	1033 Simona 8♎54'31
596 Scheila 10♊26'43	2985 Shakespeare 4♉02'12	1675 Simonida 29♈44'37
4062 Schiaparelli 9♓38'20	3408 Shalamov 12♌18'26	2426 Simonov 26♏54'05
3079 Schiller 2♎44'27	2510 Shandong 12♋30'05	3706 Sinnott 16♌34'22
1255 Schilowa 27♏39'19	1994 Shane 4♐40'47	3391 Sinon 10♓24'56
2308 Schilt 4♉04'09	2197 Shanghai 26♉43'04	3389 Sinzot 29♌50'46
3536 Schleicher 10♓40'03	3139 Shantou 12♐28'44	1009 Sirene 19♏08'54
1770 Schlesinger 21♈23'47	1881 Shao 7♏40'02	332 Siri 1♉20'59
3302 Schliemann 4♍04'26	3832 Shapiro 28♈25'54	116 Sirona 3♊31'07
922 Schlutia 24♎58'46	1123 Shapleya 19♊29'59	823 Sisigambis 14♐35'21
2234 Schmadel 5♈48'30	1902 Shaposhnikov 29♉03'39	1866 Sisyphus 3♊05'03
1743 Schmidt 9♎06'33	3694 Sharon 11♒06'53	244 Sita 28♎30'57
1782 Schneller 6♍56'55	2416 Sharonov 28♌21'06	2042 Sitarski 17♈02'58
2871 Schober 27♈54'41	3027 Shavarsh 14♎19'09	1170 Siva 0♈32'34
2959 Scholl 0♌55'32	2377 Shcheglov 22♐26'40	140 Siwa 16♋49'19
1235 Schorria 12♈24'49	1196 Sheba 10♋30'54	2619 Skalnaté Pleso 24♎07'51
1911 Schubart 15♑11'50	3996 Shekhtelia 11♋17'35	2554 Skiff 25♑58'31
2384 Schulhof 7♈38'24	2027 Shen Guo 25♉00'10	1884 Skip 23♓16'11
2018 Schuster 5♎35'00	2425 Shenzhen 22♉16'53	2431 Skovoroda 28♒37'23
4134 Schütz 14♌40'39	2036 Sheragul 15♓51'11	1130 Skuld 5♏44'13
2923 Schuyler 20♓11'20	4223 Shikoku 29♐14'10	1854 Skvortsov 8♎56'59
2119 Schwall 27♐46'34	4164 Shilov 7♏40'40	3243 Skytel 18♎50'30
2149 Schwambraniya 2♊11'20		2304 Slavia 15♎31'48
		1766 Slipher 8♎24'19

Heliocentric Nodes in Alphabetical Order
Epoch November 5, 1990   Equinox 1950.0   Planet nodes have number ####

# Name	Node	# Name	Node	# Name	Node
1807 Slovakia	25♏57'54	2238 Steshenko	3♉16'18	3564 Talthybius	23♈15'27
2047 Smetana	6♉03'37	3672 Stevedberg	13♈45'35	1089 Tama	11♊03'29
2580 Smilevskia	28♋53'38	2831 Stevin	21♊35'12	326 Tamara	1♉43'13
1613 Smiley	20♒47'23	3794 Sthenelos	12♓37'15	1084 Tamariwa	6♎39'14
3351 Smith	5♎53'02	1847 Stobbe	16♋42'07	4186 Tamashima	24♌30'35
2083 Smither	18♐38'48	4283 Stöffler	27♒27'57	3417 Tamblyn	28♊21'38
3773 Smithsonian	3♊04'43	1386 Storeria	11♍11'31	3121 Tamines	5♌03'48
3213 Smolensk	3♉39'16	1019 Strackea	23♌51'51	3403 Tammy	23♎52'36
1731 Smuts	2♍20'01	3236 Strand	6♏49'15	1497 Tampere	0♒06'44
1262 Sniadeckia	4♌01'07	1560 Strattonia	19♑09'46	2052 Tamriko	3♏32'45
2836 Sobolev	17♓45'08	1201 Strenua	22♎45'44	1641 Tana	1♓13'37
2479 Sodankylä	14♒22'24	1628 Strobel	0♎52'42	772 Tanete	3♊32'01
2864 Soderblom	14♌51'20	1422 Strömgrenia	21♎10'09	1595 Tanga	21♋49'36
1393 Sofala	26♉24'50	1124 Stroobantia	21♈57'04	825 Tanina	10♋58'57
2259 Sofievka	9♑53'14	3054 Strugatskia	25♌44'25	2102 Tantalus	3♋43'05
3279 Solon	11♎29'08	768 Struveana	8♉55'05	2127 Tanya	16♋26'35
1331 Solvejg	1♌09'09	3874 Stuart	6♊44'23	1705 Tapio	8♈13'38
2815 Soma	29♋25'19	3393 Štúr	6♍13'41	2995 Taratuta	19♍22'42
1430 Somalia	27♒06'03	964 Subamara	0♉29'01	3325 TARDIS	16♉00'00
2455 Somville	0♒30'20	1692 Subbotina	19♎16'46	1360 Tarka	1♓08'33
1293 Sonja	26♏12'35	417 Suevia	19♎14'24	3345 Tarkovskij	4♒21'28
1039 Sonneberga	11♏27'34	752 Sulamitis	24♊42'38	1109 Tata	28♐29'20
2432 Soomana	7♈31'24	563 Suleika	24♊58'46	2668 Tataria	27♉40'36
2433 Sootiyo	8♎14'16	2403 Šumava	20♑04'31	4235 Tatischckev	1♓30'10
251 Sophia	5♍49'02	2092 Sumiana	12♊02'54	769 Tatjana	8♉09'12
2921 Sophocles	29♌10'13	1090 Sumida	27♌32'18	1989 Tatry	24♈51'55
134 Sophrosyne	15♓46'54	1928 Summa	0♎13'12	3748 Tatum	3♉17'09
3864 Søren	24♈46'26	1424 Sundmania	12♉47'23	581 Tauntonia	12♋19'33
731 Sorga	16♉10'20	1656 Suomi	25♍00'56	512 Taurinensis	16♋41'46
2682 Soromundi	6♌49'48	2965 Surikov	6♌34'11	814 Tauris	28♊13'34
4039 Souseki	5♑14'09	4224 Susa	20♎39'07	2424 Tautenburg	29♈51'19
2228 Soyuz-Apollo	19♌56'04	542 Susanna	2♍39'16	2512 Tavastia	9♊05'24
4255 Spacewatch	3♋35'14	933 Susi	20♌58'04	2603 Taylor	7♉36'07
2579 Spartacus	10♑29'58	1844 Susilva	9♋12'42	2266 Tchaikovsky	19♒23'01
2459 Spellmann	6♏08'58	2532 Sutton	14♓40'47	453 Tea	11♈14'24
3282 Spencer Jones	11♍52'42	1927 Suvanto	26♈40'23	2882 Tedesco	14♒44'15
896 Sphinx	13♐44'06	2489 Suvorov	26♉05'48	604 Tekmessa	11♈40'10
2065 Spicer	28♒07'58	2719 Suzhou	5♌08'08	1749 Telamon	10♓28'20
3207 Spinrad	17♍25'54	2393 Suzuki	16♏13'05	4246 Telemann	6♉59'50
1091 Spiraea	20♊20'50	3191 Svanetia	20♉33'14	2717 Tellervo	14♍25'28
1330 Spiridonia	8♍25'56	4135 Svetlanov	19♎46'26	3808 Tempel	2♍41'52
2160 Spitzer	14♌01'11	3483 Svetlov	25♊26'03	1399 Teneriffa	11♍11'20
1564 Srbija	28♍14'18	4075 Sviridov	10♈52'25	2195 Tengström	10♋33'13
2250 Stalingrad	7♍32'46	4082 Swann	24♑13'40	2774 Tenojoki	20♑40'31
3420 Standish	25♌46'02	992 Swasey	1♏58'39	345 Tercidina	2♏13'18
4150 Starr	2♌28'16	3947 Swedenborg	13♐37'38	1189 Terentia	5♑09'26
4131 Stasik	12♑57'36	882 Swetlana	17♐14'47	478 Tergeste	23♏32'43
831 Stateira	27♍35'54	1637 Swings	21♈12'22	81 Terpsichore	0♈55'19
1147 Stavropolis	24♐45'32	2138 Swissair	15♋13'33	2399 Terradas	25♌46'20
2035 Stearns	16♊29'39	2168 Swope	13♒36'11	2244 Tesla	16♋17'59
2300 Stebbins	1♉29'44	1714 Sy	0♒23'32	2797 Teucer	9♊23'08
707 Steïna	11♑29'19	519 Sylvania	14♉32'04	1044 Teutonia	29♉35'53
1681 Steinmetz	25♋04'06	87 Sylvia	13♊05'47	1980 Tezcatlipoca	6♐05'34
2867 Šteins	25♉04'06	1104 Syringa	8♌46'06	1236 Thaïs	18♉10'54
3140 Stellafane	11♋27'28	2268 Szmytowna	29♊20'41	23 Thalia	6♊41'13
2146 Stentor	10♌37'21	721 Tabora	8♉44'19	586 Thekla	18♏47'04
3444 Stepanian	12♓55'02	3097 Tacitus	16♎36'19	24 Themis	5♉38'39
220 Stephania	17♐39'32	2469 Tadjikistan	1♍40'27	1625 The NORC	22♒56'40
566 Stereoskopia	20♊04'58	2169 Taiwan	11♊29'53	778 Theobalda	23♒08'18
995 Sternberga	11♏26'50	2514 Taiyuan	28♓19'36	440 Theodora	21♋36'43
		3151 Talbot	2♏05'40	295 Theresia	5♑53'53
				1545 Thernöe	22♉01'55

Heliocentric Nodes in Alphabetical Order
Epoch November 5, 1990　Equinox 1950.0　Planet nodes have number

1868 Thersites 17≏07'11	3532 Tracie 26♉04'20	3472 Upgren 2♐47'11
1161 Thessalia 12♊36'40	715 Transvaalia 15♉49'09	2191 Uppsala 7♐14'05
17 Thetis 5♌02'02	1537 Transylvania 19♏35'45	30 Urania 7♒17'13
405 Thia 14♐43'03	3735 Třeboň 29♑33'48	#### Uranus 13♊46'59
4173 Thicksten 16♋49'52	619 Triberga 7≏00'19	3722 Urata 21♏58'32
1586 Thiele 5♌21'54	2990 Trimberger 21♍22'49	167 Urda 15♍56'48
88 Thisbe 6♑16'38	2037 Tripaxeptalis 9♈05'41	501 Urhixidur 27♓06'35
3255 Tholen 6♓45'47	1966 Tristan 5♌13'09	1838 Ursa 13♉51'22
1023 Thomana 14≏08'45	1208 Troilus 17♉56'28	860 Ursina 9♒09'38
2555 Thomas 13♑30'46	3912 Troja 25♈44'11	375 Ursula 6♓06'04
2064 Thomsen 1♒41'53	3702 Trubetskaya 29♋34'22	2729 Urumqi 3♊55'41
299 Thora 0♐51'30	1408 Trusanda 21≏26'35	3010 Ushakov 6♋46'55
3717 Thorenia 11♋06'18	2240 Tsai 0♊25'06	634 Ute 12♌57'10
4098 Thraen 9♋22'45	2111 Tselina 17♍02'52	1282 Utopia 23♒55'40
3801 Thrasymedes 28≏45'17	2498 Tsesevich 1♓36'38	1447 Utra 5♉18'34
279 Thule 13♊10'02	4105 Tsia 24≏01'13	1351 Uzbekistania 9♈35'45
934 Thüringia 25♒12'41	1590 Tsiolkovskaja 16♏09'02	1507 Vaasa 22♑31'12
219 Thusnelda 20≏20'26	4097 Tsurugisan 19♐36'22	2096 Väinö 4♒26'22
115 Thyra 8♒35'41	2770 Tsvet 8♉20'29	2596 Vainu Bappu 18♌44'53
2209 Tianjin 0♍35'35	3511 Tsvetaeva 19♏25'39	1573 Väisälä 21≏53'14
2158 Tietjen 6≏46'17	1481 Tübingia 23♓27'17	131 Vala 5♊13'59
753 Tiflis 0♊55'34	2013 Tucapel 6♋09'54	839 Valborg 7♓46'51
2251 Tikhov 12≏42'37	1038 Tuckia 27♉43'40	262 Valda 8♑13'02
1229 Tilia 19≏38'46	2224 Tucson 21♉00'01	2793 Valdaj 26♓14'25
3272 Tillandz 3♋38'16	1323 Tugela 15♉37'35	2741 Valdivia 0♍54'59
603 Timandra 13♓04'03	1095 Tulipa 28♍18'11	447 Valentine 11♊37'41
3238 Timresovia 11♈02'21	1070 Tunica 15♍06'27	611 Valeria 9≏18'45
4056 Timwarner 22♌01'42	1425 Tuorla 5≏33'37	610 Valeska 20♑03'07
1222 Tina 5♐48'47	530 Turandot 8♌36'59	3725 Valsecchi 15♓21'04
1933 Tinchen 14♍27'43	3323 Turgenev 21♈39'58	3230 Vampilov 15♊43'09
687 Tinette 4♓12'40	2584 Turkmenia 19♉39'52	240 Vanadis 24♋44'26
4081 Tippett 13♐25'05	1496 Turku 23♑55'08	2019 Van Albada 11♐45'00
1400 Tirela 0♍19'44	1186 Turnera 12♉42'18	2370 Van Altena 9♈56'41
267 Tirza 13♊31'40	2716 Tuulikki 8♏06'05	1781 Van Biesbroeck
466 Tisiphone 20♑42'46	2610 Tuva 24≏52'44	14♉14'06
3663 Tisserand 16♋38'00	3261 Tvardovskij 22♌38'11	2413 Van de Hulst 16♍29'35
593 Titania 15♊45'21	258 Tyche 27≏16'55	1965 Van de Kamp 27♊50'37
1801 Titicaca 17♊29'58	1677 Tycho Brahe 7♓28'27	4230 Van den Bergh
1998 Titius 21♓29'36	1055 Tynka 26♌41'06	10♍06'38
1550 Tito 4♊42'54	2120 Tyumenia 12♍28'00	1663 Van den Bos 22♊51'06
732 Tjilaki 22♍48'56	4257 Ubasti 18♍40'59	3091 Van den Heuvel
3090 Tjossem 20♍28'00	1276 Ucclia 24♋14'42	18♏07'28
2478 Tokai 18♏18'12	2707 Ueferji 19♊29'43	2823 Van der Laan 8♐11'11
498 Tokio 7♋05'26	1619 Ueta 1♏06'28	2538 Vanderlinden 19♋55'31
2675 Tolkien 5♈29'18	1279 Uganda 5♓10'02	1666 Van Gent 22♐45'45
2326 Tololo 5♍36'09	2020 Ukko 28♌35'06	1752 Van Herk 26♏32'57
138 Tolosa 24♉39'06	1709 Ukraina 29♑48'36	1673 Van Houten 28≏17'37
1604 Tombaugh 9♒04'05	4128 UKSTU 22♑05'23	3401 Vanphilos 22♒04'23
1013 Tombecka 27♈12'39	909 Ulla 26♌35'35	200 Van Rhijn 20♉08'52
2443 Tomeileen 28♋24'40	885 Ulrike 28♌31'52	3098 Van Sprang 27♋21'33
2391 Tomita 12♍58'51	2471 Ultrajectum 15♈55'21	1263 Varsavia 8♍07'52
590 Tomyris 15♋53'24	2439 Ulugbek 22♋58'02	3776 Vartiovuori 9♉18'32
1266 Tone 21♒08'46	714 Ulula 23♏38'47	3930 Vasil'ev 7♉19'19
924 Toni 0♍07'11	2112 Ulyanov 3♐14'48	2014 Vasilevskis 23≏44'24
1471 Tornio 21♒42'14	1397 Umtata 17♊11'15	1312 Vassar 8♌55'48
1685 Toro 3♑45'14	160 Una 8♈25'11	416 Vaticana 27♉49'28
2104 Toronto 12♐05'25	2154 Underhill 0♈24'38	2862 Vavilov 15♏23'30
2614 Torrence 15♋10'17	92 Undina 11♋25'31	3510 Veeder 9♑36'18
3150 Tosa 19♓53'30	1585 Union 29♌57'12	3030 Vehrenberg 22♑28'16
4179 Toutatis 7♌08'32	306 Unitas 21♌27'14	2151 Velimir 8♊46'45
2787 Tovarishch 0♉06'00	905 Universitas 6♍45'20	2827 Vellamo 15♓05'50
3533 Toyota 16≏43'44	2842 Unsöld 9♒37'39	126 Velleda 22♈59'42

Heliocentric Nodes in Alphabetical Order
Epoch November 5, 1990   Equinox 1950.0   Planet nodes have number ####

487 Venetia 24♋34'21	1380 Volodia 29♓45'54	3721 Widorn 13♒49'36
2458 Veniakaverin 7♌58'33	2009 Voloshina 17♋08'22	2412 Wil 3♒16'02
#### Venus 16♊07'01	2992 Vondel 4♎49'14	1941 Wild 0♊13'26
499 Venusia 15♐51'01	2350 Von Lüde 20♌37'02	392 Wilhelmina 29♎33'16
245 Vera 1♊07'20	2916 Voronveliya 10♒37'01	4117 Wilke 18♍38'38
2265 Verbaandert 12♌54'07	2721 Vsekhsvyatskij	1688 Wilkens 5♐23'51
2545 Verbiest 22♒15'37	24♊44'51	1763 Williams 4♒04'22
2798 Vergilius 9♏14'13	635 Vundtia 3♎10'12	2465 Wilson 23♑48'18
490 Veritas 27♍55'36	2953 Vysheslavia 10♐54'17	747 Winchester 9♌34'53
2809 Vernadskij 26♓55'28	1600 Vyssotsky 0♊04'39	1556 Wingolfia 1♋31'41
612 Veronika 23♎27'59	2453 Wabash 11♈40'30	1575 Winifred 26♎20'27
3974 Verveer 20♈55'05	1704 Wachmann 19♐02'34	2044 Wirt 23♉23'13
2642 Vésale 20♎38'43	1695 Walbeck 8♏15'31	3402 Wisdom 27♓33'16
2599 Veselí 23♓05'52	1260 Walhalla 4♒26'36	717 Wisibada 14♓09'30
4 Vesta 13♋21'56	1417 Walinskia 5♋57'51	2256 Wiśniewski 25♋38'16
2011 Veteraniya 8♓11'32	877 Walküre 25♋54'42	4295 Wisse 15♒36'22
2710 Veverka 23♌58'22	1153 Wallenbergia 10♑04'59	2732 Witt 24♌43'33
2414 Vibeke 26♓45'56	2114 Wallenquist 0♈55'41	852 Wladilena 27♈02'29
3269 Vibert–Douglas	987 Wallia 22♒54'45	2155 Wodan 8♉26'55
23♓05'04	3198 Wallonia 23♊08'36	827 Wolfiana 22♍25'44
144 Vibilia 16♊06'49	256 Walpurga 2♎37'06	1795 Woltjer 12♎06'11
1097 Vicia 13♌18'26	1946 Walraven 16♈51'11	1660 Wood 2♏28'19
12 Victoria 25♏06'48	4266 Waltari 22♒10'35	2218 Wotho 6♋14'02
2644 Victor Jara 17♓13'59	3145 Walter Adams	690 Wratislavia 12♐45'15
3237 Victorplatt 10♑21'46	13♑13'07	3062 Wren 20♌09'04
2814 Vieira 3♍38'11	890 Waltraut 10♍35'21	1747 Wright 27♐49'15
397 Vienna 17♏46'51	1057 Wanda 18♐50'47	1765 Wrubel 10♊49'16
1053 Vigdis 17♈21'34	2276 Warck 4♏49'10	2705 Wu 7♈54'42
1478 Vihuri 18♒04'43	886 Washingtonia 0♊31'32	2752 Wu Chien–Shiung
2258 Viipuri 7♒07'44	2660 Wasserman 23♎43'44	6♋13'51
3507 Vilas 28♊09'32	4155 Watanabe 17♈07'11	3206 Wuhan 10♊39'58
2803 Vilho 20♈37'09	1645 Waterfield 26♐04'51	3987 Wujek 18♉14'22
2553 Viljev 29♋54'53	1822 Waterman 10♏37'35	1785 Wurm 12♑51'18
1310 Villigera 27♓13'55	729 Watsonia 4♌04'59	411 Xanthe 17♋14'49
3072 Vilnius 2♍01'48	1798 Watts 13♉50'15	156 Xanthippe 1♐36'10
2890 Vilyujsk 26♓22'12	1352 Wawel 5♎47'40	625 Xenia 7♌14'46
366 Vincentina 16♓33'07	3107 Weaver 1♑12'35	2387 Xian 22♉59'53
231 Vindobona 20♓20'14	3041 Webb 22♊07'39	2336 Xinjiang 27♊01'23
759 Vinifera 18♒01'25	4152 Weber 21♎35'50	2344 Xizang 9♋00'55
1544 Vinterhansenia	3639 Weidenschilling	1506 Xosa 24♏20'20
29♉31'30	11♏59'08	2652 Yabuuti 4♊15'21
1076 Viola 23♌24'54	3539 Weimar 21♌03'09	1653 Yakhontovia 3♒53'23
3559 Violaumayer 14♒06'05	4085 Weir 8♊15'21	2607 Yakutia 29♓19'38
557 Violetta 22♑40'53	2802 Weisell 9♌01'18	1475 Yalta 19♎41'06
50 Virginia 23♍13'45	3197 Weissman 21♋19'18	3786 Yamada 21♐30'19
1449 Virtanen 20♋21'11	2405 Welch 8♌08'39	2249 Yamamoto 27♌36'26
1887 Virton 18♓32'52	1721 Wells 17♒09'18	4260 Yanai 0♋35'07
494 Virtus 8♉08'01	1950 Wempe 9♊31'19	2693 Yan'an 29♉23'58
1030 Vitja 7♎40'44	1438 Wendeline 27♏53'05	3039 Yangel 10♎09'23
2235 Vittore 24♎43'09	2993 Wendy 13♒15'39	2273 Yarilo 6♊01'30
2558 Viv 15♉44'26	621 Werdandi 6♏57'46	2728 Yatskiv 20♎49'55
1623 Vivian 25♋17'51	226 Weringia 14♌44'02	2270 Yazhi 15♒53'38
3260 Vizbor 8♐54'54	1302 Werra 29♊51'29	3689 Yeates 21♎56'39
1724 Vladimir 13♍40'12	1945 Wesselink 22♌19'25	2956 Yeomans 21♋54'43
2967 Vladisvyat 2♉05'41	2017 Wesson 20♍51'49	990 Yerkes 23♓43'57
2374 Vladvysotskij 17♓25'44	2022 West 2♈07'34	2576 Yesenin 11♒04'11
2123 Vltava 11♒33'37	2902 Westerlund 27♏56'44	2843 Yeti 15♐42'11
1439 Vogtia 5♉26'45	930 Westphalia 10♓34'33	1972 Yi Xing 16♉19'50
1149 Volga 21♐20'25	2128 Wetherill 28♓16'19	2846 Ylppö 24♌23'29
2360 Volgo–Don 8♉02'30	1940 Whipple 23♐47'29	3823 Yorii 21♋36'42
3703 Volkonskaya 22♍29'15	2301 Whitford 19♊26'58	2910 Yoshkar–Ola 13♉52'06
1790 Volkov 1♈33'50	931 Whittemora 22♋19'04	2165 Young 18♈59'09

Heliocentric Nodes in Alphabetical Order
Epoch November 5, 1990   Equinox 1950.0   Planet nodes have number ####

2804 Yrjö	18♋59'04	
351 Yrsa	8♋56'41	
1554 Yugoslavia	6♏45'26	
2230 Yunnan	3♍30'25	
1340 Yvette	15♓18'28	
1301 Yvonne	11♍09'38	
999 Zachia	4♏35'20	
421 Zähringia	7♎01'33	
1242 Zambesia	19♓42'08	
1462 Zamenhof	24♈39'25	
2945 Zanstra	5♋26'38	
2813 Zappalà	21♏45'44	
2189 Zaragoza	8♌22'36	
1336 Zeelandia	7♋05'19	
851 Zeissia	20♌42'39	
169 Zelia	24♓18'32	
633 Zelima	27♌01'32	
654 Zelinda	7♑58'29	
3042 Zelinsky	15♏52'22	
2411 Zellner	10♌32'12	
840 Zenobia	2♑59'41	
693 Zerbinetta	21♓35'10	
531 Zerlina	17♎19'16	
438 Zeuxo	18♉44'58	
1802 Zhang Heng	22♌12'03	
2631 Zhejiang	24♈32'29	
3789 Zhongguo	26♊40'49	
1734 Zhongolovich	1♎43'15	
2903 Zhuhai	22♏23'22	
2132 Zhukov	22♊10'47	
3064 Zimmer	6♍44'52	
3100 Zimmerman	26♈39'48	
1775 Zimmerwald	15♎49'07	
689 Zita	17♍43'30	
1468 Zomba	8♒29'37	
1793 Zoya	15♏29'19	
865 Zubaida	26♍41'53	
1888 Zu Chong–Zhi	4♐19'08	
1922 Zulu	15♏53'02	
2323 Zverev	6♈09'35	
1700 Zvezdara	26♓30'18	
785 Zwetana	11♊54'02	
1803 Zwicky	6♓53'59	
2098 Zyskin	7♓17'53	

APPENDIX FOUR
Heliocentric Nodes
(in Zodiacal Order)

Heliocentric Nodes in Zodiacal Order
Epoch November 5, 1990   Equinox 1950.0   Planet nodes have number ####

2262 Mitidika	0♈09'39	1134 Kepler	5♈49'49	2370 Van Altena	9♈56'41
3447 Burckhalter	0♈10'08	359 Georgia	5♈52'16	290 Bruna	10♈02'27
671 Carnegia	0♈16'33	4007 Euryalos	6♈04'33	55 Pandora	10♈09'26
645 Agrippina	0♈18'54	551 Ortrud	6♈07'34	477 Italia	10♈09'42
209 Dido	0♈19'46	1864 Daedalus	6♈07'57	3034 Climenhaga	10♈11'55
2154 Underhill	0♈24'38	2323 Zverev	6♈09'35	2782 Leonidas	10♈19'55
1170 Siva	0♈32'34	497 Iva	6♈10'09	91 Aegina	10♈22'40
2006 Polonskaya	0♈33'00	1686 De Sitter	6♈15'21	1046 Edwin	10♈27'07
1996 Adams	0♈35'33	312 Pierretta	6♈16'30	2551 Decabrina	10♈40'47
1126 Otero	0♈38'47	3053 Dresden	6♈22'12	2501 Lohja	10♈47'51
1174 Marmara	0♈39'54	2520 Novorossijsk	6♈23'22	2045 Peking	10♈48'05
2070 Humason	0♈49'22	1453 Fennia	6♈32'13	4075 Sviridov	10♈52'25
77 Frigga	0♈53'26	3943 Silbermann	6♈33'13	2178 Kazakhstania	10♈58'46
81 Terpsichore	0♈55'19	1179 Mally	6♈33'46	3238 Timresovia	11♈02'21
1192 Prisma	0♈55'33	195 Eurykleia	6♈41'32	3056 INAG	11♈06'22
2114 Wallenquist	0♈55'41	73 Klytia	6♈43'42	453 Tea	11♈14'24
3148 Grechko	0♈59'17	3294 Carlvesely	6♈44'58	2134 Dennispalm	11♈19'29
1541 Estonia	1♈06'13	3013 Dobrovoleva	6♈49'31	3193 Elliot	11♈22'37
3607 Naniwa	1♈22'02	642 Clara	6♈49'40	2503 Liaoning	11♈25'41
746 Marlu	1♈28'07	2247 Hiroshima	6♈51'30	3432 Kobuchizawa	11♈35'21
139 Juewa	1♈32'05	1317 Silvretta	6♈51'44	2339 Anacreon	11♈36'50
1790 Volkov	1♈33'50	812 Adele	6♈52'12	604 Tekmessa	11♈40'10
1080 Orchis	1♈34'07	37 Fides	7♈08'54	2453 Wabash	11♈40'30
1035 Amata	1♈37'14	1204 Renzia	7♈14'32	1225 Ariane	11♈56'48
828 Lindemannia	1♈41'54	802 Epyaxa	7♈21'25	1768 Appenzella	12♈05'24
994 Otthild	2♈00'48	302 Clarissa	7♈22'03	2406 Orelskaya	12♈06'27
1227 Geranium	2♈04'25	66 Maja	7♈22'56	3248 Farinella	12♈07'13
2022 West	2♈07'34	3439 Lebofsky	7♈28'05	1521 Seinäjoki	12♈13'09
2876 Aeschylus	2♈29'32	2432 Soomana	7♈31'24	1235 Schorria	12♈24'49
705 Erminia	2♈29'58	2384 Schulhof	7♈38'24	1495 Helsinki	12♈45'05
94 Aurora	2♈30'03	3750 Ilizarov	7♈41'56	3673 Levy	12♈56'02
3910 Liszt	2♈30'23	2236 Austrasia	7♈46'10	3196 Maklaj	12♈58'15
2680 Mateo	2♈35'15	298 Baptistina	7♈46'14	1808 Bellerophon	13♈04'04
571 Dulcinea	2♈43'17	766 Moguntia	7♈50'25	1694 Kaiser	13♈05'01
2452 Lyot	2♈48'03	3854 George	7♈51'50	4037 Ikeya	13♈12'02
109 Felicitas	2♈49'16	2705 Wu	7♈54'42	255 Oppavia	13♈20'16
2023 Asaph	2♈49'21	927 Ratisbona	7♈56'17	615 Roswitha	13♈22'47
47 Aglaja	2♈52'53	2464 Nordenskiöld	7♈58'49	1332 Marconia	13♈42'41
3055 Annapavlova	2♈53'29	3009 Coventry	8♈06'51	3672 Stevedberg	13♈45'35
734 Benda	2♈54'27	3006 Livadia	8♈06'53	1325 Inanda	13♈55'46
1160 Illyria	3♈17'09	33 Polyhymnia	8♈13'30	2383 Bradley	13♈59'19
373 Melusina	3♈29'38	2428 Kamenyar	8♈13'39	2701 Cherson	14♈01'53
843 Nicolaia	3♈39'48	160 Una	8♈25'11	450 Brigitta	14♈08'28
3368 Duncombe	3♈50'21	1016 Anitra	8♈25'37	1908 Pobeda	14♈11'38
93 Minerva	3♈56'00	2362 Mark Twain	8♈36'07	1508 Kemi	14♈12'00
1622 Chacornac	3♈59'09	422 Berolina	8♈40'09	2788 Andenne	14♈12'40
2640 Hällström	4♈01'41	1729 Beryl	8♈41'08	186 Celuta	14♈16'16
2004 Lexell	4♈07'34	3092 Herodotus	8♈41'09	2502 Nummela	14♈22'34
208 Lacrimosa	4♈12'11	2786 Grinevia	8♈51'22	784 Pickeringia	14♈31'46
2730 Barks	4♈32'08	2010 Chebyshev	8♈53'20	1183 Jutta	14♈46'20
3508 Pasternak	4♈34'11	915 Cosette	8♈53'35	932 Hooveria	14♈46'31
2386 Nikonov	4♈46'39	1735 ITA	8♈56'07	1824 Haworth	14♈46'35
4158 Santini	4♈48'03	2037 Tripaxeptalis	9♈05'41	2057 Rosemary	14♈51'45
1188 Gothlandia	4♈59'26	3293 Rontaylor	9♈15'38	2179 Platzeck	14♈54'45
3426 Seki	5♈07'41	2905 Plaskett	9♈34'50	2008 Konstitutsiya	15♈07'12
2835 Ryoma	5♈09'59	1351 Uzbekistania	9♈35'45	697 Galilea	15♈16'22
2675 Tolkien	5♈29'18	2757 Crisser	9♈41'21	1519 Kajaani	15♈22'41
1572 Posnania	5♈34'09	2504 Gaviola	9♈43'58	1962 Dunant	15♈22'47
3624 Mironov	5♈35'44	280 Philia	9♈51'08	1527 Malmquista	15♈43'50
842 Kerstin	5♈36'03	1552 Bessel	9♈51'19	2471 Ultrajectum	15♈55'21
1707 Chantal	5♈42'52	1512 Oulu	9♈52'16	1786 Raahe	16♈09'02
2234 Schmadel	5♈48'30	2941 Alden	9♈56'27	2792 Ponomarev	16♈16'12

Heliocentric Nodes in Zodiacal Order
Epoch November 5, 1990   Equinox 1950.0   Planet nodes have number ####

1631 Kopff 16♈29'03	546 Herodias 21♈30'30	1744 Harriet 27♈03'12
1501 Baade 16♈31'42	3323 Turgenev 21♈39'58	1013 Tombecka 27♈12'39
2526 Alisary 16♈34'39	331 Etheridgea 21♈45'34	83 Beatrix 27♈13'56
2007 McCuskey 16♈40'31	2446 Lunacharsky 21♈50'36	2641 Lipschutz 27♈18'15
2156 Kate 16♈43'51	1124 Stroobantia 21♈57'04	1518 Rovaniemi 27♈21'32
1946 Walraven 16♈51'11	2574 Ladoga 21♈58'53	2151 Hadwiger 27♈39'46
855 Newcombia 16♈52'08	757 Portlandia 22♈01'37	3274 Maillen 27♈40'30
2016 Heinemann 16♈52'25	1960 Guisan 22♈02'02	2212 Hephaistos 27♈46'08
2181 Fogelin 16♈53'05	2243 Lönnrot 22♈04'27	3024 Hainan 27♈47'54
2143 Jimarnold 16♈58'57	1205 Ebella 22♈41'32	229 Adelinda 27♈54'17
795 Fini 17♈00'35	4103 Chahine 22♈45'24	2871 Schober 27♈54'41
1226 Golia 17♈02'56	435 Ella 22♈46'15	254 Augusta 28♈01'59
2042 Sitarski 17♈02'58	2113 Ehrdni 22♈52'56	4184 Berdyayev 28♈05'30
1446 Sillanpää 17♈06'57	1948 Kampala 22♈59'16	3155 Lee 28♈05'58
4155 Watanabe 17♈07'11	126 Velleda 22♈59'42	2663 Miltiades 28♈07'01
428 Monachia 17♈10'56	1099 Figneria 23♈00'16	1354 Botha 28♈16'24
1053 Vigdis 17♈21'34	1983 Bok 23♈15'19	2807 Karl Marx 28♈16'36
3167 Babcock 17♈22'14	3564 Talthybius 23♈15'27	3832 Shapiro 28♈25'54
2900 Luboš Perek 17♈30'41	2080 Jihlava 23♈25'46	341 California 28♈42'23
3489 Lottie 17♈47'12	2293 Guernica 23♈26'03	207 Hedda 28♈48'24
1368 Numidia 17♈51'31	1861 Komenský 23♈31'19	1390 Abastumani 28♈51'55
1479 Inkeri 17♈54'50	3955 Bruckner 23♈33'02	3843 OISCA 28♈53'25
2819 Ensor 17♈59'10	761 Brendelia 23♈35'13	1027 Aesculapia 28♈57'44
952 Caia 18♈09'20	4061 Martelli 23♈49'45	3714 Kenrussell 29♈08'02
161 Athor 18♈12'13	3036 Krat 23♈55'02	459 Signe 29♈08'33
2632 Guizhou 18♈19'49	250 Bettina 23♈59'08	3309 Brorfelde 29♈15'19
4096 Kushiro 18♈32'48	1366 Piccolo 24♈00'24	1797 Schaumasse 29♈16'28
361 Bononia 18♈36'17	595 Polyxena 24♈05'45	1961 Dufour 29♈17'42
1669 Dagmar 18♈37'00	4087 Pärt 24♈17'17	578 Happelia 29♈17'52
2034 Bernoulli 18♈38'44	1267 Geertruida 24♈24'22	1675 Simonida 29♈44'37
1846 Bengt 18♈39'06	1851 Lacroute 24♈25'20	1029 La Plata 29♈44'41
3372 Bratijchuk 18♈54'08	3359 Purcari 24♈27'01	2032 Ethel 29♈47'37
3720 Hokkaido 18♈54'35	2631 Zhejiang 24♈32'29	1132 Hollandia 29♈48'52
2165 Young 18♈59'09	3414 Champollion 24♈35'09	2424 Tautenburg 29♈51'19
2899 Runrun Shaw 19♈18'38	2353 Alva 24♈36'00	2315 Czechoslavakia
3688 Navajo 19♈22'17	1462 Zamenhof 24♈39'25	29♈57'23
3416 Dorrit 19♈27'23	215 Oenone 24♈40'37	2913 Horta 29♈57'26
1500 Jyväskylä 19♈28'27	3864 Søren 24♈46'26	4242 Brecher 0♉04'25
2335 James 19♈29'02	1989 Tatry 24♈51'55	2787 Tovarishch 0♉06'00
3604 Berkhuijsen 19♈33'37	2951 Perepadin 24♈52'27	1087 Arabis 0♉06'06
4097 Tsurugisan 19♈36'22	2931 Mayakovsky 24♈58'24	3775 Ellenbeth 0♉15'42
1814 Bach 19♈52'47	2305 King 25♈00'56	1081 Reseda 0♉27'40
1207 Ostenia 19♈56'53	1654 Bojeva 25♈04'51	964 Subamara 0♉29'01
610 Valeska 20♈03'07	82 Alkmene 25♈18'00	31 Euphrosyne 0♉37'21
3576 Galina 20♈08'50	3680 Sasha 25♈38'29	2761 Eddington 0♉53'10
2239 Paracelsus 20♈09'09	3849 Incidentia 25♈42'48	127 Johanna 0♉55'22
3592 Nedbal 20♈10'12	3912 Troja 25♈44'11	281 Lucretia 0♉56'55
1008 La Paz 20♈12'58	3540 Protesilaos 25♈44'42	332 Siri 1♉20'59
1696 Nurmela 20♈36'09	2072 Kosmodemyanskaya	2300 Stebbins 1♉29'44
2803 Vilho 20♈37'09	25♈51'19	326 Tamara 1♉43'13
175 Andromache 20♈50'59	1190 Pelagia 26♈01'55	3305 Ceadams 1♉44'48
3974 Verveer 20♈55'05	3220 Murayama 26♈15'56	454 Mathesis 1♉58'07
1452 Hunnia 20♈55'40	3555 Miyasaka 26♈17'31	4017 Disneya 1♉59'12
944 Hidalgo 20♈59'48	961 Gunnie 26♈24'03	2955 Newburn 2♉02'43
2492 Kutuzov 21♈01'02	3100 Zimmerman 26♈39'48	2967 Vladisvyat 2♉05'41
3068 Khanina 21♈06'03	1927 Suvanto 26♈40'23	3939 Huruhata 2♉06'24
1637 Swings 21♈12'22	3170 Dzhanibekov 26♈42'20	349 Dembowska 2♉09'10
468 Lina 21♈18'15	340 Eduarda 26♈48'48	210 Isabella 2♉22'14
1358 Gaika 21♈19'45	362 Havnia 26♈51'12	2063 Bacchus 2♉40'40
187 Lamberta 21♈21'12	2434 Bateson 26♈55'18	3078 Horrocks 2♉44'41
1770 Schlesinger 21♈23'47	1698 Christophe 26♈58'30	796 Sarita 2♉49'04
3804 Drunina 21♈29'09	852 Wladilena 27♈02'29	3583 Burdett 3♉02'20

Heliocentric Nodes in Zodiacal Order
Epoch November 5, 1990   Equinox 1950.0   Planet nodes have number ####

Name	Position	Name	Position	Name	Position
2238 Steshenko	3♉16'18	721 Tabora	8♉44'19	1664 Felix	13♉48'26
3748 Tatum	3♉17'09	768 Struveana	8♉55'05	1798 Watts	13♉50'15
2826 Ahti	3♉21'37	1757 Porvoo	9♉04'26	1838 Ursa	13♉51'22
2248 Kanda	3♉29'46	1073 Gellivara	9♉06'24	2910 Yoshkar–Ola	13♉52'06
2314 Field	3♉36'12	2880 Nihondaira	9♉16'21	68 Leto	13♉52'16
3213 Smolensk	3♉39'16	3776 Vartiovuori	9♉18'32	2839 Annette	14♉07'15
2801 Huygens	3♉56'14	2040 Chalonge	9♉29'18	1781 Van Biesbroeck	
2985 Shakespeare	4♉02'12	1253 Frisia	9♉32'59		14♉14'06
2308 Schilt	4♉04'09	1162 Larissa	9♉33'56	508 Princetonia	14♉15'11
520 Franziska	4♉08'59	680 Genoveva	9♉44'21	770 Bali	14♉15'33
912 Maritima	4♉12'44	2333 Porthan	9♉49'06	599 Luisa	14♉18'00
3437 Kapitsa	4♉13'50	152 Atala	9♉51'13	806 Gyldenia	14♉31'47
257 Silesia	4♉28'01	906 Repsolda	9♉57'27	519 Sylvania	14♉32'04
636 Erika	4♉35'46	321 Florentina	10♉00'55	4106 Nada	14♉32'48
475 Ocllo	4♉37'05	1939 Loretta	10♉06'42	3131 Mason–Dixon	
2480 Papanov	4♉44'49	3153 Lincoln	10♉09'26		14♉34'20
1813 Imhotep	4♉48'32	1840 Hus	10♉11'56	1448 Lindbladia	14♉37'58
1447 Utra	5♉18'34	2543 Machado	10♉30'42	1472 Muonio	14♉46'30
1862 Apollo	5♉18'42	698 Ernestina	10♉32'17	3448 Narbut	14♉51'34
1439 Vogtia	5♉26'45	155 Scylla	10♉36'23	3275 Oberndorfer	14♉56'33
720 Bohlinia	5♉31'03	1223 Neckar	10♉37'25	1841 Masaryk	15♉05'40
859 Bouzaréah	5♉37'48	641 Agnes	10♉39'07	1895 Larink	15♉12'15
24 Themis	5♉38'39	2255 Qinghai	10♉44'26	3247 Di Martino	15♉13'17
793 Arizona	5♉41'23	1343 Nicole	10♉49'07	722 Frieda	15♉17'37
3045 Alois	5♉51'59	965 Angelica	10♉57'13	2750 Loviisa	15♉19'35
162 Laurentia	5♉59'07	1459 Magnya	11♉03'12	2430 Bruce Helin	15♉26'55
401 Ottilia	5♉59'35	2884 Reddish	11♉03'24	26 Proserpina	15♉29'27
2047 Smetana	6♉03'37	99 Dike	11♉13'18	2321 Luznice	15♉33'58
953 Painleva	6♉06'18	104 Klymene	11♉43'33	1323 Tugela	15♉37'35
463 Lola	6♉07'05	446 Aeternitas	11♉46'14	3841 Dicicco	15♉40'38
597 Bandusia	6♉12'26	988 Appella	11♉50'35	981 Martina	15♉43'53
2193 Jackson	6♉24'03	2296 Kugultinov	11♉52'24	2558 Viv	15♉44'26
3292 Sather	6♉28'45	3840 Mimistrobell	11♉52'31	715 Transvaalia	15♉49'09
2777 Shukshin	6♉31'43	1982 Cline	12♉05'04	3289 Mitani	15♉59'21
1072 Malva	6♉32'06	1219 Britta	12♉08'15	3819 Robinson	15♉59'36
154 Bertha	6♉34'48	3157 Novikov	12♉12'42	3273 Drukar	15♉59'41
3133 Sendai	6♉43'31	3526 Jeffbell	12♉14'12	3325 TARDIS	16♉00'00
905 Universitas	6♉45'20	2364 Seillier	12♉26'53	3777 McCauley	16♉05'49
2734 Hašek	6♉54'24	300 Geraldina	12♉36'49	2966 Korsunia	16♉08'33
4246 Telemann	6♉59'50	2361 Gogol	12♉38'07	731 Sorga	16♉10'20
2337 Boubin	7♉03'02	1421 Esperanto	12♉38'53	4121 Carlin	16♉19'02
448 Natalie	7♉03'11	2226 Cunitza	12♉40'54	1972 Yi Xing	16♉19'50
272 Antonia	7♉06'05	2982 Muriel	12♉41'10	492 Gismonda	16♉23'09
3930 Vasil'ev	7♉19'19	1186 Turnera	12♉42'18	867 Kovacia	16♉27'06
2603 Taylor	7♉36'07	735 Marghanna	12♉43'50	1440 Rostia	16♉31'38
1074 Beljawskya	7♉44'50	13 Egeria	12♉44'23	2583 Fatyanov	16♉41'46
651 Antikleia	7♉51'25	1424 Sundmania	12♉47'23	1995 Hajek	16♉43'34
3015 Candy	7♉56'14	907 Rhoda	12♉49'44	2194 Arpola	16♉45'22
2360 Volgo–Don	8♉02'30	3548 Eurybates	12♉52'15	3486 Fulchignoni	16♉45'55
3396 Muazzez	8♉02'31	845 Naëma	12♉54'25	2124 Nissen	16♉50'27
718 Erida	8♉06'51	292 Ludovica	13♉06'05	2069 Hubble	17♉01'25
494 Virtus	8♉08'01	3430 Bradfield	13♉06'24	118 Peitho	17♉10'20
769 Tatjana	8♉09'12	1378 Leonce	13♉07'02	2963 Chen Jiageng	
262 Valda	8♉13'02	3343 Nedzel	13♉08'55		17♉20'42
343 Ostara	8♉18'42	1599 Giomus	13♉10'09	1429 Pemba	17♉26'40
3747 Belinskij	8♉19'03	3254 Bus	13♉35'51	2153 Akiyama	17♉28'16
2770 Tsvet	8♉20'29	1869 Philoctetes	13♉38'35	70 Panopaea	17♉32'38
975 Perseverantia	8♉26'06	1738 Oosterhoff	13♉42'50	2500 Alascattalo	17♉34'10
2155 Wodan	8♉26'55	2849 Shklovskij	13♉42'58	384 Burdigala	17♉34'40
1715 Salli	8♉29'14	3933 Portugal	13♉44'35	2369 Chekhov	17♉38'41
151 Abundantia	8♉31'26	617 Patroclus	13♉44'55	#### Mercury	17♉41'10
1155 Aënna	8♉38'18	3537 Jürgen	13♉48'16	223 Rosa	17♉50'40

Heliocentric Nodes in Zodiacal Order
Epoch November 5, 1990   Equinox 1950.0   Planet nodes have number ####

3080 Moisseiev 17♉53'07	2044 Wirt 23♉23'13	2693 Yan'an 29♉23'58
2897 Ole Römer 17♉54'07	2355 Nei Monggol 23♉32'04	1544 Vinterhansenia
1208 Troilus 17♉56'28	2678 Aavasaksa 23♉37'40	29♉31'30
344 Desiderata 17♉58'48	2573 Hannu Olavi 23♉48'42	1044 Teutonia 29♉35'53
1616 Filipoff 17♉59'52	2962 Otto 23♉55'16	1344 Caubeta 29♉39'20
947 Monterosa 18♉03'30	1978 Patrice 23♉56'39	3253 Gradie 29♉45'13
2883 Barabashov 18♉06'22	1088 Mitaka 24♉03'18	4250 Perun 29♉50'05
3203 Huth 18♉07'35	4024 Ronan 24♉04'46	1041 Asta 29♉59'47
1236 Thaïs 18♉10'54	2263 Shaanxi 24♉04'57	1600 Vyssotsky 0♊04'39
3987 Wujek 18♉14'22	1388 Aphrodite 24♉05'22	1522 Kokkola 0♊08'55
2830 Greenwich 18♉30'55	1676 Kariba 24♉10'40	1941 Wild 0♊13'26
3857 Cellino 18♉33'58	1630 Milet 24♉17'53	2240 Tsai 0♊25'06
438 Zeuxo 18♉44'58	138 Tolosa 24♉39'06	2185 Guangdong 0♊25'33
2805 Kalle 18♉53'31	2027 Shen Guo 25♉00'10	2818 Juvenalis 0♊30'09
1515 Perrotin 18♉58'43	2867 Šteins 25♉04'06	886 Washingtonia 0♊31'32
926 Imhilde 18♉59'19	1093 Freda 25♉07'33	1713 Bancilhon 0♊45'11
2703 Rodari 19♉00'51	3523 Arina 25♉14'49	425 Cornelia 0♊55'19
#### Mars 19♉03'05	1741 Giclas 25♉14'49	753 Tiflis 0♊55'34
4021 Dancey 19♉10'04	4040 Purcell 25♉27'50	1701 Okavango 0♊58'04
1193 Africa 19♉14'17	2578 Saint–Exupéry	3545 Gaffey 1♊00'50
264 Libussa 19♉20'32	25♉28'43	1619 Ueta 1♊06'28
4091 Lowe 19♉27'37	1889 Pakhmutova 25♉29'46	2332 Kalm 1♊06'39
2584 Turkmenia 19♉39'52	2515 Gansu 25♉38'32	245 Vera 1♊07'20
528 Rezia 19♉44'27	2582 Harimaya–Bashi	2341 Aoluta 1♊08'43
910 Anneliese 19♉44'52	26♉03'55	293 Brasilia 1♊10'17
2538 Vanderlinden 19♉55'31	3532 Tracie 26♉04'20	4058 Cecilgreen 1♊27'29
2657 Bashkiria 20♉01'14	2489 Suvorov 26♉05'48	2725 David Bender 1♊33'13
1202 Marina 20♉06'18	3393 Sofala 26♉24'50	2312 Duboshin 1♊33'58
2203 Van Rhijn 20♉08'52	3192 A'Hearn 26♉28'08	2837 Griboedov 1♊35'24
1849 Kresák 20♉14'54	110 Lydia 26♉39'06	157 Dejanira 1♊36'11
2790 Needham 20♉22'37	2197 Shanghai 26♉43'04	278 Paulina 1♊38'53
1957 Angara 20♉28'25	815 Coppelia 26♉48'47	1580 Betulia 1♊41'56
3191 Svanetia 20♉33'14	1119 Euboea 26♉58'39	2376 Martynov 1♊47'38
2706 Borovský 20♉34'40	1967 Menzel 27♉22'09	936 Kunigunde 1♊47'56
2401 Aehlita 20♉39'42	3461 Mandelshtam 27♉28'46	106 Dione 1♊59'31
1839 Ragazza 20♉42'49	1237 Geneviève 27♉33'33	2488 Bryan 1♊59'51
178 Belisana 20♉48'04	1327 Namaqua 27♉40'36	963 Iduberga 2♊02'06
2224 Tucson 21♉00'01	1038 Tuckia 27♉43'40	2633 Bishop 2♊02'38
2566 Kirghizia 21♉09'32	416 Vaticana 27♉49'28	4258 Ryazanov 2♊03'13
2182 Semirot 21♉09'32	1133 Lugduna 27♉51'13	1534 Näsi 2♊07'18
1567 Alikoski 21♉12'54	3568 ASCII 27♉52'38	2149 Schwambraniya
1238 Predappia 21♉30'00	567 Eleutheria 28♉01'26	2♊11'20
813 Baumeia 21♉30'40	2129 Cosicosi 28♉03'28	1305 Pongola 2♊40'30
4104 Alu 21♉34'56	4293 Masumi 28♉03'30	2695 Christabel 2♊43'28
2986 Mrinalini 21♉36'07	674 Rachele 28♉09'28	3792 Preston 2♊51'53
1899 Crommelin 21♉43'02	1753 Mieke 28♉09'44	1122 Neith 2♊58'36
3994 Ayashi 21♉49'44	3349 Manas 28♉13'23	1897 Hind 3♊01'47
2438 Oleshko 21♉50'42	1423 Jose 28♉18'30	692 Hippodamia 3♊02'29
1545 Thernöe 22♉01'55	3452 Hawke 28♉23'40	3773 Smithsonian 3♊04'43
2177 Oliver 22♉02'20	3521 Comrie 28♉28'11	1866 Sisyphus 3♊05'03
1042 Amazone 22♉08'14	1024 Hale 28♉35'59	3783 Morris 3♊12'28
941 Murray 22♉11'09	2840 Kallavesi 28♉40'37	1480 Aunus 3♊14'14
1375 Alfreda 22♉15'57	3779 Kieffer 28♉46'01	1218 Aster 3♊25'30
1071 Brita 22♉16'12	2505 Hebei 28♉52'36	2206 Gabrova 3♊27'37
2425 Shenzhen 22♉16'53	1670 Minnaert 28♉55'24	116 Sirona 3♊31'07
1540 Kevola 22♉18'16	1128 Astrid 29♉03'20	1920 Sarmiento 3♊31'20
1048 Feodosia 22♉25'16	1902 Shaposhnikov	772 Tanete 3♊32'01
2768 Gorky 22♉50'02	29♉03'39	1517 Beograd 3♊38'33
3176 Paolicchi 22♉58'23	536 Merapi 29♉07'04	991 McDonalda 3♊44'35
2387 Xían 22♉59'53	2286 Fesenkov 29♉07'19	1364 Safara 3♊46'41
2278 Götz 23♉05'59	959 Arne 29♉09'02	2699 Kalinin 3♊48'14
1563 Noël 23♉13'20	2117 Danmark 29♉19'47	2593 Buryatia 3♊50'22

Heliocentric Nodes in Zodiacal Order
Epoch November 5, 1990   Equinox 1950.0   Planet nodes have number ####

1028 Lydina 3♊52'55	3206 Wuhan 10♊39'58	3374 Namur 15♊02'14
2729 Urumqi 3♊55'41	2215 Sichuan 10♊48'49	4289 Biwako 15♊29'15
1359 Prieska 3♊57'43	1765 Wrubel 10♊49'16	977 Philippa 15♊32'59
742 Edisona 4♊09'57	3575 Anyuta 10♊50'17	3230 Vampilov 15♊43'09
1893 Jakoba 4♊14'14	1482 Sebastiana 10♊51'10	593 Titania 15♊45'21
3194 Dorsey 4♊15'11	3185 Clintford 10♊52'23	2288 Karolinum 15♊49'15
2652 Yabuuti 4♊15'21	942 Romilda 11♊00'14	2270 Yazhi 15♊53'38
3164 Prast 4♊22'39	1089 Tama 11♊03'29	3249 Musashino 15♊54'18
363 Padua 4♊29'56	3651 Friedman 11♊11'04	1032 Pafuri 15♊55'29
2003 Harding 4♊31'38	1968 Mehltretter 11♊12'42	1912 Anubis 16♊00'53
1550 Tito 4♊42'54	3718 Dunbar 11♊16'32	128 Nemesis 16♊03'18
529 Preziosa 5♊00'17	3450 Dommanget 11♊17'19	2569 Madeline 16♊05'51
1929 Kollaa 5♊04'06	2673 Lossignol 11♊20'10	144 Vibilia 16♊06'49
131 Vala 5♊13'59	1185 Nikko 11♊29'43	#### Venus 16♊07'01
1412 Lagrula 5♊41'15	2169 Taiwan 11♊29'53	455 Bruchsalia 16♊08'28
4153 Roburnham 5♊41'16	3166 Klondike 11♊32'54	2201 Oljato 16♊23'20
22 Kalliope 5♊47'44	1320 Impala 11♊37'04	4276 Clifford 16♊23'21
235 Carolina 5♊49'20	447 Valentine 11♊37'41	2035 Stearns 16♊29'39
2273 Yarilo 6♊01'30	1303 Luthera 11♊44'51	1761 Edmondson 16♊36'19
2081 Sázava 6♊04'05	1483 Hakoila 11♊48'53	164 Eva 16♊37'01
2269 Efremiana 6♊26'28	1140 Crimea 11♊49'10	3234 Hergiani 16♊39'07
481 Emita 6♊30'59	785 Zwetana 11♊54'02	145 Adeona 17♊03'56
4151 Alanhale 6♊32'20	3174 Alcock 11♊54'59	3612 Peale 17♊07'19
2571 Geisei 6♊33'33	553 Kundry 11♊57'57	1397 Umtata 17♊11'15
4157 Izu 6♊38'57	2611 Boyce 11♊59'55	2421 Nininger 17♊28'37
23 Thalia 6♊41'13	2050 Francis 12♊02'35	1801 Titicaca 17♊29'58
2681 Ostrovskij 6♊45'29	2092 Sumiana 12♊02'54	3344 Modena 17♊33'42
3215 Lapko 6♊48'03	2517 Orma 12♊03'32	1047 Geisha 17♊52'30
858 El Djezaïr 6♊50'39	4256 Kagamigawa 12♊04'27	1137 Raïssa 18♊02'33
1261 Legia 6♊56'41	196 Philomela 12♊06'02	3608 Kataev 18♊10'31
621 Werdandi 6♊57'46	966 Muschi 12♊07'09	2133 Franceswright
394 Arduina 6♊59'27	1115 Sabauda 12♊08'00	18♊11'21
2812 Scaltriti 7♊44'07	1831 Nicholson 12♊11'23	1952 Hesburgh 18♊11'44
4085 Weir 8♊15'21	2219 Mannucci 12♊18'12	1427 Ruvuma 18♊11'50
3007 Reaves 8♊27'16	1792 Reni 12♊31'37	751 Faïna 18♊21'09
9 Metis 8♊28'32	1161 Thessalia 12♊36'40	1745 Ferguson 18♊25'36
1850 Kohoutek 8♊31'03	1484 Postrema 12♊39'28	1805 Dirikis 18♊37'34
725 Amanda 8♊32'29	1012 Sarema 12♊44'57	1937 Locarno 18♊39'11
503 Evelyn 8♊39'43	1239 Queteleta 12♊46'42	2874 Jim Young 18♊45'08
3112 Velimir 8♊46'45	3262 Miune 12♊54'09	2639 Planman 18♊51'46
2024 McLaughlin 8♊52'27	2038 Bistro 13♊05'00	3173 McNaught 18♊54'13
3411 Debetencourt 8♊54'14	87 Sylvia 13♊05'47	1248 Jugurtha 19♊01'58
4042 Okhotsk 8♊59'52	279 Thule 13♊10'02	2208 Pushkin 19♊05'42
2077 Kiangsu 9♊01'45	267 Tirza 13♊31'40	2470 Agematsu 19♊11'55
940 Kordula 9♊01'50	2617 Jiangxi 13♊38'23	2904 Millman 19♊18'07
1594 Danjon 9♊03'24	1578 Kirkwood 13♊40'01	2301 Whitford 19♊26'58
2512 Tavastia 9♊05'24	#### Uranus 13♊46'59	3867 Shiretoko 19♊28'46
423 Diotima 9♊09'55	1460 Haltia 13♊57'31	2707 Ueferji 19♊29'43
946 Poësia 9♊17'38	2828 Iku–Turso 14♊00'04	1123 Shapleya 19♊29'59
3327 Campins 9♊17'39	1953 Rupertwildt 14♊05'05	776 Berbericia 19♊32'29
2797 Teucer 9♊23'08	121 Hermione 14♊05'24	767 Bondia 19♊44'14
750 Oskar 9♊28'43	2046 Leningrad 14♊15'10	3143 Genecampbell
1950 Wempe 9♊31'19	1601 Patry 14♊15'55	19♊48'10
1356 Nyanza 9♊34'54	1773 Rumpelstilz 14♊17'43	2779 Mary 19♊50'51
1693 Hertzsprung 9♊43'55	1883 Rimito 14♊24'20	222 Lucia 19♊58'00
1890 Konoshenkova	1450 Raimonda 14♊28'27	3116 Goodricke 19♊58'41
9♊56'24	2999 Dante 14♊31'52	1 Ceres 20♊01'04
564 Dudu 10♊24'48	4079 Britten 14♊35'15	782 Montefiore 20♊01'32
596 Scheila 10♊26'43	1259 Ogyalla 14♊40'37	566 Stereoskopia 20♊04'58
562 Salome 10♊31'54	1602 Indiana 14♊43'07	1091 Spiraea 20♊20'50
90 Antiope 10♊33'03	3290 Azabu 14♊53'33	1083 Salvia 20♊24'42
818 Kapteynia 10♊33'33	3057 Mälaren 14♊54'44	21 Lutetia 20♊25'13

Heliocentric Nodes in Zodiacal Order

Epoch November 5, 1990   Equinox 1950.0   Planet nodes have number ####

1667 Pels 20♊26'01	1771 Makover 25♊56'52	3565 Ojima 2♋04'20
3758 Karttunen 20♊27'47	1934 Jeffers 26♊10'24	404 Arsinoë 2♋05'03
2877 Likhachev 20♊37'13	14 Irene 26♊12'20	452 Hamiltonia 2♋13'00
311 Claudia 20♊43'53	974 Lioba 26♊13'09	274 Philagoria 2♋24'44
1294 Antwerpia 20♊56'12	3597 Kakkuri 26♊26'19	3562 Ignatius 2♋27'01
1096 Reunerta 20♊57'37	2525 O'Steen 26♊35'57	986 Amelia 2♋34'00
3449 Abell 21♊03'36	1464 Armisticia 26♊36'04	383 Janina 2♋46'57
2984 Chaucer 21♊19'45	3789 Zhongguo 26♊40'49	2287 Kalmykia 2♋52'23
197 Arete 21♊24'45	86 Semele 26♊42'25	2822 Sacajawea 3♋00'21
1511 Daléra 21♊25'17	1304 Arosa 26♊56'02	3117 Niepce 3♋01'11
2831 Stevin 21♊35'12	2336 Xinjiang 27♊01'23	1687 Glarona 3♋13'33
3671 Dionysius 21♊47'28	259 Aletheia 27♊03'35	1926 Demiddelaer 3♋14'18
1886 Lowell 21♊58'28	2568 Maksutov 27♊07'26	1078 Mentha 3♋25'59
967 Helionape 21♊59'04	629 Bernardina 27♊10'11	2816 Pien 3♋33'15
2476 Andersen 22♊00'57	2587 Gardner 27♊20'13	1582 Martir 3♋33'35
3041 Webb 22♊07'39	1348 Michel 27♊22'58	3272 Tillandz 3♋38'16
2132 Zhukov 22♊10'47	4084 Hollis 27♊25'00	2102 Tantalus 3♋43'05
728 Leonisis 22♊14'14	1566 Icarus 27♊29'41	40 Harmonia 3♋47'07
579 Sidonia 22♊27'36	2398 Jilin 27♊43'18	486 Cremona 3♋47'28
857 Glasenappia 22♊30'08	1965 Van de Kamp 27♊50'37	534 Nassovia 3♋51'56
1154 Astronomia 22♊37'01	2225 Serkowski 27♊51'55	369 Aëria 3♋57'12
1300 Marcelle 22♊38'33	2183 Neufang 27♊54'40	1681 Steinmetz 4♋06'47
1663 Van den Bos 22♊51'06	2655 Guangxi 27♊54'58	4044 Erikhøg 4♋13'53
3172 Hirst 22♊56'02	691 Lehigh 27♊55'37	3784 Chopin 4♋14'38
367 Amicitia 23♊02'07	1180 Rita 27♊57'57	27 Euterpe 4♋21'31
1680 Per Brahe 23♊06'33	3434 Hurless 28♊03'30	1504 Lappeenranta 4♋23'39
3198 Wallonia 23♊08'36	1772 Gagarin 28♊03'46	1901 Moravia 4♋25'04
971 Alsatia 23♊16'58	3032 Evans 28♊07'01	913 Otila 4♋30'37
3460 Ashkova 23♊17'28	3507 Vilas 28♊09'32	3684 Berry 4♋35'51
1357 Khama 23♊22'17	814 Tauris 28♊13'34	3049 Kuzbass 4♋35'52
2519 Annagerman 23♊23'22	3165 Mikawa 28♊16'54	2220 Hicks 4♋36'23
3985 Raybatson 23♊37'37	1817 Katanga 28♊18'51	2222 Lermontov 4♋37'46
146 Lucina 23♊41'51	3417 Tamblyn 28♊21'38	730 Athanasia 4♋41'38
471 Papagena 23♊51'00	432 Pythia 28♊23'50	3699 Milbourn 4♋42'19
237 Coelestina 23♊56'27	199 Byblis 28♊51'44	380 Fiducia 4♋49'36
2906 Caltech 24♊03'44	451 Patientia 29♊00'07	1784 Benguella 4♋51'25
42 Isis 24♊06'15	1445 Konkolya 29♊09'22	3800 Karayusuf 4♋54'54
2172 Plavsk 24♊09'27	2268 Szmytowna 29♊20'41	1063 Aquilegia 4♋55'47
3418 Izvekov 24♊15'30	1209 Pumma 29♊22'13	3111 Misuzu 5♋01'33
535 Montague 24♊18'23	786 Bredichina 29♊29'03	2058 Róka 5♋05'36
2417 McVittie 24♊18'29	521 Brixia 29♊29'20	1658 Innes 5♋09'47
3277 Aaronson 24♊30'17	2176 Donar 29♊44'59	2087 Kochera 5♋12'37
488 Kreusa 24♊32'25	348 May 29♊49'13	1852 Carpenter 5♋15'33
2073 Janáček 24♊41'00	1302 Werra 29♊51'29	2688 Halley 5♋16'42
752 Sulamitis 24♊42'38	350 Ornamenta 29♊54'46	2600 Lumme 5♋18'46
2721 Vsekhsvyatskij	2082 Galahad 29♊56'28	2945 Zanstra 5♋26'38
24♊44'51	1278 Kenya 29♊59'02	2656 Evenkia 5♋32'10
2245 Hekatostos 24♊49'04	1589 Fanatica 0♋01'26	2039 Payne–Gaposchkin
1549 Mikko 24♊51'35	1591 Baize 0♋05'00	5♋32'55
563 Suleika 24♊58'46	1634 Ndola 0♋18'32	1674 Groeneveld 5♋33'05
2511 Patterson 25♊07'15	1976 Kaverin 0♋28'38	2068 Dangreen 5♋38'44
908 Buda 25♊09'13	505 Cava 0♋34'06	2621 Goto 5♋40'18
347 Pariana 25♊19'57	4260 Yanai 0♋35'07	3169 Ostro 5♋50'38
2909 Hoshi–no–ie 25♊20'00	1156 Kira 0♋43'15	1417 Walinskia 5♋57'51
3483 Svetlov 25♊26'03	866 Fatme 0♋53'22	2013 Tucapel 6♋09'54
449 Hamburga 25♊32'30	1947 Iso–Heikkilä 1♋04'44	2218 Wotho 6♋14'02
2870 Haupt 25♊34'07	1665 Gaby 1♋09'10	261 Prymno 6♋14'25
2445 Blazhko 25♊41'43	2841 Puijo 1♋09'58	700 Auravictrix 6♋25'05
1054 Forsytia 25♊45'11	1061 Paeonia 1♋15'21	410 Chloris 6♋43'55
652 Jubilatrix 25♊46'19	1556 Wingolfia 1♋31'41	1125 China 6♋47'53
2894 Kakhovka 25♊50'35	598 Octavia 1♋40'42	323 Brucia 6♋56'13
2260 Neoptolemus 25♊55'22	346 Hermentaria 1♋47'23	1336 Zeelandia 7♋05'19

Heliocentric Nodes in Zodiacal Order

Epoch November 5, 1990   Equinox 1950.0   Planet nodes have number ####

Num	Name	Node	Num	Name	Node	Num	Name	Node
498	Tokio	7♋05'26	1391	Carelia	13♋17'04	3356	Resnik	17♋52'18
1487	Boda	7♋09'30	4	Vesta	13♋21'56	548	Kressida	18♋00'59
1270	Datura	7♋26'13	4016	Sambre	13♋23'44	2062	Aten	18♋01'38
3061	Cook	7♋37'27	1702	Kalahari	13♋38'03	2893	Peiroos	18♋05'40
2372	Proskurin	7♋51'19	1056	Azalea	13♋43'04	3204	Lindgren	18♋22'10
2485	Scheffler	7♋52'03	3019	Kulin	13♋52'40	2938	Hopi	18♋40'07
3459	Bodil	8♋11'07	413	Edburga	13♋56'37	3318	Blixen	18♋48'35
1588	Descamisada	8♋30'14	2531	Cambridge	14♋00'56	3638	Davis	18♋52'51
2636	Lassell	8♋30'53	1026	Ingrid	14♋11'04	3713	Pieters	18♋57'49
1010	Marlene	8♋33'00	504	Cora	14♋19'03	2804	Yrjö	18♋59'04
3226	Plinius	8♋36'22	1581	Abanderada	14♋26'05	3201	Sijthoff	19♋02'20
424	Gratia	8♋53'42	1461	Jean–Jacques	14♋34'57	2627	Churyumov	19♋11'27
351	Yrsa	8♋56'41	462	Eriphyla	14♋56'16	749	Malzovia	19♋21'55
580	Selene	8♋59'03	3467	Bernheim	14♋57'25	644	Cosima	19♋28'25
2344	Xizang	9♋00'55	2277	Moreau	14♋58'00	3212	Agricola	19♋32'32
2395	Aho	9♋01'43	1657	Roemera	14♋59'03	####	Pluto	19♋33'00
1052	Belgica	9♋11'30	2122	Pyatiletka	15♋01'12	2852	Declercq	19♋44'15
1844	Susilva	9♋12'42	3726	Johnadams	15♋01'15	3267	Glo	20♋05'55
1569	Evita	9♋13'01	560	Delila	15♋03'16	3062	Wren	20♋09'04
1809	Prometheus	9♋14'52	1609	Brenda	15♋03'25	3754	Kathleen	20♋10'58
2462	Nehalennia	9♋20'06	364	Isara	15♋07'03	887	Alinda	20♋13'36
4098	Thraen	9♋22'45	1141	Bohmia	15♋09'08	1449	Virtanen	20♋21'11
####	Jupiter	10♋02'47	2614	Torrence	15♋10'17	3119	Dobronravin	20♋26'28
171	Ophelia	10♋07'41	630	Euphemia	15♋12'37	1107	Lictoria	20♋27'30
3214	Makarenko	10♋09'54	2138	Swissair	15♋13'33	8	Flora	20♋28'42
1131	Porzia	10♋19'27	1684	Iguassú	15♋17'55	2924	Mitake–Mura	20♋28'46
741	Botolphia	10♋21'32	891	Gunhild	15♋31'19	2404	Antarctica	20♋29'41
1529	Oterma	10♋22'35	3855	Pasasymphonia	15♋34'51	1553	Bauersfelda	20♋34'03
2988	Korhonen	10♋29'24	758	Mancunia	15♋46'26	1558	Järnefelt	20♋34'43
1196	Sheba	10♋30'54	590	Tomyris	15♋53'24	618	Elfriede	20♋41'36
2873	Binzel	10♋33'05	1988	Delores	15♋55'52	414	Liriope	20♋48'03
2195	Tengström	10♋33'13	1592	Mathieu	15♋56'57	1815	Beethoven	20♋48'55
1075	Helina	10♋34'30	2280	Kunikov	16♋04'15	1655	Comas Solá	20♋53'04
307	Nike	10♋47'05	1904	Massevitch	16♋05'56	3589	Loyola	20♋55'11
2773	Brooks	10♋48'25	412	Elisabetha	16♋06'22	3197	Weissman	21♋19'18
825	Tanina	10♋58'57	1166	Sakuntala	16♋16'58	1022	Olympiada	21♋35'02
3772	Piaf	11♋05'02	2244	Tesla	16♋17'59	3823	Yorii	21♋36'42
3717	Thorenia	11♋06'18	2127	Tanya	16♋26'35	628	Christine	21♋37'28
3967	Shekhtelia	11♋17'35	1963	Bezovec	16♋27'34	2708	Burns	21♋38'10
3310	Patsy	11♋22'01	1210	Morosovia	16♋34'33	559	Nanon	21♋40'12
92	Undina	11♋25'31	1778	Alfvén	16♋36'41	2075	Martinez	21♋44'22
3140	Stellafane	11♋27'28	3663	Tisserand	16♋38'00	1595	Tanga	21♋49'36
1326	Losaka	11♋27'47	512	Taurinensis	16♋41'46	1703	Barry	21♋50'03
4126	Mashu	11♋36'34	1847	Stobbe	16♋42'07	2956	Yeomans	21♋54'43
2171	Kiev	11♋38'09	3670	Northcott	16♋45'20	679	Pax	22♋09'35
1789	Dobrovolsky	11♋39'26	182	Elsa	16♋48'34	2338	Bokhan	22♋18'03
2775	Odishaw	11♋49'55	140	Siwa	16♋49'19	931	Whittemora	22♋19'04
2769	Mendeleev	11♋56'44	4173	Thicksten	16♋49'52	2319	Aristides	22♋21'36
3128	Obruchev	11♋58'07	1551	Argelander	16♋54'00	4063	Euforbo	22♋50'50
464	Megaira	12♋09'38	3352	McAuliffe	16♋54'05	2163	Korczak	22♋51'23
3683	Baumann	12♋13'15	3286	Anatoliya	17♋06'09	2439	Ulugbek	22♋58'02
2089	Cetacea	12♋15'38	2009	Voloshina	17♋08'22	2720	Pyotr Pervyj	23♋02'49
3154	Grant	12♋17'35	1341	Edmée	17♋11'56	####	Saturn	23♋06'43
2261	Keeler	12♋18'32	411	Xanthe	17♋14'49	1220	Crocus	23♋07'08
581	Tauntonia	12♋19'33	511	Davida	17♋19'15	3132	Landgraf	23♋08'21
353	Ruperto–Carola	12♋22'01	532	Herculina	17♋23'46	3441	Pochaina	23♋10'07
2510	Shandong	12♋30'05	3037	Alku	17♋28'16	1925	Franklin–Adams	23♋14'40
2800	Ovidius	12♋31'49	2784	Domeyko	17♋39'40	1758	Naantali	23♋21'57
1618	Dawn	12♋33'18	3216	Harrington	17♋40'43	3760	Poutanen	23♋31'24
2482	Perkin	12♋44'29	2912	Lapalma	17♋44'24	943	Begonia	23♋42'10
638	Moira	13♋06'02				1276	Ucclia	24♋14'42

Heliocentric Nodes in Zodiacal Order
Epoch November 5, 1990   Equinox 1950.0   Planet nodes have number ####

2563 Boyarchuk	24♋15'15	268 Adorea	0♌29'25	3010 Ushakov	6♌46'55
2091 Sampo	24♋20'22	2334 Cuffey	0♌33'10	4265 Kani	6♌48'27
487 Venetia	24♋34'21	3129 Bonestell	0♌36'03	2682 Soromundi	6♌49'48
861 Aïda	24♋37'59	1015 Christa	0♌40'33	472 Roma	6♌52'34
1333 Cevenola	24♋40'28	1362 Griqua	0♌47'55	415 Palatia	6♌52'50
1633 Chimay	24♋41'38	2959 Scholl	0♌55'32	484 Pittsburghia	6♌59'24
1385 Gelria	24♋43'01	2933 Amber	0♌59'14	2394 Nadeev	7♌07'03
2891 McGetchin	24♋44'01	850 Altona	0♌59'21	100 Hekate	7♌07'13
240 Vanadis	24♋44'26	2733 Hamina	1♌02'38	4179 Toutatis	7♌08'32
4251 Kavasch	24♋49'07	296 Phaëtusa	1♌08'17	4174 Pikulia	7♌10'25
3002 Delasalle	24♋57'17	1331 Solvejg	1♌09'09	1271 Isergina	7♌12'29
4119 Miles	25♋14'45	1216 Askania	1♌09'15	625 Xenia	7♌14'46
1623 Vivian	25♋17'51	515 Athalia	1♌18'05	2844 Hess	7♌18'04
1021 Flammario	25♋21'42	3106 Morabito	1♌37'27	1720 Niels	7♌19'52
1428 Mombasa	25♋29'38	213 Lilaea	1♌39'36	816 Juliana	7♌29'27
3610 Decampos	25♋31'17	1819 Laputa	1♌59'43	2217 Eltigen	7♌33'29
868 Lova	25♋34'18	3520 Klopsteg	2♌15'52	1163 Saga	7♌40'54
2164 Lyalya	25♋34'57	2742 Gibson	2♌25'51	3209 Buchwald	7♌47'41
2256 Wiśniewski	25♋38'16	1607 Mavis	2♌27'50	387 Aquitania	7♌54'04
740 Cantabia	25♋43'50	4150 Starr	2♌28'16	1455 Mitchella	7♌54'19
877 Walküre	25♋54'42	1171 Rusthawelia	2♌31'59	2458 Veniakaverin	7♌58'33
2461 Clavel	25♋57'25	2604 Marshak	2♌33'26	3210 Lupishko	8♌03'01
2898 Neuvo	26♋14'34	3123 Dunham	2♌38'44	2858 Carlosporter	8♌06'50
1880 McCrosky	26♋34'30	1432 Ethiopia	2♌54'33	2405 Welch	8♌08'39
863 Benkoela	26♋34'30	2516 Roman	2♌55'48	2162 Anhui	8♌09'32
1548 Palomaa	26♋36'18	113 Amalthea	3♌01'19	3590 Holst	8♌11'26
2066 Palala	26♋44'23	2210 Lois	3♌04'14	4113 Rascana	8♌17'35
1105 Fragaria	26♋50'17	1689 Floris–Jan	3♌05'49	2625 Jack London	8♌17'46
522 Helga	26♋53'22	3495 Colchagua	3♌07'43	2189 Zaragoza	8♌22'36
2450 Ioannisiani	26♋54'30	1577 Reiss	3♌09'15	1127 Mimi	8♌23'04
431 Nephele	27♋01'14	1215 Boyer	3♌15'25	3162 Nostalgia	8♌24'13
3082 Dzhalil	27♋16'25	316 Goberta	3♌35'44	2672 Písek	8♌30'26
3098 Van Sprang	27♋21'33	888 Parysatis	3♌46'11	3016 Meuse	8♌30'54
1431 Luanda	27♋22'26	1800 Aguilar	3♌46'14	3766 Junepatterson	8♌34'58
3561 Devine	27♋32'28	2310 Olshaniya	3♌57'27	52 Europa	8♌36'43
2085 Henan	27♋48'28	1262 Sniadeckia	4♌01'07	530 Turandot	8♌36'59
3623 Chaplin	27♋54'06	4247 Grahamsmith	4♌04'54	3953 Perth	8♌38'44
2237 Melnikov	28♋01'23	729 Watsonia	4♌04'59	1104 Syringa	8♌46'06
820 Adriana	28♋20'35	3809 Amici	4♌23'50	4163 Saaremaa	8♌46'21
3504 Kholshevnikov		381 Myrrha	4♌56'05	166 Rhodope	8♌47'26
	28♋21'47	856 Backlunda	5♌01'16	1312 Vassar	8♌55'48
2443 Tomeileen	28♋24'40	17 Thetis	5♌02'02	2802 Weisell	9♌01'18
2887 Krinov	28♋35'33	11 Parthenope	5♌03'36	1562 Gondolatsch	9♌01'37
1017 Jacqueline	28♋35'58	3121 Tamines	5♌03'48	402 Chloë	9♌07'56
2320 Blarney	28♋37'35	2719 Suzhou	5♌08'08	3473 Sapporo	9♌09'37
938 Chlosinde	28♋40'12	817 Annika	5♌10'37	3496 Arieso	9♌22'08
2580 Smilevskia	28♋53'38	1966 Tristan	5♌13'09	928 Hildrun	9♌22'47
1725 CrAO	28♋54'17	62 Erato	5♌14'41	791 Ani	9♌29'52
2815 Soma	29♋25'19	1586 Thiele	5♌21'54	1211 Bressole	9♌34'15
3702 Trubetskaya	29♋34'22	1748 Mauderli	5♌35'57	747 Winchester	9♌34'53
1593 Fagnes	29♋34'55	745 Mauritia	5♌38'59	655 Briseïs	9♌44'18
1646 Rosseland	29♋37'35	3338 Richter	5♌41'17	1603 Neva	9♌45'08
3205 Boksenberg	29♋52'28	3859 Börngen	5♌44'56	2507 Bobone	9♌46'10
2597 Arthur	29♋53'25	1516 Henry	5♌48'13	1648 Shajna	10♌00'16
2553 Viljev	29♋54'53	3647 Dermott	5♌49'39	334 Chicago	10♌07'37
288 Glauke	0♌01'38	3478 Fanale	6♌01'46	1951 Lick	10♌07'58
537 Pauly	0♌08'14	2556 Louise	6♌01'47	2772 Dugan	10♌12'36
1914 Hartbeespoortdam		2410 Morrison	6♌04'36	4001 Ptolemaeus	10♌15'29
	0♌12'11	2161 Grissom	6♌13'30	2960 Ohtaki	10♌20'22
527 Euryanthe	0♌15'20	2213 Meeus	6♌29'50	555 Norma	10♌20'42
2863 Ben Mayer	0♌19'57	2651 Karen	6♌31'03	2411 Zellner	10♌32'12
870 Manto	0♌23'12	2965 Surikov	6♌34'11	811 Nauheima	10♌35'58

Heliocentric Nodes in Zodiacal Order
Epoch November 5, 1990   Equinox 1950.0   Planet nodes have number ####

2146 Stentor	10♌37'21	294 Felicia	15♌44'13	824 Anastasia	21♌10'50
2448 Sholokhov	10♌45'47	129 Antigone	15♌51'08	306 Unitas	21♌27'14
3642 Frieden	11♌01'32	2690 Ristiina	15♌53'56	3488 Brahic	21♌36'19
44 Nysa	11♌02'42	479 Caprera	15♌55'10	221 Eos	21♌37'09
#### Neptune	11♌12'41	2585 Irpedina	16♌08'54	3814 Hoshi–no–mura	
1329 Eliane	11♌42'20	2271 Kiso	16♌09'29		21♌37'12
738 Alagasta	11♌53'01	739 Mandeville	16♌15'48	183 Istria	21♌38'54
807 Ceraskia	11♌57'29	3301 Jansje	16♌32'05	783 Nora	21♌42'34
1011 Laodamia	12♌08'02	3208 Lunn	16♌33'06	622 Esther	21♌50'47
360 Carlova	12♌08'24	3706 Sinnott	16♌34'22	3251 Eratosthenes	21♌52'31
1111 Reinmuthia	12♌15'04	330 Adalberta	16♌37'10	287 Nephthys	21♌52'51
1629 Pecker	12♌15'39	202 Chryseïs	16♌37'36	4056 Timwarner	22♌01'42
3408 Shalamov	12♌18'26	3917 Franz Schubert		301 Bavaria	22♌03'25
889 Erynia	12♌22'04		16♌39'03	1069 Planckia	22♌05'15
3698 Manning	12♌22'07	1345 Potomac	16♌59'41	627 Charis	22♌09'15
2612 Kathryn	12♌25'37	2187 La Silla	16♌59'42	1802 Zhang Heng	22♌12'03
1860 Barbarossa	12♌26'44	4026 Beet	17♌05'01	3341 Hartmann	22♌12'37
502 Sigune	12♌28'57	4284 Kaho	17♌08'24	744 Aguntina	22♌13'23
1727 Mette	12♌29'11	1492 Oppolzer	17♌19'03	2567 Elba	22♌18'08
3681 Boyan	12♌31'58	2745 San Martin	17♌19'47	1845 Helewalda	22♌19'08
727 Nipponia	12♌35'26	526 Jena	17♌23'49	1945 Wesselink	22♌19'25
1627 Ivar	12♌37'37	357 Ninina	17♌50'34	2929 Harris	22♌21'02
4227 Kaali	12♌38'32	781 Kartvelia	17♌58'05	1539 Borrelly	22♌33'18
653 Berenike	12♌44'40	2144 Marietta	18♌11'22	3261 Tvardovskij	22♌38'11
2349 Kurchenko	12♌47'47	6 Hebe	18♌20'55	3040 Kozai	22♌54'55
2265 Verbaandert	12♌54'07	3332 Raksha	18♌26'33	4083 Jody	23♌07'42
634 Ute	12♌57'10	3802 Dornburg	18♌43'58	3780 Maury	23♌16'43
1334 Lundmarka	13♌03'10	2596 Vainu Bappu	18♌44'53	53 Kalypso	23♌23'25
2722 Abalakin	13♌08'34	3383 Koyama	18♌47'22	1414 Jérôme	23♌24'45
1624 Rabe	13♌18'20	1528 Conrada	18♌51'56	1076 Viola	23♌24'54
1097 Vicia	13♌18'26	1003 Lilofee	18♌57'47	558 Carmen	23♌28'16
2895 Memnon	13♌21'30	600 Musa	19♌00'30	2253 Espinette	23♌29'45
662 Newtonia	13♌27'00	1142 Aetolia	19♌02'06	181 Eucharis	23♌31'29
2041 Lancelot	13♌37'25	3384 Daliya	19♌09'33	1019 Strackea	23♌51'51
2714 Matti	13♌44'18	1350 Rosselia	19♌14'26	2845 Franklinken	23♌55'28
275 Sapientia	13♌44'40	2279 Barto	19♌32'51	2710 Veverka	23♌58'22
159 Aemilia	13♌47'37	2441 Hibbs	19♌38'34	28 Bellona	23♌59'51
2634 James Bradley		1085 Amaryllis	19♌40'47	234 Barbara	24♌04'11
	13♌49'19	2325 Chernykh	19♌42'25	3342 Fivesparks	24♌06'16
3125 Hay	13♌56'05	710 Gertrud	19♌43'41	3370 Kohsai	24♌10'15
3071 Nesterov	13♌58'31	2228 Soyuz–Apollo		2846 Ylppö	24♌23'29
2160 Spitzer	14♌01'11		19♌56'04	282 Clorinde	24♌28'14
1269 Rollandia	14♌18'18	2110 Moore–Sitterly		2147 Kharadze	24♌28'43
1191 Alfaterna	14♌18'34		19♌56'09	4186 Tamashima	24♌30'35
4286 Rubtsov	14♌19'07	354 Eleonora	20♌02'30	780 Armenia	24♌35'56
458 Hercynia	14♌23'28	2188 Orlenok	20♌03'49	893 Leopoldina	24♌38'01
2622 Bolzano	14♌24'10	4219 Nakamura	20♌06'49	1820 Lohmann	24♌42'09
442 Eichsfeldia	14♌26'45	2297 Daghestan	20♌09'52	2732 Witt	24♌43'33
4134 Schütz	14♌40'39	2457 Rublyov	20♌15'19	148 Gallia	24♌44'08
2086 Newell	14♌41'30	2409 Chapman	20♌17'17	206 Hersilia	24♌46'29
1711 Sandrine	14♌41'34	1251 Hedera	20♌22'19	3736 Rokoske	24♌56'25
226 Weringia	14♌44'02	2330 Ontake	20♌22'27	1148 Rarahu	25♌04'56
2864 Soderblom	14♌51'20	3355 Onizuka	20♌24'33	1871 Astyanax	25♌05'38
1903 Adzhimushkaj		1252 Celestia	20♌27'22	2121 Sevastopol	25♌13'50
	14♌59'36	2350 Von Lüde	20♌37'02	962 Aslög	25♌15'24
3615 Safronov	15♌14'58	851 Zeissia	20♌42'39	130 Elektra	25♌16'28
2918 Salazar	15♌16'56	2392 Jonathan Murray		2397 Lappajärvi	25♌22'24
3317 Paris	15♌17'50		20♌48'10	1514 Ricouxa	25♌22'53
2935 Naerum	15♌19'38	538 Friederike	20♌58'00	2284 San Juan	25♌25'25
736 Harvard	15♌27'23	933 Susi	20♌58'04	4050 Mebailey	25♌43'11
103 Hera	15♌43'24	3539 Weimar	21♌03'09	3054 Strugatskia	25♌44'25
1513 Mátra	15♌44'09	5 Astraea	21♌07'49		

Heliocentric Nodes in Zodiacal Order
Epoch November 5, 1990   Equinox 1950.0   Planet nodes have number ####

716 Berkeley	25♌45'48	2379 Heiskanen	0♍38'08	2326 Tololo	5♍36'09
3420 Standish	25♌46'02	2684 Douglas	0♍44'38	2290 Helffrich	5♍37'16
2399 Terradas	25♌46'20	3631 Sigyn	0♍47'05	251 Sophia	5♍49'02
1568 Aisleen	25♌46'25	3831 Pettengill	0♍50'48	3393 Štúr	6♍13'41
2542 Calpurnia	25♌55'52	3222 Liller	0♍51'11	269 Justitia	6♍15'03
4278 Harvey	26♌02'51	3291 Dunlap	0♍51'31	1799 Koussevitzky	6♍22'39
1986 Plaut	26♌09'18	876 Scott	0♍51'54	1164 Kobolda	6♍27'02
2373 Immo	26♌10'01	317 Roxane	0♍53'01	1533 Saimaa	6♍32'29
2616 Lesya	26♌15'09	2741 Valdivia	0♍54'59	201 Penelope	6♍34'11
3379 Oishi	26♌21'13	2731 Cucula	0♍59'26	660 Crescentia	6♍39'20
2447 Kronstadt	26♌23'17	3817 Lencarter	1♍13'16	39 Laetitia	6♍43'46
3270 Dudley	26♌28'23	3785 Kitami	1♍23'01	3064 Zimmer	6♍44'52
3315 Chant	26♌29'37	1245 Calvinia	1♍26'51	1403 Idelsonia	6♍45'01
2199 Kleť	26♌30'12	2106 Hugo	1♍34'15	2311 El Leoncito	6♍46'05
3358 Anikushin	26♌30'40	4181 Kivi	1♍35'25	2659 Millis	6♍48'30
909 Ulla	26♌35'35	2469 Tadjikistan	1♍40'27	1755 Lorbach	6♍48'45
1055 Tynka	26♌41'06	1907 Rudneva	1♍41'28	3311 Podobed	6♍52'40
1117 Reginita	26♌41'06	1742 Schaifers	1♍49'28	1782 Schneller	6♍56'55
4025 Ridley	26♌53'25	1764 Cogshall	1♍50'52	1144 Oda	6♍57'31
1830 Pogson	26♌59'44	3362 Khufu	1♍59'51	461 Saskia	6♍57'49
633 Zelima	27♌01'32	3072 Vilnius	2♍01'48	2998 Berendeya	6♍58'10
4208 Kiselev	27♌17'20	232 Russia	2♍10'01	2048 Dwornik	7♍06'05
45 Eugenia	27♌21'10	810 Atossa	2♍12'53	2309 Mr. Spock	7♍06'35
1082 Pirola	27♌28'58	1731 Smuts	2♍20'01	1283 Komsomolia	7♍17'57
1090 Sumida	27♌32'18	1434 Margot	2♍20'23	2285 Ron Helin	7♍22'46
2249 Yamamoto	27♌36'26	542 Susanna	2♍39'16	2711 Aleksandrov	7♍27'17
1999 Hirayama	27♌55'35	2723 Gorshkov	2♍40'18	871 Amneris	7♍32'18
1217 Maximiliana	27♌55'44	3808 Tempel	2♍41'52	2250 Stalingrad	7♍32'46
335 Roberta	27♌58'04	1384 Kniertje	2♍42'56	2602 Moore	7♍43'56
173 Ino	28♌01'01	667 Denise	2♍44'03	1833 Shmakova	7♍54'03
2560 Siegma	28♌03'54	2385 Mustel	2♍45'47	1993 Guacolda	7♍57'28
3499 Hoppe	28♌09'42	1615 Bardwell	2♍47'13	2550 Houssay	8♍02'11
2595 Gudiachvili	28♌11'03	2318 Lubarsky	2♍48'11	1263 Varsavia	8♍07'52
2316 Jo–Ann	28♌18'42	1816 Liberia	2♍50'30	2396 Kochi	8♍09'30
2416 Sharonov	28♌21'06	1842 Hynek	3♍01'43	1120 Cannonia	8♍10'42
2979 Murmansk	28♌28'47	2564 Kayala	3♍02'12	2796 Kron	8♍13'18
885 Ulrike	28♌31'52	2724 Orlov	3♍13'03	1759 Kienle	8♍25'17
2589 Daniel	28♌34'52	1004 Belopolskya	3♍19'14	1597 Laugier	8♍25'48
2020 Ukko	28♌35'06	185 Eunike	3♍25'35	1330 Spiridonia	8♍25'56
4107 Rufino	28♌37'52	2230 Yunnan	3♍30'25	2207 Antenor	8♍32'01
2136 Jugta	28♌38'05	4127 Kyogoku	3♍31'52	273 Atropos	8♍36'20
1094 Siberia	28♌39'04	1956 Artek	3♍33'42	304 Olga	8♍41'55
2084 Okayama	28♌39'05	2814 Vieira	3♍38'11	1733 Silke	8♍53'03
286 Iclea	28♌43'19	3227 Hasegawa	3♍54'46	194 Prokne	8♍59'13
3906 Chao	28♌44'09	3302 Schliemann	4♍04'26	3892 Dezsö	9♍01'42
2911 Miahelena	28♌52'40	809 Lundia	4♍06'17	1043 Beate	9♍02'04
2879 Shimizu	29♌00'08	3101 Goldberger	4♍21'53	191 Kolga	9♍05'08
1212 Francette	29♌05'28	2093 Genichesk	4♍25'20	149 Medusa	9♍05'14
2921 Sophocles	29♌10'13	1466 Mündleria	4♍31'57	903 Nealley	9♍17'51
2857 NOT	29♌29'00	2021 Poincaré	4♍33'24	2466 Golson	9♍18'17
1723 Klemola	29♌33'52	4149 Harrison	4♍33'25	1736 Floirac	9♍19'40
3389 Sinzot	29♌50'46	594 Mireille	4♍33'31	1874 Kacivelia	9♍23'29
16 Psyche	29♌51'39	1489 Attila	4♍39'41	97 Klotho	9♍29'52
1585 Union	29♌57'12	4285 Hulkower	4♍41'27	2422 Perovskaya	9♍31'40
873 Mechthild	29♌58'29	1617 Alschmitt	4♍42'43	163 Erigone	9♍46'49
2927 Alamosa	29♌58'31	869 Mellena	4♍48'30	794 Irenaea	9♍53'18
18 Melpomene	0♍01'19	2142 Landau	4♍51'06	1337 Gerarda	9♍56'26
2067 Aksnes	0♍01'57	2246 Bowell	5♍17'24	561 Ingwelde	9♍58'33
2381 Landi	0♍02'44	582 Olympia	5♍18'18	4230 Van den Bergh	
676 Melitta	0♍02'59	2216 Kerch	5♍19'06		10♍06'38
924 Toni	0♍07'11	65 Cybele	5♍22'53	3918 Brel	10♍13'06
2209 Tianjin	0♍35'35	1732 Heike	5♍25'44	1762 Russell	10♍21'46

Heliocentric Nodes in Zodiacal Order
Epoch November 5, 1990   Equinox 1950.0   Planet nodes have number ####

Name	Longitude	Name	Longitude	Name	Longitude
2204 Lyyli	10♍31'19	1299 Mertona	15♍16'19	688 Melanie	20♍35'56
890 Waltraut	10♍35'21	260 Huberta	15♍30'03	1410 Margret	20♍50'12
3124 Kansas	10♍36'06	2561 Margolin	15♍39'22	1221 Amor	20♍50'38
1668 Hanna	10♍39'13	1346 Gotha	15♍53'48	2017 Wesson	20♍51'49
58 Concordia	10♍50'36	805 Hormuthia	15♍55'42	3088 Jinxiuzhonghua	
3619 Nash	10♍53'51	167 Urda	15♍56'48		20♍55'43
3491 Fridolin	11♍00'28	2586 Matson	16♍04'56	2700 Baikonur	21♍00'18
3598 Saucier	11♍05'00	3033 Holbaek	16♍23'37	1938 Lausanna	21♍13'25
318 Magdalena	11♍07'58	386 Siegena	16♍28'42	1730 Marceline	21♍15'38
291 Alice	11♍08'22	2413 Van de Hulst	16♍29'35	2990 Trimberger	21♍22'49
3954 Mendelssohn	11♍08'42	1465 Autonoma	16♍38'32	2400 Derevskaya	21♍38'33
1301 Yvonne	11♍09'38	489 Comacina	16♍45'36	2605 Sahade	21♍40'49
315 Constantia	11♍10'08	1576 Fabiola	16♍55'52	379 Huenna	21♍44'57
1399 Teneriffa	11♍11'20	2111 Tselina	17♍02'52	3308 Ferreri	21♍49'48
1386 Storeria	11♍11'31	2987 Sarabhai	17♍04'31	358 Apollonia	21♍54'57
474 Prudentia	11♍18'52	2664 Everhart	17♍20'05	2980 Cameron	22♍00'05
1788 Kiess	11♍22'44	3207 Spinrad	17♍25'54	2292 Seili	22♍01'18
3569 Kumon	11♍25'21	2419 Moldavia	17♍31'38	3094 Chukokkala	22♍04'04
3516 Rusheva	11♍27'35	4060 Deipylos	17♍36'15	1335 Demoulina	22♍06'39
2624 Samitchell	11♍32'53	2534 Houzeau	17♍43'02	2907 Nekrasov	22♍18'12
1247 Memoria	11♍33'30	689 Zita	17♍43'30	2535 Hämeenlinna	22♍18'24
3108 Lyubov	11♍33'33	1722 Goffin	17♍48'27	827 Wolfiana	22♍25'44
3497 Innanen	11♍42'18	1811 Bruwer	17♍51'35	3703 Volkonskaya	22♍29'15
3104 Dürer	11♍48'08	3331 Kvistaberg	17♍54'22	2 Pallas	22♍36'47
2109 Dhotel	11♍51'41	592 Bathseba	17♍54'38	4132 Bartók	22♍37'00
3282 Spencer Jones		1636 Porter	17♍54'48	878 Mildred	22♍41'49
	11♍52'42	3223 Forsius	17♍56'19	470 Kilia	22♍46'34
246 Asporina	11♍55'29	3295 Murakami	17♍57'43	732 Tjilaki	22♍48'56
2919 Dali	11♍58'59	1974 Caupolican	17♍59'44	3915 Fukushima	23♍07'55
2435 Horemheb	12♍06'19	4196 Shuya	18♍11'43	50 Virginia	23♍13'45
1614 Goldschmidt	12♍07'02	3008 Nojiri	18♍17'10	339 Dorothea	23♍23'07
2528 Mohler	12♍19'19	3455 Kristensen	18♍19'40	1605 Milankovitch	23♍26'03
3321 Dasha	12♍21'20	4117 Wilke	18♍38'38	107 Camilla	23♍27'30
1915 Quetzálcoatl	12♍22'07	3375 Amy	18♍40'36	1691 Oort	23♍48'14
2832 Lada	12♍23'00	4257 Ubasti	18♍40'59	483 Seppina	23♍51'16
217 Eudora	12♍31'10	125 Liberatrix	18♍46'01	2299 Hanko	23♍52'47
1754 Cunningham	12♍39'25	2031 BAM	18♍48'05	3256 Daguerre	24♍03'26
864 Aase	12♍40'14	2329 Orthos	18♍51'02	1389 Onnie	24♍12'42
2949 Kaverznev	12♍43'32	2608 Seneca	18♍55'00	670 Ottegebe	24♍18'03
2496 Fernandus	12♍44'08	2291 Kevo	19♍08'56	2327 Gershberg	24♍28'05
3972 Richard	12♍45'25	3474 Linsley	19♍09'18	2173 Maresjev	24♍29'07
1025 Riema	12♍49'57	2932 Kempchinsky	19♍09'27	664 Judith	24♍38'27
2391 Tomita	12♍58'51	1379 Lomonosowa	19♍20'31	1443 Ruppina	24♍40'01
1376 Michelle	12♍58'53	2030 Belyaev	19♍20'51	434 Hungaria	24♍46'59
954 Li	12♍59'26	2995 Taratuta	19♍22'42	1451 Grano	24♍47'19
723 Hammonia	13♍03'37	601 Nerthus	19♍25'12	1774 Kulikov	24♍56'15
1898 Cowell	13♍08'32	3186 Manuilova	19♍30'10	4130 Ramanujan	24♍58'02
4175 Billbaum	13♍11'20	59 Elpis	19♍42'34	443 Photographica	
2166 Handahl	13♍31'11	2202 Pele	19♍42'46		24♍59'39
1724 Vladimir	13♍40'12	1178 Irmela	19♍44'39	1656 Suomi	25♍00'56
114 Kassandra	13♍50'06	3 Juno	19♍50'44	491 Carina	25♍02'24
2954 Delsemme	13♍58'33	1975 Pikelner	19♍55'06	3888 Hoyt	25♍09'17
2408 Astapovich	14♍16'49	3538 Nelsonia	20♍02'39	3066 McFadden	25♍09'53
4055 Magellan	14♍18'18	314 Rosalia	20♍04'32	190 Ismene	25♍23'07
799 Gudula	14♍19'43	2977 Chivilikhin	20♍06'38	892 Seeligeria	25♍28'32
2717 Tellervo	14♍25'28	2100 Ra–Shalom	20♍16'17	51 Nemausa	25♍34'03
1933 Tinchen	14♍27'43	218 Bianca	20♍18'21	2460 Mitlincoln	25♍39'07
2506 Pirogov	14♍29'46	3435 Boury	20♍21'38	2354 Lavrov	25♍41'05
1361 Leuschneria	14♍35'32	2116 Mtskheta	20♍23'45	1870 Glaukos	25♍41'42
2859 Paganini	14♍50'17	669 Kypria	20♍24'17	2148 Epeios	25♍53'52
609 Fulvia	14♍59'32	3090 Tjossem	20♍28'00	313 Chaldaea	26♍18'05
1070 Tunica	15♍06'27	2759 Idomeneus	20♍32'24	3114 Ercilla	26♍18'58

Heliocentric Nodes in Zodiacal Order
Epoch November 5, 1990 Equinox 1950.0 Planet nodes have number ####

1776 Kuiper	26♍28'12	256 Walpurga	2≏37'06	2776 Baikal	7≏11'51
865 Zubaida	26♍41'53	3079 Schiller	2≏44'27	4281 Pounds	7≏27'09
2746 Hissao	26♍44'25	3363 Bowen	2≏50'41	1878 Hughes	7≏28'00
3373 Koktebelia	26♍47'50	3218 Delphine	2≏54'35	2981 Chagall	7≏28'19
755 Quintilla	26♍52'37	3146 Dato	2≏56'36	2922 Dikan'ka	7≏28'44
1679 Nevanlinna	27♍03'51	2540 Blok	3≏00'40	4221 Picasso	7≏30'59
3005 Pervictoralex	27♍07'16	1973 Colocolo	3≏05'30	1030 Vitja	7≏40'44
1409 Isko	27♍16'12	635 Vundtia	3≏10'12	124 Alkeste	7≏44'15
4068 Menestheus	27♍16'35	834 Burnhamia	3≏12'03	2557 Putnam	7≏44'34
1671 Chaika	27♍18'58	48 Doris	3≏21'37	1917 Cuyo	7≏49'04
3189 Penza	27♍21'55	4255 Spacewatch	3≏35'14	3149 Okudzhava	7≏50'06
681 Gorgo	27♍33'03	238 Hypatia	3≏35'18	105 Artemis	7≏52'29
589 Croatia	27♍34'56	787 Moskva	3≏40'24	3480 Abante	8≏03'31
831 Stateira	27♍35'54	656 Beagle	3≏49'11	1275 Cimbria	8≏04'25
41 Daphne	27♍40'47	993 Moultona	3≏57'14	3436 Ibadinov	8≏04'39
788 Hohensteina	27♍48'35	4272 Entsuji	4≏02'46	1705 Tapio	8≏13'38
490 Veritas	27♍55'36	34 Circe	4≏05'39	2433 Sootiyo	8≏14'16
329 Svea	27♍56'17	1635 Bohrmann	4≏06'45	2861 Lambrecht	8≏14'19
2902 Westerlund	27♍56'44	1579 Herrick	4≏14'32	3046 Molière	8≏16'32
122 Gerda	28♍06'29	1828 Kashirina	4≏21'43	3225 Hoag	8≏18'20
1564 Srbija	28♍14'18	513 Centesima	4≏21'54	1766 Slipher	8≏24'19
2002 Euler	28♍14'42	4264 Karljosephine	4≏25'35	1932 Jansky	8≏29'00
1095 Tulipa	28♍18'11	737 Arequipa	4≏27'35	1872 Helenos	8≏30'48
3693 Barringer	28♍18'46	4116 Elachi	4≏32'34	1469 Linzia	8≏34'51
1394 Algoa	28♍24'52	1295 Deflotte	4≏39'55	2214 Carol	8≏35'07
1812 Gilgamesh	28♍26'32	4171 Carrasco	4≏43'13	3897 Louhi	8≏37'49
2227 Otto Struve	28♍27'41	2992 Vondel	4≏49'14	2356 Hirons	8≏38'29
1413 Roucarie	28♍38'47	1371 Resi	4≏54'14	1033 Simona	8≏54'31
2357 Phereclos	28♍43'43	365 Corduba	4≏54'24	1854 Skvortsov	8≏56'59
482 Petrina	28♍59'55	3941 Haydn	4≏59'15	1743 Schmidt	9≏06'33
2674 Pandarus	29♍12'26	2473 Heyerdahl	5≏12'53	3361 Orpheus	9≏08'20
253 Mathilde	29♍13'05	69 Hesperia	5≏13'51	1783 Albitskij	9≏10'24
754 Malabar	29♍43'23	3348 Pokryshkin	5≏22'21	1435 Garlena	9≏14'40
585 Bilkis	29♍45'29	1856 Růžena	5≏25'21	3365 Recogne	9≏15'26
533 Sara	0≏01'58	3084 Kondratyuk	5≏28'37	611 Valeria	9≏18'45
1928 Summa	0≏13'12	3113 Chizhevskij	5≏31'12	3659 Bellingshausen	
1672 Gezelle	0≏18'40	1425 Tuorla	5≏33'37		9≏24'21
3022 Dobermann	0≏19'06	2018 Schuster	5≏35'00	2289 McMillan	9≏24'42
1020 Arcadia	0≏22'24	1984 Fedynskij	5≏35'21	1570 Brunonia	9≏42'11
239 Adrastea	0≏36'14	236 Honoria	5≏37'27	2442 Corbett	10≏08'58
46 Hestia	0≏37'39	801 Helwerthia	5≏38'40	3039 Yangel	10≏09'23
1369 Ostanina	0≏44'38	1352 Wawel	5≏47'40	2689 Bruxelles	10≏10'44
1051 Merope	0≏48'11	2696 Magion	5≏52'05	3948 Bohr	10≏14'22
808 Merxia	0≏49'32	3351 Smith	5≏53'02	1606 Jekhovsky	10≏15'17
1628 Strobel	0≏52'42	2527 Gregory	5≏58'11	854 Frostia	10≏22'10
2378 Pannekoek	0≏58'36	136 Austria	6≏01'30	2367 Praha	10≏22'30
3059 Pryor	0≏59'16	495 Eulalia	6≏03'30	894 Erda	10≏23'24
2969 Mikula	1≏04'35	2348 Michkovitch	6≏04'14	874 Rotraut	10≏30'44
3617 Eicher	1≏05'45	719 Albert	6≏05'34	1855 Korolev	10≏33'53
1458 Mineura	1≏13'22	319 Leona	6≏12'06	682 Hagar	10≏36'34
950 Ahrensa	1≏17'08	2752 Wu Chien-Shiung		2135 Aristaeus	10≏45'37
308 Polyxo	1≏22'48		6≏13'51	1546 Izsák	10≏48'31
1621 Druzhba	1≏25'06	3709 Polypoites	6≏29'17	1383 Limburgia	11≏03'28
1896 Beer	1≏41'56	1084 Tamariwa	6≏39'14	3242 Bakhchisaraj	11≏07'12
1734 Zhongolovich	1≏43'15	2158 Tietjen	6≏46'17	2508 Alupka	11≏07'43
2328 Robeson	1≏43'55	3503 Brandt	6≏47'34	60 Echo	11≏23'50
289 Nenetta	1≏44'32	1796 Riga	6≏50'01	3279 Solon	11≏29'08
2577 Litva	2≏03'23	2317 Galya	6≏58'06	2499 Brunk	11≏47'22
900 Rosalinde	2≏05'20	1651 Behrens	6≏59'10	1767 Lampland	11≏53'28
1931 Čapek	2≏07'05	619 Triberga	7≏00'19	3232 Brest	12≏02'02
853 Nansenia	2≏25'18	421 Zähringia	7≏01'33	1795 Woltjer	12≏06'11
1992 Galvarino	2≏25'18	3158 Anga	7≏11'28	956 Elisa	12≏17'08

Heliocentric Nodes in Zodiacal Order

Epoch November 5, 1990   Equinox 1950.0   Planet nodes have number ####

1708 Pólit 12♎29'26	1692 Subbotina 19♎16'46	189 Phthia 23♎11'18
3531 Cruikshank 12♎30'54	836 Jole 19♎19'45	119 Althaea 23♎15'57
920 Rogeria 12♎30'57	1650 Heckmann 19♎23'04	1165 Imprinetta 23♎17'08
2251 Tikhov 12♎42'37	2049 Grietje 19♎32'27	612 Veronika 23♎27'59
2810 Lev Tolstoj 12♎49'00	1632 Sieböhme 19♎32'38	3073 Kursk 23♎39'19
1289 Kutaïssi 12♎49'20	837 Schwarzschilda	2660 Wasserman 23♎43'44
2539 Ningxia 12♎50'09	19♎35'57	2014 Vasilevskis 23♎44'24
547 Praxedis 12♎53'42	1229 Tilia 19♎38'46	724 Hapag 23♎45'11
2053 Nuki 12♎54'00	1475 Yalta 19♎41'06	518 Halawe 23♎47'11
56 Melete 13♎07'57	1935 Lucerna 19♎42'13	2972 Niilo 23♎50'36
1990 Pilcher 13♎08'07	4135 Svetlanov 19♎46'26	3403 Tammy 23♎52'36
3454 Lieske 13♎13'03	3793 Leonteus 19♎49'22	2853 Harvill 23♎53'28
485 Genua 13♎15'15	2572 Annschnell 19♎58'58	76 Freia 24♎00'04
2342 Lebedev 13♎16'29	1059 Mussorgskia 20♎04'58	4105 Tsia 24♎01'13
4027 Mitton 13♎21'09	3316 Herzberg 20♎10'33	3250 Martebo 24♎01'33
3347 Konstantin 13♎21'39	1037 Davidweilla 20♎12'16	2592 Hunan 24♎02'06
1875 Neruda 13♎28'36	1638 Ruanda 20♎14'06	2484 Parenago 24♎05'06
3668 Ilfpetrov 13♎32'55	1230 Riceia 20♎16'35	2619 Skalnaté Pleso
4110 Keats 14♎05'40	219 Thusnelda 20♎20'26	24♎07'51
2653 Principia 14♎06'36	2715 Mielikki 20♎22'42	1502 Arenda 24♎10'34
572 Rebekka 14♎07'44	176 Iduna 20♎23'16	921 Jovita 24♎42'44
1023 Thomana 14♎08'45	3654 AAS 20♎25'14	2235 Vittore 24♎43'09
2322 Kitt Peak 14♎17'38	2059 Baboquivari 20♎26'12	204 Kallisto 24♎43'24
3027 Shavarsh 14♎19'09	1286 Banachiewicza	2610 Tuva 24♎52'44
872 Holda 14♎27'24	20♎26'35	460 Scania 24♎55'38
1494 Savo 14♎33'16	2666 Gramme 20♎33'11	3202 Graff 24♎56'33
4108 Rakos 14♎49'10	3000 Leonardo 20♎36'09	1200 Imperatrix 24♎57'30
2303 Retsina 15♎02'33	2642 Vésale 20♎38'43	922 Schlutia 24♎58'46
3076 Garber 15♎03'11	4224 Susa 20♎39'07	2518 Rutllant 25♎10'07
1918 Aiguillon 15♎06'05	1910 Mikhailov 20♎44'53	2420 Čiurlionis 25♎11'49
1536 Pielinen 15♎10'23	2728 Yatskiv 20♎49'55	3677 Magnusson 25♎33'03
3882 Johncox 15♎11'29	1882 Rauma 20♎53'53	2359 Debehogne 25♎33'33
444 Gyptis 15♎18'04	1905 Ambartsumian	1309 Hyperborea 25♎38'33
1114 Lorraine 15♎22'52	20♎58'08	2493 Elmer 25♎39'41
2304 Slavia 15♎31'48	1422 Strömgrenia 21♎10'09	150 Nuwa 25♎51'55
2549 Baker 15♎39'47	3522 Becker 21♎18'37	20 Massalia 26♎01'46
875 Nymphe 15♎48'20	2192 Pyatigoriya 21♎23'22	3126 Davydov 26♎07'13
1775 Zimmerwald 15♎49'07	1408 Trusanda 21♎26'35	1150 Achaia 26♎08'28
3479 Malaparte 16♎17'49	439 Ohio 21♎31'34	2698 Azerbajdzhan 26♎13'45
2283 Bunke 16♎22'06	2533 Fechtig 21♎34'57	79 Eurynome 26♎18'31
3097 Tacitus 16♎36'19	4152 Weber 21♎35'50	1575 Winifred 26♎20'27
3533 Toyota 16♎43'44	3870 Mayré 21♎36'21	2654 Ristenpart 26♎27'12
225 Henrietta 16♎43'57	4254 Kamél 21♎37'58	168 Sibylla 26♎30'02
3815 König 16♎53'24	1101 Clematis 21♎38'42	2628 Kopal 26♎33'43
74 Galatea 17♎00'36	540 Rosamunde 21♎42'22	4222 Nancita 26♎35'49
2606 Odessa 17♎03'44	137 Meliboea 21♎52'08	2074 Shoemaker 26♎42'48
1868 Thersites 17♎07'11	1573 Väisälä 21♎53'14	242 Kriemhild 26♎47'42
3246 Bidstrup 17♎11'06	252 Clementina 21♎54'00	2529 Rockwell Kent
3385 Bronnina 17♎12'30	3689 Yeates 21♎56'39	26♎57'36
923 Herluga 17♎13'22	2727 Paton 21♎57'38	2704 Julian Loewe 27♎02'21
1873 Agenor 17♎14'18	1287 Lorcia 22♎11'47	2976 Lautaro 27♎09'50
531 Zerlina 17♎19'16	1979 Sakharov 22♎14'38	496 Gryphia 27♎10'08
2598 Merlin 17♎33'05	4216 Neunkirchen 22♎16'11	4138 Kalchas 27♎16'00
2783 Chernyshevskij	67 Asia 22♎21'06	2282 Andrés Bello 27♎16'35
17♎35'20	2934 Aristophanes 22♎28'02	258 Tyche 27♎16'55
904 Rockefellia 17♎43'04	510 Mabella 22♎32'02	2771 Polzunov 27♎19'14
2298 Cindijon 18♎13'25	1718 Namibia 22♎38'04	2061 Anza 27♎20'28
2530 Shipka 18♎35'11	1387 Kama 22♎43'21	3058 Delmary 27♎23'10
1791 Patsayev 18♎40'58	1201 Strenua 22♎45'44	848 Inna 27♎31'12
57 Mnemosyne 18♎44'50	85 Io 22♎51'01	72 Feronia 27♎31'15
2495 Noviomagum 19♎11'54	1739 Meyermann 22♎55'02	3637 O'Meara 27♎34'26
417 Suevia 19♎14'24	525 Adelaide 22♎56'50	756 Lilliana 27♎34'42

Heliocentric Nodes in Zodiacal Order

Epoch November 5, 1990   Equinox 1950.0   Planet nodes have number ####

Name	Node	Name	Node	Name	Node
3175 Netto	27♎44'24	2051 Chang	4♏57'16	1794 Finsen	11♏10'46
2679 Kittisvaara	27♎46'01	666 Desdemona	5♏05'23	3268 De Sanctis	11♏17'06
2477 Biryukov	27♎53'09	216 Kleopatra	5♏08'31	1058 Grubba	11♏24'06
2834 Christy Carol	28♎12'45	2658 Gingerich	5♏17'04	995 Sternberga	11♏26'50
1673 Van Houten	28♎17'37	1291 Phryne	5♏21'50	1039 Sonneberga	11♏27'34
244 Sita	28♎30'57	1036 Ganymed	5♏35'05	3828 Hoshino	11♏41'13
2948 Amosov	28♎37'22	1130 Skuld	5♏44'13	233 Asterope	11♏43'17
2060 Chiron	28♎39'15	3147 Samantha	5♏45'46	2175 Andrea Doria	11♏43'33
968 Petunia	28♎40'20	3377 Lodewijk	5♏54'22	4080 Galinskij	11♏43'51
305 Gordonia	28♎42'35	2468 Repin	6♏02'12	3639 Weidenschilling	
3801 Thrasymedes	28♎45'17	978 Aidamina	6♏08'50		11♏59'08
1136 Mercedes	29♎03'25	2459 Spellmann	6♏08'58	4204 Barsig	12♏18'18
1969 Alain	29♎04'17	263 Dresda	6♏11'27	2120 Tyumenia	12♏28'00
4218 Demottoni	29♎10'04	1473 Ounas	6♏11'43	3625 Fracastoro	12♏34'47
821 Fanny	29♎25'28	2820 Iisalmi	6♏15'22	3159 Prokof'ev	12♏41'34
822 Lalage	29♎31'21	1102 Pepita	6♏19'11	1377 Roberbauxa	12♏44'47
392 Wilhelmina	29♎33'16	3387 Greenberg	6♏31'40	2198 Ceplecha	12♏44'56
1281 Jeanne	29♎36'36	2925 Beatty	6♏43'34	3498 Belton	13♏07'56
377 Campania	29♎43'02	1554 Yugoslavia	6♏45'26	2590 Mourão	13♏14'43
2475 Semenov	29♎49'10	3236 Strand	6♏49'15	1328 Devota	13♏17'31
1400 Tirela	0♏19'44	614 Pia	6♏51'50	3846 Hazel	13♏29'12
102 Miriam	0♏38'37	3069 Heyrovský	7♏03'54	1167 Dubiago	14♏22'09
3826 Handel	0♏45'20	3581 Alvarez	7♏18'25	631 Philippina	14♏22'42
276 Adelheid	0♏50'25	509 Iolanda	7♏25'58	1203 Nanna	14♏31'54
19 Fortuna	0♏55'30	1881 Shao	7♏40'02	1355 Magoeba	14♏41'29
2340 Hathor	0♏59'12	771 Libera	7♏40'02	3687 Dzus	14♏43'55
2363 Cebriones	1♏12'04	4164 Shilov	7♏40'40	3574 Rudaux	14♏45'17
205 Martha	1♏30'34	2343 Siding Spring	7♏44'46	3138 Ciney	14♏49'50
1353 Maartje	1♏47'51	3977 Maxine	7♏51'24	570 Kythera	14♏57'08
1542 Schalén	1♏53'10	3320 Namba	7♏55'10	1151 Ithaka	14♏57'39
2196 Ellicott	1♏57'40	2232 Altaj	8♏05'50	2056 Nancy	15♏18'01
992 Swasey	1♏58'39	2716 Tuulikki	8♏06'05	2862 Vavilov	15♏23'30
1944 Gunter	2♏02'04	3288 Seleucus	8♏07'35	1793 Zoya	15♏29'19
3151 Talbot	2♏05'40	1168 Brandia	8♏11'37	3756 Ruscannon	15♏31'54
2490 Bussolini	2♏08'21	3909 Gladys	8♏14'35	2686 Linda Susan	15♏37'39
345 Tercidina	2♏13'18	1695 Walbeck	8♏15'31	565 Marbachia	15♏38'03
1865 Cerberus	2♏22'16	80 Sappho	8♏20'34	3042 Zelinsky	15♏52'22
4226 Damiaan	2♏27'10	2099 Öpik	8♏22'45	1922 Zulu	15♏53'02
391 Ingeborg	2♏28'07	2437 Amnestia	8♏31'56	1590 Tsiolkovskaja	16♏09'02
1660 Wood	2♏28'19	1031 Arctica	8♏41'35	2393 Suzuki	16♏13'05
393 Lampetia	2♏42'00	374 Burgundia	8♏44'24	1296 Andrée	16♏29'19
1139 Atami	2♏49'56	3527 McCord	8♏46'19	673 Edda	16♏33'13
2795 Lepage	2♏56'07	713 Luscinia	8♏50'41	2440 Educatio	16♏47'55
3306 Byron	2♏56'17	3469 Bulgakov	9♏06'41	368 Haidea	17♏02'47
1419 Danzig	3♏06'52	3692 Rickman	9♏13'40	1909 Alekhin	17♏03'33
3287 Olmstead	3♏08'22	2798 Vergilius	9♏14'13	2427 Kobzar	17♏18'07
703 Noëmi	3♏17'58	429 Lotis	9♏40'09	2205 Glinka	17♏30'45
1257 Móra	3♏21'52	320 Katharina	9♏48'09	3224 Irkutsk	17♏37'15
2052 Tamriko	3♏32'45	32 Pomona	9♏56'41	3744 Horn–d'Arturo	
4192 Breysacher	3♏34'38	3120 Dangrania	10♏24'33		17♏44'06
25 Phocaea	3♏38'37	2223 Sarpedon	10♏26'07	397 Vienna	17♏46'51
3048 Guangzhou	3♏58'42	1827 Atkinson	10♏27'56	153 Hilda	17♏47'19
798 Ruth	4♏04'25	2926 Caldeira	10♏31'25	2671 Abkhazia	17♏53'18
668 Dora	4♏08'50	1143 Odysseus	10♏35'26	3018 Godiva	18♏04'25
4029 Bridges	4♏15'50	2961 Katsurahama	10♏35'56	849 Ara	18♏05'32
1146 Biarmia	4♏22'19	1822 Waterman	10♏37'35	3091 Van den Heuvel	
3312 Pedersen	4♏26'20	3181 Ahnert	10♏38'31		18♏07'28
999 Zachia	4♏35'20	1583 Antilochus	10♏39'19	2478 Tokai	18♏18'12
1363 Herberta	4♏37'47	1442 Corvina	10♏45'40	743 Eugenisis	18♏46'20
2685 Masursky	4♏48'58	1060 Magnolia	10♏45'41	586 Thekla	18♏47'04
2276 Warck	4♏49'10	4220 Flood	10♏58'19	456 Abnoba	18♏55'17
650 Amalasuntha	4♏56'58	2107 Ilmari	10♏58'49	1347 Patria	18♏56'32

Heliocentric Nodes in Zodiacal Order

Epoch November 5, 1990   Equinox 1950.0   Planet nodes have number ####

Name	Node	Name	Node	Name	Node
419 Aurelia	19♏02'08	1315 Bronislawa	26♏03'27	4129 Richelen	5♐22'33
1009 Sirene	19♏08'54	1293 Sonja	26♏12'35	2638 Gadolin	5♐22'46
310 Margarita	19♏14'46	2306 Bauschinger	26♏32'16	1688 Wilkens	5♐23'51
2266 Tchaikovsky	19♏23'01	1752 Van Herk	26♏32'57	1243 Pamela	5♐32'33
3511 Tsvetaeva	19♏25'39	1175 Margo	26♏50'12	2221 Chilton	5♐40'56
919 Ilsebill	19♏35'06	480 Hansa	26♏51'57	2382 Nonie	5♐41'48
1537 Transylvania	19♏35'45	2426 Simonov	26♏54'05	3285 Ruth Wolfe	5♐42'28
826 Henrika	20♏05'24	1611 Beyer	27♏14'15	1943 Anteros	5♐45'26
694 Ekard	20♏06'20	1712 Angola	27♏32'31	1222 Tina	5♐48'47
3023 Heard	20♏09'31	2474 Ruby	27♏34'10	2751 Campbell	5♐50'32
1690 Mayrhofer	20♏17'03	1255 Schilowa	27♏39'19	2264 Sabrina	5♐59'38
2920 Automedon	20♏22'55	1316 Kasan	27♏43'49	1980 Tezcatlipoca	6♐05'34
712 Boliviana	20♏30'19	1256 Normannia	27♏50'32	2702 Batrakov	6♐07'22
3428 Roberts	20♏46'17	1438 Wendeline	27♏53'05	1574 Meyer	6♐14'00
3333 Schaber	20♏47'55	797 Montana	27♏58'07	248 Lameia	6♐31'37
1726 Hoffmeister	20♏53'09	3052 Herzen	28♏09'19	1172 Äneas	6♐46'37
929 Algunde	20♏54'00	1964 Luyten	28♏15'03	3534 Sax	6♐47'05
277 Elvira	21♏13'01	230 Athamantis	29♏21'04	2233 Kuznetsov	6♐47'58
979 Ilsewa	21♏22'21	1499 Pori	29♏21'57	352 Gisela	6♐49'14
4191 Assesse	21♏22'55	3050 Carrera	29♏32'00	997 Priska	6♐56'55
2813 Zappalà	21♏45'44	1647 Menelaus	29♏43'01	1277 Dolores	6♐58'32
1561 Fricke	21♏53'32	838 Seraphina	29♏56'55	2454 Olaus Magnus	7♐12'34
3553 Mera	21♏58'04	1751 Herget	0♐02'20	2191 Uppsala	7♐14'05
3722 Urata	21♏58'32	3936 Elst	0♐11'27	2983 Poltava	7♐36'17
2352 Kurchatov	22♏04'02	1728 Goethe Link	0♐21'03	1505 Koranna	7♐57'38
342 Endymion	22♏12'17	2709 Sagan	0♐38'03	3182 Shimanto	7♐59'39
1760 Sandra	22♏13'23	299 Thora	0♐51'30	2823 Van der Laan	8♐11'11
378 Holmia	22♏18'20	4066 Haapavesi	0♐51'34	418 Alemannia	8♐30'42
2755 Avicenna	22♏20'12	188 Menippe	0♐56'58	147 Protogeneia	8♐30'59
789 Lena	22♏21'55	2872 Gentelec	1♐05'57	960 Birgit	8♐44'41
2903 Zhuhai	22♏23'22	2115 Irakli	1♐10'54	3869 Norton	8♐45'26
3572 Leogoldberg	22♏26'21	1110 Jaroslawa	1♐26'38	1596 Itzigsohn	8♐52'42
957 Camelia	22♏28'31	156 Xanthippe	1♐36'10	1818 Brahms	8♐54'54
663 Gerlinde	22♏29'30	898 Hildegard	1♐40'07	430 Hybris	9♐03'45
3896 Pordenone	22♏33'12	409 Aspasia	1♐58'21	457 Alleghenia	9♐10'24
3595 Gallagher	22♏40'42	726 Joëlla	2♐08'33	2694 Pino Torinese	9♐27'39
2180 Marjaleena	23♏06'09	2588 Flavia	2♐14'31	1879 Broederstroom	9♐28'32
2908 Shimoyama	23♏07'44	2789 Foshan	2♐15'02	568 Cheruskia	9♐29'24
3837 Carr	23♏20'35	699 Hela	2♐15'04	3873 Roddy	9♐31'04
284 Amalia	23♏24'09	3259 Brownlee	2♐15'23	3376 Armandhammer	9♐37'35
1307 Cimmeria	23♏25'36	2028 Janequeo	2♐23'47	774 Armor	9♐46'58
478 Tergeste	23♏32'43	3472 Upgren	2♐47'11	396 Aeolia	9♐49'03
714 Ulula	23♏38'47	95 Arethusa	3♐01'17	3606 Pohjola	10♐11'02
2436 Hatshepsut	23♏44'39	989 Schwassmannia	3♐03'04	3322 Lidiya	10♐14'11
2257 Kaarina	23♏53'38	686 Gersuind	3♐09'01	983 Gunila	10♐26'10
1108 Demeter	24♏02'58	2112 Ulyanov	3♐14'48	2152 Hannibal	10♐44'56
1506 Xosa	24♏20'20	1716 Peter	3♐17'48	2953 Vysheslavia	10♐54'17
640 Brambilla	24♏37'08	937 Bethgea	3♐18'00	803 Picka	10♐55'33
336 Lacadiera	24♏37'15	3810 Aoraki	3♐28'03	3299 Hall	11♐17'42
1264 Letaba	24♏41'47	701 Oriola	3♐46'21	1652 Hergé	11♐17'43
3690 Larson	24♏47'09	420 Bertholda	3♐50'42	3982 Kastel	11♐28'49
2371 Dimitrov	24♏51'07	4290 Heisei	3♐58'35	790 Pretoria	11♐33'12
685 Hermia	24♏55'53	1888 Zu Chong–Zhi	4♐19'08	1014 Semphyra	11♐36'18
12 Victoria	25♏06'48	2346 Lilio	4♐26'03	2483 Guinevere	11♐37'48
3838 Epona	25♏07'06	1994 Shane	4♐40'47	2019 Van Albada	11♐45'00
4069 Blakee	25♏14'21	1311 Knopfia	4♐51'18	1177 Gonnessia	11♐53'33
266 Aline	25♏34'02	1395 Aribeda	4♐58'23	179 Klytaemnestra	11♐54'27
1857 Parchomenko	25♏36'47	976 Benjamina	4♐59'06	2104 Toronto	12♐05'25
1199 Geldonia	25♏40'36	2649 Oongaq	5♐00'49		
2692 Chkalov	25♏52'18	3353 Jarvis	5♐02'48		
1807 Slovakia	25♏57'54				

Heliocentric Nodes in Zodiacal Order
Epoch November 5, 1990   Equinox 1950.0   Planet nodes have number ####

Name		Name		Name	
643 Scheherezade	12♐06'17	7 Iris	19♐20'04	514 Armida	28♐36'11
322 Phaeo	12♐17'02	1198 Atlantis	19♐24'23	3928 Randa	28♐42'40
899 Jokaste	12♐18'27	683 Lanzia	19♐33'55	1407 Lindelöf	29♐01'43
3139 Shantou	12♐28'44	4093 Bennett	20♐09'38	4223 Shikoku	29♐14'10
2167 Erin	12♐29'34	3664 Anneres	20♐17'17	1129 Neujmina	29♐14'30
951 Gaspra	12♐39'25	1436 Salonta	20♐17'46	3796 Lene	29♐16'45
1322 Coppernicus	12♐43'58	1181 Lilith	20♐25'00	879 Ricarda	29♐47'50
690 Wratislavia	12♐45'15	4231 Fireman	20♐37'22	550 Senta	0♑15'48
1520 Imatra	13♐06'27	1420 Radcliffe	20♐46'33	1367 Nongoma	0♑23'03
441 Bathilde	13♐19'45	523 Ada	20♐47'39	1644 Rafita	0♑25'47
4081 Tippett	13♐25'05	1565 Lemaître	20♐54'31	3085 Donna	0♑30'56
3947 Swedenborg	13♐37'38	4207 Chernova	21♐01'46	241 Germania	0♑34'05
1810 Epimetheus	13♐40'37	1661 Granule	21♐16'54	1806 Derice	0♑37'17
3415 Danby	13♐43'40	1149 Volga	21♐20'25	847 Agnia	0♑51'37
896 Sphinx	13♐44'06	846 Lipperta	21♐27'18	3319 Kibi	1♑00'23
3400 Aotearoa	13♐47'58	3786 Yamada	21♐30'19	3107 Weaver	1♑12'35
1441 Bolyai	13♐50'39	2190 Coubertin	21♐52'38	1292 Luce	1♑15'41
1779 Paraná	13♐55'38	1232 Cortusa	22♐05'39	3751 Kiang	1♑24'14
1490 Limpopo	13♐58'00	3535 Ditte	22♐08'11	1213 Algeria	1♑30'23
270 Anahita	13♐58'52	4122 Ferrari	22♐10'39	2141 Simferopol	1♑36'39
3622 Ilinsky	14♐09'16	2377 Shcheglov	22♐26'40	2229 Mezzarco	1♑47'41
832 Karin	14♐16'11	3307 Athabasca	22♐44'15	1858 Lobachevskij	1♑48'18
4094 Aoshima	14♐20'22	1666 Van Gent	22♐45'45	1176 Lucidor	1♑57'54
2817 Perec	14♐24'04	675 Ludmilla	22♐59'52	3620 Platonov	2♑15'13
647 Adelgunde	14♐24'55	437 Rhodia	23♐06'21	2697 Albina	2♑28'57
823 Sisigambis	14♐35'21	880 Herba	23♐09'23	1836 Komarov	2♑34'54
1169 Alwine	14♐39'07	211 Isolda	23♐25'00	677 Aaltje	2♑43'41
405 Thia	14♐43'03	1940 Whipple	23♐47'29	840 Zenobia	2♑59'41
2736 Ops	15♐06'25	895 Helio	24♐10'45	2105 Gudy	3♑06'53
2331 Parvulesco	15♐10'45	1314 Paula	24♐13'56	1699 Honkasalo	3♑10'47
914 Palisana	15♐20'26	2145 Blaauw	24♐15'19	1750 Eckert	3♑15'33
4095 Ishizuchisan	15♐29'24	43 Ariadne	24♐21'43	3593 Osip	3♑27'48
1197 Rhodesia	15♐29'47	2423 Ibarruri	24♐44'08	3871 Reiz	3♑31'59
2170 Byelorussia	15♐30'55	1147 Stavropolis	24♐45'32	2940 Bacon	3♑37'08
2843 Yeti	15♐42'11	1498 Lahti	24♐46'50	1685 Toro	3♑45'14
499 Venusia	15♐51'01	901 Brunsia	24♐47'33	2968 Iliya	3♑59'27
1319 Disa	16♐15'27	1949 Messina	24♐48'06	1826 Miller	3♑59'46
2139 Makharadze	16♐18'30	3200 Phaethon	24♐55'02	1306 Scythia	4♑04'15
2184 Fujian	16♐23'16	1936 Lugano	25♐01'01	517 Edith	4♑23'04
3134 Kostinsky	16♐36'58	792 Metcalfia	25♐02'16	539 Pamina	4♑26'22
2513 Baetslé	17♐14'37	748 Simeïsa	25♐12'24	2780 Monnig	4♑32'39
882 Swetlana	17♐14'47	4279 De Gasparis	25♐13'50	2140 Kemerovo	4♑34'44
897 Lysistrata	17♐26'58	4261 Gekko	25♐20'52	2754 Efimov	4♑48'34
583 Klotilde	17♐29'55	2937 Gibbs	25♐23'00	2536 Kozyrev	4♑51'56
220 Stephania	17♐39'32	1535 Päijänne	26♐03'18	3195 Fedchenko	5♑00'59
1224 Fantasia	17♐45'07	1645 Waterfield	26♐04'51	1189 Terentia	5♑09'26
3381 Mikkola	17♐47'15	3392 Setouchi	26♐21'41	4039 Souseki	5♑14'09
1894 Haffner	17♐53'16	1843 Jarmila	26♐35'42	695 Bella	5♑27'34
1955 McMath	17♐54'28	1402 Eri	26♐43'36	4125 Lew Allen	5♑31'15
3367 Alex	17♐54'58	1103 Sequoia	27♐07'56	295 Theresia	5♑53'53
1365 Henyey	18♐06'47	552 Sigelinde	27♐09'09	3880 Kaiserman	5♑58'51
132 Aethra	18♐25'31	4071 Rostovdon	27♐12'06	4205 David Hughes	6♑00'01
3115 Baily	18♐27'38	1045 Michela	27♐22'57	88 Thisbe	6♑16'38
1249 Rutherfordia	18♐34'31	3369 Freuchen	27♐25'47	2635 Huggins	6♑26'43
2083 Smither	18♐38'48	3563 Canterbury	27♐32'06	1244 Deira	6♑38'34
1057 Wanda	18♐50'47	541 Deborah	27♐33'35	3874 Stuart	6♑44'23
1704 Wachmann	19♐02'34	2119 Schwall	27♐46'34	2012 Guo Shou–Jing	6♑47'09
764 Gedania	19♐02'49	1747 Wright	27♐49'15	881 Athene	6♑56'11
395 Delia	19♐05'59	1834 Palach	27♐57'01	1401 Lavonne	7♑09'05
1001 Gaussia	19♐08'31	198 Ampella	28♐07'08	2613 Plzeň	7♑23'50
3890 Bunin	19♐10'46	3573 Holmberg	28♐20'20	2029 Binomi	7♑39'31
		1109 Tata	28♐29'20		

Heliocentric Nodes in Zodiacal Order

Epoch November 5, 1990   Equinox 1950.0   Planet nodes have number ####

Asteroid	Node	Asteroid	Node	Asteroid	Node
654 Zelinda	7♑58'29	883 Matterania	15♑08'55	3759 Piironen	22♑32'09
4022 Nonna	8♑01'55	1911 Schubart	15♑11'50	1571 Cesco	22♑33'47
158 Koronis	8♑07'15	2186 Keldysh	15♑12'38	557 Violetta	22♑40'53
2524 Budovicium	8♑07'46	1530 Rantaseppä	15♑28'36	445 Edna	22♑41'25
1954 Kukarkin	8♑11'14	4051 Hatanaka	15♑31'29	15 Eunomia	22♑53'36
3093 Bergholz	8♑20'27	49 Pales	15♑33'35	1829 Dawson	22♑59'35
1531 Hartmut	8♑41'40	1214 Richilde	15♑36'54	3095 Omarkhayyam	22♑59'55
1525 Savonlinna	9♑02'53	556 Phyllis	15♑37'11	3025 Higson	23♑04'50
1626 Sadeya	9♑03'21	980 Anacostia	15♑37'37	2054 Gawain	23♑07'47
1706 Dieckvoss	9♑15'27	2444 Lederle	15♑49'13	3371 Giacconi	23♑17'06
2648 Owa	9♑30'18	476 Hedwig	15♑54'48	1280 Baillauda	23♑18'27
3510 Veeder	9♑36'18	2078 Nanking	16♑55'01	3127 Bagration	23♑30'23
398 Admete	9♑38'19	2368 Beltrovata	17♑10'29	2465 Wilson	23♑48'18
1040 Klumpkea	9♑43'11	3063 Makhaon	17♑10'57	507 Laodica	23♑51'14
639 Latona	9♑51'10	338 Budrosa	17♑13'11	1496 Turku	23♑55'08
2259 Sofievka	9♑53'14	1254 Erfordia	17♑46'55	608 Adolfine	23♑56'18
3525 Paul	10♑03'37	1543 Bourgeois	17♑48'20	4082 Swann	24♑13'40
1153 Wallenbergia	10♑04'59	969 Leocadia	17♑52'49	407 Arachne	24♑14'16
1064 Aethusa	10♑08'37	2601 Bologna	18♑02'47	4239 Goodman	24♑22'52
3577 Putilin	10♑10'37	3737 Beckman	18♑06'35	543 Charlotte	24♑51'37
704 Interamnia	10♑21'11	1643 Brown	18♑06'43	554 Peraga	25♑07'19
3237 Victorplatt	10♑21'46	4147 Lennon	18♑16'49	4183 Cuno	25♑14'02
2579 Spartacus	10♑29'58	1825 Klare	18♑26'57	3749 Balam	25♑15'30
1837 Osita	10♑31'35	3640 Gostin	18♑47'02	38 Leda	25♑26'55
1195 Orangia	10♑51'04	3700 Geowilliams	18♑50'31	3240 Laocoon	25♑31'06
2521 Heidi	10♑56'35	2676 Aarhus	19♑09'34	1740 Paavo Nurmi	25♑34'21
678 Fredegundis	11♑16'30	1560 Strattonia	19♑09'46	1297 Quadea	25♑48'00
2618 Coonabarabran	11♑23'09	3860 Plovdiv	19♑18'09	2554 Skiff	25♑58'31
1900 Katyusha	11♑27'34	763 Cupido	19♑28'29	1457 Ankara	26♑03'23
707 Steïna	11♑29'19	1067 Lunaria	19♑30'32	1273 Helma	26♑17'33
2094 Magnitka	11♑31'38	3219 Komaki	19♑36'50	3999 Aristarchus	26♑35'46
584 Semiramis	11♑50'05	702 Alauda	19♑37'13	1835 Gajdariya	26♑39'09
389 Industria	11♑58'43	500 Selinur	19♑47'59	1398 Donnera	26♑41'26
3605 Davy	12♑08'40	985 Rosina	20♑03'43	3674 Erbisbühl	26♑43'40
972 Cohnia	12♑16'24	2403 Šumava	20♑04'31	1373 Cincinnati	26♑56'17
3991 Basilevsky	12♑20'33	1246 Chaka	20♑13'57	3077 Henderson	26♑58'45
2365 Interkosmos	12♑25'42	3228 Pire	20♑17'18	1821 Aconcagua	27♑00'21
2799 Justus	12♑36'03	370 Modestia	20♑33'21	3001 Michelangelo	27♑15'52
3626 Ohsaki	12♑40'33	142 Polana	20♑40'07	427 Galene	27♑26'03
1785 Wurm	12♑51'18	2774 Tenojoki	20♑40'31	2958 Arpetito	27♑26'20
4131 Stasik	12♑57'36	466 Tisiphone	20♑42'46	657 Gunlöd	27♑28'37
1867 Deiphobus	12♑58'17	2294 Andronikov	20♑46'12	1485 Isa	27♑32'49
1509 Esclangona	12♑58'21	1339 Désagneauxa	20♑47'26	4263 Abashiri	27♑33'45
10 Hygiea	13♑02'33	1233 Kobresia	20♑52'23	775 Lumière	27♑34'24
2494 Inge	13♑08'20	1756 Giacobini	20♑52'35	1598 Paloque	27♑35'03
1173 Anchises	13♑12'08	1194 Aletta	20♑54'05	1006 Lagrangea	27♑40'17
371 Bohemia	13♑12'58	2005 Hencke	20♑54'50	2668 Tataria	27♑40'36
3145 Walter Adams	13♑13'07	1780 Kippes	21♑01'04	544 Jetta	27♑51'53
2764 Moeller	13♑21'19	1547 Nele	21♑02'05	408 Fama	28♑05'14
779 Nina	13♑29'34	549 Jessonda	21♑13'44	1313 Berna	28♑06'52
2555 Thomas	13♑30'46	3425 Hurukawa	21♑18'54	665 Sabine	28♑22'55
2947 Kippenhahn	13♑32'34	1250 Galanthus	21♑27'32	1853 McElroy	28♑29'24
1138 Attica	13♑34'13	648 Pippa	21♑35'50	1288 Santa	28♑42'29
777 Gutemberga	14♑02'51	2000 Herschel	21♑36'16	982 Franklina	28♑55'56
3549 Hapke	14♑10'02	440 Theodora	21♑36'43	696 Leonora	28♑59'29
1456 Saldanha	14♑15'30	3774 Megumi	21♑47'01	925 Alphonsina	29♑14'43
1411 Brauna	14♑28'08	4128 UKSTU	22♑05'23	2548 Leloir	29♑16'34
2670 Chuvashia	14♑35'39	3719 Karamzin	22♑09'15	576 Emanuela	29♑27'09
1959 Karbyshev	14♑38'08	2669 Shostakovich	22♑20'52	1258 Sicilia	29♑30'19
607 Jenny	14♑54'06	3030 Vehrenberg	22♑28'16	1298 Nocturna	29♑32'03
		1507 Vaasa	22♑31'12	3735 Třeboň	29♑33'48

Heliocentric Nodes in Zodiacal Order

Epoch November 5, 1990   Equinox 1950.0   Planet nodes have number ####

862 Franzia 29♑47'32	2302 Florya 7♒17'40	406 Erna 15♒44'10
1709 Ukraina 29♑48'36	123 Brunhild 7♒29'33	71 Niobe 15♒46'01
1971 Hagihara 0♒00'25	1092 Lilium 7♒30'40	588 Achilles 15♒52'23
1497 Tampere 0♒06'44	1228 Scabiosa 7♒40'27	3961 Arthurcox 16♒06'39
465 Alekto 0♒09'02	2366 Aaryn 7♒49'29	1503 Kuopio 16♒31'03
3086 Kalbaugh 0♒13'50	623 Chimaera 7♒49'40	3280 Grétry 17♒00'43
1714 Sy 0♒23'32	2763 Jeans 8♒18'57	1721 Wells 17♒09'18
3453 Dostoevsky 0♒26'08	1468 Zomba 8♒29'37	3047 Goethe 17♒14'52
2455 Somville 0♒30'20	115 Thyra 8♒35'41	3031 Houston 17♒21'49
170 Maria 0♒53'20	2467 Kollontai 8♒45'39	1321 Majuba 17♒39'01
884 Priamus 1♒00'20	64 Angelina 9♒00'20	945 Barcelona 17♒48'44
3152 Jones 1♒02'06	1604 Tombaugh 9♒04'05	1285 Julietta 17♒51'34
998 Bodea 1♒21'38	860 Ursina 9♒09'38	759 Vinifera 18♒01'25
569 Misa 1♒32'01	2842 Unsöld 9♒37'39	2878 Panacea 18♒02'00
376 Geometria 1♒37'56	1823 Gliese 9♒37'45	1478 Vihuri 18♒04'43
2064 Thomsen 1♒41'53	835 Olivia 9♒44'54	1555 Dejan 18♒07'07
2071 Nadezhda 1♒46'09	3160 Angerhofer 10♒11'48	1930 Lucifer 18♒13'00
1374 Isora 2♒12'14	2928 Epstein 10♒21'40	606 Brangäne 18♒14'36
3505 Byrd 2♒13'53	2916 Voronveliya 10♒37'01	4000 Hipparchus 18♒17'41
165 Loreley 2♒20'47	285 Regina 10♒49'37	141 Lumen 18♒24'30
646 Kastalia 2♒28'12	2026 Cottrell 10♒59'12	133 Cyrene 18♒38'24
1284 Latvia 2♒34'26	89 Julia 11♒02'24	1118 Hanskya 18♒43'15
3065 Sarahill 2♒46'47	2576 Yesenin 11♒04'11	1068 Nofretete 18♒45'38
1444 Pannonia 2♒48'34	3694 Sharon 11♒06'53	1769 Carlostorres 18♒51'31
1112 Polonia 2♒53'35	426 Hippo 11♒09'36	2097 Galle 18♒58'32
1832 Mrkos 3♒02'26	970 Primula 11♒16'23	1612 Hirose 19♒06'50
4043 Perolof 3♒10'39	2123 Vltava 11♒33'37	2691 Sersic 19♒28'18
2412 Wil 3♒16'02	1405 Sibelius 11♒39'46	2137 Priscilla 19♒46'58
2609 Kiril-Metodi 3♒26'59	3968 Koptelov 11♒40'06	3658 Feldman 19♒58'35
2762 Fowler 3♒37'54	180 Garumna 12♒05'32	3304 Pearce 20♒05'44
2345 Fučik 3♒42'50	3431 Nakano 12♒13'39	2324 Janice 20♒23'05
433 Eros 3♒44'21	3696 Herald 12♒20'35	1477 Bonsdorffia 20♒28'28
1653 Yakhontovia 3♒53'23	2824 Franke 12♒21'43	3142 Kilopi 20♒31'47
283 Emma 3♒54'42	3711 Ellensburg 12♒25'59	3354 McNair 20♒45'13
1324 Knysna 3♒56'41	1342 Brabantia 12♒32'09	1613 Smiley 20♒47'23
1876 Napolitania 3♒56'42	506 Marion 12♒40'59	949 Hel 20♒59'57
1100 Arnica 4♒00'47	54 Alexandra 12♒51'52	1266 Tone 21♒08'46
1763 Williams 4♒04'22	228 Agathe 12♒54'40	1272 Gefion 21♒10'01
1034 Mozartia 4♒09'52	1086 Nata 12♒54'44	3914 Kotogahama 21♒12'46
3345 Tarkovskij 4♒21'28	382 Dodona 13♒04'29	1433 Geramtina 21♒16'21
1234 Elyna 4♒21'30	212 Medea 13♒11'30	2033 Basilea 21♒17'19
3135 Lauer 4♒25'46	3029 Sanders 13♒15'36	4292 Aoba 21♒18'57
2096 Väinö 4♒26'22	2993 Wendy 13♒15'39	1891 Gondola 21♒32'00
1260 Walhalla 4♒26'36	2295 Matusovskij 13♒28'12	2575 Bulgaria 21♒33'30
390 Alma 4♒48'37	2168 Swope 13♒36'11	2946 Muchachos 21♒37'27
1584 Fuji 4♒54'49	1987 Kaplan 13♒48'26	96 Aegle 21♒37'59
3730 Hurban 5♒07'08	3721 Widorn 13♒49'36	3879 Machar 21♒38'43
2544 Gubarev 5♒13'37	1491 Balduinus 13♒54'29	1471 Tornio 21♒42'14
1985 Hopmann 5♒14'08	3798 De Jager 13♒57'31	2043 Ortutay 21♒42'53
111 Ate 5♒22'44	984 Gretia 14♒01'08	1241 Dysona 21♒52'49
2131 Mayall 5♒28'21	3559 Violaumayer 14♒06'05	1746 Brouwer 21♒53'27
762 Pulcova 5♒35'03	1265 Schweikarda 14♒08'07	3401 Vanphilos 22♒04'23
1370 Hella 5♒35'36	3500 Kobayashi 14♒16'37	773 Irmintraud 22♒06'52
3413 Andriana 6♒31'15	2808 Belgrano 14♒20'29	4266 Waltari 22♒10'35
2497 Kulikovskij 6♒33'52	2479 Sodankylä 14♒22'24	467 Laura 22♒13'28
1349 Bechuana 6♒47'15	2882 Tedesco 14♒44'15	2545 Verbiest 22♒15'37
1787 Chiny 6♒50'29	3485 Barucci 15♒06'12	2615 Saito 22♒42'13
1290 Albertine 7♒03'33	1437 Diomedes 15♒07'29	987 Wallia 22♒54'45
1007 Pawlowia 7♒04'13	1892 Lucienne 15♒13'12	2952 Lilliputia 22♒56'05
2258 Viipuri 7♒07'44	2474 Birgitta 15♒16'47	1625 The NORC 22♒56'40
3412 Kafka 7♒13'27	2125 Karl-Ontjes 15♒27'27	778 Theobalda 23♒08'18
30 Urania 7♒17'13	4295 Wisse 15♒36'22	1719 Jens 23♒14'07

Heliocentric Nodes in Zodiacal Order

Epoch November 5, 1990   Equinox 1950.0   Planet nodes have number ####

Name	Long.	Name	Long.	Name	Long.
112 Iphigenia	23♒16'27	1098 Hakone	28♒43'42	3546 Atanasoff	4♓47'37
1000 Piazzia	23♒21'50	1415 Malautra	28♒48'09	265 Anna	4♓59'50
1474 Beira	23♒24'34	3824 Brendalee	29♒13'56	1279 Uganda	5♓10'02
1240 Centenaria	23♒27'33	1079 Mimosa	29♒14'09	2758 Cordelia	5♓18'34
243 Ida	23♒51'30	916 America	29♒25'28	271 Penthesilea	5♓30'20
1282 Utopia	23♒55'40	1065 Amundsenia	29♒52'13	2791 Paradise	5♓34'54
1639 Bower	23♒56'12	4209 Briggs	29♒58'31	661 Cloelia	5♓38'42
2388 Gase	23♒57'59	1476 Cox	0♓06'25	1157 Arabia	5♓43'10
709 Fringilla	24♒03'36	2766 Leeuwenhoek	0♓08'29	1182 Ilona	5♓55'43
2570 Porphyro	24♒03'44	3588 Kirik	0♓11'50	3188 Jekabsons	6♓02'23
587 Hypsipyle	24♒05'52	2794 Kulik	0♓13'44	684 Hildburg	6♓05'13
3231 Mila	24♒07'30	918 Itha	0♓14'29	375 Ursula	6♓06'04
1113 Katja	24♒10'30	1493 Sigrid	0♓17'04	574 Reginhild	6♓26'23
2380 Heilongjiang	24♒10'53	1532 Inari	0♓27'57	3433 Fehrenbach	6♓29'01
200 Dynamene	24♒11'17	2964 Jaschek	0♓29'00	2973 Paola	6♓29'37
3464 Owensby	24♒13'16	1662 Hoffmann	0♓35'39	2833 Radishchev	6♓32'28
1206 Numerowia	24♒13'54	1463 Nordenmarkia	0♓57'13	1526 Mikkeli	6♓36'53
4133 Heureka	24♒14'14	1510 Charlois	1♓06'37	1620 Geographos	6♓41'25
800 Kressmannia	24♒42'03	2118 Flagstaff	1♓06'41	3255 Tholen	6♓45'47
706 Hirundo	25♒08'57	1360 Tarka	1♓08'33	1803 Zwicky	6♓53'59
1338 Duponta	25♒11'20	1697 Koskenniemi	1♓13'21	911 Agamemnon	7♓17'39
934 Thüringia	25♒12'41	1641 Tana	1♓13'37	2098 Zyskin	7♓17'53
1804 Chebotarev	25♒14'21	3924 Birch	1♓24'07	2402 Satpaev	7♓17'59
4148 McCartney	25♒14'52	4235 Tatischckev	1♓30'10	1677 Tycho Brahe	7♓28'27
4282 Endate	25♒18'44	760 Massinga	1♓34'42	63 Ausonia	7♓30'13
1682 Karel	25♒19'41	172 Baucis	1♓36'03	2254 Requiem	7♓43'49
2390 Nežárka	25♒21'23	2498 Tsesevich	1♓36'38	839 Valborg	7♓46'51
3946 Shor	25♒37'19	297 Caecilia	1♓37'05	3655 Eupraksia	7♓52'02
1885 Herero	25♒56'49	1152 Pawona	1♓37'57	3900 Knežević	7♓53'35
1467 Mashona	26♒20'15	2451 Dollfus	1♓38'07	1659 Punkaharju	8♓08'54
765 Mattiaca	26♒25'17	1848 Delvaux	1♓43'34	2011 Veteraniya	8♓11'32
1683 Castafiore	26♒25'41	3244 Petronius	1♓51'15	2848 ASP	8♓16'33
524 Fidelio	26♒26'16	602 Marianna	1♓52'33	3087 Beatrice Tinsley	8♓19'15
2892 Filipenko	26♒27'18	473 Nolli	1♓53'59	3811 Karma	8♓29'49
939 Isberga	26♒40'25	2650 Elinor	1♓57'26	4101 Ruikou	8♓42'57
1274 Delportia	26♒41'54	1977 Shura	2♓00'20	1642 Hill	8♓51'56
400 Ducrosa	26♒47'31	184 Dejopeja	2♓02'33	2662 Kandinsky	8♓58'31
372 Palma	26♒49'10	2095 Parsifal	2♓11'29	2737 Kotka	9♓23'43
2456 Palamedes	26♒51'12	1404 Ajax	2♓16'01	3778 Regge	9♓23'49
1187 Afra	26♒54'03	143 Adria	2♓41'28	3199 Nefertiti	9♓25'54
1430 Somalia	27♒06'03	819 Barnardiana	2♓44'52	2713 Luxembourg	9♓26'17
1737 Severny	27♒07'50	2351 O'Higgins	2♓45'00	4294 Horatius	9♓26'43
84 Klio	27♒10'13	1406 Komppa	2♓49'59	4062 Schiaparelli	9♓38'20
1372 Haremari	27♒12'11	1486 Marilyn	2♓59'52	2090 Mizuho	9♓40'40
1523 Pieksämäki	27♒20'33	78 Diana	3♓08'30	2562 Chaliapin	9♓42'23
2126 Gerasimovich	27♒21'06	61 Danaë	3♓22'38	2875 Lagerkvist	10♓01'43
174 Phaedra	27♒21'48	2389 Dibaj	3♓35'35	1717 Arlon	10♓02'12
2108 Otto Schmidt	27♒26'49	4038 Kristina	3♓52'53	3675 Kemstach	10♓05'41
4283 Stöffler	27♒27'57	591 Irmgard	3♓53'13	2055 Dvořák	10♓07'59
227 Philosophia	27♒29'43	545 Messalina	4♓01'15	1916 Boreas	10♓13'47
1559 Kustaanheimo	27♒42'33	2860 Pasacentennium	4♓04'57	3391 Sinon	10♓24'56
324 Bamberga	27♒50'00	2996 Bowman	4♓05'13	1749 Telamon	10♓28'20
3931 Batten	27♒50'51	3075 Bornmann	4♓05'21	930 Westphalia	10♓34'33
1106 Cydonia	27♒53'41	469 Argentina	4♓06'52	3536 Schleicher	10♓40'03
1991 Darwin	28♒00'43	2785 Sedov	4♓12'38	3594 Scotti	10♓48'11
2267 Agassiz	28♒07'29	687 Tinette	4♓12'40	733 Mocia	10♓51'41
2065 Spicer	28♒07'58	249 Ilse	4♓21'23	4203 Brucato	10♓53'41
577 Rhea	28♒25'15	1777 Gehrels	4♓26'15	120 Lachesis	10♓59'10
2076 Levin	28♒31'21	1426 Riviera	4♓38'14	3634 Iwan	11♓12'16
2431 Skovoroda	28♒37'23	3471 Amelin	4♓39'39	626 Notburga	11♓18'15
516 Amherstia	28♒43'23	2537 Gilmore	4♓44'26	830 Petropolitana	11♓20'18

Heliocentric Nodes in Zodiacal Order
Epoch November 5, 1990   Equinox 1950.0   Planet nodes have number ####

Name	Node	Name	Node	Name	Node
1062 Ljuba	11♓20'29	3233 Krišbarons	17♓13'48	2646 Abetti	22♓07'14
1231 Auricula	11♓36'28	2644 Victor Jara	17♓13'59	1454 Kalevala	22♓09'04
214 Aschera	11♓46'27	177 Irma	17♓17'08	829 Academia	22♓12'08
3903 Kliment Ohridski		804 Hispania	17♓18'11	2915 Moskvina	22♓19'54
	11♓52'00	1159 Granada	17♓23'46	2760 Kacha	22♓20'21
1050 Meta	11♓54'37	2374 Vladvysotskij	17♓25'44	1877 Marsden	22♓29'18
624 Hektor	12♓05'16	1524 Joensuu	17♓28'58	1923 Osiris	22♓32'46
2683 Brian	12♓09'11	203 Pompeja	17♓34'29	1921 Pala	22♓34'00
2231 Durrell	12♓10'19	996 Hilaritas	17♓39'14	902 Probitas	22♓34'11
605 Juvisia	12♓25'06	2836 Sobolev	17♓45'08	1416 Renauxa	22♓35'18
3390 Demanet	12♓27'31	2765 Dinant	17♓47'01	224 Oceana	22♓38'01
573 Recha	12♓36'39	3235 Melchior	17♓52'45	2079 Jacchia	22♓41'41
3794 Sthenelos	12♓37'15	2274 Ehrsson	18♓00'07	1382 Gerti	22♓43'17
3506 French	12♓45'35	2547 Hubei	18♓02'09	1997 Leverrier	22♓46'10
1538 Detre	12♓46'48	973 Aralia	18♓06'41	833 Monica	22♓48'47
1049 Gotho	12♓49'51	3281 Maupertuis	18♓07'45	3269 Vibert-Douglas	
1859 Kovalevskaya		3074 Popov	18♓20'15		23♓05'04
	12♓52'46	2917 Sawyer Hogg	18♓24'56	2599 Veselí	23♓05'52
3444 Stepanian	12♓55'02	3245 Jensch	18♓27'58	1884 Skip	23♓16'11
101 Helena	12♓55'05	117 Lomia	18♓31'35	35 Leukothea	23♓18'37
192 Nausikaa	12♓55'41	1887 Virton	18♓32'52	3350 Scobee	23♓18'54
2552 Remek	13♓02'23	844 Leontina	18♓33'09	1481 Tübingia	23♓27'17
3217 Seidelmann	13♓03'13	2978 Roudebush	18♓33'55	98 Ianthe	23♓39'23
603 Timandra	13♓04'03	2885 Palva	18♓48'50	990 Yerkes	23♓43'57
917 Lyka	13♓04'06	3243 Skytel	18♓50'30	333 Badenia	23♓44'46
958 Asplinda	13♓10'47	1005 Arago	19♓08'58	3180 Morgan	23♓46'53
2509 Chukotka	13♓19'19	2157 Ashbrook	19♓13'09	1308 Halleria	23♓51'43
672 Astarte	13♓24'47	2645 Daphne Plane		1488 Aura	24♓08'54
135 Hertha	13♓25'13		19♓19'06	388 Charybdis	24♓14'17
1002 Olbersia	13♓28'32	575 Renate	19♓20'48	841 Arabella	24♓17'16
303 Josephina	13♓40'46	193 Ambrosia	19♓37'04	3740 Menge	24♓17'27
2735 Ellen	14♓02'13	2130 Evdokiya	19♓37'24	169 Zelia	24♓18'32
2015 Kachuevskaya		2939 Coconino	19♓40'34	1906 Naef	24♓23'42
	14♓05'53	1242 Zambesia	19♓42'08	3660 Lazarev	24♓29'43
717 Wisibada	14♓09'30	1924 Horus	19♓51'01	613 Ginevra	24♓31'35
2753 Duncan	14♓16'28	3150 Tosa	19♓53'30	327 Columbia	24♓33'36
1158 Luda	14♓23'23	3552 Don Quixote	20♓04'11	1418 Fayeta	24♓40'36
2358 Bahner	14♓26'54	3067 Akhmatova	20♓04'56	2997 Cabrera	24♓45'52
1958 Chandra	14♓32'00	2748 Patrick Gene	20♓06'43	356 Liguria	24♓50'06
2532 Sutton	14♓40'47	2756 Dzhangar	20♓09'07	708 Raphaela	24♓53'05
4253 Märker	14♓42'06	108 Hecuba	20♓09'11	337 Devosa	24♓58'33
385 Ilmatar	14♓45'17	2923 Schuyler	20♓11'20	4217 Engelhardt	24♓58'50
1066 Lobelia	14♓46'40	231 Vindobona	20♓20'14	3012 Minsk	24♓59'03
325 Heidelberga	14♓46'58	659 Nestor	20♓24'26	1640 Nemo	25♓01'41
3770 Nizami	14♓58'41	1135 Colchis	20♓28'46	1557 Roehla	25♓02'46
3842 Harlansmith	15♓01'59	3043 San Diego	20♓33'31	637 Chrysothemis	25♓14'12
2200 Pasadena	15♓04'42	2101 Adonis	20♓34'32	4031 Mueller	25♓20'33
2827 Vellamo	15♓05'50	658 Asteria	20♓48'13	1184 Gaea	25♓28'11
1340 Yvette	15♓18'28	2159 Kukkamäki	20♓53'24	2726 Kotelnikov	25♓32'22
3725 Valsecchi	15♓21'04	2888 Hodgson	21♓00'01	2626 Belnika	25♓35'35
134 Sophrosyne	15♓46'54	436 Patricia	21♓01'48	2637 Bobrovnikoff	25♓41'23
2036 Sheragul	15♓51'11	955 Alstede	21♓04'50	616 Elly	25♓48'04
1077 Campanula	15♓51'42	3161 Beadell	21♓07'26	29 Amphitrite	25♓55'40
1942 Jablunka	15♓54'06	3697 Guyhurst	21♓08'03	3596 Meriones	25♓58'34
935 Clivia	16♓04'14	1678 Hveen	21♓11'53	309 Fraternitas	26♓05'42
3083 OAFA	16♓04'53	1268 Libya	21♓15'00	2591 Dworetsky	26♓08'54
399 Persephone	16♓16'27	3038 Bernes	21♓15'49	1710 Gothard	26♓13'07
1145 Robelmonte	16♓19'30	1998 Titius	21♓29'36	2793 Valdaj	26♓14'25
366 Vincentina	16♓33'07	1381 Danubia	21♓32'16	2890 Vilyujsk	26♓22'12
4076 Dörffel	16♓38'01	693 Zerbinetta	21♓35'10	1116 Catriona	26♓25'09
1863 Antinous	16♓54'09	355 Gabriella	21♓39'13	1919 Clemence	26♓27'41
2487 Juhani	17♓13'47	328 Gudrun	22♓04'42	1700 Zvezdara	26♓30'18

Heliocentric Nodes in Zodiacal Order
Epoch November 5, 1990   Equinox 1950.0   Planet nodes have number ####

1981 Midas	26♓30'41	
1608 Muñoz	26♓31'12	
2001 Einstein	26♓32'20	
4169 Celsius	26♓38'34	
632 Pyrrha	26♓43'15	
711 Marmulla	26♓43'29	
649 Josefa	26♓44'07	
2414 Vibeke	26♓45'56	
2869 Nepryadva	26♓53'58	
2809 Vernadskij	26♓55'28	
948 Jucunda	27♓06'03	
501 Urhixidur	27♓06'35	
1310 Villigera	27♓13'55	
493 Griseldis	27♓17'22	
1587 Kahrstedt	27♓25'03	
1121 Natascha	27♓32'38	
3402 Wisdom	27♓33'16	
1318 Nerina	27♓48'58	
2994 Flynn	27♓52'10	
1392 Pierre	27♓52'56	
3190 Aposhanskij	27♓56'32	
3554 Amun	28♓01'21	
2252 CERGA	28♓02'47	
36 Atalante	28♓14'22	
2128 Wetherill	28♓16'19	
2514 Taiyuan	28♓19'36	
1913 Sekanina	28♓28'54	
3676 Hahn	28♓33'16	
1470 Carla	28♓52'40	
75 Eurydike	28♓58'30	
3314 Beals	29♓00'03	
2930 Euripides	29♓05'29	
1396 Outeniqua	29♓07'27	
1018 Arnolda	29♓13'08	
2088 Sahlia	29♓17'15	
1610 Mirnaya	29♓17'50	
2607 Yakutia	29♓19'38	
2486 Metsähovi	29♓31'07	
3667 Anne–Marie	29♓38'48	
2174 Asmodeus	29♓39'07	
620 Drakonia	29♓43'55	
1380 Volodia	29♓45'54	
247 Eukrate	29♓51'15	

INDEX

RETURN CHART OPTIONS

One method of studying the current trends for an individual is with the chart of the exact moment when the Sun, Moon or a planet returns to the exact position occupied in the birth chart. This places the transits into a framework that is specific to the individual, and the theory is that the resulting chart reveals issues that will confront the person during the time period of the return.

Probably the most popular Return Chart is the Solar Return. Your Solar Return is a "birthday chart" that is interpreted for the year ahead—a personal "New Year" just for you. Many astrologers also calculate a Lunar Return Chart each month for the time that the Moon returns to its position in the natal chart, and this chart is interpreted for the (almost) one month ahead. (Since a complete lunar cycle is about 28 days, there are 13 "months" in a lunar year.)

Astro offers a two-page computer interpretation (summary) of either the Solar or Lunar Return Chart. Remember, Astro offers numerous variations on these options, so please tell the operator what "add-ons" you would like. Credit card orders call TOLL-FREE:

1-800-888-9983

Solar Return Chart only $4.00

Lunar Return Chart only $4.00

Solar Return Chart and Summary $7.00

Lunar Return Chart and Summary $7.00

P.S. *The time calculated for our Return options is highly accurate, based on a subroutine which continues computing until it calculates the precise time.*

Also by ACS Publications

All About Astrology Series of booklets

The American Atlas, Expanded Fifth Edition: US Latitudes & Longitudes,
    Time Changes and Time Zones (Shanks)

The American Book of Tables (Michelsen)

The American Ephemeris Series 1901-2000

The American Ephemeris for the 20th Century [Noon or Midnight] 1900 to 2000,
    Revised Fifth Edition

The American Ephemeris for the 21st Century 2001-2050, Revised Second Edition

The American Heliocentric Ephemeris 1901-2000

The American Midpoint Ephemeris 1991-1995

The American Sidereal Ephemeris 1976-2000

Asteroid Goddesses: The Mythology, Psychology and Astrology
    of the Reemerging Feminine (George & Bloch)

Astro-Alchemy: Making the Most of Your Transits (Negus)

Astro Essentials: Planets in Signs, Houses & Aspects (Pottenger)

Astrological Games People Play (Ashman)

Astrological Insights into Personality (Lundsted)

Basic Astrology: A Guide for Teachers & Students (Negus)

Basic Astrology: A Workbook for Students (Negus)

The Book of Neptune (Waram)

The Changing Sky: A Practical Guide to the New Predictive Astrology (Forrest)

Complete Horoscope Interpretation: Putting Together Your Planetary Profile (Pottenger)

Cosmic Combinations: A Book of Astrological Exercises (Negus)

Dial Detective: Investigation with the 90° Dial (Simms)

Easy Tarot Guide (Masino)

Expanding Astrology's Universe (Dobyns)

Hands That Heal (Burns)

Healing with the Horoscope: A Guide To Counseling (Pottenger)

Houses of the Horoscope (Herbst)

The Inner Sky: The Dynamic New Astrology for Everyone (Forrest)

The International Atlas, Revised Third Edition: World Latitudes & Longitudes,
    Time Changes and Time Zones (Shanks)

The Koch Book of Tables (Michelsen)

Midpoints: Unleashing the Power of the Planets (Munkasey)

The Only Way to... Learn Astrology, Vols. I-V (March & McEvers)

    Volume I - Basic Principles

    Volume II - Math & Interpretation Techniques

    Volume III - Horoscope Analysis

    Volume IV- Learn About Tomorrow: Current Patterns

    Volume V - Learn About Relationships: Synastry Techniques

Planetary Heredity (M. Gauquelin)

Planetary Planting (Riotte)

Planets in Solar Returns: A Yearly Guide for Transformation and Growth (Shea)

Planets in Work: A Complete Guide to Vocational Astrology (Binder)

Psychology of the Planets (F. Gauquelin)

Skymates: The Astrology of Love, Sex and Intimacy (S. & J. Forrest)

Spirit Guides: We Are Not Alone (Belhayes)

Tables of Planetary Phenomena (Michelsen)

Twelve Wings of the Eagle: Our Spiritual Evolution through the Ages of the Zodiac (Simms)

The Way of the Spirit: The Wisdom of the Ancient Nanina (Whiskers)